Illustrated Series™

Microsoft® 365
Office 2021
Intermediate

⚡ Cengage

Australia • Brazil • Canada • Mexico • Singapore • United Kingdom • United States

**Illustrated Series® Collection Microsoft® Office 365®
& Office 2021 Intermediate**
David Beskeen, Carol Cram, Lynn Wermers

SVP, Product: Erin Joyner

VP, Product: Thais Alencar

Product Director: Mark Santee

Senior Product Manager: Amy Savino

Product Assistant: Ciara Horne

Learning Designer: Zenya Molnar

Content Manager: Grant Davis

Digital Delivery Quality Partner: Jim Vaughey

Developmental Editors: Julie Boyles, Barbara
  Clemens, Mary-Terese Cozzola, Karen Porter

VP, Product Marketing: Jason Sakos

Director, Product Marketing: Danaë April

Executive Product Marketing Manager: Jill Staut

IP Analyst: Ann Hoffman

IP Project Manager: Ilakkiya Jayagopi

Production Service: Lumina Datamatics, Inc.

Designer: Erin Griffin

Cover Image Source: Getty Images

Mac Users: If you're working through this product using a Mac, some of the steps may vary. Additional information for Mac users is included with the Data files for this product.

Disclaimer: This text is intended for instructional purposes only; data is fictional and does not belong to any real persons or companies.

Disclaimer: The material in this text was written using Microsoft Windows 10 and Office 365 Professional Plus and was Quality Assurance tested before the publication date. As Microsoft continually updates the Windows 10 operating system and Office 365, your software experience may vary slightly from what is presented in the printed text.

Windows, Access, Excel, and PowerPoint are registered trademarks of Microsoft Corporation. Microsoft and the Office logo are either registered trademarks or trademarks of Microsoft Corporation in the United States and/or other countries. This product is an independent publication and is neither affiliated with, nor authorized, sponsored, or approved by, Microsoft Corporation.

Some of the product names and company names used in this book have been used for identification purposes only and may be trademarks or registered trademarks of Microsoft Corporation in the United States and/or other countries.

For product information and technology assistance, contact us at
**Cengage Customer & Sales Support, 1-800-354-9706 or
support.cengage.com.**

For permission to use material from this text or product, submit all requests online at **www.copyright.com.**

Library of Congress Control Number: 2022904735

Student Edition ISBN: 978-0-357-67496-3
K12 ISBN: 978-0-357-67498-7
Looseleaf ISBN: 978-0-357-67497-0*
*Looseleaf available as part of a digital bundle

Cengage
200 Pier 4 Boulevard
Boston, MA 02210
USA

Cengage is a leading provider of customized learning solutions with employees residing in nearly 40 different countries and sales in more than 125 countries around the world. Find your local representative at **www.cengage.com.**

To learn more about Cengage platforms and services, register or access your online learning solution, or purchase materials for your course, visit **www.cengage.com.**

Notice to the Reader

Publisher does not warrant or guarantee any of the products described herein or perform any independent analysis in connection with any of the product information contained herein. Publisher does not assume, and expressly disclaims, any obligation to obtain and include information other than that provided to it by the manufacturer. The reader is expressly warned to consider and adopt all safety precautions that might be indicated by the activities described herein and to avoid all potential hazards. By following the instructions contained herein, the reader willingly assumes all risks in connection with such instructions. The publisher makes no representations or warranties of any kind, including but not limited to, the warranties of fitness for particular purpose or merchantability, nor are any such representations implied with respect to the material set forth herein, and the publisher takes no responsibility with respect to such material. The publisher shall not be liable for any special, consequential, or exemplary damages resulting, in whole or part, from the readers' use of, or reliance upon, this material.

Printed in the United States of America
Print Number: 02   Print Year: 2022

Brief Contents

Contents

Excel 2021

Illustrated Series™

Microsoft® 365
Office 2021

Intermediate

Getting to Know Microsoft Office Versions

Cengage is proud to bring you the next edition of Microsoft Office. This edition was designed to provide a robust learning experience that is not dependent upon a specific version of Office.

Microsoft supports several versions of Office:

- **Office 365:** A cloud-based subscription service that delivers Microsoft's most up-to-date, feature-rich, modern productivity tools direct to your device. There are variations of Office 365 for business, educational, and personal use. Office 365 offers extra online storage and cloud-connected features, as well as updates with the latest features, fixes, and security updates.

- **Office 2021:** Microsoft's "on-premises" version of the Office apps, available for both PCs and Macs, offered as a static, one-time purchase and outside of the subscription model.

- **Office Online:** A free, simplified version of Office web applications (Word, Excel, PowerPoint, and OneNote) that facilitates creating and editing files collaboratively.

Office 365 (the subscription model) and Office 2021 (the one-time purchase model) had only slight differences between them at the time this content was developed. Over time, Office 365's cloud interface will continuously update, offering new application features and functions, while Office 2021 will remain static. Therefore, your onscreen experience may differ from what you see in this product. For example, the more advanced features and functionalities covered in this product may not be available in Office Online or may have updated from what you see in Office 2021.

For more information on the differences between Office 365, Office 2021, and Office Online, please visit the Microsoft Support site.

Cengage is committed to providing high-quality learning solutions for you to gain the knowledge and skills that will empower you throughout your educational and professional careers.

Thank you for using our product, and we look forward to exploring the future of Microsoft Office with you!

Using SAM Projects and Textbook Projects

SAM Projects allow you to actively apply the skills you learned live in Microsoft Word, Excel, PowerPoint, or Access. Become a more productive student and use these skills throughout your career.

To complete SAM Textbook Projects, please follow these steps:

SAM Textbook Projects allow you to complete a project as you follow along with the steps in the textbook. As you read the module, look for icons that indicate when you should download **sam**⬇ your SAM Start file(s) and when to upload **sam**⬆ the final project file to SAM for grading.

Everything you need to complete this project is provided within SAM. You can launch the eBook directly from SAM, which will allow you to take notes, highlight, and create a custom study guide, or you can use a print textbook or your mobile app. Download IOS or Download Android.

To get started, launch your SAM Project assignment from SAM, MindTap, or a link within your LMS.

Step 1: Download Files

- Click the "Download All" button or the individual links to download your **Start File** and **Support File(s)** (when available). You <u>must</u> use the SAM Start file.

- Click the Instructions link to launch the eBook (or use the print textbook or mobile app).

- Disregard any steps in the textbook that ask you to create a new file or to use a file from a location outside of SAM.

- Look for the SAM Download icon **sam**⬇ to begin working with your start file.

- Follow the module's step-by-step instructions until you reach the SAM Upload icon **sam**⬆.

- Save and close the file.

Step 2: Save Work to SAM

- Ensure you rename your project file to match the Expected File Name.

- Upload your in-progress or completed file to SAM. You can download the file to continue working or submit it for grading in the next step.

Step 3: Submit for Grading

- Upload the completed file to SAM for immediate feedback and to view the available Reports.

  - The **Graded Summary Report** provides a detailed list of project steps, your score, and feedback to aid you in revising and re-submitting the project.

  - The **Study Guide Report** provides your score for each project step and links to the associated training and textbook pages.

- If additional attempts are allowed, use your reports to assist with revising and resubmitting your project.

- To re-submit the project, download the file saved in step 2.

- Edit, save, and close the file, then re-upload and submit it again.

For all other SAM Projects, please follow these steps:

To get started, launch your SAM Project assignment from SAM, MindTap, or a link within your LMS.

Step 1: Download Files

- Click the "Download All" button or the individual links to download your **Instruction File**, **Start File**, and **Support File(s)** (when available). You must use the SAM Start file.

- Open the Instruction file and follow the step-by-step instructions. Ensure you rename your project file to match the Expected File Name (change _1 to _2 at the end of the file name).

Step 2: Save Work to SAM

- Upload your in-progress or completed file to SAM. You can download the file to continue working or submit it for grading in the next step.

Step 3: Submit for Grading

- Upload the completed file to SAM for immediate feedback and to view available Reports.

  - The **Graded Summary Report** provides a detailed list of project steps, your score, and feedback to aid you in revising and resubmitting the project.

  - The **Study Guide Report** provides your score for each project step and links to the associated training and textbook pages.

- If additional attempts are allowed, use your reports to assist with revising and resubmitting your project.

- To re-submit the project, download the file saved in step 2.

- Edit, save, and close the file, then re-upload and submit it again.

For additional tips to successfully complete your SAM Projects, please view our Common Student Errors Infographic.

Step 3: Submit for Grading

- Upload the completed file to SAM for immediate feedback and to view available Reports

- The **Graded Summary Report** provides a detailed list of project steps, your score, and feedback to aid you in revising and resubmitting the project.

- The **Study Guide Report** provides your score for each project step and links to the associated training and textbook pages.

- If additional attempts are allowed, use your reports to assist with revising and resubmitting your project.

- To re-submit the project, download the file saved in step 2.

- Edit, save, and close the file, then re-upload and submit it again.

- For additional tips to successfully complete your SAM Projects, please view our Common Student Errors infographic.

Formatting Tables and Documents

CASE You are preparing a prospectus for an advertising campaign aimed at the New York market. The goal of the ad campaign is to promote JCL Talent to employers and job seekers in the office support industries. You format the budget information in the prospectus as a table, so that it is easy to read and analyze, and then add headers and footers and a cover page to the prospectus.

Module Objectives

After completing this module, you will be able to:

- Modify character spacing
- Work with indents
- Insert a section break
- Modify a table
- Modify rows and columns
- Sort table data
- Split and merge cells
- Perform calculations in tables
- Modify table style options
- Customize a table format
- Insert a cover page

Files You Will Need

IL_WD_4-1.docx
IL_WD_4-2.docx
IL_WD_4-3.docx

Modify Character Spacing

A powerful way to change the appearance of text is to modify character spacing. **Character spacing** is formatting that changes the scale (or width) of characters, expands or condenses the amount of space between characters, raises or lowers characters relative to the line of text, and adjusts the kerning of characters. **Kerning** is the space between standard combinations of letters. You use the Advanced tab in the Font dialog box to modify character spacing. **CASE** ▶ *You enhance the appearance of the headings in the prospectus by modifying the character spacing.*

STEPS

1. **sam↓** Start Word, open the file IL_WD_4-1.docx **from the location where you store your Data Files, save it as** IL_WD_4_Prospectus, **then drag the** Zoom slider **to 120**

2. **Select the heading** Executive Summary, **click the** Font Size arrow **on the Mini toolbar, then click** 48

   The font size of the heading is enlarged to 48.

3. **Click the** Launcher ⬚ **in the Font group on the Home tab to open the Font dialog box, click the** Small caps check box **in the Effects area on the Font tab, then click** OK

   The lowercase characters change to small capital characters. You can use the options on the Font tab to apply other font effects, as well, including Subscript, Superscript, and Strikethrough.

4. **Click the** Launcher ⬚ **in the Font group, then click the** Advanced tab **in the Font dialog box**

   The Advanced tab in the Font dialog box is shown in FIGURE 4-1. You use the options on the Advanced tab to change the scale and spacing of characters, or to raise or lower the characters.

5. **Click the** Scale arrow, **click** 80%, **click the** Spacing arrow, **click** Expanded, **then click** OK

   Decreasing the scale of the characters makes them narrower and gives the text a tall, thin appearance. Expanding the spacing increases the amount of white space between characters.

6. **Click the** Font Size arrow ⬚ **in the Font group, click** 24, **double-click the** Format Painter button ⬚ **in the Clipboard group, then move the pointer over the document text to see** ⬚

   The font size of the heading changes to 24. The Format Painter is turned on and the pointer changes to ⬚.

7. **Scroll down, select the headings** Development Timeline and Projected Budget, **click the** Format Painter button ⬚ **to turn off the Format Painter, press** CTRL+HOME, **then save your changes**

   The headings are formatted the same; they are 24-point, small caps, character scale of 80%, with character spacing expanded by 1 point, as shown in FIGURE 4-2.

FIGURE 4-1: Advanced tab in Font dialog box

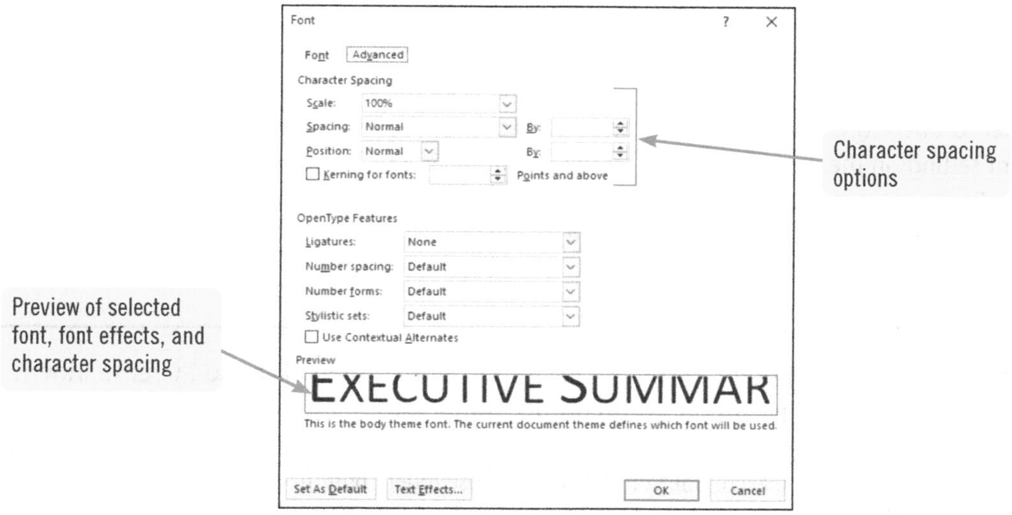

Character spacing options

Preview of selected font, font effects, and character spacing

24-point headings with a small caps effect and a character scale of 80% expanded by 1 point

FIGURE 4-2: Font and character spacing effects applied to text

Researching job roles and job skills with the Resume Assistant

The Resume Assistant in Word can help you research job roles and the types of skills they typically require. The Resume Assistant is available when you enable Intelligent Services in your Office installation. To open Resume Assistant, click the Review tab, and then click the Resume Assistant button in the Resume group. In the Resume Assistant pane, type keywords for a job role, such as "medical assistant," and an industry, such as "hospital" or "mental health care," you wish to explore. Descriptions of work experience from the LinkedIn public profiles of users with similar

job and industry titles will appear in the Resume Assistant pane. If you want to learn more about the job skills typically related to the role, click the Filter examples by top skills arrow to see the top job skills for the role (as identified by LinkedIn). The descriptions of work experience and top job skills you find using the Resume Assistant might be helpful to you as inspiration for writing descriptions of your own work experience for your résumé. Keep in mind that Resume Assistant is for reference use only. It's important that your résumé be original content that is unique to you.

Work with Indents

Learning
Outcomes
• Increase and
  decrease list levels
• Change bullet
  characters

When you indent a paragraph, you move its edge in from the left or right margin. Dragging an indent marker to a new location on the ruler is one way to change the indentation of a paragraph, changing the indent settings in the Paragraph group on the Layout tab is a second way, and using the indent buttons in the Paragraph group on the Home tab is a third. **CASE** *You format the development timeline as a bulleted list and apply indents to better organize the information.*

STEPS

1. **Place the insertion point in the first body paragraph, then click the Increase Indent button** ⬚ **in the Paragraph group on the Home tab**

   The entire paragraph is indented ½" from the left margin. The left indent marker also moves to the ½" mark on the horizontal ruler. Each time you click the Increase Indent button, the left edge of a paragraph moves another ½" to the right.

2. **Click the Decrease Indent button** ⬚ **in the Paragraph group**

   The left edge of the paragraph moves ½" to the left, and the indent marker moves back to the left margin.

3. **Scroll until the Development Timeline heading is at the top of your document window, select the eleven-line list that begins with Budget and resources, click the Bullets arrow** ⬚ **in the Paragraph group, then click the black round bullet**

   The 11 paragraphs are formatted as a bulleted list using the black round bullet symbol, as shown in FIGURE 4-3.

4. **Click a bullet in the list to select all the bullets, click the Font Color arrow** ⬚ **in the Font group, then click Blue, Accent 1**

   The bullet characters all change to blue.

5. **Click to place the insertion point in Preliminary budget is drafted in the bulleted list, then click the Increase Indent button** ⬚

   The list item is indented ½" and the bullet character changes to an open circle.

6. **Click to place the insertion point in Marketing approval due in the bulleted list, click the** ⬚ **three times, then click** ⬚ **once**

   The list item is indented further and the bullet character changes to a square, as shown in FIGURE 4-4. You promote and demote items in a bulleted list using the Increase Indent and Decrease Indent buttons. Each time you promote or demote an item, the bullet character changes.

7. **Click** ⬚ **to indent the items in the bulleted list to match** FIGURE 4-5, **then save your changes**

Creating multilevel lists

You can create lists with hierarchical structures by applying a multilevel list style to a list. To create a multilevel list, also called an outline, begin by applying a multilevel list style using the Multilevel List arrow ⬚ in the Paragraph group on the Home tab, then type your outline, pressing ENTER after each item. To demote items to a lower level of importance in the outline, place the insertion point in the item, then click the Increase Indent button ⬚ in the Paragraph group on the Home tab. Each time you indent a paragraph, the item is demoted to a lower level in the outline. Similarly, you can use the Decrease Indent button ⬚ to promote an item to a higher level in the outline. You can also create a hierarchical structure in any bulleted or numbered list by using ⬚ and ⬚ to demote and promote items in the list. To change the multilevel list style applied to a list, select the list, click ⬚ and then select a new style.

FIGURE 4-3: Bulleted list

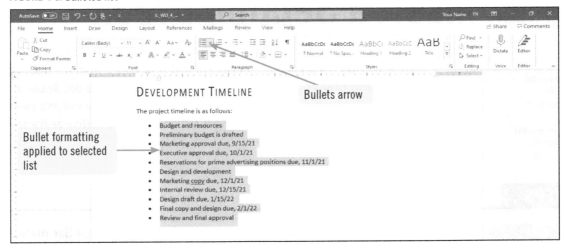

FIGURE 4-4: Demoted items in list

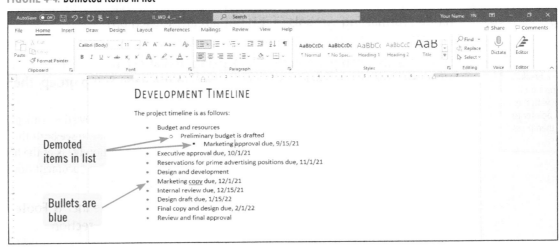

FIGURE 4-5: Multilevel list

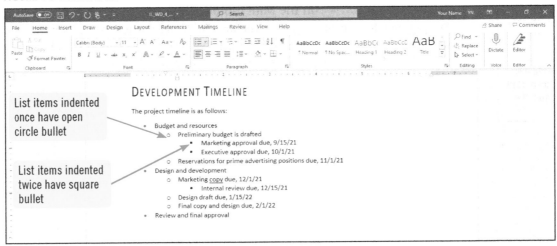

Insert a Section Break

Learning Outcomes
- Customize the status bar
- Insert section breaks
- Manage headers and footers

Dividing a document into sections allows you to format each section of the document with different page layout settings. A **section** is a portion of a document that is separated from the rest of the document by section breaks. **Section breaks** are formatting marks that you insert in a document to show the end of a section. **CASE** *You insert a next page section break to divide the document into two sections, and then insert a page number in the footer. Before inserting a section break, you customize the status bar to display section information.*

STEPS

QUICK TIP

Use the Customize Status Bar menu to turn on and off the display of information in the status bar.

1. **Right-click the** status bar, **click** Section **on the Customize Status Bar menu that opens (if it is not already checked), then click the document to close the menu**

   The status bar indicates the insertion point is located in Section 1 of the document.

2. **Click the** Show/Hide ¶ button ¶ **in the Paragraph group to show paragraph marks and hidden formatting symbols (if it is not already turned on)**

   Turning on formatting marks allows you to see the section breaks you insert in a document.

QUICK TIP

To delete a break, click to the left of the break with the selection pointer to select it, then press DELETE.

3. **Place the insertion point in the blank paragraph above the Projected Budget heading, click the** Layout tab, **click the** Breaks button **in the Page Setup group, then click** Next Page **in the Section Breaks section**

   Word inserts a next page section break, shown as a dotted double line, above the blank paragraph above the heading, as shown in FIGURE 4-6. You might need to scroll or zoom out to see both the section break and the insertion point in your document window. When you insert a section break at the beginning of a paragraph, Word inserts the break at the end of the previous paragraph. The document now has two sections. Notice that the status bar indicates the insertion point is in Section 2.

4. **Click the** Insert tab, **click the** Page Number button **in the Header & Footer group, point to** Bottom of Page, **then click** Plain Number 3 **in the Simple section**

   A page number field containing the number 2 is right-aligned in the Footer area at the bottom of page 2 of the document. The document text is dimmed.

QUICK TIP

To change the location or formatting of page numbers, click the Page Number button, point to a page number location, then select a format from the gallery.

5. **Select the** page number, **click the** Bold button B **on the Mini toolbar, click the** Font Color button A **on the Mini toolbar, then save your changes**

   The page number is bold and blue. If you want to change the numbering format or start page numbering with a different number, you can simply click the Page Number button, click Format Page Numbers, and then choose from the options in the Page Number Format dialog box.

FIGURE 4-6: **Next Page section break**

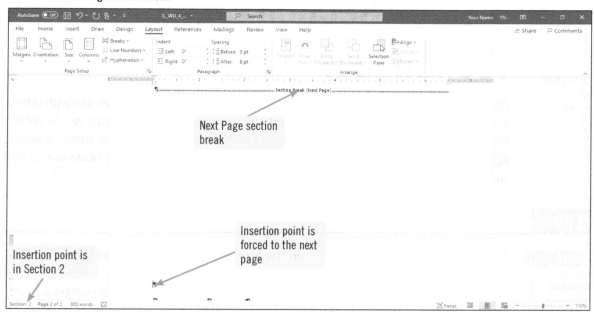

FIGURE 4-6: **Next Page section break**

Using sections to vary the layout of a document

Dividing a document into sections allows you to vary the layout of a document. In addition to applying different column settings to sections, you can apply different margins, page orientation, paper size, vertical alignment, header and footer, page numbering, footnotes, endnotes, and other page layout settings. For example, if you are formatting a report that includes a table with many columns, you might want to change the table's page orientation to landscape so that it is easier to read. To do this, you would insert a section break before and after the table to create a section that contains only the table, and then you would change the page orientation of the section that contains the table to landscape. If the table does not fill the page, you could also change the vertical alignment of the table so that it is centered vertically on the page. To do this, use the Vertical alignment arrow on the Layout tab of the Page Setup dialog box.

To check or change the page layout settings for an individual section, place the insertion point in the section, then open the Page Setup dialog box. Select any options you want to change, click the Apply to arrow, click This section, then click OK. When you select This section, the settings are applied to the current section only. When you select This point forward, the settings are applied to the current section and all sections that follow it. If you select Whole document, the settings are applied to all the sections in the document. Use the Apply to arrow in the Columns dialog box or the Footnote and Endnote dialog box to change those settings for a section.

(Continued)

Insert a Section Break (Continued)

**Learning
Outcomes**
- Manage headers and footers
- Insert property controls

Once you have divided a document into sections, you can format each section with different header and footer, column, margin, page orientation, and other page layout settings. By default, a document is formatted as a single section, but you can divide a document into as many sections as you like. **CASE** *You insert a Quick Part property control in the header and format the header using a built-in header style.*

STEPS

TROUBLE
If the Header & Footer contextual tab is not showing, click the Header & Footer tab.

1. **Click the** Go to Header button **in the Navigation group, click the** Quick Parts button **in the Insert group, point to** Document Property, **then click** Title

   A property control for the Title property is added to the header. A **property control** is a content control that contains document property information, such as title, company, or author. You can assign or update a document property by typing directly in a property control or by typing in the Properties boxes on the Info screen.

2. **Type** Advertising Campaign Prospectus **in the Title property control**

   The document title is added to the header. When you assign or update a document property by typing in a property control, all controls of the same type in the document are updated with the change, as well as the corresponding property field on the Info screen.

QUICK TIP
To remove a header, click in the Header or Footer area, click the Header button in the Header & Footer group, then click Remove Header. To remove a footer, click the Footer button, then click Remove Footer.

3. **Click the** Header button **in the Header & Footer group, scroll down the gallery, click** Integral, **then scroll until the bottom of page 1 and the top of page 2 are visible in the document window**

   The header design changes to the Integral design, as shown in FIGURE 4-7. The headers and footers are the same in Section 1 and Section 2. If you wanted to create different headers and footers for different sections, you would need to break the link between sections by clicking the Link to Previous button in the Navigation group. The Link to Previous button is a toggle button that you can use to link and unlink headers and footers between sections in a multi-section document.

4. **Click the** Close Header and Footer button **in the Close group**

   The header and footer areas close and are dimmed. The body of the document is now active.

5. **Click the** Home tab, **click the** Show/Hide ¶ button ¶, **then save your changes**

FIGURE 4-7: Integral header

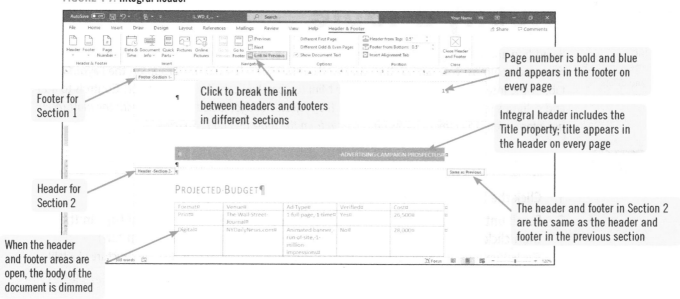

Footer for Section 1 ← Footer -Section 1-

Click to break the link between headers and footers in different sections

Page number is bold and blue and appears in the footer on every page

Integral header includes the Title property; title appears in the header on every page

ADVERTISING·CAMPAIGN·PROSPECTUS

Header for Section 2 ← Header -Section 2-

Same as Previous

The header and footer in Section 2 are the same as the header and footer in the previous section

PROJECTED·BUDGET¶

Format¤	Venue¤	Ad·Type¤	Verified¤	Cost¤	¤
Print¤	The·Wall·Street·Journal¤	1·full-page,·1·time¤	Yes¤	26,500¤	¤
Digital¤	NYDailyNews.com¤	Animated·banner,·run-of-site,·1-million-impressions¤	No¤	28,000¤	¤

When the header and footer areas are open, the body of the document is dimmed

Adding a custom header or footer to the gallery

When you design a header that you want to use again in other documents, you can add it to the Header gallery by saving it as a building block. Building blocks are reusable pieces of formatted content or document parts, including headers and footers, page numbers, and text boxes, that are stored in galleries. **Building blocks** include predesigned content that comes with Word, as well as content that you create and save for future use. For example, you might create a custom header that contains your company name and logo and is formatted using the fonts, border, and colors you use in all company documents.

To add a custom header to the Header gallery, select all the text in the header, including the last paragraph mark, click the Header button, and then click Save Selection to Header Gallery. In the Create New Building Block dialog box that opens, type

a unique name for the header in the Name box, click the Gallery arrow and select the appropriate gallery, verify that the Category is General, and then type a brief description of the new header design in the Description box. This description appears in a ScreenTip when you point to the custom header in the gallery. When you are finished, click OK. The new header appears in the Header gallery under the General category.

To remove a custom header from the Header gallery, click the Header button in the Header & Footer group, scroll to the new header, right-click it in the Header gallery, click Organize and Delete, make sure the appropriate building block is selected in the Building Blocks Organizer that opens, click Delete, click Yes, and then click Close. You can follow the same process to add or remove a custom footer to the Footer gallery.

Modify a Table

By adding and deleting rows and columns, you can modify the structure of a table. To add and remove rows and columns, you can use the commands in the Rows & Columns group on the Layout contextual tab, or the Insert and Delete buttons on the Mini toolbar. You can also use the Insert Controls to add rows and columns to a table. **CASE** *You edit the Projected Budget table to update it with the most recent budget information. You remove a row and column from the table and add two rows.*

STEPS

1. **Click the** View tab, **then click** Page Width **in the Zoom group**

2. **Scroll until the table is at the top of the document window, click** Taxi tops **in the table, then click the** Layout contextual tab **(to the right of the Table Design tab)**
   The buttons on Layout tab (the contextual tab for tables) can be used to alter the structure of a table.

3. **Click the** Delete button ▦ **in the Rows and Columns group, then click** Delete Rows
   The Taxi tops row is deleted from the table.

4. **Place the pointer over the** Verified column top border **until the pointer changes to ↓, then click**
   The entire Verified column is selected, as shown in **FIGURE 4-8**.

5. **Click the** Delete button ▦ **on the Mini toolbar, then click** Delete Columns
   The Verified column is deleted from the table.

6. **Place the** ⬈ **pointer at the left edge of the table over the border between the** NYDailyNews.com **and** NYPost.com **rows to display the Insert Control, then click the Insert Control**
   A new row is added between the NYDailyNews.com and NYPost.com rows.

7. **Click in the** first cell **in the new row, type** Sign, **press TAB, type** Subway cars, **press TAB, type** 1000 panels, 2 weeks, **press TAB, type** 18,000, **then save your changes**
   Text is added to the new row, as shown in **FIGURE 4-9**.

Copying and moving rows and columns

You can copy and move rows and columns within a table in the same manner you copy and move text. Select the row or column you want to move, then use the Copy or Cut button to place the selection on the Clipboard. Place the insertion point in the location where you want to insert the row or column, then click the Paste button to paste the selection. Rows are inserted above the row containing the insertion point; columns are inserted to the left of the column containing the insertion point. You can also copy or move columns and rows by selecting them and using the pointer to drag them to a new location in the table. To copy or move an entire table, select the entire table and then use the Cut, Copy, and Paste commands.

FIGURE 4-8: **Column is selected**

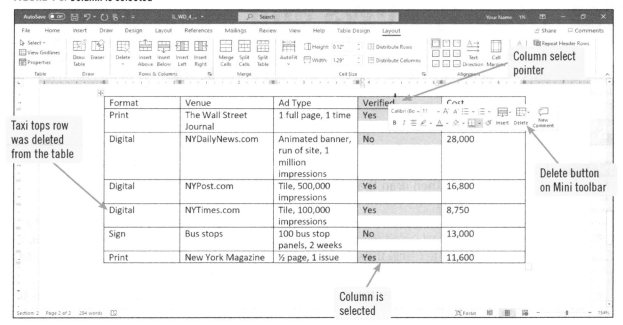

Taxi tops row
was deleted
from the table

Column select
pointer

Delete button
on Mini toolbar

Column is
selected

FIGURE 4-9: **New row in table**

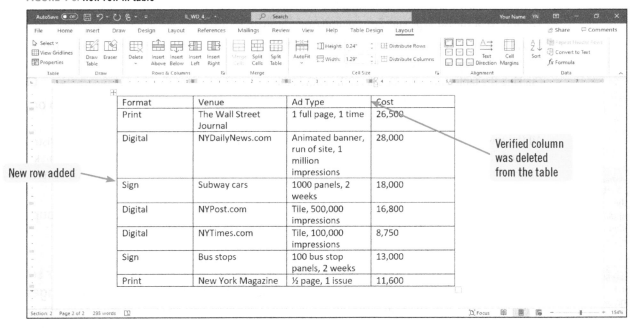

New row added

Verified column
was deleted
from the table

Word

Modify Rows and Columns

Once you create a table, you can easily adjust the size of columns and rows to make the table easier to read. You can change the width of columns and the height of rows by dragging a border, by using the AutoFit command, or by setting precise measurements in the Cell Size group on the Layout contextual tab. **CASE** *You adjust the size of the columns and rows to make the table more attractive and easier to read. You also center the text vertically in each table cell.*

STEPS

1. **Position the pointer over the** border between Format and Venue **until the pointer changes to** ◄‖► **then drag the** border **left to approximately the** ½" **mark on the horizontal ruler**

   The dotted line that appears as you drag represents the border. Dragging the column border changes the width of the first and second columns: the first column is narrower and the second column is wider. When dragging a border to change the width of an entire column, make sure no cells are selected in the column. You can also drag a row border up or down to change the height of the row above it.

2. **Position the pointer over the** Venue column right border **until the pointer changes to** ◄‖► **then double-click**

   Double-clicking a column border automatically resizes the column to fit the text.

3. **Double-click the** Ad Type column right border **with the** ◄‖► **pointer, then double-click the** Cost column right border **with the** ◄‖► **pointer**

   The widths of the Ad Type and Cost columns are adjusted.

4. **Move the pointer over the** table, **then click the** table move handle ⊞ **that appears outside the upper-left corner of the table**

   Clicking the table move handle selects the entire table.

5. **With the** table **selected, click the** Distribute Rows button ⊞ **in the Cell Size group on the Layout contextual tab, then click in the table to deselect it**

   All the rows in the table become the same height, as shown in FIGURE 4-10. You can also use the Distribute Columns button to make all the columns the same width, or you can use the AutoFit button to make the width of the columns fit the text, to adjust the width of the columns so the table is justified between the margins, or to set fixed column widths.

6. **Click in the** Ad Type column, **click the** Table Column Width box **in the Cell Size group, type** 3.5, **then press** ENTER

   The width of the Ad Type column changes to 3.5".

7. **Click the** Select button **in the Table group, click** Select Table, **click the** Align Center Left button ▤ **in the Alignment group, click to deselect the table, then save your changes**

   The text is centered vertically in each table cell, as shown in FIGURE 4-11. You can use the alignment buttons in the Alignment group to change the vertical and horizontal alignment of the text in selected cells or in the entire table.

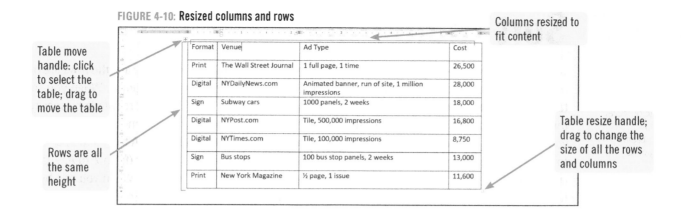

FIGURE 4-10: Resized columns and rows

Columns resized to fit content

Table move handle: click to select the table; drag to move the table

Table resize handle; drag to change the size of all the rows and columns

Rows are all the same height

Format	Venue	Ad Type	Cost
Print	The Wall Street Journal	1 full page, 1 time	26,500
Digital	NYDailyNews.com	Animated banner, run of site, 1 million impressions	28,000
Sign	Subway cars	1000 panels, 2 weeks	18,000
Digital	NYPost.com	Tile, 500,000 impressions	16,800
Digital	NYTimes.com	Tile, 100,000 impressions	8,750
Sign	Bus stops	100 bus stop panels, 2 weeks	13,000
Print	New York Magazine	½ page, 1 issue	11,600

FIGURE 4-11: Text centered vertically in cells

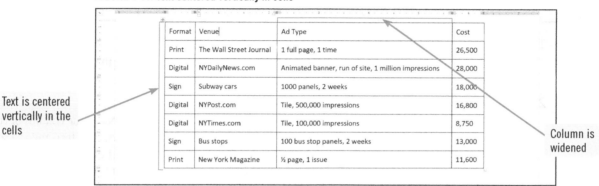

Text is centered vertically in the cells

Column is widened

Format	Venue	Ad Type	Cost
Print	The Wall Street Journal	1 full page, 1 time	26,500
Digital	NYDailyNews.com	Animated banner, run of site, 1 million impressions	28,000
Sign	Subway cars	1000 panels, 2 weeks	18,000
Digital	NYPost.com	Tile, 500,000 impressions	16,800
Digital	NYTimes.com	Tile, 100,000 impressions	8,750
Sign	Bus stops	100 bus stop panels, 2 weeks	13,000
Print	New York Magazine	½ page, 1 issue	11,600

Word

Setting advanced table properties

When you want to wrap text around a table, indent a table, or set other advanced table properties, you click the Properties command in the Table group on the Layout tab to open the Table Properties dialog box, shown in FIGURE 4-12. Using the Table tab in this dialog box, you can set a precise width for the table, change the horizontal alignment of the table between the margins, indent the table, and set text wrapping options for the table. You can also click Options on the Table tab to open the Table Options dialog box, which you use to customize the table's default cell margins and the spacing between table cells. Alternatively, click Borders and Shading on the Table tab to open the Borders and Shading dialog box, which you can use to create a custom format for the table.

The Row, Column, and Cell tabs in the Table Properties dialog box allow you to set an exact height for rows, to specify an exact width for columns, and to indicate an exact size for individual cells. The Alt Text tab is used to add alternative text for a table, such as a description of its content, so that the table can be understood by a person using a screen reader.

FIGURE 4-12: Table Properties dialog box

Table Properties   ? ×

Table   Row   Column   Cell   Alt Text

Size
☑ Preferred width: 98.5%   Measure in: Percent

Alignment
Left   Center   Right   Indent from left: 0"

Text wrapping
None   Around   Positioning...

Borders and Shading...   Options...

OK   Cancel

Sort Table Data

Tables are often easier to interpret and analyze when the data is **sorted**, which means the rows are organized in alphabetical or sequential order based on the data in one or more columns. When you sort a table, Word arranges all the table data according to the criteria you set. You set sort criteria by specifying the column (or columns) you want to sort by and indicating the sort order—ascending or descending—you want to use. **Ascending order** lists data alphabetically or sequentially (from A to Z, 0 to 9, or earliest to latest). **Descending order** lists data in reverse alphabetical or sequential order (from Z to A, 9 to 0, or latest to earliest). You can sort using the data in one column or multiple columns. When you sort by multiple columns, you must select primary, secondary, and tertiary sort criteria. You use the Sort command in the Data group on the Layout tab to sort a table. **CASE** *You sort the table so that all ads of the same format type are listed together. You also add secondary sort criteria so that the ads within each format type are listed in descending order by cost.*

STEPS

1. **Click to place the insertion point anywhere in the table**

   To sort an entire table, you simply need to place the insertion point anywhere in the table. If you want to sort specific rows only, then you must select the rows you want to sort.

2. **Click the Sort button in the Data group on the Layout tab**

   The Sort dialog box opens, as shown in FIGURE 4-13. You use this dialog box to specify the column or columns you want to sort by, the type of information you are sorting (text, numbers, or dates), and the sort order (ascending or descending). Column 1 is selected by default in the Sort by list box. Since you want to sort your table first by the information in the first column—the Format type (Print, Digital, or Sign)—you don't change the Sort by criteria.

3. **Click the Header row option button in the My list has section to select it**

   The table includes a **header row**, which is the first row of a table that contains the column headings. You must select the Header row option button first when you do not want the header row included in the sort.

4. **Click the Descending option button in the Sort by section**

   The information in the Format column will be sorted in descending—or reverse alphabetical—order, so that the "Sign" ads will be listed first, followed by the "Print" ads, and then the "Digital" ads.

5. **Click the Then by arrow in the first Then by section, click Cost, verify that Number appears in the Type box, then click the Descending option button**

   Within the Digital, Print, and Sign groups, the rows will be sorted by the cost of the ad, which is the information contained in the Cost column. The rows will appear in descending order within each group, with the most expensive ad listed first.

6. **Click OK, then deselect the table**

   The rows in the table are sorted first by the information in the Format column and second by the information in the Cost column, as shown in FIGURE 4-14. The first row of the table, which is the header row, is not included in the sort.

7. **Save your changes to the document**

FIGURE 4-13: **Sort dialog box**

Select the primary sort column

Include or exclude the header row in the sort

Select the type of data in the sort column

Choose the sort order

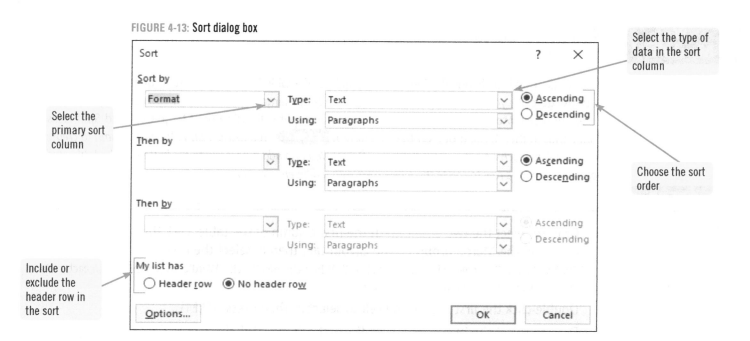

FIGURE 4-14: **Sorted table**

Header row is not included in the sort

First, rows are sorted by type in descending order

Second, within each type, rows are sorted by cost in descending order

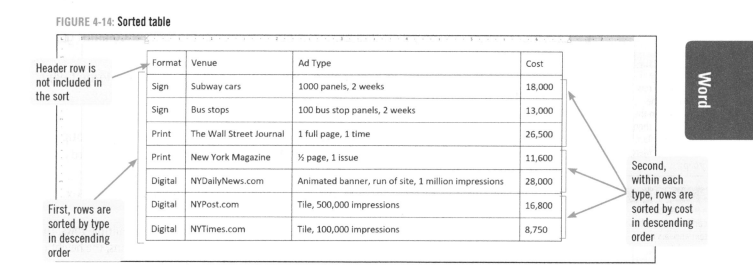

Format	Venue	Ad Type	Cost
Sign	Subway cars	1000 panels, 2 weeks	18,000
Sign	Bus stops	100 bus stop panels, 2 weeks	13,000
Print	The Wall Street Journal	1 full page, 1 time	26,500
Print	New York Magazine	½ page, 1 issue	11,600
Digital	NYDailyNews.com	Animated banner, run of site, 1 million impressions	28,000
Digital	NYPost.com	Tile, 500,000 impressions	16,800
Digital	NYTimes.com	Tile, 100,000 impressions	8,750

Word

Sorting lists and paragraphs

In addition to sorting table data, you can use the Sort command to alphabetize text or sort numerical data. When you want to sort data that is not formatted as a table, such as lists and paragraphs, you use the Sort command in the Paragraph group on the Home tab. To sort lists and paragraphs, select the items you want included in the sort, then click the Sort button. In the Sort Text dialog box, use the Sort by arrow to select the sort by criteria (such as paragraphs or fields), use the Type arrow to select the type of data (text, numbers, or dates), and then click the Ascending or Descending option button to choose a sort order.

When sorting text information in a document, the term "fields" refers to text or numbers that are separated by a character, such as a tab or a comma. For example, you might want to sort a list of names alphabetically. If the names you want to sort are listed in "Last name, First name" order, then last name and first name are each considered a field. You can choose to sort the list in alphabetical order by last name or by first name. Use the Options button in the Sort Text dialog box to specify the character that separates the fields in your lists or paragraphs, along with other sort options.

Split and Merge Cells

A convenient way to change the format and structure of a table is to merge or split the table cells. When you **merge** cells, you combine adjacent cells into a single larger cell. When you **split** a cell, you divide an existing cell into multiple cells. You can merge and split cells using the Merge Cells and Split Cells commands in the Merge group on the Layout tab. **CASE** *You merge cells in the first column to create a single cell for each ad type—Sign, Print, and Digital. You also add a new row to the bottom of the table, and split the cells in the row to create three new rows with a different structure.*

STEPS

TROUBLE
If you click below the table to deselect it, the active tab changes to the Home tab. If necessary, click in the table, then click the Layout tab to continue with the steps in this lesson.

1. **Drag to select the two** Sign cells **in the first column of the table, click the** Merge Cells button **in the Merge group on the Layout tab, then deselect the text**

   The two Sign cells merge to become a single cell. When you merge cells, Word converts the text in each cell into a separate paragraph in the merged cell.

2. **Double-click the first** Sign **in the cell to select it, then press** DELETE

3. **Drag to select the two** Print cells **in the first column, click the** Merge Cells button, **type** Print, **drag to select the three** Digital cells, **click the** Merge Cells button, **then type** Digital

   The two Sign cells merge to become one cell, the two Print cells merge to become one cell, and the three Digital cells merge to become one cell.

4. **Click the** NYTimes.com cell, **then click the** Insert Below button **in the Rows & Columns group**

   A row is added to the bottom of the table.

QUICK TIP
To split a table in two, click the row you want to be the first row in the second table, then click the Split Table button in the Merge group.

5. **Drag to select the** first three cells **in the new last row of the table, click the** Merge Cells button, **then deselect the cell**

   The three cells in the row merge to become a single cell.

6. **Click the** first cell in the last row, **then click the** Split Cells button **in the Merge group**

   The Split Cells dialog box opens, as shown in FIGURE 4-15. You use this dialog box to split the selected cell or cells into a specific number of columns and rows.

QUICK TIP
If the cell you split contains text, all the text appears in the upper-left cell.

7. **Type** 1 **in the Number of columns box, press** TAB, **type** 3 **in the Number of rows box, click** OK, **then deselect the cells**

   The single cell is divided into three rows of equal height. When you split a cell into multiple rows, the width of the original column does not change. When you split a cell into multiple columns, the height of the original row does not change.

8. **Click the** last cell **in the Cost column, click the** Split Cells button, **type** 1 **in the Number of columns box, press** TAB, **type** 3 **in the Number of rows box, click** OK, **then save your changes**

   The cell is split into three rows, as shown in FIGURE 4-16. The last three rows now have only two columns.

Changing cell margins

By default, table cells have .08" left and right cell margins with no spacing between the cells, but you can adjust these settings for a table using the Cell Margins button in the Alignment group on the Layout tab. First, place the insertion point in the table, and then click the Cell Margins button to open the Table Options dialog box. Enter new settings for the top, bottom, left, and right cell margins in the boxes in the Default cell margins section of the dialog box, or select the Allow spacing between cells check box and then enter a setting in the Cell spacing section to increase the spacing between table cells. You can also deselect the Automatically resize to fit contents check box in the Options section of the dialog box to turn off the setting that causes table cells to widen to fit the text as you type. Any settings you change in the Table Options dialog box are applied to the entire table.

FIGURE 4-15: **Split Cells dialog box**

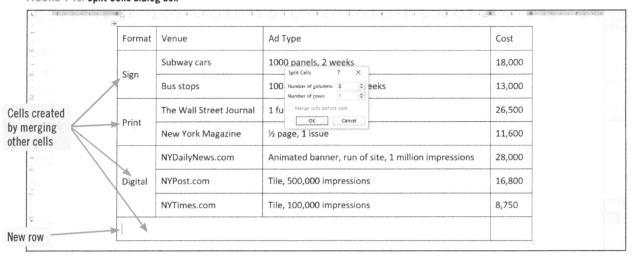

FIGURE 4-15: **Split Cells dialog box**

Cells created by merging other cells

New row

FIGURE 4-16: **Cells split into three rows**

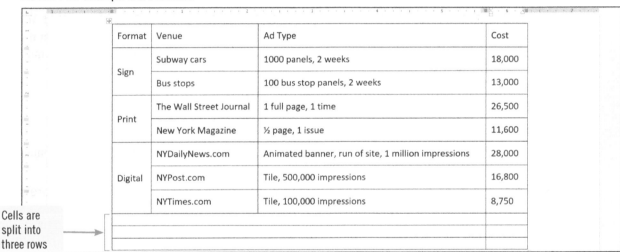

Cells are split into three rows

Using tables to lay out a page

Tables are often used to display information for quick reference and analysis, but you can also use tables to structure the layout of a page. You can insert any kind of information in the cell of a table—including graphics, bulleted lists, charts, and other tables (called **nested tables**). For example, you might use a table to lay out a résumé, a newsletter, or a webpage. When you use a table to lay out a page, you generally remove the table borders to hide the table structure from the reader. After you remove borders, it can be helpful to display the table gridlines on screen while you work. **Gridlines** are dotted lines that show the boundaries of cells, but do not print. If your document will be viewed online—for example, if you are planning to email your résumé to potential employers—you should turn off the display of gridlines before you distribute the document so that it looks the same online as it looks when printed. To turn gridlines off or on, click the View Gridlines button in the Table group on the Layout tab.

Word

Perform Calculations in Tables

Learning
Outcomes
• Sum numbers in
a table
• Update a field
• Insert a formula

If your table includes numerical information, you can perform simple calculations in the table. The Formula command allows you to quickly total the numbers in a column or row, and to perform other simple calculations, such as averages. When you calculate data in a table using formulas, you use cell references to refer to the cells in the table. Each cell has a unique **cell reference** composed of a letter and a number; the letter represents its column and the number represents its row. For example, the cell in the third row of the fourth column is cell D3. FIGURE 4-17 shows the cell references in a simple table. **CASE** *You use the Formula command to calculate the total cost of the New York ad campaign. You also add information about the budgeted cost, and create a formula to calculate the difference between the total and budgeted costs.*

STEPS

QUICK TIP
You must type a zero in any blank cell in a row or column before using the SUM function.

1. **Click the first blank cell in column 1, type** Total Cost, **press TAB, then click the** Formula **button in the Data group on the Layout tab**

   The Formula dialog box opens, as shown in FIGURE 4-18. The SUM function appears in the Formula box followed by the reference for the cells to include in the calculation, (ABOVE). The formula =SUM(ABOVE) indicates that Word will sum the numbers in the cells above the active cell.

2. **Click OK**

   Word totals the numbers in the cells above the active cell and inserts the resulting sum as a field. You can use the SUM function to quickly total the numbers in a column or a row. If the cell you select is at the bottom of a column of numbers, Word totals the column. If the cell is at the right end of a row of numbers, Word totals the row.

3. **Select** 8,750 **in the cell above the total, then type** 9,500

   If you change a number that is part of a calculation, you must recalculate the field result.

4. **Press DOWN ARROW, right-click the cell, then click** Update Field

   The resulting sum in the cell is updated. When the insertion point is in a cell that contains a formula, you can also press F9 to update the field result.

5. **Press TAB, type** Budgeted **in the cell below Total Cost, press TAB, type** 125,000, **press TAB, type** Difference **in the cell below Budgeted, then press TAB**

   The insertion point is in the last cell of the table.

6. **Click the** Formula **button**

   The Formula dialog box opens. Word proposes to sum the numbers above the active cell, but you want to insert a formula that calculates the difference between the total and budgeted costs. You can type simple custom formulas using a plus sign (+) for addition, a minus sign (–) for subtraction, an asterisk (*) for multiplication, and a slash (/) for division.

QUICK TIP
Cell references are determined by the number of columns in each row, not by the number of columns in the table. Rows 9 and 10 have only two columns: A and B.

7. **Select** =SUM(ABOVE) **in the Formula box, then type** =B9–B10

   You must type an equal sign (=) to indicate that the text following the equal sign (=) is a formula. You want to subtract the budgeted cost in the second column of row 10 from the total cost in the second column of row 9; therefore, you type a formula to subtract the value in cell B10 from the value in cell B9.

8. **Click OK, then save your changes**

   The difference appears in the cell, as shown in FIGURE 4-19.

Formatting Tables and Documents

FIGURE 4-17: **Cell references in a table**

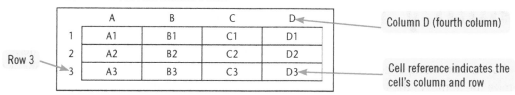

FIGURE 4-18: **Formula dialog box**

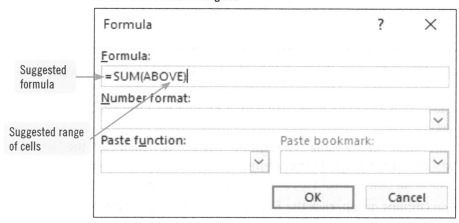

FIGURE 4-19: **Difference calculated in table**

Format	Venue	Ad Type	Cost
Sign	Subway cars	1000 panels, 2 weeks	18,000
	Bus stops	100 bus stop panels, 2 weeks	13,000
Print	The Wall Street Journal	1 full page, 1 time	26,500
	New York Magazine	½ page, 1 issue	11,600
Digital	NYDailyNews.com	Animated banner, run of site, 1 million impressions	28,000
	NYPost.com	Tile, 500,000 impressions	16,800
	NYTimes.com	Tile, 100,000 impressions	9,500
Total Cost			123,400
Budgeted			125,000
Difference			-1,600

Cell A9
Cell A10
Cell B9
Cell B10
B9–B10= –1600

Working with formulas

In addition to the SUM function, Word includes formulas for averaging, counting, and rounding data, to name a few. To use a Word formula, delete any text in the Formula box, type =, click the Paste function arrow in the Formula dialog box, select a function, and then insert the cell references of the cells you want to include in the calculation in parentheses after the name of the function. When entering formulas, you must separate cell references by a comma. For example, if you want to average the values in cells A1, B3, and C4, enter the formula =AVERAGE(A1,B3,C4). You must separate cell ranges by a colon. For example, to total the values in cells A1 through A9, enter the formula =SUM(A1:A9). To display the result of a calculation in a particular number format, such as a decimal percentage (0.00%), click the Number format arrow in the Formula dialog box and select a number format. Word inserts the result of a calculation as a field in the selected cell.

Word

Word Module 4

Modify Table Style Options

Learning Outcome
- Format a table
- Align cells in a table

Applying a table style is a fast way to format a table using borders, shading, fonts, alignment, colors, and other formatting effects. Once you apply a table style, you can use the table style options to customize the format of the table, and the alignment buttons to adjust the position of text within the table. **CASE** *You want to enhance the appearance of the table, so you apply a table style to the table, adjust the table style options, and then change the alignment of text in the table cells.*

STEPS

1. **Scroll so the top of the table is at the top of the document window, then click the Table Design tab**
   The Table Design tab includes buttons for applying table styles and for adding, removing, and customizing borders and shading in a table.

> **QUICK TIP**
> Click Clear in the gallery of table styles to remove all borders, shading, and other style elements from the table.

2. **Click the More button in the Table Styles group, scroll down, then click the List Table 2 – Accent 1 style (the second style in the second row of the List Tables section)**
   This style makes some of the table data easier to read but is confusing, as shown in FIGURE 4-20.

3. **In the Table Style Options group, click the First Column check box to clear it, click the Banded Rows check box to clear it, then click the Banded Columns check box to select it**
   The bold formatting is removed from the first column, the shading is removed from the table rows, and shading is added to the table columns. When the banded columns or banded rows setting is active, the odd columns or rows are formatted differently from the even columns or rows.

4. **Click the First Column check box to select it, then click the Banded Columns check box to clear it**
   The bold formatting is restored to the first column, and the shading is removed from the table columns, making the data easier to read. You can also use the check boxes in the Table Style Options group to change the Header row, Total row, and Last Column formatting in a table.

> **TROUBLE**
> The Colors button is located on the Design tab, not the Table Design tab.

5. **Click the Design tab, click the Colors button, then click Green**
   The color palette for the document changes to Green.

6. **Click the Layout contextual tab, then click the View Gridlines button in the Table group to display table gridlines if they are not already displayed**
   The View Gridlines button is a toggle button. You use it to turn the display of table gridlines on and off. Gridlines display on screen but do not print. You want the gridlines to be turned on.

> **TROUBLE**
> When you select the Format column, the first column in the last three rows is also selected.

7. **Click the table move handle, click the Align Center Left button in the Alignment group, select the Format column, click the Align Center button, select the Cost column, then click the Align Center Right button**
   First, the data in the table is left-aligned and centered vertically, then the data in the Format column is centered, and finally the data in the Cost column is right-aligned.

8. **Select the last three rows of the table, click the Bold button B on the Mini toolbar twice, then click the Align Center Right button in the Alignment group on the Layout tab on the Ribbon**
   The text in the last three rows is right-aligned and bold is applied.

> **QUICK TIP**
> You can also use the alignment buttons in the Paragraph group on the Home tab to change the alignment of text in a table.

9. **Select the first row of the table, click the Center button on the Mini toolbar, click the Font Size arrow on the Mini toolbar, click 12, deselect the row, then save your changes**
   The text in the header row is centered and enlarged, as shown in FIGURE 4-21.

FIGURE 4-20: **List Table 2 - Accent 1 style applied to table**

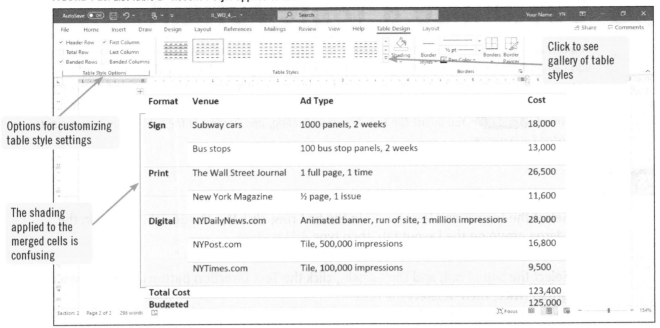

Options for customizing table style settings

Click to see gallery of table styles

The shading applied to the merged cells is confusing

FIGURE 4-21: **Table format modified with table style options**

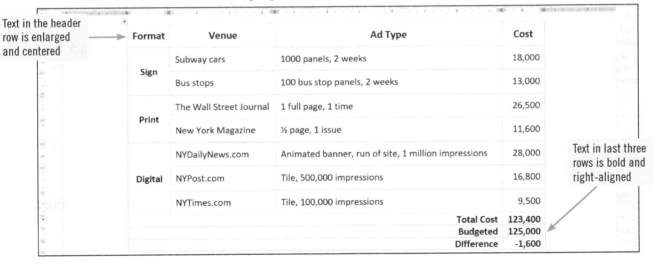

Text in the header row is enlarged and centered

Text in last three rows is bold and right-aligned

Word

Formatting Tables and Documents

WD 4-21

Customize a Table Format

You can also use the formatting tools available in Word to create your own table designs. For example, you can add or remove borders and shading; vary the line style, thickness, and color of borders; and change the orientation of text from horizontal to vertical. In addition, if a table is located at the top of a document, you can press ENTER at the beginning of a table to move the table down one line in the document. **CASE** ▶ *You adjust the text direction, shading, and borders in the table to make it easier to understand at a glance.*

STEPS

1. **Select the Format and Venue cells in the first row, click the Merge Cells button in the Merge group on the Layout tab, then type Ad Location**

   The two cells are combined into a single cell containing the text "Ad Location".

2. **Select the Sign, Print, and Digital cells, click the Text Direction button in the Alignment group twice, then deselect the cells**

   The text in each cell is rotated 270 degrees.

3. **Position the pointer over the Sign cell right border until the pointer changes to ◄‖►, then drag the border left to approximately the ¼" mark on the horizontal ruler**

   The width of the column containing the vertical text narrows.

4. **Click Sign to place the insertion point in the Sign cell, click the Table Design tab, then click the Shading arrow in the Table Styles group**

   The gallery of shading colors for the Green theme color palette opens.

5. **Click Lime, Accent 2 in the gallery as shown in FIGURE 4-22, click the Print cell, click the Shading arrow, click Dark Teal, Accent 4, click the Digital cell, click the Shading arrow, then click Turquoise, Accent 6**

   Colored shading is applied to each cell.

6. **Select the header row, click the Shading arrow ◇▾ on the Mini toolbar, click Green, Accent 1, click the Font color arrow A on the Mini toolbar, then click White, Background 1**

   Shading is applied to the header row and the font color changes to white for better contrast.

7. **Click the Borders arrow in the Borders group, click View Gridlines to turn off the display of gridlines, select the last three rows of the table, click the Borders arrow, click No Border on the Borders menu, then click in the table to deselect the rows**

   The top, bottom, left, and right borders are removed from each cell in the selected rows.

8. **Select the Total Cost row, click the Borders arrow, click Top Border, click the 125,000 cell, click the Borders arrow, then click Bottom Border**

   The active border color is black. A black top border is added to the Total Cost row, and a black bottom border is added below 125,000. You can use the buttons in the Borders group to change the active color, line weight, line style, and border style settings before adding a border to a table.

9. **Select the Total Cost row, click the Borders arrow, click Borders and Shading, click the Color arrow, click Green, Accent 1, click the top border in the Preview area, click OK, deselect the row, then save your changes**

   The top border changes to green. The completed table is shown in FIGURE 4-23.

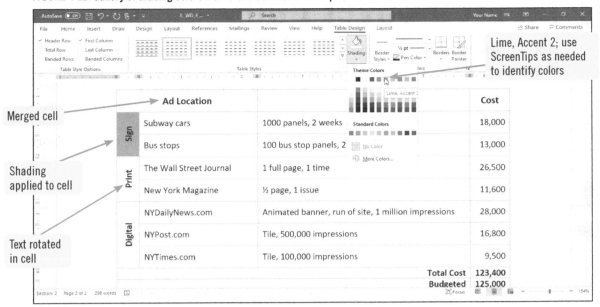

FIGURE 4-23: **Completed table**

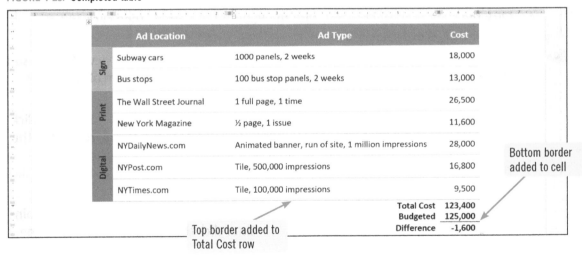

Drawing a table

The Word Draw Table feature allows you to draw table cells exactly where you want them. To draw a table, click the Table button on the Insert tab, and then click Draw Table. If a table is already started, you can click the Draw Table button in the Draw group on the Layout tab to turn on the Draw pointer, and then click and drag to draw a cell. Using the same method, you can draw borders within the cell to create columns and rows, or draw additional cells attached to the first cell. Click the Draw Table button to turn off the draw feature. The borders you draw are added using the active line style, line weight, and pen color settings found in the Borders group on the Table Design tab.

If you want to remove a border from a table, click the Eraser button in the Draw group to activate the Eraser pointer, and then click the border you want to remove. Click the Eraser button to turn off the erase feature. You can use the Draw pointer and the Eraser pointer to change the structure of any table, not just the tables you draw from scratch.

Insert a Cover Page

Learning
Outcomes
• Manage a cover
  page
• Add a watermark

To quickly finalize a report, you can insert one of the many predesigned cover pages that come with Word. Cover page designs range from conservative and business-like to colorful and attention grabbing. Each cover page design includes placeholder text and property controls that you can replace with your own information. You can also customize a document by adding a watermark. A **watermark** is a WordArt or other graphic object that appears lightly shaded behind text in a document. **CASE** ▶ *You finalize the project report by inserting an eye-catching cover page that mirrors the design of the report. You also add a "Confidential" watermark.*

STEPS

QUICK TIP
Click the Blank Page button in the Pages group to insert a blank page at the insertion point.

1. **Click the** View tab, **then click the** Multiple Pages button
   Both pages of the document appear in the document window.

2. **Click the** Insert tab, **then click the** Cover Page arrow **in the Pages group**
   The gallery of cover pages opens. Each page design includes placeholder text and property controls. The page designs are shown using the active color palette, which is Green.

QUICK TIP
To remove a cover page, click the Cover Page arrow, then click Remove Current Cover Page.

3. **Scroll down the gallery, then click** Semaphore
   The Semaphore cover page is added at the beginning of the document. Notice that the document title was added automatically to the Title property control.

4. **Click the** Date property control, **click the** Publish Date arrow, **then click** Today
   The date changes to the current date.

TROUBLE
If your name is not entered in the Author property control, right-click the Author control, click Remove Content Control, select the text that remains, then type your name.

5. **Click the** View tab, **click the** Page Width button, **then scroll down to view the title, subtitle, author, company name, and company address controls at the bottom of the page**
   Your name is already entered in the Author property control.

6. **Click the** Document Subtitle property control, **type** JCL Talent, New York, **right-click the** Company Name property control, **click** Remove Content Control, **right-click the** Company address property control, **then click** Remove Content Control
   The Company Name and Company address controls are removed from the cover page, as shown in FIGURE 4-24.

7. **Click the** View tab, **click the** Multiple Pages button, **click to place the insertion point in the middle of** page 2, **click the** Design tab, **then click the** Watermark button **in the Page Background group**
   A gallery of watermarks opens. You can apply one of the preformatted watermarks or create a custom watermark.

QUICK TIP
To remove a watermark, click the Watermark button, then click Remove Watermark.

8. **Click** Confidential 1, **then save your changes**
   The word "Confidential" appears lightly shaded behind the text on each page of the document, but not the cover page. The completed document is shown in FIGURE 4-25.

9. **sam** ⬆ **Submit the document to your instructor, close the file, then exit Word.**

FIGURE 4-24: Semaphore cover page

Title property

Subtitle property

Author property

FIGURE 4-25: Completed document

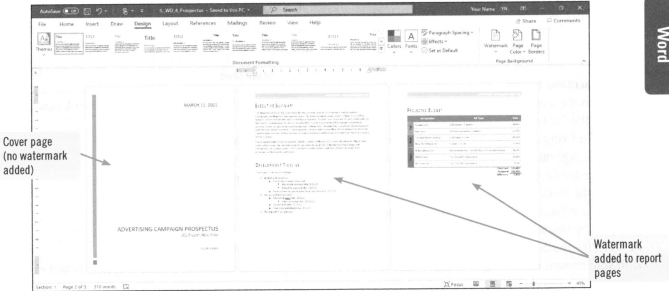

Cover page
(no watermark
added)

Watermark
added to report
pages

Practice

Skills Review

1. Modify character spacing.

a. Start Word, open the file IL_WD_4-2.docx from the location where you store your Data Files, then save it as **IL_WD_4_CarInsurance**.

b. Select the heading Car Insurance Rates Vary By State, then change the font size to 36.

c. Format the heading in small caps, then change the character scale to 80% and the character spacing to Expanded by 1 point.

d. Change the font size of the heading to 24, then use the Format Painter to copy the formatting of the heading to the headings "The New England States" and "Car Insurance Rates in New England".

e. Turn off Format Painter and save your changes.

2. Work with indents.

a. Scroll up, select the list that begins with "Age" and ends with "State laws", then apply square bullets to the list.

b. Change the font color of the bullet characters to Blue, Accent 1.

c. Using the Increase and Decrease Indent buttons, create the multilevel list shown in FIGURE 4-26, then save your changes.

FIGURE 4-26

- Age
- Gender
- Location
    - Crime rate
    - Claim rates for your local area
    - Percentage of uninsured drivers
    - Weather- and climate-related disaster rate
        - Blizzards, hurricanes, and tornados
        - Wildfires
        - Earthquakes
- Model and year of the car you drive
- Driving record
    - Moving violations and accidents
    - Your personal claim rate
- State laws

3. Insert a section break.

a. Turn on the display of formatting marks, scroll down, then insert a continuous section break in the blank paragraph above the Car Insurance Rates in New England heading.

b. Delete the continuous section break, then insert a next page section break at the same location.

c. Insert a page number at the bottom of the page using the Accent Bar 2 design.

d. Change the font color of the page number in the footer area to Blue, Accent 1.

e. Go to the header, then, using the Quick Parts command, insert a Title property control.

f. Type **Car Insurance Rates: New England** in the Title property control.

g. Open the Header gallery, then remove the header.

h. Open the Header gallery again, then insert a header using the Filigree design.

i. If your name is not the name in the Author property control, replace the text in the Author property control with your name.

j. Close the header area, turn off the display of formatting marks, then save your changes.

Skills Review (continued)

4. **Modify a table.**
   a. Scroll to page 2 to display the table in your document window.
   b. Insert a table row above the Rhode Island row, then type the following text in the new row:

Maine	2506	2038	1176	1199	1116	1163	1189

   c. Delete the New York row, then delete the 65+ column.
   d. Insert a column to the right of the 45F column, type **Nat'l Rank** in the header row, then enter the following numbers in each cell in the column: **39, 51, 47, 5, 38, 4.**
   e. Move the Nat'l Rank column to the right of the State column, then save your changes.

5. **Modify rows and columns.**
   a. Double-click the border between the first and second columns to resize the columns.
   b. Drag the border between the second and third columns left to resize the column.
   c. Double-click the right border of the Nat'l Rank, 45M, and 45F columns to resize the columns.
   d. Select the 16M, 16F, 30M, 30F, 45M, and 45F columns, then distribute the columns evenly.
   e. Select rows 2–7, set the row height to exactly .3", then save your changes.

6. **Sort table data.**
   Perform three separate sorts, making sure to select that your list has a header row, as follows:
   a. Sort the table data in descending order by the information in the 45F column, then click OK.
   b. Sort the table data by state in alphabetical order then click OK.
   c. Sort the table data in ascending order by national rank, click OK, then save your changes.

7. **Split and merge cells.**
   a. Insert a row above the header row, then merge the first cell in the new row with the State cell.
   b. Merge the second cell in the new row with the Nat'l Rank cell.
   c. Merge the six remaining blank cells in the first row into a single cell, then type **Average Annual Premium** in the merged cell.
   d. Select the second column (from Nat'l Rank to 51), open the Split Cells dialog box, clear the Merge cells before split check box, then split the cells into two columns.
   e. Type **PD Rank** as the heading for the new column, then enter the following text in the remaining cells in the column: **4, 8, 45, 5, 27,** and **37.**
   f. Add a new row to the bottom of the table.
   g. Merge the first three cells in the new row, then type **Average Premium** in the merged cell.
   h. AutoFit the content of the table to fit the window, then save your changes.

8. Perform calculations in tables.

  a. Place the insertion point in the last cell in the 16M column.

  b. Open the Formula dialog box, delete the text in the Formula box, type **=average(above)**, click the Number format arrow, scroll down, click 0, then click OK.

  c. Repeat Step b to insert the average premium in the last cell in the 16F, 30M, 30F, 45M, and 45F columns.

  d. Change the value of the 16M premium for Vermont from 1986 to **2500**.

  e. Recalculate the average premium for 16M. (*Hint*: Right-click the cell and select Update Field, or use F9.)

  f. Type **$** in front of every number in the last row of the table, then save your changes.

9. Modify table style options.

  a. Click the Table Design tab, then apply the Grid Table 5 Dark – Accent 1 style to the table.

  b. Remove the style from First Column and Banded Rows.

  c. Add the Total Row, Last Column, and Banded Columns styles.

  d. Add the First Column and Banded Rows styles.

  e. Remove all table styles options except the Header Row option.

  f. Clear all formatting from the table.

  g. Apply the Table Grid Light style (top row) to the table.

  h. Apply bold to the 16M, 16F, 30M, 30F, 45M, and 45F column headings, and to the bottom row of the table.

  i. Center the table title Car Insurance Rates in New England, then save your changes.

10. Customize a table format.

  a. Use the Align Center button in the Alignment group on the Layout tab for the table to center the text in every cell vertically and horizontally.

  b. Center right-align the numbers in columns 4–9.

  c. Center left-align the state names in column 1, but not the column heading.

  d. Center right-align the text in the bottom row. Make sure the text in the header row is still centered.

  e. Select all the cells in the header row, including the 16M, 16F, 30M, 30F, 45M, and 45F column headings, apply Blue, Accent 1 shading, then change the font color to White, Background 1.

  f. Apply Blue, Accent 1, Lighter 60% shading to the Connecticut, Massachusetts, and Vermont rows.

  g. Change the font color of the bottom row to Blue, Accent 1.

  h. Add a ½-point white bottom border to the Average Annual Premium cell in the header row, then save your changes. (*Hint*: Click in the cell, then, using the buttons in the Borders group on the Table Design tab, verify that the line style is a single line, verify that the weight is ½ pt, change the pen color to white, click the Border Painter button to turn off the Border Painter, then use the Borders button to apply the bottom border.)

Skills Review (continued)

11. Insert a cover page.

  a. Change the view to multiple pages, then insert the Filigree cover page.

  b. Remove the Filigree cover page, then insert the Banded cover page.

  c. Zoom in on the cover page, verify that the name in the Author property control is your name. If not, remove the property control, select the text that remains, then replace it with your name.

  d. Remove the Company Name and Company address controls.

  e. Click Title in the Title property control to select the title, change the font size to 48, use the Change Case button to change the case to Capitalize Each Word, then deselect the Title control.

  f. Zoom out to see both pages of the document, click page 2, then insert the Confidential 1 watermark.

  g. Remove the watermark, insert the Do Not Copy 1 watermark, then save your changes.

  h. Compare your document to FIGURE 4-27, then make any necessary adjustments.

  i. Save your changes, submit a copy to your instructor, close the file, then exit Word.

FIGURE 4-27

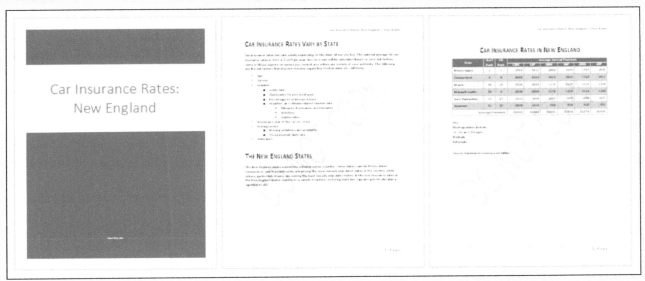

Independent Challenge 1

You work at the Riverwalk Medical Clinic. In preparation for a meeting of the board of directors, you create a summary report that shows quarterly client visits by department for fiscal year 2021. You format the information as a table and prepare the document for presentation to the board.

a. Start Word, then save a new blank document as **IL_WD_4_ClientVisits** to the location where you store your Data Files.

b. Type the table heading **Quarterly Client Visits, Fiscal Year 2021** at the top of the document, then press ENTER.

c. Insert a table with five columns and four rows, then enter the data shown in FIGURE 4-28 into the table, adding rows as necessary. (*Note: Do not format the text or the table at this time.*)

FIGURE 4-28

Department	Q1	Q2	Q3	Q4
Mental Health	345	276	421	389
Pediatrics	1168	834	782	1340
Pharmacy	2145	1973	1989	2346
Adult Family Care	867	593	772	1048
Dental	357	298	423	359
Health & Wellness	473	385	381	447
Insurance & Other Support	636	722	578	1245

d. Resize the columns to fit the text.

e. Sort the table rows in alphabetical order by Department.

f. Add a new row to the bottom of the table, type **Total** in the first cell, then enter a formula in each remaining cell in the new row to calculate the sum of the cells above it.

g. Add a new column to the right side of the table, type **Total** in the first cell, then enter a formula in each remaining cell in the new column to calculate the sum of the cells to the left of it. (*Hint:* Make sure the formula you insert in each cell sums the cells to the left, not the cells above. In the last cell in the last column, you can sum the cells to the left or the cells above; either way, the total should be the same.)

h. Apply a table style to the table. Select a style that enhances the information contained in the table, and adjust the Table Style Options to suit the content.

i. Right-align the numerical data in the table, then adjust the alignment of the text in the header row and first column to suit the design of the table.

j. Enhance the table with fonts, font colors, shading, and borders to make the table attractive and easy to read at a glance.

k. Increase the font size of the table heading to 18 points, change the character scale to 80%, expand the character spacing by 1 point, then center the table heading on the page.

l. Center the table on the page, then adjust the row height so the table is easy to read.

m. Add a header to the document that includes the title property. Type **Riverwalk Medical Clinic** in the Title property control.

n. Add the Ion (Light) cover page to the document. Type **Quarterly Report, Fiscal Year 2021** for the subtitle, add your name as the author, and add the current year for the date.

o. Save your changes, submit the file to your instructor, close the file, then exit Word.

Independent Challenge 2

A well-written and well-formatted résumé gives you an advantage when it comes to getting a job interview. In a winning résumé, the content and format support your career objective and effectively present your background and qualifications. One simple way to create a résumé is to lay out the page using a table. In this exercise you research guidelines for writing and formatting résumés and search for descriptions of job roles that align with your career objective. You then create your own résumé using a table for its layout.

a. Use your favorite search engine to search the web for information on writing and formatting résumés. Use the keywords **resume advice**.

b. Find helpful advice on writing and formatting résumés from at least two websites.

c. Think about the information you want to include in your résumé. The header should include your name, address, telephone number, email address, and other contact information. The body should include your career objective and information on your education, work experience, and skills. You may want to add additional information.

d. Sketch a layout for your résumé using a table as the underlying grid. Include the table rows and columns in your sketch.

e. Start Word, open a new blank document, then save it as **IL_WD_4_Resume** to the location where you store your Data Files.

f. If Intelligent Services is enabled on your system, use the Resume Assistant in Word to research job roles in the industries that interest you. Take note of the top job skills for the job role you would like to have. (*Hint*: Enable Intelligent Services through the Word Options dialog box.)

g. Set appropriate margins, then insert a table to serve as the underlying grid for your résumé. Split and merge cells and adjust the size of the table columns as necessary. FIGURE 4-29 shows a sample layout for a résumé that uses a table for an underlying structure.

h. Type your résumé in the table cells. Take care to use a professional tone and keep your language to the point.

i. Format your résumé with fonts, bullets, and other formatting features. Adjust the spacing between sections by resizing the table columns and rows.

j. When you are satisfied with the content and format of your résumé, remove the borders from the table, then hide the gridlines if they are visible. You may want to add some borders back to the table to help structure the résumé for readers.

k. Check your résumé for spelling and grammar errors.

l. Save your changes, preview your résumé, submit a copy to your instructor, close the file, then exit Word.

FIGURE 4-29

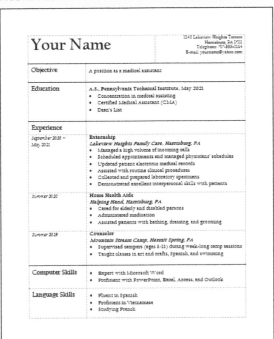

Visual Workshop

Open the file IL_WD_4-3.docx from the location where you store your Data Files, save it as **IL_WD_4_ProjectedSales**, then format document as shown in FIGURE 4-30. The headings are formatted with 80% character scale and character spacing expanded by 0.1 point. The Plain Table 5 table style is applied to the table. The theme colors are Marquee. Add a total row and total column to the table. Sort the table rows by Total in descending order. Use a formula to insert the totals in the Total column and Total row. Type your name in the header, save the document, then submit a copy to your instructor.

FIGURE 4-30

Your Name

The Laghari–Agarwal Group

Projected Sales in Millions, Fiscal Year 2022

	Q1	Q2	Q3	Q4	Total
Mumbai	$8.42	$7.81	$9.82	$9.43	$35.48
Melbourne	$8.81	$8.51	$6.89	$7.46	$31.67
Frankfurt	$8.90	$5.86	$4.95	$9.81	$29.52
Dubai	$5.47	$7.44	$5.94	$8.28	$27.13
Hong Kong	$5.82	$7.28	$4.77	$8.23	$26.10
Mexico City	$6.71	$8.96	$4.68	$4.92	$25.27
Seoul	$7.93	$6.83	$3.89	$6.22	$24.87
Total	$52.06	$52.69	$40.94	$54.35	$200.04

Formatting Tables and Documents

Working with Styles, Themes, and Building Blocks

CASE ▶ You are preparing a Frequently Asked Questions (FAQ) sheet for JCL Talent. You create a customized style and theme for the FAQ document and then simplify the process of designing the layout of the document by using predesigned building blocks. You save the reusable customized theme and content you created so that you can use easily them again in other JCL Talent documents.

Module Objectives

After completing this module, you will be able to:

- Add hyperlinks
- Modify page margins
- Create paragraph styles
- Format with themes
- Customize a theme

- Insert Quick Parts
- Create building blocks
- Insert building blocks
- Use a document template
- Work with PDF files in Word

Files You Will Need

IL_WD_5-1.docx	IL_WD_5-5.docx
IL_WD_5-2.docx	IL_WD_5-6.docx
IL_WD_5-3.docx	IL_WD_5-7.docx
IL_WD_5-4.docx	

Add Hyperlinks

Learning Outcomes
• Insert a hyperlink
• Share documents

A **hyperlink** is text or a graphic that, when clicked, "jumps" the viewer to a different location or program. When a document is viewed on screen, hyperlinks allow readers to link (or jump) to a webpage, an email address, a file, or a specific location in a document. When you create a hyperlink in a document, you select the text or graphic you want to use as a hyperlink, and then you specify the location you want to jump to when the hyperlink is clicked. You create a hyperlink using the Link button in the Links group on the Insert tab. Text that is formatted as a hyperlink appears as colored, underlined text. **CASE** ▶ *JCL clients will receive the FAQ document by email or view it on the JCL website. To make it easier for these people to access additional information, you add several hyperlinks to the document.*

STEPS

1. **sam ↓ Start Word, open the file IL_WD_5-1.docx from the location where you store your Data Files, save it as IL_WD_5_EmployerFAQ, then drag the Zoom slider to 120**
   The document includes FAQ (Frequently Asked Questions), the JCL logo, and a preformatted sidebar. A **sidebar** is a text box that is positioned adjacent to the body of a document and contains auxiliary information.

   QUICK TIP
   By default, Word automatically creates a hyperlink to an email address or URL when you type an email address or a URL in a document.

2. **Select send us an email in the first body paragraph, click the Insert tab, then click the Link button in the Links group**
   The Insert Hyperlink dialog box opens, as shown in **FIGURE 5-1**. You use this dialog box to specify the location you want to jump to when the hyperlink—in this case, "send us an email"—is clicked.

3. **Click E-mail Address in the Link to section**
   The Insert Hyperlink dialog box changes so you can create a hyperlink to an email address.

4. **Type your email address in the E-mail address box, type Employer Inquiry in the Subject box, then click OK**
   As you type, Word automatically adds mailto: in front of your email address. After you close the dialog box, the hyperlink text—send us an email—is formatted in blue and underlined. Before distributing a document, it's important to test any hyperlinks you added.

   TROUBLE
   If an email message does not open, close any window that opens and continue with Step 7.

5. **Press and hold CTRL, then click the send us an email hyperlink**
   An email message addressed to you with the subject "Employer Inquiry" opens in the default email program.

6. **Close the email message window, clicking No if you are prompted to save**
   The hyperlink text changed color, indicating the hyperlink has been followed.

   QUICK TIP
   To remove a hyperlink, right-click it, then click Remove Hyperlink. Removing a hyperlink removes the link, but the text remains.

7. **Scroll down, select Find an office near you in the second paragraph, click the Link button, click Existing File or Web Page in the Link to section of the Insert Hyperlink dialog box, type www.jcltalent.com in the Address box, then click OK**
   As you type the web address, Word automatically adds "http://" in front of "www." The text "Find an office near you" is formatted as a hyperlink to the JCL Talent home page www.jcltalent.com. When clicked, the hyperlink will open the webpage in the default browser window. If you point to a hyperlink in Word, the link to the location appears in a ScreenTip. You can edit ScreenTip text to make it more descriptive.

   QUICK TIP
   You can also edit the hyperlink destination or the hyperlink text.

8. **Right-click office in the Find an office near you hyperlink, click Edit Hyperlink, click ScreenTip in the Edit Hyperlink dialog box, type Search for JCL Talent locations in the ScreenTip text box, click OK, click OK, save your changes, then point to the Find an office near you hyperlink in the document**
   The ScreenTip you created appears above the Find an office near you hyperlink, as shown in **FIGURE 5-2**.

FIGURE 5-1: Insert Hyperlink dialog box

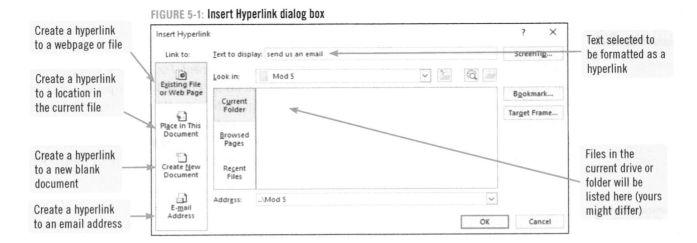

Create a hyperlink to a webpage or file

Create a hyperlink to a location in the current file

Create a hyperlink to a new blank document

Create a hyperlink to an email address

Text selected to be formatted as a hyperlink

Files in the current drive or folder will be listed here (yours might differ)

FIGURE 5-2: Hyperlinks in the document

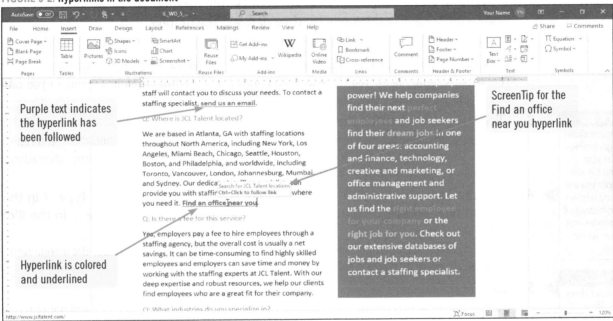

Purple text indicates the hyperlink has been followed

Hyperlink is colored and underlined

ScreenTip for the Find an office near you hyperlink

Sharing documents from Word and checking compatibility

Word includes several options for distributing and sharing documents over the Internet directly from within Word, including saving a document to OneDrive for others to view and edit, emailing a document, presenting a document online so others can view it in a web browser, sending an Adobe pdf to others for review, and posting a document to a blog. To share a document, open the file in Word, click the File tab, click Share, then click one of the Share options. You can also use the Share button on the title bar to save a document to an online location.

When you email a document from within Word, the document is sent as an attachment to an email message using your default email program. You can choose to attach the document as a Word file, a .pdf file, or an .xps file, or to send it as an Internet fax. When you click an option, a message window opens that includes the filename of the current file as the message subject and the file as an attachment. Type the email address(es) of the recipient(s) in the To and Cc boxes, type any message you want in the message window, then click Send. The default email program sends a copy of the document to each recipient. Note that faxing a document directly from Word requires registration with a third-party Internet fax service.

Before you share a document with others, it's a good idea to check it for compatibility with previous versions of Word. Click the File tab, click Info, click Check for Issues, click Check Compatibility, select the versions you want to check for in the Microsoft Word Compatibility Checker dialog box, then click OK.

Modify Page Margins

The Page Setup options enable you to change the layout of a document. For example, you can change the margins in a document to control the amount of text that fits on a page. The margins of a document are the blank areas between the edge of the text and the edge of the page. When you create a document in Word, the default margins are 1" at the top, bottom, left, and right sides of the page, but you can increase or decrease the size of any margin to create custom margins. **CASE** ▸ *You reduce the size of the document margins so that more text fits on each page. You also move a table column and resize the text within the table so the table fits better within the new margins on the page.*

STEPS

1. **Scroll to the top of the page, click the** JCL Talent logo **to select the graphic, click the** Picture Format tab, **click the** Position button **in the Arrange group, click** Position in Top Right with Square Text Wrapping, **then deselect the graphic**

   The logo graphic is now a floating graphic that aligns with the top and right margins of the document.

2. **Click the** Layout tab, **then click the** Margins button **in the Page Setup group**

   The Margins menu opens. You can select predefined margin settings from this menu, or you can click Custom Margins to create different margin settings.

3. **Click** Custom Margins **on the Margins menu**

   The Page Setup dialog box opens with the Margins tab displayed, as shown in FIGURE 5-3. You can use the Margins tab to change the top, bottom, left, or right document margin, to change the orientation of the pages from portrait to landscape, and to alter other page layout settings.

4. **Click the** Top down arrow **three times until** 0.7" **appears, press** TAB, **type** .7 **in the Bottom box, press** TAB, **type** .7 **in the Left box, press** TAB, **then type** .7 **in the Right box**

   The top, bottom, left, and right margins of the report will all be .7". You can change the margin settings by using the arrows or by typing a value in the appropriate box.

5. **Click** OK

   The document margins change to .7". The location of each margin (right, left, top, and bottom) is shown on the horizontal and vertical rulers at the intersection of the white and shaded areas.

6. **Scroll until the Sample Timesheet table on page 2 is at the top of the document window, then click the** Home tab

7. **Place the pointer over the top of the** second column **in the table, click to select the** Day column, **click the** Cut button **in the Clipboard group, click in the** Date cell, **then click the** Paste button **in the Clipboard group**

   The Day column moves to become the first column in the table.

8. **Click in the** table, **click the** Layout contextual tab **for tables, click the** AutoFit button **in the Cell Size group, click** AutoFit Window, **click the** View tab, **click the** Multiple Pages button **in the Zoom group, then save your changes**

   The table is resized to fit the new margin settings, as shown in FIGURE 5-4.

FIGURE 5-3: Margins tab in Page Setup dialog box

Default margin settings →

Select page orientation →

Set mirror margins and other page layout options

Preview of margin settings

Select part of document to apply settings to

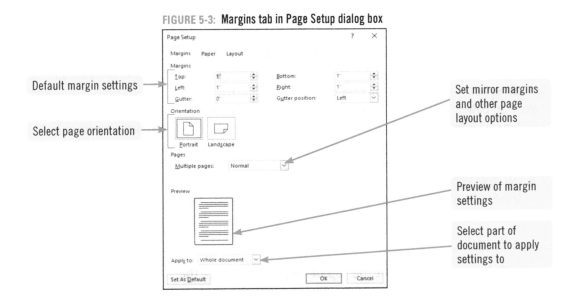

FIGURE 5-4: Document with smaller margins

Logo positioned in top right with square text wrapping

Ruler shows location of top margin

Document margins are narrower than the original default margins

Ruler shows location of right margin

Table is AutoFit to the margins

Ruler shows location of left margin

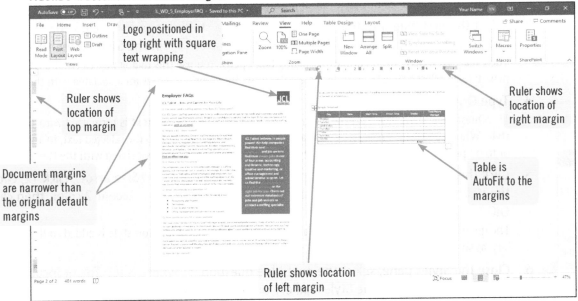

Word

Changing vertical alignment

By default, text is aligned vertically at the top margin of a document, but you can change the vertical alignment of text to align with the bottom margin, to be centered between the top and bottom margins, or to be justified. To change the vertical alignment of text, click the Layout tab in the Page Setup dialog box, click the Vertical alignment arrow, then click the alignment option you want. Using the Apply to arrow on the Layout tab, you can choose to apply the vertical alignment settings to the whole document, to the current section, or to the current section and all sections that follow it. When you are finished, click OK.

Create Paragraph Styles

Applying a style to text allows you to apply multiple format settings to text in one easy step. In addition to using built-in styles, you can create your own styles. You can base a new style on an existing style or you can base it on no style. When you base a style on an existing style, both the formatting associated with the existing style and any new formatting you apply are associated with the new style. One type of style you can create is a paragraph style. A **paragraph style** is a combination of character and paragraph formats that you name and store as a set. You can create a paragraph style and then apply it to any paragraph. **CASE** *You apply two built-in styles to title text in the document and then create a new paragraph style called Question and apply it to the FAQ questions in the document.*

STEPS

1. **Click** Employer FAQs **at the top of page 1, then click the** 100% button **in the Zoom group**

2. **Select the title** Employer FAQs, **click the** Home tab, **click** Title **in the Styles group, select the subtitle** JCL Talent – Jobs and Careers for Your Life, **then click** Subtitle **in the Styles group**

   The built-in Title and Subtitle styles are applied to the selected text.

3. **Select the first blue question** Q: I've never used a staffing agency..., **click the** Styles group Launcher 🔲, **then click the** New Style button 𝖠₊ **in the Styles pane that opens**

   The Create New Style from Formatting dialog box opens. You use this dialog box to enter a name for the new style, to select a style type, and to select the formatting options you want associated with the new style.

4. **Type** Question **in the Name box**

   The Question style is based on the Normal style because the selected text is formatted with the Normal style. When you create a new style, you can base it on the style applied to the selected text, to another style, or to no preset style. You want the new style to include the formatting associated with the Heading 1 style.

5. **Click the** Style based on arrow, **click** Heading 1, **click the** Font Size arrow, **click** 12, **click the** Italic button, **click the** Font Color arrow, **click the** Orange, Accent 2 color, **then click** OK

   The question is formatted in 12-point italic orange, and the new Question style is added to the Styles gallery, as shown in **FIGURE 5-5**.

6. **Close the Styles pane, select the next blue question** Q: Where is JCL Talent located?, **then click** Question **in the Styles gallery on the Ribbon**

   The new Question style is applied to the selected text.

7. **Scroll down and apply the** Question style **to the remaining five** blue questions **in the document, then press** CTRL+HOME

   The new Question style is applied to every FAQ question in the document.

8. **Click in the** first orange question, **then press** SHIFT+F1

   The Reveal Formatting pane opens, as shown in **FIGURE 5-6**. This pane lists exactly which styles and formats are applied to the character, paragraphs, and section of the selected text.

9. **Click several other paragraphs, notice the format settings in the Reveal Formatting pane for each paragraph, close the Reveal Formatting pane, close all other panes if necessary, then save your changes**

FIGURE 5-5: New style in Styles gallery

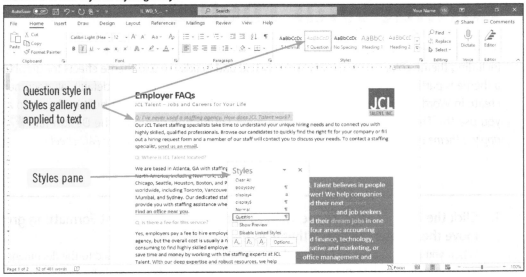

Question style in Styles gallery and applied to text

Styles pane

FIGURE 5-6: Reveal Formatting pane

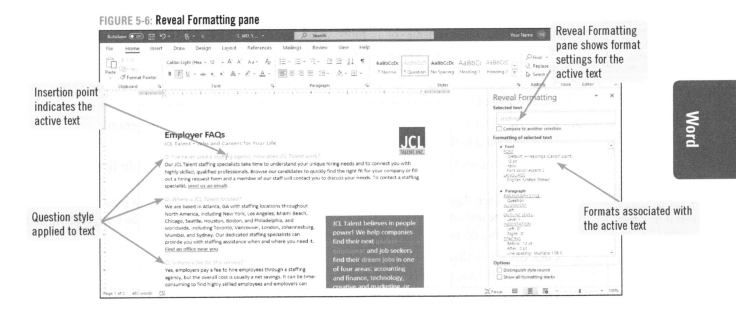

Reveal Formatting pane shows format settings for the active text

Insertion point indicates the active text

Question style applied to text

Formats associated with the active text

Saving a document as a webpage

Creating a webpage and posting it on the Internet or an intranet is a powerful way to share information with other people. You can design a webpage from scratch in Word, or you can use the Save As command to save an existing document in HTML format so it can be viewed with a browser. When you save an existing document as a webpage, Word converts the content and formatting of the Word file to HTML and displays the webpage in Web Layout view, which shows the webpage as it will appear in a browser. Any formatting that is not supported by web browsers is either converted to similar supported formatting or removed from the webpage.

To save a document as a webpage, open the Save As dialog box, and then select a Web Page format in the Save as type list. You have the option of saving the document in Single File Web Page (.mht or .mhtml) format, or in Web Page or Web Page, Filtered (.htm or .html) format. In a single file webpage, all the elements of the webpage, including the text and graphics, are saved together in a single MIME encapsulated aggregate HTML (MHTML) file, making it simple to publish your webpage or send it via email. By contrast, if you choose to save a webpage as an .htm file, Word automatically creates a supporting folder in the same location as the .htm file. This folder has the same name as the .htm file plus the suffix files, and it houses the supporting files associated with the webpage, such as graphics.

Format with Themes

Learning Outcomes
- Apply a theme
- Change the style set
- Change the default theme

Applying a theme to a document is a quick way to apply a unified set of design elements to a document, including theme colors, theme fonts for body text and headings, and theme effects for graphics. Applying a theme is particularly effective if a document is formatted with styles. By default, all documents that you create in Word are formatted with the Office theme. To apply a different built-in theme to a document, you use the Themes command in the Document Formatting group on the Design tab. **CASE** *You apply a theme that suits the professional message you want to convey with the FAQ sheet.*

STEPS

1. **Click the Design tab, click the Themes button in the Document Formatting group, then move the pointer over each theme in the gallery**

   When you point to a theme in the gallery, a preview of the theme is applied to the document. Notice that the font colors and the fonts for the body text and headings to which a style has been applied change when you preview each theme.

2. **Click the Slice theme**

   A complete set of new theme colors, fonts, styles, and effects is applied to the document, as shown in FIGURE 5-7. Keep in mind that changing the document theme does not affect the formatting of text to which font formatting has been applied. Only document content that uses theme colors, text that is formatted with a style (including default body text), and table styles and graphic effects change when a new theme is applied.

3. **Click the View tab, then click the Multiple Pages button in the Zoom group**

   The style applied to the table at the bottom of the last page reflects the Slice theme.

4. **Click the Design tab, click the Themes button, then point to each built-in theme in the gallery**

   Notice how each theme affects the formatting of the text, sidebar, and table, and, in some cases, the pagination of the document. It's important to choose a theme that not only mirrors the tone, content, and purpose of your document, but also meets your goal for document length.

5. **Click the Basis theme**

   The Basis theme is applied to the document as shown in FIGURE 5-8.

6. **Click the View tab, click the 100% button in the Zoom group, press CTRL+HOME, then save your changes**

Changing the style set

Applying a different style set is another quick way to change the look of an entire document. Style sets include font and paragraph settings for headings and body text so that when you apply a new style set to a document, all the body text and all the headings that have been formatted with a style change to the format settings for the active style set. You apply styles to a document using the styles available in the Styles group on the Home tab.

You apply a style set using the style sets available in the Document Formatting group on the Design tab.

You can also save a group of font and paragraph settings as a new style set. To do this, click the More button in the Document Formatting group, then click Save as a New Style Set. If you want to return a document to its original style set, click the More button, then click Reset to the Default Style Set.

FIGURE 5-7: **Slice theme applied to document**

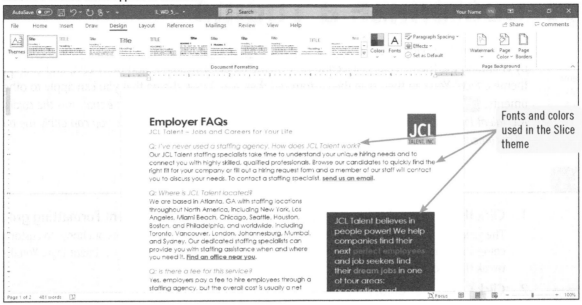

FIGURE 5-8: **Basis theme applied to document**

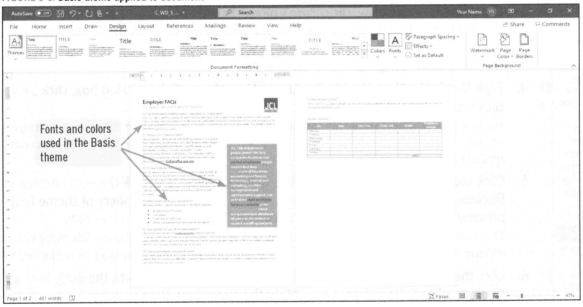

Changing the default theme

By default, all new documents created in Word are formatted with the Office theme, but you can change your settings to use a different theme as the default. To change the default theme to a different built-in theme, press CTRL+N to open a new blank document, click the Themes button in the Document Formatting group on the Design tab, and then click the theme you want to use as the default. If you want to customize the theme before saving it as the new default, use the Colors, Fonts, and Effects buttons in the Document Formatting group to customize the settings for theme colors, fonts, and effects. Alternatively, click the More button in the Document Formatting group then select a new style set to use in the new default theme. When you are satisfied with the settings for the new default theme, click the Set as Default button in the Document Formatting group. The Themes gallery will be updated to reflect your changes.

Customize a Theme

When one of the built-in Word themes is not quite right for your document, you can customize the theme by changing the theme colors, selecting new theme fonts for headings and body text, and changing the theme effects. You can then save the customized theme as a new theme that you can apply to other documents. **CASE** > *You tweak the theme colors and fonts to create a new theme that uses the colors of the JCL Talent logo and is easy to read. You then save the settings as a new theme so you can apply the theme to all documents related to FAQ questions.*

STEPS

1. **Click the Design tab, then click the Colors button in the Document Formatting group**

   The gallery of theme colors opens. You can select a new palette of built-in colors or choose to customize the colors in the active palette. You want a palette that picks up the colors of the JCL Talent logo. You decide to tweak the colors in the Basis theme palette.

2. **Click Customize Colors**

   The Create New Theme Colors dialog box opens and shows the color palette from the Basis theme, as shown in FIGURE 5-9. You use this dialog box to change the colors in the active palette and to save the set of colors you create with a new name.

3. **Click the Accent 2 arrow, click More Colors, click the Custom tab in the Colors dialog box if it is not the active tab, type 0 in the Red box, type 51 in the Green box, type 153 in the Blue box, then click OK**

   The Accent 2 color changes from dark orange to blue.

4. **Type FAQ in the Name box in the Create New Theme Colors dialog box, click Save, then click the Colors button**

   The new color scheme is saved with the name FAQ, the orange questions in the document change to blue, and the FAQ color scheme appears in the Custom section in the Colors gallery. The FAQ colors can now be applied to any document.

5. **Click the document to close the Colors gallery if necessary, click the Fonts button in the Document Formatting group, point to several options in the gallery of theme fonts to preview those fonts applied to the document, then click Customize Fonts**

   The Create New Theme Fonts dialog box opens, as shown in FIGURE 5-10. You use this dialog box to select different fonts for headings and body text, and to save the font combination as a new theme font set.

6. **Click the Heading font arrow, scroll up, click Century Gothic, click the Body font arrow, scroll up, click Calibri Light, type FAQ in the Name box, then click Save**

   The font of the headings in the report changes to Century Gothic, the font of the body text changes to Calibri Light, and the FAQ theme font set is added to the Custom section of the Fonts gallery.

7. **Click the Themes button, click Save Current Theme, type FAQ in the File name box in the Save Current Theme dialog box, then click Save**

   The FAQ theme colors and FAQ theme fonts are saved together as a new theme called FAQ in the default location for document themes.

8. **Save your changes, then click the Themes button**

   The new theme appears in the Custom section of the Themes gallery, as shown in FIGURE 5-11.

QUICK TIP

To remove a custom color palette from the gallery, right-click the palette, then click Delete.

QUICK TIP

To change the line and paragraph spacing applied to a document, click the Paragraph Spacing button in the Document Formatting group, then click a Built-In style or click Custom Paragraph Spacing to enter custom settings in the Manage Styles dialog box.

QUICK TIP

To customize theme effects, click the Effects button in the Document Formatting group, then select an effect from the gallery.

QUICK TIP

To remove a custom theme from the gallery, right-click the theme, then click Delete.

FIGURE 5-9: Create New Theme Colors dialog box

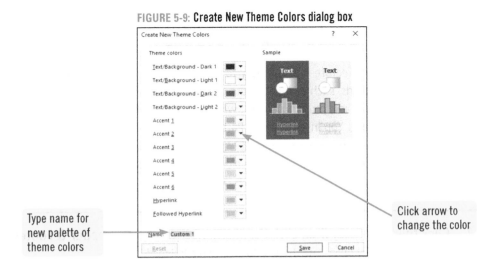

Type name for new palette of theme colors

Click arrow to change the color

FIGURE 5-10: Create New Theme Fonts dialog box

Select font for headings

Select font for body text

Preview fonts

Type name for new set of theme fonts

FIGURE 5-11: Custom theme in the Themes gallery

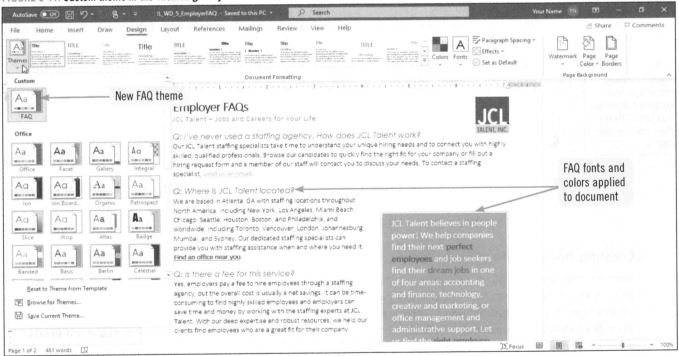

New FAQ theme

FAQ fonts and colors applied to document

Insert Quick Parts

Learning Outcomes
- Insert headers and footers
- Update a document property
- Insert and delete a property control

The Word Quick Parts feature makes it easy to insert reusable pieces of content into a document. Quick Parts items include fields, such as for the date or a page number; document properties, such as the document title or author; and building blocks, which are customized content that you can create, format, and save for future use. You insert a Quick Part into a document using the Quick Parts command on the Insert tab or on the Header & Footer tab. **CASE** *You finalize the design of the FAQ document by adding a header building block and a footer building block to the document. You then customize the footer by adding a document property to it using the Quick Parts command.*

STEPS

1. **Click the Insert tab, then click the Header button in the Header & Footer group**

   The Header gallery opens and displays the list of predesigned headers.

2. **Scroll down the Header gallery, then click Integral**

   The Integral header is added to the document and the Header area opens. The Integral header includes a property control for the Document Title. A **property control** is a content control that contains document property information, such as title, company, or author. You can assign or update a document property by typing directly in a property control or by typing in the Properties boxes on the Info screen.

3. **Click in the property control to select the Document Title property control, then type Frequently Asked Questions from Employers**

   The document title is added to the header, as shown in FIGURE 5-12. The text appears as all capital letters because the All caps effect from the Effects section of the Font dialog box is applied to the property control as part of the Integral header style. When you assign or update a document property by typing in a property control, all controls of the same type in the document are updated with the change, as well as the corresponding property field on the Info screen.

4. **Click the Footer button in the Header & Footer group, scroll down the Footer gallery, then click Integral**

   The Integral footer includes an Author property control and a page number field. Notice that this footer is formatted as a table; you can see the table move handle on the left side of the footer.

5. **Click Author to select the Author property control, press DELETE to delete the Author property control, click the Quick Parts button in the Insert group, point to Document Property, then click Company**

   The Company property control is added to the footer.

6. **Type JCL Talent, Inc.**

   The Company property is updated to become JCL TALENT, INC., as shown in FIGURE 5-13.

7. **Close the Footer area, press CTRL+END, type your name, press CTRL+HOME, save your changes, click the View tab, then click the Multiple Pages button**

   The completed Employer FAQ document is shown in FIGURE 5-14.

Creating customized bullet characters

When you create a bulleted list, you can choose to format the list using a bullet character from the Bullet Library, or you can create a customized bullet character using a symbol or a picture. To create a custom bullet character, click the Bullets button in the Paragraph group on the Home tab, then click Define New Bullet. In the Define New Bullet dialog box, click Symbol to open the Symbol gallery, double-click the symbol you want to use as a bullet, then click OK in the Define New Bullet dialog box. The symbol is added to the active paragraph as a bullet and added to the Bullet Library.

FIGURE 5-12: Document Title property control in Integral header

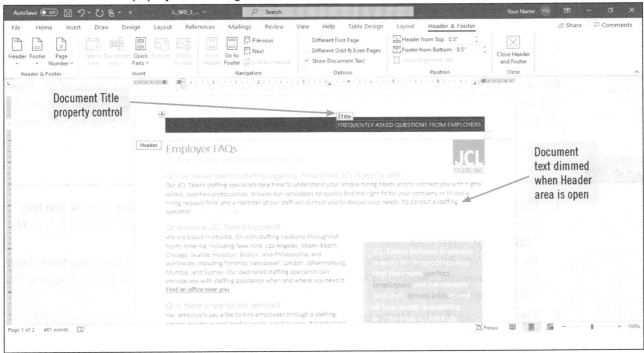

Document Title property control

Document text dimmed when Header area is open

FIGURE 5-13: Company property control in Integral footer

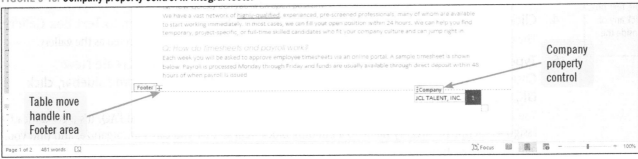

Company property control

Table move handle in Footer area

FIGURE 5-14: Completed Employers FAQ document

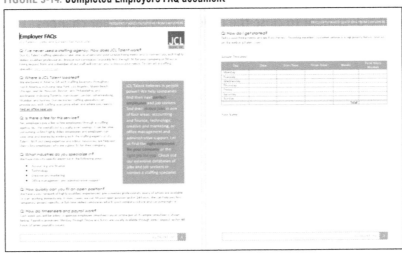

Create Building Blocks

Building blocks are the reusable pieces of formatted content or document parts that are stored in galleries, including headers and footers, cover pages, and text boxes. When you design a piece of content that you want to use again in other documents, you can save it as a building block in one of the Word galleries. You save an item as a building block using the Quick Parts command. **CASE** *You save the JCL Talent logo and the sidebar as building blocks so that you can easily include them in other FAQ documents.*

STEPS

1. **Click the** View tab, **click the** 100% button **in the Zoom group, click the** logo **at the top of page 1 to select it, click the** Insert tab, **click the** Explore Quick Parts button 📧 ▾ **in the Text group, then click** Save Selection to Quick Part Gallery

   The Create New Building Block dialog box opens, as shown in FIGURE 5-15. You use this dialog box to enter a unique name and a description for the item and to specify the gallery where you want it to appear. You want the logo to appear in the Quick Parts gallery.

2. **Type** JCL Logo **in the Name box, click the** Description box, **type** JCL logo in top-right corner of page, **then click** OK

   The logo is added to the Quick Parts gallery.

3. **Click the edge of the** green sidebar **to select it**

   A solid line and sizing handles surround the box so you know the box is selected.

4. **Click the** Text Box button **in the Text group, then click** Save Selection to Text Box Gallery

   The Create New Building Block dialog box opens with Text Box automatically selected as the gallery.

5. **Type** FAQ Sidebar **in the Name box, click the** Category arrow, **click** Create New Category, **type** FAQ, **click** OK, **click the** Description box, **type** JCL promo sidebar, **click** OK, **then click anywhere in the document to deselect the box**

   You added the sidebar to the Text Box gallery and created a new category called FAQ. It's a good idea to assign a descriptive category name to a building block item so that you can sort, organize, and find your building blocks easily.

6. **Click the** Text Box button **in the Text group, then scroll to the bottom of the gallery**

   The FAQ Sidebar building block is displayed in the Text Box gallery in the FAQ category, as shown in FIGURE 5-16.

7. **Click the document to close the gallery, then save your changes**

FIGURE 5-15: Create New Building Block dialog box

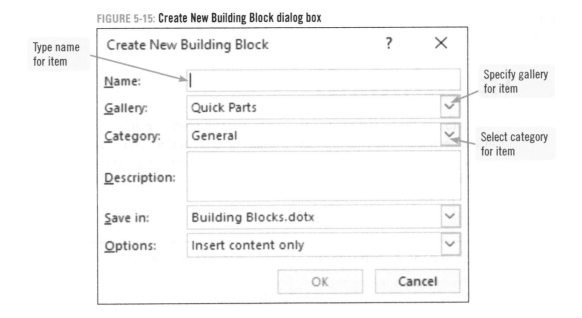

Type name for item

Specify gallery for item

Select category for item

FIGURE 5-16: New building block in Text Box gallery

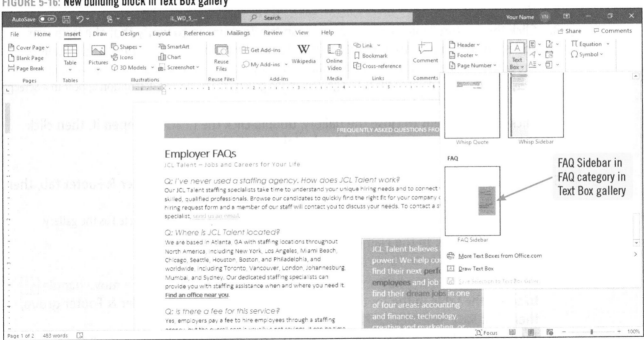

FAQ Sidebar in FAQ category in Text Box gallery

Inserting icons in a document

Word includes hundreds of icon images that you can insert into documents to visually communicate using symbols. To insert an icon in a document, click the Icons button in the Illustrations group on the Insert tab, scroll the gallery of icons in the Insert Icon dialog box, select an icon, then click Insert. The icon is inserted as a graphic object at the location of the insertion point. Like any graphic object, you can use the options on the Graphics Format tab to size, position, and format the icon graphic.

Create Building Blocks (continued)

It is useful to save the customized headers and footers you create as building blocks so that you can reuse them in other documents. When you save a header or footer as a building block, it is added to the Header or Footer gallery. You can save a header or footer as a building block using the Header or Footer button. **CASE** ▸ *You save the sample timesheet table and the header and footer as building blocks so that you can easily include them in other FAQ documents.*

STEPS

1. **Scroll to page 2, then click the** Sample timesheet table move handle ⊞ **to select the table**

2. **Click the** Insert tab **if necessary, click the** Explore Quick Parts button 🔲▾ **in the Text group, click** Save Selection to Quick Part Gallery, **type** Sample Timesheet **in the Name box, click the** Category arrow, **click** Create New Category, **type** FAQ, **click** OK, **then click** OK
   The Sample Timesheet table is saved in the Quick Parts gallery in the FAQ category.

3. **Click the** Explore Quick Parts button 🔲▾ **in the Text group to verify that the item was added to the gallery, then point to (but do not click) the** JCL Logo **item in the gallery**
   The gallery includes the JCL Logo item in the General category and the Sample Timesheet item in the FAQ category. When you point to the JCL Logo item in the gallery, the name and description appear in a Screen-Tip, as shown in FIGURE 5-17.

4. **Click the document to close the gallery, double-click the** header **to open it, then click the** table move handle ⊞ **to select the table in the header**
   The information in the header area is formatted as a table.

5. **Click the** Header button **in the Header & Footer group on the Header & Footer tab, then click** Save Selection to Header Gallery
   The Create New Building Block dialog box opens with Headers automatically selected as the gallery.

6. **Type** FAQ Header **in the Name box, then click** OK
   The header is added to the Header gallery under the General category.

7. **Click the** Go to Footer button **in the Navigation group, click the** table move handle ⊞ **to select the table in the footer, click the** Footer button **in the Header & Footer group, then click** Save Selection to Footer Gallery
   The Create New Building Block dialog box opens with Footers automatically selected as the gallery.

8. **Type** FAQ Footer **in the Name box, click** OK, **then close the Header and Footer**
   The footer is added to the Footer gallery under the General category. You now will be able to insert the building blocks you created into a different FAQ document.

9. **sam⬆ Save the document, submit it, then close the document without exiting Word**

FIGURE 5-17: Items in Quick Parts gallery

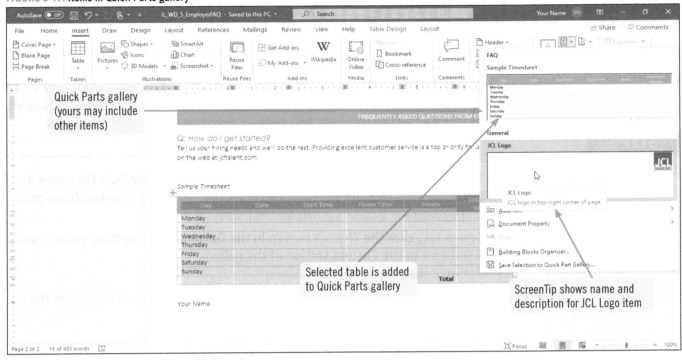

Quick Parts gallery (yours may include other items)

Selected table is added to Quick Parts gallery

ScreenTip shows name and description for JCL Logo item

Renaming a building block and editing other properties

You can edit the properties of a building block at any time, including changing its name, gallery location, category, and description. To modify building block properties, simply right-click the item in a gallery, then click Edit Properties. In the Modify Building Block dialog box that opens, edit the item's name or

description, or assign it to a new gallery or category. When you are finished, click OK, then click Yes in the warning box that opens. You can also modify the properties of a building block by selecting the item in the Building Blocks Organizer, then clicking Edit Properties.

Insert Building Blocks

Once you have created customized building blocks, it is easy to insert them in your documents. You can insert a building block directly from a gallery, or you can use the Building Blocks Organizer to sort, preview, insert, delete, and edit the properties of building blocks. **CASE** *You need to create a FAQ document for Job Seekers. You open the Job Seeker FAQ file, apply the FAQ theme, and then insert the building blocks you created so that all the FAQ documents have common content and a consistent look and feel.*

STEPS

1. **Open the file** IL_WD_5-2.docx **from the location where you store your Data Files, save it as** IL_WD_5_JobSeekerFAQ, **click the** View tab, **then click the** 100% button **in the Zoom group**
   The Job Seeker FAQ document includes text formatted with styles.

2. **Click the** Design tab, **click the** Themes button **in the Document Formatting group, then click the** FAQ theme **in the Custom section of the gallery**
   The FAQ theme you created is applied to the document.

3. **Press** CTRL+HOME, **click the** Insert tab, **click the** Explore Quick Parts button 🗐▾ **in the Text group, then click the** JCL Logo **item in the Quick Part gallery**
   The logo is added to the upper-right corner of the first page.

4. **Press** CTRL+END, **click the** Explore Quick Parts button 🗐▾, **then click the** Sample Timesheet **item in the Quick Part gallery**
   The Sample Timesheet table is added to the end of the document.

QUICK TIP
To edit the content of a building block, insert the item in a document, edit the item, then save the selection to the same Quick Parts gallery using the same name.

5. **Click anywhere on page 1, click the** Header button **in the Header & Footer group, scroll down the Header gallery, click** FAQ Header **in the General section, click the** Footer button, **scroll down the Footer gallery, click** FAQ Footer **in the General section, then click the** Close Header and Footer button
   The custom header and footer you created are added to pages 1 and 2. The property information that appears in the header and footer, in this case the document title and the company name, are the property information for the current document.

6. **Click the** Q: Where is JCL Talent located? **paragraph, click the** Insert tab, **click the** Explore Quick Parts button 🗐▾ **in the Text group, then click** Building Blocks Organizer
   The Building Blocks Organizer opens, as shown in FIGURE 5-18. The Building Blocks Organizer includes a complete list of the built-in and customized building blocks from every gallery. You use the Building Blocks Organizer to sort, preview, insert, delete, and edit the properties of building blocks.

QUICK TIP
To delete a building block, select it in the Building Blocks Organizer, then click Delete.

7. **Click the** Category column heading **in the list of building blocks**
   The building blocks are sorted and grouped by category.

8. **Scroll down the list to locate the items in the FAQ category, click the** FAQ Sidebar **item to select it, then click** Insert
   The FAQ Sidebar is inserted on page 1. The sidebar is anchored to the Q: Where is JCL Talent located paragraph, which is the current position of the insertion point.

TROUBLE
If you are working on your personal computer and you want to save the building blocks you created, click Save to save the Building Blocks.dotx file.

9. **With the sidebar selected, click the** Shape Format tab, **click the** Position button **in the Arrange group, click** Position in Middle Left with Square Text Wrapping, **click the** View tab, **click the** Multiple Pages button, **press** CTRL+END, **press** ENTER, **then type your name**
   The sidebar is moved to the left of the text, and your name is added to the end of the document. The completed Job Seekers FAQ document is shown in FIGURE 5-19.

10. **Save your changes, submit the document, then close the file without exiting Word**

FIGURE 5-18: Building Blocks Organizer

Click a column heading to sort the building blocks by that criterion

Complete list of building blocks (your order may differ)

Preview of selected building block

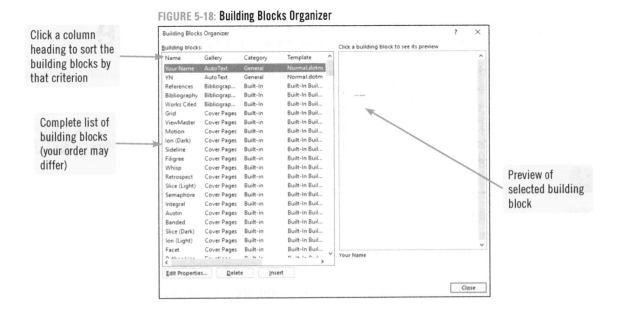

FIGURE 5-19: Completed Job Seekers FAQ document

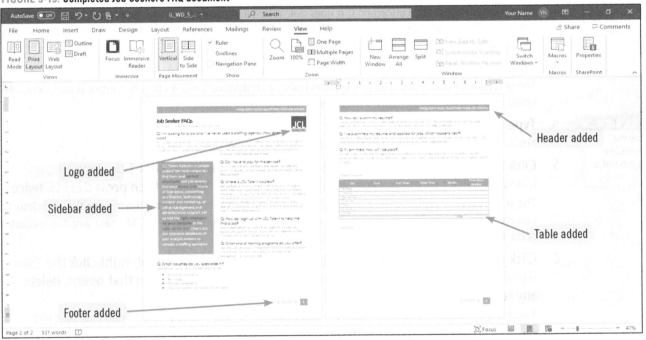

Logo added

Sidebar added

Footer added

Header added

Table added

Working with Styles, Themes, and Building Blocks

Use a Document Template

**Learning
Outcomes**
• Customize a
template
• Use content
controls

Word includes many templates that you can use to create letters, reports, brochures, calendars, and other professionally designed documents quickly. A **template** is a formatted document that contains placeholder text and graphics, which you replace with your own text and graphics. To create a document that is based on a template, you use the New command on the File tab in Backstage view, and then select a template to use. You can then customize the document and save it with a new filename. **CASE** *You use a template to create a cover letter for a contract you will send to a client.*

STEPS

QUICK TIP
You must have an
active Internet con-
nection to search for
templates.

1. **Click** File**, then click** New

   The New screen opens in Backstage view, as shown in FIGURE 5-20. You can select a template from the gallery shown in this window or use the search box and the links in the Suggested searches section to find other templates.

TROUBLE
Templates change
over time. If this
template is not avail-
able, select another
Cover Letter tem-
plate or just read the
steps to understand
how to work with
templates.

2. **Click** Resumes and Cover Letters **in the Suggested searches section, scroll down until you find the** Cover letter (blue) **thumbnail on the New screen, click it, preview the template in the preview window that opens, click** Create**, then change the zoom level to** 100%

   The Cover Letter (blue) template opens as a new document in the document window. It contains placeholder text, which you can replace with your own information. Your name might appear at the top of the document. Don't be concerned if it does not. When a document is created using this template, Word automatically enters the user name from the Word Options dialog box at the top of the document and in the signature block.

3. **Click** Date **in the document**

   The placeholder text is selected and appears inside a content control. A content control is an interactive object that you use to customize a document with your own information.

QUICK TIP
As you type the
month, AutoCom-
plete suggests text to
insert.

4. **Type today's date**

   The current date replaces the placeholder text.

5. **Click** Recipient Name **in the address block, type** Ms. Sara Bay**, click** Title**, type** Hiring Manager**, click** Company**, type** Simpson and Co.**, click** Address**, then press DELETE twice**

   The text you type replaces the placeholder text, and the Address content control for the recipient is removed from the document. Notice that when you typed the recipient name, Ms. Sara Bay, the recipient name information was updated in the greeting line.

6. **Click your name in the content control at the top of the document, right-click the** Your Name **content control, click** Remove Content Control **on the menu that opens, delete any text that remains, then type** JCL Talent, Inc.

   Removing the content control changes the text to static text that you can replace with your own text.

7. **Click** Address **in the letterhead, type** www.jcltalent.com**, click** Telephone**, type** 555-555-0789**, click** Email**, then type** jcl@jcltalent.com

8. **Scroll down, select the three paragraphs of placeholder body text, type** Enclosed please find a copy of our contract for staffing services. We look forward to working with you.**, then, if the name in the signature block is not your name, select the text in the content control and type your name**

   The text you type replaces the placeholder text, as shown in FIGURE 5-21.

9. **Save the document as** IL_WD_5_ContractLetter **to the location where you store your Data Files**

FIGURE 5-20: **New screen in Backstage view**

Click to navigate to and open an existing document

Click to create a new blank document

Types of templates available with an active Internet connection

Search for a template

Cover letter (blue) template (scroll to find it if necessary)

Your templates may differ

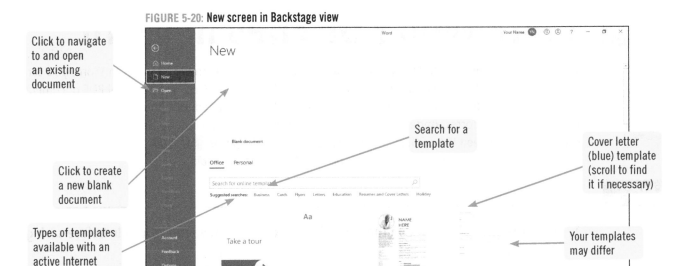

FIGURE 5-21: **Document created using the Cover Letter (blue) template**

Static text replaces content control

Placeholder text is replaced with customized text

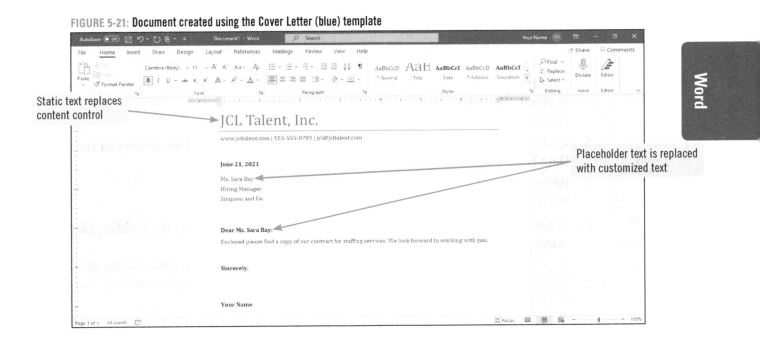

Word

Work with PDF Files in Word

Learning Outcomes
- Export a document to PDF
- Open and edit a PDF document

You can save any file you create in Word as a Portable Document Format (PDF) file. In Word, you can also open a file that has been saved as a PDF file and edit the file in Word. If the original PDF document contains only text, the document will look almost identical in Word as it does in the original PDF, although the page to page correspondence may not be exact. If the PDF document includes graphics, some discrepancies between the original and the Word version may appear. **CASE** *You save the letter as a PDF file for distribution to the client. You then open the PDF document to edit it.*

STEPS

1. **Click the** Save button 🖫 **on the Quick Access toolbar to save the Word file before saving it as a PDF file**

2. **Click the** File tab, **click** Export, **click** Create PDF/XPS Document **in the list below Export if it is not already selected, then click the** Create PDF/XPS button

   The Publish as PDF or XPS dialog box opens.

3. **Click the** Open file after publishing check box **if it is not already selected, then click Publish**

   In a few moments, the document is saved as IL_WD_5_ContractLetter.pdf and it opens in an Adobe Acrobat window or an Edge browser window if Acrobat is not installed. Another way to save a file as a PDF is to click the File tab, click Save As, navigate to the location where you want to save the file, click the Save as type arrow in the Save As dialog box, click PDF as the Save as type, then click Save. The file will be saved as a PDF document.

4. **Click the** Close button ⨯ **to exit Adobe (or the Edge browser window), click the** File tab **in Word, then click** Close

   The PDF file closes in Adobe and the Word file closes in Word.

5. **Click the** File tab, **click** Open, **click** Browse, **navigate to the location where you store your Data Files, then double-click** IL_WD_5_ContractLetter.pdf

TROUBLE
It may take up to a minute before the document is open and ready for editing.

6. **When the message shown in** FIGURE 5-22 **appears, click** OK

   The PDF file opens in Word, as shown in FIGURE 5-23.

7. **Submit the file, close the file, close Word, then click** Don't Save **in the Building Block warning box that opens**

   You removed the customized building blocks you created in this session from the Building Blocks Organizer. If you wanted to use the customized building blocks at a later time, you would save them when prompted when exiting Word.

FIGURE 5-23: PDF file open in Word

Opening non-native files directly in Word

By default, Microsoft Word saves files in one of its proprietary formats. The saved file is called a native Word file because it is saved in a file format that is native to Word, such as .docx for Word documents and .dotx for Word templates. A Word file may not be recognized by other software programs.

Sometimes you may need to open a file in Word that is a non-native file—that is, a file created with a different software program. Depending on the program used to create the original file, you may not be able to open the non-native file in Word. For example, you will get an error message if you attempt to open an Excel or PowerPoint file in Word.

When you are working with a different program and you want to work with that file in Word, you can save the file as a PDF file, as a txt, or as an rtf file. You can open and work on any of these three non-native file formats in Word. For example, you can save an Excel file as a PDF file, then open and work on the file in Word.

Practice

Skills Review

1. Add hyperlinks.

a. Start Word, open the file IL_WD_5-3.docx from the location where you store your Data Files, then save it as **IL_WD_5_EnergyHome**.

b. Select the bold text "Contact us" in the fourth paragraph, then open the Insert Hyperlink dialog box.

c. Create a hyperlink to your email address with the subject **Home Energy Consultation**.

d. Test the contact us hyperlink, then close the message window that opens and click No if a message window opens. (*Hint*: Press and hold CTRL then click the hyperlink.)

e. Scroll down, select "Energy Star" in the Source line under the table, then create a hyperlink to the webpage with the URL **www.energystar.gov**.

f. Right-click the Energy Star hyperlink, then edit the hyperlink ScreenTip to become **Information on Energy Star products and standards**.

g. Point to the Energy Star hyperlink to view the new ScreenTip, then save your changes.

2. Modify page margins.

a. Change the top and bottom margins to **.75**".

b. Change the left and right margins to **.6**".

c. In the table, select the Approximate cost per bulb table row, cut it, then paste it above the Average lifespan in hours row. (*Hint*: If necessary, use your mouse to manually adjust the column borders of the pasted row to match the rest of the table.)

d. AutoFit the table to the contents, then center the table between the margins. (*Hint*: With the table selected, click Properties in the Table group on the Layout contextual tab, then click Center.) Save your changes.

3. Create paragraph styles.

a. Apply the Title style to the "Energy Saving Measures for Homeowners" heading, then change the font color to Green, Accent 6.

b. Apply the Subtitle style to the "Reducing greenhouse gas emissions at home" heading, then click the Increase Font Size button twice.

c. Apply the Heading 1 style and Green, Accent 6 font color to the red headings: "Small Steps to Take in Your Home and Yard" and "Use Green Power."

d. Select the purple heading "Change light bulbs," click the Launcher in the Styles group, then click the New Style button in the Styles pane to open the Create New Style from Formatting dialog box.

e. Create a new style called **Small Steps** that is based on the Heading 2 style, is italic, and has a Blue, Accent 1 font color.

f. Apply the Small Steps style to each purple heading.

g. Open the Reveal Formatting pane, examine the format settings applied to several paragraphs, close all open panes, then save your changes.

4. Format with themes.

a. Change the view to Multiple Pages, then change the Style Set to Basic (Simple). (*Hint*: Use the Style Sets gallery in the Document Formatting group on the Design tab.)

b. Open the Themes gallery, apply the Slice theme (or any other theme), then zoom in to view each page.

c. Apply the Metropolitan theme, scroll to see it applied to both pages, zoom out to 50%, then save your changes.

5. Customize a theme.

a. Click the Theme Colors button, then change the theme colors to Marquee.

b. Click the Theme Colors button again, click Customize Colors, click the Accent 4 arrow, click More Colors, click the Custom tab if it is not the active tab, type **215** in the Red box, type **212** in the Green box, type **71** in the Blue box, then click OK. The Accent 4 color is now yellow green.

c. Name the palette of new theme colors **Small Steps**, then save it.

d. Change the theme fonts to Candara, change the theme effects to Smokey Glass, then change the paragraph spacing to Open. (*Hint*: Use the Theme Fonts, Effects, and Paragraph Spacing buttons in the Document Formatting group on the Design tab.)

e. Save the current theme with the name **Small Steps**, then save your changes.

6. Insert Quick Parts.

a. Change the view to 100%, then insert the Retrospect header from the Header gallery.

b. Click the Document Title property control, then type **Small Steps Toward Energy Efficiency**.

c. Press TAB, remove the Date control, insert a Company property control, then type **PKG Consultants**.

d. Insert the Retrospect footer from the Footer gallery, then click the Footer from Bottom down arrow in the Position group on the Header & Footer tab twice.

e. Type your name in the Author property control, close headers and footers, then save your changes.

7. Create Building Blocks.

a. Change the view to Multiple Pages, click the edge of the chart object on page 2 to select it, click the Insert tab, then use the Explore Quick Parts button to save the selection as a Quick Part. (*Note*: Sizing handles and a solid border appear around the chart object when it is selected.)

b. Name the building block **Pie Chart**, assign it to the Quick Parts gallery, create a new category called **Small Steps**, then click OK twice.

c. Zoom in on page 1, turn on the display of paragraph and other formatting marks, select the block of text and table beginning with the heading Change light bulbs through the end of the Energy Star hyperlink, including the paragraph mark after the hyperlink, save the selected block of text and table as a Quick Part, name the building block **Change light bulbs**, assign it to the Quick Parts gallery, assign it to the Small Steps category, then click OK.

d. Open the Header area, click the Table move handle to select the entire header, then save the header to the Header Gallery, using the name **Small Steps header**, creating a **Small Steps category**, then clicking OK twice.

e. Move to the Footer area, click the Table move handle to select the entire footer, then save the footer to the Footer Gallery, using the name **Small Steps footer**, creating a **Small Steps category**, then clicking OK twice.

f. Close the Header and Footer areas, save your changes, submit the document, then close the file without exiting Word. The completed document is shown in FIGURE 5-24.

FIGURE 5-24

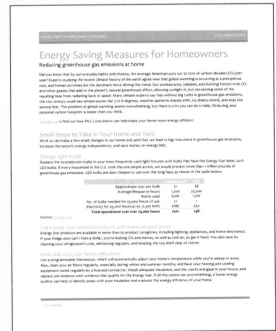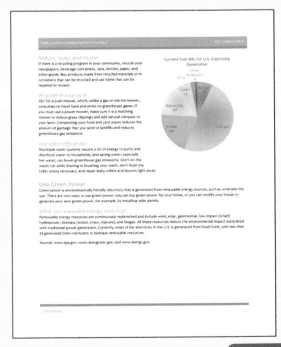

Word

8. Insert Building Blocks.

a. Open the file IL_WD_5-4.docx from the location where you store your Data Files, save it as **IL_WD_5_EnergyWork**, then apply the Small Steps theme.

b. Insert the Small Steps header from the Small Steps category in the Header gallery.

c. Insert the Small Steps footer from the Small Steps category in the Footer gallery and replace the information in the Author control with your name if necessary.

d. Click the title on page 1, open the Quick Parts gallery, then insert the Pie Chart from the Small Steps category. Select the pie chart object, then position it in bottom left with square text wrapping. (*Hint*: Take care to select only the chart object and not any elements inside the chart object.)

e. Zoom in to page 2, click in front of Manage office equipment... to position the insertion point, then open the Building Blocks Organizer.

f. Click the Category heading to sort the items by category, scroll to locate the items in the Small Steps category, click the Change light bulbs item, then click Insert.

g. Adjust the placement of the items, if necessary, then apply Red, Accent 6 font color to the title "Energy Saving Measures for Workers" and the headings "Small Steps to Take for Commuters" and "Small Steps to Take at Your Office or School."

h. Save your changes, then submit the document. The completed document is shown in FIGURE 5-25.

i. Close the file without exiting Word.

FIGURE 5-25

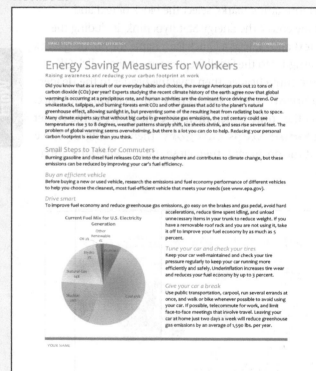

9. Use a document template.

a. Click the File tab, click New, then scroll the gallery of templates.

b. Create a new document using the Invoice (Timeless Design) template. (*Hint*: Use the Search box to find the template, if necessary.)

c. Open the header area, click the "Company" placeholder text, type **PKG Consultants**, click the "Street Address..." placeholder, type **45 Westview Highway, Syracuse, NY 13219**, click the "phone" placeholder, type **555-555-0998**, delete the word Fax and the "fax" placeholder, delete the logo graphic placeholder, then close the header area.

   d. After "Invoice No.", type **13**, then replace the Date placeholder with **July 8,** and the current year.

   e. Type your name and address in the Bill to section.

   f. In the first cell in the Description column, type **Home energy audit, initial assessment**, press TAB twice, then type **$250**.

   g. Scroll down, click the "Date" placeholder in the Total due by cell, type **August 8**, press TAB, then type **$250**.

   h. Save the document with the filename **IL_WD_5_Invoice13** to the location where you store your Data Files, clicking OK if a warning box opens.

10. Work with PDF files in Word.

   a. Click the File tab, click Export, click the Create PDF/XPS button, then click Publish.

   b. View the invoice in Adobe or your browser, then click to exit Adobe or your browser.

   c. Submit the Word file, click the File tab in Word, then click Close.

   d. Click the File tab, click Open, navigate to the location where you store your Data Files, then open **IL_WD_5_Invoice13.pdf**.

   e. Submit the PDF file, close the file, do not save changes to the Building Blocks.dotx file if prompted, then exit Word.

Independent Challenge 1

You work in public outreach at the Riverwalk Medical Clinic. You have written the text for a report on annual giving to the Clinic, and now you need to format the report. You'll use styles, themes, and Quick Parts to give the report a cohesive and professional look.

   a. Start Word, create a new document using the Report design (blank) template, then save it as **IL_WD_5_RMCGiving**.

   b. Insert a Sideline cover page. Type **Riverwalk Medical Clinic Annual Giving** in the Title property control, then type **An Invitation to Donors** in the Subtitle property control.

   c. Remove the Company property control, type your name in the Author property control, then remove the Date property control.

   d. Scroll to the next page (contains "Title"), select all the body text on the page under the Heading 1 heading (starting with "To get started..."), insert the text file IL_WD_5-5.docx from the location where you store your Data Files. (*Hint*: Click the Object button arrow in the Text group on the Insert tab, click Text from file, then locate and insert the text file.)

   e. Scroll up to view the format and content of the report. Press CTRL+HOME, scroll to the second page (contains "Title"), select Title, type **Riverwalk Medical Clinic Annual Giving**, select Heading 1, type **An Invitation to Donors**, then format the following headings in the Heading 1 style: Capital Campaign Exceeds Its Goal, Types of Gifts, and The Cambridge Society.

   f. Change the style set of the document to Lines (Stylish), then reduce the font size of the title at the top of the second page of the document (not on the cover page) to 28 points.

   g. See how different styles change the look of a document by applying the following heading styles to the Annual Fund Gifts subheading under the Types of Gifts heading: the Heading 1 style, the Heading 2 style, then the Heading 3 style. (*Hint*: Open the Styles pane, click Options, then click All Styles in the Select styles to show box).

   h. Apply the Heading 3 style to the following subheadings: Memorial Gifts, Charitable Gifts, Named Endowments.

   i. Insert a Next Page section break after the end of the last paragraph above the chart (ends with "...requests for anonymity"), switch to multiple pages view, select the chart object on the last page, open the Page Setup dialog box from the Layout tab, then change the vertical alignment of the page containing the chart to Center.

   j. Using the Cover Page command, remove the current cover page, then use the Cover Page command again to insert a different cover page for the report from the Built-in category. Update or remove the content and property controls as necessary. (*Hint*: Scroll as needed to see the Built-in options.)

Independent Challenge 1 (continued)

k. Starting on the first page of the report (contains the text of the report), add a footer to the report that includes a page number and your name. Navigate to the footer on the last page of the report (contains the chart), click the Different First Page check box in the Options group on the Header & Footer ribbon to deselect it, click Page Number in the Header & Footer group, click Format Page Numbers, then click the Continue from previous section option button. Close the footer and verify that the three pages of the report text (not including the cover page) are numbered 1, 2, and 3 similar to the sample report shown in FIGURE 5-26.

l. Experiment with different themes, theme colors, theme fonts, theme effects, and paragraph spacing, then use these tools to customize the look of the report.

m. Adjust the elements of the report as necessary to make sure each page has a cohesive and professional look and the text fits comfortably on four pages. Figure 5-26 shows a sample finished report using the Gallery theme, the Facet built-in cover page, and the Integral built-in footer.

n. Save your changes to the document, submit the document to your instructor, close the document, then exit Word.

FIGURE 5-26

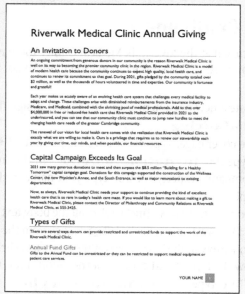

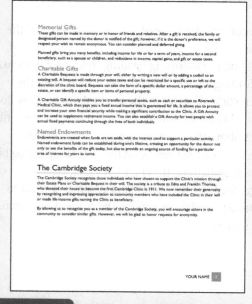

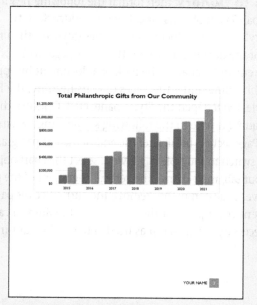

Independent Challenge 2

The Education department at the university where you work publishes a blog each month on a different topic in education. The blog is published on the university website and distributed electronically to a mailing list of subscribers. It's your job to format the blog posts and prepare them for electronic distribution. In this exercise you design a layout for a blog post, add hyperlinks to it, then save the document as a PDF file and as a webpage.

a. Start Word, open the file IL_WD_5-6.docx from the location where you store your Data Files, then save it as **IL_WD_5_LiteracyBlog** to the location where you store your Data Files.

b. In the third line of the document, replace YOUR NAME with your name.

c. Replace each instance of green text in the document with a hyperlink to the appropriate website for each source, shown in the table below. Include a ScreenTip in each hyperlink.

Source	Website URL	ScreenTip
UNESCO	www.unesco.org	United Nations Educational, Cultural, and Scientific Organization
ProLiteracy	www.proliteracy.org	Research and data on adult literacy worldwide
National Bureau of Economic Research	www.nber.org	Research and data on public policy
American Journal of Public Health	www.ajph.org	American Public Health Association
American Library Association	www.ala.org/advocacy/literacy	Key resources from the ALA

d. Test each link to make sure it works, then make any necessary adjustments.

e. Apply styles to the document. Format the first three lines of text using styles of your choice, then apply a heading style to each red heading in the document.

f. Apply a style set to the document.

g. Apply a theme to the document. Customize the theme fonts, theme colors, and paragraph spacing to achieve the look you want. FIGURE 5-27 shows a sample layout.

h. Create a new bullet character using a symbol and apply the new symbol bullet to the two bulleted lists in the document.

i. Adjust the margins, alignment, colors, and other formatting so the blog post is readable and the layout is attractive, then save your changes and submit the file.

j. Check the document for compatibility with earlier versions of Word.

k. Save the document as a PDF file, submit the PDF file, then close Adobe or your browser.

l. Save document as a Single File Web Page, view the webpage in Word, submit the webpage file, then save your changes.

m. Close all open files, then exit Word.

FIGURE 5-27

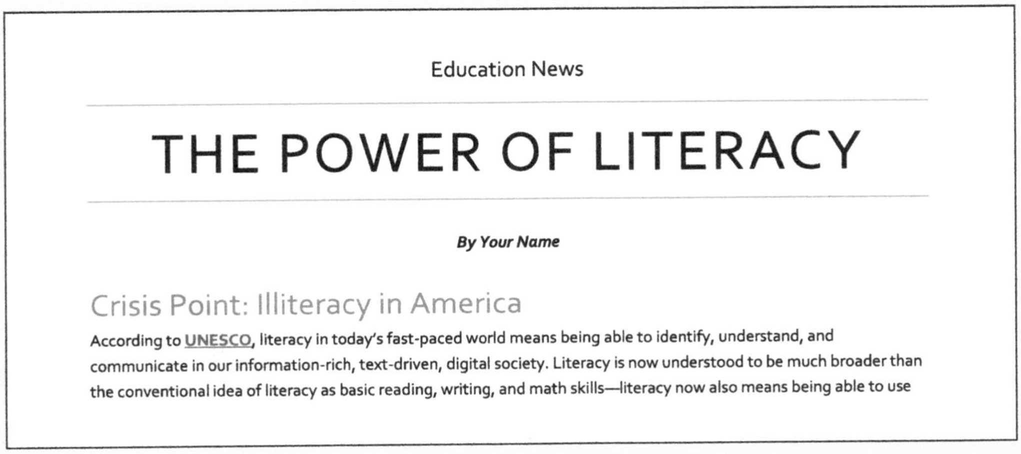

Education News

THE POWER OF LITERACY

By Your Name

Crisis Point: Illiteracy in America

According to UNESCO, literacy in today's fast-paced world means being able to identify, understand, and communicate in our information-rich, text-driven, digital society. Literacy is now understood to be much broader than the conventional idea of literacy as basic reading, writing, and math skills—literacy now also means being able to use

Visual Workshop

Create the letter shown in FIGURE 5-28. Start with the Modern Capsules letterhead template. Replace the logo placeholder with an icon. (*Hint*: Right-click the logo placeholder, point to Change Picture, click From Icons, then search for Headset and select the icon shown in the figure.) Resize the icon to be .7" tall and wide. Replace the placeholder text with the text shown in Figure 5-28. For the body of the letter, insert the text file **IL_WD_5-7.docx** from the location where you store your Data Files. (*Hint*: Use the Object arrow on the Insert tab, then click Text from File.) In the address block, remove the space after the paragraphs. Remove any hyperlinks from the letter. Apply the Slice theme and change the theme fonts to Corbel. (*Hint*: If the Slice theme is not available, select a different theme.) Save the document as **IL_WD_5_ArtisanLetter**.

FIGURE 5-28

Artisan Customer Service Agency
1550 East 9th Avenue, Escondido, CA 92025
www.artisancustomerservice.com
Tel: 442-555-0243

August 31, 2021

Ms. Lydia Paulo
Vice President
Cityside Auto Insurance
35 North Tulip Street
Escondido, CA 92029

Dear Ms. Paulo,

Thank you for choosing the Artisan Customer Service Agency to represent Cityside Auto Insurance in your customer service needs. Your business and your customers are in good hands with us.

Our trained customer service representatives are available 24 hours a day to assist your customers in a friendly, efficient, and professional manner. We look forward to working with you to achieve your customer service goals.

Warm regards,

Your Name
President
yourname@artisancustomerservice.com

Working with Styles, Themes, and Building Blocks

Merging Word Documents

CASE You need to send a letter to people who signed up for one of the job search workshops offered by the Seattle branch of JCL Talent, Inc. The letter confirms their reservation and receipt of a nonrefundable deposit. You also need to send a general information packet to all the people participating in upcoming JCL Talent workshops. You use mail merge to create a personalized form letter for people who recently signed up for a workshop and mailing labels for the information packet.

Module Objectives

After completing this module, you will be able to:

- Understand mail merge
- Create a main document
- Design a data source
- Enter and edit records
- Add merge fields

- Work with merge rules
- Merge data
- Create labels
- Sort and filter records

Files You Will Need

IL_WD_6-1.docx

Support_WD_6_LabelsData.accdb

IL_WD_6-2.docx

IL_WD_6-3.docx

IL_WD_6-4.docx

Support_WD_6_MuseumData.accdb

Understand Mail Merge

Learning Outcomes
• Identify the elements of a mail merge
• State the benefits of performing a mail merge

When you perform a **mail merge**, you merge a standard Word document with a file that contains customized information for many individuals or items. The standard document is called the **main document**. The file with the unique data for individual people or items is called the **data source**. Merging the main document with a data source results in a **merged document** that contains customized versions of the main document, as shown in FIGURE 6-1. The Mail Merge pane steps you through the process of setting up and performing a mail merge. You can also perform a mail merge using the commands on the Mailings tab. **CASE** *You decide to use the Mail Merge pane to create your form letters and the commands on the Mailings tab to create your mailing labels. Before beginning, you explore the steps involved in performing a mail merge.*

DETAILS

- **Create the main document**

  The main document contains the text—often called **boilerplate text**—that appears in every version of the merged document. The main document also includes the merge fields, which indicate where the customized information is inserted when you perform the merge. You insert the merge fields in the main document after you have created or selected the data source. You can create a main document using one of the following: a new blank document, the current document, a template, or an existing document.

- **Create a data source or select an existing data source**

  The data source is a file that contains the unique information for each individual or item, such as a person's name. It provides the information that varies in every version of the merged document. A data source is composed of data fields and data records. A **data field** is a category of information, such as last name, first name, street address, city, or postal code. A **data record** is a complete set of related information for an individual or an item, such as one person's name and address. Think of a data source file as a table: the header row contains the names of the data fields (the **field names**), and each row in the table is an individual data record. You can create a new data source or you can use an existing data source, such as a data source created in Word, an Outlook contact list, an Access database, or an Excel worksheet.

- **Identify the fields to include in the data source and enter the records**

  When you create a new data source, you must first identify the fields to include, such as first name, last name, and street address if you are creating a data source that will include addresses. It is also important to think of and include all the fields you will need (not just the obvious ones) before you begin to enter data. For example, if you are creating a data source that includes names and addresses, you might need to include fields for a person's middle name, title, apartment number, department name, or country, even if some records in the data source will not include that information. Once you have identified the fields and set up your data source, you are ready to enter the data for each record.

- **Add merge fields to the main document**

  A **merge field** is a placeholder that you insert in the main document to indicate where the data from each record should be inserted when you perform the merge. For example, you insert a ZIP Code merge field in the location where you want to insert a ZIP Code. The merge fields in a main document must correspond with the field names in the associated data source. Merge fields must be inserted, not typed, in the main document. The Mail Merge pane and the Mailings tab provide access to the dialog boxes you use to insert merge fields.

- **Merge the data from the data source into the main document**

  Once you have established your data source and inserted the merge fields in the main document, you are ready to perform the merge. You can merge to a new file, which contains a customized version of the main document for each record in the data source, or you can merge directly to a printer or an email message.

FIGURE 6-1: **Mail Merge Process**

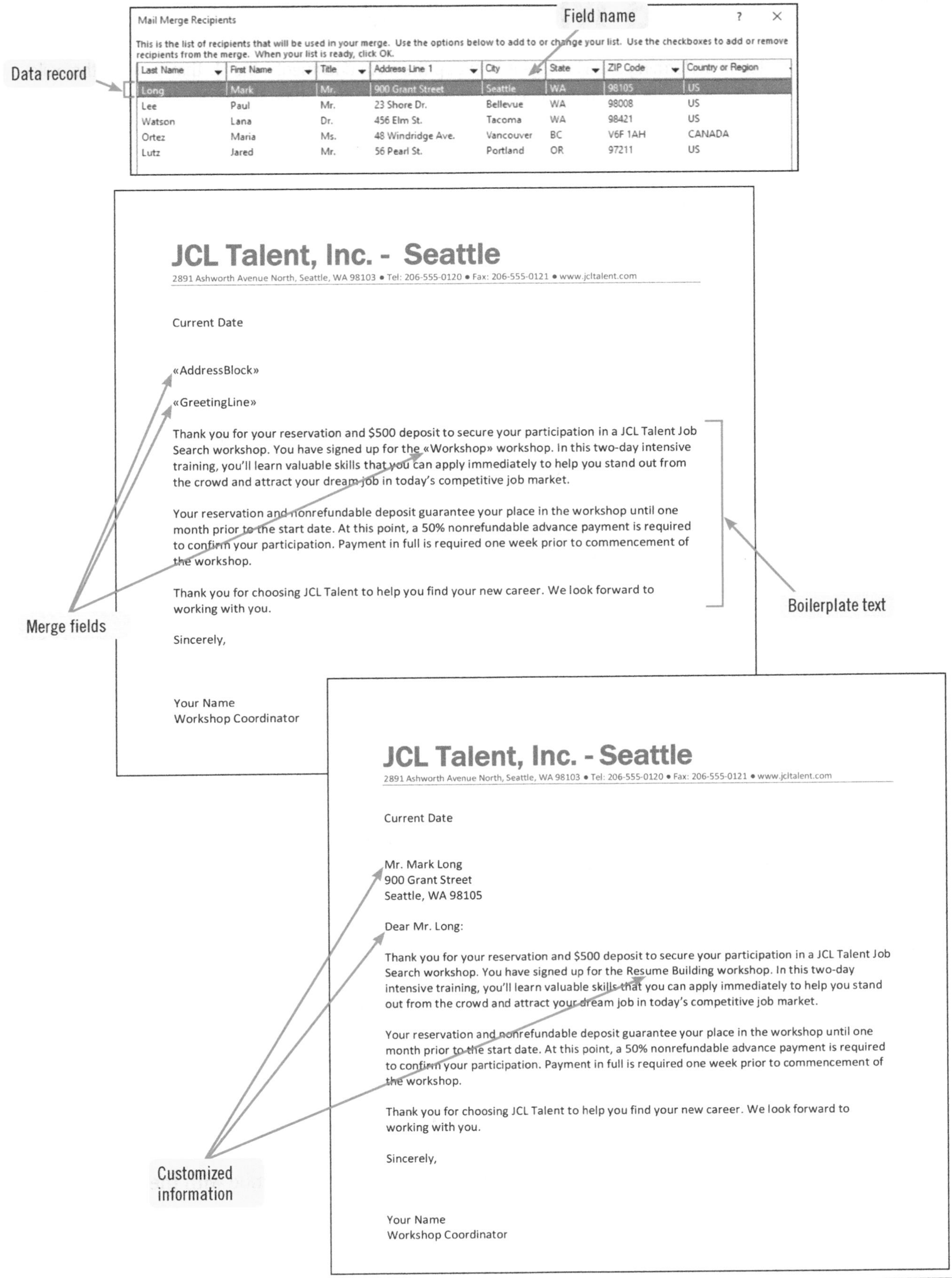

Field name

Mail Merge Recipients   ?   ×

This is the list of recipients that will be used in your merge. Use the options below to add to or change your list. Use the checkboxes to add or remove
recipients from the merge. When your list is ready, click OK.

Data record

Last Name	First Name	Title	Address Line 1	City	State	ZIP Code	Country or Region
Long	Mark	Mr.	900 Grant Street	Seattle	WA	98105	US
Lee	Paul	Mr.	23 Shore Dr.	Bellevue	WA	98008	US
Watson	Lana	Dr.	456 Elm St.	Tacoma	WA	98421	US
Ortez	Maria	Ms.	48 Windridge Ave.	Vancouver	BC	V6F 1AH	CANADA
Lutz	Jared	Mr.	56 Pearl St.	Portland	OR	97211	US

JCL Talent, Inc. - Seattle

2891 Ashworth Avenue North, Seattle, WA 98103 ● Tel: 206-555-0120 ● Fax: 206-555-0121 ● www.jcltalent.com

Current Date

«AddressBlock»

«GreetingLine»

Thank you for your reservation and $500 deposit to secure your participation in a JCL Talent Job
Search workshop. You have signed up for the «Workshop» workshop. In this two-day intensive
training, you'll learn valuable skills that you can apply immediately to help you stand out from
the crowd and attract your dream job in today's competitive job market.

Your reservation and nonrefundable deposit guarantee your place in the workshop until one
month prior to the start date. At this point, a 50% nonrefundable advance payment is required
to confirm your participation. Payment in full is required one week prior to commencement of
the workshop.

Thank you for choosing JCL Talent to help you find your new career. We look forward to
working with you.

Sincerely,

Your Name
Workshop Coordinator

Merge fields

Boilerplate text

JCL Talent, Inc. - Seattle

2891 Ashworth Avenue North, Seattle, WA 98103 ● Tel: 206-555-0120 ● Fax: 206-555-0121 ● www.jcltalent.com

Current Date

Mr. Mark Long
900 Grant Street
Seattle, WA 98105

Dear Mr. Long:

Thank you for your reservation and $500 deposit to secure your participation in a JCL Talent Job
Search workshop. You have signed up for the Resume Building workshop. In this two-day
intensive training, you'll learn valuable skills that you can apply immediately to help you stand
out from the crowd and attract your dream job in today's competitive job market.

Your reservation and nonrefundable deposit guarantee your place in the workshop until one
month prior to the start date. At this point, a 50% nonrefundable advance payment is required
to confirm your participation. Payment in full is required one week prior to commencement of
the workshop.

Thank you for choosing JCL Talent to help you find your new career. We look forward to
working with you.

Sincerely,

Your Name
Workshop Coordinator

Customized
information

Word

Create a Main Document

The first step in performing a mail merge is to set up the main document—the file that contains the boiler-plate text. You can create a main document from scratch, save an existing document as a main document, or use a mail merge template to create a main document. When you start with an existing document, you modify the page setup before you save the document as a main document. You then open the Mail Merge pane, which walks you through the process of selecting the type of main document you want to create.

CASE > *You decide to use an existing form letter for your main document. You modify the page setup by changing the page orientation, then start the mail merge process by opening the Mail Merge pane.*

STEPS

1. **sam ↓ Open IL_WD_6-1.docx from the location where you store your Data Files, then save it as IL_WD_6_ConfirmLetter**
   The document containing the text of the letter you want to send is formatted in Landscape orientation. You change the orientation to Portrait.

2. **Click the Layout tab, click Orientation in the Page Setup group, then click Portrait**

3. **Save and close the document, but do not exit Word**

4. **Open a new blank document in Word, click the Mailings tab, click the Start Mail Merge button in the Start Mail Merge group, then click Step-by-Step Mail Merge Wizard**
   The Mail Merge pane opens, as shown in FIGURE 6-2, and displays information for the first step in the mail merge process: Select document type, which is the type of merge document to create. Options for documents include E-mail messages, Envelopes, Labels, and Directory.

5. **Make sure the Letters option button is selected, then click Next: Starting document to continue with the next step**
   The Mail Merge pane displays the options for the second step: Select starting document, which is the main document. You can use the current document, start with a mail merge template, or use an existing file.

6. **Select the Start from existing document option button, make sure (More files...) is selected in the Start from existing box, then click Open**
   The Open dialog box opens.

7. **Navigate to the location where you stored the document you created at the beginning of this lesson, select the file IL_WD_6_ConfirmLetter.docx, then click Open**
   Notice the filename in the title bar is Document1. When you create a main document that is based on an existing document, Word gives the main document a default temporary filename.

8. **Click the Save button 🖫 on the Quick Access toolbar, then save the main document as IL_WD_6_ConfirmLetterMain to the location where you store your files**
   It's a good idea to include "main" in the filename so that you can easily recognize the file as a main document.

9. **Replace Current Date at the beginning of the document with the current date, scroll to and select Keisha Dunbar in the signature line at the end of the letter, type your name, press CTRL+HOME, then save your changes**
   The edited main document is shown in FIGURE 6-3.

10. **Click Next: Select recipients in the Mail Merge pane to continue with the next step**
    You continue with Step 3 of 6 in the next lesson.

FIGURE 6-2: Step 1 of 6 Mail Merge pane

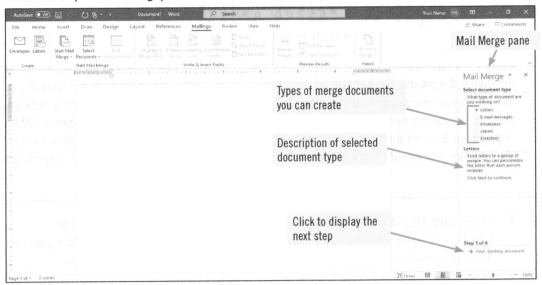

- Mail Merge pane
- Types of merge documents you can create
- Description of selected document type
- Click to display the next step

FIGURE 6-3: Main document with Step 2 of 6 Mail Merge pane

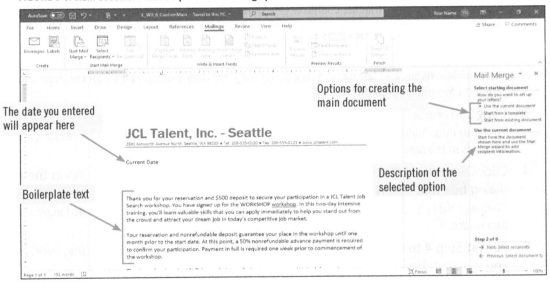

- Options for creating the main document
- The date you entered will appear here
- Description of the selected option
- Boilerplate text

Using a mail merge template

If you are creating letters or faxes, you can use a mail merge template to start your main document. Each template includes placeholder text, which you can replace, and merge fields, which you can match to the field names in your data source. To create a main document that is based on a mail merge template, click the File tab, click New, type "mail merge" in the Search for online templates box, click the Start searching button, select one of the mail merge templates to use as your main document, and then click Create. You can then use the Mail Merge pane or the Ribbon to begin a mail merge using the current document. In the Step 2 of 6 Mail Merge pane, click the Use the current document option

button, and then click Next. Once you have created the main document, you can customize the main document with your own information: edit the placeholder text; change the document format; or add, remove, or modify the merge fields.

Before performing the merge, make sure to match the names of the merge fields used in the template with the field names used in your data source. To match the field names, click the Match Fields button in the Write & Insert Fields group on the Mailings tab, and then use the arrows in the Match Fields dialog box to select the field name in your data source that corresponds to each address field component in the main document.

Design a Data Source

Learning Outcomes
• Create a data source
• Add and remove fields in a data source

Once you have set up and created the main document, the next step in the mail merge process is to identify the data source, the file that contains the information that is used to customize each version of the merge document. You can use an existing data source that already contains the records you want to include in your merge, or you can create a new data source. When you create a new data source, you must determine the fields to include—the categories of information, such as a first name, last name, city, or postal code—and then add the records. **CASE** ▸ *You create a new data source that includes fields for the workshop participant's name and address, and the name of the workshop booked by the participant.*

STEPS

QUICK TIP
Data sources created and saved as an Access database use the .accdb file extension; data sources created and saved in Word as part of the Mail Merge process use the .mdb file extension.

1. **Make sure Step 3 of 6 is displayed at the bottom of the Mail Merge pane**

   Step 3 of 6 involves selecting a data source to use for the merge. You can use an existing data source from Access, use a list of contacts created in Microsoft Outlook, or create a new data source.

2. **Select the Type a new list option button, then click Create**

   The New Address List dialog box opens, as shown in FIGURE 6-4. You use this dialog box both to design your data source and to enter records. The column headings in the Type recipient information... section of the dialog box are fields that are commonly used in form letters, but you can customize your data source by adding and removing columns (fields) from this table. A data source can be merged with more than one main document, so it's important to design a data source to be flexible. The more fields you include in a data source, the more flexible it is. For example, if you include separate fields for a person's title, first name, middle name, and last name, you can use the same data source to create an envelope addressed to "Mr. John Montgomery Smith" and a form letter with the greeting "Dear John".

3. **Click Customize Columns**

   The Customize Address List dialog box opens. You use this dialog box to add, delete, rename, and reorder the fields in the data source.

4. **Click Company Name in the list of field names, click Delete, then click Yes in the warning dialog box that opens**

   Company Name is removed from the list of field names. The Company Name field is no longer a part of the data source.

5. **Repeat Step 4 to delete the following fields: Address Line 2, Home Phone, Work Phone, and E-mail Address**

   The fields are removed from the data source.

6. **Click Add, type Workshop in the Add Field dialog box, then click OK**

   A field called "Workshop", which you will use to indicate the workshop booked by the participant, is added to the data source.

7. **Make sure Workshop is selected in the list of field names, then click Move Up until Workshop is at the top of the list**

   The field name "Workshop" is moved to the top of the list, as shown in FIGURE 6-5. Although the order of field names does not matter in a data source, it's convenient to arrange the field names logically to make it easier to enter and edit records.

8. **Click OK**

   The New Address List dialog box shows the customized list of fields, with the Workshop field first in the list. The next step is to enter each record you want to include in the data source. You add records to the data source in the next lesson.

FIGURE 6-4: **New Address List dialog box**

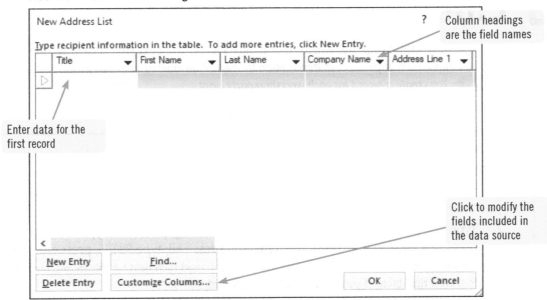

Enter data for the first record

Column headings are the field names

Click to modify the fields included in the data source

FIGURE 6-5: **Customize Address List dialog box**

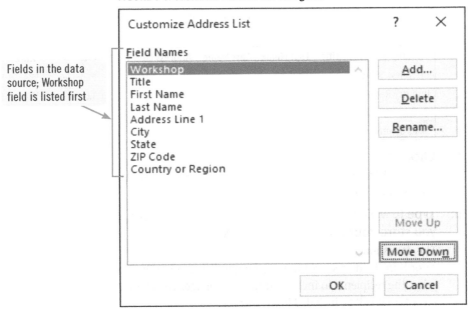

Fields in the data source; Workshop field is listed first

Merging with an Outlook data source

If you maintain lists of contacts in Microsoft Outlook, you can use one of your Outlook contact lists as a data source for a merge. To merge with an Outlook data source, click the Select from Outlook contacts option button in the Step 3 of 6 Mail Merge pane, then click Choose Contacts Folder to open the Choose Profile dialog box. In this dialog box, use the Profile Name arrow to select the profile you want to use, then click OK to open the Select Contacts dialog box. In this dialog box, select the contact list you want to use as the data source, and then click OK. All the contacts included in the selected folder appear in the Mail Merge Recipients dialog box. Here, you can refine the list of recipients to include in the merge by sorting and filtering the records. When you are satisfied, click OK in the Mail Merge Recipients dialog box.

Enter and Edit Records

Learning
Outcomes
• Add records
• Edit a recipient list

Once you have established the structure of a data source, the next step is to enter the records. Each record includes the complete set of information for each individual or item you include in the data source. **CASE** ▸ *You create a record for each workshop participant.*

STEPS

QUICK TIP
Be careful not to add spaces or extra punctuation after an entry in a field, or these will appear when the data is merged.

1. **Verify the insertion point is in the Workshop box in the New Address List dialog box, type Resume Building, then press TAB**

   "Resume Building" appears in the Workshop field, and the insertion point moves to the next column, the Title field.

2. **Type Mr., press TAB, type Mark, press TAB, type Long, press TAB, type 900 Grant Street, press TAB, type Seattle, press TAB, type WA, press TAB, type 98105, press TAB, then type US**

   Data is entered in all the fields for the first record. You used each field for this record, but you can choose to leave a field blank if you do not need it for a record.

QUICK TIP
You can also press TAB at the end of the last field to start a new record.

3. **Click New Entry**

   The record for Mark Long is added to the data source, and the New Address List dialog box displays empty fields for the next record, as shown in FIGURE 6-6.

4. **Enter the following four records, pressing TAB to move from field to field, and clicking New Entry at the end of each record except the last:**

Workshop	Title	First Name	Last Name	Address Line 1	City	State	ZIP	Country
Interview Skills	Mr.	Paul	Lee	23 Shore Dr.	Bellevue	WA	98008	US
Industry Research	Ms.	Lana	Watson	456 Elm St.	Tacoma	WA	98421	US
Resume Building	Ms.	Maria	Ortez	48 Windridge Ave.	Vancouver	BC	V6F 1AH	CANADA
Skills Inventory	Mr.	Jared	Lutz	56 Pearl St.	Portland	OR	97211	US

TROUBLE
If a check mark appears in the blank record under Jared Lutz, click the check mark to eliminate the record from the merge.

5. **Click OK**

   The Save Address List dialog box opens. Data sources are saved by default in the My Data Sources folder in Microsoft Office Address Lists (*.mdb) format.

6. **Type IL_WD_6_WorkshopData in the File name box, navigate to the location where you store your Data Files, then click Save**

   The data source is saved, and the Mail Merge Recipients dialog box opens. The dialog box shows the records in the data source in table format. You can use the dialog box to sort and filter records, and to select the recipients to include in the mail merge. The check marks in the second column indicate the records that will be included in the merge.

7. **Click IL_WD_6_WorkshopData.mdb in the Data Source box at the bottom of the dialog box as shown in FIGURE 6-7**

8. **Click Edit to open the Edit Data Source dialog box**

   You use this dialog box to edit a recipient list, including adding and removing fields, editing field names, adding and removing records, and editing existing records.

QUICK TIP
If you want to add new records or modify existing records, click Edit recipient list in the Mail Merge pane.

9. **Click Ms. in the Title field of the Lana Watson record to select it, then type Dr. as shown in FIGURE 6-8**

10. **Click OK in the Edit Data Source dialog box, click Yes, then click OK in the Mail Merge Recipients dialog box**

    The file type and filename of the data source attached to the main document now appear under Use an existing list heading in the Mail Merge pane.

Merging Word Documents

FIGURE 6-6: Record in New Address List dialog box

Click to add a new record

Data for the first record in the data source

Enter the data for the second record

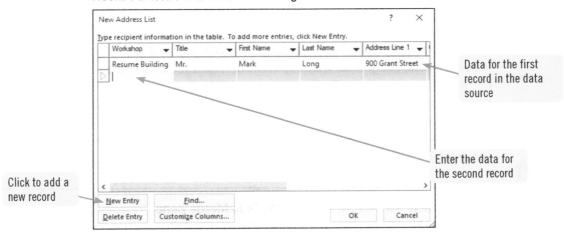

FIGURE 6-7: Data Source selected in the Mail Merge Recipients dialog box

Click to include all records in the merge

Click to enable the Edit button

Edit button

Records

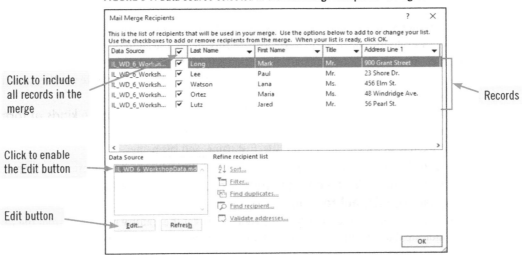

FIGURE 6-8: Edit Data Source dialog box

Type edits directly in the record

Click to search for a record

Click to delete the selected record

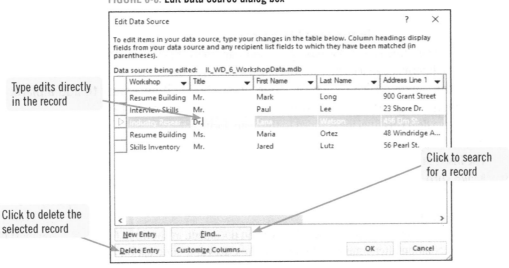

Word

Add Merge Fields

Learning Outcomes
• Insert merge fields
• Customize an address block and greeting field

After you have created and identified the data source, the next step is to insert the merge fields in the main document. Merge fields serve as placeholders for text that is inserted when the main document and the data source are merged. The names of merge fields correspond to the field names in the data source. You can insert merge fields using the Mail Merge pane or the Address Block, Greeting Line, and Insert Merge Field buttons in the Write & Insert Fields group on the Mailings tab. You cannot type merge fields into the main document. **CASE** ▶ *You use the Mail Merge pane to insert merge fields for the inside address and greeting of the letter. You also insert a merge field for the workshop in the body of the letter.*

STEPS

1. **Click** Next: Write your letter **in the Mail Merge pane**

   The Mail Merge pane shows the options for Step 4 of 6: Write your letter. During this step, you write or edit the boilerplate text and insert the merge fields in the main document. Since your form letter is already written, you are ready to add the merge fields to it.

2. **Click the blank line above the first body paragraph, then click** Address block **in the Mail Merge pane**

   The Insert Address Block dialog box opens, as shown in FIGURE 6-9. You use this dialog box to specify the fields you want to include in an address block. In this merge, the address block is the inside address of the form letter. An address block automatically includes fields for the recipient's title, name, street, city, state, and ZIP code, but you can select the format for the recipient's name and indicate whether to include a company name or country in the address.

3. **Scroll the list of formats for a recipient's name to get a feel for the kinds of formats you can use, then click** Mr. Joshua Randall Jr. **if it is not already selected**

   The selected format uses the recipient's title, first name, and last name.

4. **Make sure the** Only include the country/region if different than: option button **is selected, select** United States **in the box (or another country name if entered), then type** US **or the appropriate country abbreviation**

   You only need to include the country in the address block if the country is different from the United States, so you indicate that all entries in the Country field in your data source, except "US", should be included in the printed address.

5. **Deselect the** Format address according to the destination country/region check box, **click** OK, **then press** ENTER **twice**

   The merge field AddressBlock is added to the main document. Chevrons (<< and >>) surround a merge field to distinguish it from the boilerplate text.

6. **Click** Greeting line **in the Mail Merge pane**

   The Insert Greeting Line dialog box opens. You want to use the format "Dear Mr. Randall:" for a greeting. The default format uses a comma instead of a colon, so you have to change the comma to a colon.

7. **Click the , arrow, click :, click** OK, **then press** ENTER, **if necessary to add a blank line between the greeting line and the first paragraph of the letter**

   The merge field GreetingLine is added to the main document.

8. **In the body of the letter select** WORKSHOP, **then click** More items **in the Mail Merge pane**

   The Insert Merge Field dialog box opens and displays the list of field names included in the data source.

9. **Make sure** Workshop **is selected in the dialog box, click** Insert, **click** Close, **press** SPACEBAR **to add a space between the merge field and "workshop" if there is no space, then save your changes**

   The Workshop merge field is inserted in the main document, as shown in FIGURE 6-10. You must type spaces and punctuation after a merge field if you want spaces and punctuation to appear in that location in the merged documents.

FIGURE 6-9: Insert Address Block dialog box

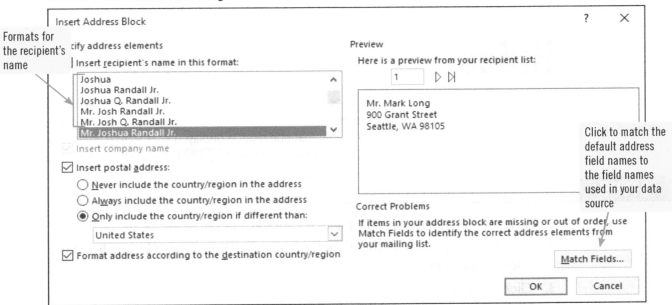

Formats for the recipient's name

FIGURE 6-10: Merge fields in the main document

Matching fields

The merge fields you insert in a main document must correspond with the field names in the associated data source. If you are using the Address Block merge field, you must make sure that the default address field names correspond to the field names used in your data source. If the default address field names do not match the field names in your data source, click Match Fields in the Insert Address Block dialog box, then use the arrows in the Match Fields dialog box to select the field name in the data source that corresponds to each default address field name. You can also click the Match Fields button in the Write & Insert Fields group on the Mailings tab to open the Match Fields dialog box.

Work with Merge Rules

Learning
Outcomes
• Specify a merge
  rule
• Use an IF field
• Modify field
  properties

You can specify that certain merge rules be applied to the merge process. One of the most useful of these merge rules is the If…Then…Else merge rule. This rule inserts an IF merge field into a main document. You use an IF field when you need to specify that one result is displayed if a specific condition is met and another result is displayed if the specific condition is *not* met. **CASE** *You select and then customize the If…Then…Else merge rule, and then toggle and format a field code.*

STEPS

1. **Select** two-day **in the second line of paragraph 1 of the letter**

2. **Click the** Rules button **in the Write & Insert Fields group to display the list of merge rules as shown in** FIGURE 6-11

3. **Click** If…Then…Else…
   The Insert Word Field: IF dialog box opens. In this dialog box, you enter the IF criteria.

4. **Enter criteria for the If…Then…Else rule as shown in** FIGURE 6-12**, click** OK**, then press** SPACEBAR **to add a space between "two-day" and "intensive", if necessary**
   You specify that "two-day" will appear as the workshop duration in every letter to people participating in the Resume Building seminar, and "three-day" will appear in every letter to people participating in any of the other seminars. The If…Then…Else rule turns "two-day" into an IF Merge field that you can view using the Toggle feature.

5. **Select** two-day **(it turns gray, indicating it is a field and not regular text), click the** right mouse button**, then click** Toggle Field Codes
   The IF merge field is displayed as shown in FIGURE 6-13. You notice that the font of the merge field does not match the font of the letter text.

6. **Click the** right mouse button**, click** Toggle Field Codes **to view "two-day", then select** two-day **if necessary (it becomes a darker gray)**

7. **Click the** right mouse button**, click** Font**, select** Calibri **in the Font box, then click** OK
   The merge field "two-day" now matches the rest of the letter. You only know it is a merge field if you click on it to view the gray shading.

8. **Save the document**
   In the next lesson, you will preview and then complete the merge.

FIGURE 6-11: List of merge rules

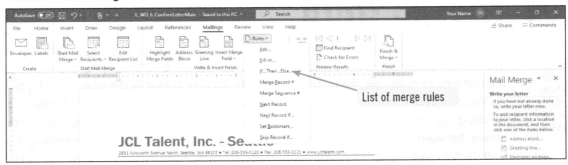

List of merge rules

FIGURE 6-12: Insert Word Field: IF dialog box

The Workshop field name is compared to "Resume Building"

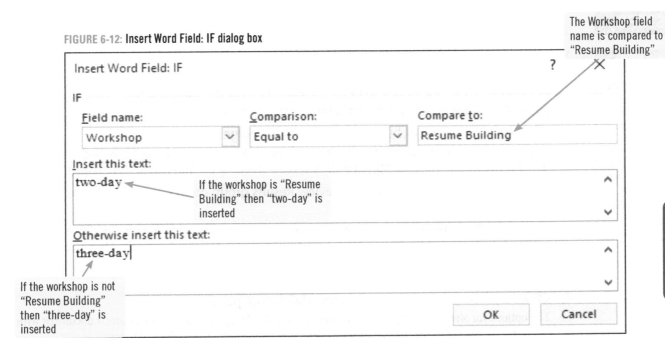

If the workshop is "Resume Building" then "two-day" is inserted

If the workshop is not "Resume Building" then "three-day" is inserted

FIGURE 6-13: Toggled IF merge field

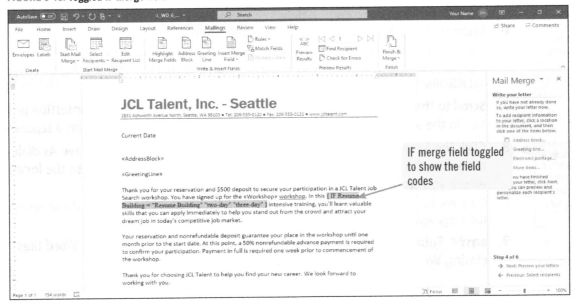

IF merge field toggled to show the field codes

Merge Data

**Learning
Outcomes**
• Preview a merge
• Merge data to a
  new document
• Customize a
  merged document

Once you have added records to your data source and inserted merge fields and selected merge rules in the main document, you are ready to perform the merge. Before merging, you should preview the merged data to make sure the printed documents will appear exactly the way in which you want them to. You can preview the merge using the Mail Merge pane or the Preview Results button in the Preview Results group on the Mailings tab. When you merge the main document with the data source, you must choose between merging to a new file or directly to a printer. **CASE** ▶ *Before merging the form letter with the data source, you preview the merge to make sure the data appears in the letter as you intended. You then merge the two files to a new document.*

STEPS

QUICK TIP
To adjust the main document, click the Preview Results button in the Preview Results group on the Mailings tab, then make any necessary changes. Click the Preview Results button again to preview the merged data.

1. **Click** Next: Preview your letters **in the Mail Merge pane**

   The data from the first record in the data source appears in place of the merge fields in the main document, as shown in FIGURE 6-14. Always preview a document to verify that the merge fields, punctuation, page breaks, and spacing all appear as you intend before you perform the merge.

2. **Click the** Next Recipient button ⟩⟩ **in the Mail Merge pane**

   The data from the second record in the data source appears in place of the merge fields. Notice that "two-day" has changed to "three-day" because Mr. Paul Lee is attending the Interview Skills workshop.

3. **Click the** Go to Record box **in the Preview Results group on the Mailings tab, type** 4, **then press** ENTER

   The data for the fourth record appears in the document window. The non-US country name, in this case CANADA, is included in the address block, just as you specified. You can also use the **First Record** ◁|, **Previous Record** ◁, **Next Record** ▷, and **Last Record** |▷| buttons in the Preview Results group to preview the merged data. TABLE 6-1 describes other commands on the Mailings tab.

4. **Click** Next: Complete the merge **in the Mail Merge pane**

   The options for Step 6 of 6 appear in the Mail Merge pane. Merging to a new file creates a document with one letter for each record in the data source. This allows you to edit the individual letters.

QUICK TIP
If your data source contains many records, you can merge directly to a printer to avoid creating a large file.

5. **Click** Edit individual letters **to merge the data to a new document**

   The Merge to New Document dialog box opens. You can use this dialog box to specify the records to include in the merge.

6. **Make sure the** All option button **is selected, then click** OK

   The main document and the data source are merged to a new document called Letters1, which contains a customized form letter for each record in the data source. You can now further personalize the letters without affecting the main document or the data source.

7. **Scroll to the fourth letter (addressed to Ms. Maria Ortez), place the insertion point before V6F in the address block, then press** ENTER **to place the postal code on a separate line**

QUICK TIP
Print only one letter if you are required to submit a printed document to your instructor.

8. **Click the Save button** 🖫 **on the Quick Access toolbar to open the Save As dialog box, then save the merged document as** IL_WD_6_ConfirmLetterMerge **to the location where you store your Data Files**

   Once you have created the main document and the data source, you can create the letters by performing the merge again.

9. **sam**▲ **Submit the document to your instructor, then close all open Word files without closing Word, saving changes to the files if prompted**

FIGURE 6-14: Preview of merged data

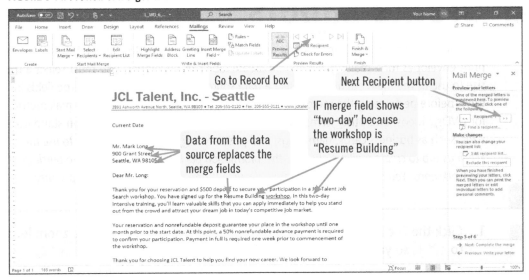

TABLE 6-1: Commands on the Mailings tab

command	use to
Envelopes	Create and print an individual envelope
Labels	Create and print an individual label
Start Mail Merge	Select the type of mail merge document to create and start the mail merge process
Select Recipients	Attach an existing data source to a main document or create a new data source
Edit Recipient List	Edit, sort, and filter the associated data source
Highlight Merge Fields	Highlight the merge fields in the main document
Address Block	Insert an Address Block merge field in the main document
Greeting Line	Insert a Greeting Line merge field in the main document
Insert Merge Field	Insert a merge field from the data source in the main document
Rules	Set rules to control how Word merges the data in the data source with the main document
Match Fields	Match the names of address or greeting fields used in a main document with the field names used in the data source
Update Labels	Update all the labels in a label main document to match the content and formatting of the first label
Preview Results	Switch between viewing the main document with merge fields or with merged data
Find Recipient	Search for a specific record in the merged document
Check for Errors	Check for and report errors in the merge
Finish & Merge	Specify whether to merge to a new document or directly to a printer or to email, then complete the merge

Opening Merge Files

The Word file you have designated as "Main" in the filename is linked to the data source that you attached to it. When you open the Word file, a message appears advising you that "Opening this document will run the following SQL command:". When you click Yes, the data from the data source attached to the merge file will be placed in the document. If you wish to run the merge again, you need to click Yes when this message is displayed.

Create Labels

Learning Outcomes
- Create a label main document
- Merge with an existing data source
- Update mailing labels

You can also use the Mail Merge pane or the commands on the Mailings tab to create mailing labels or print envelopes for a mailing. When you create labels or envelopes, you must select a label or envelope size to use as the main document, select a data source, and then insert the merge fields in the main document before performing the merge. In addition to mailing labels, you can use mail merge to create labels for DVDs, videos, and other items, and to create documents that are based on standard or custom label sizes, such as business cards, name tags, and postcards. **CASE** ▶ *You decide to use the commands on the Mailings tab to create mailing labels for the information packet you need to send to participants about upcoming workshops. You create a new label main document and attach an existing data source.*

STEPS

QUICK TIP

To create an envelope mail merge, click Envelopes to open the Envelope Options dialog box, and then select from the options.

1. **Click the** File tab, **click** New, **click** Blank document, **make sure the zoom level is set to** 120% **so you can easily see the label text, then click the** Mailings tab

   A blank document must be open for the commands on the Mailings tab to be available.

2. **Click the** Start Mail Merge button **in the Start Mail Merge group, click** Labels, **click the** Label vendors arrow **in the Label Options dialog box, then click** Microsoft **if Microsoft is not already displayed**

   The Label Options dialog box opens, as shown in FIGURE 6-15. You use this dialog box to select a label size for your labels and to specify the type of printer you plan to use. The name Microsoft appears in the Label vendors box. You can use the Label vendors arrow to select other brand name label vendors, such as Avery, Staples, or Office Depot. Many standard-sized labels for mailings, business cards, postcards, and other types of labels are listed in the Product number box. The type, height, width, and page size for the selected product are displayed in the Label information section.

QUICK TIP

If your labels do not match FIGURE 6-16, click the Undo button ↺ on the Quick Access toolbar, then repeat Step 3, making sure to click the second instance of 30 Per Page.

3. **Click the second instance of** 30 Per Page **in the Product number list, click** OK, **click the** Layout contextual tab **(to the right of the Table Design tab), click the** View Gridlines button **in the Table group to turn on the display of gridlines if they are not displayed, then click the** Mailings tab

   A table with gridlines appears in the main document, as shown in FIGURE 6-16. Each table cell is the size of a label for the label product you selected.

TROUBLE

Click Enable Content if it appears in a yellow bar in the Access window.

4. **Save the label main document with the filename** IL_WD_6_WorkshopLabelsMain **to the location where you store your Data Files**

   Next, you need to select a data source for the labels. You open a data source in Microsoft Access and resave it with a new name, then attach it to the main document.

5. **Open** File Explorer, **navigate to the location where you store your Data Files, then double-click** Support_WD_6_LabelsData.accdb

   The data source opens in Access, which is a database program often used to create recipient lists for mail merges.

QUICK TIP

To create or change the return address for an envelope mail merge, click the File tab, click Options, click Advanced in the left pane of the Word Options dialog box, then scroll down the right pane and enter the return address in the Mailing address box in the General section.

6. **Click the** File tab, **click** Save As, **click the** Save As button, **navigate to the location where you store your Data Files, change the name of the file to** IL_WD_6_LabelsDataSource, **click** Save, **then click the** ✕ **in the top right corner of the Access window to exit Access**

7. **Return to the labels document in Word, click the** Select Recipients button **in the Start Mail Merge group, then click** Use an Existing List

   The Select Data Source dialog box opens.

8. **Navigate to the location where you store your Data Files, open the file** IL_WD_6_LabelsDataSource.accdb, **then save your changes**

   The data source file is attached to the label main document, and <<Next Record>> appears in every cell in the table except the first cell, which is blank. In the next lesson, you sort and filter the records before performing the mail merge.

FIGURE 6-15: Label Options dialog box

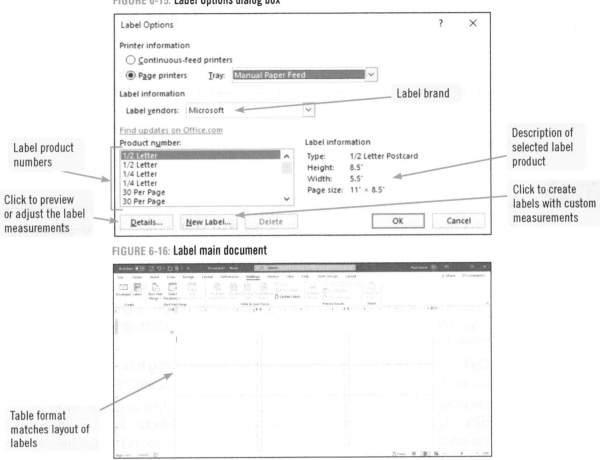

Label product numbers

Click to preview or adjust the label measurements

Label brand

Description of selected label product

Click to create labels with custom measurements

FIGURE 6-16: Label main document

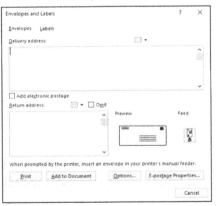

Table format matches layout of labels

FIGURE 6-17: Envelopes and Labels dialog box

Printing individual envelopes and labels

The Mail Merge feature enables you to easily print envelopes and labels for mass mailings, but you can also quickly format and print individual envelopes and labels using the Envelopes or Labels commands in the Create group on the Mailings tab. Simply click the Envelopes button or Labels button to open the Envelopes and Labels dialog box. On the Envelopes tab, shown in FIGURE 6-17, type the recipient's address in the Delivery address box and the return address in the Return address box. Click Options to open the Envelope Options dialog box, which

you use to select the envelope size, change the font and font size of the delivery and return addresses, and change the printing options. When you are ready to print the envelope, click Print in the Envelopes and Labels dialog box. The procedure for printing an individual label is similar to printing an individual envelope: enter the label text in the Address box on the Labels tab, click Options to select a label product number, click OK, and then click Print. Be sure to have envelopes loaded into your printer.

Sort and Filter Records

Learning Outcomes
- Filter a data source
- Sort records in a data source
- Find a mail merge recipient

If you are using a large data source, you might want to sort and/or filter the records before performing a merge. **Sorting** the records determines the order in which the records are merged. **Filtering** the records pulls out the records that meet specific criteria and includes only those records in the merge. You can use the Mail Merge Recipients dialog box both to sort and to filter a data source. **CASE** *You apply a filter to the data source so only United States addresses are included in the merge and sort those records in ZIP Code order.*

STEPS

1. **Click the** Edit Recipient List button **in the Start Mail Merge group, scroll right to display the Country field, then click the** Country column heading
   The records are sorted in ascending alphabetical order by country, with Canadian records listed first.

2. **Click the** Country column heading arrow, **then click** US **on the menu that opens**
   A filter is applied to the data source so only the records with "US" in the Country field will be merged. The grayish-blue arrow in the Country column heading indicates that a filter has been applied to the column. To remove a filter, click a column heading arrow, then click (All).

QUICK TIP

Use the options on the Filter Records tab to apply more than one filter to the data source.

3. **Click** Sort **in the Refine recipient list section of the dialog box**
   You use the Filter and Sort dialog box to apply more advanced sort and filter options to the data source.

4. **Click the** Sort by arrow, **click** ZIP Code, **click the first** Then by arrow, **click** Last Name, **click** OK, **compare the Mail Merge Recipients dialog box to** FIGURE 6-18, **then click** OK
   The sort and filter criteria you set are saved for the current merge. You can use the Find feature to quickly find and then edit a mail merge recipient's record.

QUICK TIP

Sorting and filtering a data source does not alter the records in a data source; it simply reorganizes the records for the current merge only.

5. **Click** Edit Recipient List, **click** Find recipient, **type** Graton, **click** Find Next, **then click** Cancel
   You need to open the data source to make a change to a record.

6. **Double-click the filename in the Data Source box, click** Find, **type** Graton, **click** Find Next, **click** Cancel, **verify that** Graton **is selected, type** San Francisco, **click** OK, **click** Yes, **then click** OK
   With your recipients list filtered, sorted, and edited, you are ready to complete the merge.

QUICK TIP

To change the font or paragraph formatting of merged data, format the merge fields, including the chevrons, before performing a merge.

7. **Click the** Address Block button **in the Write & Insert Fields group, then click** OK **in the Insert Address Block dialog box to add the Address Block merge field to the first label**

8. **Click the** Update Labels button **in the Write & Insert Fields group to copy the merge field from the first label to every label in the main document**

9. **Click the** Preview Results button **in the Preview Results group**
   A preview of the merged label data appears in the main document, as shown in FIGURE 6-19. Only US addresses are included, and the labels are organized in ZIP Code order, with recipients with the same ZIP Code listed in alphabetical order by Last Name.

10. **Click the** Finish & Merge button **in the Finish group, click** Edit Individual Documents, **click** OK **in the Merge to New Document dialog box, replace** Mr. David Friar **with your name in the first label, save the document as** IL_WD_6_WorkshopLabels_USZipMerge, **submit the labels, then save and close all open files and exit Word**

FIGURE 6-18: **US records sorted in zip code order**

Click a column heading
to sort the records

Click a column
heading arrow to
filter the records

All records with a US
address are sorted
first by ZIP Code in
ascending order,
then alphabetically
by Last Name

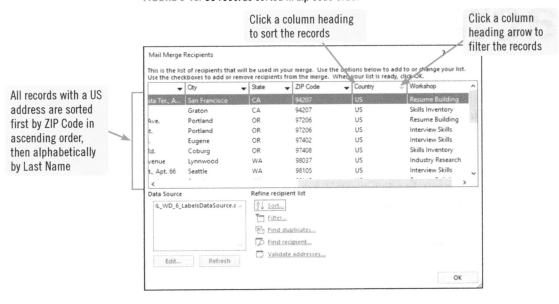

FIGURE 6-19: **Merged labels**

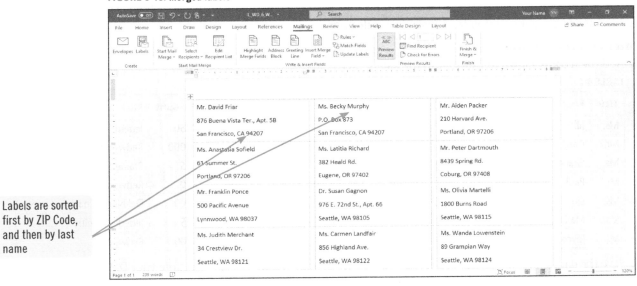

Labels are sorted
first by ZIP Code,
and then by last
name

Inserting individual merge fields

You must include proper punctuation, spacing, and blank lines between the merge fields in a main document if you want punctuation, spaces, and blank lines to appear between the data in the merge documents. For example, to create an address line with a city, state, and ZIP Code, you insert the City merge field, type a comma and a space, insert the State merge field, type a space, and then insert the ZIP Code merge field: <<City>>, <<State>> <<ZIP Code>>.

You can insert an individual merge field by clicking the Insert Merge Field arrow in the Write & Insert Fields group and

then selecting the field name from the menu that opens. Alternatively, you can click the Insert Merge Field button to open the Insert Merge Field dialog box, which you can use to insert several merge fields at once by clicking a field name in the dialog box, clicking Insert, clicking another field name, clicking Insert, and so on. When you have finished inserting the merge fields, click Close to close the dialog box. You can then add spaces, punctuation, and lines between the merge fields you inserted in the main document.

Practice

Skills Review

1. Create a main document.

a. Open IL_WD_6-2.docx from the location where you store your Data Files, then save it as **IL_WD_6_RedwoodLetter**

b. Change the orientation of the document to Portrait.

c. Save and close the document, but do not exit Word.

d. Start a new blank document, then use the Mail Merge pane to create a letter main document from the file you just saved.

e. Replace Current Date with today's date.

f. Type your name where indicated in the signature line.

g. Save the mail merge main document as **IL_WD_6_RedwoodLetterMain**.

2. Design a data source.

a. Click Next: Select recipients, select the Type a new list option button in the Step 3 of 6... pane, then click Create.

b. Click Customize Columns in the New Address List dialog box, then remove these fields from the data source: Company Name, Address Line 2, Country or Region, Home Phone, Work Phone, and E-mail Address.

c. Add an **Amount** field and a **Park** field to the data source. Be sure these fields follow the ZIP Code field.

d. Click OK to close the Customize Address List dialog box.

3. Enter and edit records.

a. Add the records shown in TABLE 6-2 to the data source.

TABLE 6-2

Title	First Name	Last Name	Address Line 1	City	State	ZIP Code	Amount	Park
Ms.	Jill	Wade	35 Oak St.	Eureka	CA	95501	$250	Jedediah Smith
Mr.	Cary	Poon	223 Elm St.	Redding	CA	96001	$1000	Redwood
Ms.	Grace	Park	62 Main St.	Redding	CA	96002	$25	Prairie Creek Redwoods
Mr.	Paul	Jones	987 Ocean Rd.	Mendocino	CA	95460	$50	Redwood
Ms.	Lin	Juarez	73 Bay Rd.	Eureka	CA	95501	$500	Del Norte Coast Redwoods
Ms.	Maria	Shad	67 Cove Rd.	San Francisco	CA	94121	$75	Jedediah Smith
Ms.	Joyce	Leblanc	287 Concord Rd.	Sausalito	CA	94965	$100	Redwood

b. Save the data source as **IL_WD_6_RedwoodData** to the location where you store your Data Files.

c. Change the park for record 2 (Cary Poon) from Redwood to **Jedediah Smith**.

d. Click OK as needed to close all dialog boxes.

4. Add merge fields.

a. Click Next: Write your letter, then in the blank line between the date and the first body paragraph, insert an Address block merge field, then click OK.

b. Press ENTER twice, then insert a Greeting Line merge field using the default greeting line format.

c. In the first body paragraph, replace AMOUNT with the Amount merge field.

d. In the second body paragraph, replace PARK with the Park merge field. (*Note*: Make sure to insert a space before or after each merge field as needed.) Save your changes to the main document.

5. Work with merge rules.

a. Select National Park at the end of paragraph 2, then select the If...Then...Else merge rule.

b. Select Park as the field name, then enter criteria for the rule so that when "Redwood" is the record in the Park field, "National Park" is displayed, and if not, then "State Park" is displayed.

    c. Toggle the field codes and verify the code is { IF { MERGEFIELD Park } = "Redwood" "National Park" "State Park" }.

    d. Change the font of the field code to Garamond.

6. Merge data.

    a. Click Next: Preview your letters to preview the merged data, then use the Next Record button to scroll through each letter, examining it carefully for errors. Check that the merge rule worked.

    b. Click the Preview Results button on the Mailings tab, make any necessary adjustments to the main document, save your changes, then click the Preview Results button to return to the preview of the document.

    c. Click Next: Complete the merge, click Edit individual letters, then merge all the records to a new file.

    d. Save the merged document as **IL_WD_6_RedwoodLetterMerge** to the location where you store your Data Files. The fourth letter is shown in FIGURE 6-20. Submit the file or a copy of the last letter per your instructor's directions, then save and close all open files but not Word.

FIGURE 6-20

Redwood Conservation Project
455 Watson Street, Redding, CA 96003; Tel: 530-555-0166; www.redwoodconservation.org

Current Date

Mr. Paul Jones
987 Ocean Rd.
Mendocino, CA 95460

Dear Mr. Jones,

We are delighted to receive your generous contribution of $50 to the Redwood Conservation Project (RCP).

Whether we are helping to protect our beautiful state's natural resources or bringing nature and environmental studies into our public schools, senior centers, and communities, RCP depends upon private contributions to ensure that free public environmental programs continue to flourish in Redwood National Park.

Sincerely

Your Name
Executive Director

7. Create labels.

    a. Open a new blank document, click the Start Mail Merge button in the Start Mail Merge group on the Mailings tab, then create a Labels main document.

    b. In the Label Options dialog box, select Avery US Letter, select 5160 Address Labels, then click OK.

    c. Click the Select Recipients button, then open the IL_WD_6_RedwoodData.mdb file you created.

    d. Save the label main document as **IL_WD_6_RedwoodLabelsMain** to the location where you store your Data Files.

8. Sort and filter records.

    a. Click the Edit Recipient List button, filter the records so that only the records with Redwood in the Park field are included in the merge, sort the records in City order, then click OK as needed to return to the labels document.

    b. Insert an Address Block merge field using the default settings, update the labels, then click the Preview Results button.

    c. Open the Recipient List, find the record for Maria Shad, then change the Park to Redwood.

FIGURE 6-21

Mr. Paul Jones	Ms. Maria Shad	Ms. Joyce Leblanc
987 Ocean Rd.	67 Cove Rd.	287 Concord Rd.
Mendocino, CA 95460	San Francisco, CA 94121	Sausalito, CA 94965

    d. Verify that Maria's record appears, examine the merged data for errors, then correct any mistakes.

    e. Click the Finish & Merge button, then click the Edit Individual Documents to merge all the records to an individual document, shown in FIGURE 6-21.

    f. Save the merged file as **IL_WD_6_RedwoodLabelsRedwoodOnlyMerge** to the location where you store your Data Files.

    g. In the first label, change Mr. Paul Jones to your name, submit the document to your instructor, save and close all open Word files, then exit Word.

Word

Independent Challenge 1

As an administrator at Riverwalk Medical Clinic in San Antonio, you handle all the correspondence for the Dental Department, including sending reminders to patients for dental cleaning. You'll use Mail Merge to create the letter and a sheet of labels.

a. Start Word, open IL_WD_6-3.docx from the location where you store your Data Files, save the document as **IL_WD_6_DentalLetter**, change the page orientation to Portrait, add the current date, replace Your Name with your name in the signature block, then save and close the file.

b. Start a new blank document in Word, then using either the Mailings tab or the Mail Merge pane, create a letter main document using the document you just saved. Save the main document as **IL_WD_6_DentalLetterMain**.

c. Create a new recipient list using the data shown below. Remove any field names that are not included.

Title	First Name	Last Name	Address Line 1	City	State	ZIP Code	CHECKUP	DENTIST
Ms.	Anna	Sanchez	35 Oak St.	San Antonio	TX	78215	three-month	Dr. Haven
Mr.	Rick	Leung	223 Cherry St.	San Antonio	TX	78207	annual	Dr. Singh
Ms.	Maria	Ortez	62 Main St.	Austin	TX	78745	six-month	Dr. Singh
Ms.	Helen	May	987 State Rd.	Devine	TX	78016	annual	Dr. Haven
Ms.	Emer	O'Toole	73 River Rd.	San Antonio	TX	78214	three-month	Dr. Singh

d. Name the data source **IL_WD_6_DentalData**.

e. Sort the data source by Last Name, then edit the data by changing the address for Ms. Helen May to **600 County Rd**.

f. Insert an Address Block and a Greeting Line merge field in the main document.

g. Customize the Greeting Line merge field by selecting Joshua as the greeting line format. When the merge is run, "Dear" will be followed by the first name of the recipient.

h. Replace "CHECKUP" and "DENTIST" with the appropriate merge fields.

i. Preview the merged letters, make any spacing adjustments required, merge all the records to a new document, save it as **IL_WD_6_DentalLetterMerge**, then close the document.

j. Save and close **IL_WD_6_DentalLetterMain**.

k. Open a new blank document, then using the Mail Merge pane on the Mailings tab, select Labels as the main document and select the label type **Microsoft** and the second instance of 30 Per Page.

l. Select recipients from the IL_WD_6_DentalData.mdb file you just created.

m. Save the label main document as **IL_WD_6_DentalLabelsMain** to the location where you store your Data Files.

n. Insert an Address Block merge field using the default settings, update the labels, then preview the results.

o. Filter the records so that only the records with Dr. Singh in the Dentist field are included in the merge, then sort the records in City order.

p. In the data source, find the record for Rick Leung, then change "Rick" to **Richard**.

q. Examine the merged data for errors, then correct any mistakes. The three labels should appear as shown in FIGURE 6-22.

r. Merge all the records to an individual document, save the merged file as **IL_WD_6_DentalLabelsSinghOnlyMerge** to the location where you store your Data Files.

s. Change the name in the first label to your name.

t. Submit the files or a copy of the label sheet and the first merge letter per your instructor's directions, close all open Word files, saving changes, and then exit Word. Note that Rick Leung's name will appear as "Richard Leung" in both the DentalLetterMain and the DentalLabelsMain documents. His name will appear as "Rick Leung" in the DentalLetterMerge document because the merged letters are not linked to the data source and so were not updated.

FIGURE 6-22

Ms. Maria Ortez
62 Main St.
Austin, TX 78745

Ms. Emer O'Toole
73 River Rd.
San Antonio, TX 78214

Mr. Richard Leung
223 Cherry St.
San Antonio, TX 78207

Independent Challenge 2

As the director of the Lake Country Museum in Minnesota, you are hosting an exhibit of old photographs from pioneer times. You want to send a letter to all museum donors with a Minnesota address to advise them of a discount in the museum gift store according to their donation amount and to invite them to the opening of the exhibition. You'll use Mail Merge to create the letter and create an envelope for one letter.

a. Start Word, open a blank document, then using either the Mailings tab or the Mail Merge pane, create a letter main document using the file IL_WD_6-4.docx from the location where you store your Data Files.

b. Replace Current Date with the current date and Your Name with your name in the signature block, then save the main document as **IL_WD_6_MuseumLetterMain**.

c. Use the file **Support_WD_6_MuseumData.accdb** from the location where you store your Data Files as the data source.

d. Sort the data source by Last Name, then filter the data so that only records with MN as the state are included in the merge.

e. Insert an Address Block and a Greeting Line merge field in the main document (separate with a blank line).

f. Replace "AMOUNT" with the Amount merge field.

g. Select 15% discount, then use the If...Then...Else merge rule to change 15% discount to **20% discount** if the Amount field is greater than or equal to "100." (*Hint*: You need to modify the Comparison operator to select Greater Than or Equal To.)

h. Toggle the field code to verify the IF field is correct.

i. Toggle off the field code, select "20% discount," then apply Bold formatting.

j. Preview results, then scroll through the letters to verify that the merge rule worked.

k. Merge all the records to a new document, then save it as **IL_WD_6_MuseumLetterMerge**.

l. Select the recipient address in the first merge letter, then click the Envelopes button in the Create group on the Mailings tab to open the Envelopes and Labels dialog box. (*Note*: You will create one envelope and include it as part of the merge document. If you were doing a mail merge, you would create a separate envelope merge.)

m. On the Envelopes tab in the Envelopes and Labels dialog box, verify that the Omit check box is not selected, then in the Return address box, type your name followed by a comma and **Lake Country Museum**, press ENTER, then type the address **541 Newtown Street, Minneapolis, MN 55404** on one line.

n. Click Options to open the Envelope Options dialog box, click the Envelope Options tab if it is not the active tab, then make sure the Envelope size is set to Size 10.

o. Click the Printing Options tab, select the appropriate Feed method for your printer, then click OK.

p. Click Add to Document, click No if a message box opens asking if you want to save the new return address as the default return address. The dialog box closes without printing the envelope and the envelope is added as the first page of the merge document as shown in FIGURE 6-23.

q. Submit the file or a copy of the envelope and the first merge letter per your instructor's directions, close all open Word files, saving changes, and then exit Word.

FIGURE 6-23

Visual Workshop

Using mail merge, create the data source shown in FIGURE 6-24 for the postcard main document shown in FIGURE 6-25. Use Avery US Letter 3263 Postcards labels for the main document. Save the data source as **IL_WD_6_InvestorData**, save the merge document as **IL_WD_6_InvestorReminderMerge**, and save the main document as **IL_WD_6_InvestorReminderMain**, all to the location where you store your Data Files. Notice that the postcard label main document is formatted as a table. To lay out the postcard, insert a nested table with two columns and one row in the upper-left postcard; add the text and merge field to the nested table; and then remove the outside borders on the nested table. The font is Book Antiqua. Submit a copy of the postcards to your instructor.

FIGURE 6-24

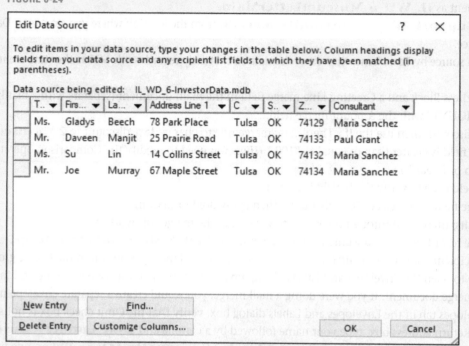

FIGURE 6-25

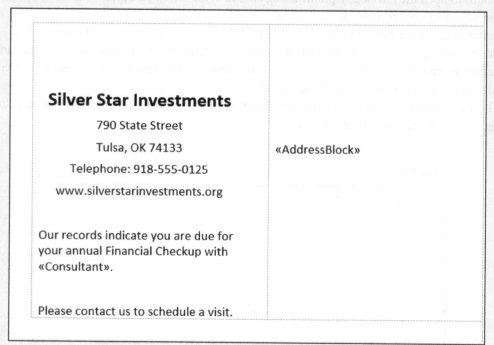

Illustrating Documents with Graphics

CASE > You have been asked to edit and finalize a two-page information sheet that will be distributed to clients and job seekers who visit the Vancouver office of JCL Talent, Inc. The information sheet includes short articles about the job market, information about the branch staff, and tips for job seekers.

Module Objectives

After completing this module, you will be able to:

- Use the Office Clipboard
- Create sections and columns
- Create SmartArt graphics
- Modify SmartArt graphics
- Crop and rotate a picture
- Position a graphic
- Create WordArt
- Create a text box
- Insert a Word file

Files You Will Need

IL_WD_7-1.docx
Support_WD_7_References.docx
Support_WD_7_Utilities.jpg
Support_WD_7_Accounts.jpg
Support_WD_7_Interviews.docx
Support_WD_7_Chicago.docx
IL_WD_7-2.docx
Support_WD_7_Risk.docx
Support_WD_7_Quiz.docx
Support_WD_7_Coins.jpg
Support_WD_7_Disaster.jpg

Support_WD_7_RiskReport_WatsonFinancial.docx
IL_WD_7-3.docx
Support_WD_7_Brain.jpg
Support_WD_7_Class.jpg
Support_WD_7_Donations.jpg
Support_WD_7_Education.docx
IL_WD_7-4.docx
Support_WD_7_RemoteWorking.docx
Support_WD_7_DraftReport.docx
IL_WD_7-5.docx

Use the Office Clipboard

Learning Outcomes
- Copy and cut items to the Clipboard
- Paste items from the Clipboard

You can use the Office Clipboard to collect text and graphics from files created in any Office program and then insert them into your Word documents. The Office Clipboard (the Clipboard) holds up to 24 items at a time. To display the Clipboard, you simply click the launcher in the Clipboard group on the Home tab. You add items to the Clipboard using the Cut and Copy commands. The last item you collect is always added at the top of the Clipboard. **CASE** *You use the Clipboard to store text and a picture that you move within the information sheet.*

STEPS

QUICK TIP
You can set the Clipboard pane to open automatically when you cut or copy two items consecutively by clicking Options on the Clipboard pane and then selecting Show Office Clipboard Automatically.

1. **saɪɪ⬇ Start Word, open IL_WD_7-1.docx from the location where you store your Data Files, save it as IL_WD_7_InformationSheet, then click the Launcher ▣ in the Clipboard group on the Home tab**

   The Office Clipboard opens in the Clipboard pane. In this pane, each object and text selection you copied or cut in a current Office session is listed. The Clipboard pane will be empty if you have not copied or pasted anything recently.

2. **If items appear in the Clipboard pane, click Clear All, then select the two lines of text at the top of the document from Prepared by Your Name at JCL Talent . . . to the company phone number**

   With the text selected, you can choose to either copy it or cut it. You want to move this text to the document footer, so you need to cut it.

QUICK TIP
If you add a 25th item to the Clipboard, the first item you collected is deleted.

3. **Click the Cut button ✂ in the Clipboard group**

   The text is removed from the document and placed in the Clipboard as shown in FIGURE 7-1. The icon next to the item indicates it is cut or copied from a Word document. You can continue to cut or copy additional items to the Clipboard, including objects such as charts and pictures.

QUICK TIP
You may see a Pre-view Not Available icon instead of the picture, depending on the settings.

4. **Click the picture of the city and mountains, then click the Cut button in the Clipboard group**

   The picture is displayed at the top of the Clipboard pane because it is the most recent item collected. As new items are collected, the existing items move down the Clipboard. Clicking an item on the Clipboard pastes the item in the document at the location of the insertion point. Items remain on the Clipboard until you delete them or close all open Office programs.

5. **Press CTRL+HOME to move to the top of the document, press ENTER two times, press Up Arrow ↑ two times to move to the first line in the document, then click the picture in the Clipboard**

   The picture is inserted at the top of your document.

QUICK TIP
To delete an individual item from the Clipboard, click the arrow next to the item, then click Delete.

6. **Click the Insert tab, click the Footer button in the Header & Footer group, click the Blank style, click Prepared by ... in the Clipboard, then press BACKSPACE and DELETE as needed to remove any extra blank lines**

7. **Press CTRL+E to center the text as shown in FIGURE 7-2, replace Your Name with your name, click the Close Header and Footer button in the Close group, then click the Close button ☒ on the Clipboard pane**

   The text is pasted into the footer and will appear on both pages of the information sheet.

FIGURE 7-1: **Text copied to the Clipboard**

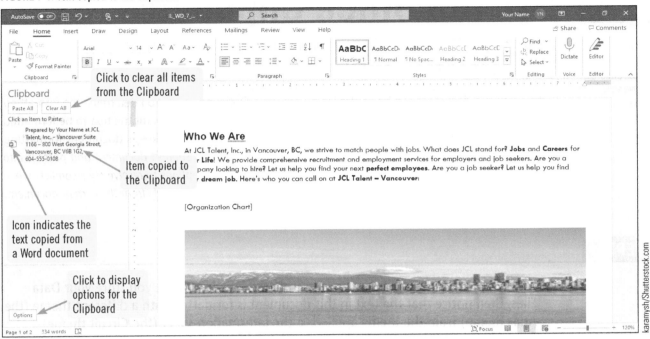

FIGURE 7-2: **Footer text copied and formatted**

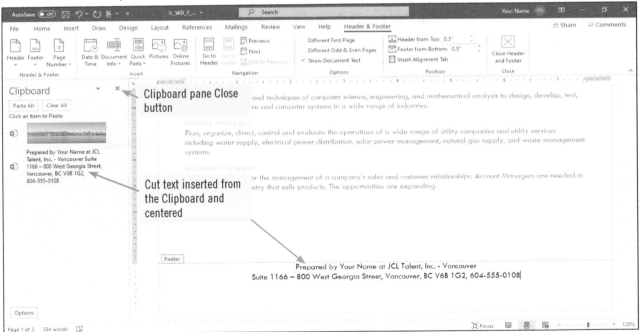

(Continued)

Use the Office Clipboard (Continued)

Pasting text in a document can be controlled by the Paste Options feature. You determine the formatting for the pasted text by clicking the Paste arrow and then selecting how you want the text to be formatted when placed in the document. Pasting text with the destination theme keeps document formatting consistent. **CASE** ▶ *You use text copied into the Clipboard from a support document and paste it into the Information sheet using the Paste Options button. You use paste options to resolve style conflicts when you paste text copied from another Word document that is formatted differently from the current document.* TABLE 7-1 *describes the Paste options available.*

STEPS

1. **Open** Support_WD_7_References.docx **from the location where you store your Data Files, then notice that the text in this document is formatted with a different theme (the Atlas theme) from the theme applied to the information sheet (the Circuit theme)**
   When you copy text from another Word document that is formatted with a theme different from the theme of your current document, you use Paste options to choose how you want the pasted text formatted.

2. **Press CTRL+A to select the heading** References **and the paragraph following, click the** Copy **button in the Clipboard group, then close the document**

3. **Click the blank line above Top Jobs!, then click the** Paste **arrow in the Clipboard group to display the list of Paste options as shown in** FIGURE 7-3

4. **Move your mouse pointer over each option to see how the pasted text appears**
   As you can see by exploring the Paste options, the Destination theme options will keep the document formatting consistent throughout.

5. **Click the** Use Destination Theme (H) **button**

6. **Save the document**
   The text is copied into the current document and is formatted with the Circuit theme.

FIGURE 7-3: **Paste options**

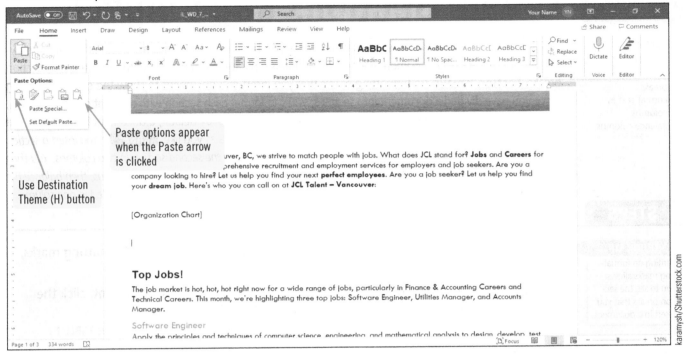

TABLE 7-1: **Paste options**

paste option	description
Use Destination Theme	The formatting applied to text copied from a source file is changed to match the formatting applied to text in the destination file.
Keep Source Formatting	The formatting applied to the copied text in the source file is retained, even if the formatting is different from the formatting applied to text in the destination file.
Merge Formatting	The copied text takes on the style characteristics of the paragraph where it is pasted.
Picture	The copied text is pasted as a picture that you can resize and move like any graphic object.
Keep Text Only	Only the text, with no formatting, is pasted into the destination file.

Create Sections and Columns

Learning
Outcomes
• Insert section
  breaks
• Format text in
  columns
• Balance columns

Dividing a document into sections allows you to format each section of the document with different page lay-out settings. A **section** is a portion of a document that is separated from the rest of the document by section breaks. **Section breaks** are formatting marks that you insert in a document to show the end of a section. Once you have divided a document into sections, you can format each section with different column, margin, page orientation, header and footer, and other page layout settings. By default, a document is formatted as a single section, but you can divide a document into as many sections as you like. **CASE** *You insert a section break to divide the document into two sections and format the text in the second section in two columns. You then insert a Next Page section break to create a third section, format text in Section 3 in three columns, then balance the three columns so they are all similar in height. Finally, you create a fourth section that is formatted in one column.*

STEPS

QUICK TIP
Turning on format-ting marks allows you to see the sec-tion breaks that you insert in a document.

1. **Click the** Show/Hide ¶ **button** ¶ **in the Paragraph group to turn on formatting marks, if necessary**

2. **Click to the left of the heading** Who We Are **near the top of the document, click the** Layout tab, **then click the** Breaks button **in the Page Setup group**
   The Breaks menu opens. You use this menu to insert different types of section breaks. See TABLE 7-2.

3. **Click** Continuous
   Word inserts a continuous section break, shown as a dotted double line below the picture and above the "Who We Are" heading. See FIGURE 7-4. When you insert a section break at the beginning of a paragraph, Word inserts the break at the end of the previous paragraph. The section break stores the formatting infor-mation for the previous section. The status bar indicates the insertion point is in Section 2.

TROUBLE
If you do not see Section 2 in the status bar in the lower-left corner of your screen, right-click the status bar, then click **Section** to add a check mark next to it.

4. **Click the** Columns button **in the Page Setup group, then click** More Columns

5. **Select** Right **in the Presets section, click the** Spacing down arrow **twice until 0.3" appears, select the** Line between check box, **compare the dialog box to** FIGURE 7-5, **then click** OK
   Section 2 is formatted in two unequal columns with .3" of spacing and a vertical line between columns.

QUICK TIP
When you delete a section break, you delete the section formatting of the text before the break. That text becomes part of the following section and assumes the formatting of that section.

6. **Click the** View tab, **click** Multiple Pages **to show both pages of the information sheet, click to the left of** Top Jobs **in column 1, click the** Layout tab, **click** Breaks, **then click** Next Page
   Top Jobs and its accompanying text move to the top of page 2 and Section 3 appears on the status bar. Page 2 looks odd at this point, but you'll fix the spacing soon.

7. **Click the** Columns button, **click** More Columns, **click** Three, **change the spacing between columns to .2" and click the** Line between check box **to deselect it, then click** OK
   All the text and pictures on the page are formatted in three narrow columns.

8. **Return to** 100% view, **click to the left of the paragraph mark following** expanding. **at the end of the description of the Accounts Manager position toward the bottom of the first column on page 2, click the** Layout tab, **click** Breaks **in the Page Setup group, then click** Continuous
   You inserted a Continuous section break to balance the columns only in the "Top Jobs" section so each col-umn is approximately the same height. Text in the balanced columns flows automatically from the bottom of one column to the top of the next column.

9. **Verify that the insertion point appears to the left of the paragraph mark above the heading** Find New Opportunities **and below the beginning of the** Software Engineer **paragraph, click the** Columns button **in the Page Setup group, click** One, **then save the document**
   You create another section (Section 4) because you want the remaining information in the document to extend the full width of the page.

FIGURE 7-4: Continuous section break

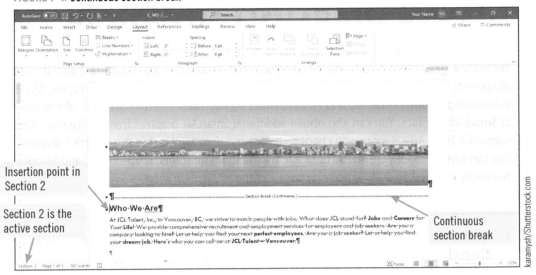

Insertion point in Section 2

Section 2 is the active section

Continuous section break

karamysh/Shutterstock.com

FIGURE 7-5: Columns dialog box

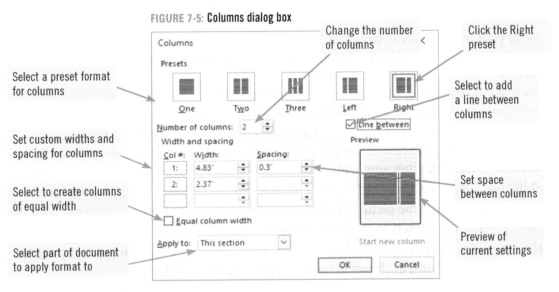

Change the number of columns

Click the Right preset

Select a preset format for columns

Select to add a line between columns

Set custom widths and spacing for columns

Select to create columns of equal width

Set space between columns

Select part of document to apply format to

Preview of current settings

TABLE 7-2: Types of section breaks

section	function
Next page	Begins a new section and moves the text following the break to the top of the next page
Continuous	Begins a new section on the same page
Even page	Begins a new section and moves the text following the break to the top of the next even-numbered page
Odd page	Begins a new section and moves the text following the break to the top of the next odd-numbered page

Changing page layout settings for a section

Dividing a document into sections allows you to vary the layout of a document. In addition to applying different column settings to sections, you can apply different margins, page orientation, paper size, vertical alignment, header and footer, page numbering, footnotes, endnotes, and other page layout settings. To check or change the page layout settings for an individual section, place the insertion point in the section, then open the Page Setup dialog box.

Select any options you want to change, click the Apply to arrow, click This section, then click OK. When you select This section in the Apply to box, the settings are applied to the current section only. When you select This point forward, the settings are applied to the current section and all sections that follow it. If you select Whole document in the Apply to box, the settings are applied to all the sections in the document.

Create SmartArt Graphics

Learning Outcomes
- Create a picture SmartArt Graphic
- Change the SmartArt layout

You create a SmartArt graphic when you want to provide a visual representation of information. A **SmartArt graphic** is a customizable diagram that combines shapes with text and is used to pictorially present lists, processes, and relationships. SmartArt categories include List, Process, Cycle, Hierarchy, Relationship, Matrix, Pyramid, and Picture. TABLE 7-3 describes when to use each of the eight categories of SmartArt graphics. You can also obtain additional SmartArt graphics from Office.com. Once you have selected a SmartArt category, you choose a layout and then type text in the SmartArt shapes or text pane. You can further modify a SmartArt graphic by changing fill colors, shape styles, and layouts. **CASE** You create a picture SmartArt graphic on page 2 of the information sheet.

STEPS

1. **Click the** picture of the woman at the computer **on page 2, click the** Picture Format tab, **then click the** Picture Layout button **in the Picture Styles group**

   A selection of picture SmartArt layouts is displayed. You can create a picture SmartArt graphic from any picture inserted in a document, and then you can add additional pictures.

2. **Move your mouse pointer over each layout, click the** Bending Picture Caption layout **(second row, second column), click the** Add Shape button **in the Create Graphic group, then click the** Add Shape button **again**

   The SmartArt Design tab is active and the text pane opens. The picture SmartArt graphic now consists of three shapes, only one of which currently contains a picture.

3. **Click the** picture content control **for the blank shape to the right of the picture of the woman in the top row of the SmartArt graphic, click** From a File, **navigate to the location where you store your Data Files, double-click** Support_WD_7_Utilities.jpg, **click in the** last shape, **click** From a File, **then double-click** Support_WD_7_Accounts.jpg

4. **Click a blank area of the picture SmartArt graphic, click next to the** top bullet **in the text pane if necessary, then type** Software Engineer

5. **Use** Down Arrow ↓ **to enter** Utilities Manager **and** Accounts Manager **in the text pane for the other two pictures as shown in** FIGURE 7-6, **then close the text pane**

6. **Click the** More button **in the Layouts group on the SmartArt Design tab, then click the** Bending Picture Blocks layout **(second row, fifth column)**

   You can experiment with how you want the SmartArt graphic to appear by selecting different picture layouts. You set a precise height and width for the SmartArt graphic.

7. **Click the** Format tab, **click the** Size button **to show the Height and Width boxes if necessary, select the measurement in the** Height box, **type** 3.8, **press** TAB **to select the measurement in the Width box, type** 5.7, **then press** ENTER

   You can also format the appearance of each shape in a SmartArt graphic.

8. **Click away from the picture SmartArt graphic to deselect it, click the** woman picture, **press and hold** SHIFT, **then click the other two pictures so all three pictures in the picture SmartArt graphic are selected**

9. **Click the** Shape Effects button **in the Shape Styles group on the Format tab, point to** Bevel, **click** Angle **(first column, second row in the Bevel section), click away from the picture SmartArt graphic to deselect it, then save the document**

   The picture SmartArt graphic appears as shown in FIGURE 7-7.

FIGURE 7-6: Data for the picture

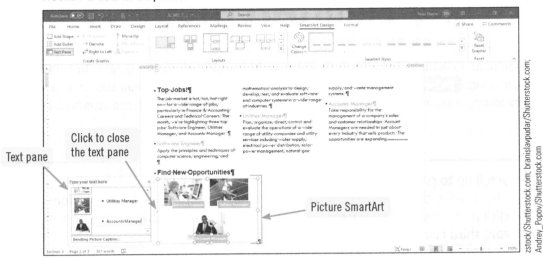

FIGURE 7-7: Sized and formatted picture SmartArt graphic

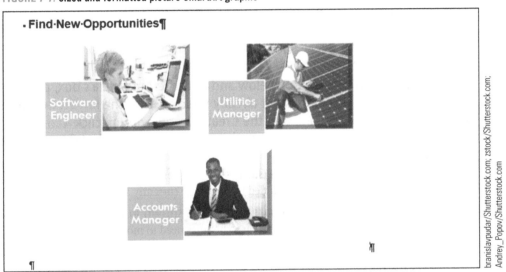

TABLE 7-3: Eight categories of SmartArt graphics

category	when to use	category	when to use
List	To show nonsequential information	Relationship	To illustrate connections between the shapes in the graphic
Process	To show steps in a process or timeline	Matrix	To show how parts relate to a whole
Cycle	To show a continual process	Pyramid	To show proportional relationships with the largest component on the bottom
Hierarchy	To show an organization chart or decision tree	Picture	To use pictures to convey or emphasize visual content

Inserting a picture into a SmartArt shape

You can fill any shape in a SmartArt graphic with a picture, even if the shape does not include a Picture content control. Click the shape, click the Format tab, click the Shape Fill arrow, click Picture, click From a File, navigate to the location of the picture, then click Insert. The picture is inserted into the shape.

Modify SmartArt Graphics

SmartArt graphics provide you with many options to graphically display information in ways that are meaningful to readers. Sometimes you may need to modify a SmartArt graphic to better convey the information. **CASE** *You insert an organization chart on page 1 of the information sheet and then modify it by adding, removing, and resizing individual shapes in the SmartArt graphic, and applying 3-D effects.*

STEPS

1. **Scroll up to page 1 of the information sheet, select the** [Organization Chart] **placeholder, click the** Insert tab, **click the** SmartArt button **in the Illustrations group, click** Hierarchy **in the left pane, select the** Name and Title Organization Chart style **(first row, third column), then click** OK

   An organization chart from the Hierarchy category is inserted into the document. You use charts in the Hierarchy category to show the chain of command within a company or organization.

2. **Close the Text pane if it is open, increase the zoom to** 200%, **scroll to see the whole graphic, click in the** top box, **type** Sheila Leung, **click in the** box below Sheila, **then type** Branch Manager

   By default, an assistant box is attached to the top box in the Organization chart. Space is limited on the page, so you remove the assistant box and add two subordinates to one of the Level 2 boxes.

3. **Click the edge of the** green box **below and to the left of Sheila's box, press** DELETE, **click the** SmartArt Design tab **if it is not already selected, click the** far-left box **in the bottom row, click the** Add Shape arrow **in the Create Graphic group, click** Add Shape Below, **then click the** Add Shape button **(not the arrow) to add another shape to the right of the shape you just inserted**

   The Add Shape menu provides options (such as below, after, and above) for adding more shapes to your SmartArt graphic. The new shapes are added based on the currently selected box and the menu selection.

4. **Enter text so the organization chart appears as shown in** FIGURE 7-8

   After entering text in a SmartArt graphic, you sometimes need to modify the text wrapping.

5. **Click the** Branch Manager box, **then drag the** lower-right handle **to the right to increase the width of the text box so the text does not wrap**

   You can also rearrange the shapes in a SmartArt graphic.

6. **Click the** Anna Ricard box, **then click the** Move Down button **in the Create Graphic group**

   The Move Down command moves the box to the right and on the same level as the other two boxes. The two subordinate boxes attached to Anna's box are also moved. TABLE 7-4 explains the different ways in which you can move shapes in a SmartArt graphic.

7. **Click the** Change Colors button **in the SmartArt Styles group, select** Colorful – Accent Colors **(first selection in the Colorful section), click the** More button ▼ **in the SmartArt Styles group, then click** Inset **(second selection in the 3-D section)**

8. **Click a blank area of the chart, click the** Format tab, **click the** Size button, **type** 2.7 **in the Height box, type** 4.5 **in the Width box, then press** ENTER

9. **Click the** Jasjit Singh box, **press and hold** SHIFT, **click the remaining four subordinate boxes:** Anna Ricard, Gary Ng, Mary Warr, **and** Phil Banks, **release** SHIFT, **click the** Size button, **type** 1 **in the Width box, press** ENTER, **return to** 100% **view, click away from the chart, then save the document**

   The width of all the boxes in the Organization chart is decreased to 1" as shown in FIGURE 7-9.

FIGURE 7-8: **Text for the organization chart**

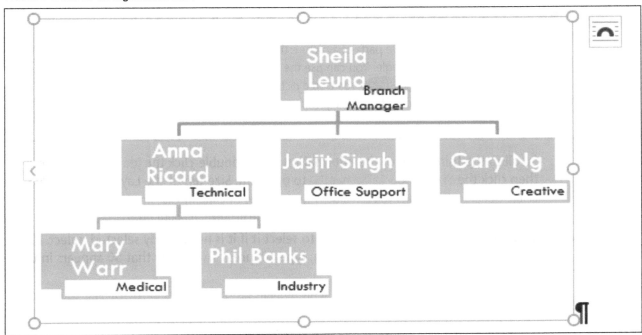

FIGURE 7-9: **Completed organization chart**

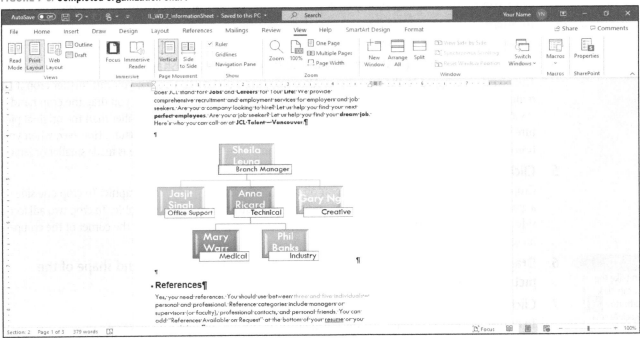

TABLE 7-4: **Options for moving shapes in a SmartArt graphic**

option	click to move
Promote	a subordinate box up one level
Demote	a subordinate box down one level
Right to Left	a box to the far left or right of the current row of boxes
Move Up	a box to the left of the adjacent box on the current row
Move Down	a box to the right of the adjacent box on the current row

Crop and Rotate a Picture

Learning Outcomes
• Crop a picture
• Rotate a picture

You use the Crop tool to remove parts of a picture that you do not want. You can also crop a graphic to a shape such as a circle or triangle. You can use the mouse to rotate a graphic to an approximate value or enter a specific number. **CASE** *You crop a picture to a shape and then crop additional portions of the picture. Finally, you use the mouse to rotate a picture.*

STEPS

1. **Scroll to the third page of the information sheet, double-click the jumping man picture, then click the Size group Launcher 🖾 to open the Size tab of the Layout dialog box**
   Before cropping the picture, you can modify its size either by entering exact measurements or scaling the graphic to a percentage. You decide to scale the graphic to maintain proportions.

   TROUBLE
   Make sure you enter 50 in the Scale section toward the bottom of the Size dialog box.

2. **Click the Lock aspect ratio check box to select it if it is not already selected, select 100% in the Height box in the Scale section, type 50, press TAB, verify that 50 appears in the Width box, then click OK**
   The scale of the width changes to 50% and the Absolute measurements in the Height and Width sections increase proportionally. The picture also moves up to page 2. When the Lock aspect ratio check box is selected, you need to enter only a height or width measurement. Word calculates the other measurement so that the resized graphic is proportional.

3. **With the picture still selected, click the Crop arrow in the Size group, then point to Crop to Shape**
   A selection of shapes is displayed as shown in FIGURE 7-10. You can crop any picture to any shape.

4. **Click the Oval shape (first selection in the first row of Basic Shapes)**
   The picture is cropped to the oval shape. After cropping a picture to a shape, you can further crop it to remove portions of the picture that you do not want. When you crop a picture, you drag the crop handle associated with the part of the picture you want to crop. A cropped picture is smaller than the original picture because you take away content from the top, bottom, and/or sides of the picture. However, when you resize a picture, the content of the picture stays the same even though the picture is made smaller or larger.

5. **Click the Crop button to show the crop marks**
   Cropping handles (solid black lines) appear on all four corners and sides of the graphic. To crop one side of a graphic, drag a side cropping handle inward to where you want to trim the graphic. To crop two adjacent sides at once, drag a corner cropping handle inward to the point where you want the corner of the cropped image to be.

   QUICK TIP
   If you don't like the crop, you can click the Undo button 🔙 on the Quick Access Toolbar to undo your last crop action.

6. **Drag the right-side and bottom-middle crop marks to set the size and shape of the picture as shown in FIGURE 7-11**

7. **Click the Crop button again to turn off the crop feature**
   To further modify the graphic, you use the mouse to rotate it to an approximate value.

8. **Click the Rotate handle ⟳ at the top of the picture, drag the mouse to rotate the picture so it appears similar to FIGURE 7-12, click away to deselect the picture, then save the document**

FIGURE 7-10: Shapes for cropping a picture to

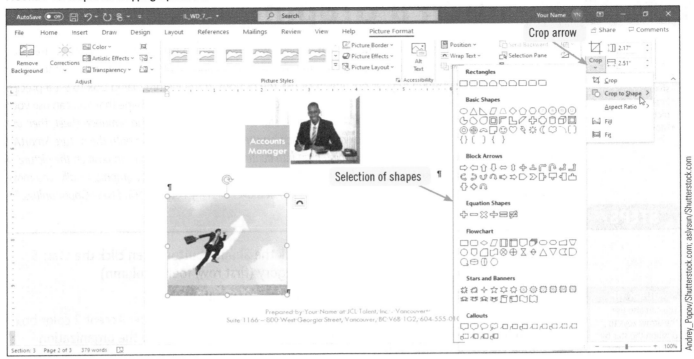

FIGURE 7-11: Cropping a picture

Drag crop handles to
remove portions of the
picture you don't want

FIGURE 7-12: Rotating a picture

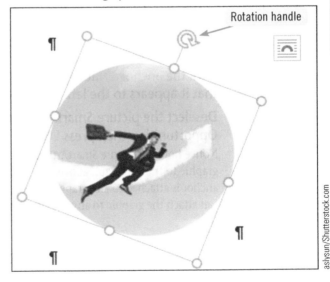

Rotation handle

Position a Graphic

**Learning
Outcomes**
- Position a floating shape
- Position a floating picture
- Move an anchor

By default, a picture inserted into a document is inline with text, which means that you cannot use your mouse to move the picture. You need to convert the picture to a floating graphic so that you can either move it to an approximate position in your document or use the options in the Picture dialog box to set a precise location on the page. A shape that you draw is automatically inserted as a floating shape that you can use your mouse to position on the page. **CASE** *You draw a star shape on page 1 of the information sheet, then use the mouse to move the shape to an approximate position on the page. You then make both the picture SmartArt graphic on page 2 and the picture of the jumping man into floating graphics so that you can position the picture of the jumping man at a precise location on the page with relation to the picture SmartArt graphic. Finally, you move the anchor attached to the picture SmartArt graphic so that it moves with the heading "Find New Opportunities."*

STEPS

1. Press CTRL+HOME, **click the** Insert tab, **click the** Shapes button, **then click the** Star: 5 Points shape **in the Stars and Banners category (first row, fourth column)**

2. **Draw a star approximately .5" wide next to the organization chart**

3. **Click the** Shape Fill arrow **in the Shape Styles group, click the** Orange, Accent 2 color box **(top row), then use your mouse to position the star with relation to the organization chart SmartArt as shown in** FIGURE 7-13

4. **Scroll to page 2 of the information sheet, then double-click a** white area **of the picture SmartArt graphic**

5. **Click the** Format tab, **click the** Arrange button, **click the** Wrap Text button **in the Arrange group, then click** Through

   You change the wrap setting to Through so that you can layer the jumping man picture under the picture SmartArt graphic.

6. **Click the** anchor ⚓ **at the top left of the picture SmartArt graphic, then drag it up so that it appears to the left of** Find New Opportunities **as shown in** FIGURE 7-14

7. **Deselect the picture SmartArt graphic, click the** first paragraph mark **below Find New Opportunities, then press** ENTER

   Notice how the picture SmartArt graphic does not move. Because you moved the anchor up to attach the graphic to the paragraph above, the graphic only moves when you also move its attached paragraph. An anchor is attached to any graphic object such as a picture, SmartArt, or shape that you insert in Word. You can attach the graphic to any paragraph by moving its anchor.

FIGURE 7-13: Star shape filled and positioned

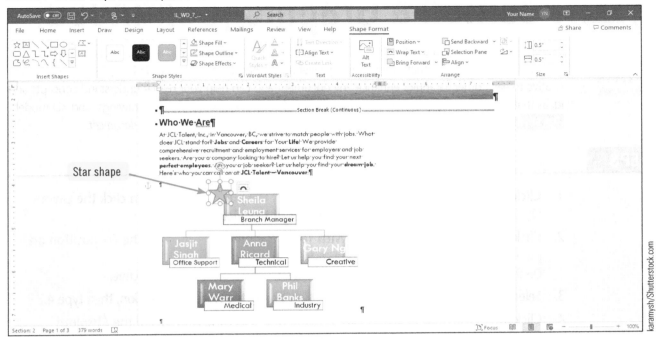

Star shape

karamysh/Shutterstock.com

FIGURE 7-14: Anchor repositioned

Anchor attached to the picture SmartArt is moved up so the picture SmartArt is now attached to the "Find New Opportunities" heading

branislavpudar/Shutterstock.com; Andrey_Popov/Shutterstock.com; zstock/Shutterstock.com; aslysun/Shutterstock.com

(*Continued*)

Word

Position a Graphic (Continued)

Learning Outcomes
- Position a picture
- Insert 3D models

Working with layouts and deciding where and how to insert images and graphics in a document is a creative process. You have many options for wrapping, layering, and positioning objects and graphics in a document relative to each other. Graphics enhance any document and can help your reader understand concepts and ideas that you are trying to convey. Graphics include SmartArt graphics, photos, drawings, and 3D models.

CASE *You continue to work with the layout options to best place the picture in the document.*

STEPS

1. **Click in the lower-right area of the** picture of the jumping man, **then click the** Layout Options button ⌐̂ **at the top-right corner of the picture**

2. **Click the** Through button **in the With Text Wrapping section, click the** Fix position on page option button, **then click** See more

   On the Position tab in the Layout dialog box, you set a precise position for the picture.

3. **Select the contents of the** Absolute position box **in the Horizontal section, then type** 4.2

4. **Click the** to the right of arrow, **click** Left Margin, **select the contents of the** Absolute position box **in the Vertical section, then type** 5

5. **Click the** below arrow, **click** Top Margin, **compare the Layout dialog box to** FIGURE 7-15, **then click** OK

   The position of the picture is now set 4.2" to the right of the left margin and 5" from the top margin. The picture slightly overlaps the picture SmartArt graphic and the Job Search Text wraps around the SmartArt graphic. When you make changes to text wrapping options for graphics and pictures, you often need to readjust the position of surrounding text.

6. **Click to the left of one of the paragraph marks above Job Search Tips, then add or remove paragraph marks** ¶ **so the Job Search Tips heading and paragraph appear at the bottom of page 2 below the picture SmartArt graphic**

7. **Click the** picture SmartArt graphic, **click the** Format tab, **click the** Arrange button **to show the selection of Arrange options if necessary, click the** Bring Forward arrow **in the Arrange group, click** Bring to Front, **then save the document**

Inserting and Editing 3D Models

You can use 3D models to creatively enhance your documents. You create a 3D model by either inserting a 3D model file or selecting a 3D model from the stock 3D models provided online. To insert a 3D model, click the Insert tab, then click the 3D Models arrow to show two options: This Device and Stock 3D Models. To select a stock 3D model, click Stock 3D Models, click the model category you require, click the model you wish to use, then click Insert. FIGURE 7-16 shows the 3D model of a parrot from the Animals category.

Once you have inserted a 3D model, you use the options on the 3D Model tab to add additional models, return the model to its original settings, change the 3D model view, add Alt text, arrange the position of the 3D model with relation to other objects on the page, and modify the size of the 3D model. FIGURE 7-17 shows how the 3D model of the parrot has been edited.

FIGURE 7-15: Layout dialog box

Absolute Horizontal
position set at 4.2
inches to the right
of the Left Margin

Absolute Vertical
position set at 5
inches below the
Top Margin

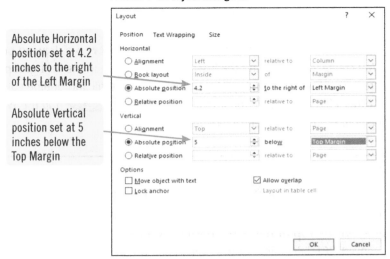

FIGURE 7-16: 3D Model tab

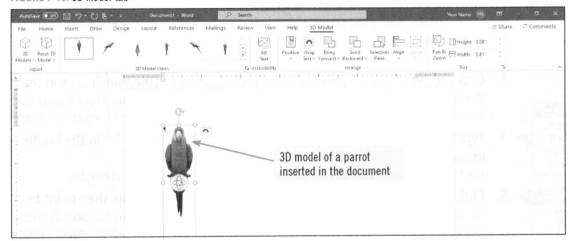

3D model of a parrot
inserted in the document

FIGURE 7-17: Editing and enhancing the 3D model

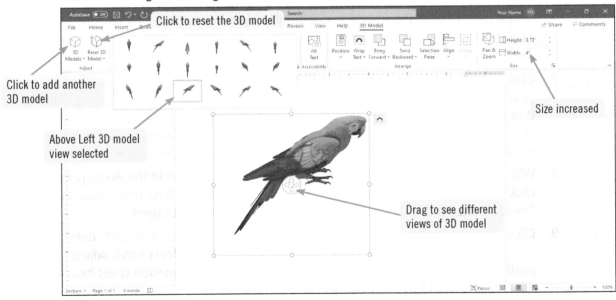

Click to reset the 3D model

Click to add another
3D model

Above Left 3D model
view selected

Size increased

Drag to see different
views of 3D model

Word

Create WordArt

Another way to enhance your documents is to use WordArt. **WordArt** is a drawing object that contains decorative text. You create WordArt using the Insert WordArt button in the Text group on the Insert tab. Once you have created a WordArt object, you can change its font, fill and outline colors, borders, shadows, shape, and other effects to create the impact you desire. **CASE** *You use WordArt to create an impressive heading from existing text for the information sheet.*

STEPS

1. **Double-click in the Footer area, select JCL Talent, Inc. – Vancouver, click the Home tab, click the Copy button in the Clipboard group, double-click anywhere in the document to exit the footer area, press CTRL+HOME, press ENTER, press Up Arrow ↑ to position the insertion point at the top of the page, then click the Paste button in the Clipboard group**
   You want to convert "JCL Talent, Inc. – Vancouver" into a WordArt object.

2. **Select the text JCL Talent, Inc. – Vancouver, click the Insert tab, then click the Insert WordArt button ⟨4·⟩ in the Text group**
   The WordArt gallery opens as shown in FIGURE 7-18 with styles you can choose for your WordArt. You can convert existing text to a WordArt object or you can click the Insert tab and click the Insert WordArt button in the text group to insert a WordArt object that you type.

3. **Click Fill: White; Outline Blue, Accent color 5; Shadow (the fourth style in the first row)**
   The WordArt object appears at the location of the insertion point, and the Shape Format tab becomes the active tab. By default, the WordArt object is inserted as a floating graphic with Square text wrapping.

QUICK TIP
You can change the font or font size of WordArt text using the Mini toolbar.

4. **Type .7 in the Height box in the Size group, press TAB, type 7.5 in the Width box, then press ENTER**
   The WordArt object is enlarged to span the page between the left and right margins.

QUICK TIP
Use the Text Effects and Typography button in the Font group on the Home tab to apply text effects to regular text.

5. **Click the Text Effects button ⟨A·⟩ in the WordArt Styles group, then point to Transform**
   The Text Effects button is used to apply a shadow, reflection, glow, bevel, or 3-D rotation to the text. It is also used to change the shape of the text. The Transform gallery shows the available shapes for WordArt text.

6. **Click Warp Up in the Warp section (fourth row, third column), click the Launcher ⟨回⟩ in the WordArt Styles group to open the Format Shape pane, click Shadow in the Format Shape pane to view the ways you can modify a shadow applied to a WordArt object, click the Presets button, then click Offset: Bottom Left in the Outer section (first row, third column)**

7. **Click Glow in the Format Shape pane, click the Presets button, click Glow: 5 point; Orange, Accent color 2 (first row, second column), click the Text Fill arrow ⟨A·⟩ in the WordArt Styles group, then click Orange, Accent 2, Lighter 80%**
   The customized settings and the new fill effects applied to the WordArt are shown in FIGURE 7-19. You want the WordArt object to appear on top of the picture. The wrapping for both objects must be changed to Through.

8. **With the WordArt object selected, click the Wrap Text button in the Arrange Group, click Through, double-click the picture of the city, click the Wrap Text button again, click Through, then move the picture up so it covers the WordArt object**

9. **Click the Send Backward arrow in the Arrange group, click Send to Back, delete the paragraph mark below the picture, close the Format Text Effects pane, adjust the positions of the WordArt object and the picture so the information sheet header appears as shown in FIGURE 7-20, then save the document**

FIGURE 7-18: **WordArt gallery**

Selected text for WordArt
WordArt gallery

FIGURE 7-19: **Formatted WordArt object**

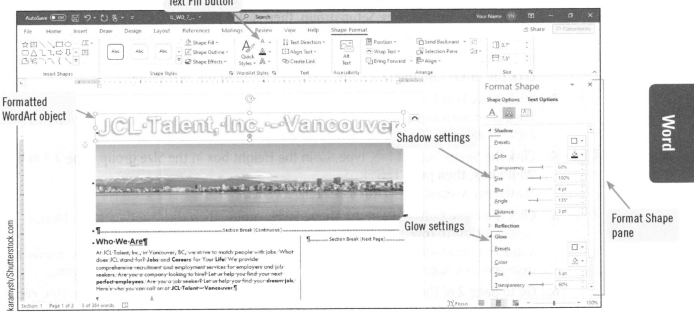
Text Fill button
Formatted WordArt object
Shadow settings
Glow settings
Format Shape pane

FIGURE 7-20: **Completed header**

Illustrating Documents with Graphics

Create a Text Box

A **text box** is a container that you can fill with text and graphics. A text box can be resized; formatted with colors, lines, and text wrapping; and positioned anywhere on a page. You can insert a preformatted text box that you customize with your own text, draw an empty text box and then fill it with text, or select existing text and then draw a text box around it. You use the Text Box button in the Text group, or the Shapes button in the Illustrations group to create a text box. A **drop cap** is a large initial capital letter that is often used to set off the first paragraph of an article in documents such as information sheets, newsletters, and books. **CASE** ➤ *You draw a text box in column 2 on page 1 of the information sheet, resize and position the text box on the page, then fill it with text and format it using a text box style. You then insert a preformatted text box on page 2 of the information sheet and add a drop cap to the first paragraph of text on page 1.*

STEPS

1. **Press** CTRL+END, **select the text from** Job Search Tips **to the end of the document, click the** Cut button **in the Clipboard group, scroll up to page 1 and click after them. and to the left of the paragraph mark at the bottom of column 1, click the** Layout tab, **click the** Breaks button **in the Page Setup group, then click** Column

   The insertion point is positioned at the top of column 2 on page 1 where you want to draw the text box.

2. **In column 2, click the** Home tab, **click the** Paste button, **select the text you just pasted, click the** Insert tab, **then click the** Text Box button **in the Text group**

3. **Click** Draw Text Box

   The selected text is formatted as a text box in column 2 on page 1 as shown in FIGURE 7-21. When you draw a text box around existing text or graphics, the text box becomes a floating object.

4. **Click the** Shape Format tab, **type** 6.2 **in the Height box in the Size group, type** 2.3 **in the Width box, then press** ENTER

   The text box is resized to be exactly 6.2" tall and 2.3" wide.

5. **Click the** More button ⬇ **in the Shape Styles group, then click** Subtle Effect – Lime, Accent 1 **(fourth row, second column)**

   A style that includes light green shading and a thin green border is applied to the text box. You can also create your own designs using the Shape Fill and Shape Outline buttons in the Shape Styles group.

6. **Go to page 2 of the information sheet, click to the left of** Find New Opportunities, **click the** Insert tab, **click the** Text Box button **in the Text group, then click the** Austin Quote **preformatted style (middle selection in the first row)**

7. **Drag the** left-middle sizing handle **to the right to reduce the width of the text box to approximately** 2", **move the** text box **to the right to a blank area, click in the** text box, **type** Contact Anna Ricard or Phil Banks for information about current job opportunities in these sectors., **then use your mouse to size and position the text box as shown in** FIGURE 7-22

8. **Click away from the text box, press** CTRL+HOME, **click in the paragraph below the** Who We Are **heading in Column 1, click the** Insert tab, **click the** Drop Cap button ⬛ **in the Text group, then click** Dropped

   A drop cap is added to the paragraph. You can modify the size and font of the drop cap.

9. **With the drop cap still selected, click the** Drop Cap button ⬛, **click** Drop Cap Options, **click the** Lines to drop down arrow **to show** 2, **click** OK, **deselect the drop cap, then save the document**

FIGURE 7-21: Text enclosed in a text box

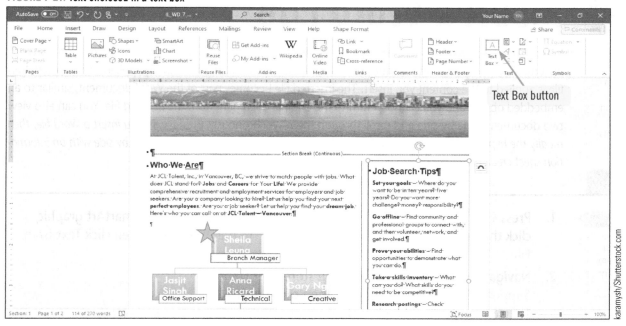

Text Box button

karamysh/Shutterstock.com

FIGURE 7-22: Text box sized and positioned

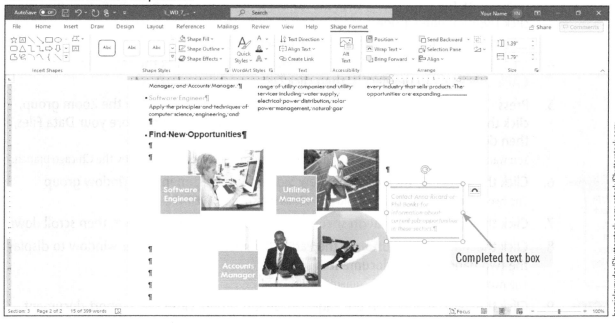

Completed text box

branislavpudar/Shutterstock.com; zstock/Shutterstock.com;
Andrey_Popov/Shutterstock.com; aslysun/Shutterstock.com

Linking text boxes

If you are working on a longer document, you might want text to begin in a text box on one page and then continue in a text box on another page. By creating a **link** between two or more text boxes, you can force text to flow automatically from one text box to another, allowing you to size and format the text boxes any way you wish. To link two or more text boxes, you must first create the original text box, fill it with text, and then create a second, empty text box. Then, to create the link, select the first text box, click the Create Link button in the Text group on the Shape Format tab to activate the pointer, and then click the second text box with the pointer. Any overflow text from the first text box flows seamlessly into the second text box. As you resize the first text box, the flow of text adjusts automatically between the two linked text boxes. If you want to break a link between two linked text boxes so that all the text is contained in the original text box, select the original text box, and then click the Break Link button in the Text group.

Illustrating Documents with Graphics

Insert a Word File

You use the Text from File command on the Insert tab to add a Word document to another Word document. When you insert an entire Word file into a document, the formatting applied to the destination file is applied to the content you insert. The inserted file becomes part of the Word document, similar to an embedded object, and you cannot return to the original document from the inserted file. You can also view two documents side by side and scroll through them synchronously. **CASE** *You insert a Word file, then modify the hyphenation options. Finally, you view the completed information sheet side by side with an information sheet created by the Chicago branch of JCL Talent to compare them.*

STEPS

TROUBLE
Do not to select the graphic. If you do, click away from the graphic and try again

1. **Press** CTRL+END, **click the** paragraph mark **just below the picture SmartArt graphic, click the** Insert tab, **click the** Object arrow 🔲 ▾ **in the Text group, then click** Text from File

2. **Navigate to the location where you store your Data Files, click** Support_WD_7_Interviews.docx, **then click** Insert
   The file Support_WD_7_Interviews.docx, formatted with the Circuit theme, is inserted.

3. **Delete extra hard returns above and below the text so the document fits on two pages, click the** Layout tab, **click the** Hyphenation arrow **in the Page Setup group, then click** Hyphenation Options
   You can choose to hyphenate a document automatically or manually.

4. **Click the** Automatically hyphenate document check box, **click the** Hyphenate words in CAPS check box **to deselect it, then click** OK

5. **Press** CTRL+HOME, **click the** View tab, **click the** One Page button **in the Zoom group, click the** File tab, **click** Open, **navigate to the location where you store your Data Files, then double-click** Support_WD_7_Chicago.docx
   You want to compare this finished document to an information sheet produced by the Chicago branch.

QUICK TIP
By default, the Vertical page movement option is selected, which means that page 1 of both documents appears side by side.

6. **Click the** View tab, **then click the** View Side by Side button **in the Window group**
   The two information sheets appear side by side as shown in FIGURE 7-23.

7. **Click the** Chicago information sheet **(left window), click the** scroll bar, **then scroll down**

8. **Click the** Side to Side button **in the Page Movement group in either window to display the two pages of each document**
   The two pages of the support document are displayed.

QUICK TIP
You need to select the Vertical page movement option to continue working normally in Word.

9. **Click the** Vertical button **in the Page Movement group, close the Support document, make any spacing adjustments necessary so your document matches** FIGURE 7-24, **then click the** Vertical button **in the Page Movement group if necessary**

10. **sam ↑ Save your changes, submit a copy to your instructor, then close the file and exit Word**

Configuring line numbers

To add line numbers to selected text, click the Line Numbers button in the Page Setup group on the Layout tab. You can then choose to number lines continuously, restart numbering on each new page or section, or suppress for the current paragraph. You can also choose to display the numbers at intervals. Word counts the number of lines in a document. This is helpful if you want to refer to a specific line in a document such as in a legal contract.

Illustrating Documents with Graphics

FIGURE 7-23: Two documents viewed side by side

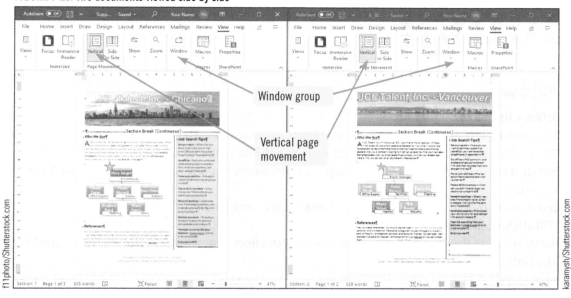

FIGURE 7-24: Completed information sheet

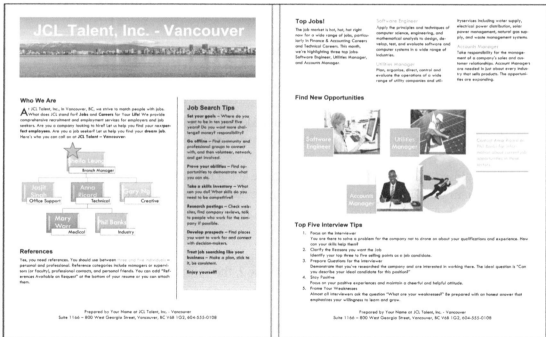

Inserting online videos and online pictures in a document

You can also illustrate your documents with graphics and media that you have found on the web and have permission to use. The Online Video command in the Media group on the Insert tab allows you to insert videos found on the web into your Word documents and play them. Click the Online Video button, type the URL or embed code in the Insert Video dialog box, then click Insert. Use the Pictures button in the Illustrations group to insert images from the web. Click Online Pictures on the Pictures button menu to open the Online Pictures window, type a keyword or phrase in the search box for the image you want to find, then press ENTER. Select an image from the search results, click Insert to add it to the document, then format the item as you would any other graphic object. Videos inserted in a document include a play button that you can click to view the video right in Word.

Word

Practice

Skills Review

1. Use the Office Clipboard.

  a. Start Word, open IL_WD_7-2.docx from the location where you store your Data Files, save it as **IL_WD_7_RiskReport**, open the Clipboard, then clear all items currently listed.

  b. Select and then cut the two lines of text at the top of the document (starting with "Prepared by Your Name . . .) to the Clipboard.

  c. Select and then cut the picture of the man's two hands on the block puzzle to the Clipboard.

  d. Press CTRL+HOME, then paste the picture.

  e. Open the footer, paste the text in the footer, remove any extra lines, center the text, replace "Your Name" with your name, then exit the footer.

  f. Open Support_WD_7_Risk.docx from the location where you store your Data Files, select and copy all the text, then close the document.

  g. Click the blank line below the "Organization Chart" placeholder, paste the text using the Use Destination Theme paste option, close the Clipboard, then save the document.

2. Create sections and columns.

  a. Turn on formatting marks, if necessary.

  b. Place the insertion point to the left of the heading "Risk Management Team", press ENTER, then insert a continuous section break.

  c. In Section 2, turn on columns with the following settings: Right preset, spacing between set at .4", and the Line between option selected.

  d. In Multiple Pages view, insert a Next Page section break to the left of "Risk Questions".

  e. In Section 3, turn on columns with the following settings: Three, spacing between at .2", and the Line between option deselected.

  f. Return to 100% view, insert a Continuous section break to the left of the paragraph mark following "maintenance?" at the bottom of column 1 to balance the columns containing the Risk Questions text.

  g. Click the paragraph mark above the picture of the blocks in column 1 on page 2, turn on one column (Section 4), then save the document.

3. Create SmartArt graphics.

  a. Click the picture of the woman teaching at the bottom of page 2, then create a picture SmartArt graphic using the Bending Picture Blocks layout.

  b. Add two shapes to the picture SmartArt.

  c. Insert **Support_WD_7_Coins.jpg** in the first blank shape, then insert **Support_WD_7_Disaster.jpg** in the second blank shape.

  d. Expand the text pane, if necessary, label the three boxes as follows: **Employee Training, Financial Reserves**, and **Disaster Preparation**, then close the text pane. (*Hint:* Press the down arrow, *not* ENTER, to move to the next bullet. If you press ENTER, click the Undo button.)

  e. Change the layout to Bending Picture Caption (second row, second column).

  f. Set the height of the picture SmartArt graphic to 3.3" and the width to 5.7".

  g. Use SHIFT to select the three pictures in the picture SmartArt graphic, apply the Slant bevel shape effect (first row, fourth column), then save the document.

4. Modify SmartArt graphics.

  a. On page 1 of the Risk Report, select the "Organization Chart" placeholder, then insert a Hierarchy SmartArt graphic using the Name and Title Organization Chart style.

  b. Click a white area of the chart, then set the height of the organization chart at 2.8" and the width at 4.7".

  c. Add and remove shapes and text so the organization chart appears as shown in FIGURE 7-25.

  d. Use the Move Down command to move the box for Edie Quinn so it and its subordinate boxes appear in the middle of row 2.

  e. Change the colors of the chart to Colored Fill – Accent 4 (red).

  f. Apply the Cartoon SmartArt style from the 3-D section.

FIGURE 7-25

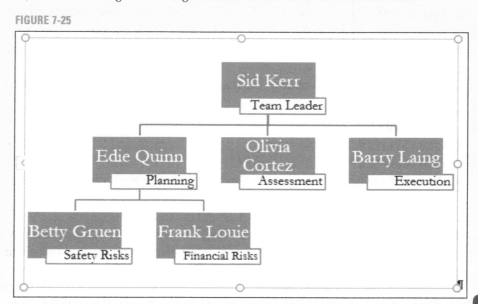

  g. Select all five of the subordinate boxes, set the width at 1.1", then save the document.

5. Crop and rotate a picture.

  a. Scroll to page 2 of the report, double-click the picture of the three hands and block tower, then scale the picture to 75%. (*Hint:* Remember to verify that the Lock aspect ratio check box is selected so the picture is resized proportionally.)

  b. Crop the picture to the Cloud shape (third row, third selection from the right in the Basic Shapes category).

  c. See FIGURE 7-26. Further crop the picture and use the mouse to slightly rotate it to the left.

  d. Deselect the picture, then save the document.

FIGURE 7-26

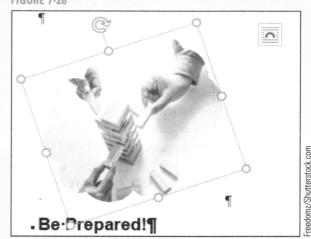

6. Position a graphic.

  a. Scroll down to view the picture SmartArt graphic, then draw a Lightning Bolt shape that is approximately 1" in height.

  b. Fill the lightning bolt with Gold, Accent 6, Lighter 40%.

  c. Position the lightning bolt shape in the lower left corner of the picture SmartArt graphic, slightly overlapping the Disaster Preparation box. Refer to the completed document in FIGURE 7-27.

  d. On page 1, change the wrapping of the organization chart to Through. Don't worry that text will wrap around it.

Word

Skills Review (continued)

e. Drag the anchor for the chart up so it appears to the left of the paragraph of text that starts "We have embarked upon ...".

f. Scroll down and click the cloud-shaped picture, cut the picture, then paste it at the paragraph mark above the "Risk Dimensions" heading on page 1 of the report.

g. Change the wrapping of the cloud shape to Through, then on the Position tab in the Layout dialog box, set the position of the picture at .5" to the right of the Page and 5" below the Top Margin.

h. Click the organization chart, then change the layering to Bring to Front so that the chart slightly overlaps the cloud picture.

i. Click the paragraph mark above "Risk Dimensions", press ENTER until the "Risk Dimensions" paragraph is moved below the organization chart, then save the document.

7. Create WordArt.

a. Press CTRL+HOME to move to the top of the document, press ENTER, press CTRL+HOME, then type **Risk Management Plan**.

b. Convert the text "Risk Management Plan" to a WordArt object using the Fill: Red, Accent color 4; Soft Bevel WordArt style (last selection in row 1).

c. Set the height of the WordArt object at .9" and the width at 7.5".

d. Transform the WordArt object with the Wave: Down effect (first column, fifth row in the Warp section).

e. Add the Offset: Left shadow effect to the WordArt object (second row, third column in the Outer section), then apply the Glow: 5 point; Gold, Accent color 6 glow effect (first row, last column).

f. Change the fill color of the WordArt object to White, Background 1 (top left color box).

g. Change the wrap setting to Through, then change the wrap setting of the wide picture below to Through.

h. Adjust the WordArt object and picture so the WordArt object appears in front of the picture at the top of the document as shown in the completed report in FIGURE 7-27.

i. Delete the extra paragraph mark below the first picture in the document, then save the document.

8. Create a text box.

a. Scroll to and select the text from "Risk Categories" to the end of the document, then cut it.

b. Scroll up to page 1, click after "monitor it" at the end of the Risk Dimensions paragraph at the bottom of column 1 on page 1, press ENTER, insert a column break, then paste the copied text in the new column.

c. Select the text again, then insert it into a text box using the Draw Text Box option.

d. Set the height of the text box to 7" and the width to 2.2".

e. Apply the Moderate Effect – Red, Accent 4 shape style to the text box.

f. If necessary, remove any extra hard returns following the text box so that page 2 moves up, change the wrapping to Through for the picture SmartArt graphic, then send it behind the lightning bolt.

g. Remove the two paragraph marks above "Be Prepared," then insert a text box using the Austin Quote preformatted text box.

h. Size and position the text box, then type **Contact Betty Gruen for information about company-wide emergency procedures and to obtain emergency kits for each department.** as shown in the completed report in FIGURE 7-27.

i. On page 1 of the report, insert a drop cap that is dropped 2 lines in the paragraph under the "Risk Management Team" heading.

j. Save the document.

Skills Review (continued)

9. Insert a Word file.

   a. Double-click below the picture SmartArt graphic on page 2 to position the insertion point, then insert the Word file **Support_WD_7_Quiz.docx** from the location where you store your Data Files.

   b. Remove any extra hard returns so that the document fits on two pages.

   c. Change the hyphenation options so that the text in the document is automatically hyphenated and words in CAPS are *not* hyphenated.

   d. Press CTRL+HOME, then view the document in One Page view.

   e. Open Support_WD_7_RiskReport_WatsonFinancial.docx from the location where you store your Data Files.

   f. View the two documents side by side, then change the page movement to Side to Side.

   g. Return the page movement to Vertical, close the Support document, then make any spacing adjustments necessary so that the two pages of the Risk Management Report appear as shown in FIGURE 7-27.

   h. Save the document, submit a copy to your instructor, then close the file and exit Word.

FIGURE 7-27

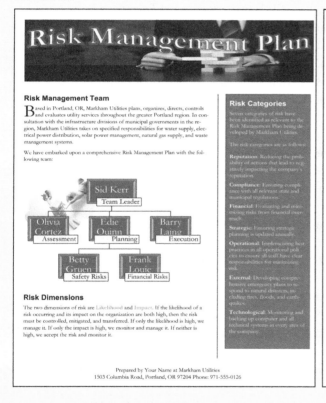

Word

Independent Challenge 1

At Riverwalk Medical Clinic in Cambridge, MA, you've been asked to take over the writing and formatting of the clinic's quarterly news bulletin. The two pages of the bulletin are printed on both sides of one page and distributed to staff. In addition, a PDF of the bulletin can be downloaded from the clinic's website. You open a draft of the Spring bulletin and format it in sections with columns, and then add graphic objects, including text boxes, a picture, a SmartArt graphic, a WordArt object, and a picture cropped to a shape.

a. Start Word, open the file IL_WD_7-3.docx from the location where you store your Data Files, save it as **IL_WD_7_RiverwalkSpringBulletin**, then show formatting marks.

b. Create "Spring Bulletin" as a WordArt object using the Fill: White; Outline: Red, Accent color 2; Hard Shadow: Red, Accent color 2 WordArt style (third row, fourth column).

c. Increase the width of the WordArt object to 5", change the wrapping to Through, then modify the WordArt object using the following settings:
   - Shadow: Offset: Bottom Left in the Outer section
   - Glow: 5 point; Green, Accent color 1
   - Transform: Double Wave: Down-Up (fifth row in the third column in the Warp section)

d. Crop the picture of the river scene at the top of the document to the Flowchart: Punched Tape shape (second row, fourth column in the Flowchart section), then set the height of the cropped picture at 1.3" and the width at 6.5". (*Hint:* deselect the Lock aspect ratio check box in the Size dialog box so the shape is not resized proportionally.)

e. Change the text wrapping of the cropped shape to Through, then use layering and your mouse to position the WordArt object in front of the cropped shape at the top of the page as shown in the completed bulletin in FIGURE 7-28.

f. Open the Clipboard, clear the contents, select the text from the "Giving Back" heading to the end of the paragraph under "Donation Hearts", then cut it to the Clipboard.

g. Cut the picture of the women in pink shirts to the Clipboard.

h. Paste the cut text at the second paragraph mark below the "Spring Bulletin" heading and picture, then paste the picture following the text you just pasted.

i. Press ENTER to move the "Clinic News" heading to a new line, if necessary, then insert a Next Page Section break to move the heading to Section 2 at the top of a new page.

j. Scroll up, then insert a Continuous section break at the paragraph mark below the "Spring Bulletin" header and picture.

k. Click to the left of the "Giving Back" heading, then turn on columns with the following settings: Two, .3 spacing between, and a line between.

l. Balance the two columns by inserting a Continuous section break after "$2,000." at the end of the "Donation Hearts" paragraph.

m. Make the picture of the women in pink shirts a picture SmartArt graphic using the Bending Picture Blocks layout, then add two shapes.

n. Fill the first new shape with the picture file **Support_WD_7_Brain.jpg** and the second new shape with the picture file **Support_WD_7_Donations.jpg**.

o. Change the layout of the picture SmartArt graphic to Captioned Pictures, then with the picture SmartArt graphic selected, select One column and modify the width of the picture SmartArt graphic to 6.7" so that it extends in one line of boxes across the bottom of the page as shown in FIGURE 7-28. Enter the required captions.

p. On page 2 of the document, make the text "Congratulations" and the paragraph that follows it into a text box formatted with the Subtle Effect – Yellow, Accent 5 shape style.

q. Anchor the text box to the paragraph above it ("New Emergency Room Procedures") by dragging the anchor currently attached to the text box up so it appears to the left of the paragraph above.

r. Add a blank line below the text box, then insert the Word file **Support_WD_7_Education.docx**.

s. Insert the picture **Support_WD_7_Class.jpg**, then format it as follows:

- Crop the picture to the Oval shape.
- Further crop the top and bottom of the picture if necessary so it appears as shown in FIGURE 7-28.
- Change the width of the picture to 2.41".
- Change the text wrapping to Through, then slightly rotate the picture and position it next to the inserted Word file as shown in FIGURE 7-28. *(Hint:* Switch to One Page view if necessary so you can see where to position the picture.)

t. View the bulletin in Multiple Pages view, then compare it to FIGURE 7-28 and make any spacing adjustments.

u. Save your changes, submit a copy to your instructor, close the document, then exit Word.

FIGURE 7-28

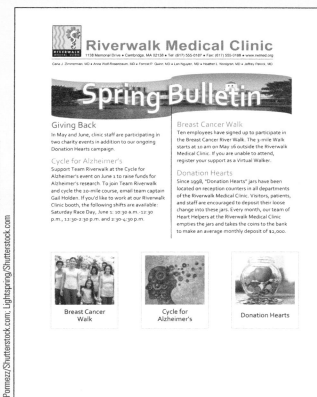

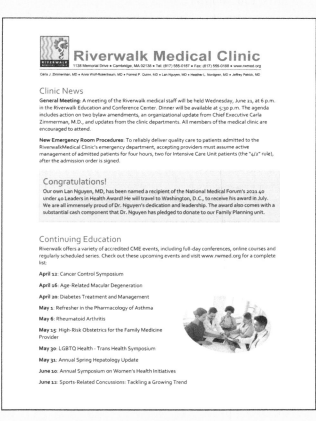

Independent Challenge 2

You have just started working for Rose Management, a management consulting firm created by Margaret Rose and based in Vermont. You've been asked to prepare a short report for distribution at an upcoming meeting of the board of directors. First, you create a graphic for use on the company's revamped website, then you create an organization chart to show the company personnel. Finally, you paste information from another document and format it as a text box that includes drop caps, and then view the document side by side with another report.

a. Start Word, open the file IL_WD_7-4.docx from the drive and folder where you store your Data Files, then save it as **IL_WD_7_RoseManagementReport**.

b. Create a graphic that includes the rose picture and a WordArt object as follows:

- Crop the rose picture to remove as much of the white background as possible so the rose fills the space.
- Change the text wrapping to Through. Press ENTER to move down the text related to the organization chart so you have room to work.
- Type **Rose Management** at the paragraph mark above the rose picture, then create a WordArt object from the text using the Fill: White; Outline: Blue, Accent color 2; Hard Shadow: Blue, Accent color 2 WordArt style (last row, fourth column).
- Format the WordArt with the Arch Transform effect (first selection in the Follow Path section).
- Reduce the height of the rose picture to 2.4", then set the exact position of the rose picture on the page at 1" to the right of Column and 3" below Page.
- Compare the graphic to the completed report in FIGURE 7-29.

FIGURE 7-29

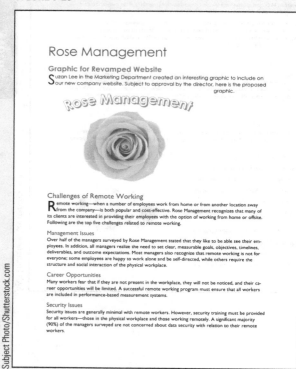

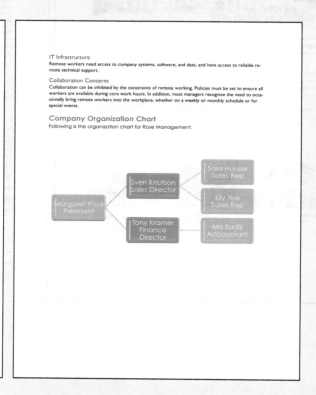

Independent Challenge 2 (continued)

c. Scroll down to the Company Organization Chart heading, insert a page break to move the Company Organization Chart heading to the next page, then use the information contained in the table to create a SmartArt graphic organization chart that uses the Horizontal Hierarchy style in the Hierarchy category. (*Hint*: Press SHIFT+ENTER after you type a name so that you can enter the position.)

d. Apply the Polished SmartArt style from the 3-D section of the SmartArt style, then apply the Colorful - Accent Colors color scheme.

e. Apply the Cutout Bevel style to all the boxes in the organization chart.

f. When you have entered the names and positions for the organization chart, delete the table containing the text for the chart.

g. Open Support_WD_7_RemoteWorking.docx, copy all the text, then paste it to the left of the page break on page 1 (below the rose graphic) using the Keep Source Formatting paste option.

h. Delete the page break.

i. Insert a drop cap in paragraph 1 below "Graphic for Revamped Website" and set the dropped to 2, then insert another drop cap with the same settings in the paragraph below "Challenges of Remote Working."

j. Open Support_WD_7_DraftReport.docx, view the draft report side by side with the completed report, scroll the two documents, then close Support_WD_7_DraftReport and return the Page Movement to Vertical.

k. Set the hyphenation options so that text in the document is automatically hyphenated.

l. Type your name in the document footer if requested to do so, save the document, submit the document to your instructor, then close the document and exit Word.

Word

Visual Workshop

Open IL_WD_7-5.docx from the drive and folder where you store your Data Files, then save the document as **IL_WD_7_CommunityTransportationPlan**. Format the text and graphics in the document to match **FIGURE 7-30**. You will need to move text, create a WordArt object and a picture SmartArt graphic, format selected text in columns, and enclose some of the text in a text box. The WordArt object is formatted with the Fill: Red, Accent color 1; Shadow WordArt style with the Square Transform effect applied and the height of the object reduced to 1". To create the picture SmartArt graphic from the four pictures, create a graphic from the first picture (the walker), add three shapes, then cut and paste each picture into a shape. Select the Bending Picture Semi-Transparent Text layout, a height of 3.7" and a width of 6". Apply the Subtle Effect, Red, Accent 1 style to the text box. Remember you can move the anchor icon attached to a graphic to help you move objects and text on the page. Save the document, submit a copy to your instructor, then close the document and exit Word.

FIGURE 7-30

Community Transportation Master Plan

Following the vision and policies set out in the Official Community Plan, the Community Transportation Master Plan (CTMP) will integrate planning for:

- Multiple modes of transportation

- Transportation and land use
- Demand management

The CTMP will be built upon a community vision to create a more efficient and sustainable transportation system for the community.

Walking Paths

Cycling Routes

Bus Routes

Improved Roads

The CTMP project for Courtney Lake, MI, consists of five phases taking place over one and a half years:

1. Review Existing Plans and Studies
2. Gather Information for Existing Conditions
3. Engage Stakeholders to Identify Key Issues and Solutions
4. Create Alternatives and Refine Strategies
5. Finalize the Plan for Adoption

Get involved! Check the website regularly for upcoming engagement initiatives.

Illustrating Documents with Graphics

Working with Tables

CASE JCL uses tables to analyze placement data using placement dates, divisions, and commissions. The manager of the Boston office, Cheri McNeil, asks you to help her build and manage a table of information about the office's placements for the year. You will create the table, add information, organize it so it is easy to view, and perform calculations that help Cheri understand how the Boston office performed.

Module Objectives

After completing this module, you will be able to:

- Create and format a table
- Add and delete table data
- Sort table data
- Use formulas in a table

- Filter a table
- Look up values in a table
- Summarize table data
- Validate table data

Files You Will Need

IL_EX_5-1.xlsx IL_EX_5-4.xlsx
IL_EX_5-2.xlsx IL_EX_5-5.xlsx
IL_EX_5-3.xlsx

Create and Format a Table

Learning
Outcomes
• Create a table
• Format a table

You can analyze and manipulate data in a table structure to take advantage of Excel tools and features designed specifically for tables. An Excel **table** is an organized collection of rows and columns of similarly structured data on a worksheet. Tables offer a convenient way to understand and manage large amounts of information. A table is organized into rows of data called **records**, each of which represents a complete set of field values for a specific person, place, object, event, or idea. A **field** is a column containing a specific property for each record, such as a person's last name or street address. Each field has a field name, which is a column label, such as "Address," that describes its contents. The **header row** is the first row of the table, and it contains the field names. After you create a table you can add preset formatting combinations of fill color, borders, type style, and type color by applying a table style. **CASE** ▶ *You begin building the placement table by creating it using worksheet data and applying a table style.*

STEPS

1. **sam** ⬇ **Start Excel, open IL_EX_5-1.xlsx from the location where you store your Data Files, then save it as IL_EX_5_BostonPlacements**

2. **With cell A1 selected, click the Insert tab on the ribbon, click the Table button in the Tables group, in the Create Table dialog box verify that the range $A$1:$H$65 appears in the Where is the data for your table? box and the My table has headers check box contains a checkmark, as shown in FIGURE 5-1, then click OK**

   The data range is now defined as a table and is selected. **Filter list arrows**, which let you display portions of your data, appear next to each field name in the table. When you create a table, Excel automatically applies a table style. The default table style has a dark blue header row and alternating light and dark blue data rows. The Table Design tab appears, and the Table Styles group displays a gallery of table formatting options.

3. **Click the Table Styles More button ⬇ on the Table Design tab, scroll and view all of the table styles, then move the pointer over several styles without clicking**

   The Table Styles gallery on the Table Design tab contains three style categories—Light, Medium, and Dark—each of which includes numerous designs. The designs use the current workbook theme colors so the table coordinates with your existing workbook content. If you select a different workbook theme and color scheme in the Themes group on the Page Layout tab, the Table Styles gallery uses those colors.

4. **Click the Green, Table Style Light 14 table style (the first style in the third row under Light), then click cell A1**

5. **Position the pointer in the column heading area for column A until it changes to ⬇, drag to select columns A and B, press CTRL, then drag ⬇ to select the column headings for columns F, G, and H**

6. **Click the Home tab on the ribbon, click the Format button in the Cells group, click Column Width, in the Column Width dialog box type 15.57 in the Column width box, then click OK**

7. **Position the pointer in the column D heading area until it changes to ⬇, drag to select columns D and E, click the Format button in the Cells group, click Column Width, in the Column Width dialog box type 9.43 in the Column width box, then click OK**

8. **Click cell A1, compare your table to FIGURE 5-2, then save your work**

FIGURE 5-1: **Create Table dialog box**

Verify the table range →

Create Table ? ✕

Where is the data for your table?

= $A$1:$H$65

☑ **M**y table has headers

Verify that this check box contains a checkmark →

OK   Cancel

FIGURE 5-2: **Formatted table**

	Account #	Employer ID	Division	Posting Date	Filled Date	Position Type	Commission	Preferred Employer
2	6686	69661	Finance & Accounting	10/13/21	11/10/21	Full-time	$16,171	Yes
3	6488	49734	Creative	4/5/21	4/14/21	Consultant	$9,546	No
4	5499	88302	Office Support	12/22/21	12/29/21	Full-time	$10,098	Yes
5	4438	51467	Technical	3/26/21	5/3/21	Full-time	$15,751	Yes
6	7569	30405	Creative	2/3/21	3/13/21	Full-time	$13,764	No
7	7803	99768	Technical	2/24/21	3/29/21	Consultant	$8,547	No
8	7701	26988	Office Support	8/14/21	9/13/21	Consultant	$5,324	No
9	2886	30993	Office Support	1/15/21	2/16/21	Consultant	$7,984	Yes
10	9017	82305	Finance & Accounting	7/8/21	8/7/21	Full-time	$20,724	Yes
11	4507	22043	Finance & Accounting	10/14/21	11/23/21	Full-time	$5,693	No
12	5801	64998	Creative	2/8/21	3/12/21	Consultant	$2,478	No
13	4890	37262	Creative	5/1/21	6/1/21	Consultant	$824	No
14	3117	93040	Technical	4/26/21	5/17/21	Full-time	$18,434	Yes
15	3100	85601	Office Support	8/2/21	8/24/21	Full-time	$14,277	Yes
16	4302	74521	Technical	7/2/21	8/9/21	Full-time	$16,976	No
17	6488	49734	Creative	4/5/21	4/14/21	Consultant	$9,546	No
18	1262	26610	Office Support	4/16/21	5/5/21	Consultant	$6,321	No

Division Info
Division
Technic
Total Com
Number of Pla

Changing table style options

You can change a table's appearance by using the check boxes in the Table Style Options group on the Table Design tab, as shown in FIGURE 5-3. You can use the check boxes to turn on or turn off the following options: Header Row, which displays or hides the header row; Total Row, which calculates totals for each column; Banded Rows, which applies or removes **banding**, a type of fill formatting in alternating rows or columns; and First Column and Last Column, which applies or removes special formatting in the first and last columns. You can display or hide the filter arrows on a table using the Filter Button check box; removing the checkmark removes the arrows.

You can also create your own table style by clicking the Table Styles More button, then clicking New Table Style at the bottom of the Table Styles Gallery. In the New Table Style dialog box, enter a name for the style in the Name box, click an item in the Table Element list, then click Format to format the selected element. You can also set a custom style as the default style for your tables by adding a checkmark to the Set as default table style for this document check box. You can remove a table style from the currently selected table by clicking Clear at the bottom of the Table Styles gallery.

FIGURE 5-3: **Table Style Options group**

Table Design tab

Filter list arrows

Filter button check box

Division Info
Division
Technica
Total Com
Number of Pla

Table Style Options group

Excel

Add and Delete Table Data

Learning Outcomes
- Add a row to a table
- Delete a table row
- Add a column to a table
- Remove duplicate data from a table

To keep a table up to date, you need to periodically add and remove records. You also need to check a table for duplicate records so that you can remove unnecessary duplication. You can add records and columns to a table by typing data directly below the last row of the table or directly to the right of the last table column. You can also expand a table by dragging the sizing handle in a table's lower-right corner; drag down to add rows and drag to the right to add columns. **CASE** ▶ *A recruiter informs you of an additional placement, so you need to update the table. Cheri also wants the table to display the number of days a placement was posted before it was filled.*

STEPS

1. **Scroll down to the last table row, click cell** A66, **enter the data shown below, then press** [Enter]

Account #	Employer ID	Division	Posting Date	Filled Date	Position Type	Commission	Preferred Employer
9408	32231	Creative	12/13/2021	12/23/2021	Consultant	$8,125	Yes

As you scroll down, notice that the table headers are visible at the top of the table as long as the active cell is inside the table. The new placement is now part of the table.

2. **Click cell** I1, **type** Days Posted, **press** ENTER, **then resize the width of column** I **to** 10.00
The new field becomes part of the table, and the header formatting extends to the new field name, as shown in FIGURE 5-4. The table range is now A1:I66.

3. **Click the** inside left edge of cell A3 **to select the table row, click the** Delete arrow **in the Cells group, then click** Delete Table Rows
The placement in row 3 is deleted, and the placement in row 4 moves up to row 3. You can also delete a table row or a column by right-clicking the row or column, then clicking Delete.

4. **Click the** Table Design tab **on the ribbon, then click the** Remove Duplicates button **in the Tools group**
The table is selected, and the Remove Duplicates dialog box opens, as shown in FIGURE 5-5.

5. **Make sure the** My data has headers check box **contains a checkmark, click** Unselect All **to deselect all the check boxes, click the** Account # check box **to add a checkmark, then click** OK
Excel checks the table for any duplicates in the Account # field. A message box opens, telling you one duplicate record has been found and removed, leaving a total of 64 rows in the table, including the header row.

6. **Click** OK, **enter your name in the center section of the footer, then save the workbook**

FIGURE 5-4: **New table column**

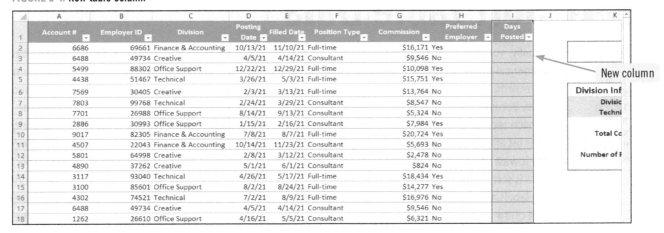

	Account #	Employer ID	Division	Posting Date	Filled Date	Position Type	Commission	Preferred Employer	Days Posted
2	6686	69661	Finance & Accounting	10/13/21	11/10/21	Full-time	$16,171	Yes	
3	6488	49734	Creative	4/5/21	4/14/21	Consultant	$9,546	No	
4	5499	88302	Office Support	12/22/21	12/29/21	Full-time	$10,098	Yes	
5	4438	51467	Technical	3/26/21	5/3/21	Full-time	$15,751	Yes	
6	7569	30405	Creative	2/3/21	3/13/21	Full-time	$13,764	No	
7	7803	99768	Technical	2/24/21	3/29/21	Consultant	$8,547	No	
8	7701	26988	Office Support	8/14/21	9/13/21	Consultant	$5,324	No	
9	2886	30993	Office Support	1/15/21	2/16/21	Consultant	$7,984	Yes	
10	9017	82305	Finance & Accounting	7/8/21	8/7/21	Full-time	$20,724	Yes	
11	4507	22043	Finance & Accounting	10/14/21	11/23/21	Consultant	$5,693	No	
12	5801	64998	Creative	2/8/21	3/12/21	Consultant	$2,478	No	
13	4890	37262	Creative	5/1/21	6/1/21	Consultant	$824	No	
14	3117	93040	Technical	4/26/21	5/17/21	Full-time	$18,434	Yes	
15	3100	85601	Office Support	8/2/21	8/24/21	Full-time	$14,277	No	
16	4302	74521	Technical	7/2/21	8/9/21	Full-time	$16,976	No	
17	6488	49734	Creative	4/5/21	4/14/21	Consultant	$9,546	No	
18	1262	26610	Office Support	4/16/21	5/5/21	Consultant	$6,321	No	

New column

Division Inf
Divisio
Techni

Total Co

Number of F

FIGURE 5-5: **Remove Duplicates dialog box**

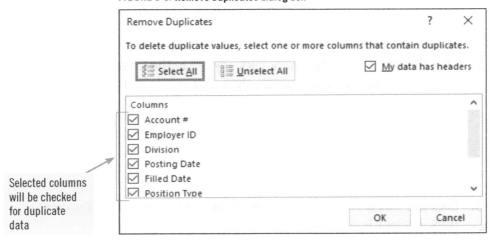

Selected columns will be checked for duplicate data

Selecting table elements

When working with tables you often need to select rows, columns, and even the entire table. Clicking to the right of a row number, inside column A, selects the table row. You can select a table column by clicking the top edge of the column. Be careful not to click a column letter or row number, however, because this selects the entire worksheet row or column. You can select the entire table by clicking the upper-left corner of the top-left table cell. When selecting a column or a table, the first click selects only the data in the column or table. If you click a second time, you add the headers to the selection.

Excel

Sort Table Data

Usually, you add table records in the order in which you receive information, rather than in alphabetical or numerical order, so new records commonly appear at the bottom of the table. You can change the order of records, or **sort** them, which organizes data in ascending or descending order, based on criteria such as date. Because the data is structured as a table, Excel changes the order of the records while keeping the data in each record, or row, together. You can sort a table in ascending or descending order on a field using the filter list arrows next to the field name, or using the Sort & Filter button on the ribbon. In **ascending order**, the lowest value (the beginning of the alphabet or the earliest date) appears at the top of the table, because data is sorted from lowest to highest, earliest to more recent, or alphabetically from A to Z; in a field containing labels and numbers, numbers appear first in the sorted list. In **descending order**, the highest value (the end of the alphabet or the latest date) appears at the top of the table because data is sorted from highest to lowest, most recent to earliest, or from Z to A; in a field containing labels and numbers, labels appear first. TABLE 5-1 provides examples of ascending and descending sorts. **CASE** ▶ *Cheri wants the table sorted by the date the placement was filled, with placements that were filled the earliest at the top of the table.*

STEPS

1. **Click the** Filled Date filter list arrow, **then click** Sort Oldest to Newest

   Excel rearranges the records in ascending order by filled date, as shown in FIGURE 5-6. The Filled Date filter list arrow displays a small up arrow indicating that an ascending sort in this field has been applied.

2. **Click the** Home tab **if necessary, click any cell in the** Commission column, **click the** Sort & Filter button **in the Editing group, then click** Sort Largest to Smallest

   Excel sorts the table, placing records with higher commissions at the top. The Commission filter list arrow now displays a small down arrow, indicating the descending sort order. You can also rearrange table data using a **multilevel sort**, which reorders records using more than one column or field at a time; each field is considered a different level, based on its importance in the sort. In a two-level sort, for instance, the records are sorted by the first field, and then within each grouping created by that first sort they are sorted by the second field.

3. **Click the** Sort & Filter button **in the Editing group, then click** Custom Sort

   The Sort dialog box opens, as shown in FIGURE 5-7.

4. **Click the** Sort by arrow, **click** Division, **click the** Order arrow, **click** A to Z, **click** Add Level, **click the** Then by arrow, **click** Commission, **click the second** Order arrow, **click** Smallest to Largest **if necessary, then click** OK

   As shown in FIGURE 5-8, the table is sorted alphabetically in ascending order (A–Z) by Division and, within each division grouping, in ascending order by the Commission (smallest amount to largest).

5. **Save the workbook**

TABLE 5-1: Sort order options and examples

option	alphabetic	numeric	date	alphanumeric
Ascending	A, B, C	7, 8, 9	1/1, 2/1, 3/1	12A, 99B, DX8, QT7
Descending	C, B, A	9, 8, 7	3/1, 2/1, 1/1	QT7, DX8, 99B, 12A

FIGURE 5-6: Table sorted by filled date

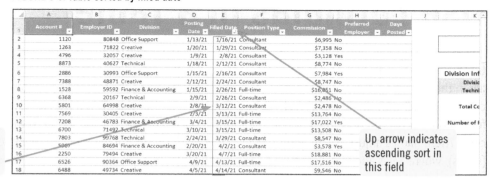

Records are sorted by filled date in ascending order

Up arrow indicates ascending sort in this field

FIGURE 5-7: Sort dialog box

Click to delete sort levels

Click to add additional sort levels

Click to display fields

FIGURE 5-8: Table sorted using two levels

First-level sort arranges records by division

Second-level sort arranges records within each division by commission

Sorting conditional formatted data

You can emphasize top-ranked or bottom-ranked values in a field or column by applying conditional formatting to the sorted data. To highlight the top or bottom values in a field, select the field data, click the Conditional Formatting button in the Styles group on the Home tab, point to Top/Bottom Rules, click a rule, if necessary modify the percentage or number of cells you want to format, select the desired formatting, then click OK. You can also format your worksheet or table data using color scales based on the cell values. A **color scale** is a formatting scheme that uses a color set or shades of color to convey relative values of data. For example, you could use red fill to indicate cells that have higher values and green fill to signify lower values. To add a color scale, select a data range, click the Home tab, click the Conditional Formatting button in the Styles group, then point to Color Scales. On the submenu, you can select preformatted color sets or click More Rules to create your own color sets. If conditional formats have been applied to a table or worksheet data, you can sort the table using conditional formatting to arrange the rows. For example, if cells are conditionally formatted with color, you can use the Sort dialog box to sort a field on Cell Color, using the color with the order of On Top or On Bottom in the Sort dialog box.

Specifying a custom sort order

You can identify a custom sort order in the Sort dialog box if the standard alphabetic and numeric sort orders do not meet your needs. For example, you might want to sort records by days of the week (Sun, Mon, Tues, Wed, etc.); an alphabetic sort would not sort these items properly. In the Sort dialog box, first specify the field you want to sort on, click the Order arrow, then click Custom List. In the Custom Lists dialog box that opens, click an item under Custom lists, view the list entries, then click OK. To build your own custom list, click NEW LIST, click Add, type the desired list under List entries, then click OK.

Use Formulas in a Table

The Excel table calculation features help you summarize table data so you can see important patterns and trends. After you enter a single formula into a table cell, the **calculated column** feature automatically fills in the remaining cells in the column with formula results, using the formula you entered. The column continues to fill with the formula results as you enter rows in the table. This makes it easy to update your formulas because you only need to edit the formula once, and the change fills in to the other column cells. These names adjust as you add or delete table fields. An example of a table reference is =[Sales]– [Costs], where Sales and Costs are field names in the table. You can also add a **table total row** to the bottom of a table for calculations on the table data. Clicking a cell in this row displays an arrow you can click to open a list of functions that can be used for the column calculation. The table total row adapts to any changes in the table size. **CASE** ▶ *Cheri asks you to calculate the number of days each placement was posted before being filled. You will also add summary information to the end of the table.*

STEPS

1. **Click cell I2, then type =[**

   A list of the table field names opens, as shown in FIGURE 5-9. The **structured reference** feature allows table formulas to refer to table columns by names that are automatically generated when the table is created. You can choose a field name by clicking it and pressing TAB or by double-clicking it.

2. **Double-click @ - This Row, click Filled Date, press TAB, then type]**

   Excel begins the formula, placing [@[Filled Date]] in the cell, in blue, and framing the Filled Date value in cell E2 in a blue border. The @ sign means to use the data in the same row as the formula. The formula uses an extra set of square brackets to enclose a field name that contains a space.

3. **Type -[@, double-click Posting Date, then type]**

   Excel places [@[Posting Date]] in the cell in red and outlines the Posting Date value in cell D2 in a red border.

4. **Click the Enter button ☑ on the Formula Bar**

   The formula result, 31, is displayed in cell I2. The table column also fills with the formula, displaying the number of days each placement was posted before being filled. The AutoCorrect Options button provides an option to turn off calculated columns. Because the calculated columns option saves time, you decide to leave the feature on.

5. **Click the Table Design tab on the ribbon, then click the Total Row check box in the Table Style Options group to add a checkmark**

   A total row appears at the bottom of the table, and the sum of the number of days posted, 1367, is displayed in cell I65.

6. **Click cell I65, click the cell list arrow on the right side of the cell, click Average, click the Home tab on the ribbon, then click the Decrease Decimal button ⁰⁰→ in the Number group five times**

7. **Click cell G65 (in the Commission column), click the cell list arrow, then click Sum**

   The total row shows the average of days a placement was posted and the total amount of commissions earned by the office this year.

8. **Click cell A65, press DELETE, click cell F65 (in the Position Type column), type Total Commissions, click ☑, click cell H65, type Average Days, click ☑, widen column F to fully display the label in cell F65, compare your total row to FIGURE 5-10, then save your work**

FIGURE 5-9: Table field names

Field names list

FIGURE 5-10: Table with total row

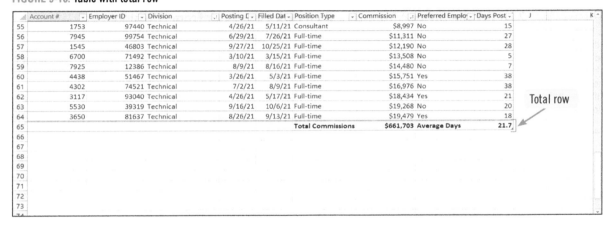

Total row

Excel

Filter a Table

Learning Outcomes
- Filter records using AutoFilter
- Filter records using a custom filter

In addition to sorting records, you can **filter** them, specifying a set of restrictions to only display specific records. You can filter quickly by using the **AutoFilter** feature to click a column's filter list arrow and then sort on or view selected values. **CASE** *Cheri asks you to display only the creative division's records. She also asks for information about the most lucrative placements, and placements that were posted in the second quarter.*

STEPS

QUICK TIP

If you add data to a table where a filter is applied, you can reapply the filter to include the new data either by clicking the Home tab, clicking the Sort & Filter button in the Editing group, and clicking Reapply, or by clicking the Reapply button in the Sort & Filter group on the Data tab.

1. **Click the** Division filter list arrow, **in the list of divisions for the field click** Select All **to clear the checkmarks, click** Creative, **then click** OK

   Only those records containing "Creative" in the Division field appear, as shown in FIGURE 5-11. The row numbers for the matching records change to blue, and the list arrow for the filtered field displays a filter icon 🔽 . Both indicate that there is a filter in effect and that some of the records are temporarily hidden.

2. **Click the** Division list arrow, **then click** Clear Filter From "Division"

   You have cleared the Division filter, and all the records reappear.

3. **Click the** Commission filter list arrow, **point to** Number Filters, **click** Top 10, **select** 10 **in the middle box, type** 5, **click the** Items arrow, **click** Percent, **then click** OK

   Excel displays the records for the top five percent in the Commission field, as shown in FIGURE 5-12.

4. **Click the** Sort & Filter button **in the Editing group on the Home tab, then click** Clear

   You have cleared the filter and all the records reappear.

5. **Click the** Filled Date filter list arrow, **point to** Date Filters, **then click** Custom Filter

   The Custom AutoFilter dialog box allows you to create more detailed filters by entering your criteria in the text boxes. Your criteria can contain comparison operators such as greater than or less than. You can also use **logical conditions** such as And to display records that meet both a criterion in a field *and* another criterion in that same field, and you can use Or to display records that meet either criterion in a field.

QUICK TIP

When specifying criteria in the Custom Filter dialog box, you can use the (?) wildcard to represent any single character and the (*) wildcard to represent any series of characters.

6. **Click the** left text box arrow **on the first line, click** is after or equal to, **type** 4/1/2021 **in the right text box on the first line, verify that the** And option button **is selected, click the** left text box arrow **on the second line, click** is before or equal to, **type** 6/30/2021 **in the right text box on the second line, then click** OK

   Only the placements filled in the second quarter, after 4/1/2021 and before 6/30/2021, appear in the worksheet, as shown in FIGURE 5-13.

7. **Click the** Filled Date filter list arrow, **then click** Clear Filter From "Filled Date"

   You have cleared the filter and all the records reappear.

8. **Save the workbook**

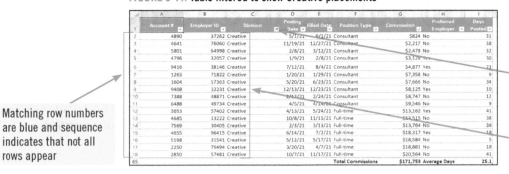

FIGURE 5-11: Table filtered to show Creative placements

Account #	Employer ID	Division	Posting Date	Filled Date	Position Type	Commission	Preferred Employer	Days Posted
4890	37262	Creative	5/1/21	6/1/21	Consultant	$824	No	31
4641	76060	Creative	11/19/21	12/27/21	Consultant	$2,217	No	38
5801	64998	Creative	2/8/21	3/12/21	Consultant	$2,478	No	32
4796	32057	Creative	1/9/21	2/8/21	Consultant	$3,128	Yes	30
9416	38146	Creative	7/12/21	8/4/21	Consultant	$4,877	Yes	23
1263	71822	Creative	1/20/21	1/29/21	Consultant	$7,358	No	9
1604	57363	Creative	5/20/21	6/23/21	Consultant	$7,666	No	34
9408	32231	Creative	12/13/21	12/23/21	Consultant	$8,125	Yes	10
7388	48871	Creative	2/12/21	2/24/21	Consultant	$8,747	No	12
6488	49734	Creative	4/5/21	4/14/21	Consultant	$9,546	No	9
3653	57402	Creative	4/13/21	5/24/21	Full-time	$13,162	Yes	41
4685	13222	Creative	10/8/21	11/15/21	Full-time	$13,515	No	38
7569	30405	Creative	2/3/21	3/13/21	Full-time	$13,764	No	38
4655	96415	Creative	6/14/21	7/2/21	Full-time	$18,317	Yes	18
5198	31541	Creative	5/12/21	5/17/21	Full-time	$18,584	No	5
2250	79494	Creative	3/20/21	4/7/21	Full-time	$18,881	No	18
2850	57481	Creative	10/7/21	11/17/21	Full-time	$20,564	No	41
					Total Commissions	$171,753	Average Days	25.1

List arrow changed to filter icon

Matching row numbers are blue and sequence indicates that not all rows appear

Filter displays only creative division records

FIGURE 5-12: Table filtered with top 5% of commissions

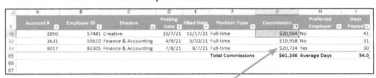

Account #	Employer ID	Division	Posting Date	Filled Date	Position Type	Commission	Preferred Employer	Days Posted
2850	57481	Creative	10/7/21	11/17/21	Full-time	$20,564	No	41
3631	55610	Finance & Accounting	4/9/21	5/10/21	Full-time	$19,958	No	31
9017	82305	Finance & Accounting	7/8/21	8/7/21	Full-time	$20,724	Yes	30
					Total Commissions	$61,246	Average Days	54.0

Only records containing the top 5% in commissions appear

FIGURE 5-13: Results of custom filter

Account #	Employer ID	Division	Posting Date	Filled Date	Position Type	Commission	Preferred Employer	Days Posted
4890	37262	Creative	5/1/21	6/1/21	Consultant	$824	No	31
1604	57363	Creative	5/20/21	6/23/21	Consultant	$7,666	No	34
6488	49734	Creative	4/5/21	4/14/21	Consultant	$9,546	No	9
3653	57402	Creative	4/13/21	5/24/21	Full-time	$13,162	Yes	41
5198	31541	Creative	5/12/21	5/17/21	Full-time	$18,584	No	5
2250	79494	Creative	3/20/21	4/7/21	Full-time	$18,881	No	18
7511	79106	Finance & Accounting	6/14/21	6/29/21	Consultant	$3,314	No	15
5867	84694	Finance & Accounting	2/20/21	4/2/21	Consultant	$3,578	Yes	41
1803	89294	Finance & Accounting	6/3/21	6/21/21	Full-time	$14,398	Yes	18
8806	76870	Finance & Accounting	4/22/21	5/18/21	Full-time	$19,035	No	26
3631	55610	Finance & Accounting	4/9/21	5/10/21	Full-time	$19,958	No	31
1949	55639	Office Support	4/5/21	5/3/21	Consultant	$5,447	No	28
1262	26610	Office Support	4/16/21	5/5/21	Consultant	$6,321	No	19
6526	90364	Office Support	4/9/21	4/13/21	Full-time	$17,516	No	4
3700	64735	Technical	5/19/21	6/3/21	Consultant	$5,968	Yes	15
2511	12281	Technical	4/1/21	4/17/21	Consultant	$7,642	No	16
1753	97440	Technical	4/26/21	5/11/21	Consultant	$8,997	No	15
4438	51467	Technical	3/26/21	5/3/21	Full-time	$15,751	Yes	38
3117	93040	Technical	4/26/21	5/17/21	Full-time	$18,434	Yes	21
					Total Commissions	$215,022	Average Days	22.4

Placement dates are between 4/1 and 6/30

Using an advanced filter

When you want to see table data that meets a detailed set of conditions, you can use the Advanced Filter feature. This feature lets you specify data that you want to display from the table using And and Or conditions. Rather than entering the criteria in a dialog box, you enter the criteria in a criteria range on your worksheet. A **criteria range** is a location separate from the table that you use to list specific search specifications. This range is usually a copy of the column labels with at least one additional row beneath the labels that contains the criteria you want to match. Placing all criteria in the same row specifies an **And condition**, which searches only for records where all the entered criteria are matched. Placing criteria in different rows specifies an **Or condition**, which searches for records where at least one entered criterion is matched. To apply an advanced filter, add the criteria range to the worksheet, click any cell in the table, click the Data tab, click the Advanced button in the Sort & Filter group, in the Advanced Filter dialog box verify the table range in the List range box, click the Criteria range text box, select your criteria range on the worksheet, then click OK. The default setting under Action is to filter the table in its current location ("in-place") rather than copy it to another location. You can move the filtered table data to a different area of the worksheet or to a new worksheet. FIGURE 5-14 shows a worksheet with the And criteria range located in the range $A$67:$I$68 and the filtered results of consultant positions with commissions greater than $7,000.

FIGURE 5-14: Results of advanced filter

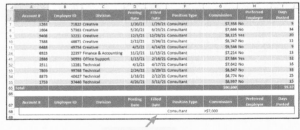

Account #	Employer ID	Division	Posting Date	Filled Date	Position Type	Commission	Preferred Employer	Days Posted
1263	71822	Creative	1/20/21	1/29/21	Consultant	$7,358	No	9
1604	57363	Creative	5/20/21	6/23/21	Consultant	$7,666	No	34
9408	32231	Creative	12/3/21	12/23/21	Consultant	$8,125	Yes	20
7388	48871	Creative	2/12/21	2/24/21	Consultant	$8,747	No	12
6488	49734	Creative	4/5/21	4/14/21	Consultant	$9,546	No	9
6923	22397	Finance & Accounting	11/2/21	11/15/21	Consultant	$7,214	No	13
2860	30593	Office Support	1/15/21	2/16/21	Consultant	$7,584	Yes	32
2511	12281	Technical	4/1/21	4/17/21	Consultant	$7,642	No	16
7809	99768	Technical	2/24/21	3/29/21	Consultant	$8,547	No	33
8873	40627	Technical	1/18/21	2/12/21	Consultant	$8,774	No	25
1753	97440	Technical	4/26/21	5/11/21	Consultant	$8,997	No	15
Total						$90,000		19.5?

Account #	Employer ID	Division	Posting Date	Filled Date	Position Type	Commission	Preferred Employer	Days Posted
					Consultant	>$7,000		

Criteria range

Look Up Values in a Table

Learning
Outcomes
• Use table ref-
erences in a
XLOOKUP formula
• Find table
information using
XLOOKUP

The Excel XLOOKUP function helps you locate specific values in a table or range. XLOOKUP searches a column or row of a table, then returns the value corresponding to the first match it finds. For example, you might want to look up a phone number based on an employee's name. **CASE** *Cheri wants to be able to find a division responsible for a placement by entering the account #. You will use the XLOOKUP function to accomplish this task. You begin by viewing the table name so you can refer to it in a lookup function.*

STEPS

1. **Click the Formulas tab on the ribbon, then click the Name Manager button in the Defined Names group**

   The table name appears in the Name Manager dialog box, as shown in FIGURE 5-15. The Excel structured reference feature automatically created the table name of Table1 when the table was created.

2. **Click Close, click cell L2, enter 2850, click cell L3, click the Lookup & Reference button in the Function Library group, then click XLOOKUP**

   The Function Arguments dialog box opens, with boxes for each of the XLOOKUP arguments.

3. **With the insertion point in the Lookup_value text box click cell L2, click the Lookup_array text box, then type Table1[Account '#]**

   Because the value you want to find is in cell L2, L2 is the Lookup_value. The range you want to search, the Account # column in Table1, is the Lookup_array. Be sure to include the apostrophe (') to indicate # is a special character.

QUICK TIP
Instead of typing
the Table_array
argument, you
can select the
range A2:A64 to
have Excel insert
Table1[Account '#]
in the Table_array
text box. You
can also enter
the Return_array
argument by
selecting the
range C2:C64 to
have Excel insert
Table1[Division] in
the Return_array
text box.

4. **Click the Return_array text box, then type Table1[Division]**

   The column containing the information that you want to find and display in cell L3 is the Division column in Table1. The other two arguments are optional. You use the Match_mode argument to set an exact or approximate match. Because an exact match is the default, you do not need to specify this argument. Your completed Function Arguments dialog box should match FIGURE 5-16.

5. **Click OK**

   Excel searches down the Account # column of the table until it finds an account # that matches the one in cell L2. It then looks in the Division column of the table and finds the division for that record, Creative, and displays it in cell L3.

6. **Click cell L2, type 6234, then click the Enter button ☑ on the formula bar**

   The XLOOKUP function returns the value of Technical in cell L3. You can use this function to determine the division for other account numbers.

7. **Press CTRL+HOME, then save the workbook**

FIGURE 5-15: Named ranges in the workbook

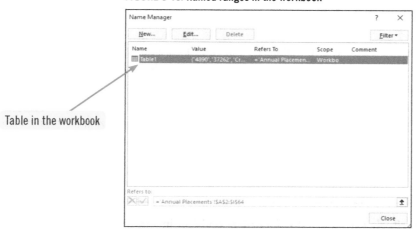

Table in the workbook

FIGURE 5-16: Completed Function Arguments dialog box for XLOOKUP

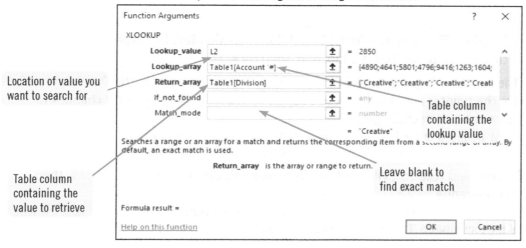

Location of value you
want to search for

Table column
containing the
value to retrieve

Table column
containing the
lookup value

Leave blank to
find exact match

Using other LOOKUP functions

VLOOKUP searches vertically (V) down the far-left column of a table, then reads across the row to find the value you specify. You provide a Lookup_value, the value you want to find, and a Table_array, the table you want to search. The Lookup_value must appear in the far-left column of the table. You set a Col_index_num to identify the column containing the information you want to find and display. For example, a Col_index_num of 3 means the third column from the left in the table range. When your data is arranged horizontally in rows instead of vertically in columns, use the HLOOKUP (Horizontal Lookup) function. HLOOKUP searches horizontally across the upper row of a table until it finds the matching value, then looks down the number of rows you specify. The arguments are identical to those for the VLOOKUP function, except that instead of a Col_index_number, HLOOKUP uses a Row_index_number, which indicates the location of the row you want to search. When you want to know the position of an item in a range, you can use the MATCH function. The MATCH function uses the syntax: MATCH (lookup_value,lookup_array,match_ type)

where the lookup_value is the value you want to match in the lookup_array range. The match_type can be 0 for an exact match, 1 for matching the largest value that is less than or equal to the lookup_value, or −1 for matching the smallest value that is greater than or equal to the lookup_value. The INDEX function is often used with the MATCH function, using the position obtained from the MATCH function and returning a value from a table or range. The syntax for the Index function is: INDEX(range, row_num, column_num). For example, =INDEX(A1:D7, 3, 4) returns the value in the cell located at the intersection of the third row and fourth column in the range A1:D7. The MATCH function can be used to find the row for an INDEX function. For example:

$$=INDEX(A1:B5,MATCH(3250,E1:E4),2)$$

Here, the match function searches the database E1:E4 and finds the position of the value 3250. This position becomes the row value for the index function while 2 is the column position in the database A1:B5.

Summarize Table Data

An Excel table acts as a simple type of database, and you can use database functions to summarize table data in a variety of ways. When working with a sales activity table, for example, you can use Excel to count the number of client contacts by sales representative or to total the amount sold to specific accounts by month. TABLE 5-2 lists commonly used database functions for summarizing table data. **CASE** *Cheri is reviewing the yearly performance of each division. She needs your help in analyzing the total number of placements and commissions for each division.*

STEPS

1. **Review the criteria range for the Technical division in the range** K7:K8

   The criteria range in K7:K8 tells Excel to summarize records with the entry "Technical" in the Division column.

2. **Click cell** K11**, click the** Formulas tab **on the ribbon, click the** Insert Function button **in the Function Library group, in the Search for a function text box type** database**, click** Go**, click** DSUM **under Select a function, then click** OK

3. **In the Function Arguments dialog box, with the insertion point in the** Database text box **move the pointer over the upper-left corner of cell A1 until the pointer changes to** ↘**, click once, then click again**

   The first argument of the DSUM function is the table, or database. The first click selects the table's data range, and the second click selects the entire table, including the header row.

4. **Click the** Field text box**, click cell** G1 (Commission)**, click the** Criteria text box**, then select the range** K7:K8

   The second argument of the DSUM function is the label for the column that you want to sum. You want to total the commissions. The last argument for the DSUM function is the criteria that will be used to determine which values to total. Your completed Function Arguments dialog box should match FIGURE 5-17.

5. **Click** OK**, click the** Home tab **on the ribbon, click the** Accounting Number Format button **$ in the Number group, then click the** Decrease Decimal button **twice**

   The result in cell K11 is $200,255. Excel totaled the information in the Commission column for those records that meet the criterion of Division equals Technical.

6. **Click cell** K13**, click the** Insert Function button *fx* **on the formula bar, in the Search for a function text box type** database**, click** Go**, then double-click** DCOUNTA **in the Select a function list**

   The DCOUNT and the DCOUNTA functions can help you determine the number of records meeting specified criteria in a database field. DCOUNTA counts the number of nonblank cells.

7. **With the insertion point in the** Database text box **move the pointer over the upper-left corner of cell A1 until it changes to** ↘**, click once, click again to include the header row, click the** Field text box**, click cell** C1**, click the** Criteria text box **and select the range** K7:K8**, then click** OK

   The result in cell K13 is 18, and it indicates that the technical division had 18 placements over the past year.

8. **Click cell** K8**, type** Office Support**, click the** Enter button ✓ **on the formula bar, then save your work**

   The formulas in cells K11 and K13 are updated to reflect the new criteria. FIGURE 5-18 shows that the office support division had 13 placements and commissions of $112,230 over the past year.

FIGURE 5-17: Completed Function Arguments dialog box for DSUM

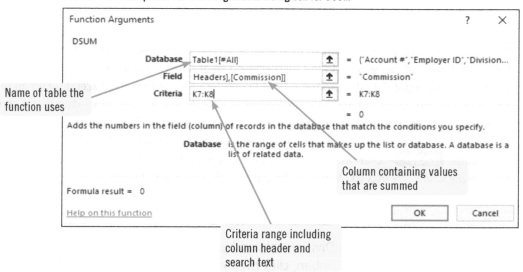

FIGURE 5-18: Result generated by database functions

	Employer ID	Division	Posting Date	Filled Date	Position Type	Commission	Preferred Employer	Days Posted
2	37262	Creative	5/1/21	6/1/21	Consultant	$824	No	31
3	76060	Creative	11/19/21	12/27/21	Consultant	$2,217	No	38
4	64998	Creative	2/8/21	3/12/21	Consultant	$2,478	No	32
5	32057	Creative	1/9/21	2/8/21	Consultant	$3,128	Yes	30
6	38146	Creative	7/12/21	8/4/21	Consultant	$4,877	Yes	23
7	71822	Creative	1/20/21	1/29/21	Consultant	$7,358	No	9
8	57363	Creative	5/20/21	6/23/21	Consultant	$7,666	No	34
9	32231	Creative	12/13/21	12/23/21	Consultant	$8,125	Yes	10
10	48871	Creative	2/12/21	2/24/21	Consultant	$8,747	No	12
11	49734	Creative	4/5/21	4/14/21	Consultant	$9,546	No	9
12	57402	Creative	4/13/21	5/24/21	Full-time	$13,162	Yes	41
13	13222	Creative	10/8/21	11/15/21	Full-time	$13,515	No	38
14	30405	Creative	2/3/21	3/13/21	Full-time	$13,764	No	38
15	96415	Creative	6/14/21	7/2/21	Full-time	$18,317	Yes	18
16	31541	Creative	5/12/21	5/17/21	Full-time	$18,584	No	5
17	79494	Creative	3/20/21	4/7/21	Full-time	$18,881	No	18
18	57481	Creative	10/7/21	11/17/21	Full-time	$20,564	No	41

Information for office support division

Account #
Division

Division Information
Division
Office Support

Total Commissions:
$ 112,230
Number of Placements:
13

TABLE 5-2: Common database functions

function	result
DGET	Extracts a single record from a table that matches criteria you specify
DSUM	Totals numbers in a given table column that match criteria you specify
DAVERAGE	Averages numbers in a given table column that match criteria you specify
DCOUNT	Counts the cells that contain numbers in a given table column that match criteria you specify
DCOUNTA	Counts the cells that contain nonblank data in a given table column that match criteria you specify

Validate Table Data

Learning Outcomes
- Use data validation to restrict data entry to specified values
- Insert table data using data validation
- Add print titles to a table

When setting up tables, you want to help ensure accuracy when you or others enter data. The Data Validation feature allows you to do this by specifying what data users can enter in a range of cells. Once you've specified what data the program should consider valid for that cell, Excel displays an error message when invalid data is entered and can prevent users from entering any other data that it considers to be invalid. When printing tables, you may have more rows than can fit on a page. In that case, you can define the first row of the table (containing the field names) as the **print title**, which prints at the top of every page. **CASE** *Cheri wants to make sure that information in the Division column is entered consistently in the future. She asks you to restrict the entries in that column to the office's divisions.*

STEPS

QUICK TIP
You can paste cell validation in a worksheet by copying a cell with data validation, right-clicking the destination cell, clicking Paste Special in the Paste Options, then selecting the Validation button in the Paste Special dialog box.

1. **Click the** top edge **of the Division column header to select the table data in this column, click the** Data tab **on the ribbon, click the** Data Validation button 📊▾ **in the Data Tools group, on the Settings tab of the Data Validation dialog box click the** Allow arrow, **click** List, **click the** Source box, **type** Creative, Finance & Accounting, Office Support, Technical, **verify that the** In-cell dropdown check box **contains a checkmark, then click** OK

2. **Click the** Home tab **on the ribbon, click any** cell **in the last table row, click the** Insert arrow **in the Cells group, click** Insert Table Row Below, **click the** Division cell **in this row, then click its** list arrow

   A list of valid list entries opens, based on the values entered in the Data Validation dialog box, as shown in **FIGURE 5-19**.

3. **Click the** list arrow **to close the list, type** Medical, **press ENTER, click** Cancel **in the warning dialog box, click the** list arrow, **then click** Creative

   The cell accepts the valid entry.

4. **Click the** Delete arrow **in the Cells group, click** Delete Table Rows, **click the** File tab **on the ribbon, click** Print, **in the Preview window click** No Scaling **under Settings, then click** Fit All Columns on One Page

   Below the table you see 1 of 2, which indicates you are viewing page 1 of a 2-page document.

5. **Click the** Next Page button ▶ **in the Preview area**

   The rows continue onto page 2, though you cannot see the field names.

QUICK TIP
You can choose to print an entire workbook or a selected area of the worksheet by clicking the Print Active Sheets button in the Settings list, then clicking Print Entire Workbook or Print Selection.

6. **Return to the worksheet, click the** Page Layout tab **on the ribbon, click the** Print Titles button **in the Page Setup group, click inside the** Rows to repeat at top text box **under Print titles, in the worksheet scroll up to row 1 if necessary, click any** cell **in row 1 of the table, click the** Print Preview button **in the Page Setup dialog box, then click** ▶ **in the preview window to view the second page**

   A print title that repeats row 1 shows the field names at the top of each printed page.

7. **Return to the worksheet, click the** Insert tab, **click the** Text button, **click the** Header & Footer button, **click the** left header section text box **if necessary, type** 2021 Boston Office Placements, **click any** cell **on the worksheet, click the** Normal button ⊞ **in the status bar, then press CTRL+HOME**

8. **sam'⬆ Save the table, preview it, close the workbook, close Excel, then submit the workbook to your instructor**

   Compare your printed table with **FIGURE 5-20**.

FIGURE 5-19: Entering data in restricted cells

	Employer ID	Division	Posting D	Filled Dat	Position Type	Commission	Preferred Emplo	Days Post
52	12281	Technical	4/1/21	4/17/21	Consultant	$7,642	No	16
53	99768	Technical	2/24/21	3/29/21	Consultant	$8,547	No	33
54	40627	Technical	1/18/21	2/12/21	Consultant	$8,774	No	25
55	97440	Technical	4/26/21	5/11/21	Consultant	$8,997	No	15
56	99754	Technical	6/29/21	7/26/21	Full-time	$11,311	No	27
57	46803	Technical	9/27/21	10/25/21	Full-time	$12,190	No	28
58	71492	Technical	3/10/21	3/15/21	Full-time	$13,508	No	5
59	12386	Technical	8/9/21	8/16/21	Full-time	$14,480	No	7
60	51467	Technical	3/26/21	5/3/21	Full-time	$15,751	Yes	38
61	74521	Technical	7/2/21	8/9/21	Full-time	$16,976	No	38
62	93040	Technical	4/26/21	5/17/21	Full-time	$18,434	Yes	21
63	39319	Technical	9/16/21	10/6/21	Full-time	$19,268	No	20
64	81637	Technical	8/26/21	9/13/21	Full-time	$19,479	Yes	18
65								0
66		Creative			Total Commissions	$661,703	Average Days	21.4
67		Finance & Accounting						
68		Office Support						
69		Technical						

List

FIGURE 5-20: Printed table

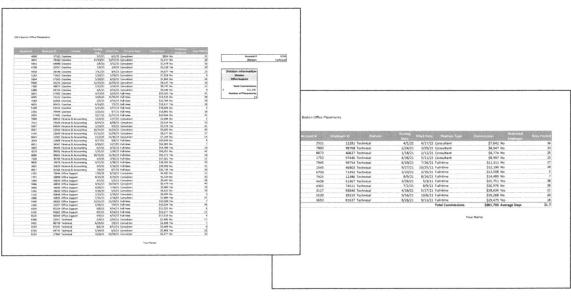

Restricting cell values and data length

In addition to providing an in-cell dropdown list for data entry, you can use data validation to restrict the values that are entered into cells. For example, you might want to restrict cells in a selected range to values less than a certain number, date, or time. To do so, click the Data tab, click the Data Validation button in the Data Tools group, on the Settings tab click the Allow arrow, select Whole number, Decimal, Date, or Time, click the Data arrow, select less than, then in the bottom text box, enter the maximum value. You can also limit the length of data entered into cells by choosing Text length in the Allow list, clicking the Data arrow and selecting less than, then entering the maximum length in the Maximum text box.

Adding input messages and error alerts

You can customize the way data validation works by adding input messages and setting alert styles. To do so, click the Input Message tab in the Data Validation dialog box, enter a message title and message, then click OK. To set an alert style, which controls how a user can proceed when entering invalid data, click the Error Alert tab, then click the Style arrow. The Information style displays your message with the information icon but allows the user to proceed with data entry. The Warning style displays your information with the warning icon and gives the user the option to proceed with data entry or not. The Stop style, which you used in this lesson, is the default; it displays your message and only lets the user retry or cancel data entry for that cell.

Practice

Skills Review

1. Create and format a table.

a. Start Excel, open IL_EX_5-2.xlsx from the location where you store your Data Files, then save it as **IL_EX_5_Scientific**.

b. Using the data in the range A1:I17, create a table.

c. Apply a table style of Red, Table Style Light 14.

d. Enter your name in the center section of the worksheet footer, enter **EOR Scientific Consulting** in the center section of the header, then activate cell A1.

e. Save the workbook.

2. Add and delete table data.

a. Insert a worksheet row below the table, then add a new record at the bottom of the table for Carlos Hurdo. Carlos's employee number is 2442. He was hired on 4/2/2021 to work in the Chicago office with a monthly salary of $5,120.

b. Add a column to the table by entering the label **Annual Compensation** in cell J1. Widen the column as necessary to fully display the label on two lines.

c. Delete the record for Hank Gole in row 6.

d. Remove duplicate data in the table by checking for matching employee numbers.

e. Save the file.

3. Sort table data.

a. Sort the table by Monthly Salary in descending (largest to smallest) order.

b. Sort the table again by Last Name in ascending (A to Z) order.

c. Perform a custom, multilevel sort by sorting the table first by Office in A to Z order, and then by Hire Date in Oldest to Newest order.

d. Review the results of the multilevel sort to make sure the records are sorted first by Office and then by Hire Date.

e. Save the file.

4. Use formulas in a table.

a. In cell J2, enter a formula, using structured references, to calculate an employee's annual compensation by totaling the annual salary, annual bonus, and annual benefits columns.

b. Check the table to make sure that the formula from cell J2 filled into the cells in column J, and that the annual compensation is calculated for the cells in the column.

c. Add a total row to display the total annual compensation for all employees.

d. Change the function in the total row to display the average annual compensation. Change the label in cell A17 from Total to **Average**.

e. Save your work.

5. Filter a table.

   a. Filter the table to list only records for employees in the Dallas branch.

   b. Clear the filter.

   c. Use AutoFilter to list only the three employees with the highest annual compensation. (*Hint:* Find the top three items.)

   d. Redisplay all the records.

   e. Create a Custom AutoFilter showing employees hired in 2020. (*Hint:* Use the criteria after or equal to 1/1/2020 and before or equal to 12/31/2020.)

   f. Redisplay all the records and save your work.

6. Look up values in a table.

   a. Open the Name Manager using a button on the Formulas bar, view named tables in the workbook, then close the Name Manager.

   b. Enter the employee number **1322** in cell B22.

   c. In cell C22, use the XLOOKUP function and enter **B22** as the Lookup_value, **Table1[Employee Number]** as the Lookup_array, and **Table1[Annual Compensation]** as the Return_array; observe the compensation displayed for that employee number, then check it against the table to make sure it is correct.

   d. Replace the existing Employee Number in cell B22 with **1080** and view the annual compensation for that employee.

   e. Format cell C22 with the Accounting format with the $ symbol and no decimal places.

   f. Save the workbook.

7. Summarize table data.

   a. In cell F22, use the DAVERAGE function to find the average benefits for the Dallas office. (*Hint:* Click the upper-left corner of cell A1 twice to select the table and its header row as the Database, select cell I1 for the Field, and select the range E21:E22 for the Criteria.)

   b. Verify that the average Dallas benefit amount is 13,938.

   c. Test the function further by entering the text **Chicago** in cell E22. When the criterion is entered, verify that the average Chicago benefit amount is 11,534.04.

   d. Format cell F22 in the Accounting format with the $ symbol and no decimal places.

   e. Save the workbook.

8. Validate table data.

   a. Select the table data in column E and set a validation criterion specifying that you want to allow a list of valid options.

   b. Enter a list of valid options that restricts the entries to **LA**, **Chicago**, and **Dallas**. Remember to use a comma between each item in the list.

   c. Confirm that the options will appear in an in-cell dropdown list, then close the dialog box.

   d. Add a row to the bottom of the table. Select cell E17, open the dropdown list, then click Chicago.

   e. Complete the new record by adding an Employee Number of **1119**, a First Name of **Cate**, a Last Name of **Smith**, a Hire Date of **10/1/2021**, Office of **Chicago**, and a monthly salary of **$5,000**. Compare your screen to FIGURE 5-21.

Excel

FIGURE 5-21

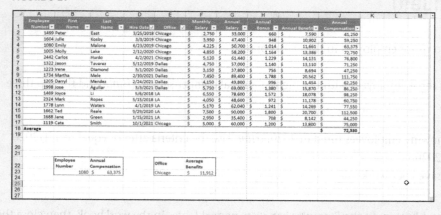

	Employee Number	First Name	Last Name	Hire Date	Office	Monthly Salary	Annual Salary	Annual Bonus	Annual Benefits	Annual Compensation
1										
2	1499 Peter	East		3/25/2018	Chicago	$ 2,750	$ 33,000	$ 660	$ 7,590	$ 41,250
3	1604 Julie	Kosby		3/3/2019	Chicago	$ 3,950	$ 47,400	$ 948	$ 10,902	$ 59,250
4	1080 Emily	Malone		6/23/2019	Chicago	$ 4,225	$ 50,700	$ 1,014	$ 11,661	$ 63,375
5	1005 Molly	Lake		2/12/2020	Chicago	$ 4,850	$ 58,200	$ 1,164	$ 13,386	$ 72,750
6	2442 Carlos	Hurdo		4/2/2021	Chicago	$ 5,120	$ 61,440	$ 1,229	$ 14,131	$ 76,800
7	1322 Jason	Tavarez		5/12/2019	Dallas	$ 4,750	$ 57,000	$ 1,140	$ 13,110	$ 71,250
8	1223 Irene	Diamond		3/1/2020	Dallas	$ 3,150	$ 37,800	$ 756	$ 8,694	$ 47,250
9	1734 Martha	Mele		2/10/2021	Dallas	$ 7,450	$ 89,400	$ 1,788	$ 20,562	$ 111,750
10	1205 Darryl	Mendez		2/24/2021	Dallas	$ 4,150	$ 49,800	$ 996	$ 11,454	$ 62,250
11	1998 Jose	Aguilar		3/3/2021	Dallas	$ 5,750	$ 69,000	$ 1,380	$ 15,870	$ 86,250
12	1469 Joyce	Li		5/6/2018	LA	$ 6,550	$ 78,600	$ 1,572	$ 18,078	$ 98,250
13	2324 Mark	Ropes		5/15/2018	LA	$ 4,050	$ 48,600	$ 972	$ 11,178	$ 60,750
14	1778 Lynn	Waters		4/1/2019	LA	$ 5,170	$ 62,040	$ 1,241	$ 14,269	$ 77,550
15	1662 Ted	Reale		9/29/2020	LA	$ 7,500	$ 90,000	$ 1,800	$ 20,700	$ 112,500
16	1688 Jane	Green		1/15/2021	LA	$ 2,950	$ 35,400	$ 708	$ 8,142	$ 44,250
17	1119 Cate	Smith		10/1/2021	Chicago	$ 5,000	$ 60,000	$ 1,200	$ 13,800	$ 75,000
18	Average								$	72,590

	Employee Number	Annual Compensation		Office	Average Benefits
22	1080	$ 63,375		Chicago	$ 11,912

f. Add column A as a print title that repeats at the left of each printed page.

g. Save the worksheet, then preview the worksheet to verify that the employee number column appears on both pages.

h. Submit your workbook to your instructor. Close the workbook, then close Excel.

Independent Challenge 1

As the assistant to the clinic director at Riverwalk Medical Clinic, you have been asked to organize the billing information for the physical therapy department. Using data in an Excel worksheet, you will create a table and analyze the procedure data to help with the January billing.

a. Start Excel, open IL_EX_5-3.xlsx from the location where you store your Data Files, then save it as **IL_EX_5_RiverwalkPT**.

b. Using the data in the range A1:G64 on the January Procedures worksheet, create a table and format the table with the table style Blue-Gray, Table Style Medium 7. Widen the columns as necessary to fully display the field names.

c. Remove the banding of the table rows. (*Hint:* Use the Table Style Options group on the Table Design tab.)

d. Add the record shown below to the end of the table:

Procedure Code	Procedure	Date	Amount Billed	Payment	Provider	Patient ID
601Q	Therap Proc 2	1/15/2021	$65	$30	Rubin	1189

e. Delete the record in row 8 for procedure code 251D.

f. Remove any duplicate records by checking for matching procedure codes.

g. Add a new column to the table by entering a field named **Balance** in cell H1. Calculate the balance for each procedure using structured references to subtract the payment from the amount billed. Format the balance amounts in column H in Accounting format with the $ symbol and no decimal places.

h. Sort the table by Balance in ascending order.

i. Use a custom sort to sort the table first by the procedure in descending order, and then within each procedure by the provider in ascending order.

Independent Challenge 1 (continued)

j. Filter the table to show only Martin's procedures, then copy the filtered records to the Martin Procedures worksheet. Do not copy the field names. Clear the filter from the table on the January Procedures worksheet.

k. Filter the table to show only records where the amount billed is greater than or equal to $80 and less than or equal to $200. Copy the filtered records to the >= 80 <=200 worksheet. Do not copy the field names. Remove the filter from the table on the January Procedures worksheet.

l. On the January Procedures worksheet, enter **467B** in cell J2. Enter an XLOOKUP function in cell J4 to retrieve the procedure based on the procedure code entered in cell J2. Make sure you have an exact match with the procedure code. Test the function by changing the procedure code in cell J2 to **331E**.

m. Use the database function DSUM in cell J10 to total the amount billed for Rubin using the criteria in J7:J8. Format cell J10 in the Accounting format with the $ symbol and no decimal places.

n. Using the criteria in J7:J8, enter a database function in cell J12 to count the number of procedures performed by Rubin. (*Hint:* Use the DCOUNTA function.)

o. Use the Data Validation dialog box to add an in-cell dropdown list to the cells in the provider column that restricts entries to Axel, Martin, and Rubin. Check the list by clicking any cell in column F. Compare your table to FIGURE 5-22.

p. Add print titles to repeat the first row at the top of each printed page, enter your name in the center section of the worksheet footer, enter **January Procedures** in the center section of the header, then activate cell A1.

q. Save the workbook, preview it, then submit the workbook to your instructor.

r. Close the workbook, then close Excel.

FIGURE 5-22

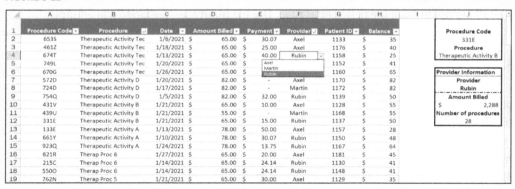

Excel

Independent Challenge 2

As the director of development at a small, private independent college, you are responsible for managing alumni donations. The past two years' donation information is organized in a worksheet. You will analyze this information using table features.

a. Start Excel, open IL_EX_5-4.xlsx from the location where you store your Data Files, then save it as **IL_EX_5_Donations**.

b. Using the data in the range A1:E92, create a table and format the table with the table style Blue, Table Style Light 9. Widen the columns, as necessary, to fully display the field names.

c. Delete the record in row 5 for donor #18574. Check the table for duplicates, using the Donor # field, and check to see if there are any duplicate records.

d. Add a field named **% Increase** in cell F1. Widen the columns as necessary to display all field names.

e. Enter a table formula in cell F2 that calculates the percent increase in the donation amount from 2019 to 2020. Check that the formula was filled into the other column cells. Format the values in column F in the Percent Style format with two decimal places. (*Hint:* A % increase is calculated by subtracting the old value from the new value and then dividing that difference by the old value. Remember to use parentheses when calculating the difference between the old and new values.)

f. Use a custom filter for the Class field to find donations from the classes of years 2010 - 2020. Copy the results, including the field names, and paste them on a new sheet named **2010 - 2020 Classes**. Widen the columns as necessary to fully display all of the worksheet data. Return to the 2019 - 2020 Donations sheet and remove the filter from the Class field.

g. Use the Data Validation dialog box to create an in-cell dropdown list that restricts entries in the School column to Business, Arts & Sciences, Engineering, and Health Sciences.

h. Use the Error Alert tab of the Data Validation dialog box to set the alert style to the Warning style with the error message "Data is not valid." Do not include the period after *valid*. Use the Input Message tab to add an input message of "Select the school." Do not include the period after *school*.

i. Add a new row at the end of the table and test the validation in the table with a valid entry. Use the new row to add a record for Donor # 10050, a graduate in the class of 1998 from the Engineering school, who donated $50 in 2019 and $100 in 2020.

j. Test the data validation by entering **Graduate** in cell B92. Verify the correct error message is displayed, then click Cancel to keep the existing valid data.

k. Add a total row to the table to display the total donations for 2019 and 2020. Delete any other total amounts in the row.

l. Apply conditional formatting to the % Increase column to show the values less than 0% in Light Red Fill with Dark Red Text. (*Hint:* Use Highlight Cell Rules with the criteria of Less than 0%.)

Independent Challenge 2 (continued)

m. Sort the records on the % Increase column, to display the Light Red Fill color cells at the top of the column. (*Hint:* Use a custom sort to sort by cell color with fill on top.)

n. Add print titles to repeat the first row at the top of each printed page, enter your name in the center section of the worksheet footer, enter **2019 - 2020 Donations** in the center section of the header, then activate **cell A1**.

o. Save the workbook, preview it, then compare your table to FIGURE 5-23.

p. Submit the workbook to your instructor, close the workbook, then close Excel.

FIGURE 5-23

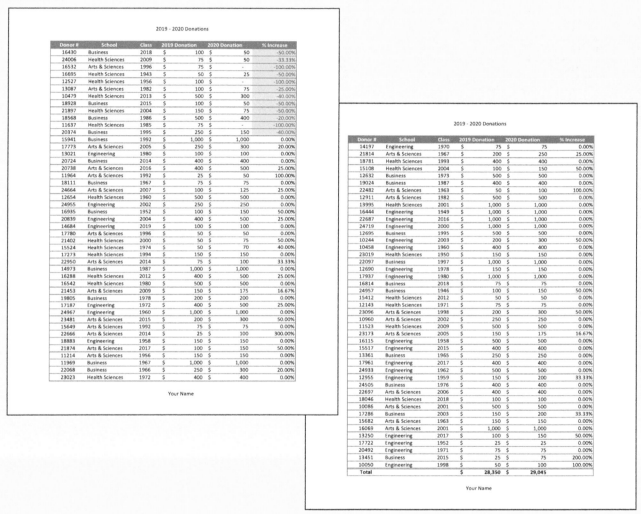

Excel

Visual Workshop

Open IL_EX_5-5.xlsx from the location where you store your Data Files, then save it as **IL_EX_5_Billings**. Create a table with the default table style. Sort, summarize, add a column, build a table formula, and add data validation so that your screen matches the table shown in FIGURE 5-24. Enter your name in the center section of the worksheet footer. Save the workbook, preview the table, close the workbook, submit the workbook to your instructor, then close Excel.

FIGURE 5-24

	Account #	Attorney	Office	Service	Referral	Billed	Paid	Balance				Attorney Billings	
2	1008	Castro	Austin	Real Estate	Friend/Family	$ 1,200	$ 1,000	200				Attorney	
3	1272	Castro	Austin	Real Estate	Other	$ 300	$ 200	100				Castro	
4	1659	Castro	Austin	Real Estate	Chamber of Commerce	$ 1,200	$ -	1200				Billed	$ 2,950
5	1663	Castro	Austin	Small Business	Friend/Family	$ 250	$ 100	150					
6	1762	Rousseau	Dallas	Bankruptcy	Friend/Family	$ 4,500	$ 4,500	0				Referral Billings	
7	1498	Tavarez	Dallas	Bankruptcy	Chamber of Commerce	$ 300	$ 100	200				Referral	
8	1085	Rousseau	Dallas	Bankruptcy	Online Search	$ 500	$ 400	100				Chamber of Commerce	
9	1992	Rousseau	Dallas	Civil Litigation	Social Media	$ 500	$ -	500				Billed	$ 7,800
10	1214	Rousseau	Dallas	Civil Litigation	Social Media	$ 3,000	$ 1,000	2000					
11	1153	Rousseau	Dallas	Civil Litigation	Online Search	$ 500	$ 500	0					
12	1696	Tavarez	Dallas	Real Estate	Other	$ 500	$ 100	400					
13	1512	Tavarez	Dallas	Real Estate	Other	$ 2,050	$ -	2050					
14	1035	Rousseau	Dallas	Real Estate	Online Search	$ 1,500	$ 500	1000					
15	1559	Rousseau	Dallas	Small Business	Online Search	$ 1,500	$ 1,500	0					
16	1266	Tavarez	Dallas	Small Business	Chamber of Commerce	$ 300	$ 300	0					
17	1063	Tavarez	Dallas	Small Business	Other	$ 500	$ -	500					
18	1484	Lewis	Houston	Bankruptcy	Friend/Family	$ 2,050	$ 2,000	50					
19	1742	Lewis	Houston	Bankruptcy	Social Media	$ 500	$ 500	0					
20	1134	Lewis	Houston	Civil Litigation	Chamber of Commerce	$ 4,500	$ 1,000	3500					
21	1300	Lewis	Houston	Estate Planning	Online Search	$ 3,000	$ 3,000	0					
22	1167	Lewis	Houston	Small Business	Chamber of Commerce	$ 1,500	$ 500	1000					

Friend/Family
Online Search
Chamber of Commerce
Social Media
Other

Managing Workbook Data

CASE ▶ Ellie Schwartz, the vice president of finance at JCL, asks for your help in analyzing yearly sales revenues from the North America and worldwide offices. When the analysis is complete, she will distribute the workbook for office managers to review.

Module Objectives

After completing this module, you will be able to:

- View and arrange worksheets
- Protect worksheets and workbooks
- Save custom views of a worksheet
- Prepare a workbook for distribution
- Insert hyperlinks
- Save a workbook for distribution
- Work with grouped data
- Work with grouped worksheets

Files You Will Need

View and Arrange Worksheets

Learning Outcomes
- Compare worksheet data by arranging worksheets
- View and hide instances of a workbook

As you work with workbooks made up of multiple worksheets, you might need to compare data in the various sheets. To do this, you can view each worksheet in its own workbook window, called an **instance**, and display the windows in an arrangement that makes it easy to compare data. When you work with worksheets in separate windows, you are working with different views of the same workbook; the data itself remains in one file. **CASE** ▶ *Ellie asks you to compare the monthly revenue totals for the worldwide and North America locations. Because the revenue totals are on different worksheets, you want to arrange the worksheets side by side in separate instances.*

STEPS

1. **sam↓ Start Excel, open** IL_EX_6-1.xlsx **from the location where you store your Data Files, then save it as** IL_EX_6_Revenue

2. **With the Worldwide sheet active, click the** View **tab on the ribbon, then click the** New Window **button in the Window group**

   There are now two instances of the Revenue workbook open, each in their own workbook window.

3. **Point to the** Excel icon **on the taskbar**

   Two window thumbnails open, IL_EX_6_Revenue - 1 and IL_EX_6_Revenue - 2.

> **QUICK TIP**
> You can use the View Side by Side button in the Window group to arrange windows next to each other and also activate the Synchronous Scrolling button below the View Side by Side button. Synchronous scrolling allows you to scroll through the arranged worksheets simultaneously.

4. **In the current instance, click the** North America sheet tab, **click the** View **tab on the ribbon, click the** Switch Windows button **in the Window group, then click** 1 IL_EX_6_Revenue - 1

   The IL_EX_6_Revenue - 1 instance moves to the front. The Worldwide sheet is active in this instance, and the North America sheet is active in the IL_EX_6_Revenue - 2 instance.

5. **Click the** Arrange All button **in the Window group**

   The Arrange Windows dialog box, shown in FIGURE 6-1, lets you choose how to display the instances. You want to view the workbooks next to each other.

6. **Click the** Vertical option button, **then click** OK

   The windows are arranged next to each other, as shown in FIGURE 6-2. The second instance of the workbook opens at a zoom of 100%, not the 120% zoom of the first instance. You can activate a workbook by clicking one of its cells.

7. **Scroll horizontally to view the data in the** IL_EX_6_Revenue - 1 workbook, click **anywhere in the** IL_EX_6_Revenue - 2 workbook, scroll horizontally and view the data, **then click the** Hide Window button ▱ **in the Window group**

   When you hide the second instance, only the IL_EX_6_Revenue - 1 workbook is visible.

> **QUICK TIP**
> You can hide a worksheet in a workbook by right-clicking its sheet tab and clicking Hide on the shortcut menu. To display the hidden sheet, right-click any sheet tab, click Unhide, in the Unhide dialog box select the sheet, then click OK.

8. **In the** IL_EX_6_Revenue - 1 window, **click the** Unhide Window button ▭ **in the Window group, then with the** IL_EX_6_Revenue – 2 worksheet selected in the Unhide dialog box **click** OK

9. **Click the** Close button ✕ **in the title bar of the** IL_EX_6_Revenue - 2 instance, **then maximize the** IL_EX_6_Revenue.xlsx workbook

   Closing the IL_EX_6_Revenue – 2 instance leaves only the first instance open. Its name in the title bar returns to IL_EX_6_Revenue. When closing an instance of a workbook, it is important to use the Close button and not the Close command on the File menu, which closes the workbook.

FIGURE 6-1: Arrange Windows dialog box

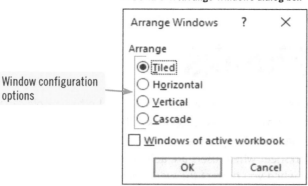

Window configuration options

FIGURE 6-2: Window instances displayed vertically

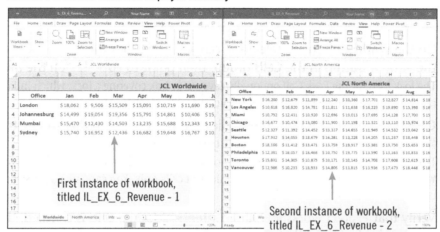

First instance of workbook, titled IL_EX_6_Revenue - 1

Second instance of workbook, titled IL_EX_6_Revenue - 2

Splitting the worksheet into multiple panes

Excel lets you split the worksheet area into vertical and/or horizontal **panes**, or sections of columns and rows. You can then click inside any one pane and scroll to locate information while the other panes remain in place, as shown in **FIGURE 6-3**. To split a worksheet area into multiple panes, click a cell below and to the right of where you want the split to appear, click the View tab on the ribbon, then click the Split button in the Window group. You can also split a worksheet into only two panes by selecting the row or column below or to the right of where you want the split to appear, clicking the View tab on the ribbon, then clicking Split in the Window group. To remove a split, click the View tab, then click Split in the Window group.

FIGURE 6-3: Worksheet split into four panes

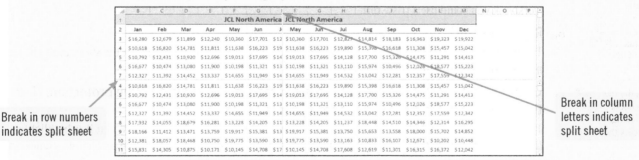

Break in row numbers indicates split sheet

Break in column letters indicates split sheet

Excel

Protect Worksheets and Workbooks

Learning Outcomes
- Protect a worksheet
- Create a data entry area on a worksheet by unlocking cells
- Protect a workbook

To protect information, Excel lets you **lock** one or more cells so that other people can view the values and formulas in those cells, but not make changes. Excel locks all cells by default, but this locking does not take effect until you activate the protection feature. A common worksheet protection strategy is to create an unlocked portion of a worksheet where users are able to enter and change data, sometimes called the **data entry area**. Then, when you protect the worksheet, the unlocked areas can still be changed.

CASE ▶ *Because the worldwide revenue figures for January through March have been finalized, Ellie asks you to protect that worksheet area. That way, users cannot change the figures for those months.*

STEPS

1. **On the Worldwide sheet, select the range E3:M6, click the Home tab on the ribbon, click the Format button in the Cells group, then point to Lock Cell on the menu**

   The lock icon for the Lock Cell option displays a gray box covering a lock, which indicates the cells are currently locked, as shown in FIGURE 6-4, so clicking will unlock them.

2. **Click Lock Cell to unlock the cells, click the Review tab on the ribbon, then click the Protect Sheet button in the Protect group**

   The Protect Sheet dialog box opens, as shown in FIGURE 6-5. The default options protect the worksheet while allowing users to select locked or unlocked cells only. You can enter a password in the Password to unprotect sheet box.

3. **Verify that Protect worksheet and contents of locked cells is checked, that the password text box is blank, and that the Select locked cells and Select unlocked cells check boxes contain checkmarks, then click OK**

4. **Click cell B3, type 1 to confirm that locked cells cannot be changed, click OK, click cell F3, type 1, notice that Excel lets you begin the entry, press ESC to cancel the entry, then save your work**

   When you try to change a locked cell on a protected worksheet, a dialog box, shown in FIGURE 6-6, reminds you of the protected cell's status and provides instructions to unprotect the worksheet.

5. **Click the Protect Workbook button in the Protect group, in the Protect Structure and Windows dialog box make sure the Structure check box contains a checkmark, verify that the password text box is blank, then click OK**

   The workbook's structure is protected from changes. If you wanted to provide additional protection to the workbook you could use a password.

6. **Right-click the Worldwide sheet tab**

   The Insert, Delete, Rename, Move or Copy, Tab Color, Hide, and Unhide options on the shortcut menu are not available because the structure is protected.

7. **Click the Protect Workbook button in the Protect group to turn off the protection, click the Unprotect Sheet button, then save your changes**

   The Protect Workbook button is a toggle, which means it's like an on/off switch. When it is highlighted, the workbook is protected. Clicking it again removes the highlighting, indicating the protection is removed from the workbook.

FIGURE 6-4: Lock Cell option

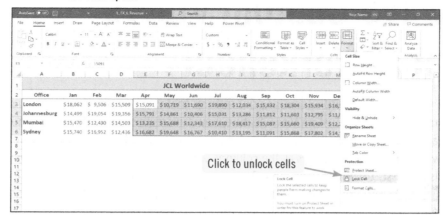

FIGURE 6-5: Protect Sheet dialog box

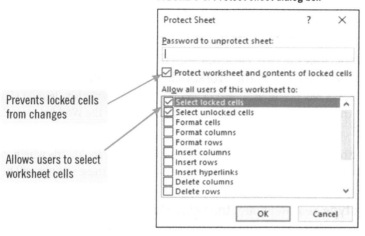

FIGURE 6-6: Reminder of protected worksheet status

Creating edit ranges

You can allow users to edit certain ranges on a worksheet by selecting the range, clicking the Review tab on the ribbon, clicking the Allow Edit Ranges button in the Protect group, clicking New in the Allow User to Edit Ranges dialog box, entering an optional title for the range and a password to edit it, confirming the password, clicking Protect Sheet, then clicking OK.

Freezing rows and columns

A **pane** is a section of columns and/or rows that you can **freeze**, or set so that they remain visible as you scroll through your worksheet. To freeze panes, click the first cell in the area you want to scroll, click the View tab on the ribbon, click the Freeze Panes button in the Window group, then click Freeze Panes. Excel freezes the columns to the left and the rows above the selected cell, as shown in **FIGURE 6-7**. You can also select Freeze Top Row or Freeze First Column to freeze the top row or left worksheet column. To unfreeze panes, click the View tab, click Freeze Panes, then click Unfreeze Panes.

FIGURE 6-7: Worksheet with top two rows and left column frozen

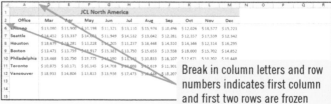

Break in column letters and row numbers indicates first column and first two rows are frozen

Save Custom Views of a Worksheet

Learning
Outcomes
• Create different
views of worksheet
data using custom
views
• Display different
views of worksheet
data using custom
views

A **view** is a set of display and/or print settings that you can name and save, and then access at a later time. By using the Custom Views feature, you can create several different views of a worksheet without having to create separate sheets. For example, if you often hide columns in a worksheet, you can create two views, one that displays all the columns and another with the columns hidden. You set the worksheet display first, then name the view. Then you can open the view whenever you want, using the name.
CASE *Because Ellie wants to generate a revenue report from the final revenue data for January through March, she asks you to create a custom view that shows only the first-quarter revenue data.*

STEPS

1. **With the Worldwide sheet active, click cell A1, click the** View tab **on the ribbon, then click the** Custom Views button **in the Workbook Views group**

   The Custom Views dialog box opens, as shown in FIGURE 6-8. Any previously defined views for the active worksheet appear in the Views box. No views are currently defined for the Worldwide worksheet.

2. **Click** Add

   The Add View dialog box opens. Here, you enter a name for the view and decide whether to include print settings and/or hidden rows, columns, and filter settings. By default, these settings will be included in the new view.

3. **In the Name box type** Year Revenue, **then click** OK

   You have created a view called Year Revenue that displays all the worksheet columns.

QUICK TIP
Clicking Hide on
the shortcut menu
will similarly hide
selected worksheet
rows. To unhide
columns and rows,
select the columns
or rows on both
sides of the hidden
ones, right-click the
selected area, then
click Unhide on the
shortcut menu.

4. **Select columns** E through M, **right-click the selected area, then click** Hide **on the shortcut menu**

   The April through December columns are hidden.

5. **Click cell A1, click the** Custom Views button **in the Workbook Views group, click** Add, **in the Name box type** First Quarter, **then click** OK

6. **Click the** Custom Views button **in the Workbook Views group, click** Year Revenue **in the Views list, then click** Show

   The Year Revenue custom view displays all the months' revenue data.

TROUBLE
If you receive the
message "Some view
settings could not
be applied," turn
off worksheet pro-
tection by clicking
the Unprotect Sheet
button in the Protect
group of the Review
tab.

7. **Click the** Custom Views button **in the Workbook Views group, then with** First Quarter **in the Custom Views dialog box selected, click** Show

   Only the January through March revenue figures appear on the screen, as shown in FIGURE 6-9.

8. **Click the** Custom Views button, **click** Year Revenue, **click** Show, **then save your work**

FIGURE 6-8: Custom Views dialog box

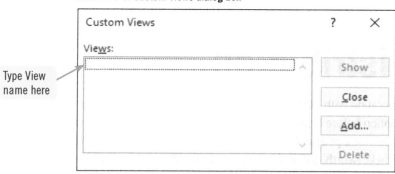

FIGURE 6-9: First Quarter view

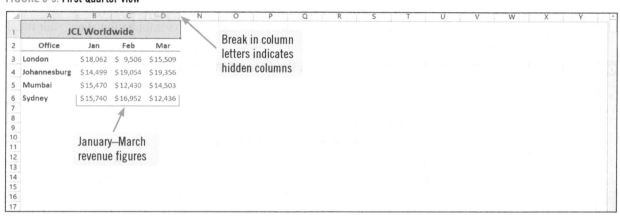

Using Page Break Preview

The vertical and horizontal dashed lines in the Normal view of worksheets represent page breaks. Excel automatically inserts a page break when your worksheet data doesn't fit on one page. These page breaks are **dynamic**, which means they adjust automatically when workbook content changes, such as when rows and columns are added, deleted, or resized. Everything to the left of the first vertical dashed line and above the first horizontal dashed line is printed on the first page. You can manually add or remove page breaks by clicking the Page Layout tab on the ribbon, clicking the Breaks button in the Page Setup group, then clicking Insert Page Break, Remove Page Break, or Reset All Page Breaks. Clicking Insert Page Break adds a page break above and

to the left of a selected cell, and clicking Remove Page Break removes page breaks above and to the left of a cell. Reset All Page Breaks resets page breaks back to the default setting. You can also view and change page breaks manually by clicking the View tab on the ribbon, then clicking the Page Break Preview button in the Workbook Views group, or by clicking the Page Break Preview button on the status bar. You can drag the blue page break lines to the desired location. Some cells may temporarily display ##### while you are in Page Break Preview. If you drag a page break to the right to include more data on a page, Excel shrinks the type to fit the data on that page. To exit Page Break Preview, click the Normal button in the Workbook Views group.

Prepare a Workbook for Distribution

If you are collaborating with others and want to share a workbook with them, you might want to remove sensitive information before distributing the file. On the other hand, you might want to add details about a file, called **document properties**, to the file to help others identify, understand, and locate it. Properties might include keywords, the author's name, a title, the status, and comments. **Keywords**, also called **tags**, are terms you add to the file's properties that users can use when searching to help them locate your workbook. Properties are also called **metadata**, descriptive information that is used by Microsoft Windows in document searches. In addition, to ensure that others do not make unauthorized changes to your workbook, you can mark a file as final. This makes it a read-only file, which discourages others from making changes to it. **CASE** ▸ *Ellie wants you to protect the workbook and prepare it for distribution.*

STEPS

1. **Click the File tab on the ribbon, then click Info on the navigation bar**

   Backstage view opens and displays the Info pane, which displays information about your file. It also includes tools you can use to check for security issues.

2. **Click the Check for Issues button in the Inspect Workbook area, then click Inspect Document**

   The Document Inspector dialog box opens, as shown in FIGURE 6-10. It lists items that Excel can check in the file. All the options are selected by default.

3. **Click Inspect, then scroll to view the inspection results**

   Areas containing data have a red "!" in front of them. If areas are flagged as having data that you can remove from this dialog box, you can click the Remove All button. Some data cannot be removed from this dialog box; for example, hidden names are created by Excel and can't be deleted without running a special program.

4. **Click Close, click the Properties list arrow on the right side of the Info pane, then click Advanced Properties**

   The file's Properties dialog box opens with the Summary tab active, as shown in FIGURE 6-11. This tab allows you to enter identifying, and searchable, information for the file.

5. **In the Title text box type Revenue, in the Keywords text box type Worldwide North America Revenue, then in the Comments text box type The first-quarter figures are final., then click OK**

6. **Click the Protect Workbook button on the left side of the Info pane, click Mark as Final, click OK, then click OK again**

   The workbook is marked as final and "Read-Only" appears in the title bar indicating the workbook is saved as a read-only file. A yellow bar also appears below the tabs indicating the workbook is marked as final. The yellow bar also includes an Edit Anyway button.

7. **Click cell B3, type 1 to confirm that the cell cannot be changed, click the Edit Anyway button above the formula bar, then save the workbook**

   By clicking Edit Anyway, you removed the read-only status, making the workbook editable again. Marking a workbook as final is not a strong form of workbook protection because a workbook recipient can remove this Final status.

FIGURE 6-10: **Document Inspector dialog box**

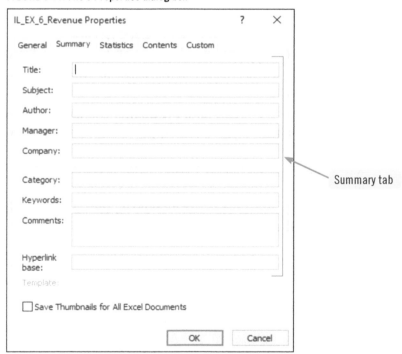

FIGURE 6-11: **File's Properties dialog box**

Adding a worksheet background

You can make your Excel data more attractive on the screen by adding a picture to the worksheet background. To add a worksheet background, click the Page Layout tab on the ribbon, click the Background button in the Page Setup group, choose From a file, Bing Image Search, or a OneDrive account in the

Insert Pictures dialog box, click the image file in the next dialog boxes, then click Insert. The image appears tiled, repeating as necessary to fill the background behind the worksheet data on the screen. A worksheet background will not print with the worksheet.

Excel

Insert Hyperlinks

Learning
Outcomes
• Add a hyperlink in
  a worksheet
• Add ScreenTips to
  a hyperlink

As you manage the content and appearance of your workbooks, you might want the workbook user to view related information that exists in another location. A **hyperlink** is a specially formatted word, phrase, or graphic which, when clicked or tapped, displays a webpage on the Internet, another file, an email, or another location within the same file. The document, webpage, or place to which the hyperlink connects is called the **target**. You can also specify a ScreenTip that users see when they point to a hyperlink in your workbook. **CASE** ▸ *Ellie wants the office managers who view the Revenue workbook to also be able to view the division totals for their offices. She asks you to create a hyperlink to a file with this information for the London manager.*

STEPS

1. **Click cell A3 on the Worldwide worksheet**

2. **Click the Insert tab on the ribbon, then click the Link button in the Links group**

   The Insert Hyperlink dialog box opens. The icons under "Link to" on the left side of the dialog box let you specify the type of location to where you want the link to jump: an existing file or webpage, a place in the same document, a new document, or an email address.

3. **Click the Existing File or Web Page button if necessary, click the Look in list arrow, navigate to where you store your Data Files if necessary, then click Support_EX_6-2.xlsx**

   The filename you selected and its path appear in the Address text box, as shown in FIGURE 6-12. Your path to the Support_EX_6-2.xlsx file may be different depending on how you set up your files on your computer. This is the file users will see when they click the hyperlink.

4. **Click ScreenTip, type Division revenue, click OK, then click OK again**

   Cell A3 now contains underlined blue text, indicating that it is a hyperlink. The default color of a hyperlink depends on the current theme colors.

5. **Point to the London text until the pointer changes to 🖑, view the ScreenTip, then click once; if a dialog box opens asking you to confirm the file is from a trustworthy source, click OK**

   After you click, the Support_EX_6-2.xlsx workbook opens, displaying the London revenue data, as shown in FIGURE 6-13.

6. **Close the Support_EX_6-2.xlsx workbook, click Don't Save if necessary, then save your changes to the IL_EX_6_Revenue workbook**

FIGURE 6-12: **Insert Hyperlink dialog box**

Locations to
which a hyperlink
can jump

Click to link to a
place in the file

Click to link to
a new file

Click to link to an
email address

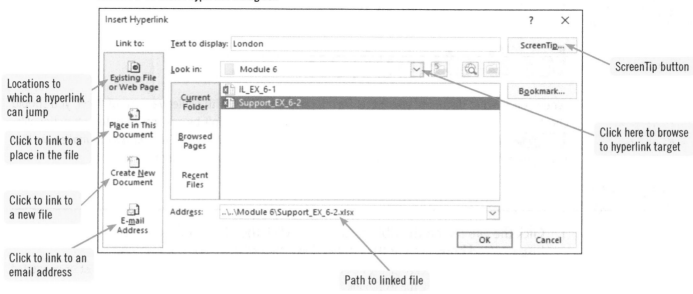

ScreenTip button

Click here to browse
to hyperlink target

Path to linked file

FIGURE 6-13: **Target document**

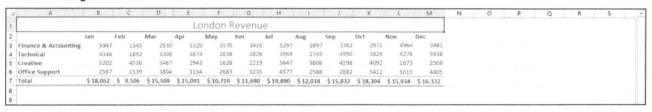

Excel

Save a Workbook for Distribution

Learning
Outcomes
• Check workbook
  compatibility
• Check
  compatibility
  for different
  Excel versions

When you need to distribute your Excel files to people working with earlier versions of Excel, you should check the compatibility of your workbook to make sure there won't be any loss of data or functionality.

CASE ▶ *Ellie asks you to check the workbook's compatibility with earlier Excel formats to make sure that managers running an earlier version of Excel can accurately view the revenue data.*

STEPS

1. **Click the** File tab **on the ribbon, click** Info, **click the** Check for Issues button **in the Inspect Workbook area of Backstage view, then click** Check Compatibility

   The Compatibility Checker dialog box opens, alerting you to the features that will be lost or converted when saving or opening the workbook in earlier versions of Excel. The Summary box displays a warning titled "Minor loss of fidelity," indicating that some of the worksheet's formatting either might not be available or might appear differently in earlier versions of Excel. Minor loss of fidelity warnings won't result in lost data or worksheet functionality.

2. **Click the** Select versions to show arrow, **then click** Excel 97-2003 **to deselect it**

   The warning in the Summary box is no longer displayed, as shown in FIGURE 6-14, because it applies only to 97-2003 versions of Excel.

3. **Click the** Select versions to show arrow, **click** Excel 97-2003 **to select it, then click** OK

4. **Click the** Home tab **on the ribbon, click the** Find & Select button **in the Editing group, click** Go To, **type** LL1 **in the Reference box, click** OK, **type** 1 **in cell** LL1, **then press** ENTER

5. **Click the** File tab **on the ribbon, click** Info, **click the** Check for Issues button **in the Inspect Workbook area of Backstage view, then click** Check Compatibility

   The Compatibility Checker now displays a "Significant loss of functionality warning," as shown in FIGURE 6-15. This type of warning indicates a loss of data or functionality when a workbook is opened in an earlier Excel version. The data that was entered in cell LL1 could be lost because column LL is outside the limit of 256 columns in the 97-2003 versions of Excel.

6. **Click** OK **to close the Compatibility Checker, click cell** LL1, **press** DEL **to remove the data from the cell, then press** CTRL+HOME

7. **Click the** File tab, **click** Info, **click the** Check for Issues button **in the Inspect Workbook area of Backstage, click** Check Compatibility, **verify there is no longer a significant loss of functionality, then click** OK

8. **Save the workbook**

FIGURE 6-14: Compatibility Checker dialog box

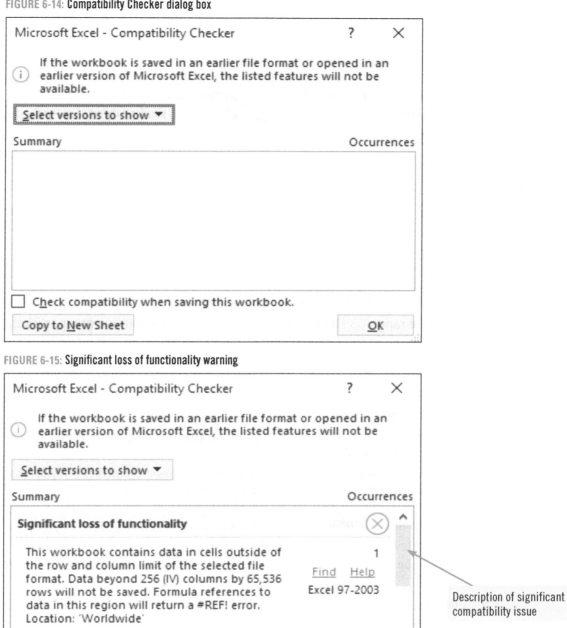

FIGURE 6-15: Significant loss of functionality warning

Exporting a workbook to other file types

You can export Excel workbooks to many other formats. Clicking File, then clicking Export opens the Export pane, where you can either Create a PDF/XPS Document or Change File Type. PDFs and XPS files have the advantage of preserving formatting, fonts, and images, and making it difficult to change the file. These files can be opened and viewed in free viewers available online. To select this option, click Create PDF/XPS in the Create PDF/XPS Document section, choose the file type in the Save as type box, then click Publish. If you click Change File Type in the Export pane you can choose from several file types, including Macro Enabled Workbook, Excel 97-2003 workbook, Template, OpenDocument Spreadsheet (which can be used with OpenOffice), Text, special types of text file such as CSV and Formatted Text, or a Binary workbook that is optimized for fast loading and saving. Click the format you want, click Save As, then click Save in the Save As dialog box.

Work with Grouped Data

Learning Outcomes
• Group worksheet data
• Apply symbols to view outlined data

You can create groups of rows and columns on a worksheet to manage your data and make it easier to work with and view. The Excel grouping feature displays outline symbols that allow you to easily expand and collapse groups to show or hide selected worksheet data. You can turn off the outline symbols if you are using the condensed data in a report. **CASE** ▶ *Ellie asks you for a report showing the quarterly revenue totals for all JCL offices.*

STEPS

1. **Click the International sheet, select the range C3:E16, click the Data tab on the ribbon, click the Group button in the Outline group, click the Columns option button in the Group dialog box, then click OK**

   The first-quarter data details are grouped. The quarter summary data isn't contained in the group to allow for that summary information to be displayed. The **outline symbols** that let you hide and display details appear over the grouped columns, as shown in FIGURE 6-16.

QUICK TIP
You can create an outline using the Auto Outline feature by selecting the entire range, C3:R17, clicking the Group arrow in the Outline group, then clicking Auto Outline.

2. **Select the range G3:I16, click the Group button in the Outline group, click the Columns option button in the Group dialog box, click OK, select the range K3:M16, click the Group button in the Outline group, click the Columns option button in the Group dialog box, click OK, select the range O3:Q16, click the Group button in the Outline group, click the Columns option button in the Group dialog box, click OK, then click cell A1**

   All four quarters are grouped.

3. **Click the Collapse Outline button ⊟ above the column F label, then click the Expand Outline button ⊞ above the column F label**

   Clicking the (–) symbol temporarily hides the Q1 detail columns, and the (–) symbol changes to a (+) symbol. Clicking the (+) symbol expands the Q1 details and redisplays the hidden columns. The numbered Outline symbols in the upper-left corner of the worksheet are used to display and hide levels of detail across the entire worksheet.

4. **Click the level 1 Outline Symbol button ①**

   All the group details, considered Level 2, collapse, and only the quarter totals, considered Level 1, are displayed.

5. **Click the level 2 Outline Symbol button ②**

   You see the quarter details again. Ellie asks you to hide the quarter details and the outline symbols for the summary report.

QUICK TIP
You can ungroup a range of cells by clicking Ungroup in the Outline group. You can clear an outline by clicking the Ungroup arrow and clicking Clear Outline.

6. **Click ①, click the File tab, click Options, click Advanced in the category list, scroll down to Display options for this worksheet, verify that International is displayed as the worksheet name, click the Show outline symbols if an outline is applied check box to deselect it, then click OK**

   The worksheet displays quarter totals without outline symbols, as shown in FIGURE 6-17.

7. **Save the workbook**

FIGURE 6-16: First-quarter data grouped

Outline symbols

Column-level buttons

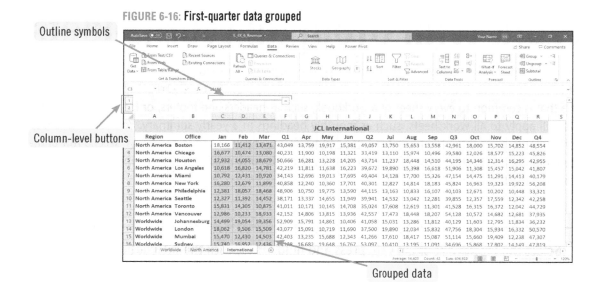

Grouped data

FIGURE 6-17: Quarterly summary

Breaks in column letter sequence indicate data is grouped

	A	B	F	J	N	R
1		JCL International				
2	Region	Office	Q1	Q2	Q3	Q4
3	North America	Boston	43,049	49,057	42,961	48,554
4	North America	Chicago	40,231	33,419	39,580	45,826
5	North America	Houston	50,666	43,714	44,195	42,955
6	North America	Los Angeles	42,219	39,672	51,906	41,807
7	North America	Miami	34,143	49,404	47,154	40,179
8	North America	New York	40,858	40,301	45,824	56,208
9	North America	Philadelphia	48,906	44,115	40,103	33,321
10	North America	Seattle	38,171	39,941	39,855	42,258
11	North America	Toronto	41,011	35,024	41,528	44,729
12	North America	Vancouver	42,152	42,557	54,128	37,935
13	Worldwide	Johannesburg	52,909	41,058	40,129	36,232
14	Worldwide	London	43,077	37,500	47,756	50,570
15	Worldwide	Mumbai	42,403	41,266	51,114	47,307
16	Worldwide	Sydney	45,128	53,097	34,696	47,819
17						

Creating Subtotals

The Excel Subtotals feature provides a quick, easy way to group and summarize a range of data. It lets you create not only subtotals using the SUM function, but other statistics as well, including COUNT, AVERAGE, MAX, and MIN. In order to get meaningful statistics, data must be sorted on the field on which you will group. To create subtotals, first select the range of data you want to subtotal, click the Data tab on the ribbon, click the Subtotal button in the Outline group, click the At each change in arrow in the Subtotal dialog box, select the field by which you want to group the data, such as region, click the Use function arrow, click the function you want to use, select the fields that you want to subtotal in the "Add subtotal to" list, then click OK. FIGURE 6-18 shows data grouped by region and summed on each quarter.

FIGURE 6-18: Worksheet subtotals and grand total

Subtotal rows

Grand Total row

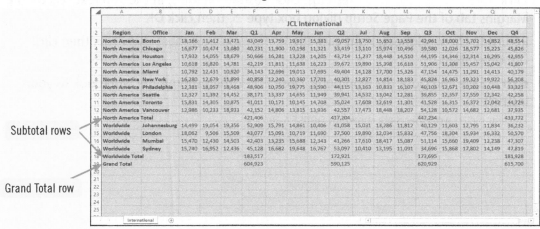

Excel

Work with Grouped Worksheets

Learning Outcomes
- Group worksheets
- Add custom margins to worksheets

You can group worksheets to work on them as a collection. When you enter data into one grouped worksheet, that data is also automatically entered into all the worksheets in the group. This is useful for data that is common to every sheet of a workbook, such as headers and footers, or for column headings that will apply to all worksheets, such as monthly headings in a yearly summary. You can also group worksheets to print them all at one time. **CASE** *Ellie asks you to add text in a new, second row of the Worldwide, North America, and International worksheets. You also need to adjust the margin at the top of these worksheets.*

STEPS

QUICK TIP
You can group non-contiguous worksheets by pressing and holding CTRL while clicking only the sheet tabs you want to include.

1. **Select the** Worldwide sheet tab, **press and hold** SHIFT, **click the** International sheet tab, **then release** SHIFT
   The Worldwide, North America, and International sheets are selected, and the title bar now displays "IL_EX_6_Revenue.xlsx - Group" to indicate that the worksheets are grouped together and this is the first group in the workbook. Now, any changes you make to the Worldwide sheet will also be made to the other sheets.

2. **Select row** 2, **click the** Home tab **on the ribbon, click the** Insert button **in the Cells group, click cell** A2, **enter** Revenue, **click the** Enter button ✓ **on the Formula bar, select the range** A2:M2, **then click the** Merge & Center button **in the Alignment group**
   FIGURE 6-19 shows the Worldwide worksheet with the new Revenue row.

3. **Right-click the** Worldwide sheet tab, **click** Ungroup Sheets **on the shortcut menu, then verify the revenue label appears on the North America and International sheets**

QUICK TIP
If you want to customize the status bar, right-click it, then click the options that you want.

4. **Select the** Worldwide sheet tab, **press and hold** SHIFT, **click the** International sheet, **release** SHIFT, **click the** Insert tab **on the ribbon, click the** Header & Footer button **in the** Text group, **enter your name in the** center header section, **click any cell on the worksheet, click the** Normal button ▦ **on the status bar, then press** CTRL+HOME

5. **With the worksheets still grouped, click the** File tab, **click** Print, **click** No Scaling under **Settings, click** Fit All Columns on One Page, **preview the first page, then click the** Next Page button ▶ **to preview the other two pages**
   Because the worksheets are grouped, all worksheets are ready to print and all pages contain the header with your name.

6. **Click** Normal Margins under **Settings, click** Custom Margins, **in the Top text box on the Margins tab of the Page Setup dialog box type** .5, **then click** OK

7. **Return to the worksheet, right-click the** Worldwide worksheet sheet tab, **then click** Ungroup Sheets

8. **sam⬆ Save and close the workbook, close** Excel, **then submit the workbook to your instructor**
   The completed worksheets are shown in FIGURE 6-20.

FIGURE 6-19: Worldwide worksheet with Revenue label

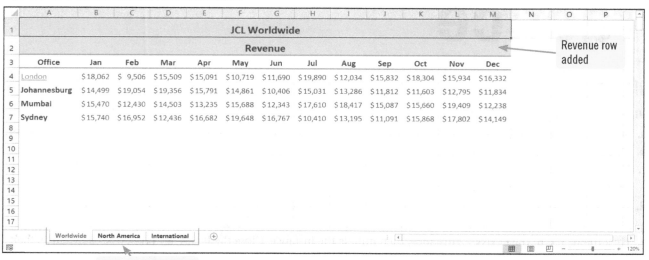

Grouped worksheets

FIGURE 6-20: Completed worksheets

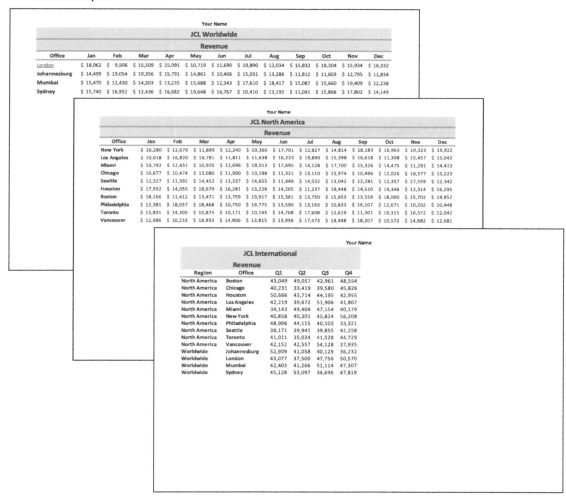

Excel

Practice

Skills Review

1. View and arrange worksheets.

a. Start Excel, open IL_EX_6-3.xlsx from the location where you store your Data Files, then save it as **IL_EX_6_Travel**.

b. Open a new window that contains another instance of the workbook.

c. Verify the Business sheet is active in the IL_EX_6_Travel.xlsx - 1 instance of the workbook. Activate the Personal sheet in the IL_EX_6_Travel.xlsx - 2 instance.

d. Use the Arrange Windows dialog box to view the IL_EX_6_Travel.xlsx - 1 and IL_EX_6_Travel.xlsx - 2 workbook windows tiled horizontally, then compare the workbooks in a vertical arrangement.

e. Hide the IL_EX_6_Travel.xlsx - 2 instance, then unhide the instance. Close the IL_EX_6_Travel.xlsx - 2 instance, then maximize the IL_EX_6_Travel.xlsx workbook.

2. Protect worksheets and workbooks.

a. On the Business sheet, unlock the expense data in the range B12:F19.

b. Protect the sheet without using a password, accepting the default settings in the Protect Sheet dialog box.

c. To make sure the other cells are locked, attempt to make an entry in cell D4 and verify that you receive an error message.

d. Change the first-quarter real estate expense in cell B12 to **15,000**.

e. Protect the workbook's structure without applying a password.

f. Right-click the Business and Personal sheet tabs to verify that you cannot insert, delete, rename, move, copy, hide or unhide the sheets, or change their tab color.

g. Unprotect the workbook. Unprotect the Business worksheet.

h. Save the workbook.

3. Save custom views of a worksheet.

a. With the Business sheet active, create a custom view of the entire worksheet called **Entire Business Budget**.

b. Hide rows 10 through 23, then create a new custom view called **Business Income** that shows only the current data.

c. Use the Custom Views dialog box to display the Entire Business Budget view of the Business worksheet.

d. Use the Custom Views dialog box to display only the Business Income view of the Business worksheet.

e. Return to the Entire Business Budget view.

f. Save the workbook.

4. Prepare a workbook for distribution.

a. Use the Info pane in Backstage view to check for issues in the workbook, then use the Document Inspector to remove all document properties and personal data.

b. Use the Summary tab of the file's Properties dialog box to add a title of **Quarterly Budget** and the keyword **travel**.

c. Mark the workbook as final, then verify that "Read-Only" appears in the title bar.

d. Remove the final status using the Edit Anyway button, then save the workbook.

5. Insert hyperlinks.

a. On the Business worksheet, make cell I1 a hyperlink to cell A22 on the worksheet. (*Hint:* In the Insert Hyperlink dialog box, use the Place in This Document button and enter the target cell reference in the Type the cell reference box.)

b. Test the link.

c. Edit the hyperlink in cell I1 to add a ScreenTip that reads **Cash Flow by Quarter**, then verify that the ScreenTip opens.

d. Remove the hyperlink in cell I1, then delete the text in the cell.

e. Save the workbook.

Skills Review (continued)

6. Save a workbook for distribution.

a. Check the compatibility of the IL_EX_6_Travel.xlsx with all previous versions of Excel.

b. Review the Minor loss of fidelity issue in the Compatibility Checker.

c. Deselect the Excel 97-2003 version in the Select versions to show list, then verify that the Minor loss of fidelity warning no longer appears.

d. Select the Excel 97-2003 version in the Select versions to show list.

e. Save the workbook.

7. Work with grouped data.

a. Activate the Business sheet, then group the income information in the range A5:G9 as rows.

b. Group the expenses information in the range A11:G20 as rows.

c. Collapse the income details in rows 5 through 9.

d. Collapse the expenses details in rows 11 through 20.

e. Expand the income and expenses details.

f. Save the workbook.

8. Work with grouped worksheets.

a. Group the Business and Personal worksheets.

b. Add your name to the center footer section of the grouped worksheets.

c. Add a 1.25" custom margin to the top and bottom of the grouped worksheets.

d. Preview the sheets, then ungroup the sheets.

e. Save the workbook, then compare your Business worksheet to FIGURE 6-21.

f. Submit IL_EX_6_Travel.xlsx file to your instructor, close all open files, then close Excel.

FIGURE 6-21

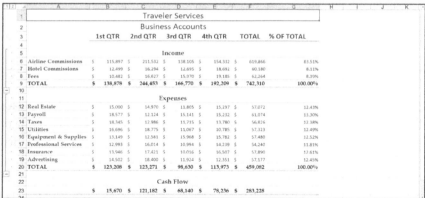

Independent Challenge 1

As the assistant to the CFO at Riverwalk Medical Clinic, you have been asked to analyze the annual insurance reimbursement data for the departments. After you complete your analysis, you will distribute the workbook to the clinic's vice presidents.

a. Start Excel, open IL_EX_6-4.xlsx from the location where you store your Data Files, then save it as **IL_EX_6_RiverwalkReimbursements**.

b. Display each worksheet in its own window, arrange the two sheets horizontally, then compare the data in the two windows.

Independent Challenge 1 (continued)

c. Hide the window displaying the Acute sheet. Unhide the Acute sheet window, then close this window.

d. Maximize the Elective window. Unlock the data in cells B5:D8.

e. Protect the worksheet without using a password. Verify the protection by trying to edit a locked cell, such as F5. Verify that you can edit the data in an unlocked cell, such as B5, but do not change the data.

f. Unprotect the Elective worksheet.

g. Protect the workbook without using a password.

h. Verify the protection by trying to change the Elective sheet name.

i. Unprotect the workbook.

j. On the Elective sheet, create a custom view called **Annual Reimbursements** that displays all the worksheet data. Hide columns F through Q. Create a custom view displaying the data in A1:E8, named **First Quarter Reimbursements**. Display all the data using a custom view. Display only the first-quarter reimbursement data using a custom view. Use a custom view to view all the reimbursement data for the year.

k. Insert a hyperlink in cell A5 on the Elective worksheet to the file Support_EX_6-5.xlsx. (*Hint:* If necessary, navigate to the location where you store your Data Files to locate and select the target file.) Add a ScreenTip that reads **Reimbursement by Procedure**, then test the hyperlink. Compare your screen to FIGURE 6-22.

FIGURE 6-22

	A	B
1	Ophthalmology	
2	Elective Procedures	
3	Procedure	Reimbursements
4	CK	$898,812
5	Lasik	$1,463,456
6	PRK	$797,425
7	LTK	$1,023,456
8	Intacs	$1,005,187

l. Close the Support_EX_6_5.xlsx file. Change the font of cell A5 to Calibri, to match the worksheet data.

m. Inspect the workbook for issues, then remove all document properties and personal data. Add a title property of **RMC Reimbursements** and keywords **acute** and **elective**. Mark the workbook as final, then remove the final status.

n. Check the compatibility of the workbook with previous Excel versions.

o. On the Elective worksheet, group the reimbursement data by quarters. (*Hint:* Group the monthly data by columns; do not include the quarter totals.) Use the outline buttons to collapse the monthly details and display only the quarter totals.

p. Group the two worksheets, add your name to the center footer section of the worksheets, then add 1.25" custom margins to the top of the worksheets.

q. Preview the worksheets, ungroup the worksheets, then save the workbook.

r. Submit the IL_EX_6_Riverwalk Reimbursements.xlsx file to your instructor, close the workbook, then close Excel.

Independent Challenge 2

As the Director of Finances at LPR Business Services, you need to review the US monthly billings for the regions and industries the company serves. With two months of data in a workbook, you will create formatted monthly worksheets with subtotals for each region. The reports will be distributed to the regional managers.

a. Start Excel, open IL_EX_6-6.xlsx from the location where you store your Data Files, then save it as **IL_EX_6_BusinessServices**.

b. Group the US January and US February worksheets.

c. With the worksheets grouped, add a row at the top of the worksheet with the title **LPR Business Services** merged and centered across columns A through G.

d. Format the title in row 1 using the Title cell style. Format the column headings in row 2 using the Heading 3 cell style. Format the worksheet data with the font color Blue, Accent 1, Darker 50% (the fifth color from the left in the last row of theme colors).

e. Ungroup the worksheets. Arrange the worksheets as necessary to verify that both have the same title row and worksheet formatting. When you are finished, hide any unnecessary instances of the workbook.

f. On the US January worksheet, sort the data in A to Z order on the region field.

g. On this sheet, create subtotals for the billed amount and balance for each region. (*Hint:* In the Subtotals dialog box, select Region in the At each change in list and add subtotals to both the Billed Amount and Balance fields.) Widen column G to fully display the balance totals.

h. Remove the page break from the US January worksheet. (*Hint:* Use Page Break Preview to drag the blue page break line to the bottom of the worksheet data.)

i. Inspect the workbook and remove all document properties and personal information. Add the keywords, or tags, **business** and **consulting** to the workbook's summary properties.

j. Freeze the first two rows of the US January worksheet. Scroll down to row 40 to verify the first two rows appear at the top of the screen. Unfreeze the rows.

k. Check the compatibility of the workbook with earlier versions of Excel.

l. Group the two worksheets. With the worksheets grouped, change the custom top margin to .5".

m. With the worksheets grouped, add a header that includes your name in the left section and the sheet name in the center section. (*Hint:* To add a field that displays the current sheet name, click the Sheet Name button in the Header and Footer Elements group of the Header & Footer tab.)

n. Ungroup the worksheets, then prepare the workbook for distribution by marking as final. Save the workbook, close the workbook, reopen the workbook, and enable editing.

o. Use the outline symbols on the US January worksheet to display only the regional totals and the grand total. Compare your US January worksheet to FIGURE 6-23.

p. Save the workbook, submit the workbook to your instructor, then close Excel.

FIGURE 6-23

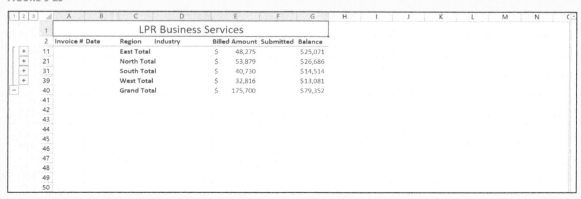

Visual Workshop

Open IL_EX_6-7.xlsx from the location where you store your Data Files, then save it as **IL_EX_6_BusinessCommunications**. Use the skills you learned in this module to complete the worksheet so it looks like the one shown in FIGURE 6-24. The text in cell A6 is a hyperlink to the Support_EX_6-8.xlsx workbook in the location where you store your Data Files. (*Hint:* You will first need to add columns and formulas to calculate each quarter's total; you can then group the worksheets and use the outline symbols to display only the necessary information.) Resize columns as necessary, and adjust merged and centered data to include any new columns. Enter your name in the center footer section, save the workbook, submit your work to your instructor as directed, close the workbook, then close Excel.

FIGURE 6-24

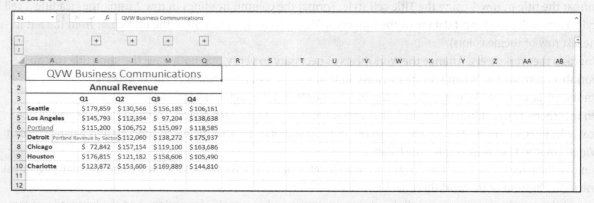

Working with Images and Integrating with Other Programs

CASE ▶ Ellie Schwartz, the vice president of finance, is researching the possible purchase of Tech Career Services (TCS), a small company specializing in technology career placements. Ellie needs to review the organization's files and develop a presentation on the feasibility of acquisition. To create the necessary documents, she asks you to create data exchanges between Excel and other programs.

Module Objectives

After completing this module, you will be able to:

- Plan a data exchange
- Import a text file
- Import data from another workbook
- Import a database table

- Link worksheet data to a Word document
- Link an Excel chart to a PowerPoint slide
- Import Excel data into Access
- Insert a graphic file in a worksheet

Files You Will Need

Support_EX_7-1.txt	Support_EX_7-8.txt	Support_EX_7-15.xlsx
Support_EX_7-2.xlsx	Support_EX_7-9.xlsx	Support_EX_7-16.txt
Support_EX_7-3.accdb	Support_EX_7-10.accdb	Support_EX_7-17.accdb
IL_EX_7-4.docx	IL_EX_7-11.docx	Support_EX_7-18.jpg
IL_EX_7-5.pptx	IL_EX_7-12.pptx	Support_EX_7-19.txt
Support_EX_7-6.xlsx	Support_EX_7-13.xlsx	IL_EX_7-20.xlsx
Support_EX_7-7.jpg	Support_EX_7-14.jpg	IL_EX_7-21.pptx

Plan a Data Exchange

Learning
Outcomes
• Plan a data
exchange between
Microsoft 365 apps
• Develop an
understanding of
data exchange
vocabulary

Because the tools available in Microsoft 365 apps are designed to be compatible, exchanging data between Excel and other Microsoft 365 apps is easy. The first step in each data exchange involves planning what you want to accomplish. **CASE** *Ellie asks you to use the following guidelines to plan data exchanges between Excel and other apps to support her business analysis of Tech Career Services.*

DETAILS

To plan an exchange of data:

- ### Identify the data you want to exchange, its file type, and, if possible, the app used to create it

  Whether the data you want to exchange is a graphics file, database file, worksheet, or simply a text file, it is important to identify its **source program** (the program used to create the data you are linking or embedding) and file type. Once you identify the source program, you can determine options for exchanging the data with Excel. Ellie needs to analyze a text file containing the TCS revenue data. A file that contains data but no formatting is sometimes called an **ASCII file** or a **text file**.

- ### Determine the app with which you want to exchange data

  Besides knowing which program created the data you want to exchange, you must also identify the program that will receive the data, called the **destination program**. This determines the procedure you use to perform the exchange. Ellie received a database table created with the Access database app. You decide to import the database file into Excel so Ellie can analyze it using Excel tools.

- ### Determine the method of your data exchange

  In this module, you use queries to import data into an Excel workbook. A **query** is a request for information from a data source. You can use Excel's Get & Transform tools to import data from other sources. Get & Transform creates a dynamic connection between an Excel workbook and a data source. After connecting to a data source, you can use the **Power Query** tool, which is a BI, or Business Intelligence, tool to query almost any kind of data source in order to transform the data into a more desirable format. For example, you can remove a column, remove a row, split a column, or change a data type in the Query Editor before you manipulate the data in the worksheet window. FIGURE 7-1 shows data to be imported in the Power Query Editor. You may have multiple queries in a workbook.

  Windows supports a technology called **object linking and embedding (OLE)**, which lets you share information among the Microsoft 365 apps, copying from a source file and pasting, embedding, or linking into a destination file. The data to be exchanged, called an **object**, may consist of text, a worksheet, or any other type of data. You can copy Excel data and paste it in other applications using OLE. The copied data can be linked or embedded in the destination file. When you **embed**, you simply insert a copy of the original object into the destination document; you can later, if necessary, edit this embedded data separately from the source document. You **link** when you want the information you insert to be updated automatically if the data in the source document changes. FIGURE 7-2 shows an Excel chart that is linked to a PowerPoint slide. You will use object linking when pasting Excel data in other applications so any changes in the Excel data will be updated in the destination files.

FIGURE 7-1: Data to be imported in the Power Query Editor

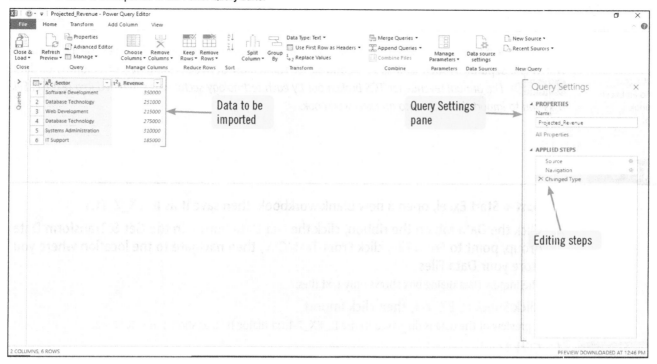

FIGURE 7-2: Excel chart linked to a PowerPoint slide

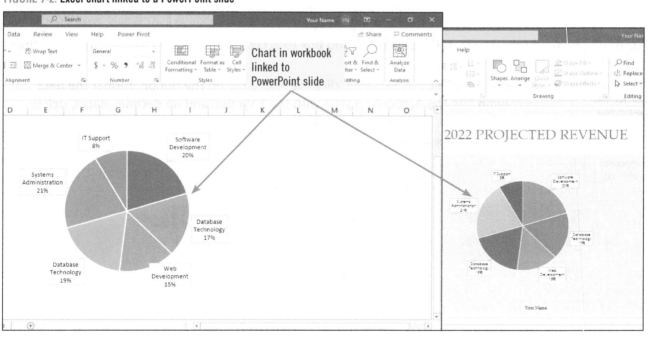

Import a Text File

Learning
Outcomes
• Import a text
  file into an Excel
  workbook
• Format imported
  data

You can import text data into Excel and save the imported data in Excel format. Text files use a **delimiter**, which is a separator, such as a space, comma, or semicolon between elements, or columns of data.
CASE ▶ *The annual revenue for TCS broken out by each technology sector was submitted in a text file. Ellie asks you to import that data into an Excel workbook.*

STEPS

1. **sam** ⬇ **Start Excel, open a new blank workbook, then save it as** IL_EX_7_TCS

2. **Click the** Data tab **on the ribbon, click the** Get Data button **in the Get & Transform Data group, point to** From File, **click** From Text/CSV, **then navigate to the location where you store your Data Files**

   The Import Data dialog box shows only text files.

3. **Click** Support_EX_7-1, **then click** Import

   A preview of the data is displayed in the IL_EX_7-1.txt dialog box, as shown in FIGURE 7-3.

QUICK TIP
Clicking Transform
Data in the
Support_EX_7-1.txt
dialog box opens the
Power Query Editor
and allows you to
edit the data.

4. **Click** Load

   The data appears in table format on a new sheet in the workbook. The Queries & Connections pane opens on the right with the Queries tab showing the file name and the number of rows loaded into the worksheet. Because text editors do not have spell-checking functionality, text files are more likely to contain spelling errors.

5. **Close the Queries & Connections pane, click the** Review tab **on the ribbon, then click the** Spelling button **in the Proofing group**

6. **Click** Change **in the Spelling dialog box to accept the correction for** Development, **then click** OK

QUICK TIP
A Comma Separated
Values, CSV, file is
a text file that uses
commas to separate
data. CSV files have
the extension .csv
and are imported
using the same
steps as importing
text files with .txt
extensions.

7. **Rename the sheet** TCS Revenue, **click the** Home tab **on the ribbon, format the data in column B in the Accounting style with the $ symbol and no decimal places, delete** Sheet1, **click cell A1, then save your work**

   FIGURE 7-4 shows the worksheet with the data you imported into Excel.

FIGURE 7-3: **Preview of data from text file**

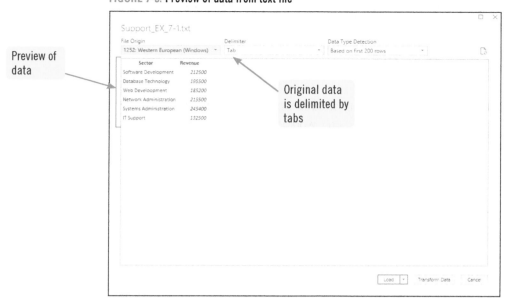

Preview of
data

Original data
is delimited by
tabs

FIGURE 7-4: **Worksheet with imported and formatted text file data**

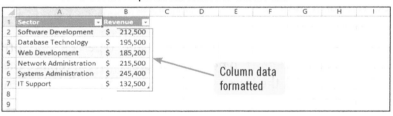

Column data
formatted

Importing text files using the Text Import Wizard

Another way to import a text file into Excel is to use the Text Import Wizard. Click the File tab, click Open, then navigate to the location where you store your Data Files. By default, the Open dialog box displays only Excel files. To import a text file, you need to change your view so you see the file you want to open. To do this, click All Excel Files, click Text Files, click the name of the desired text file, then click Open. The Text Import Wizard opens, where you can complete the import by completing each step of the Wizard.

Import Data from Another Workbook

You can import worksheet data from another workbook into Excel. If you use the Get & Transform tool, any changes you later make in the source workbook are updated when you refresh the destination workbook. **CASE** > *The human resources office at TCS has provided an Excel file listing the employees and their positions. You will import that information into the workbook containing the revenue information.*

STEPS

1. **Open the workbook** Support_EX_7-2 **from the location where you store your Data Files, then save it as** IL_EX_7_Staff

2. **Activate the** IL_EX_7_TCS **workbook, click the** Data tab **on the ribbon, click the** Get Data **button in the Get & Transform Data group, point to** From File, **click** From Workbook, **then navigate to the location where you store your Data Files**

3. **Click** IL_EX_7_Staff, **then click** Import
   The Navigator dialog box opens.

4. **Click** Sheet1 **in the Navigator dialog box**
   The data in Sheet1 is displayed in the preview area on the right side of the dialog box, as shown in FIGURE 7-5.

5. **Click** Transform Data
   The Query Settings pane opens.

6. **Double-click** Sheet1 **in the Query Settings pane, type** TCS Staff, **press** ENTER, **double-click the heading** Column1, **type** Position, **press** ENTER, **replace the** Column2 **heading with** Employee, **click the** Home tab **if necessary, then click the** Close & Load button **in the Close group**

7. **Close the Queries & Connections pane**

8. **Activate the** IL_EX_7_Staff workbook, **change Ashley McFadden's name in cell** B5 **to** Ashley Elwell, **then save and close the** IL_EX_7_Staff **workbook**

9. **In the** IL_EX_7_TCS workbook **click the** Data tab, **click the** Refresh All button **in the Queries & Connections group, then save your work**
   FIGURE 7-6 shows the worksheet with the updated staff data.

FIGURE 7-5: Preview of worksheet data in dialog box

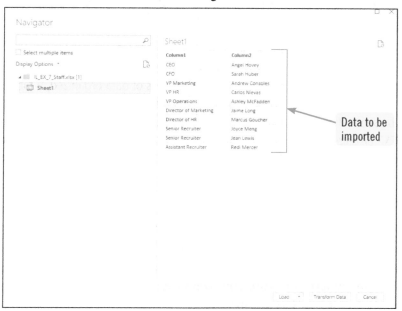

FIGURE 7-6: Refreshed and updated worksheet data

Converting text to columns

You can convert text into columns if, for example, you want to split a column of first and last names into two separate columns. To do so, select the range containing the names, click the Data tab on the ribbon, click the Text to Columns button in the Data Tools group, click the Space check box as the delimiter in the second step of the Convert Text to Columns Wizard dialog box, then click Finish.

Excel

Import a Database Table

You can import data from database tables into Excel. A **database table** is a set of data organized using columns and rows, which is created in a database program. A **database program** is an application, such as Microsoft Access, that lets you manage large amounts of data organized in tables. To import data from an Access table into Excel you will use the Get & Transform tool, so that any changes in the Access database can be seen when the workbook is refreshed. **CASE** ▶ *Ellie received a database table in Access containing TCS's projected revenue for the year ahead. She asks you to import this table into the Excel workbook containing the TCS revenue and staff data. The data has a column that needs to be removed and Ellie would like you to transform the data before it is imported.*

STEPS

1. **Click the Data tab on the ribbon, click the Get Data button in the Get & Transform Data group, point to From Database, click From Microsoft Access Database, then navigate to the location where you store your Data Files**

2. **Click Support_EX_7-3, then click Import**
   The Navigator dialog box opens, showing the Access file and the Projected Revenue table on the left and a preview window on the right.

3. **Click Projected Revenue in the Navigator dialog box**
   The data in the Projected Revenue table is displayed in the preview area, as shown in FIGURE 7-7.

4. **Click Transform Data, then in the Power Query Editor with the ID column selected click the Remove Columns button in the Manage Columns group on the Home tab**
   The Power Query Editor allows you to edit data before importing it into Excel. In the Power Query Editor's Query Settings pane on the right, the editing steps are listed in the Applied Steps area.

5. **Click the Close & Load button in the Close group**
   The Access data is imported into the worksheet as a table, and the Queries & Connections pane confirms that six rows were loaded using the Projected Revenue query.

6. **Format the data in column B in the Accounting format and no decimal places**
   Your formatted worksheet should match FIGURE 7-8.

7. **Change the sheet name to TCS Projected Revenue**

8. **Click the TCS Revenue worksheet, hold SHIFT, click the TCS Projected Revenue worksheet, release SHIFT, click the Insert tab on the ribbon, click the Text button, click the Header & Footer button, enter your name in the center header section, click any cell on the worksheet, click the Normal button ▦ in the status bar, press CTRL+HOME, right-click any worksheet, then click Ungroup Sheets**

9. **Save your work**

FIGURE 7-7: **Preview of Access data**

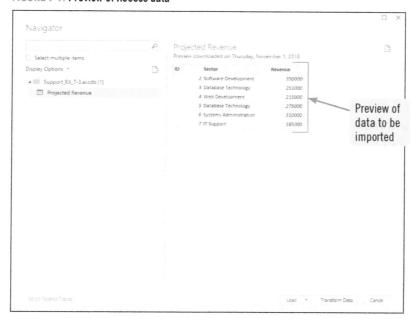

FIGURE 7-8: **Formatted worksheet containing imported data**

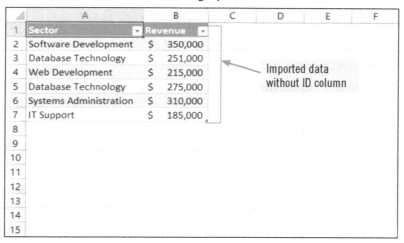

Link Worksheet Data to a Word Document

When you link worksheet data to a Word document, the link contains a connection to the workbook so that any changes you make to the workbook are reflected in the linked object. **CASE** ▶ *Ellie wants to update the CEO of JCL on the project status. She asks you to prepare a Word memo that includes the projected revenue workbook data. To ensure that any workbook changes will be reflected in the memo, you decide to link the workbook data.*

STEPS

1. **Open a File Explorer window, navigate to the location where you store your Data Files, then double-click the Word document** IL_EX_7-4

   Microsoft Word starts, and the memo opens in Word.

2. **Click the** File tab **on the ribbon, click** Save As, **navigate to the location where you store your Data Files, replace the text in the File name text box with** IL_EX_7_TCSMemo, **then click** Save

3. **Activate the** IL_EX_7_TCS workbook, **then copy the data in the range** A1:B7 **on the** TCS Projected Revenue sheet

   The workbook data is copied to the Clipboard.

4. **Activate the** Word memo, **then press** CTRL+END

   The insertion point moves to the end of the memo.

5. **Click the** Home tab **on the ribbon if necessary, click the** Paste arrow **in the Clipboard group, then click the** Link & Use Destination Styles button 📋 **under Paste Options**

6. **If the revenue data and $ sign wrap to two lines, point to the** right edge of the table **until the** column resize pointer ✛ **appears, then drag the** right edge **to the right, so your screen matches** FIGURE 7-9

7. **Activate the** IL_EX_7_TCS workbook, **on the TCS Projected Revenue worksheet click cell** B2, **type** 300,000, **then click the** Enter button ✓ **on the Formula Bar**

8. **Activate the** IL_EX_7_TCSMemo document, **select the** table, **right-click the** table, **then click** Update Link

   The table data is updated to reflect the change in the linked Excel workbook, as shown in FIGURE 7-10.

9. **Click the** Insert tab **on the ribbon, click the** Header button **in the Header & Footer group, click** Edit Header, **type your name in the Header area, click the** Close Header and Footer button **in the Close group, save the Word file, close the Word document, then close Word**

FIGURE 7-9: Memo with linked worksheet data

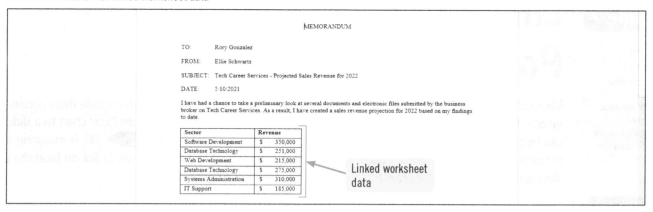

FIGURE 7-10: Memo with updated table data

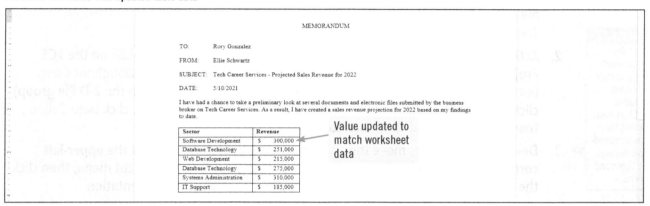

Managing and breaking links

When you open a Word document containing linked data, you are asked if you want to update the linked data. You can manage the updating of links by clicking the File tab on the ribbon, clicking Info, then clicking Edit Links to Files in the right pane. The Links dialog box opens, allowing you to change a link's update method from the default setting of automatic to manual. The Links dialog box also allows you to change the link source, permanently break a link, open the source file, or manually update a link. If you send your linked files to another user, the links will be broken because the linked file path references the local computer where you inserted the links. Because the file path will not be valid on the recipient user's device, the links will no longer be updated when the user opens the destination document. To correct this, recipients who have both the destination and source documents can use the Links dialog box to change the link's source in the destination document to their own device. Then, the links will be automatically updated when they open the destination document in the future. If you are managing links in an Excel workbook you can click the Data tab, then click the Edit Links button in the Queries & Connections group to open the Edit Links dialog box.

Link an Excel Chart to a PowerPoint Slide

Learning Outcomes
- Insert a linked chart in a PowerPoint slide
- Configure automatic links in a PowerPoint file

Microsoft PowerPoint is a **presentation graphics** program that you can use to create slide show presentations. PowerPoint slides can include a mix of text, data, and graphics. Adding an Excel chart to a slide can help to illustrate data and give your presentation more visual appeal. **CASE** ▸ *Ellie is preparing a presentation for JCL management about the potential acquisition of TCS. She asks you to link an Excel chart illustrating the 2022 revenue projection for TCS to one of her PowerPoint slides.*

STEPS

1. **Click the** Start button **on the Windows taskbar, begin typing** PowerPoint **in the Search box, click** PowerPoint **in the list that opens, click** Open **on the left side of the Open pane, navigate to where you store your Data Files, double-click** IL_EX_7-5, **then save the file as** IL_EX_7_ManagementPresentation
   The presentation appears in Normal view, as shown in FIGURE 7-11.

> **TROUBLE**
> If you don't see Copy on the shortcut menu, you may have clicked the Plot area rather than the Chart area. Right-clicking the white area surrounding the pie displays the Copy command on the menu.

2. **Activate the** IL_EX_7_TCS **workbook, select the data in the range** A2:B7 **on the TCS Projected Revenue sheet, click the** Insert tab, **click the** Insert Pie or Doughnut Chart **button** 🥧▾ **in the Charts group, click the** Pie chart **(the first chart in the 2-D Pie group), click the** Chart Elements button ⊞, **click the** Data Labels arrow ▸, **click** Data Callout, **then click the** Legend check box **to deselect it**

3. **Delete the** chart title, **move the** chart **until its upper-left corner is at the upper-left corner of cell D1, right-click the** Chart Area, **click** Copy **on the shortcut menu, then click the** PowerPoint program button **on the taskbar to display the presentation**

> **QUICK TIP**
> You can click the Use Destination Theme & Embed workbook button 📋 to place a copy of, or embed, the chart object. You can edit the embedded object by double-clicking it. You can also embed a chart in PowerPoint by clicking the Insert tab, clicking the Object button 📄 in the Text group, clicking the Create from file option button, browsing to the desired file, then clicking OK.

4. **Click** Slide 2 **in the Thumbnails pane, right-click** Slide 2 **in the Slide pane, then click the** Use Destination Theme & Link Data button 📋 **in the Paste Options group**
   A pie chart illustrating the projected revenue appears in the slide. The chart matches the colors and fonts in the presentation that is the destination document.

5. **Click the** File tab **on the ribbon, click** Info, **click** Edit Links to Files **at the bottom of the right pane, in the Links dialog box click the** Automatic Update check box **to add a checkmark, click** Close **in the dialog box, click the** Back button ⬅ **at the top of the left pane, then in the presentation click the** Save button 💾 **on the Quick Access Toolbar**
   The default setting for updating links in a PowerPoint file is Manual, but you have changed it so that the links will be automatically updated if the Excel file changes.

6. **Switch to** Excel, **type** 125,000 **in cell B7, click the** Enter button ✓ **on the Formula bar, then click the** PowerPoint program button **on the taskbar to display the presentation**
   The IT Support percentage decreases from 12% to 8%, reflecting the change in the Excel data.

7. **Click the** Slide Show button 🖵 **on the status bar**
   Slide Show view shows the slide full screen, the way the audience will see it, as shown in FIGURE 7-12.

8. **Press** ESC **to return to Normal view, with** Slide 2 **selected click the** Insert tab **on the ribbon, click the** Header & Footer button **in the Text group, add a checkmark in the** Footer check box, **type your name in the** Footer text box, **click** Apply to All, **save and close the presentation, then close PowerPoint**

FIGURE 7-11: **Presentation in Normal view**

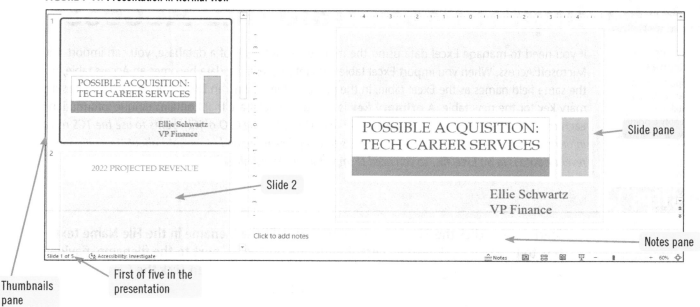

Thumbnails pane

First of five in the presentation

Slide pane

Slide 2

Notes pane

FIGURE 7-12: **Completed slide**

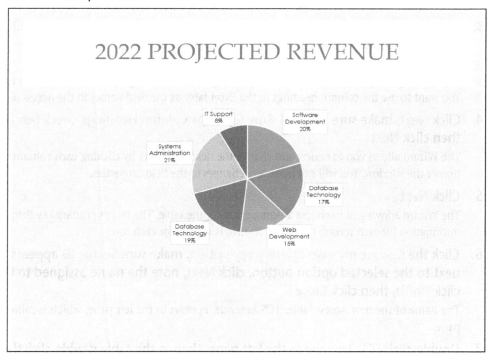

Excel

Import Excel Data into Access

Learning
Outcomes
• Import Excel data
  into an Access
  database
• Identify a primary
  key for a database

If you need to manage Excel data using the more extensive tools of a database, you can import it into Microsoft Access. When you import Excel table data into Access, the data becomes an Access table, using the same field names as the Excel table. In the process of importing an Excel table, Access specifies a primary key for the new table. A **primary key** is a field in a database that contains unique information for each record, or set of information. **CASE** ▶ *Rory Gonzales, the CEO of JCL, wants to use the TCS revenue information in an Access database, where he is tracking inventory and other data about the company. This revenue data is in an Excel file, so you need to import it into Microsoft Access.*

STEPS

1. **Start** Access, **click the** Blank database button, **edit the filename in the File Name text box to** IL_EX_7_TCSRevenue, **click the** Browse button 🖿 **next to the filename, navigate to where you store your Data Files, click** OK, **click** Create, **then click the** Close Table1 button ⊠ **on the Table1 tab (Do not close Access)**

   The IL_EX_7_Revenue database is created, and Table1 is removed from the database.

2. **Click the** External Data tab **on the ribbon, click the** New Data Source button **in the** Import & Link group, **click** From File, **then click** Excel

   The Get External Data - Excel Spreadsheet dialog box opens, as shown in FIGURE 7-13. This dialog box allows you to specify how you want the data to be stored in Access.

3. **Click** Browse, **navigate to where you store your Data Files, click** Support_EX_7-6, **click** Open, **if necessary click the** Import the source data into a new table in the current database. option button, **then click** OK

   The first Import Spreadsheet Wizard dialog box opens, with a sample of the sheet data in the lower section. You want to use the column headings in the Excel table as the field names in the Access database.

4. **Click** Next, **make sure the** First Row Contains Column Headings check box **is selected, then click** Next

   The Wizard allows you to review and change the field properties by clicking each column in the lower section of the window. You will not make any changes to the field properties.

5. **Click** Next

   The Wizard allows you to choose a primary key for the table. The table's primary key field contains unique information for each record; the Sector ID field is unique for each row.

QUICK TIP
Specifying a primary
key allows you to
retrieve data more
quickly in the future.

6. **Click the** Choose my own primary key option, **make sure** Sector ID **appears in the box next to the selected option button, click** Next, **note the name assigned to the new table, click** Finish, **then click** Close

   The name of the new Access table, TCS Revenue, appears in the left pane, which is called the Navigation pane.

7. **Double-click** TCS Revenue **in the left pane, then in the table double-click the** border **between the** Sector **and the** Revenue **column headings**

   The Sector column widens. The Access table is shown in FIGURE 7-14.

8. **Click in the last** row **of the table, in the Sector ID column type** 9999, **press TAB, then type your name in the Sector column**

9. **Click the** Save button 🖫 **on the Quick Access Toolbar, close the file, then close Access**

FIGURE 7-13: **Get External Data - Excel Spreadsheet dialog box**

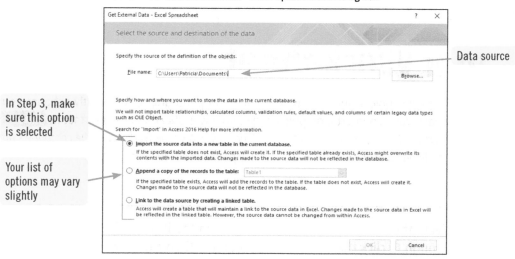

FIGURE 7-13: **Get External Data - Excel Spreadsheet dialog box**

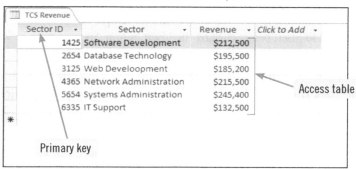

FIGURE 7-14: **Completed Access table with data imported from Excel**

Adding SmartArt graphics

SmartArt graphics provide another way to visually communicate information on a worksheet. Each SmartArt type communicates a kind of information or relationship, such as a list, process, or hierarchy. Each type has various layouts you can choose. To insert a SmartArt graphic into a worksheet, click the Insert tab, then click the Insert a SmartArt Graphic button 🔲 in the Illustrations group. In the Choose a SmartArt Graphic dialog box, choose from eight SmartArt types: List, Process, Cycle, Hierarchy, Relationship, Matrix, Pyramid, and Picture. There is also a link for SmartArt available on Office.com. The dialog box describes the type of information that is appropriate for each selected layout. After you choose a layout and click OK, a SmartArt object appears on your worksheet. FIGURE 7-15 shows examples of SmartArt graphics. You can enter text directly in the placeholders or use the SmartArt text pane. If this pane is in your way, you can close it by clicking the Close button in the upper-right corner of the pane. As you enter text, the font is automatically resized to fit the graphic. You can change the layout by selecting the SmartArt, then clicking a different layout in the Layouts group on the SmartArt Design tab.

FIGURE 7-15: **Examples of SmartArt graphics**

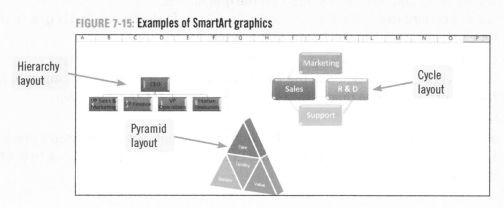

Excel

Insert a Graphic File in a Worksheet

Learning Outcomes
- Insert an image into an Excel worksheet
- Add a style to an image

Adding a graphic object, such as a drawing, logo, or photograph, can greatly enhance your worksheet's visual impact. You can insert a graphic image into a worksheet and then format it. **CASE** *Ellie wants you to insert the JCL logo at the top of the TCS Projected Revenue worksheet. The company's graphic designer created the image and saved it in JPG (commonly pronounced "jay-peg") format.*

STEPS

QUICK TIP
You can insert a screenshot of an open window on your worksheet by clicking the Insert tab, clicking the Take a Screenshot button in the Illustrations group, then clicking one of the windows in the gallery. You can also click the Screen Clipping button in the gallery to select and paste an area from an open window.

1. **Activate the** TCS Projected Revenue sheet **in the** IL_EX_7_TCS **workbook, select rows 1 through 6, click the** Home tab **if necessary, then click the** Insert button **in the Cells group**

   Six blank rows appear at the top of the worksheet, leaving space to insert column headings for the workbook data and the logo. If you need to insert multiple rows or columns, it saves time to select the number you need to insert before clicking the Insert button. Six rows were inserted because you selected six rows before clicking the button.

2. **Click cell A6, enter** TCS Projected Revenue, **click the** Enter button ☑ **on the Formula bar, click the** Cell Styles button **in the Styles group, then click** Title

3. **Click cell A1, click the** Insert tab **on the ribbon, click the** Illustrations button **in the Illustrations group, click the** Pictures button, **then click** This Device

   The Insert Picture dialog box opens. Because you specified that you want to insert a picture, the dialog box displays only files that contain graphics file extensions, such as .jpg.

4. **Navigate to where you store your Data Files if necessary, click** Support_EX_7-7, **then click** Insert

   Excel inserts the image and displays the Picture Format tab. The small circles around the picture's edge are sizing handles. Sizing handles appear when a picture is selected; you use them to change the size of a picture.

QUICK TIP
To correct a selected image, click the Corrections button in the Adjust group on the Picture Format tab, then click an option in the Sharpen/Soften or Brightness/Contrast section.

5. **Position the** pointer **over the** sizing handle **in the logo's lower-right corner until the pointer becomes** ⬉**, then drag the** sizing handle **up and to the left so that the logo's outline fits within rows 1 through 5**

   Compare your screen to FIGURE 7-16.

6. **With the image selected, click the** More button ▼ **in the Picture Styles group, point to several styles and observe the effect on the graphic, click the** Bevel Rectangle style **(the last in the third row), click the** Picture Border button **in the Picture Styles group, then click** Green, Accent 6 **in the Theme Colors group**

QUICK TIP
You can copy the formatting of a selected image by clicking the Format Painter button in the Clipboard group of the Home tab, then clicking the image to apply the formatting.

7. **Click the** Picture Effects button **in the Picture Styles group, click** Glow, **click** More Glow Colors, **click** Green, Accent 6 **in the Theme Colors group, resize the logo again to fit it in rows 1 through 5, then drag it to center it over the data in columns A and B**

   Compare your worksheet to FIGURE 7-17.

8. **sam̃ ⬆ Save the workbook, change the worksheet orientation to landscape, preview the worksheet, close the workbook, close Excel, then submit the workbook to your instructor**

FIGURE 7-16: **Resized logo**

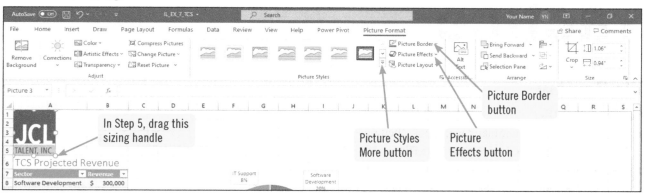

FIGURE 7-17: **Worksheet with formatted picture**

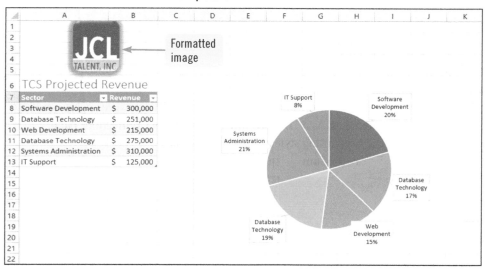

Working with SmartArt graphics

You can add shapes to a SmartArt graphic by selecting the position where the shape will appear, clicking the Add Shape arrow in the Create Graphic group of the SmartArt Design tab, then selecting the desired position. Also in the Create Graphic group are the Promote and Demote buttons, which you can use to increase or decrease the level of a selected shape. The SmartArt Design tab lets you choose color schemes and styles for your SmartArt. You can add shape styles, fills, outlines, and other shape effects to SmartArt graphics using choices on the Format tab. Clicking the Shape Fill button in the Shape Styles group of this tab, then clicking Picture inserts a picture in a shape. You can also add fills, outlines, and other effects to text using this tab. You can change the size of a SmartArt shape by selecting the shape, then clicking the Larger button or the Smaller button in the Shapes group on the Format tab. You can resize an entire SmartArt graphic by clicking it and dragging a resizing handle. To resize a graphic proportionally, drag any corner sizing handle. If you drag an edge sizing handle instead, the graphic will be resized nonproportionally. You can align multiple SmartArt graphics at once by selecting them, clicking Align in the Arrange group on the Shape Format tab, then selecting the alignment option. (This also aligns other objects on a worksheet.)

Practice

Skills Review

1. Import a text file.

a. Start Excel, create a new blank workbook, then save the workbook in the location where you store your Data Files as **IL_EX_7_OLP**.

b. Use the Get & Transform tool to import the text file Support_EX_7-8 from the location where you store your Data Files. The data is delimited using tabs.

c. Format the data in column B using the Accounting style and no decimal places.

d. Rename the sheet tab **May**, then delete Sheet1.

e. Add a table total row to show the total expenses, as shown in FIGURE 7-18.

f. Save the workbook.

FIGURE 7-18

FIGURE 7-18

	A	B	C
1	Category	Expenses	
2	Compensation	$ 323,060	
3	Facility	$ 317,638	
4	Supplies	$ 251,461	
5	Equipment	$ 271,334	
6	**Total**	**$ 1,163,493**	
7			
8			

2. Import data from another workbook.

a. Use the Get & Transform tool to import the data on the April Expenses sheet in the Excel file Support_EX_7-9 from the location where you store your Data Files.

b. In the Power Query Editor, change the column labels to **Category** and **Expenses**. Close and load the edits.

c. Rename the sheet with the imported data **April**, then close the Queries & Connections pane.

d. Format the expense data using the Accounting style and no decimal places.

e. Add a total row to the table to display the sum of the expense amounts.

f. Save the workbook.

3. Import a database table.

a. Use the Get & Transform tool to import the data on the Expenses table in the Access Data File Support_EX_7-10 from the location where you store your Data Files.

b. Rename the sheet with the imported data **May Details**.

c. Format the amount data in column D using the Accounting style and no decimal places.

d. Add a total row to the table to display the sum of the expense amounts. Autofit column D if necessary to display all the data.

e. Scroll down to see the entire table, save the workbook, then compare your screen to FIGURE 7-19.

FIGURE 7-19

	A	B	C	D	E
1	Category	Item	Month	Amount	
2	Compensation	Benefits	May	$ 50,000	
3	Compensation	Bonuses	May	$ 40,000	
4	Compensation	Commissions	May	$ 35,000	
5	Compensation	Conferences	May	$ 42,000	
6	Compensation	Promotions	May	$ 65,048	
7	Compensation	Payroll Taxes	May	$ 18,954	
8	Compensation	Salaries	May	$ 63,514	
9	Compensation	Training	May	$ 8,544	
10	Facility	Lease	May	$ 42,184	
11	Facility	Maintenance	May	$ 63,214	
12	Facility	Other	May	$ 11,478	
13	Facility	Rent	May	$ 80,214	
14	Facility	Telephone	May	$ 62,584	
15	Facility	Utilities	May	$ 57,964	
16	Supplies	Food	May	$ 61,775	
17	Supplies	Computer	May	$ 43,217	
18	Supplies	General Office	May	$ 47,854	
19	Supplies	Other	May	$ 56,741	
20	Supplies	Outside Services	May	$ 41,874	
21	Equipment	Computer	May	$ 49,874	
22	Equipment	Other	May	$ 43,547	
23	Equipment	Cash Registers	May	$ 55,987	
24	Equipment	Software	May	$ 63,147	
25	Equipment	Telecommunications	May	$ 58,779	
26	**Total**			**$1,163,493**	

Working with Images and Integrating with Other Programs

4. Link worksheet data to a Word document.

  a. With the May Details sheet active, copy the range A1:D26.

  b. Open a File Explorer window, then double-click the Word file IL_EX_7-11 from the location where you store your Data Files. When the file opens in Word, save it as **IL_EX_7_OLPMemo**.

  c. At the end of the memo body, use the Paste menu to paste the copied worksheet data by linking it and using the destination styles. Widen the Amount column if necessary to display the values on one line.

  d. Note that the first compensation value in the memo is currently $50,000. Switch to Excel, activate the May Details worksheet in the IL_EX_7_OLP workbook, press ESC to deactivate the copied range, then change the value in cell D2 to **$35,000**.

  e. Activate the IL_EX_7_OLPMemo document in Word, update the linked data, then verify that the first compensation value has changed to $35,000, as shown in FIGURE 7-20. (*Hint:* To update the link, right-click the table in the memo, then click Update Link.)

  f. Use a tool on the Insert tab of the ribbon to edit the header, enter your name in the header, save your changes to the IL_EX_7_OLPMemo document, preview the memo, close the document, then close Word.

FIGURE 7-20

Category	Item	Month	Amount
Compensation	Benefits	May	$ 35,000
Compensation	Bonuses	May	$ 40,000
Compensation	Commissions	May	$ 35,000
Compensation	Conferences	May	$ 42,000
Compensation	Promotions	May	$ 65,048
Compensation	Payroll Taxes	May	$ 18,954
Compensation	Salaries	May	$ 63,514
Compensation	Training	May	$ 8,544
Facility	Lease	May	$ 42,184
Facility	Maintenance	May	$ 63,214
Facility	Other	May	$ 11,478
Facility	Rent	May	$ 80,214
Facility	Telephone	May	$ 62,584
Facility	Utilities	May	$ 57,964
Supplies	Food	May	$ 61,775
Supplies	Computer	May	$ 43,217
Supplies	General Office	May	$ 47,854
Supplies	Other	May	$ 56,741
Supplies	Outside Services	May	$ 41,874
Equipment	Computer	May	$ 49,874
Equipment	Other	May	$ 43,547
Equipment	Cash Registers	May	$ 55,987
Equipment	Software	May	$ 63,147
Equipment	Telecommunications	May	$ 58,779
Total			$ 1,148,493

5. Link an Excel chart to a PowerPoint slide.

  a. Start PowerPoint, open the presentation IL_EX_7-12 from the location where you store your Data Files, then save it as **IL_EX_7_OLPPresentation**.

  b. Switch to Excel, activate the May worksheet in the IL_EX_7_OLP workbook, then using the data in the range A2:B5, create a 2-D pie chart. Delete the chart title, add data callouts, then delete the chart legend. Move the chart so its upper-left corner is at the upper-left corner of cell D1.

  c. Copy the chart, activate the PowerPoint file, then display Slide 6, May Expenses. (*Hint:* Click slide 6 in the Thumbnails pane.)

  d. Link the copied chart to Slide 6, using the theme of the destination file. Notice that Compensation is currently 28% of total expenses.

Skills Review (continued)

e. Open the Info pane on the File tab, then edit the file's links to automatically update. Return to the presentation.

f. Switch to Excel, then change the compensation amount in cell B2 of the May worksheet to **$500,000**. Notice in the pie chart that Compensation is now 37% of total expenses.

g. Activate the IL_EX_7_OLPPresentation file, then verify the Compensation percentage in the chart on Slide 6 changed to 37%.

h. Enlarge the chart and re-center it if necessary under the title, so it matches FIGURE 7-21.

i. Use a tool on the Insert tab to add a footer containing your name to all of the slides.

j. Save the presentation, close the presentation, then close PowerPoint.

FIGURE 7-21

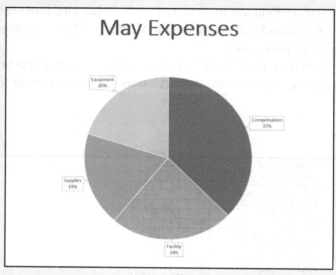

6. **Import Excel data into Access.**

a. Start Access, then create a blank database named **IL_EX_7_RevisedMay** in the location where you store your Data Files. Close Table1.

b. Use the External Data tab to import the Excel table in the Support_EX_7-13 file from the location where you store your Data Files. In the Get External Data dialog box, choose the first option to import the source data into a new Access table. Step through the Import Spreadsheet Wizard, making sure the First Row Contains Column Headings check box is selected, and accepting the default assignment of field names. Identify a primary key by letting Access add one. Accept the default table name, and do not save the import steps.

c. Open the Revised May Expenses table in Access, then compare your screen to FIGURE 7-22.

d. Enter your name in the Category column of row 5 in the table, save the database file, then close Access.

FIGURE 7-22

ID	Category	Expenses	Click to Add
1	Compensation	$312,500	
2	Facility	$307,851	
3	Supplies	$235,487	
4	Equipment	$251,487	
*	(New)		

Skills Review (continued)

7. **Insert a graphic file in a worksheet.**

   a. Activate the April worksheet in the IL_EX_7_OLP file. Select rows 1 through 4, then use a tool on the Home tab of the ribbon to insert four blank rows above row 1 to create space for an image.

   b. In rows 1 through 4, insert the picture file Support_EX_7-14.jpg from the location where you store your Data Files.

   c. Resize and reposition the logo as necessary to make it fit in rows 1 through 4.

   d. Apply the Beveled Matte, White Picture Style, then change the picture border color to Green, Accent 6 in the Theme colors.

   e. Resize the picture to fit the image and the border in the first four rows. Move the picture to center it between columns A and B. Compare your worksheet to FIGURE 7-23.

   f. Group the worksheets, change the orientation of the worksheets to landscape, add your name to the center section of the footer, preview the workbook, ungroup the worksheets, save and close the workbook, then submit the workbook to your instructor.

FIGURE 7-23

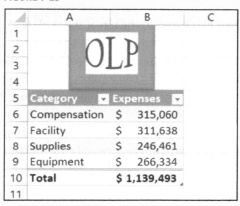

Excel

Independent Challenge 1

You have started a new position managing the respiratory therapy clinic at Riverwalk Medical Center. The previous manager left important data for the first quarter of the year in various text, workbook, and database files. You need to bring the data from all these sources into an Excel workbook, so you can analyze it together.

a. Start Excel, create a new workbook, then save it as **IL_EX_7_RiverwalkQ1** in the location where you store your Data Files.
b. Use the Get & Transform tool to import the data from Sheet1 of the Excel workbook file Support_EX_7-15. Rename the worksheet **Jan**, then delete Sheet1.
c. Format the billing data in column B using the Accounting number format and no decimal places.
d. Use the Get & Transform tool to import the data from the tab delimited text file Support_EX_7-16. Rename the worksheet **Feb**.
e. Format the billing data in column B using the Accounting number format and no decimal places.
f. Use the Get & Transform tool to import the data from the March Billings table in the Access file Support_EX_7-17. Rename the worksheet **Mar**, then close the Queries & Connections pane.
g. Delete column A in the Mar worksheet, then format the Billings data in column B as Accounting with no decimal places.
h. Activate the Jan worksheet. Insert four blank rows at the top of the worksheet.
i. Insert the Support_EX_7-18 image file and resize it to fit in rows 1 through 4.
j. Apply the Center Shadow Rectangle Picture Style (second row, second from the right), then change the picture border color to Green, Accent 6, Darker 50% in the Theme colors. Resize the picture to fit the image and the border in the first four rows. Move the picture so it appears centered above the range A1:C1.
k. Compare your Jan worksheet to **FIGURE 7-24**.
l. Group the worksheets, add the sheet name to the center header section, add your name to the center section of the footer, preview the workbook, ungroup the worksheets, save and close the workbook, then submit the workbook to your instructor.

FIGURE 7-24

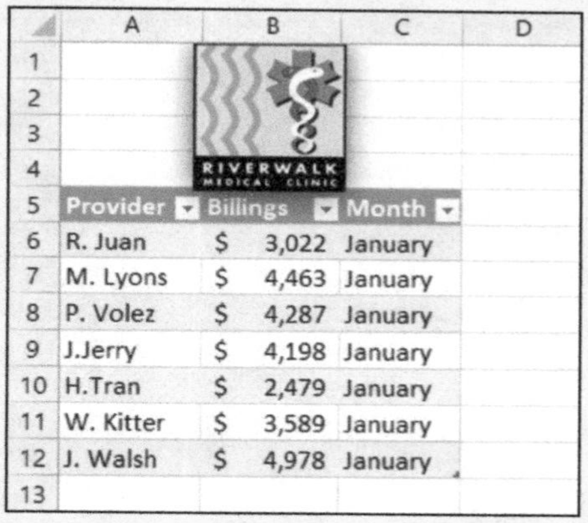

	A	B	C	D
1				
2				
3				
4				
5	Provider	Billings	Month	
6	R. Juan	$ 3,022	January	
7	M. Lyons	$ 4,463	January	
8	P. Volez	$ 4,287	January	
9	J.Jerry	$ 4,198	January	
10	H.Tran	$ 2,479	January	
11	W. Kitter	$ 3,589	January	
12	J. Walsh	$ 4,978	January	
13				

Independent Challenge 2

You are the executive assistant for the CEO of a national credit institution. The CEO has asked for an organizational chart of the company's upper management. The employee data is stored in a text file that you will import into Excel.

a. Start Excel, create a new workbook, then save it as **IL_EX_7_OrgChart** in the location where you store your Data Files.
b. Use the Get & Transform tool to import the data from the Support_EX_7-19 text file.

Independent Challenge 2 (continued)

c. Delete Sheet1, then rename the sheet with the imported data **Hierarchy**.

d. Use the Edit button in the Edit group of the Query tab to open the Power Query Editor, then rename the first column header **Employee** and the second column header **Position**.

e. Click any cell outside the data, then insert a SmartArt graphic, choosing the first Organization Chart in the Hierarchy category. (*Hint:* Click the Insert tab on the ribbon, then click the SmartArt button in the Illustrations group.)

f. Close the Queries & Connections pane, then move the SmartArt graphic to line up the upper-left corner with the upper-left corner of cell C1.

g. Referring to the imported data, enter the employee name, **Seth Werthen**, and the position, **CEO**, in the top shape of the SmartArt graphic, with the name appearing in the first line and the position in the second line. (*Hint:* Press ENTER to move to the next line in a shape.)

h. In the shape on the second level, enter Julie Hadley's information using the same format of name on the first line and position on the second line.

i. In the leftmost box on the third level, enter the information for Justin Phillips using the same format used for the previous shapes.

j. In the middle box on the third level, enter the information for Katelyn Wolff using the same format used for the previous shapes.

k. In the box farthest to the right on the third level, enter the information for Connor Ogah using the same format used for the previous shapes.

l. Add a shape below Justin Phillips, then enter Lucille Fischer's information in the new shape. (*Hint:* You can add a shape below a selected shape by clicking the Add Shape arrow and clicking Add Shape Below.)

m. Add a shape below Katelyn Wolff, then enter Christine Hassan's information in the new shape. Add a shape below Connor Ogah, then enter Huiwei Phillip's information in the new shape.

n. Change the SmartArt style to Subtle Effect.

o. Change the SmartArt colors to Gradient Loop – Accent 6. (*Hint:* Use the Change Colors tool on the SmartArt Design tab.)

p. Resize the SmartArt graphic proportionally to line up the lower-right corner with the lower-right corner of cell J16, then compare your worksheet to FIGURE 7-25.

q. Enter your name in the worksheet footer, change the orientation to landscape, preview the workbook, save and close the workbook, then submit the workbook to your instructor.

FIGURE 7-25

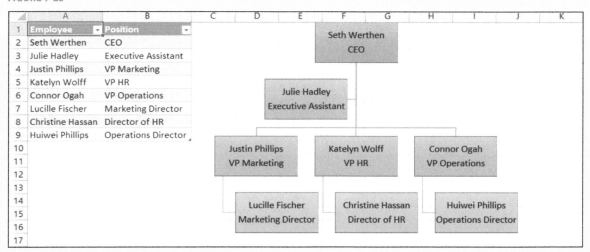

Visual Workshop

Open IL_EX_7-20.xlsx from the location where your Data Files are stored, then save it as **IL_EX_7_Systems**. Start PowerPoint, open the presentation IL_EX_7-21.pptx from the location where your Data Files are stored, then save it as **IL_EX_7_Northern**. Edit the Annual Revenue slide to match FIGURE 7-26 by creating the pie chart in the IL_EX_7_Systems file, showing data labels with the category names and percentages on the outside end of the data series and linking the chart on slide 2 of the IL_EX_7_Northern file. (*Hint:* The chart links to the Excel file and uses the destination theme.) Add a footer of your name to all the slides, save the worksheet and presentation, close the presentation and workbook, then close PowerPoint and Excel. Submit the PowerPoint file to your instructor.

FIGURE 7-26

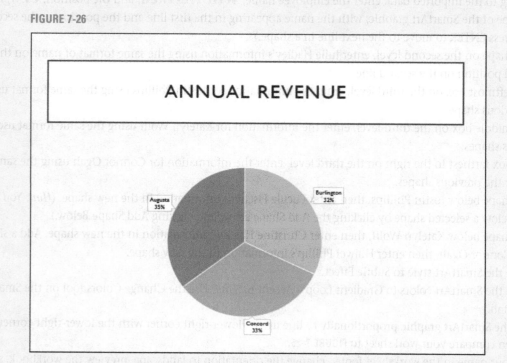

Analyzing Data with PivotTables

CASE ▸ JCL uses PivotTables to analyze revenue data. Ellie Schwartz is preparing for the annual directors' meeting and asks you to analyze revenue in JCL's Northeast offices over the past year. You will create a PivotTable to summarize last year's revenue data by quarter, position, office, and division. You will also illustrate the information using a PivotChart.

Module Objectives

After completing this module, you will be able to:

- Plan and design a PivotTable report
- Create a PivotTable report
- Change a PivotTable's summary function and design
- Filter PivotTable data

- Explore PivotTable Data Relationships
- Create a PivotChart report
- Update a PivotTable report
- Use the GETPIVOTDATA function

Files You Will Need

IL_EX_8-1.xlsx   IL_EX_8-4.xlsx

IL_EX_8-2.xlsx   IL_EX_8-5.xlsx

IL_EX_8-3.xlsx

Plan and Design a PivotTable Report

The PivotTable Report feature lets you summarize large amounts of worksheet data in a compact table format. Then you can freely rearrange, or "pivot," PivotTable rows and columns to explore the relationships within your data. Before you begin creating a PivotTable report (often called a PivotTable), you need to review the data and consider how a PivotTable can best summarize it. **CASE** ➤ *Ellie asks you to design a PivotTable to display JCL's revenue information for its offices in the Northeast. You begin by reviewing guidelines for creating PivotTables.*

DETAILS

Before you create a PivotTable, think about the following guidelines:

- **Review the source data**

  Before you can effectively summarize data in a PivotTable, you need to understand the source data's scope and structure. The source data does not have to be defined as a table, but it should be in a table-like format; that is, it should have column headings and the same type of data in each column, and it should not have any blank rows or columns. To create a meaningful PivotTable, make sure that at least one of the fields has repeated information so that the PivotTable can effectively group it. Also, be sure to include numeric data that the PivotTable can total for each group. The data columns represent categories of data, which are called fields, just as in a table. You are working with revenue information that Ellie received from JCL's Northeastern office managers, shown in FIGURE 8-1. Information is repeated in the Position ID, Division, Office, and Quarter Columns, and numeric information is displayed in the revenue column, so you will be able to summarize this data effectively in a PivotTable.

- **Determine the purpose of the PivotTable**

  The purpose of your PivotTable is to summarize revenue information by quarter across various offices.

- **Identify the fields you want to include**

  You want your PivotTable to summarize the data in the Position ID, Division, Office, Quarter, and Revenue columns, so you need to include those fields in your PivotTable.

- **Determine which field contains the data you want to summarize and which summary function you want to use**

  The JCL offices are organized into divisions, such as Technical, Finance & Accounting, Creative, and Office Support. You want to summarize revenue information by summing that field for each division in an office by quarter. You'll do this by using the Sum function.

- **Decide how you want to arrange the data**

  The PivotTable layout you choose determines the information you want to communicate. Position ID values will appear in the PivotTable columns, office and quarter numbers will appear in rows, and the PivotTable will summarize revenue figures, as shown in FIGURE 8-2.

- **Determine the location of the PivotTable**

  You can place a PivotTable in any worksheet of any workbook. Placing a PivotTable on a separate worksheet makes it easier to locate and prevents you from accidentally overwriting parts of an existing sheet. You decide to create the PivotTable as a new worksheet in the current workbook.

FIGURE 8-1: Revenue data

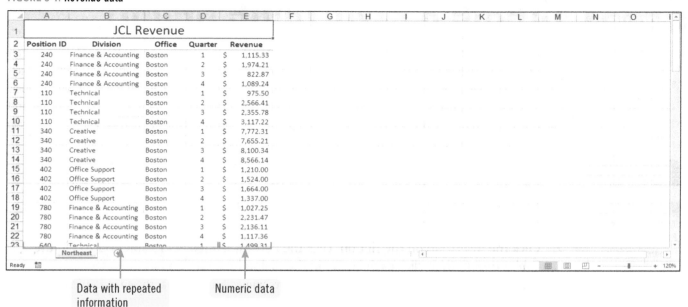

Data with repeated information

Numeric data

Position IDs are column labels

FIGURE 8-2: PivotTable report based on revenue data

Offices and quarters are row labels

PivotTable summarizes revenue figures by position ID, office, and quarter

Create a PivotTable Report

Learning
Outcomes
• Create a
PivotTable
• Move PivotTable
fields to rearrange
data

Once you've planned and designed your PivotTable report, you are ready to create it. Then, you can **populate** it by adding fields to areas in the PivotTable. A PivotTable has four areas: the Report Filter, which is the field by which you want to filter the PivotTable; the Row Labels, which contain the fields whose labels will describe the values in the rows; the Column Labels, which appear above the PivotTable values and describe the columns; and the Values, which summarize the numeric data. **CASE** ➤ *With the planning and design stage complete, you are ready to create a PivotTable that summarizes revenue information.*

STEPS

QUICK TIP

To create a blank PivotTable without reviewing recommended ones, click the PivotTable button in the Tables group, verify your data range or enter an external data source such as a database, specify a PivotTable location, then click OK.

1. **sam** ⬇ **Start Excel, open IL_EX_8-1.xlsx from the location where you store your Data Files, then save it as IL_EX_8_NERevenue**

2. **Click the Insert tab on the ribbon, click the Recommended PivotTables button in the Tables group, then click each layout in the dialog box, scrolling as necessary**
   The Recommended PivotTables dialog box displays recommended layouts, as shown in **FIGURE 8-3**.

3. **Click Blank PivotTable at the bottom of the dialog box**
   A new, blank PivotTable appears on the left side of the worksheet and the PivotTable Fields List appears in a pane on the right, as shown in **FIGURE 8-4**. To populate the PivotTable, you can click field check boxes in the PivotTable Fields List pane, often simply called the Field List. The diagram area at the bottom of the pane represents the main PivotTable areas and helps you track field locations as you populate the PivotTable. You can also drag fields among the diagram areas to change the PivotTable layout.

QUICK TIP

To remove a field from a PivotTable, click the field's check box to remove the checkmark.

4. **Click the Office field check box in the Field List**
   Because the office field is a text, rather than a numeric, field, Excel adds the offices to the Rows area of the PivotTable and adds the Office field name to the Rows area in the PivotTable Fields pane.

5. **Click the Position ID check box in the Field List**
   The Position ID information is automatically added to the PivotTable, and "Sum of Position ID" appears in the Values area in the diagram area. Because the data type of the Position ID field is numeric, the field is added to the Values area of the PivotTable and the Position ID values are summed, which is not meaningful in this case. Instead, you want the Position IDs as column headers in the PivotTable.

6. **Click the Sum of Position ID arrow in the Values area at the bottom of the PivotTable Fields List pane, then click Move to Column Labels**
   The Position ID field becomes a column label, so the Position ID values appear as column headers.

QUICK TIP

PivotTables containing a data field can be filtered by date. You need to click the PivotTable Analyze tab, then click the Insert Timeline button in the Filter group.

7. **Drag the Quarter field from the PivotTable Fields List pane and drop it below the Office field in the Rows area, then click the Revenue field check box in the pane to add a checkmark**
   You have created a PivotTable that totals revenue, with the position IDs as column headers, and offices and quarters as row labels. Sum is the Excel default function for data fields containing numbers, so Excel automatically calculates the sum of the revenue. The PivotTable tells you that Philadelphia revenue of position #110 (Technical) was twice the New York revenue and more than three times the Boston revenue. Position #340 (Creative) had the highest overall revenue, as shown in the Grand Total row in **FIGURE 8-5**.

8. **Click the Collapse button ⊟ to the left of the Boston label, then click the Expand button ⊞**
   The quarterly total details for Boston are hidden, then redisplayed. When you have two levels of data in the rows or columns area, you can drill down and drill up in the data to expand or collapse the second-level field details below the top field.

FIGURE 8-3: Recommended PivotTables dialog box

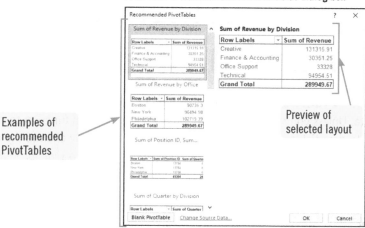

Examples of recommended PivotTables

Preview of selected layout

FIGURE 8-4: Empty PivotTable ready to receive field data

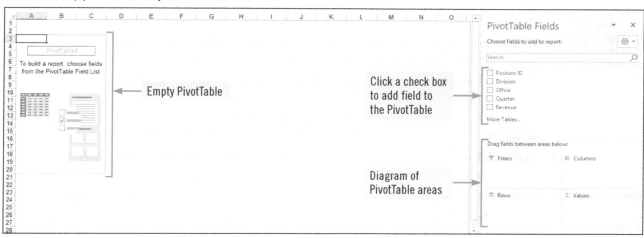

Empty PivotTable

Click a check box to add field to the PivotTable

Diagram of PivotTable areas

FIGURE 8-5: New PivotTable with fields in place

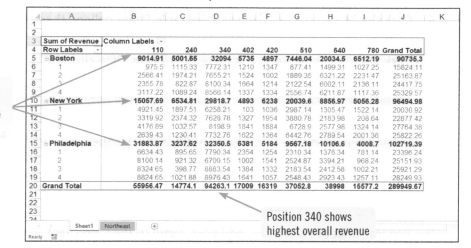

Philadelphia revenue for position 110 is twice as high as New York and three times Boston's revenue

Position 340 shows highest overall revenue

Changing a PivotTable layout

The default layout for PivotTables is the compact form; the row labels are displayed in a single column, and the second-level field items (such as the quarters in the JCL example) are indented for readability. You can change the layout of your PivotTable by clicking the Design tab, clicking the Report Layout button in the Layout group, then clicking either Show in Outline Form or Show in Tabular Form. The tabular form and the outline form show each row label in its own column. The tabular and outline layouts take up more space on a worksheet than the compact layout.

Analyzing Data with PivotTables

EX 8-5

Excel

Change a PivotTable's Summary Function and Design

Learning
Outcomes
• Change a Pivot-
Table's summary
function
• Format a
PivotTable

A PivotTable's **summary function** determines what type of calculation Excel applies, or uses to summarize the table data. Unless you specify otherwise, Excel applies the Sum function to numeric data and the Count function to data fields containing text. However, you can easily change the default summary functions. **CASE** ▶ *Ellie wants you to explore using the average function to summarize the revenue for the Northeast offices. She would like you to improve the appearance of the PivotTable for her presentation.*

STEPS

QUICK TIP
You can also change
the summary
function by clicking
the Field Settings
button in the Active
Field group on the
PivotTable Analyze
tab.

1. **Right-click cell A3, then point to** Summarize Values By **in the shortcut menu**
   The shortcut menu shows that the Sum function is selected by default, as shown in FIGURE 8-6.

2. **Click** Average
   The data area of the PivotTable shows the average revenue for each position by office and quarter, and cell A3 now contains "Average of Revenue."

3. **Click the** Design tab **on the ribbon, click the** Subtotals button **in the Layout group, then click** Do Not Show Subtotals
   The subtotals are removed from the PivotTable. After reviewing the data, you decide that it would be more useful to sum the revenue information than to average it, and to see subtotals.

4. **Right-click cell A3, point to** Summarize Values By **on the shortcut menu, then click** Sum
   Excel recalculates the PivotTable, now summing the revenue data instead of averaging it.

QUICK TIP
You can control the
display of grand
totals by clicking
the Design tab, then
clicking the Grand
Totals button in the
Layout group.

5. **Click the** Design tab **on the ribbon if necessary, click the** Subtotals button **in the Layout group, then click** Show all Subtotals at Top of Group
   Just as Excel tables have styles that let you quickly format them, PivotTables have a gallery of styles from which to choose.

6. **Click the** More button ⊽ **in the PivotTable Styles gallery, then click** White, Pivot Style Light 3

7. **Click the** PivotTable Analyze tab **on the ribbon, then click the** Field Headers button **in the Show group to deselect it**
   The unnecessary headers "Column Labels" and "Row Labels" are removed.

8. **Click any** revenue value **in the PivotTable, click the** Field Settings button **in the Active Field group, click** Number Format **in the Value Field Settings dialog box, click** Currency **in the Category list, make sure Decimal places is 2 and Symbol is $, click** OK**, click** OK **again, AutoFit any columns if necessary to display all the data, then compare your PivotTable to** FIGURE 8-7
   The revenue values are formatted as currency.

9. **Rename Sheet1** PivotTable, **add your name to the worksheet** footer, **then save the workbook**

FIGURE 8-6: Shortcut menu showing Sum function selected

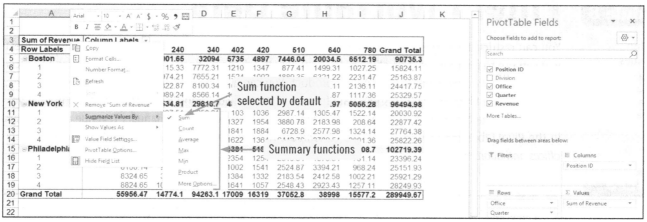

FIGURE 8-7: Formatted PivotTable

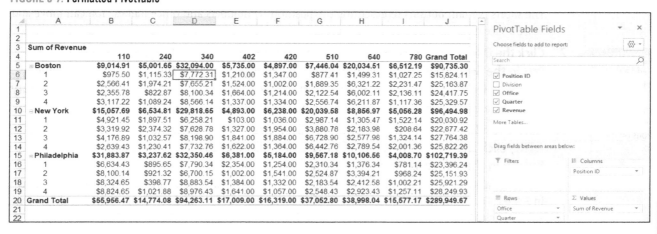

Using the Show buttons

To display and hide PivotTable elements, you can use the toggle buttons in the Show group on the PivotTable Analyze tab. For example, clicking the Field List button hides or displays the PivotTable Fields List pane. Clicking the +/– button hides or displays the Expand and Collapse Outline buttons, and clicking the Field Headers button hides or displays the Row and Column Label headers on the PivotTable.

Filter PivotTable Data

**Learning
Outcomes**
• Filter a PivotTable
  using a slicer
• Filter a PivotTable
  using a report
  filter

You can restrict the display of PivotTable data using slicers and report filters. A **slicer** is a graphic object you can use to filter data in a PivotTable, to show only the data you need. For example, you can use slicer buttons to show only data about a specific product. You can also filter a PivotTable using a **report filter**, which lets you filter the data to show data for one or more fields, using a list arrow. For example, if you add a month field to the Filters area, you can filter a PivotTable so that only January revenue data appears in the PivotTable. **CASE** ▶ *Ellie wants to compare revenue data about specific positions across specific offices and quarters.*

STEPS

1. **Click any cell in the PivotTable, click the PivotTable Analyze tab on the ribbon if necessary, click the Insert Slicer button in the Filter group, in the Insert Slicers dialog box click the Position ID check box and the Office check box to add checkmarks to both fields, click OK, then drag both slicers to the right of the PivotTable**

   The slicers contain buttons representing the position ID numbers and office names. You can move and resize a slicer similarly to other graphic objects.

QUICK TIP
You can add a slicer
style, edit a slicer
caption, and change
the button order
using the buttons
and options on the
Slicer tab.

2. **Click the Office slicer, click the Slicer tab on the ribbon if necessary, type 1.18 in the Height box in the Size group, type 2 in the Width box if necessary, click the Position ID slicer, type 2.6 in the Height box in the Size group if necessary, then type 2 in the Width box if necessary**

   The slicers are just large enough to display a button for each value, as shown in FIGURE 8-8.

3. **Click the 110 button in the Position ID slicer, press CTRL, click the 510 button, release CTRL, click the New York button in the Office slicer, press CTRL, click the Philadelphia button in the Office slicer, then release CTRL**

   The PivotTable displays only the data for position IDs 110 and 510 in New York and Philadelphia, as shown in FIGURE 8-9. In the slicers, the Filter symbol changes, indicating the PivotTable is filtered to display the selected fields.

4. **Click the Clear Filter button 🏷 in the Position ID slicer, click 🏷 in the Office slicer, click the top of the Office slicer, press CTRL, click the top of the Position ID slicer, release CTRL, right-click the Position ID slicer, then click Remove Slicers on the shortcut menu**

   The filters are cleared and the slicers are removed.

TROUBLE
If the PivotTable
Fields List pane is
not visible, click the
PivotTable Analyze
tab, then click the
Field List button in
the Show group.

5. **In the PivotTable Fields List pane, click the Quarter field arrow in the Rows area, then click Move to Report Filter in the list that opens**

   The Quarter field moves to cell A1, and a list arrow and the word "(All)" appears in cell B1. The list arrow lets you filter the data in the PivotTable by Quarter. "(All)" indicates that the PivotTable currently shows data for all quarters.

6. **Click the cell B1 list arrow, click 4, click OK, then save your work**

   The PivotTable filters the revenue data to display the fourth quarter only, as shown in FIGURE 8-10. The Quarter field list arrow changes to a filter symbol. A filter symbol also appears to the right of the Quarter field in the PivotTable Fields List pane, indicating that the PivotTable is filtered and summarizes only a portion of the PivotTable data.

FIGURE 8-8: Slicers for Position ID and Office fields

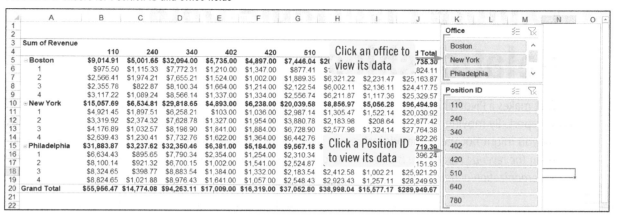

FIGURE 8-9: PivotTable filtered by Position ID and Office

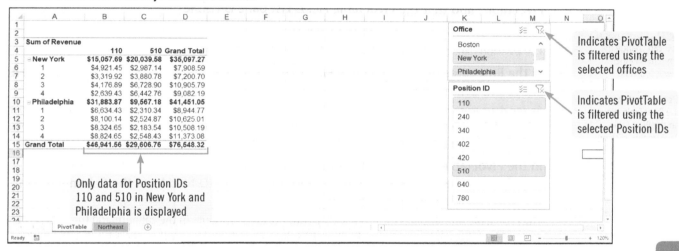

FIGURE 8-10: PivotTable filtered by fourth quarter

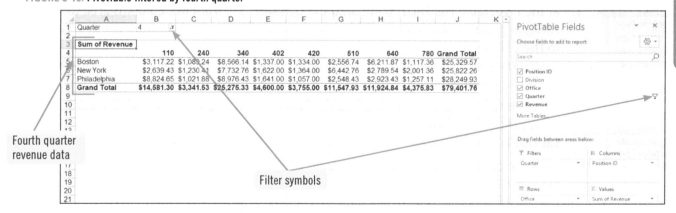

Filtering PivotTables using multiple values

Instead of using slicers to display multiple values when filtering a PivotTable report, you can use a report filter. After clicking a field's report filter list arrow in the top section of the PivotTable Fields List pane or in cell B1 on the PivotTable itself, click the Select Multiple Items check box at the bottom of the filter selections. You can then select multiple values for the filter. For example, selecting quarters 1 and 2 as the report filter in a PivotTable with quarters displays all the data for those quarters. You can also select multiple values for the row and column labels by clicking the PivotTable Analyze tab, clicking the Field Headers button in the Show group, clicking the Row Labels list arrow or the Column Labels list arrow in cells A4 and B3 on the PivotTable, then selecting the data items that you want to display.

Explore PivotTable Data Relationships

Learning
Outcomes
• Change a PivotTable's organization
• Add fields to a PivotTable

What makes a PivotTable such a powerful analysis tool is the ability to change the way data is organized in the report. By moving fields to different positions in the report, you can explore relationships and trends that you might not see in the original report structure. **CASE** ▸ *Ellie asks you to include division information in the revenue report. She is also interested in viewing the PivotTable in different arrangements to find the best organization of data for her presentation.*

STEPS

1. **Make sure that the PivotTable sheet is active, that the active cell is anywhere inside the PivotTable, and that the PivotTable Fields List pane is visible**

2. **Click the Division check box in the Field List**
The Division data is added to the Rows area below the corresponding office data.

3. **In the Rows area of the PivotTable Fields List pane, drag the Division field up and drop it above the Office field**

As you drag, a green bar shows where the field will be inserted. The division field is now the outer or upper field, and the office field is the inner or lower field. The PivotTable is restructured to display the revenue data first by division and then by office, as shown in **FIGURE 8-11**.

4. **In the PivotTable Fields List pane drag the Division field from the Rows area to anywhere in the Columns area, then drag the Position ID field from the Columns area to the Rows area below the Office field**

The PivotTable now displays the revenue data with the division values in the columns and the position IDs grouped by offices in the rows. The Position ID values are indented below the offices because the Position ID field is the inner row label.

5. **In the PivotTable Fields List pane drag the Division field from the Columns area to the Filters area above the Quarter field, then drag the Position ID field from the Rows area to the Columns area**

The PivotTable now has two report filters. The upper report filter, Division, summarizes data using the position IDs for all four divisions.

6. **Click the cell B1 list arrow of the PivotTable, click Creative, click OK, click the cell B2 list arrow, click (All), then click OK**
The PivotTable displays revenue totals for the creative division for all quarters.

7. **Click the cell B1 list arrow, click (All), then click OK**
The completed PivotTable appears, as shown in **FIGURE 8-12**.

8. **Save the workbook, change the page orientation of the PivotTable sheet to landscape, then preview the PivotTable**

FIGURE 8-11: PivotTable structured by offices within divisions

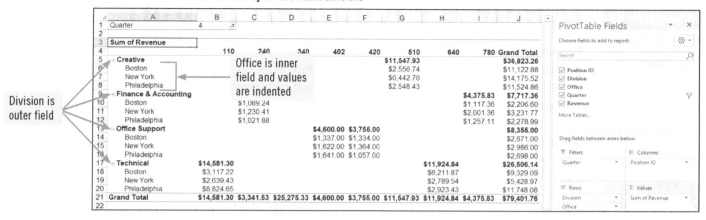

FIGURE 8-12: Completed PivotTable report

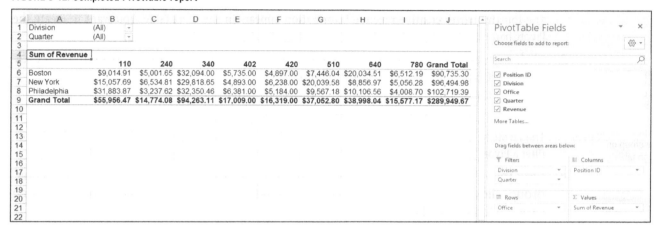

Grouping PivotTable data

You can group PivotTable data to analyze specific values in a field as a unit. For example, you may want to group revenue data for quarters 1 and 2 to analyze the first half of the year. To group PivotTable data, first select the Rows and Columns that you want to group, click the PivotTable Analyze tab, then click the Group Selection button in the Group group. The default group name of Group1 can be edited by entering the new name in the cell with

the default name. Once data is grouped, it can be expanded or collapsed to show the grouped details using the Collapse button ⊟ or the Expand button ⊞ next to the group name.
FIGURE 8-13 shows a PivotTable grouped by quarters with the first two quarters expanded and the last two quarters collapsed. To ungroup data, select the Group name in the PivotTable, then click the Ungroup button in the Group group.

FIGURE 8-13: Grouped PivotTable data

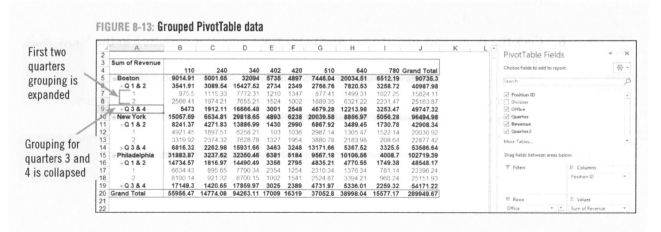

Create a PivotChart Report

Learning
Outcomes
• Create a
  PivotChart
• Format a
  PivotChart

A **PivotChart report** is a chart that you create from data or from a PivotTable report that lets you summarize and rearrange to explore new data relationships. TABLE 8-1 describes how the elements in a PivotTable report correspond to the elements in a PivotChart report. When you create a PivotChart directly from data, Excel automatically creates a corresponding PivotTable report. If you change a PivotChart report by filtering the charted elements, Excel updates the corresponding PivotTable report to show the new data values. You can move the fields of a PivotChart using the PivotChart Fields List window; the new layout will be reflected in the PivotTable. **CASE** *For her presentation, Ellie wants you to chart the fourth quarter creative revenue for all offices and the Boston office's yearly creative revenue.*

STEPS

1. **Click the cell B1 list arrow, click Creative, click OK, click the Quarter list arrow, click 4, then click OK**

   The fourth quarter creative revenue information appears in the PivotTable. You want to create the PivotChart from the PivotTable information you have displayed.

2. **Click any cell in the PivotTable, click the PivotTable Analyze tab on the ribbon, then click the PivotChart button in the Tools group**

   The Insert Chart dialog box opens and shows a gallery of chart types.

QUICK TIP
You can change a PivotChart's type by clicking the Change Chart Type button in the Type group on the Design tab.

3. **Click the Clustered Column chart if necessary, then click OK**

   The PivotChart appears on the worksheet, as shown in FIGURE 8-14. The chart has field buttons that let you filter a PivotChart in the same way you do a PivotTable. You can also add a slicer to filter a PivotChart.

4. **Click the PivotChart Analyze tab on the ribbon, click the Insert Slicer button in the Filter group, click the Office check box, click OK, move the slicer to the right of the chart, then click Boston in the slicer**

   Only the Boston revenue data is shown in the chart.

QUICK TIP
You can add a chart style to a PivotChart by clicking a style in the Chart Styles group on the Design tab.

5. **Click the PivotChart to select it, click the Design tab on the ribbon, click the Move Chart button in the Location group, click the New sheet option button, type PivotChart in the text box, then click OK**

6. **Click the Quarter field button at the top of the PivotChart, click All, then click OK**

   The chart now represents the Boston office's creative revenue for the year, as shown in FIGURE 8-15.

QUICK TIP
If you have more than one field in the Axis area, you can drill up or down in a PivotChart using the Collapse button ⊟ to hide the details of the second field and the Expand button ⊞ to display the second field details. If the buttons are not visible, click the Field Buttons button in the Show/Hide group on the PivotChart Analyze tab.

7. **Click the Design tab, click the Quick Layout button in the Chart Layouts group, click Layout 3, click the Chart Title element to select it, type Annual Creative Revenue, then press ENTER**

   You are finished filtering the chart data.

8. **Click the PivotChart Analyze tab, then click the Field Buttons button in the Show/Hide group**

   Removing the field buttons improves the chart's appearance.

9. **Enter your name in the center section of the PivotChart sheet footer, save the workbook, then preview the PivotChart report**

   The final PivotChart report displaying Boston's creative revenue for the year is shown in FIGURE 8-16.

FIGURE 8-14: **PivotChart with fourth quarter creative revenue**

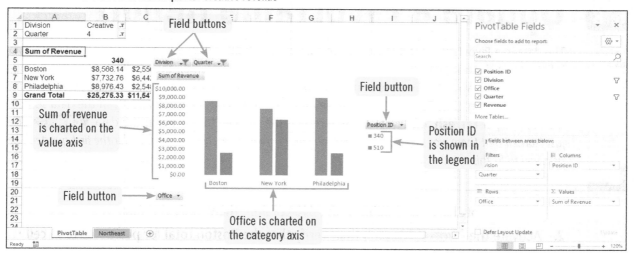

FIGURE 8-15: **PivotChart displaying Boston's creative revenue for the year**

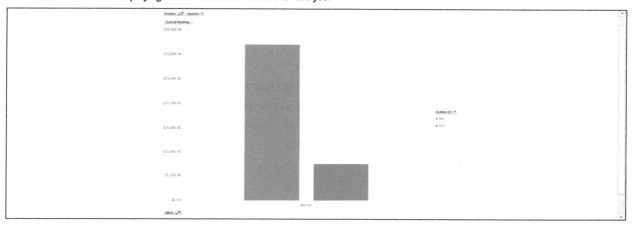

FIGURE 8-16: **Completed PivotChart report**

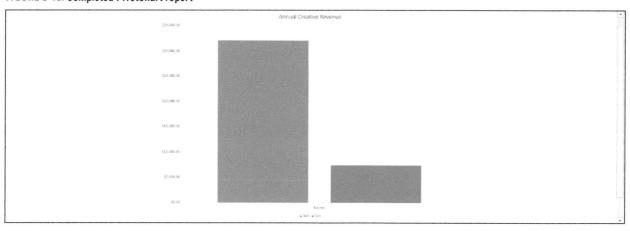

TABLE 8-1: **PivotTable and PivotChart elements**

PivotTable items	PivotChart items
Row labels	Axis fields
Column labels	Legend fields
Report Filters	Report Filters

Update a PivotTable Report

- Edit data in a PivotTable data source
- Refresh a PivotTable

The data in a PivotTable report looks like typical worksheet data. However, because the PivotTable data is linked to a **data source** (the data you used to create the PivotTable), the results it displays are read-only. That means you cannot move or modify a part of a PivotTable by inserting or deleting rows, editing results, or moving cells. To change PivotTable data, you must edit the items directly in the data source, then update, or **refresh**, the PivotTable so it reflects the changes to the underlying data. **CASE** *Ellie just learned that there was an error in the Boston office's creative revenue information for the first quarter. She asks you to fix this error.*

STEPS

1. **On the PivotChart sheet point to the** 510 **column, then verify the value is** $7,446.04

2. **Activate the** PivotTable **sheet, then verify that the Boston total for position 510 in cell C6 is $7,446.04**

QUICK TIP

If you want to change a PivotTable's source data range, click the PivotTable Analyze tab, then click the Change Data Source button in the Data group.

3. **Click the** Northeast **sheet tab, click cell** E27**, enter** 6000**, then press** ENTER

4. **Click the** PivotTable **sheet tab, then verify that the Boston total for position 510 in cell C6 is $7,446.04**

   The PivotTable does not yet reflect the changed data.

5. **Click anywhere within the PivotTable if necessary, click the** PivotTable Analyze **tab on the ribbon, then click the** Refresh button **in the Data group**

   The PivotTable now shows Boston's 510 total as $12,568.63, as shown in FIGURE 8-17.

6. **Activate the** PivotChart **sheet, point to the** 510 **column, then verify the value is updated to $12,568.63**

QUICK TIP

If you want Excel to refresh a PivotTable or PivotChart report automatically when you open a workbook, click the PivotTable/ PivotChart Analyze tab on the ribbon, click the Options button in the PivotTable/ PivotChart group, click the Data tab in the PivotTable Options dialog box, click the Refresh data when opening the file check box, then click OK.

7. **Save the workbook**

FIGURE 8-17: Updated PivotTable report

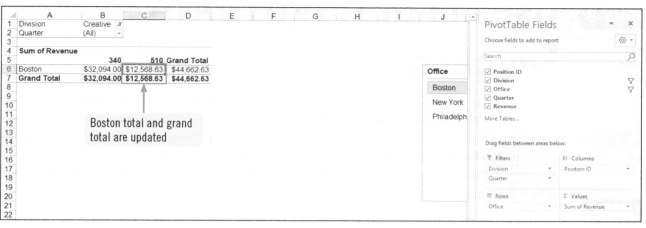

Adding a calculated field to a PivotTable and a PivotChart

You can use formulas to analyze PivotTable and PivotChart data in a field by adding a calculated field. A calculated field appears in the PivotTable's or PivotChart's Field List and can be manipulated like other PivotTable fields. To add a calculated field, click any cell in the PivotTable, click the PivotTable Analyze tab, click the Fields, Items, & Sets button in the Calculations group, then click Calculated Field. The Insert Calculated Field dialog box opens. Enter the field name in the Name text box, click in the Formula text box, click a field name in the Field list that you want to use in the formula, and click Insert Field. Use standard arithmetic operators to enter the formula you want to use. For example, you can enter a formula such as =Revenue*1.2 to increase the revenue data by 20 percent. After entering the formula in the Insert Calculated Field dialog box, click Add, then click OK. The new field with the formula results appears in the PivotTable and the PivotChart, and the field is added to the PivotTable and PivotChart Fields List pane. FIGURE 8-18 shows a calculated field added to a PivotTable.

FIGURE 8-18: PivotTable with calculated field

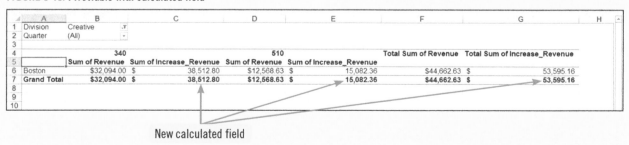

Use the GETPIVOTDATA Function

**Learning
Outcomes**
• Analyze the
GETPIVOTDATA
function
• Retrieve infor-
mation using the
GETPIVOTDATA
function

Because you can rearrange a PivotTable so easily, you can't use an ordinary cell reference when you want to reference a PivotTable cell in another worksheet. The reason is that if you change the way data is displayed in a PivotTable, the data moves, making an ordinary cell reference incorrect. Instead, to retrieve summary data from a PivotTable, you need to use the Excel GETPIVOTDATA function. See FIGURE 8-19 for the GETPIVOTDATA function format. **CASE** *Ellie wants to include the yearly revenue total for the Boston office in the Northeast sheet. You use the GETPIVOTDATA function to retrieve this information.*

STEPS

1. **Activate the PivotTable sheet**

   The revenue figures in the PivotTable are filtered to show only the creative positions.

2. **Click the Division filter arrow in cell B1, click (All), then click OK**

   The PivotChart report displays revenue information for all Boston positions.

3. **Activate the Northeast sheet, click cell G1, type Total Boston Revenue, click the Enter button ✓ on the formula bar, click the Home tab on the ribbon if necessary, click the Align Right button ☰ in the Alignment group, click the Bold button B in the Font group, then adjust the width of column G to display the new label**

4. **Click cell G2, type =, click the PivotTable sheet tab, click cell J6 on the PivotTable, then click ✓**

   Cell J6 on the PivotTable contains the data you want to display on the Northeast sheet. The GETPIVOTDATA function, along with its arguments, is inserted into cell G2 of the Northeast sheet. You want to format the revenue total.

5. **Click the Accounting Number Format button $ in the Number group**

   The current revenue total for the Boston office is $95,857.89 as shown in FIGURE 8-20. This is the same value displayed in cell J6 of the PivotTable.

6. **Add your name to the Northeast sheet custom footer, save the workbook, then preview the Northeast worksheet**

7. **sam✦ Close the file, close Excel, then submit the workbook to your instructor**

   The Northeast worksheet is shown in FIGURE 8-21.

FIGURE 8-19: Format of GETPIVOTDATA function

=GETPIVOTDATA("Revenue",PivotTable!$A$4,"Office","Boston")

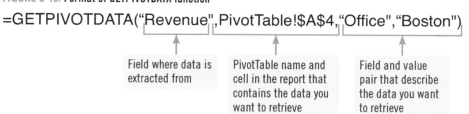

Field where data is extracted from

PivotTable name and cell in the report that contains the data you want to retrieve

Field and value pair that describe the data you want to retrieve

FIGURE 8-20: GETPIVOTDATA function in the Northeast sheet

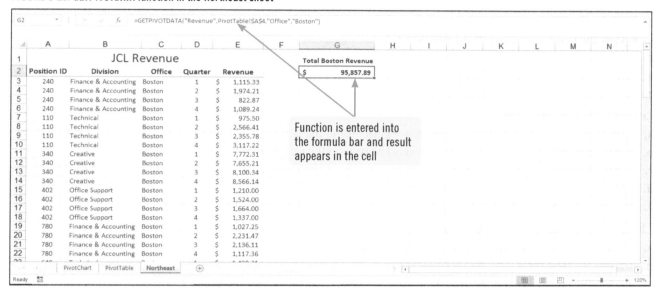

FIGURE 8-21: Completed Northeast worksheet showing total Boston revenue

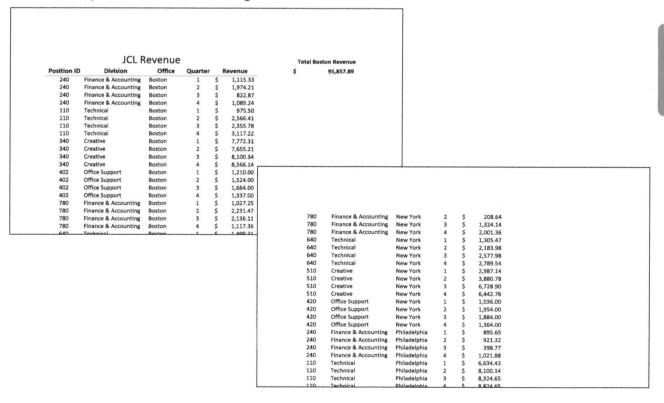

Practice

Skills Review

1. Plan and design a PivotTable report.

a. Start Excel, open IL_EX_8-2.xlsx from the location where you store your Data Files, then save it as **IL_EX_8_Pharma**.

b. Review the fields and values in the worksheet.

c. Verify that the worksheet contains repeated values in one or more fields.

d. Verify that there are not any blank rows or columns in the range A1:E25.

e. Verify that the worksheet contains a field that can be summed in a PivotTable.

2. Create a PivotTable report.

a. Create a blank PivotTable report on a new worksheet using the January Expenses worksheet data in the range A1:E25.

b. Add the Division field in the PivotTable Fields List pane to the Columns area.

c. Add the Expenses field in the PivotTable Fields List pane to the Values area.

d. Add the Location field in the PivotTable Fields List pane to the Rows area.

e. Add the Manager field in the PivotTable Fields List pane to the Rows area below the Location field.

3. Change a PivotTable's summary function and design.

a. Change the PivotTable summary function to Average.

b. Rename the new sheet **Jan Expenses PT**.

c. Change the PivotTable Style to Light Orange, Pivot Style Light 14. Format the expense values in the PivotTable as currency with a $ symbol and no decimal places.

d. Enter your name in the center section of the PivotTable report footer, then save the workbook.

e. Change the summary function back to Sum. Use a tool on the PivotTable Analyze tab to hide the field headers.

4. Filter PivotTable data.

a. Use slicers to filter the PivotTable to display expenses for the production division only in the Basel and Pittsburgh locations.

b. Clear the filters and delete the slicer.

c. Add the Product area field to the Filters area in the PivotTable Fields List pane. Use the filter list arrow to display expenses for only the Consumer Health product area.

d. Display expenses for all product areas.

e. Save the workbook.

5. Explore PivotTable data relationships.

a. In the PivotTable Fields List pane, drag the Division field from the Columns area to the Rows area below the Manager field. Drag the Manager field from the Rows area to the Columns area.

b. Drag the Location field from the Rows area to the Filters area below the Product Area field. Drag the Division field back to the Columns area.

c. Drag the Location field back to the Rows area.

d. Remove the Manager field from the PivotTable.

e. Compare your completed PivotTable to FIGURE 8-22, then save the workbook.

FIGURE 8-22

	A	B	C	D	E	F
1						
2	Product Area	(All)				
3						
4	Sum of Expenses					
5		Production	R & D	Support	Grand Total	
6	Basel	$60,986	$57,453	$41,629	$160,068	
7	Pittsburgh	$51,709	$60,550	$29,597	$141,856	
8	Seattle	$53,466	$58,527	$38,355	$150,348	
9	Singapore	$35,170	$54,153	$30,461	$119,784	
10	Grand Total	$201,331	$230,683	$140,042	$572,056	
11						
12						

Skills Review (continued)

6. **Create a PivotChart report.**

   a. Use the existing PivotTable data to create a Clustered Column PivotChart report.

   b. Move the PivotChart to a new worksheet, then name the sheet **PivotChart**.

   c. Apply the Quick Layout, Layout 1, to the PivotChart. Add the title **January Expenses** to the chart.

   d. Filter the chart to display only expense data for the Crop Science product area. Display the expense data for all product areas. Hide the field buttons.

   e. Add your name to the center section of the PivotChart custom sheet footer. Compare your PivotChart with FIGURE 8-23, then save the workbook.

   FIGURE 8-23

   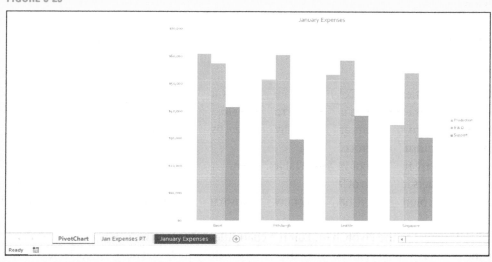

7. **Update a PivotTable report.**

   a. Activate the Jan Expenses PT sheet, then note the Seattle total for production.

   b. Activate the January Expenses sheet and change the Expenses value in cell D14 to **$30,000**.

   c. Refresh the PivotTable so it reflects the new value.

   d. Verify that the Seattle total for production increased to $60,287 on both the PivotTable and the PivotChart.

   e. Save the workbook.

8. **Use the GETPIVOTDATA function.**

   a. In cell D27 of the January Expenses sheet type =, click the Jan Expenses PT sheet, click the cell that contains the grand total for Pittsburgh, then press ENTER.

   b. Review the GETPIVOTDATA function that was entered in cell D27, then format the value in cell D27 in Accounting Number format and no decimal places.

   c. Enter your name in the January Expenses sheet footer, compare your January Expenses sheet to FIGURE 8-24, save the workbook, then preview the January Expenses worksheet.

   d. Close the workbook, then close Excel.

   e. Submit the workbook to your instructor.

   FIGURE 8-24

	A	B	C	D	E	F
1	Division	Product Area	Location	Expenses	Manager	
2	Production	Consumer Health	Basel	$ 29,518	C. Berwick	
3	R & D	Consumer Health	Basel	$ 30,234	C. Berwick	
4	Support	Consumer Health	Basel	$ 23,971	C. Berwick	
5	Production	Crop Science	Basel	$ 31,468	J. Allen	
6	R & D	Crop Science	Basel	$ 27,219	J. Allen	
7	Support	Crop Science	Basel	$ 17,658	J. Allen	
8	Production	Consumer Health	Pittsburgh	$ 22,075	D. Macey	
9	R & D	Consumer Health	Pittsburgh	$ 31,355	D. Macey	
10	Support	Consumer Health	Pittsburgh	$ 15,940	D. Macey	
11	Production	Crop Science	Pittsburgh	$ 29,634	T. Holland	
12	R & D	Crop Science	Pittsburgh	$ 29,195	T. Holland	
13	Support	Crop Science	Pittsburgh	$ 13,657	T. Holland	
14	Production	Consumer Health	Seattle	$ 30,000	L. Bartlet	
15	R & D	Consumer Health	Seattle	$ 32,443	L. Bartlet	
16	Support	Consumer Health	Seattle	$ 26,603	L. Bartlet	
17	Production	Crop Science	Seattle	$ 30,287	S. Simpson	
18	R & D	Crop Science	Seattle	$ 26,084	S. Simpson	
19	Support	Crop Science	Seattle	$ 11,752	S. Simpson	
20	Production	Consumer Health	Singapore	$ 13,056	P. Lee	
21	R & D	Consumer Health	Singapore	$ 24,883	P. Lee	
22	Support	Consumer Health	Singapore	$ 16,957	P. Lee	
23	Production	Crop Science	Singapore	$ 22,114	L. Williams	
24	R & D	Crop Science	Singapore	$ 29,270	L. Williams	
25	Support	Crop Science	Singapore	$ 13,504	L. Williams	
26						
27		Pittsburgh Expenses for January:		$ 141,856		
28						

Excel

Independent Challenge 1

As the office manager for the occupational therapy clinic at the Riverwalk Medical Clinic, you have been asked to review the billings for the month of February. The CFO of the clinic has asked you to analyze the hours being spent on the various categories of occupational therapy and how the services are paid.

a. Start Excel, open IL_EX_8-3.xlsx from the location where you store your Data Files, then save it as **IL_EX_8_RiverwalkOT**.

b. Create a blank PivotTable on a separate worksheet that sums hours by Provider and Division, using **FIGURE 8-25** as a guide.

c. Name the new sheet **PivotTable**, and apply the White, Pivot Style Light 5 PivotTable style.

d. Change the summary function of the PivotTable to average.

e. Add slicers to the PivotTable for the category and provider data. Display only data for Jolan's and Ryan's level 1 and 2 procedures. Remove the filters and remove the slicers.

f. Add the Procedure # field to the Columns area under the Category field. Move the Procedure # field to the Rows area under the Provider field.

g. Add the Billing field to the Filters area of the PivotTable. Display only the PivotTable data for insurance procedures.

h. Change the summary function of the PivotTable to sum.

i. Hide the field headers in the PivotTable.

j. Create a clustered column PivotChart that shows the insurance hours. Move the PivotChart to a new sheet named **PivotChart**.

k. Apply Quick Layout 3 to the PivotChart. Edit the chart title to **Insurance Hours**.

l. Activate the February OT sheet and change the hours in cell E4 to 2. Update the PivotTable to reflect this change.

m. Activate the February OT sheet, then use the GETPIVOTDATA function to display the total number of insurance hours in cell A29.

n. Add your name to the center section of the three worksheet footers, then save the workbook. Preview the three worksheets, comparing them to **FIGURE 8-26**.

o. Close the workbook, then close Excel. Submit the workbook to your instructor.

FIGURE 8-25

FIGURE 8-26

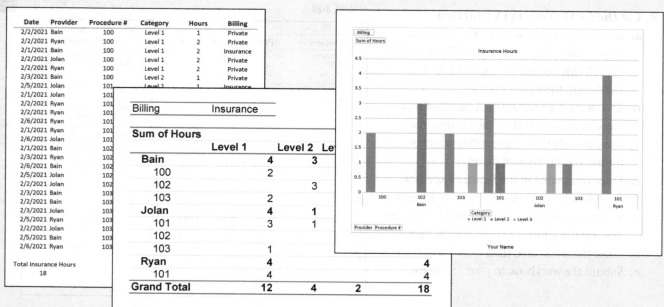

Independent Challenge 2

You are the assistant to the CFO of an international hotel group with properties in North America, Europe, and Asia. The properties in your collection cater to both business and leisure travelers. You want to create a PivotTable to analyze and graph the revenue in each quarter by purpose and region.

a. Start Excel, open IL_EX_8-4.xlsx from the location where you store your Data Files, then save it as **IL_EX_8_Accommodations**.

FIGURE 8-27

b. Create a PivotTable on a new worksheet named **PivotTable** that sums the revenue amount for each region across the rows and each purpose down the columns. Add the quarter field as an inner row label. Use FIGURE 8-27 as a guide.

c. Widen column C of the PivotTable if necessary to fully display the grand total value for that column.

d. Group the first two quarters (*Hint:* Select the first two quarter cells in any region, then click the Group Selection button in the Group group on the PivotTable Analyze tab.)

e. Rename the Group1 label **First Half**. (*Hint:* Enter the new name in any cell with the Group1 label.)

f. Group the third and fourth quarters, then name this new group **Last Half**.

g. Collapse both the First Half and Last Half groups.

h. Turn off the grand totals for the Columns. (*Hint:* Click the Grand Totals button in the Layout group on the Design tab, then click On for Rows Only.)

i. Format the revenue values using the Currency format with the $ symbol and no decimal places.

j. On the Revenue worksheet, change the North America Quarter 1 Business Revenue value in cell D2 to **$50,000,000**. Update the PivotTable to reflect this increase in revenue.

k. Create a stacked column PivotChart report for the revenue data for all three regions. (*Hint:* Choose the first Stacked Column Chart type in the dialog box.)

l. Move the PivotChart to a new sheet, and name the chart sheet **PivotChart**.

m. Apply a quick layout of Layout 4 to the PivotChart.

n. Use the Region field button at the bottom of the PivotChart to filter the chart to display only Europe and North America properties.

o. Add a Quarter 2 slicer to the PivotTable. Use the slicer to display the revenue for the first half of the year only.

p. Check the PivotChart to be sure it displays only the filtered data.

q. On the PivotTable sheet, change the slicer caption to **Grouped Quarters**. (*Hint:* Use the Slicer group on the Slicer tab.)

r. Add a slicer style of Light Blue, Slicer Style Dark 1, then move the slicer below the Pivot Table.

FIGURE 8-28

s. Using FIGURE 8-28 as a guide, configure the slicer so the buttons appear side by side and there is space above and below the text in each button. Resize the slicer if necessary. (Hint: Use the Buttons and Size groups on the Slicer tab.)

t. Add your name to the center section of the three worksheet footers, save the workbook, then preview the PivotTable and the PivotChart. Close the workbook and close Excel. Submit the workbook to your instructor.

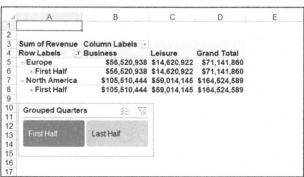

Excel

Visual Workshop

Open IL_EX_8-5.xlsx from the location where you store your Data Files, then save it as **IL_EX_8_Insurance**. Using the data on the First Quarter worksheet, create the PivotTable and slicer shown in FIGURE 8-29 on a new worksheet named **PivotTable**. Format the table, slicer, and data as necessary to match the figure. (*Hint:* The PivotTable has been formatted using the Ice Blue, Pivot Style Medium 9 Pivot Style.) Add your name to the PivotTable footer, then preview the PivotTable. Save the workbook, close the workbook, close Excel, then submit the workbook to your instructor.

FIGURE 8-29

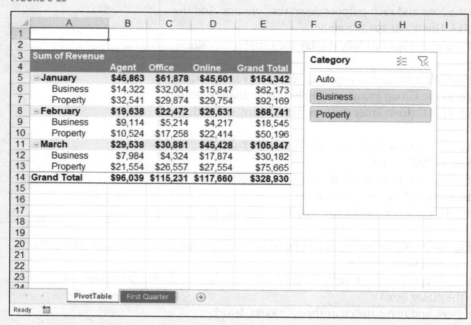

Analyzing Data with PivotTables

Integrating Word and Excel

CASE ▶ You are working with Lydia Snyder, the vice president of operations for JCL Talent, Inc. Lydia asks you to link a Word document containing a summary of company activities with data created in an Excel workbook.

Module Objectives

After completing this module, you will be able to:

- Use Paste Special to modify formatting
- Create a hyperlink between Word and Excel
- Create an Excel spreadsheet in Word
- Embed an Excel file in Word
- Change link sources

Files You Will Need

IL_INT_4-1.docx	IL_INT_4-5.docx
IL_INT_4-2.xlsx	IL_INT_4-6.xlsx
IL_INT_4-3.docx	IL_INT_4-7.docx
IL_INT_4-4.xlsx	IL_INT_4-8.xlsx

Use Paste Special to Modify Formatting

When you paste an object into an Office program, you can specify how you want that object to appear. FIGURE 4-1 shows all the Paste options available and how each option formats the pasted value of $15.00. Notice that the paragraph marks are turned on so you can easily see where the paste option adds paragraph breaks and extra spaces. Paste options will vary, depending on the type of data that is selected.

CASE ▶ *Lydia Snyder, the vice president of operations at JCL Talent, Inc., asks you to link a summary of current company activities in a Word document to data in an Excel workbook.*

STEPS

1. **Start Word, open the file** IL_INT_4-1.docx **from the location where you store your Data Files, save it as** IL_INT_4_CompanyActivities_FirstQuarter, **start Excel, open the file** IL_INT_4-2.xlsx **from the location where you store your Data Files, then save it as** IL_INT_4_CompanyData

2. **Select the range A3:F8, click the** Copy **button in the Clipboard group, switch to Word, select** EMPLOYMENT STATS, **click the** Paste **arrow in the Clipboard group, then move the mouse pointer over the available paste options to see how the formatting changes**

   None of the options will paste the spreadsheet data into a table that is both easy to modify and linked to the source file. You need to explore options in the Paste Special dialog box.

3. **Click** Paste Special, **click the** Paste link **option button, click** Microsoft Excel Worksheet Object, **then click** OK

   The pasted object is too large for the space. One of the reasons you select the Microsoft Excel Worksheet Object option is because you can easily modify the size of the pasted object.

4. **Click the pasted object, right-click, click** Picture, **click the** Size **tab, select the contents of the Width text box, type** 6 **as shown in** FIGURE 4-2, **then click** OK

5. **Switch to Excel, click cell F8, click the** Copy **button, switch to Word, then select** XX **in the paragraph below the pasted worksheet object**

6. **Click the** Paste **button, click the** Paste Options (Ctrl) **button** 🖹 (Ctrl) ▾ **next to the pasted object, then click the** Link & Merge Formatting **button** 🖺

   The Link & Merge Formatting button added paragraph breaks. You can remove these manually.

7. **Click to the left of the pasted amount, press** BACKSPACE **to move the amount up a line, click after the pasted amount, then press** DELETE **and add a space if necessary**

   You need to test the links.

8. **Switch to Excel, change the number of Not Yet Employed job seekers looking for Finance & Accounting Careers to** 40 **and press** ENTER, **switch to Word, right-click the worksheet object, click** Update Link, **right-click** 81% **in the paragraph, then click** Update Link

   The percentage of successful job seekers in cell D4 is now 84%. Each time you update a link pasted with the Link & Merge Formatting paste option, you need to adjust the spacing.

9. **Adjust the spacing around the percentage again, save the document, switch to Excel, then save and close the workbook**

FIGURE 4-1: Paste and Paste Special Options from Excel to Word

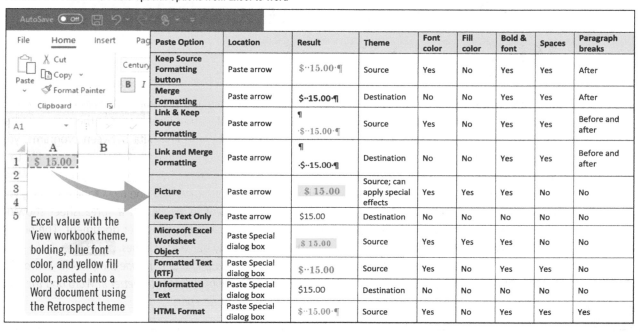

Paste Option	Location	Result	Theme	Font color	Fill color	Bold & font	Spaces	Paragraph breaks
Keep Source Formatting button	Paste arrow	$··15.00·¶	Source	Yes	No	Yes	Yes	After
Merge Formatting	Paste arrow	$··15.00·¶	Destination	No	No	Yes	Yes	After
Link & Keep Source Formatting	Paste arrow	¶ ·$··15.00·¶	Source	Yes	No	Yes	Yes	Before and after
Link and Merge Formatting	Paste arrow	¶ ·$··15.00·¶	Destination	No	No	Yes	Yes	Before and after
Picture	Paste arrow	$ 15.00	Source; can apply special effects	Yes	Yes	Yes	No	No
Keep Text Only	Paste arrow	$15.00	Destination	No	No	No	No	No
Microsoft Excel Worksheet Object	Paste Special dialog box	$ 15.00	Source	Yes	Yes	Yes	No	No
Formatted Text (RTF)	Paste Special dialog box	$··15.00	Source	Yes	No	Yes	Yes	No
Unformatted Text	Paste Special dialog box	$15.00	Destination	No	No	No	No	No
HTML Format	Paste Special dialog box	$··15.00·¶	Source	Yes	No	Yes	Yes	Yes

Excel value with the View workbook theme, bolding, blue font color, and yellow fill color, pasted into a Word document using the Retrospect theme

FIGURE 4-2: Size tab in the Format Object dialog box

Create a Hyperlink Between Word and Excel

Learning Outcomes
- Insert a hyperlink in Word
- Change the color of a followed hyperlink

You can create hyperlinks to access data from other documents and programs. A **hyperlink** is a text element or graphic that you click to display another place in a file, other files created in the same or other programs, or a location on the Internet. When you copy, paste, and link data between programs, you actually bring the data into the destination file. But when you click a hyperlink from a source file to a location in a destination file, the destination file opens. You often create hyperlinks between two files that you plan to send electronically. Instead of combining all the information into one file in one program, you can create two documents, such as a letter or other document in Word and a spreadsheet showing calculations in Excel, and insert a hyperlink in one document that opens the other document. The person who receives the two files can use the hyperlinks to switch quickly between the files. **CASE** *Lydia plans to send an electronic copy of the Word report to the marketing department and include the Excel file containing all the data referenced in the report. She asks you to create a hyperlink between the letter in Word and the Excel workbook so the client can view the Excel data directly from the Word report.*

STEPS

1. **In Word, select the words** Excel spreadsheet **in the sentence below the worksheet object**

2. **Click the** Insert tab, **click the** Link button **in the Links group, then click** Existing File or Web Page **if it is not already selected**

    In the Insert Hyperlink dialog box, you can create a link to an existing file or to a place in the current document, or you can create a hyperlink that opens a new document, or opens an email program so you can send an email. The Insert Hyperlink dialog box lists the files in the current folder, which in this case includes the Excel data file.

3. **Click the filename** IL_INT_4_CompanyData.xlsx

    You can include text in a ScreenTip that appears when users point to the hyperlink. This text can advise users what will happen when they click the hyperlink.

4. **Click** ScreenTip **in the Insert Hyperlink dialog box, type** This link opens the Company Data workbook in Excel, **click** OK, **then click** OK **again**

    The phrase "Excel spreadsheet" becomes blue and underlined, indicating that it is now a hyperlink that, when clicked, will open another document, which in this case is the Excel Company Data file.

5. **Move the mouse pointer over** Excel spreadsheet, **read the ScreenTip that appears as shown in** FIGURE 4-3, **press** CTRL, **then click** Excel spreadsheet

    The link opens the IL_INT_4_CompanyData file.

6. **Close the workbook and save changes if requested, then in Word notice that the words "Excel spreadsheet" now appear in light blue**

    You can change the color assigned to a followed hyperlink.

7. **Click the** Design tab, **click the** Colors button **in the Document Formatting group, then click** Customize Colors

    In the Create New Theme Colors dialog box, you can change the colors assigned to text in the theme currently used in the document. This document is formatted with the Parallax theme.

8. **Click the** arrow **next to the color box for Followed Hyperlink, click the** Lavender, Accent 6 color box **as shown in** FIGURE 4-4, **then click** Save

    The followed hyperlink is now lavender, which is easier to read.

9. **Save the document**

FIGURE 4-3: Viewing the ScreenTip

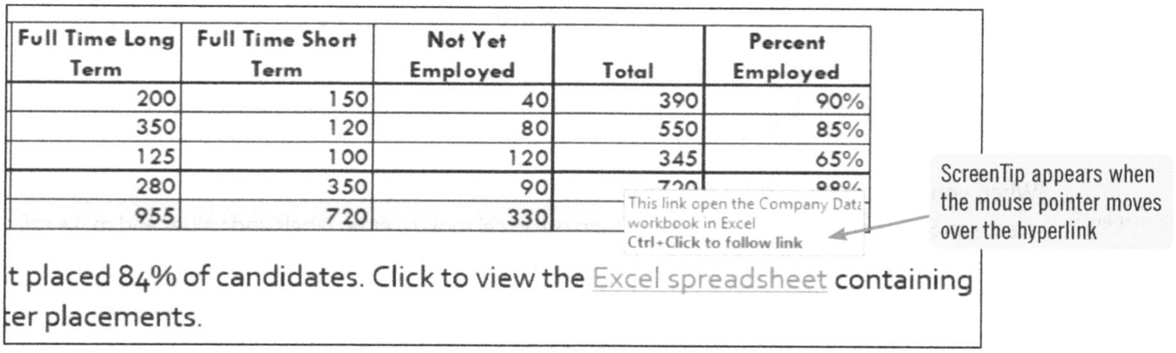

Full Time Long Term	Full Time Short Term	Not Yet Employed	Total	Percent Employed
200	150	40	390	90%
350	120	80	550	85%
125	100	120	345	65%
280	350	90	720	88%
955	720	330		

This link open the Company Data workbook in Excel
Ctrl+Click to follow link

ScreenTip appears when the mouse pointer moves over the hyperlink

t placed 84% of candidates. Click to view the Excel spreadsheet containing

er placements.

FIGURE 4-4: Changing the color of a followed hyperlink

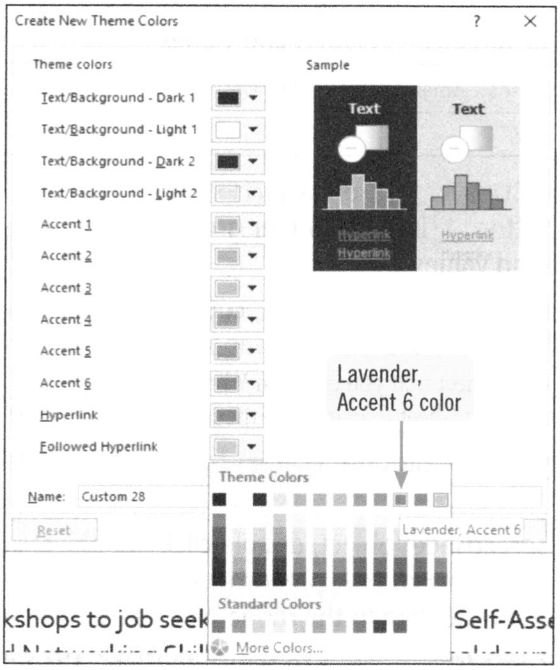

Create New Theme Colors

Theme colors

Text/Background - Dark 1
Text/Background - Light 1
Text/Background - Dark 2
Text/Background - Light 2
Accent 1
Accent 2
Accent 3
Accent 4
Accent 5
Accent 6
Hyperlink
Followed Hyperlink

Name: Custom 28

Reset

Sample

Text   Text

Hyperlink   Hyperlink
Hyperlink

Lavender, Accent 6 color

Theme Colors

Lavender, Accent 6

Standard Colors

More Colors...

kshops to job seek   Self-Asse

Editing and removing a hyperlink

To edit a hyperlink, right-click the underlined text, then click Edit Hyperlink. In the Edit Hyperlink dialog box, you can change the destination of the hyperlink, modify the ScreenTip, or remove the hyperlink. You can also remove a hyperlink by right-clicking it and then clicking Remove Hyperlink. When you remove a hyperlink, the underlining that identifies the text as a hyperlink is removed; however, the text itself remains.

Integration

Create an Excel Spreadsheet in Word

Learning Outcomes
• Create an Excel spreadsheet in Word
• Edit and format an Excel spreadsheet in Word

When you don't need to store spreadsheet data in a separate Excel file, you can use the Table command to create an Excel spreadsheet in Word and then use Excel tools to enter labels and values and make calculations. The Excel spreadsheet object is an embedded object in the Word file. To modify it, you double-click it and then use Excel tools that become available inside of the Word program window. **CASE** ▸ *You want the summary to include revenue information about the job seeker workshops. You create the data in an embedded Excel spreadsheet so you can use Excel tools to make calculations and apply formatting.*

STEPS

1. **In Word, select** WORKSHOPS **below the Workshop Revenue paragraph, click the** Insert **tab, click the** Table button **in the Tables group, then click** Excel Spreadsheet

   A blank Excel spreadsheet appears in the Word document, and Excel tools appear in the Ribbon. However, the Word document name still appears in the title bar, indicating that you are working in Excel from within the Word program.

2. **Enter the following spreadsheet labels and values**

Resume Writing	Self-Assessment	Interview Skills	Networking	Total Revenue
120000	130000	110000	90000	

3. **Click cell** E2, **type** =SUM(A2:D2), **press** ENTER, **select cells** A2:E2, **click the** Accounting Number Format button $\boxed{\$}$ **in the Number group, then if necessary adjust column widths to show all labels and values**

4. **Click cell** A3, **enter the formula** =A2/$E$2, **copy the formula to the range** B3:D3, **then with the cells still selected, click the** Percent Style button $\boxed{\%}$ **in the Number group**

   By default, an Excel spreadsheet that you create in Word is formatted with the default theme. You want the labels and values in the spreadsheet to match the theme applied to the rest of the Word document.

5. **Click the** Page Layout tab, **click the** Themes button **in the Themes group, then click the** Parallax **theme**

6. **Click outside the spreadsheet object, double-click the** object **again, then if necessary, drag the lower-right corner of the spreadsheet object up and to the left to reduce its size so it displays only the data in the range** A1:E3 **as shown in** FIGURE 4-5

7. **Click outside the spreadsheet object to return to Word, then delete** WORKSHOPS, **if necessary**

8. **Double-click the** spreadsheet object, **click cell** C2, **type** 200000, **press** ENTER, **select the range** A1:E3, **click the** Format as Table button **in the Styles group, select** Lavender, Table Style Medium 7, **click** OK, **click** Convert to Range **in the Tools group, then click** Yes

   The total is updated to reflect the change in the revenue from the Interview Skills workshop, the table is converted to a range, and the data is formatted with a table style.

9. **Click outside the spreadsheet object, click the** Home tab, **compare your screen to** FIGURE 4-6, **then save the document**

FIGURE 4-5: Spreadsheet object resized

Following is the current employment status of registered job seekers at the end of the First Quarter.

Employment Sector	Full Time Long Term	Full Time Short Term	Not Yet Employed	Total	Percent Employed
Finance & Accounting Careers	200	150	40	390	90%
Creative Careers	350	120	80	550	85%
Technical Careers	125	100	120	345	65%
Office Support Careers	280	350	90	720	88%
Totals	955	720	330	2005	84%

In the First Quarter, JCL Talent placed 84% of candidates. Click to view the Excel spreadsheet containing information about First Quarter placements.

Workshop Revenue

JCL Talent offers several workshops to job seekers: Resume Writing, Self-Assessment, Interview Preparation and Practice, and Networking Skills. Following is the breakdown of revenue generated

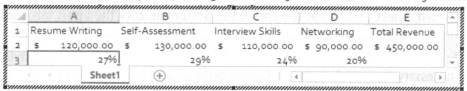

	A	B	C	D	E
1	Resume Writing	Self-Assessment	Interview Skills	Networking	Total Revenue
2	$ 120,000.00	$ 130,000.00	$ 110,000.00	$ 90,000.00	$ 450,000.00
3	27%	29%	24%	20%	

Sheet1

Corporate Clients

Five new corporate clients signed on with JCL Talent in the First Quarter. Each of these clients maintains

FIGURE 4-6: Completed Excel spreadsheet embedded in Word

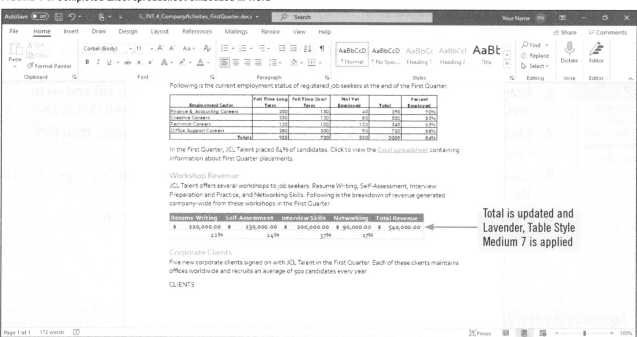

Following is the current employment status of registered job seekers at the end of the First Quarter.

Employment Sector	Full Time Long Term	Full Time Short Term	Not Yet Employed	Total	Percent Employed
Finance & Accounting Careers	200	150	40	390	90%
Creative Careers	350	120	80	550	85%
Technical Careers	125	100	120	345	65%
Office Support Careers	280	350	90	720	88%
Totals	955	720	330	2005	84%

In the First Quarter, JCL Talent placed 84% of candidates. Click to view the Excel spreadsheet containing information about First Quarter placements.

Workshop Revenue

JCL Talent offers several workshops to job seekers: Resume Writing, Self-Assessment, Interview Preparation and Practice, and Networking Skills. Following is the breakdown of revenue generated company-wide from these workshops in the First Quarter.

Resume Writing	Self-Assessment	Interview Skills	Networking	Total Revenue
$ 120,000.00	$ 130,000.00	$ 200,000.00	$ 90,000.00	$ 540,000.00
22%	24%	37%	17%	

Total is updated and Lavender, Table Style Medium 7 is applied

Corporate Clients

Five new corporate clients signed on with JCL Talent in the First Quarter. Each of these clients maintains offices worldwide and recruits an average of 500 candidates every year.

CLIENTS

Embed an Excel File in Word

**Learning
Outcomes**
• Embed an Excel
file in Word
• Change work-
sheets in an
embedded
Excel file

In Integration Module 1, you learned that when you embed a Word file in an Excel spreadsheet, the original Word formatting is retained. You then edit the embedded file by double-clicking it and using Word tools to make changes to the text and formatting. You use the same procedure to embed an Excel file in Word. In general, when you create a file in one program and embed it into another program, the formatting of the original file is retained. TABLE 4-1 summarizes the integration tasks you performed in this unit. **CASE** ▶ *You want the summary to include a list of five new corporate clients. This list is included in one of the worksheets in the IL_INT_4_CompanyData workbook.*

STEPS

1. **In Word, select** CLIENTS **at the end of the document, click the** Insert tab, **click the** Object button **in the Text group, then click the** Create from File tab

2. **Click** Browse, **navigate to the location where you stored IL_INT_4_CompanyData.xlsx, if necessary, then click** IL_INT_4_CompanyData.xlsx

3. **Click** Insert, **then click** OK

   You do not anticipate needing to update the list of clients, so you insert the Excel file into the Word document as an Excel object that is not linked to the source file. Any changes you make to the Excel file in Word are not made to the source file in Excel.

4. **Delete** CLIENTS, **then double-click the** Excel object

   The object is embedded, so you edit it by double-clicking it and using the source program tools. The Excel Ribbon and tabs replace the Word ones; however, the title bar shows that you are still working in the Word document and using Excel tools only to modify the embedded Excel file. You need to view the worksheet that contains information about the new clients and apply the Parallax theme applied to the Word document.

5. **Scroll down in Word so you can see the Excel sheet tabs if necessary, then click the** New Clients sheet tab

QUICK TIP
You can also drag
the lower-right
corner of the spread-
sheet object to resize
it proportionally.

6. **Drag the right side and bottom side of the spreadsheet object to the left and up to modify its size so it displays only the data in the range A1:D7 as shown in** FIGURE 4-7

7. **Click the** Page Layout tab, **click the** Themes button **in the Themes group, then click** Parallax

8. **Click outside the embedded object, click the** View tab, **then click the** One Page button **in the Zoom group**

9. **Enter your name where indicated in the footer, then save the document**

   The completed document appears as shown in FIGURE 4-8.

Formatting pasted, embedded, and linked objects

When you work with Copy and Paste Special options, as you did in the first lesson of this module, you select options in the Paste Special dialog box to format the copied object. With embedded objects, you double-click them in the destination program and then use tools in the source program to change the content or formatting. For linked objects, such as a chart or a worksheet range, you modify the object in the source program, which is then automatically updated in the destination program. The exception occurs when you link an entire file to a document in a destination program. In that case, you can modify the object either by double-clicking it in the destination program or by changing it in the source program.

FIGURE 4-7: Excel file inserted into Word and resized

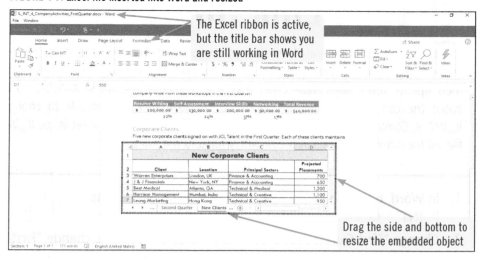

The Excel ribbon is active, but the title bar shows you are still working in Word

Drag the side and bottom to resize the embedded object

FIGURE 4-8: Completed document

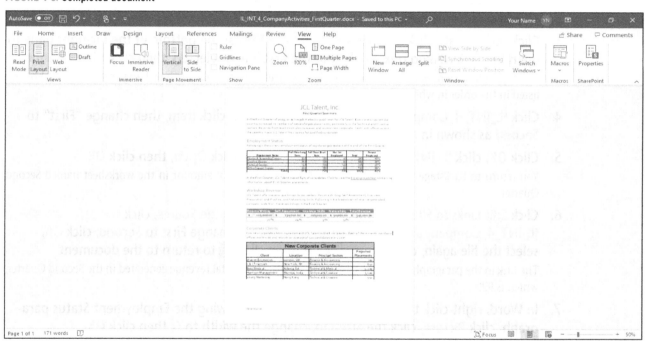

TABLE 4-1: Module 4 integration tasks

object	command	source program	destination program	result	connection type	page no.
Excel range	Copy/Paste Special/Paste Link	Excel	Word	Microsoft Excel Worksheet Object	Link	2
Excel cell	Copy/Paste using the Link & Merge Formatting option	Excel	Word	Formatted text with line breaks	Link	2
Excel file	Insert/Hyperlink/Existing File or Web Page	Excel	Word	Underlined word that users click to view source document	Hyperlink	4
Excel spreadsheet object	Insert/Table/Excel spreadsheet	Excel	Word	Embedded Excel spreadsheet object	Embed	6
Excel spreadsheet file	Insert/Object/Create from File/ Browse	Excel	Word	Embedded Excel spreadsheet file	Embed	8

Change Link Sources

Learning
Outcome
• Edit links in the
  Edit Links
  dialog box

You can change the source of any link that you create between two files, even when the files are created in different source programs. You use the Links dialog box to change link sources and then update links. **CASE** ▸ *Lydia asks you to modify the Word summary to include information about the company activities in Quarter 2. To save time, you decide to change the links in the IL_INT_4_CompanyActivities_FirstQuarter file so they reference a new sheet in the IL_INT_4_CompanyData file. All the other information in the summary remains the same.*

STEPS

1. **In Word, return to 100% view, then save the document as IL_INT_4_CompanyActivities_SecondQuarter**

2. **Change "First Quarter" to Second Quarter in the subtitle, change "First Quarter of 2019" to Second Quarter of 2019 in the first paragraph, then use Find and Replace to find every instance of First and replace it with Second**

   You will make five replacements.

3. **Click the File tab, click Info, click Edit Links to Files at the bottom of the far-right pane to open the Links dialog box, verify that the first link is selected, then click Change Source**

   The top link references the Microsoft Excel worksheet object. Links in the Change source dialog box are listed in the order in which they appear in the document.

4. **Click IL_INT_4_CompanyData.xlsx in the list of files, click Item, then change "First" to Second as shown in FIGURE 4-9**

5. **Click OK, click IL_INT_4_CompanyData.xlsx again, click Open, then click OK**

   You return to Backstage view. The link now references the total amount in the worksheet named Second Quarter.

6. **Click Edit Links to Files, click the second link, click Change Source, click IL_INT_4_CompanyData.xlsx, click the Item button, change First to Second, click OK, select the file again, click Open, click OK, then click ⬅ to return to the document**

   The link in the paragraph below the table now references the total revenue generated in the Second Quarter, which is 92%.

7. **In Word, right-click the Excel worksheet object following the Employment Status paragraph, click Picture, click the Size tab, change the width to 6, then click OK**

   Each time you open the Word document, the size of the copied Excel worksheet object reverts to the original size.

QUICK TIP
To adjust spacing, click to the left of the total and press BACKSPACE, then click to the right of the total and press DELETE.

8. **Adjust the spacing so the percentage in the sentence below the worksheet object (92%) is part of the text**

   The spacing of the pasted percentage changes because you originally selected the Link & Merge Formatting paste option, which inserts paragraph breaks.

9. **Save the document, submit the file to your instructor, then close the document and exit Word and Excel**

   The completed document appears as shown in FIGURE 4-10.

FIGURE 4-9: Changing the source location of a link

First changed to Second →

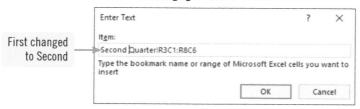

FIGURE 4-10: Completed document

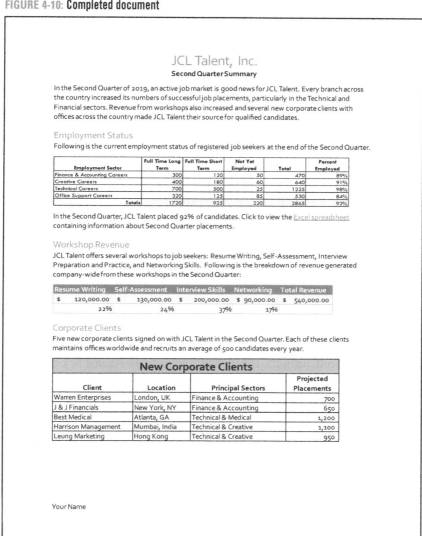

Reestablishing links

When you open a Word file that is linked to an Excel file, you receive the following message: "This document contains links that may refer to other files. Do you want to update this document with the data from the linked files?" If you created the files on your own computer, you can click "Yes" to reestablish the links between the two files. If you have sent the files to another person, such as your instructor, they will need to click "No" to open the Word file without linking to the Excel file. Note that you will need to adjust the spacing and sizes of some of the pasted Excel objects, depending on how they were pasted into Word.

Practice

Skills Review

1. **Use Paste Special to modify formatting.**
   a. Start Word, open the file IL_INT_4-3.docx from the location where you store your Data Files, save it as **IL_INT_4_RenfrewCollegeFoodServices_Fall**, start Excel, open the file IL_INT_4-4.xlsx from the location where you store your Data Files, then save it as **IL_INT_4_FoodServicesData**.
   b. Copy the range A3:F10, switch to Word, then paste the copied range as a linked Microsoft Excel Worksheet Object to replace "FOOD SERVICES."
   c. Open the Format Object dialog box, and change the width of the object to **6.5**.
   d. In Excel, copy cell F10, then paste it using the Link & Merge Formatting option, replacing "XX" in the paragraph below the copied Excel object and then adjusting spacing. (*Hint*: Click to the left of the total and press BACKSPACE, then click to the right of the total and press DELETE.)
   e. In Excel, change the average weekly revenue for the Main Cafeteria to **12,000**.
   f. In Word, update the link to the Microsoft Excel Worksheet Object, then update the total and adjust spacing. Verify the new total is $672,000.00.
   g. Save and close the Excel workbook, then save the Word document.

2. **Create a hyperlink between Word and Excel.**
   a. In Word, select "Excel spreadsheet" in the second sentence of the second paragraph (below the pasted Excel worksheet object).
   b. Open the Insert Hyperlink dialog box, then verify that Existing File or Web Page is selected.
   c. Select IL_INT_4_FoodServicesData.xlsx.
   d. Create a ScreenTip that uses the text **This link opens the Food Services Data workbook in Excel.**, then return to the document.
   e. Test the hyperlink.
   f. Close the workbook and return to Word, open the Create New Theme Colors dialog box from the Design tab, then change the color assigned to Followed Hyperlink to Purple, Accent 4.
   g. Save the document.

3. **Create an Excel spreadsheet in Word.**
   a. In Word, select SPREADSHEET after the New Food Trucks paragraph, then insert a new Excel spreadsheet from the Tables group on the Insert tab.
   b. Enter the following labels and values in the worksheet:

Food Truck	Weekly Revenue	Weeks	Totals
Belle BBQ	4200	16	
Fresh Bowls	4200	16	
Asian Fusion	6600	16	

Skills Review (continued)

  c. For the first item, calculate the Total as the product of the Weekly Revenue multiplied by Weeks. Copy the formula as necessary.

  d. Apply the Accounting Number format to the appropriate cells and widen columns as needed.

  e. Reduce the size of the object so only the data appears, click outside the spreadsheet object to return to Word, then delete SPREADSHEET.

  f. Edit the spreadsheet object by changing the weekly revenue for the Fresh Bowls food truck to 7200.

  g. Apply the Gallery theme to the worksheet, then format the data using the Red, Table Style Medium 2 table style and convert the table to a range.

  h. Close the Excel worksheet to return to Word, then save the Word document.

4. Embed an Excel file in Word.

  a. In Word, insert the IL_INT_4_FoodServicesData.xlsx file as an embedded object from a file to replace EVENTS below the last paragraph.

  b. Double-click the inserted object, and show the Events sheet tab.

  c. Resize the spreadsheet object so it displays only the data in the range A1:C7, and apply the Gallery theme.

  d. In Word, enter your name where indicated in the footer, then save the document.

5. Change link sources.

  a. In Word, save the document as **IL_INT_4_RenfrewCollegeFoodServices_Spring**, change "Fall" to **Spring** in the subtitle, then change "September and December of 2019" to **January and April of 2020** in the first paragraph.

  b. Open the Links dialog box from Backstage view, then open the Change Source dialog box for the first link.

  c. Select the IL_INT_4_FoodServicesData.xlsx, then use the Item button to change "Fall" to **Spring**.

  d. Click OK, click the filename, click Open, then click OK.

  e. Change the second link so it also references the Spring worksheet.

  f. In Word, reduce the width of the Microsoft Excel Worksheet Object to **6.5**, then adjust spacing so the linked total is part of the text.

  g. Verify the new total is $712,000.00.

  h. Save the document, submit the file to your instructor, then close the document and exit Word and Excel. The completed document for the Spring term appears as shown in FIGURE 4-11.

FIGURE 4-11

Renfrew College

Summary of Food Services – Spring Term

Renfrew College in Baltimore, Maryland, contracted with Maryland Catering to provide food services on campus between January and April of 2020. Following is the list of food services provided.

Campus Location	Food Service	Category	Average Weekly Revenue	Weeks	Total
Main Cafeteria	Full Cafeteria Service	Cafeteria	$ 11,000.00	16	$ 176,000.00
Humanities Building	Coffee Kiosk	Kiosk	$ 8,000.00	16	$ 128,000.00
Sciences Building	Taco Food Truck	Food Truck	$ 4,200.00	16	$ 67,200.00
Main Library	Coffee Kiosk	Kiosk	$ 5,500.00	16	$ 88,000.00
Central Campus	Pizza Food Truck	Food Truck	$ 2,800.00	16	$ 44,800.00
Residences	Full Cafeteria Service	Cafeteria	$ 13,000.00	16	$ 208,000.00
					$ 712,000.00

Food Services at Renfrew College generated revenue of $ 712,000.00 from all locations. Click to view the Excel spreadsheet containing detailed information about the food services.

New Food Trucks

Renfrew College plans to work with Maryland Catering to offer licenses to three new food trucks in the 2020/2021 academic term. Following are projected revenues from the food trucks based on results from other campuses of a similar size to Renfrew College:

Food Truck	Weekly Revenue	Weeks	Totals
Belle BBQ	$ 4,200.00	16	$ 67,200.00
Fresh Bowls	$ 7,200.00	16	$ 115,200.00
Asian Fusion	$ 6,600.00	16	$ 105,600.00

Special Events

Renfrew College provides food services for these events annually.

Renfrew College		
Food Services - Special Events		
Event	**Category**	**Per Person Price**
Spring Graduation	Buffet	$ 70.00
Student Orientation	Buffet	$ 50.00
Awards Ceremony	Formal Dinner	$ 125.00
Alumni Reception	Appetizers	$ 50.00

Your Name

Independent Challenge 1

You assist the office manager at Riverwalk Medical Clinic, a large outpatient medical facility that provides a wide range of medical and health services and programs to community members. You have been asked to create a summary about the revenue generated from the various therapy services available at the clinic. You open the summary in Word and then add objects from data stored in an Excel worksheet.

a. In Word, open the file IL_INT_4-5.docx from the location where you store your Data Files, then save it as **IL_INT_4_RiverwalkClinicTherapies**.

b. In Excel, open the file IL_INT_4-6.xlsx from the location where you store your Data Files, then save it as **IL_INT_4_TherapistData**.

c. In Excel, calculate the weekly revenue generated by each of the six therapists, then calculate the total weekly revenue in cell E10. Notice how the chart is filled in when you copy the formula because the chart was created from data in columns A and E.

d. Copy cells A3:E9, then paste them using the Link & Use Destination Styles paste option to the left of THERAPISTS following paragraph 1 in the Word document.

e. Select the pasted table, open the Table Design tab, then apply the Grid Table 4, Accent 2 table style.

f. Adjust the width of the columns where needed so that none of the information in the data rows 2 through 6 wraps, then delete THERAPISTS.

g. In Excel, copy the value for total revenue and paste it using the Link and Merge Formatting option to replace "XX". Adjust spacing as needed, then in Excel, save and close the workbook.

h. Create a hyperlink to the Excel file from "here" in the Weekly Revenue by Therapy paragraph. Enter **This link opens an Excel workbook containing revenue data about the therapists.** as the ScreenTip.

i. Test the hyperlink to reopen the Excel workbook, then in Word assign the Red, Accent 5 color to Followed Hyperlink.

j. In Word, replace COSTS below the Therapy Costs paragraph with a new Excel spreadsheet using the data below.

Item	Weeks	Cost	Total
Maintenance	4	500	
Support Staff	4	5000	
Utilities	4	200	
Therapists	4	18000	

Use formulas to determine the total cost of each item. Format all dollar amounts with the Currency format, and resize the worksheet object so only the data in cells A1:D5 appears.

k. Change the workbook theme to Facet, then apply the Dark Green, Medium 3 table style, convert the table to a range, and widen columns as needed.

l. Follow the hyperlink to view the Excel workbook, then change Gary Larsen's name to **Gary Morelli** and his Hourly Rate to **$160**.

m. In Word, verify that the data has been updated or update the links. Adjust spacing as needed.

n. Enter your name where indicated in the footer, save the document, submit it to your instructor, then close the document.

o. In Excel, enter your name in cell A32, save the workbook, submit it to your instructor, then close the workbook.

Visual Workshop

Start Word, open the file IL_INT_4-7.docx from the location where you store your Data Files, then save it as **IL_INT_4_UniversityChoir**. Start Excel, open the file IL_INT_4-8.xlsx, add your name where indicated, click cell A1, save it as **IL_INT_4_TourData**, then close it. In Word, insert the Excel file as a linked object below the paragraph. (*Hint*: In the Object dialog box, click the Link to file check box on the Create from File tab.) Edit the Excel file by double-clicking it, show the US Budget worksheet and then update the link in Word (*Hint*: Right-click the Excel object, click Update Link and keep the worksheet open. You will know the object is updated because the unit cost for Accommodations changes from $150 to $110). Apply the Quotable theme to the worksheet and format the data with Dark Teal, Table Style Medium 9 and convert it to a range, then save and close the Excel file. Update the link in Word. Edit the Word document by replacing "Europe" with "the United States" and "Paris" with "Atlanta" as shown in FIGURE 4-12. Open the Links dialog box, then click Break Link to break the link between the Word document and the Excel workbook. Include your name where shown in the Word document, submit it to your instructor, then close the document.

FIGURE 4-12

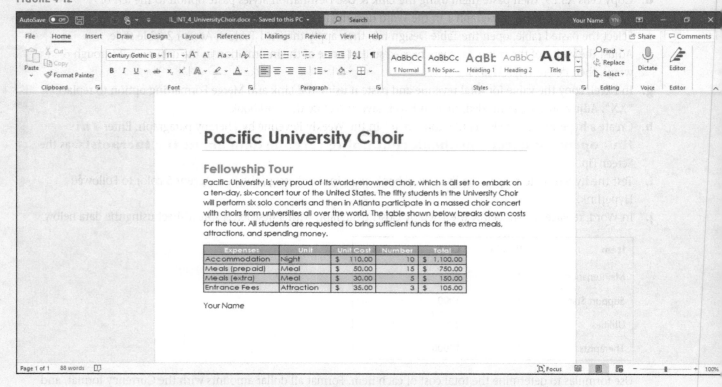

Improving Tables and Creating Advanced Queries

CASE ▶ You are working with Lydia Snyder, vice president of operations at JCL Talent, to build a research database to manage industry, company, and job data. In this module, you'll improve tables and build advanced queries.

Module Objectives

After completing this module, you will be able to:

- Create Lookup fields
- Modify Lookup fields
- Modify Validation and Indexed properties
- Create Attachment and Hyperlink fields
- Create Long Text fields
- Create Top Values queries
- Create parameter queries
- Set properties in queries
- Find unmatched records
- Create summary queries
- Create crosstab queries

Files You Will Need

IL_AC_5-1.accdb
Support_AC_5_aba.png
IL_AC_5-2.accdb
Support_AC_5_employee.jpg

IL_AC_5-3.accdb
Support_AC_5_nurse.png
IL_AC_5-4.accdb
IL_AC_5-5.accdb

Create Lookup Fields

**Learning
Outcomes**
• Create a Lookup
field
• Edit data in a
Lookup field

Lookup fields provide a list of values for a field. The values can be stored in another table or entered in the **Row Source** Lookup property of the field. Fields that are good candidates for Lookup properties are those that contain a defined set of values such as State, Gender, or Department. You can set Lookup properties for a field in Table Design View using the **Lookup Wizard.** **CASE** *The names and two-character postal abbreviations for the 50 United States, 13 Canadian provinces, and Washington, D.C., are stored in the StatesAndProvinces table. You will use the Lookup Wizard to look up information from this table for the State field in the Companies table.*

STEPS

1. **sanf↓ Start Access, open the** IL_AC_5-1.accdb database **from the location where you store your Data Files, save it as** IL_AC_5_Jobs, **enable content if prompted, right-click the Companies table in the Navigation Pane, then click** Design View
   The Lookup Wizard is included in the Data Type list.

2. **Click the** Short Text data type **for the State field, click the** Data Type list arrow, **then click** Lookup Wizard
   The Lookup Wizard starts and prompts you for information about where the Lookup column will get its values. You want to look up values from an existing table.

3. **Click** Next, **click** Table: StatesAndProvinces, **click** Next, **click the** Select All Fields button **>>** , **click** Next, **click the** first field sort arrow, **click** StateAbbrev, **click** Next, **click the** Hide key column check box **to uncheck it, click** Next, **click** Next to accept the **StateAbbrev field to store, click the** Enable Data Integrity check box, **click** Finish **to complete the Lookup Wizard, then click** Yes **to save the table and relationship**
   Note that the data type for the State field is still Short Text. The Lookup Wizard is a process for setting Lookup property values for a field, not a data type itself. The last dialog box of the Lookup Wizard established a one-to-many relationship between the StatesAndProvinces and the Companies tables using the common State field.

4. **Click the** Lookup tab **in the Field Properties pane to observe the new Lookup properties for the State field, as shown in** FIGURE 5-1
   The Lookup Wizard helped you enter Lookup property values for the State field.

5. **Click the** View button **to switch to Datasheet View, press** TAB **five times to move to the State field, then click the** State list arrow, **as shown in** FIGURE 5-2
   The State field now provides a list of values from the StatesAndProvinces table. The first column with the two-character state or province abbreviation contains the data that is saved in the State field of the Companies table. Note that the first column is wider than needed. You will modify Lookup field properties such as column widths in the next lesson.

6. **Navigate to the record for CompanyID 8 (Bank of the Midwest), click the** State list arrow, **click** MO **for Missouri, then close the Companies table**

FIGURE 5-1: Viewing Lookup properties in Table Design View

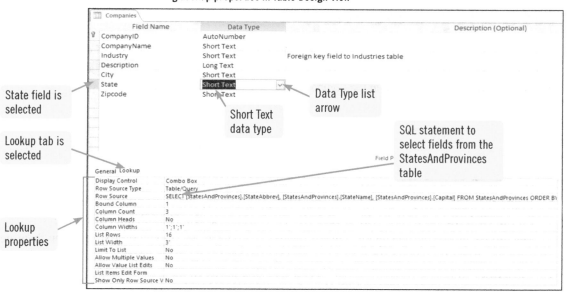

State field is selected

Lookup tab is selected

Lookup properties

Data Type list arrow

Short Text data type

SQL statement to select fields from the StatesAndProvinces table

FIGURE 5-2: Using a Lookup field in a datasheet

CompanyID	CompanyName	Industry	Description	City	State	Zipcode	Click to Add
1	ABA Solutions	Healthcare	ABA Solutions is an American managed health care company, which sells traditional and consumer directed health care insurance plans and related services, such as	Atlanta	GA	30301	
2	Accent Group	Transportation	Accent Group solves our clients' toughest challenges by providing unmatched services in transportation strategy, consulting, digital, technology and operations.	Charleston			
3	AIT Group	Consulting	AIT Group is a premier provider of IT Consulting Engineering Consulting Management Solutions	Baltimore			
4	Addcore Partners	Personnel Services	Addcore Partners the world.	Raleigh			
5	Alark Inc	Information	Alark Inc is an American computing company	Kansas City			
6	Artwell Corp	Transportation	Artwell Corp designs solutions.	Chicago			
7	Bower Pet Hospital	Healthcare	Bower Pet Hospital is a privately owned company that operates veterinary clinics.	Scottsdale	AZ	85252	
8	Bank of the Midwest	Banking	Bank of the Midwest is a multinational banking and financial services corporation.	Kansas City	MO	64102	

Row Source dropdown showing:
GA	Georgia	Atlanta
HI	Hawaii	Honolulu
IA	Iowa	Des Moines
ID	Idaho	Boise
IL	Illinois	Springfield
IN	Indiana	Indianapolis
KS	Kansas	Topeka
KT	Kentucky	Frankfort
LA	Louisiana	Baton Rouge
MA	Massachusetts	Boston
MB	Manitoba	Winnepeg
MD	Maryland	Annapolis
ME	Maine	Augusta
MI	Michigan	Lansing
MN	Minnesota	St. Paul
MO	Missouri	Jefferson City

Row Source property selects three fields from the StatesAndProvinces table and sorts the records in ascending order on the StateAbbrev field

Record: I◄ 1 of 30 ►I ►I T. No Filter Search

Multivalued fields

In a datasheet or form, a **multivalued field** presents check boxes next to the values in the list. The check boxes allow you to select more than one value to store in the field. The drawback, however, is that it is more difficult to find and filter for individual values when more than one value is stored in the same field. Many relational database designers prefer to create a child table with a one-to-many relationship to the parent table to store multiple values for a field rather than using a multivalued field. To create a multivalued field, enter Yes in the **Allow Multiple Values** Lookup property.

Modify Lookup Fields

Lookup properties determine how the Lookup field works. See TABLE 5-1 for a list of common Lookup properties. Like all field properties, you can manually edit Lookup properties. **CASE** ▸ *You modify the Lookup properties of the State field in the Company table to make it easier to use.*

STEPS

1. **Right-click the** Companies table **in the Navigation Pane, click** Design View **on the shortcut menu, click the** State field, **then click the** Lookup tab **in the Field Properties pane**

   The first column of the lookup list contains the two-character abbreviation for the state. Given there are only two characters in that field, it does not need to be as wide as the other columns.

2. **Click the** Column Widths property, **then edit the entry to be** 0.5"; 2"; 1.5"

   With the individual column widths modified, you'll modify the overall width of the combo box using the List Width property.

3. **Click the** List Width property, **then edit the entry to be** 4"

   You also want to show more than 16 rows in the list, which will reduce the amount of scrolling for users.

4. **Click the** List Rows property, **then edit the entry to be** 30

   You decide to show the field names as column headings in the list.

5. **Double-click the** Column Heads property **to change the value from No to Yes, as shown in** FIGURE 5-3, **click the** Property Update Options button ⌐, **click** Update all lookup properties everywhere State is used, **then click** OK

   It is best to set all field properties in Table Design View before building queries, forms, and reports, but if you revise a field's properties after creating other objects, the **Property Update Options button** ⌐ appears to help you propagate property changes to other objects that use that field.

   You also want to modify the **Caption** property of the CompanyName field to shorten it to "Company" when the field appears in a datasheet, form, or report.

6. **Click the** CompanyName field, **click the** General tab **in the Field Properties pane, click the** Caption property, **then type** Company

   With the modifications made to the Companies table, you are ready to work with the data.

7. **Click the** View button ⊞ **to switch to Datasheet View, click** Yes **when prompted to save the table, press** TAB **five times to move to the State field, then click the** State list arrow, **as shown in** FIGURE 5-4

8. **Close the Companies table**

FIGURE 5-3: Changing Lookup properties

State field is selected

Lookup tab is selected

Property Update Options button

Column Heads

Column Widths

List Rows

List Width

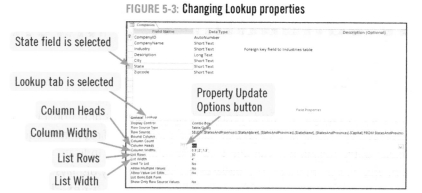

FIGURE 5-4: Modified Lookup field

Company is used as the Caption for the CompanyName field

Column Width and List Width are modified

List Rows set to 30 to minimize scrolling

Column Heads (field names) are displayed

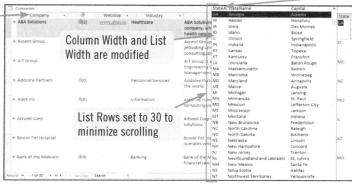

TABLE 5-1: Common Lookup properties

property name	description	property values
Display Control	Determines the type of control used to display this field on forms	Text Box, List Box, or Combo Box; if set to Text Box, all other Lookup properties are removed
Row Source Type	Identifies the type of source for the control's data	Table/Query, Value List, or Field List
Row Source	Identifies the source of the control's data	Table name, query name, or SQL statement
Bound Column	Identifies the list column that is bound to the Lookup field	1 by default, but can be set to any number based on the number of fields selected in the Row Source
Column Count	Identifies the number of columns to display in the list	1 by default, but can be set to any number based on the number of fields selected in the Row Source
Column Heads	Determines whether to display field names as the first row in the list	Yes or No; No by default
Column Widths	Sets the column widths in the list	1" by default, but if the Row Source identifies more than one column, column widths are separated by semicolons such as: 1"; 1"; 1"
List Rows	Sets the number of rows to display in the list	16 by default, but can be set to any number
List Width	Sets the overall width of the list	1" by default
Limit To List	Determines whether you can enter a new value into the field or whether the entries are limited to the drop-down list	Yes or No. No by default
Allow Multiple Values	Determines whether you can select more than one value for a field	Yes or No; No by default
Allow Value List Edits	Determines whether users can add or edit the list	Yes or No; No by default
List Items Edit Form	Identifies the name of the form to open and use if allowing users to edit the values in the list	The form name of a form saved in the current database
Show only Row Source Values	Shows only values that match the current row source when Allow Multiples Values is set to Yes	Yes or No; No by default

Modify Validation and Index Properties

**Learning
Outcomes**
- Modify the
  Validation Rule
  and Validation
  Text properties
- Define Validation
  Rule expressions
- Modify the
  Indexed property

The **Validation Rule** and Validation Text field properties help you prevent unreasonable data from being entered into the database. For example, a validation rule for a Date/Time field might require date entries on or after a particular date. A validation rule for a Currency field might indicate that valid entries fall between a minimum and maximum value. The **Validation Text** property displays an explanatory message when a user tries to enter data that breaks the validation rule. The **Indexed** property helps you speed up sorts and searches on fields commonly used for those purposes. **CASE** ▸ *Lydia Snyder reminds you that the database will be tracking job postings that have a minimum annual salary of $35,000. You can use the validation properties to establish this rule for the StartingSalary field in the Jobs table. Given you are commonly sorting and searching on the StartingSalary field, you will also establish an index for it.*

STEPS

QUICK TIP

You can also set validation properties in Table Datasheet View using the Validation button on the Fields tab.

1. **Right-click the** Jobs table **in the Navigation Pane, click** Design View, **click the** StartingSalary field, **click the** Validation Rule property box, **then type** >=35000

   This entry restricts all values in the StartingSalary field to be equal to or greater than $35,000. See TABLE 5-2 for more examples of Validation Rule expressions. The Validation Text property provides a helpful message to the user when the entry in the field breaks the rule entered in the Validation Rule property.

2. **Click the** Validation Text box, **then type** Value must be greater than or equal to $35,000

   Design View of the Jobs table should now look like FIGURE 5-5.

QUICK TIP

The Test Validation Rules button tests the Validation Rule, Required, and Allow Zero Length properties.

3. **Save the table, then click** Yes **when asked to test the existing data with new data integrity rules**

   Because no values in the StartingSalary field are less than $35,000, Access finds no errors in the current data and saves the table.

QUICK TIP

Click the Indexes button on the Design tab to view, add, or modify the indexes for the fields in that table.

4. **Double-click the** Indexed property **to change the value from No to** Yes (Duplicates OK)

   An **index** on a field will speed up the sort and search process for that field. Because the indexing process takes some overhead, be careful to add an index to only those fields that are commonly used for sorting and searching. The Indexed property is automatically set to Yes (No Duplicates) for the primary key field in the table and Yes (Duplicates OK) for other fields in the table that end in "ID".

5. **Click the** View button ▦ **to display the datasheet, click** Yes **when prompted to save the table, press** TAB **four times to move to the StartingSalary field, type** 29000, **then press** TAB

   Because you tried to enter a value that evaluated false for the Validation Rule expression in the StartingSalary field, a dialog box opens and displays the Validation Text entry, as shown in FIGURE 5-6.

6. **Click** OK **to close the validation message, press** ESC **to reject the invalid entry in the StartingSalary field, then close the Jobs table**

FIGURE 5-5: Setting Validation and Indexed properties

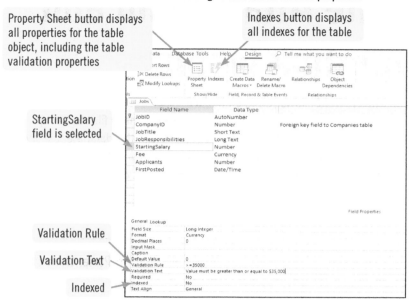

Property Sheet button displays all properties for the table object, including the table validation properties

Indexes button displays all indexes for the table

StartingSalary field is selected

Validation Rule

Validation Text

Indexed

FIGURE 5-6: Validation Text message

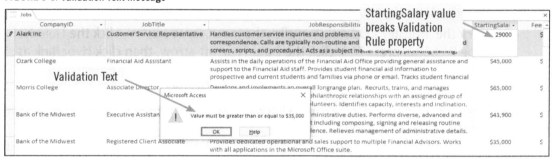

Validation Text

StartingSalary value breaks Validation Rule property

TABLE 5-2: Validation Rule expressions

data type	validation rule expression	description
Number or Currency	>0	Number must be positive
Number or Currency	>10 And <100	Number must be greater than 10 and less than 100
Number or Currency	10 Or 20 Or 30	Number must be 10, 20, or 30
Short Text	"AZ" Or "CO" Or "NM"	Entry must be AZ, CO, or NM
Date/Time	>=#7/1/19#	Date must be on or after 7/1/2019
Date/Time	>#1/1/10# And <#1/1/30#	Date must be greater than 1/1/2010 and less than 1/1/2030

Table validation properties

If your validation rule includes more than one field, open the Property Sheet for the table by clicking the Properties button on the Design tab in Table Design View. Enter the validation rule expression in the table's Validation Rule property. For example, a validation rule that includes two fields might be [ShipDate]>=[SaleDate], and the accompanying Validation Text property might be "The ShipDate value must be greater than or equal to the SaleDate value".

Create Attachment and Hyperlink Fields

Learning Outcomes
- Create an Attachment field
- Attach and view a file in an Attachment field
- Create a Hyperlink field
- Enter a webpage address in a Hyperlink field

An **Attachment field** allows you to embed a file such as a photo, Word document, PowerPoint presentation, or Excel workbook with a record. You may insert as many files to a single Attachment field as desired. If you would rather link to a file than store a copy of it in the database, use a **Hyperlink field**. Hyperlink fields are also used when you want to link to an external webpage or an email address. **CASE** ▶ *You decide to add an Attachment field to store company images and a Hyperlink field to store the home webpage address for each company in the Companies table.*

STEPS

1. **Right-click the** Companies table **in the Navigation Pane, then click** Design View
   You can insert a new field anywhere in the list.

2. **Click the** Industry field selector, **click the** Insert Rows button **on the Design tab, click the** Field Name cell, **type** Logo, **press TAB, click the** Data Type list arrow, **then click** Attachment
   You will add the Hyperlink field below the new Logo Attachment field.

3. **Click the** Industry field selector, **click the** Insert Rows button, **click the** Field Name cell, **type** WebSite, **press TAB, click the** Data Type list arrow, **then click** Hyperlink **as shown in** FIGURE 5-7
   Now that you've created the new fields, you're ready to add data to them in Datasheet View.

4. **Click the** Save button 🖫 **on the Quick Access toolbar, then click the** View button 🎛 **to switch to Datasheet View**
   An Attachment field cell displays a small paper clip icon with the number of files attached to the field in parentheses. At this point, each record shows zero (0) file attachments.

5. **Double-click the** attachment icon 🔘 **for the first record (CompanyID 1 ABA Solutions) to open the Attachments dialog box, click** Add, **navigate to the location where you store your Data Files, double-click** Support_AC_5_aba.png, **then click** OK
   The Support_AC_5_aba.png file is now included with the first record, and the Attachment field reflects that one (1) file has been added. You can attach more than one file and different types of files to the same field. Some file types, such as .png or .jpg files, automatically display their contents (an image) in forms and reports.

6. **Double-click the** attachment icon 🔘 **for the ABA Solutions record to open the Attachments dialog box shown in** FIGURE 5-8, **then click** Open
   The image opens in the program that is associated with the .png extension on your computer such as Windows Photos.

7. **Close the window that displays the Support_AC_5_aba.png image, click** Cancel **in the Attachments dialog box, press TAB to move to the WebSite field, type** www.abas.example.com, **then close the Companies table**
   Hyperlink fields store paths to files and webpages, not the files or webpages themselves. If you click www.abas.example.com (or any hyperlink) in the datasheet, your computer attempts to open that link, which in this case would be a website.

FIGURE 5-7: Adding Attachment and Hyperlink fields

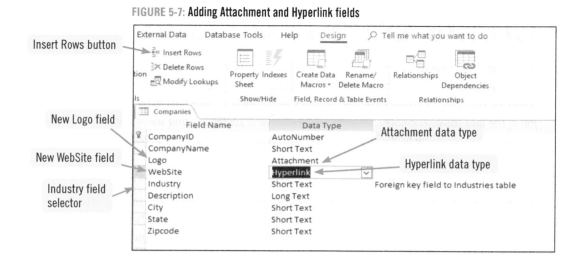

Insert Rows button

New Logo field

New WebSite field

Industry field selector

Attachment data type

Hyperlink data type

Foreign key field to Industries table

FIGURE 5-8: Opening an attached file

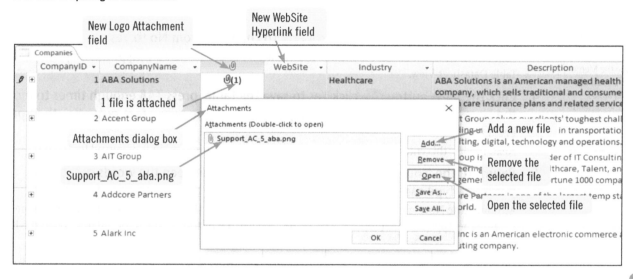

New Logo Attachment field

New WebSite Hyperlink field

1 file is attached

Attachments dialog box

Support_AC_5_aba.png

Add a new file

Remove the selected file

Open the selected file

Create Long Text Fields

**Learning
Outcomes**
• Create a Long Text
field
• Set the Append
Only property

If you want to enter more than 255 characters in a field (the maximum Field Size for a field with a Short Text data type) or retain all of the edits to a field over time, you must create a field with a **Long Text** data type that provides for these advanced features. **CASE** ▶ *Lydia wants to be able to enter notes about each job in the Jobs table. The notes may be as long as several sentences, and she also wants to retain all historical edits for the field. A new field with a Long Text data type will meet these requirements.*

STEPS

1. **Right-click the** Jobs table **in the Navigation Pane, then click** Design View

   You can also add new fields of all types in Table Datasheet View, but Table Design View provides a complete list of field properties and is therefore the generally preferred way to add and modify fields.

2. **Click the first blank** Field Name cell**, type** Notes **for the new field name, press** TAB**, click the** Data Type arrow, **then click** Long Text

   The Field Properties pane at the bottom of Table Design View changes to display properties associated with a Long Text field such as the **Append Only** property. Setting the Append Only property to Yes retains all historical edits and entries to the field.

3. **Double-click the** Append Only property **to change it from No to** Yes

   Your screen should look like **FIGURE 5-9**. To test the new Long Text field and Append Only property, work in Table Datasheet View.

4. **Click the** View button **▦, click** Yes **to save the table, press** TAB **enough times to move to the** Notes field **for the first record, type** Entry level job with great potential, **then press** ENTER

   Next, modify this entry and then observe how the historical information is preserved for the field.

5. **Return to the** Notes field **for the first record, click between the words** great **and** potential, **type** career, **then press** ENTER

   Although the Notes field only shows the last entry or edit to the field, all historical values are preserved because the Append Only property is set to Yes. To view the historical values for the field, open the History window.

6. **Right-click the** Notes field **for the first record, then click** Show column history **as shown in FIGURE 5-10**

   Each time you change the Notes field, a new line is added to the History for Notes dialog box to time-stamp the new field value.

7. **Click** OK **in the History for Notes dialog box, then close the** Jobs table

FIGURE 5-9: Creating a Long Text field

Notes field

Long Text data type

Append Only property set to Yes

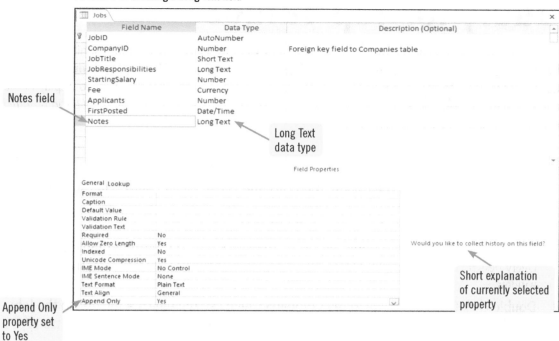

FIGURE 5-10: Viewing the History for a Long Text field

Notes field

History for Notes

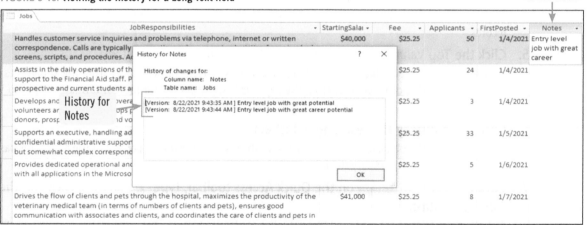

Allow Zero Length property

The **Allow Zero Length** property is available for both Short Text and Long Text fields. Yes is the default value and means that the field will accept an **intentional zero length value** when you enter two consecutive quotation marks (""). You may want to enter an intentional zero length value in a table that stores client information. For example, some clients may not want to provide personal information such as their phone number or email address. To indicate that those fields are intentionally blank, you'd enter an intentional zero length value, "". Intentional zero length values are often confused with **null** values, which mean that the field is empty for no particular reason. Both intentional zero length and null values appear blank, which can create confusion in a query. You query for intentional zero length values using two consecutive quotation marks "" as the criterion. You query for null values using **Is Null** as the criterion.

Query for Top Values

After you enter many records into a database, you may want to select only the most significant records by choosing a subset of the highest or lowest values from a sorted query. Use the **Top Values** feature in Query Design View to specify a number or percentage of sorted records that you want to display in the query's datasheet. CASE ▶ *Lydia Snyder asks you to create a listing of the top 10 percent of the jobs, sorted in descending order based on StartingSalary.*

STEPS

1. **Click the** Create tab **on the ribbon, then click the** Query Design button **in the Queries group**

   You want fields from both the Companies and the Jobs tables.

2. **Double-click** Companies, **double-click** Jobs, **then click** Close **in the Show Table dialog box**

   Query Design View displays the field lists of the Companies and Jobs tables in the upper pane of the query window.

3. **Double-click** CompanyName **in the Companies field list, double-click** JobTitle **in the Jobs field list, double-click** StartingSalary **in the Jobs field list, then click the** View button 🔲 **to switch to Datasheet View**

   The datasheet shows 82 total records. You want to know the top 10 percent of jobs based on the highest starting salaries. The next task in a Top Values query is to sort the records in the desired order.

4. **Click the** View button ⬓ **to switch to Query Design View, click the** Sort cell for the StartingSalary field, **click the** Sort list arrow, **then click** Descending

   With the records sorted in the desired order, you use the Top Values feature to display a subset of the "top" records.

5. **Click the** Top Values box **in the Query Setup group, then type** 10%

   Your screen should look like FIGURE 5-11. You can choose a value or percentage from the Top Values list or enter another value or percentage from the keyboard. See TABLE 5-3 for more information on Top Values options.

6. **Click** 🔲 **to display the resulting datasheet**

   Your screen should look like FIGURE 5-12. The datasheet shows the top 10 percent of the 82 records based on the values in the StartingSalary field.

7. **Click the** Save button 🖫 **on the Quick Access toolbar, type** TopSalaries, **click** OK, **then close the datasheet**

   As with all queries, if you enter additional job records into this database, the statistics in the TopSalaries query are automatically updated.

FIGURE 5-11: Creating a Top Values query

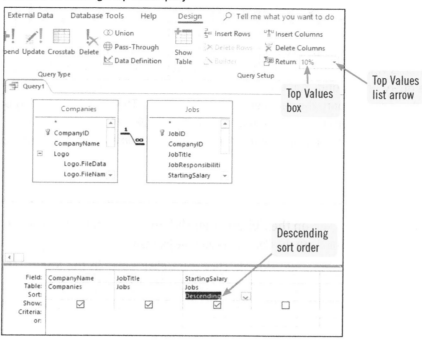

FIGURE 5-12: Top Values datasheet

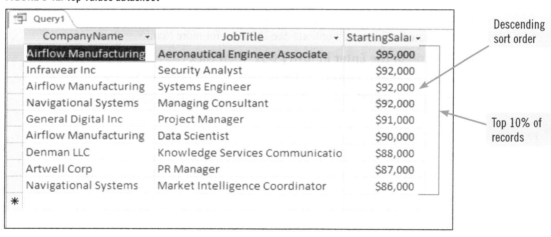

TABLE 5-3: Top Values options

action	displays
Click 5, 25, or 100 in the Top Values list	Top 5, 25, or 100 records
Enter a number, such as 10, in the Top Values box	Top 10, or whatever value is entered, records
Click 5% or 25% in the Top Values list	Top 5 percent or 25 percent of records
Enter a percentage, such as 10%, in the Top Values text box	Top 10 percent, or whatever percentage is entered, of records
Click All	All records

Create a Parameter Query

**Learning
Outcomes**
• Enter parameter
criteria
• Describe Like
operator criteria

A **parameter query** displays a dialog box that prompts you for field criteria. Your entry in the dialog box determines which records appear on the final datasheet, just as if you had entered that criteria directly in the query design grid. You can also build a form or report based on a parameter query. When you open the form or report, the parameter dialog box opens. The entry in the dialog box determines which records the query selects for the form or report. **CASE** ▶ *Lydia Snyder asks you to create a query to display the courses for an individual industry that you enter each time you run the query. To do so, you will create a parameter query.*

STEPS

QUICK TIP
You can also drag
a table from the
Navigation Pane into
Query Design View.

1. **Click the** Create tab **on the ribbon, then click the** Query Design button **in the Queries group**
   You want fields from both the Companies and the Jobs tables.

2. **Double-click** Companies, **double-click** Jobs, **click** Close **in the Show Table dialog box, double-click** CompanyName **in the Companies field list, double-click** Industry **in the Companies field list, double-click** JobTitle **in the Jobs field list, then double-click** StartingSalary **in the Jobs field list**

QUICK TIP
To enter a long
criterion, right-click
the Criteria cell, then
click Zoom.

3. **Click the** Industry field Criteria cell, **type** [Enter industry:], **then click** ▦ **to display the Enter Parameter Value dialog box, as shown in** FIGURE 5-13
   In Query Design View, you enter each parameter criterion within [square brackets], and it appears as a prompt in the Enter Parameter Value dialog box. The entry you make in the Enter Parameter Value dialog box is used as the final criterion for the field. You can combine logical operators such as greater than (>) or less than (<) as well as the keyword Like and wildcard characters such as an asterisk (*) with parameter criteria to create flexible search options. See TABLE 5-4 for more examples of parameter criteria.

QUICK TIP
Query criteria are
not case sensitive,
so "banking,"
"Banking," and
"BANKING" all yield
the same results.

4. **Type** Banking **in the Enter industry box, then click** OK
   Only those records with "Banking" in the Industry field are displayed as shown in FIGURE 5-14.

5. **Save the query with the name** IndustryParameter, **then close it**

FIGURE 5-13: **Creating a parameter query**

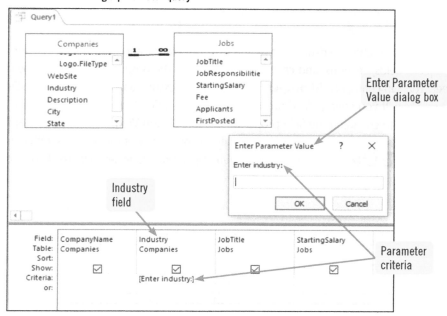

FIGURE 5-14: **Running a parameter query**

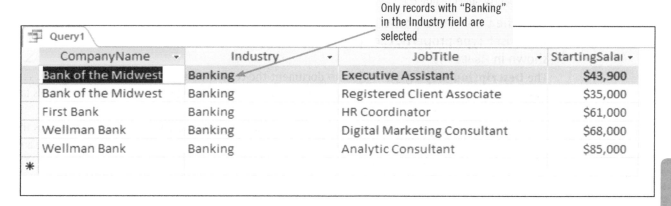

TABLE 5-4: **Examples of parameter criteria**

field data type	parameter criteria	description
Date/Time	>=[Enter start date:]	Searches for dates on or after the entered date
Date/Time	>=[Enter start date:] and <=[Enter end date:]	Prompts you for two date entries and searches for dates on or after the first date and on or before the second date
Short Text	Like [Enter the first character of the last name:] & "*"	Searches for any name that begins with the entered character
Short Text	Like "*" & [Enter any character(s) to search by:] & "*"	Searches for words that contain the entered characters anywhere in the field

Modify Properties in Queries

Learning Outcomes
- Copy and paste a query
- Modify query Description and Recordset properties
- Modify a field's Caption and Format properties in a query
- Modify a field list's Alias property

Properties are characteristics that define the appearance and behavior of items in the database, such as objects, fields, sections, and controls. You can view the properties for an item by opening its Property Sheet. You can change **field properties**, those that describe a field, in either Table Design View or Query Design View. If you change field properties in Query Design View, they are modified for that query only (as opposed to changing the field properties in Table Design View, which affects that field's characteristics throughout the database). You can also modify the properties of the field lists within a query as well as the query itself. **CASE** ▶ *You copy a query and modify several properties to better describe and present the data.*

STEPS

1. **Right-click the** JobSalaries query **in the Navigation Pane, click** Copy, **right-click in the** Navigation Pane, **click** Paste, **type** JobData **in the Paste As dialog box, then press** ENTER
   Copying and pasting a query is a fast way to build a new, similar query.

2. **Right-click the** JobData query, **click** Design View, **click the** Property Sheet button **in the** Show/Hide group, **then click in the upper portion of Query Design View (but not on a field list)**
   The Property Sheet dialog box opens to show you the properties that describe the entire query.

3. **Click the** Description property, **type** For Lydia's weekly meeting, **click** Dynaset **in the** Recordset Type property, **click the** Recordset Type list arrow, **then click** Snapshot **as shown in** FIGURE 5-15
   The **Description** property allows you to document the content, purpose, or author of a query. The Description property also appears on **Database Documenter** reports, a feature on the Database Tools tab that helps you create reports with information about the database.
       The **Recordset Type** property has two common choices: Snapshot and Dynaset. **Snapshot** locks the recordset, which prevents the data from being updated using this query. **Dynaset** is the default value and allows updates to data in this query.

QUICK TIP
"Selection type" at the top of the Property Sheet indicates what properties you are viewing.

4. **Click the** FirstPosted field **in the query grid, click the** Caption property **in the Property Sheet, type** Posted, **click the** Format property, **click the** Format property list arrow, **then click** Medium Date
   If you modify the field properties in a table, the properties apply to all objects in the database. You can override those settings by changing the properties for a field in a query, but property updates to a field made in a query apply to that query only.

5. **Click the** title bar of the Companies field list, **double-click** Companies in the Alias property in the Property Sheet, **then type** Organizations **as shown in** FIGURE 5-16
   The **Alias** property renames the field list in Query Design View. The Alias property doesn't change the actual name of the underlying table, but it can be helpful when you are working with a database that uses technical or outdated names for tables or queries.

QUICK TIP
To add a description to an object in the Navigation Pane, right-click the object, then click View Properties on the shortcut menu.

6. **Save and close the** JobData query

FIGURE 5-15: Setting query properties

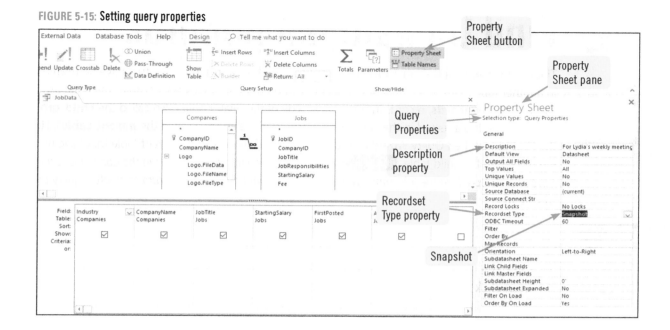

FIGURE 5-16: Setting field list properties

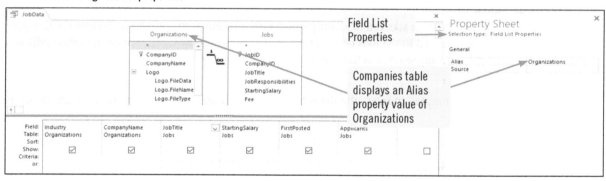

Find Unmatched Records

The **Find Unmatched Query Wizard** helps you find the records in a table that have no related records in another table. With referential integrity enforced on a one-to-many relationship, the database will not allow **orphan records**, records in the "many" side of the relationship (also called the **child table**) that are not related to a record in the "one" side of the relationship (also called the **parent table**). However, the Find Unmatched Query Wizard can still help you find records in the parent table that have no matching records in the child table. **CASE** ▶ *Lydia Snyder wonders if any records in the Companies table do not have related records in the Jobs table. You use the Find Unmatched Query Wizard to create a query to answer this question.*

STEPS

1. **Click the** Create tab, **click the** Query Wizard button, **click** Find Unmatched Query Wizard, **then click** OK

   The Find Unmatched Query Wizard starts, prompting you to select the table or query that may contain no related records. TABLE 5-5 describes the other query wizards. All queries may be modified in Query Design View regardless of whether they are initially created with a wizard or directly in Query Design View.

2. **Click** Table: Companies, **then click** Next

   You want to find which companies have no related records in the Jobs table.

3. **Click** Table: Jobs, **then click** Next

   The next question asks you to identify which field is common to both tables. Because the Companies table is already related to the Jobs table in the Relationships window via the common CompanyID field, those fields are already selected as the matching fields, as shown in FIGURE 5-17.

4. **Click** Next

   You are prompted to select the fields from the Companies table that you want to display in the query datasheet.

5. **Click the** Select All Fields button >>

6. **Click** Next, **type** CompaniesWithoutJobs, **then click** Finish

   The query selects one record as shown in FIGURE 5-18.

7. **Save and close the CompaniesWithoutJobs query**

FIGURE 5-17: Find Unmatched Query Wizard

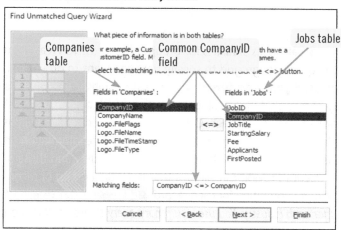

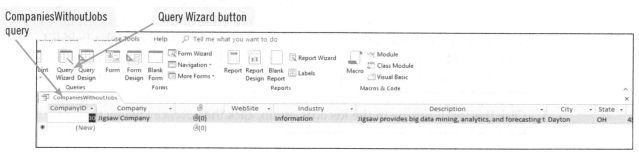

FIGURE 5-18: CompaniesWithoutJobs query in Datasheet View

TABLE 5-5: Query wizards

name	description
Simple Query Wizard	Helps you build a select query
Crosstab Query Wizard	Helps you build a crosstab query
Find Duplicates Query Wizard	Helps you find duplicate records in a table
Find Unmatched Query Wizard	Helps you find records in one table that have no related records in another table

Reviewing referential integrity

Recall that you can establish, or enforce, **referential integrity** between two tables when joining tables in the Relationships window. Referential integrity applies a set of rules to the relationship that ensures that no orphaned records currently exist, are added to, or are created in the database. A table has an **orphan record** when information in the foreign key field of the "many" table doesn't have a matching entry in the primary key field of the "one" table. The term "orphan" comes from the analogy that the "one" table contains **parent records**, and the "many" table contains **child records**. Referential integrity means that a Delete query would not be able to delete records in the "one" (parent) table that has related records in the "many" (child) table.

Build Summary Queries

Learning
Outcomes
• Create a summary
query
• Define aggregate
functions

A **summary query** calculates statistics for groups of records. To create a summary query, you add the **Total row** to the query design grid to specify how you want to group and calculate the records using aggregate functions. **Aggregate functions** calculate a statistic such as a subtotal, count, or average on a field in a group of records. Some aggregate functions, such as Sum or Avg (Average), work only on fields with Number or Currency data types. Other functions, such as Min (Minimum), Max (Maximum), or Count, also work on Short Text fields. TABLE 5-6 provides more information on aggregate functions. A key difference between the statistics displayed by a summary query and those displayed by calculated fields is that summary queries provide calculations that describe a group of records, whereas calculated fields provide a new field of information for each record. **CASE** ▸ *Lydia Snyder asks you to summarize the number of applicants for each industry. You use a summary query to answer this question.*

STEPS

1. **Click the Create tab on the ribbon, click the Query Design button, double-click Companies, double-click Jobs, then click Close in the Show Table dialog box**

QUICK TIP
The Total row for a datasheet works the same way for both tables and queries.

2. **Use the resize pointer ↕ to drag the bottom edge of the Companies field list down to display all of the fields, use ↕ to drag the bottom edge of the Jobs field list down to display all of the fields, double-click the Industry field in the Companies field list, double-click the Applicants field in the Jobs field list, then click the View button ▦**

   Eighty-two records are selected. You can add a Total row to any table or query datasheet to calculate grand total statistics for that datasheet.

3. **Click the Totals button in the Records group, click the Total cell below the Applicants field, click the Total list arrow, then click Sum**

   The Total row is added to the bottom of the datasheet and displays the total number of applicants for all jobs, 1,715. Other Total row statistics include Average, Count, Maximum, Minimum, Standard Deviation, and Variance. To create subtotals per industry, you need to group the records with the same Industry value together, a task you complete in Query Design View.

4. **Click the View button ⊠ to return to Query Design View, click the Totals button in the Show/Hide group, click Group By in the Applicants column, click the Group By list arrow, click Sum, double-click the JobID field in the Jobs table to add it to the grid, click Group By in the JobID column, click the Group By list arrow, then click Count**

   The Total row is added to the query grid below the Table row. To calculate summary statistics for each industry, the Industry field is the Group By field, as shown in FIGURE 5-19. You are also subtotaling the Applicants field using the Sum operator and counting the JobID field using the Count operator to calculate the number of jobs in each industry.

5. **Click ▦ to display the datasheet, use the column resize pointer ↔ to widen each column as needed to view all field names, click in the Total row for the SumOfApplicants field, click the list arrow, click Sum, click in the Total row for the CountOfJobID field, click the list arrow, then click Sum**

   The Energy industry leads all others with a count of 238 applicants. There are still 1,715 total applicants for 82 different jobs, as shown in FIGURE 5-20, but now each record represents a subtotal for all of the jobs in each industry instead of one record per job.

TROUBLE
To delete or rename any object, close it, then right-click it in the Navigation Pane and click Delete or Rename on the shortcut menu.

6. **Click the Save button ▤ on the Quick Access toolbar, type IndustryApplicants, click OK, then close the query**

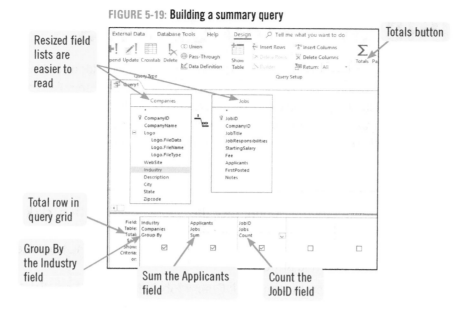

FIGURE 5-19: Building a summary query

Resized field lists are easier to read

Totals button

Total row in query grid

Group By the Industry field

Sum the Applicants field

Count the JobID field

FIGURE 5-20: Summary query in Datasheet View

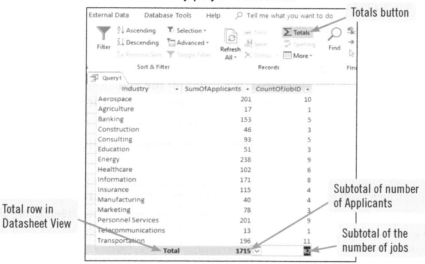

Totals button

Total row in Datasheet View

Subtotal of number of Applicants

Subtotal of the number of jobs

TABLE 5-6: Aggregate functions

aggregate function	used to find the...
Sum	Total of values in a field
Avg	Average of values in a field
Min	Minimum value in a field
Max	Maximum value in a field
Count	Number of values in a field (not counting null values)
StDev	Standard deviation of values in a field
Var	Variance of values in a field
First	Field value from the first record in a table or query
Last	Field value from the last record in a table or query

Build Crosstab Queries

A **crosstab query** subtotals a field by grouping records by two other fields placed in the column heading and row heading positions. You can use the **Crosstab Query Wizard** to guide you through the steps of creating a crosstab query, or you can build the crosstab query from scratch using Query Design View.

CASE ▶ *Lydia Snyder asks you to continue your analysis of jobs per industry by summarizing the number of jobs per industry within each state. A crosstab query works well for this request.*

STEPS

1. **Click the Create tab on the ribbon, click the Query Wizard button, click Crosstab Query Wizard, then click OK in the New Query dialog box**
   The fields you need for your crosstab query come from the Companies and Jobs table, which were previously selected in the JobsByIndustry query.

2. **Click the Queries option button, click Query: JobsByIndustry, then click Next**
   The Crosstab Query Wizard prompts you for the field to use in the row headings position.

3. **Double-click State, then click Next**
   The Crosstab Query Wizard prompts you for the field to use in the column headings position.

4. **Click Industry, then click Next**
   The Crosstab Query Wizard prompts you for the calculated field. You want to count the number of jobs for each intersection of the State row and the Industry column.

5. **Click JobTitle in the Fields list, click Count in the Functions list, click Next, accept the default query name of JobsByIndustry_Crosstab, then click Finish as shown in FIGURE 5-21**
   After creating a query, you modify it in Query Design View.

6. **Click the Home tab on the ribbon, then click the View button ⊠ to switch to Query Design View**
   Note the Total row and the Crosstab rows were added to the query grid. The **Total row** helps you determine which fields group or summarize the records, and the **Crosstab row** identifies which of the three positions each field takes in the crosstab report: Row Heading, Column Heading, or Value. The **Value field** is the field within the intersection of each column and row. You decide to switch the Row and Column Heading fields.

7. **Click Row Heading in the Crosstab row for the State field, click the list arrow, click Column Heading, click Column Heading in the Crosstab row for the Industry field, click the list arrow, then click Row Heading as shown in FIGURE 5-22**

8. **Click ▦ to review the new crosstab datasheet**
   The updated datasheet summarizes the same records but the Column Heading and Row Heading fields have been switched.

9. **sam᠈ ⬆ Save and close the JobsByIndustry_Crosstab query, compact and close the IL_AC_5_Jobs.accdb database, then close Access**
   Crosstab queries appear with a crosstab icon to the left of the query name in the Navigation Pane.

FIGURE 5-21: JobsByIndustry_Crosstab query in Datasheet View

State field is in the Row Heading position

Industry field is in the Column Heading position

Aerospace

Education

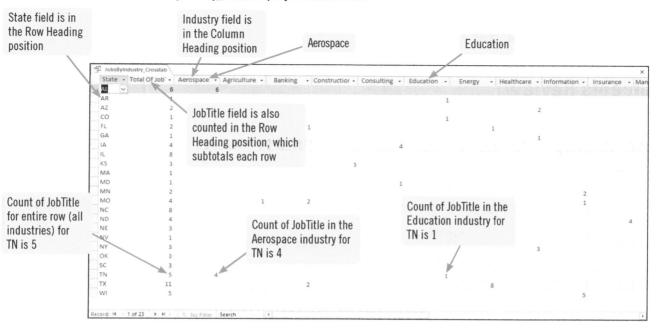

JobTitle field is also counted in the Row Heading position, which subtotals each row

Count of JobTitle for entire row (all industries) for TN is 5

Count of JobTitle in the Aerospace industry for TN is 4

Count of JobTitle in the Education industry for TN is 1

FIGURE 5-22: JobsByIndustry_Crosstab query in Design View

Crosstab query button is selected

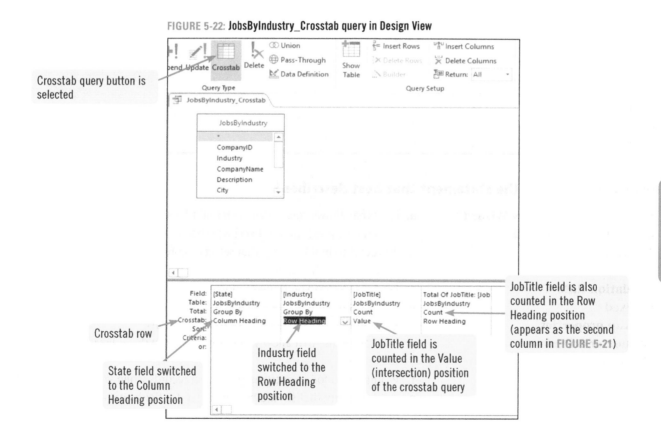

JobTitle field is also counted in the Row Heading position (appears as the second column in FIGURE 5-21)

Crosstab row

State field switched to the Column Heading position

Industry field switched to the Row Heading position

JobTitle field is counted in the Value (intersection) position of the crosstab query

Practice

Concepts Review

Explain the purpose for each Lookup property identified in FIGURE 5-23.

FIGURE 5-23

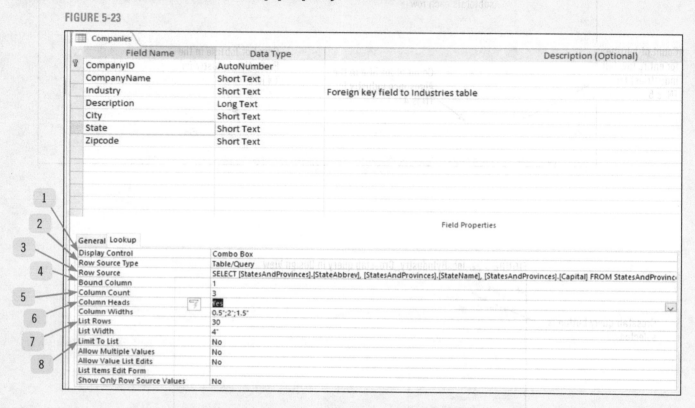

Match each term with the statement that best describes it.

9. **Find Unmatched Query Wizard**

10. **Crosstab Query Wizard**

11. **Attachment field**

12. **Hyperlink field**

13. **Validation Rule**

14. **Indexed**

15. **Lookup properties**

16. **Parameter criteria**

17. **Multivalued field**

a. Field that allows you to store external files such as a Word document, PowerPoint presentation, Excel workbook, or JPEG image

b. A process to build a query that selects records that have no related records in another table

c. Field that allows you to make more than one choice from a drop-down list

d. A process to build a query that summarizes data using two different fields in the row and column heading positions

e. Field properties that allow you to supply a drop-down list of values for a field

f. Prompts you for an entry used to select records when you run the query

g. Field property that should be considered for fields that are commonly used for searching and sorting

h. Field property that prevents unreasonable data entries for a field by testing the entry against an expression

i. Field that links to external resources such as webpages

Select the best answer from the list of choices.

18. **Which of the following fields is a good candidate for a Long Text data type?**
    a. Comments
    b. LastName
    c. City
    d. Department

19. **Which of the following is *not* true about queries?**
    a. New queries can be created in Query Design View or with a Query Wizard.
    b. Existing queries can be modified in Query Design View or with a Query Wizard.
    c. Existing queries can be copied and pasted to create a new query.
    d. New queries can be created on existing queries.

20. **What is the purpose of enforcing referential integrity?**
    a. To require an entry for each field of each record
    b. To prevent incorrect entries in the primary key field
    c. To prevent orphan records from being created
    d. To force the application of meaningful validation rules

Skills Review

1. **Create Lookup fields.**
   a. Start Access, open the IL_AC_5-2.accdb database from the location where you store your Data Files, and save it with the name **IL_AC_5_SupportDesk**. Enable content if prompted.
   b. Open the Employees table in Design View, then start the Lookup Wizard for the Department field.
   c. The lookup field will get its values from the Departments table. Select the Department field and do not specify a sort field.
   d. Do not adjust column widths. Use the default Department label, click the Enable Data Integrity check box, click Finish to finish the Lookup Wizard, then click Yes to save the table.
   e. Display the Employees table in Datasheet View, then add a new record with *your name* in the LastName and FirstName fields, **7700** in the Phone Extension field, **Marketing** in the Department Lookup field, **$55,000** in the Salary field, **1** in the Dependents field, and **(555) 111-1234** in the EmergencyPhone field.
   f. Save and close the Employees table.

2. **Modify Lookup fields.**
   a. Open the Departments table in Datasheet View and add a new record with the Department value of **Information Systems**.
   b. Add a new field named **Extension** with a Short Text data type and the values shown in FIGURE 5-24.
   c. Save and close the Departments table, then open the Employees table in Table Design View.
   d. Click the Department field, click the Lookup tab in the Field Properties pane, then modify the following properties:
      - Row Source: **SELECT Departments.Department, Departments.Extension FROM Departments;** (*Hint*: You can edit the SQL SELECT statement directly in the property or click the Build button and add the Extension field to the query.)
      - Column Count: **2**
      - Column Heads: **Yes**
      - Column Widths: **1.5"; 0.5"**
      - List Width: **2"**
      - Limit to List: **Yes**
   e. Save the Employees table, switch to Datasheet View, then modify the Department value for your name from Marketing to **Information Systems**.
   f. Close the Employees table.

FIGURE 5-24

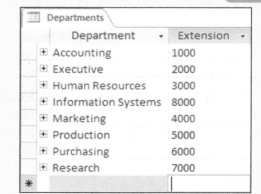

Department	Extension
Accounting	1000
Executive	2000
Human Resources	3000
Information Systems	8000
Marketing	4000
Production	5000
Purchasing	6000
Research	7000

Skills Review (continued)

3. **Modify validation and index properties.**

   a. Open the Calls table in Design View.

   b. Click the CallMinutes field name, then type **>=1** in the Validation Rule box.

   c. Click the Validation Text box, then type **CallMinutes value must be greater than or equal to 1** as the Validation Text.

   d. Save and test the changes, then open the Calls table in Datasheet View.

   e. Test the Validation Text and Validation Rule properties by tabbing to the CallMinutes field and entering **0**. Click OK when prompted with the Validation Text message, then press ESC to remove the invalid CallMinutes field entry.

   f. Return to Table Design View, then double-click the Indexed property for the CallMinutes field to toggle it from No to Yes (Duplicates OK).

   g. Click the Indexes button in the Show/Hide group to display all of the indexes for the table. Given you do not often search or sort on the CaseID field, click the selector button to the left of the first index named CaseID, which is set on the CaseID field, then press DELETE.

   h. Click the Indexes button to toggle off the Indexes dialog box, then save and close the Calls table.

4. **Create Attachment and Hyperlink fields.**

   a. Open the Employees table in Design View, then add a new field after the EmergencyPhone field with the field name **Photo** and an Attachment data type. Enter **Company photo for ID badge** for the field's Description.

   b. Add another new field after the Photo field with the field name **Email** and a Hyperlink data type.

   c. Save the Employees table, display it in Datasheet View, then attach a .jpg or .png file of yourself to the Attachment field for the record with your name or use the **Support_AC_5_employee.jpg** file provided in the location where you store your Data Files.

   d. Enter your school email address in the Email field for the record that contains your name. Close the Employees table.

   e. Use the Form Wizard to create a form based on all of the fields in the Employees table. Use a Columnar layout, and title the form **Employees Entry Form**.

   f. Navigate to the last record that contains your information, and if requested by your instructor, print only that record, then close the Employees Entry Form.

5. **Create Long Text fields.**

   a. Open the Cases table in Table Design View.

   b. Add a new field named **Comments** with a Long Text data type just below the ResolvedDate field.

   c. Modify the Allow Zero Length property for the Comments field from Yes to **No**.

   d. Modify the Append Only property for the Comments field from No to **Yes**.

   e. Save and close the Cases table.

6. **Create Top Values queries.**

   a. Create a new query in Query Design View with the CallID and CallMinutes fields from the Calls table and the CaseTitle and Category fields from the Cases table.

   b. Sort the records in descending order by the CallMinutes field.

   c. Enter **20%** in the Top Values list box to display the top 20% of records with the largest values in the CallMinutes field.

   d. Save the query as **Top20Percent**, display it in Datasheet View to view the top seven records with the greatest number of CallMinutes, then close the Top20Percent datasheet.

7. **Create parameter queries.**

   a. Create a new query in Query Design View with the FirstName and LastName fields from the Employees table, the CaseTitle field from the Cases table, and the CallMinutes field from the Calls table.

   b. Add the parameter criteria **>=[Enter minimum minutes]** in the Criteria cell for the CallMinutes field.

   c. Specify descending sort order on the CallMinutes field.

Skills Review (continued)

d. Click the Datasheet View button, then enter **20** in the Enter Parameter Value dialog box. The query should select 16 records.

e. Save the query as **CallMinutesParameter**, then close it.

8. Set properties in queries.

a. Right-click the CallMinutesParameter query in the Navigation Pane, click Object Properties, then add the following description: **Prompts for a minimum CallMinutes value**.

b. Close the CallMinutesParameter Properties dialog box, then open the CallMinutesParameter query in Query Design View.

c. Right-click the CallMinutes field in the query grid, then click Properties on the shortcut menu to open the Property Sheet for the Field Properties. Enter **Minutes** for the Caption property, then change the Format property to **Standard**.

d. Click the title bar of the Calls field list, then enter **Call Details** in the Alias property.

e. Save and close the CallMinutesParameter query.

9. Find unmatched records.

a. Start the Find Unmatched Query Wizard.

b. Select the Employees table, then the Cases table, to indicate that you want to view the Employees records that have no related records in the Cases table.

c. Confirm that the two tables are related by the EmployeeID field.

d. Select all of the fields from the Employees table in the query results.

e. Name the query **EmployeesWithoutCases**, then view the results. There should be nine records in the datasheet including the record with your name.

f. If requested by your instructor, print the EmployeesWithoutCases query, then close it.

10. Create summary queries.

a. Create a new select query in Query Design View using the Cases and Calls tables.

b. Add the following fields: CaseTitle from the Cases table, and CallMinutes from the Calls table.

c. Add the Total row to the query design grid, then change the aggregate function for the CallMinutes field from Group By to Sum.

d. Add the CallMinutes field to the grid again, and change the aggregate function for the CallMinutes field from Group By to Avg.

e. Add the CallMinutes field to the grid for a third time, and change the aggregate function for the CallMinutes field from Group By to Count.

f. Save the query as **CallAnalysis**, view the datasheet, widen all columns so that all data is clearly visible as shown in FIGURE 5-25, then save and close the query.

11. Create crosstab queries.

a. Use Query Design View to create a select query with the Department field from the Employees table, the Category field from the Cases table, and the CallMinutes field from the Calls table. Save the query as **CallsCrosstab**, then view the datasheet to see all 32 individual records.

b. Return to Query Design View, then click the Crosstab button in the Query Type group on the Design tab

FIGURE 5-25

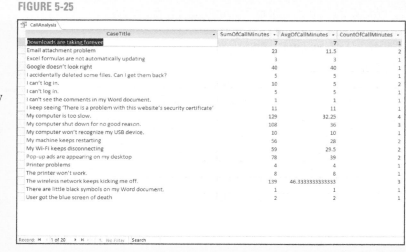

CaseTitle	SumOfCallMinutes	AvgOfCallMinutes	CountOfCallMinutes
Downloads are taking forever	7	7	1
Email attachment problem	23	11.5	2
Excel formulas are not automatically updating	3	3	1
Google doesn't look right	40	40	1
I accidentally deleted some files. Can I get them back?	5	5	1
I can't log in.	10	5	2
I can't log in.	5	5	1
I can't see the comments in my Word document.	1	1	1
I keep seeing 'There is a problem with this website's security certificate'	11	11	1
My computer is too slow.	129	32.25	4
My computer shut down for no good reason.	108	36	3
My computer won't recognize my USB device.	10	10	1
My machine keeps restarting	56	28	2
My Wi-Fi keeps disconnecting	59	29.5	2
Pop-up ads are appearing on my desktop	78	39	2
Printer problems	4	4	1
The printer won't work.	8	8	1
The wireless network keeps kicking me off.	139	46.3333333333333	3
There are little black symbols on my Word document.	1	1	1
User got the blue screen of death	2	2	1

Record: 1 of 20 No Filter Search

Access

Skills Review (continued)

to add the Total and Crosstab rows to the query design grid.

FIGURE 5-26

c. Specify Department as the crosstab Row Heading field, Category as the crosstab Column Heading field, and Sum CallMinutes as the crosstab Value field.

d. View the datasheet as shown in FIGURE 5-26, then save and close the CallsCrosstab query.

Department	Computer	Internet	Local Netwo	MS Office	Printer
Accounting	108	125		23	
Executive				139	1
Human Resources	127				
Marketing				4	12
Production	12	11	10		
Purchasing	5				
Research	58		64		

e. Compact and close the IL_AC_5_SupportDesk.accdb database, then exit Access.

Independent Challenge 1

As the manager of Riverwalk, a multispecialty health clinic, you have created a database to manage the schedules that connect each healthcare provider with the nurses that provider needs to efficiently handle patient visits. In this exercise, you will modify the tables to improve the database.

a. Start Access. Open the IL_AC_5-3.accdb database from the location where you store your Data Files and save it as **IL_AC_5_Riverwalk**. Click Enable Content if a yellow Security Warning message appears.

b. You want to add Lookup properties to the NurseNo field in the ScheduleItems table. First you will make sure it is not currently participating in any relationships as the Lookup Wizard will not work on a field that is currently used in a relationship. Open the Relationships window, right-click the existing relationship between the Nurses and ScheduleItems tables, click Delete and Yes to delete the existing relationship, then save and close the Relationships window.

c. Open the ScheduleItems table in Design View, then start the Lookup Wizard for the NurseNo field. Select all of the fields from the Nurses table and sort them ascending order on the NurseLName field. Hide the key column, enable data integrity, and use **Nurse** as the label. Click Yes when prompted to save the table. The field name changed from NurseNo to Nurse in Design View of the ScheduleItems table and in the Relationships window, and a one-to-many relationship with referential integrity was established between the Nurses and ScheduleItems tables.

d. Close the Relationships window and the ScheduleItems table. Open the Nurses table in Datasheet View and add your own name as a new record.

e. Close the Nurses table and open the ScheduleItems table in Datasheet View. Add your name to the Nurse lookup field for the first record (TransactionNo 28), then close the ScheduleItems table.

f. Open the Providers table in Design View. The DrPA field has only four valid entries: MD, DO, PA, or NP. (MD stands for medical doctor, DO for doctor of osteopathic medicine, PA for physician assistant, and NP for nurse practitioner.) You will use the Lookup Wizard to add these values to a lookup list. Start the Lookup Wizard for the DrPA field, choose the "I will type in the values that I want" option, then click Next.

g. In Col1, enter four rows as shown in FIGURE 5-27. Change the title to **Degree** and check the Limit to List check box.

h. Save and view the Providers table in Datasheet View. Add your own last name to the datasheet with a Degree value of **DO**, then save and close the Providers table.

i. Open the ScheduleDate table in Design view and add >=#8/26/2021# as a Validation Rule to the ScheduleDate field which requires all entries to be on or after 8/26/2021. Add the text **All entries must**

FIGURE 5-27

Lookup Wizard

What values do you want to see in your lookup field? Enter the number of columns you want in the list, and then type the values you want in each cell.

To adjust the width of a column, drag its right edge to the width you want, or double-click the right edge of the column heading to get the best fit.

Number of columns: [1]

Col1
MD
DO
PA
NP

[Cancel] [< Back] [Next >] [Finish]

Independent Challenge 1 (continued)

be on or after 8/26/2021 as the Validation Text property. Save and test the data, then close the ScheduleDate table.

j. Open the Nurses table in Design View and change the Indexed property to **Yes (Duplicates OK)** for the NurseLName field.

k. Add a field named **NursePhoto** with an Attachment data type and a field named **NurseEmail** with a Hyperlink data type to the end of the field list.

l. Save the Nurses table and switch to Datasheet View. In the record with your name, attach a photo of yourself or the **Support_AC_5_nurse.png** file found in your Data Files to the NursePhoto Attachment field. Add your school email address to the NurseEmail field.

m. Close the Nurses table, compact and close the IL_AC_5_Riverwalk database, then exit Access.

Independent Challenge 2

You are working for a city to coordinate a series of community-wide preparedness activities. You have created a database to track the activities and volunteers who are attending the activities. In this exercise, you will create and modify queries to analyze data.

a. Start Access, open the IL_AC_5-4.accdb database from the location where you store your Data Files, save it as **IL_AC_5_Volunteers**, then enable content if prompted.

b. Create a query in Query Design View with the LastName field from the Volunteers table, and the ActivityName and ActivityHours from the Activities table. (*Hint*: You need to add the Attendance table to Query Design View so that the Volunteers and Activities tables are joined.)

c. Use the Totals button to group the records by the ActivityName, count the LastName field, and sum the Activity-Hours field.

d. Save the query with the name **TotalActivityHours**, display it in Datasheet View as shown in FIGURE 5-28, then close the TotalActivityHours query.

FIGURE 5-28

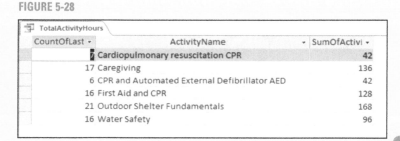

e. Open the Volunteers table and add *your name* as a new record. Use your school's address for the Street field, **66215** for the Zipcode, and **1/1/89** for the Birthday field. Close the Volunteers table.

f. Start the Find Unmatched Query Wizard. Find the records in the Volunteers table that have no matching records in the Attendance table based on the common VolunteerID field. Select all of the fields from the Volunteers table, name the query **VolunteersWithoutAttendance**, view it in Datasheet View (it should contain one record, the record you entered with your own information in the previous step), then close the query.

g. Create a new query in Query Design View with the FirstName and LastName fields from the Volunteers table and the City and State fields from the Zipcodes table.

h. Add **[Enter desired state]** parameter criteria in the State field, then save the query with the name **StateParameter**.

i. Open the StateParameter query in Datasheet View using **IA** as the criterion. The query should return four records for volunteers who live in Iowa. Return to Query Design View and run the query again using **MO** as the criteria. The query should return seven records for volunteers who live in Missouri. Close the StateParameter query.

j. Compact and close the IL_AC_5_Volunteers.accdb database, then exit Access.

Visual Workshop

Open the IL_AC_5-5.accdb database from the location where you store your Data Files, save it with the name **IL_AC_5_CollegeCourses**, then enable content if prompted. Create a new query in Query Design View with the Department field from the Professors table, and the Grade and StudentID fields from the Enrollments table. (*Hint*: Add the Sections table to connect the Professors and Enrollments tables). Save the query with the name **GradesByDepartment**, view it in Datasheet View, then close it. Using the Crosstab Query Wizard, create a new crosstab query from the GradesByDepartment query. Use Department for the row heading field, Grade for the column heading field, and count the StudentID field for each row and column intersection. Accept the default name for the query, **GradesByDepartment_Crosstab**, then view it in Datasheet View as shown in **FIGURE 5-29**. Close the query, compact and close the IL_AC_5_CollegeCourses database, then exit Access.

FIGURE 5-29

GradesByDepartment_Crosstab

Department	Total Of Stuc	A	B	C	D	F	W
ACCT	9	3	4	1	1		
BUS	9	2	4	1		1	1
CIS	22	9	9	2		1	1
ECON	3	1	1		1		
ENGR	10	3	5	2			
MATH	8		4		1	3	
MKT	11	1	7			3	

Creating Forms

CASE ▶ You are working with Lydia Snyder, vice president of operations at JCL Talent, to build a research database to manage industry, company, and job data. In this module, you'll create and modify forms, which are used to find, enter, and edit information.

Module Objectives

After completing this module, you will be able to:

- Add labels and text boxes
- Resize and align controls
- Create calculations on forms
- Add check boxes and toggle buttons
- Add option groups
- Add combo boxes to enter data
- Add combo boxes to find records
- Add lines and rectangles

- Add hyperlink controls
- Add command buttons
- Modify tab order
- Add images
- Create a split form
- Add subforms
- Add tab controls
- Modify form properties

Files You Will Need

IL_AC_6-1.accdb
Support_AC_6_jcl.png
Support_AC_6_confidential.jpg
Support_AC_6_man.jpg
Support_AC_6_woman.jpg
IL_AC_6-2.accdb

Support_AC_6_computer.png
Support_AC_6_draft.jpg
IL_AC_6-3.accdb
IL_AC_6-4.accdb
IL_AC_6-5.accdb

Add Labels and Text Boxes

Learning Outcomes
- Add labels to a form
- Add text boxes to a form
- Modify labels and text boxes on a form

Adding and deleting **controls**, the different individual items on a form, is a common activity. Controls can be used to enter and edit data, clarify information, or make the form easier to use. **Labels**, descriptive text that does not change as you navigate from record to record, are the most common type of unbound control. **Text boxes**, input boxes that provide a user with a location to enter and edit a field's value, are the most common type of bound control. TABLE 6-1 describes common form controls. **CASE** ▸ *Lydia Snyder asks you to improve the JobsEntry form. You add and modify labels and text boxes to handle this request.*

STEPS

1. **sam ↓ Start Access, open the** IL_AC_6-1.accdb database **from the location where you store your Data Files, save it as** IL_AC_6_Jobs, **enable content if prompted, right-click the** JobsEntry form, **then click** Layout View

   You can add and modify controls in either Form Layout or Form Design View. The benefit of using Form Design View is that all form modification features are available including ruler and form section information. The benefit of using Form Layout View is that live data is displayed. The Controls group on the Design tab displays the different types of controls that you can add to a form.

   QUICK TIP
   If you want to add a label only, use the Label button *Aa* in the Controls group.

2. **Click the** Text Box button ⊞ **in the Controls group, click the** form, **then use the move pointer ⁺↖ to move the new text box below the Applicants text box (which currently displays 50)**

   When you add a new text box to a form, Access automatically adds a label to the left of the text box. **Label** controls describe the data that the text box displays. You can modify a label control directly on the form or change the text using the label's **Caption property**.

   QUICK TIP
   The number portion of the caption of a new label (such as Text19) is based on the number of previous controls added to the form. The instructions use ## to indicate any number.

3. **Double-click** Text## **in the label to select it, type** Posted, **then press** ENTER

   To bind the new text box to a field in Form Layout View, use the **Control Source** property of the text box. Recall that a **property** is a characteristic of the form or control that can be modified. All of a control's properties are stored in the control's **Property Sheet**.

   TROUBLE
   Click the Property Sheet button on the Design tab to open the Property Sheet if it is not already visible.

4. **Click the** new text box **to select it, click the** Data tab **in the Property Sheet, click the** Control Source property list arrow, **click** FirstPosted, **click the** Default Value property, **then enter** =Date() **as shown in** FIGURE 6-1

   The **Default Value** property value is automatically entered in a field for new records using this form. =Date() is an expression that uses the built-in Access function **Date()** to return the current date. The Property Sheet shows all properties for the selected control in both Layout View and Design View.

5. **Right-click the** JobsEntry form tab, **click** Design View, **then click the** Close command button **in the Form Header section**

   The Property Sheet changes to show the properties of the selected command button.

6. **Click the** Format tab **on the ribbon, click the** Quick Styles button, **click the** Colored Fill – Blue, Accent 1 option **(second column, second row), click the** Change Shape button, **then click the** Oval shape **(second column, third row)**

   Changes you make using the ribbon are updated in the Property Sheet and vice versa.

   TROUBLE
   Be sure to click the text boxes on the right, not the labels on the left.

7. **Click the** JobID text box, **double-click the** Enabled property **in the Property Sheet, click the** Fee text box, **then double-click the** Locked property **as shown in** FIGURE 6-2

   The **Enabled** property determines whether that control can have the focus in Form View. The **focus** determines where the user will enter or edit data, and is visually identified by a blinking I-beam insertion point. A user may not edit the data in an AutoNumber field, so there is no need for it to receive the focus. The **Locked** property determines whether the field can be edited, which allows a user to copy the data. When the Locked property is set to Yes, a user cannot change the data.

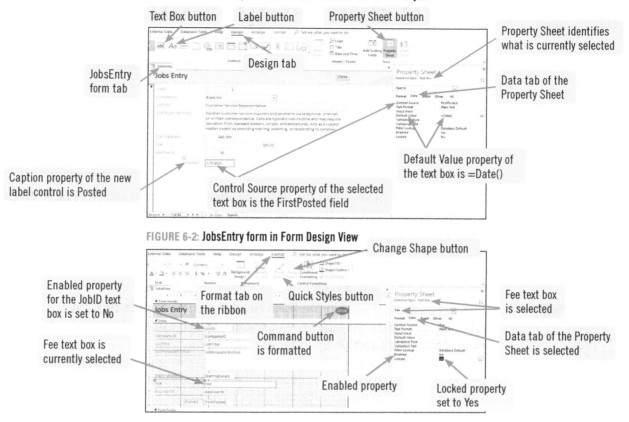

FIGURE 6-1: JobsEntry form with new label and text box in Layout View

Text Box button   Label button   Property Sheet button

Property Sheet identifies what is currently selected

JobsEntry form tab

Data tab of the Property Sheet

Caption property of the new label control is Posted

Control Source property of the selected text box is the FirstPosted field

Default Value property of the text box is =Date()

FIGURE 6-2: JobsEntry form in Form Design View

Change Shape button

Enabled property for the JobID text box is set to No

Format tab on the ribbon   Quick Styles button

Fee text box is selected

Fee text box is currently selected

Command button is formatted

Data tab of the Property Sheet is selected

Enabled property

Locked property set to Yes

TABLE 6-1: Common form controls

name	button	used to	bound or unbound
Label	Aa	Provide consistent descriptive text as you navigate from record to record; the most common type of unbound control and can also be used as a hyperlink to another database object, external file, or webpage	Unbound
Text box	abl	Display, edit, or enter data for each record from an underlying record source; the most common type of bound control	Bound
List box		Display a list of possible data entries for a field	Bound
Combo box		Display a list of possible data entries for a field, and provide a text box for an entry from the keyboard; combines the list box and text box controls	Bound
Combo box		Find a record. (When a combo box is used to find a record versus enter or edit data, it functions as an unbound control.)	Unbound
Tab control		Create a three-dimensional aspect on a form	Unbound
Check box	✓	Display "yes" or "no" answers for a field; if the box is checked, it means "yes"	Bound
Toggle button		Display "yes" or "no" answers for a field; if the button is pressed, it means "yes"	Bound
Option button	●	Display a value for a field within an option group	Bound
Option group	XYZ	Display and organize choices (usually presented as option buttons) for a field	Bound
Line and Rectangle		Draw lines and rectangles on the form	Unbound
Command button	xxxx	Provide an easy way to initiate a command or run a macro	Unbound

Resize and Align Controls

Learning Outcomes
- Resize controls and sections
- Align controls
- Work with control layouts

When you modify form controls, you change their properties. All of a control's properties are stored in the control's **Property Sheet**. Properties are categorized in the Property Sheet on the Format, Data, Event, and Other tabs. **CASE** *Lydia asks you to make other control modifications to better size and align the controls on the JobsEntry form.*

STEPS

1. **Click the** Close button ☒ **on the Property Sheet to toggle it off, then point to the** right edge of the form **and use the resize pointer ↔ to drag the right edge of the form to the left as far as possible**

   It's a good idea to regularly check the width of the form to make it as narrow as possible to eliminate unnecessary scroll bars and extra sheets of paper if you print the form. The minimum width of a form is determined by the right edge of the right-most control.

TROUBLE

Use the Undo button ↶ to undo multiple actions in Form Design View.

2. **Click the** Jobs Entry label **in the Form Header section, double-click any** sizing handle **to automatically resize the label, then use the vertical resize pointer ↨ to drag the top edge of the Detail section up as far as possible**

   TABLE 6-2 identifies the mouse pointer shapes that guide your actions in Form Design View. Eliminating unnecessary blank space in a form section is a common task. You also want to align the labels in the first column. Selecting all of the labels together allows you to modify their properties at the same time.

TROUBLE

You may need to click ☰ twice to right-align the text within the labels.

3. **Click the** JobID label **in the first column, press and hold** CTRL, **click** each of the other labels **in the first column to select them together, release** CTRL, **click the** Format tab **on the ribbon, click the** Align Right button ☰ **in the Font group, click the** Arrange tab **on the ribbon, click the** Align button, **then click** Right **as shown in** FIGURE 6-3

   The **Align Right button** ☰ right-aligns the text *within* the control whereas the **Right command** on the Align menu right-aligns the right *edges* of the selected controls. Many other options on the Arrange tab of the ribbon control the positioning of controls on the form, as described in TABLE 6-3.

   When you create new forms or add controls to the form in Layout View, they are often organized in a **layout**, an invisible grid that aligns and sizes controls within the layout. See TABLE 6-4 for more information on layouts. The Posted label and FirstPosted text box are in a layout.

4. **Click the** layout selector ⊞ **in the upper-left corner of the Posted label to select the layout, then click the** Remove Layout button **in the Table group on the Arrange tab**

   With the layout removed, you can modify the individual controls within the layout.

5. **Click the** StartingSalary text box, **press and hold** CTRL, **click the** Fee text box, **click the** Applicants text box, **click the** FirstPosted text box, **release** CTRL, **click the** Size/Space button **on the Arrange tab, then click** To Narrowest

   The four text boxes have been resized to the narrowest of the four.

6. **Click the** Save button 🖫 **on the Quick Access Toolbar, right-click the** JobsEntry form tab, **then click** Form View

FIGURE 6-3: Resizing and aligning controls on the JobsEntry form

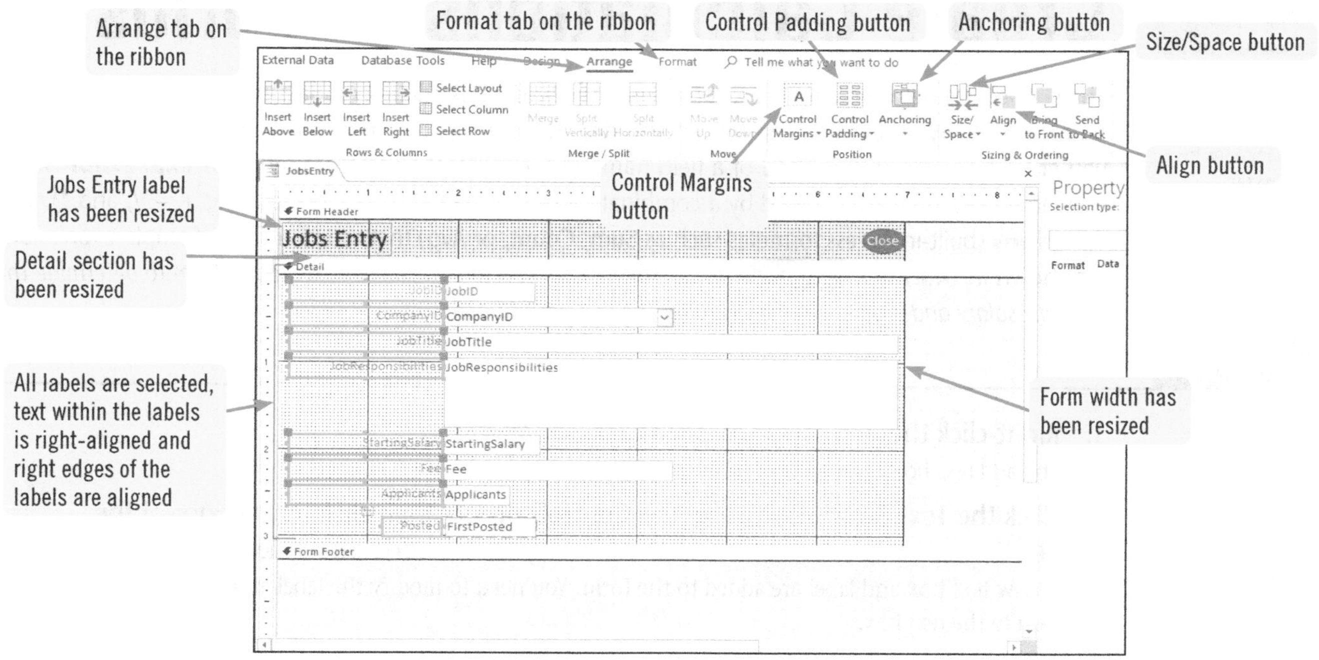

TABLE 6-2: Mouse pointer shapes in Form Design View

shape	when does this shape appear?	action
⌖	When you point to any unselected control on the form (the default mouse pointer)	Single-clicking with this mouse pointer selects a control
✛	When you point to the upper-left corner or edge of a selected control in Form Design View or the middle of the control in Form Layout View	Dragging with this mouse pointer moves the selected control(s)
↕ ↔ ↗ ↙	When you point to any sizing handle (except the larger one in the upper-left corner in Form Design View)	Dragging with one of these mouse pointers resizes the control

TABLE 6-3: Features that help position controls

button name	icon	description
Control Margins	A	Determines the **margin** of selected controls, the space between the content inside the control and the outside border of the control
Control Padding	▦	Determines the **padding** between selected controls, the space between the outside borders of the controls
Anchoring	▣	Determines the **anchor** position of selected controls, the position of the controls with respect to the edge or corner of the form
Size/Space	▤	**Sizes** selected controls to options such as the tallest, shortest, widest, or narrowest control. **Spaces** selected controls with options such as giving them equal, more or less horizontal or vertical space Also includes options to position controls to a grid or to **group** controls together so they move, resize, and format as a single control
Align	▥	Aligns the top, right, bottom, or left edges of selected controls

TABLE 6-4: Control layouts

layout	description
Tabular	Controls are arranged in rows and columns like a spreadsheet, with labels across the top
Stacked	Controls are arranged vertically as on a paper form, with a label to the left of each control

Access

Create Calculations on Forms

Learning Outcomes
- Use functions in expressions
- Build calculations on a form

The connection between a text box control and the field whose data it displays is defined by the **Control Source** property. A text box control can also display a calculation. To create a calculation in a text box, you enter an expression instead of a field name in the Control Source property. An **expression** starts with an equal sign (=) followed by a combination of field names, operators (such as +, −, /, and *), and **functions** (built-in Access formulas such as Sum, Count, or Avg) that return a value. Sample expressions are shown in TABLE 6-5. **CASE** *Lydia Snyder asks you to add calculations to the form to determine the monthly salary and a date two months after the first posting date.*

STEPS

1. **Right-click the** JobsEntry tab, **then click** Design View
   You add text box controls on a form to display calculations.

2. **Click the** Text Box button [abl] **in the Controls group, then click to the** right of the StartingSalary text box at about the 5" mark **on the horizontal ruler**
   A new text box and label are added to the form. You need to modify the label and add the desired expression to the text box.

QUICK TIP
The number portion of the default caption of a new label is based on the number of previous controls added to the form. The instructions use ## to indicate any number.

3. **Double-click** Text## **in the new label, type** Monthly Salary, **press** ENTER, **click** Unbound **in the new text box, type** =[StartingSalary]/12, **then press** ENTER
   All expressions start with an equal sign (=). When referencing a field name within an expression, [square brackets]—(not parentheses) and not {curly braces}—surround the field name. In an expression, you must type the field name exactly as it was created in Table Design View, but you do not need to match the capitalization.

QUICK TIP
You can also add a text box or any other control to a form in Form Layout View.

4. **Click** [abl] **in the Controls group, click to the** right of the FirstPosted text box at about the 5" mark **on the horizontal ruler, double-click** Text## **in the new label, type** 2 Months Later, **press** ENTER, **click** Unbound **in the new text box, type** =[FirstPosted]+60, **then press** ENTER
   To calculate the number of days between the current date and the FirstPosted date, the expression would be =Date()-[FirstPosted]. Recall that **Date()** is a built-in Access function that returns the current date.

QUICK TIP
Press an arrow key to move a selected control in the desired direction.

5. **Use the horizontal resize pointer ↔ to widen the text boxes that contain expressions to display the entire expression as shown in** FIGURE 6-4
   With the expressions in place, you are ready to view the data in Form View.

6. **Click the** Save button [💾] **on the Quick Access Toolbar, right-click the** JobsEntry form tab, **click** Form View, **navigate to the second record for JobID 3 as shown in** FIGURE 6-5, **then close the JobsEntry form**

Bound versus unbound controls

Recall that controls are either bound or unbound. **Bound controls** such as text boxes display values from a field and are used to enter data. **Unbound controls** describe data, enhance the appearance of the form, or make the form easier to use.

Labels are the most common type of unbound control, but other unbound controls include lines, images, tabs, command buttons, and combo boxes used to find records. Bound controls can also be bound to an expression.

FIGURE 6-4: Creating calculations in Form Design View

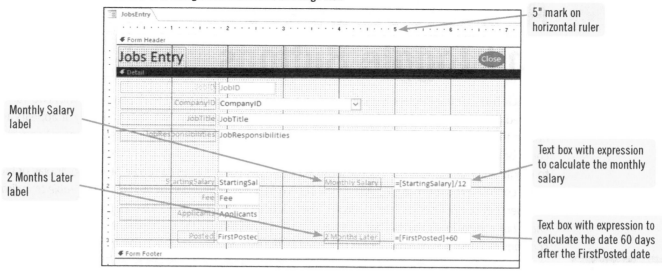

FIGURE 6-4: Creating calculations in Form Design View

Monthly Salary label

2 Months Later label

5" mark on horizontal ruler

Text box with expression to calculate the monthly salary

Text box with expression to calculate the date 60 days after the FirstPosted date

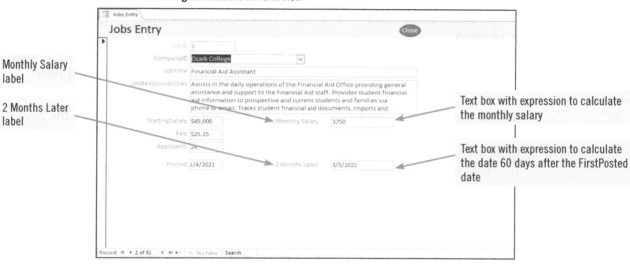

FIGURE 6-5: Viewing calculations in Form View

Monthly Salary label

2 Months Later label

Text box with expression to calculate the monthly salary

Text box with expression to calculate the date 60 days after the FirstPosted date

TABLE 6-5: Sample expressions

sample expression	description
=Sum([Salary])	Uses the **Sum function** to add the values in the Salary field
=[Price] * 1.05	Multiplies the Price field by 1.05 (adds 5% to the Price field)
=[Subtotal] + [Shipping]	Adds the value of the Subtotal field to the value of the Shipping field
=Avg([Freight])	Uses the **Avg function** to display an average of the values in the Freight field
=Date()	Uses the **Date function** to display the current date in the form of mm-dd-yy
="Page" &[Page]	Displays the word Page, a space, and the result of the **Page field**, a built-in Access field that contains the current page number
=[FirstName]& " " &[LastName]	Displays the value of the FirstName and LastName fields in one control, separated by a space
=Left([ProductNumber],2)	Uses the **Left function** to display the first two characters in the ProductNumber field

Add Check Boxes and Toggle Buttons

Learning
Outcomes
• Add a check box
  to a form
• Add a toggle
  button to a form

A **check box** control displays a small box that is checked or not checked to display fields with two values: checked (Yes) or not checked (No). A **toggle button** control also has two states. Visually, it appears as a button that is either pressed ("on") or not pressed ("off"). While the controls can be used interchangeably, check boxes are most commonly bound to a Yes/No field whereas toggle buttons are most commonly used to toggle on or off some feature of the form. For example, you could use a toggle button to display or hide other controls on a form. **CASE** *A new Yes/No field has been added to the Companies table to indicate whether that company offers internships for college students. You modify the CompanyEntry form by adding a check box control to display this data. Lydia also asks you to simplify the CompanyEntry form to not show the company description information unless requested by the user. You use a toggle button to handle this request.*

STEPS

1. **Double-click the** CompanyEntry form **to view it in Form View, right-click the** CompanyEntry tab, **then click** Design View **to display it in Design View**

   The check box control is in the Controls group on the Design tab, but typically doesn't fit on the first row of the ribbon.

2. **Click the** More button ⬇ **in the Controls group, click the** Check Box button ☑, **then click** below the Description text box at about the 2" mark **on the horizontal ruler**

   A check box control and an accompanying label have been added to the form.

3. **Double-click** Check##, **type** Internships offered?, **press ENTER, double-click the** new check box **to open its Property Sheet, click the** Data tab **in the Property Sheet, click the** Control Source list arrow, **then click** Internships

   The check box control is now bound to the Internships field in the Companies table as shown in FIGURE 6-6. Next, add the toggle button control to show and hide the Description information.

4. **Click the** More button ⬇ **in the Controls group, click the** Toggle Button 🔲, **then click in the** upper-right corner of the Detail section **just below the Close button**

   A toggle button control is added to the form. You connect the toggle button's **On Click** property to a macro named ShowHideDescription that was previously created in this database. The ShowHideDescription macro contains the instructions to show or hide the Description information.

5. **Click the** Event tab **in the Property Sheet, click the** On Click list arrow, **click** ShowHideDescription, **click the** Format tab **in the Property Sheet, click the** Caption property, **type** More, **then press ENTER as shown in** FIGURE 6-7

   With both the check box and toggle controls in place, you view and test them in Form View.

6. **Click the** Save button 🖫 **on the Quick Access Toolbar, right-click the** CompanyEntry tab, **click** Form View, **navigate to the second record, click the** Internships offered? check box, **then click the** More toggle button **several times**

   Clicking the More toggle button alternatively shows or hides the Description label and Description text box. The toggle button also changes appearance when it is "on" and "off." In a later module, you will learn how to create macros.

7. **Right-click the** CompanyEntry tab, **then click** Close

FIGURE 6-6: **Adding a check box to a form**

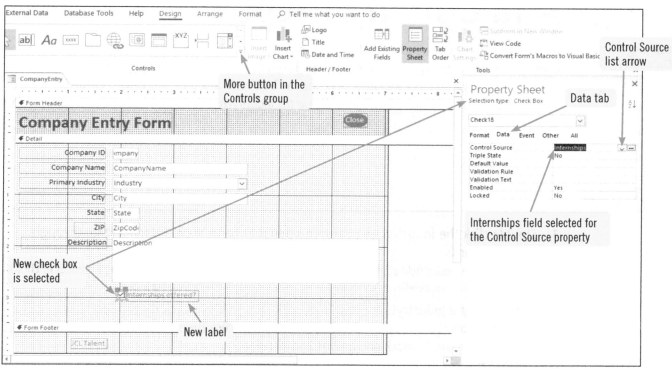

FIGURE 6-7: **Adding a toggle button to a form**

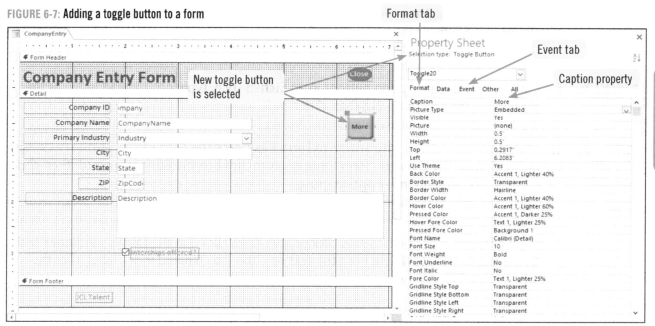

Add Option Groups

An **option group** is a bound control used when only a few values are available for a field. You add one **option button** control within the option group box for each possible field value. Option buttons within an option group are mutually exclusive; only one can be chosen at a time. **CASE** *You decide to use an option group to select a Job Demand Index value in the IndustryEntry form given only five values are possible for that field.*

STEPS

1. **Double-click the** IndustryEntry form **to open it in Form View, then navigate through several records**

   The JobDemandIndex field contains values that range from one to five. Given the small number of choices for that field, it is an excellent candidate for an option group with option buttons.

2. **Right-click the** IndustryEntry form tab, **click** Design View, **click the** Option Group button [XYZ] **in the Controls group on the Design tab, then click** below the JobDemandIndex text box at about the 2" mark **on the horizontal ruler**

   The Option Group Wizard starts. The only valid entries for the JobDemandIndex fields are 1, 2, 3, 4, or 5. You will use these values as the label names.

3. **Type** 1, **press** TAB, **type** 2, **press** TAB, **type** 3, **press** TAB, **type** 4, **press** TAB, **then type** 5 **as shown in** FIGURE 6-8

   The Option Group Wizard walks you through the process of creating both the option group and option buttons within the group.

4. **Click** Next, **click the** No, I don't want a default option button, **click** Next, **click** Next **to accept Values 1 through 5, click the** Store the Value in this field: list arrow, **click** JobDemandIndex, **then click** Next

   The Values 1–5 correspond with the **Option Value property** for each of the five option buttons. The Label Names 1–5 will become labels attached to each option button. Option buttons can be added or modified in Form Design View just like any other control.

5. **Click** Next **to accept Option buttons in an Etched style, type** Job Demand Index **as the caption for the option group, then click** Finish

   You work with the new option group and option buttons in Form View.

6. **Click the** View button [▦] **to switch to Form View, click the** Next record button [▶] **in the navigation bar for the main form three times to move to the Business record, then click** 4 **in the Job Demand Index option group**

   Your screen should look like FIGURE 6-9. Now that the JobDemandIndex value can be quickly recorded using option buttons in an option group, you no longer need the same information displayed in a text box.

7. **Right-click the** IndustryEntry tab, **click** Layout View, **click** 4 **in the JobDemandIndex text box, press** DELETE **to delete both the text box and Job Demand Index label, click the** Save button [💾], **right-click the** IndustryEntry tab, **then click** Close

FIGURE 6-8: Building an option group with the Option Group Wizard

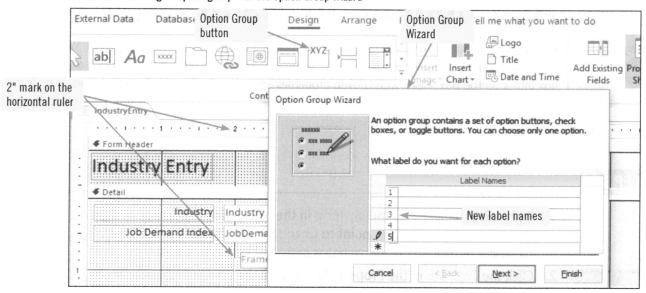

FIGURE 6-9: Using an option group in Form View

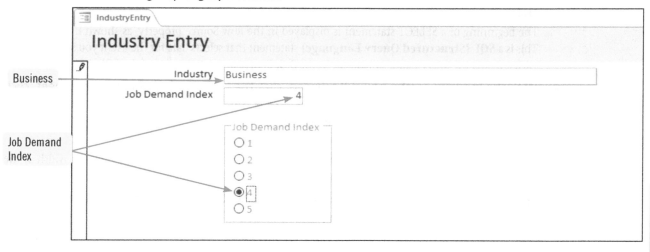

Add Combo Boxes to Enter Data

**Learning
Outcomes**
- Add a combo box
  to a form
- Modify combo
  box properties
- Use a combo box
  for data entry

A **combo box** control works as a text box that provides a list of possible values for a field. You can create a combo box by adding the control to Form Design or Form Layout View, or by changing an existing text box into a combo box. Fields with Lookup properties are automatically added as combo boxes on forms.

CASE ▸ *Lydia asks you to modify the JobsByCompany form to change the Industry text box into a combo box.*

STEPS

1. **Right-click the** JobsByCompany form **in the Navigation Pane, click** Design View, **right-click the** Industry text box, **point to** Change To, **then click** Combo Box

   You modify the properties of the combo box to define the values for the list.

QUICK TIP
A brief description of
the property appears
in the status bar.

2. **Click the** Data tab **in the Property Sheet, click the** Row Source property box, **click the** Build button ⌐, **then click** Yes

   Clicking the Build button for the **Row Source property** opens the Query Builder window, which allows you to select the field values you want to display in the combo box list. You want to select the Industry and JobDemandIndex fields for the list from the Industries table.

3. **Double-click** Industry **in the Industries field list to add it to the query grid, double-click** JobDemandIndex, **click the** Close button **on the Design tab, then click** Yes **to save the changes**

   The beginning of a SELECT statement is displayed in the Row Source property, as shown in FIGURE 6-10. This is a **SQL (Structured Query Language)** statement that selects data for the list. If you save the query with a name, the query name will appear in the Row Source property instead of the SQL statement.

4. **With the Industry combo box still selected, click the** Format tab **in the Property Sheet, click the** Column Count property, **change 1 to** 2, **click the** Column Widths property, **type** 2; 0.5, **click the** List Width property **and change Auto to** 2.5, **click the** Save button ⊟, **right-click the** JobsByCompany form tab, **then click** Form View

   Entering 2; 0.5 sets the width of the first column in the combo box list to 2 inches and the width of the second column to 0.5 inches. Test the new combo box.

5. **Navigate to the third record for CompanyID 3 (AIT Group), click the** Industry list arrow, **then click** Information **as shown in** FIGURE 6-11

   If you do not want the user to choose any values other than those provided by the list, you can modify a combo box's **Limit to List** property to Yes.

FIGURE 6-10: Adding a combo box in Form Design View

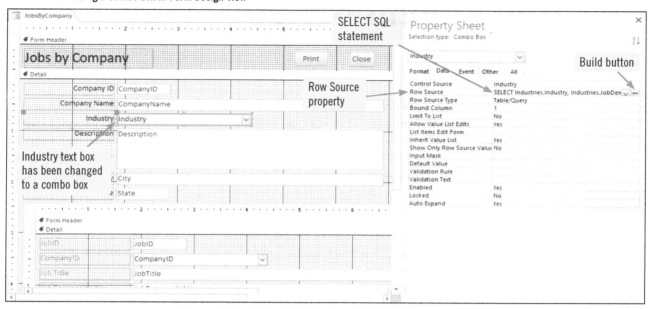

FIGURE 6-11: Using a combo box to change data in Form View

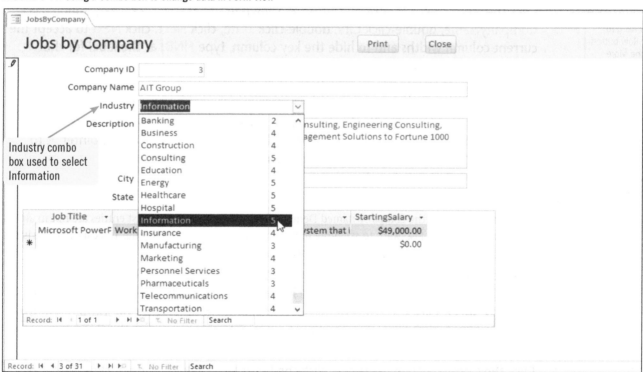

Choosing between a combo box and a list box

The list box and combo box controls are very similar, but the combo box is more popular for two reasons. While both provide a list of values from which the user can choose to make an entry in a field, the combo box also functions as a text box allowing users to make an entry that is not on the list (unless the Limit To List property for the combo box is set to Yes). More important, however, is that most users like the drop-down list action of the combo box.

Add Combo Boxes to Find Records

Learning
Outcomes
• Add a combo box
  to find records
• Modify the List
  Rows property
• Search for data
  with a combo box

Most combo boxes are bound controls used to enter data; however, you can also use a combo box as an unbound control to find records. Often, controls used for navigation are placed in the Form Header section to make them easy to find. **Form sections** determine where controls appear on the screen and print on paper. See TABLE 6-6 for more information on form sections. **CASE** ▸ *Lydia suggests that you add a combo box to the Form Header section of the JobsByCompany form to quickly locate a specific company.*

STEPS

1. **Right-click the** JobsByCompany form tab, **click** Design View, **click the** Combo Box button in the Controls group, **then click in the** Form Header section at about the 3.5" mark on the horizontal ruler

   The **Combo Box Wizard** is a tool that helps you add a new combo box and can be used in either Form Design or Form Layout View. The first two options are for combo boxes that are used to enter and edit data in a field. The difference between the first two options is where the drop-down list gets its values. The third option creates an unbound combo box that is used to find records.

2. **Click the** Find a record... option button **as shown in** FIGURE 6-12, **click** Next, **double-click** CompanyName, **double-click** City, **double-click** State, **click** Next, **click** Next **to accept the current column widths and to hide the key column, type** FIND: **as the label for the combo box, then click** Finish

   The new combo box is placed in the Form Header section. Because a combo box can be used to either enter data into a field or to find a record, a clear label to identify its purpose is very important.

3. **Click the** FIND: label, **click the** Home tab, **click the** Font Color arrow ▲ ⁃, **click** Red (second column, last row in the Standard colors palette), **use the move pointer** ↖ **to drag the label closer to the combo box, then click the** View button

   Test the new combo box in Form View.

4. **Click the** FIND: list arrow, **then click** Denman LLC

   The combo box finds the company named Denman LLC, but the combo box list entries are not in alphabetical order, and you also want to see more rows in the list to minimize scrolling. You can fix these issues in Form Design View by working with the Property Sheet of the combo box.

5. **Right-click the** JobsByCompany form tab, **click** Design View, **double-click the** Unbound combo box **in the Form Header to view its Property Sheet, click the** Format tab **in the Property Sheet, click the** List Rows property, **change** 16 to 30, **click the** Data tab **in the Property Sheet, click** SELECT **in the Row Source property, then click the** Build button

   The Query Builder opens, allowing you to modify the list of values provided by the combo box.

6. **Click the** CompanyName Sort cell, **click the** list arrow, **click** Ascending, **click the** Close button **on the Design tab, click** Yes **when prompted to save changes, click the** View button, **then click the** FIND: list arrow

   This time, the combo box list is sorted in ascending order by company name, and 30 versus 16 rows are displayed, as shown in FIGURE 6-13.

7. **Click** Cross Team **to find the Cross Team company record, click the** Save button **on the Quick Access Toolbar, right-click the** JobsByCompany form tab, **then click** Close

FIGURE 6-12: Combo Box Wizard

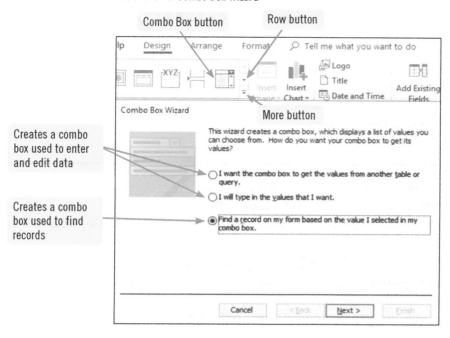

FIGURE 6-12: **Combo Box Wizard**

FIGURE 6-13: **Using a combo box to find records**

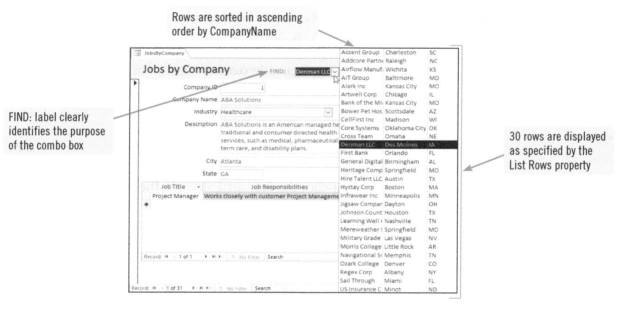

TABLE 6-6: **Form sections**

section	description
Detail	Appears once for every record
Form Header	Appears at the top of the form and often contains command buttons or a label with the title of the form
Form Footer	Appears at the bottom of the form and often contains command buttons or a label with instructions on how to use the form
Page Header	Appears at the top of a printed form with information such as page numbers or dates
Page Footer	Appears at the bottom of a printed form with information such as page numbers or dates

Access

Add Lines and Rectangles

Learning
Outcomes
• Add lines to a
  form
• Add rectangles to
  a form

Line or **rectangle** controls are often added to a form or report to highlight or clarify information. For example, you can use short lines to indicate subtotals and grand totals, which are especially common on reports. You can use rectangles to visually group controls together, which is common on forms. **CASE** *Lydia asks you to improve the ContactsEntry form. You will use line and rectangle controls to make the contact versus company information more obvious.*

STEPS

1. **Double-click the** ContactsEntry form **in the Navigation Pane to view it in Form View, right-click the** ContactsEntry tab, **then click** Design View

   You decide to add a line to separate the Form Header from the information provided about each contact in the Detail section.

2. **Click the** More button ⯆ **in the Controls group, click the** Line button ◇, **press and hold** SHIFT, **drag from the** bottom of the left edge of the Form Header section to the right edge, **then release** SHIFT

   Pressing SHIFT while dragging a line control draws a perfectly horizontal line. With the header information visually separated from the rest of the form, you decide to use rectangle controls to clarify the contact versus the company information.

3. **Click the** More button ⯆, **click the** Rectangle button ▭, **then drag a selection box from the** upper-left corner of the ContactID label to the lower-right corner of the ContactEmail text box **as shown in** FIGURE 6-14

   Pressing SHIFT while dragging a rectangle control creates a perfect square, but in this case, you want a rectangular shape. You add a second rectangle around the company information.

   QUICK TIP
   Adding lines and rectangles works the same way for reports.

4. **Click the** More button ⯆, **click the** Rectangle button ▭, **then drag a selection box from the** upper-left corner of the CompanyID label to the lower-right corner of the ZipCode text box **to completely surround the company controls**

   If you do not create the rectangle in the desired shape or size on your first try, delete it and try again, use the Undo button ↩, or use the mouse to resize the control.

5. **Click the** Save button 🖫, **right-click the** ContactsEntry tab, **then click** Form View

   The ContactsEntry form should look like FIGURE 6-15. Return to Form Design or Form Layout View to move or resize your line and two rectangle controls as needed.

6. **Right-click the** ContactsEntry tab, **click** Close, **then click** Save **if prompted**

FIGURE 6-14: **Creating line and rectangle controls in Form Design View**

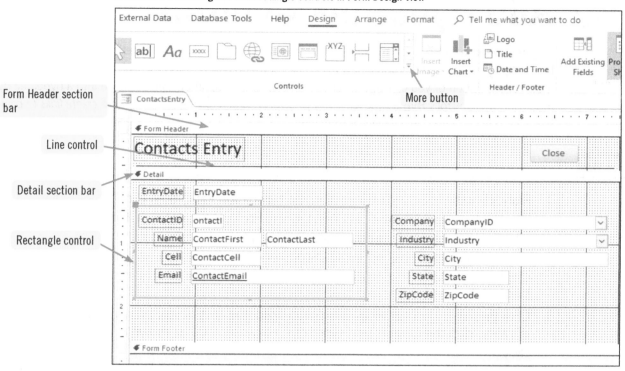

FIGURE 6-15: **Viewing line and rectangle controls in Form View**

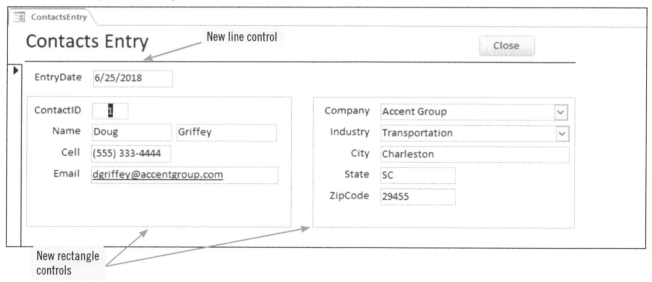

Line troubles

Sometimes lines are difficult to find in Form or Report Design View because they are placed against the edge of a section or the edge of other controls. To find lines that are positioned next to the edge of a section, drag the section bar to expand the section and expose the line. To draw a perfectly horizontal or vertical line, you hold SHIFT while creating or resizing the line. Also, it is easy to accidentally widen a line beyond the form or report margins, thus creating extra unwanted pages in a printout. To fix this problem, narrow any controls that extend beyond the margins of the printout, and drag the right edge of the form or report to the left. Note that the default left and right margins for an 8.5 × 11-inch sheet of paper are often 0.25 inches each, so a form or report in portrait orientation must be no wider than 8 inches. In landscape orientation they must be no wider than 10.5 inches.

Add Hyperlink Controls

**Learning
Outcomes**
• Add a label as a
  hyperlink
• Add a command
  button as a
  hyperlink

A **hyperlink control** is a control on a form that when clicked works like a hyperlink to redirect the user to a webpage or file. You can add a new hyperlink control to a form using the Link button in the Controls group of the ribbon or you can convert an existing label, command button, or image into a hyperlink by modifying the control's **Hyperlink Address property.** **CASE** ▶ *Lydia asks you to create links to commonly accessed resources on the IndustryEntry form.*

STEPS

1. **Right-click the** IndustryEntry form **in the Navigation Pane, then click** Design View

   You will add two new hyperlink controls in the Form Header, to the right of the Industry Entry label.

2. **Click the** Link button 🌐 **in the Controls group**

   The Insert Hyperlink dialog box opens, which allows you to link to an existing file or webpage, another object in the database, or an email address. You want to link to the federal government's Department of Labor website.

3. **Click the** Existing File or Web Page button, **click the** Text to display box, **type** Department of Labor, **click the** Address box, **type** https://www.dol.gov **as shown in** FIGURE 6-16, **then click** OK

   The new hyperlink control is positioned in the upper-left corner of the Detail section. You move it to the Form Header section.

4. **Use the move pointer** 🕂 **to drag the** new hyperlink control **to the** Form Header section at about the 3" mark **on the horizontal ruler**

   If you opened the Property Sheet for this control, you would see that the control is actually a label with a hyperlink value in the **Hyperlink Address property**. Other controls such as command buttons can work like hyperlinks, too.

5. **Click the** Button button ▭ **in the Controls group, click in the** Form Header section at about the 5" mark **on the horizontal ruler, then click** Cancel **if the Command Button Wizard starts**

   You modify the Caption and the Hyperlink Address properties for the new command button to convert it into a hyperlink control.

TROUBLE
You may need to
scroll in the Property
Sheet to find the
Hyperlink Address
property.

6. **In the Property Sheet for the new command button, click the** All tab, **select** Command## in the Caption property, **type** Glassdoor, **click the** Hyperlink Address property, **type** https://www.glassdoor.com, **then press** ENTER

   With the new hyperlinks in place, you'll test them in Form View.

7. **Click the** Save button 💾, **right-click the** IndustryEntry form tab, **click** Form View, **click the** Department of Labor label, **close the browser to return to Access, click the** Glassdoor command button, **close your browser to return to the IndustryEntry form as shown in** FIGURE 6-17, **then close the IndustryEntry form**

FIGURE 6-16: Insert Hyperlink dialog box

Link button

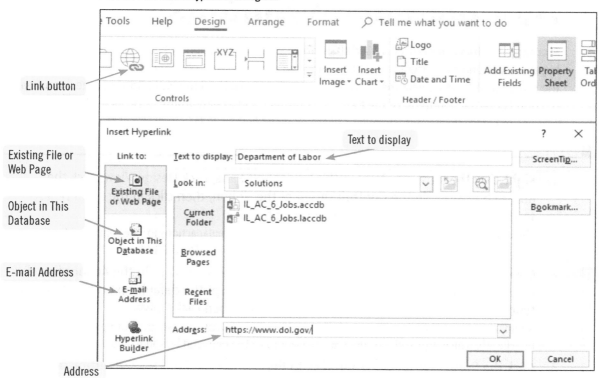

Existing File or
Web Page

Object in This
Database

E-mail Address

Address

FIGURE 6-17: IndustryEntry form with two hyperlink controls

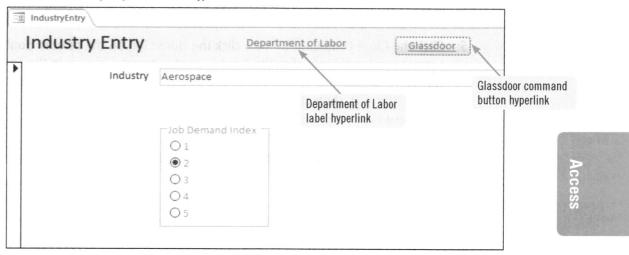

Department of Labor
label hyperlink

Glassdoor command
button hyperlink

Add Command Buttons

Learning
Outcome
• Add a command
button to a form

A **command button** control is used to perform a common action in Form View such as opening a hyperlink, printing the current record, or closing the current form. Command buttons can be added with the **Command Button Wizard**. Form designers often organize command buttons in the Form Header or Form Footer section to make the forms as consistent and as easy-to-use as possible. **CASE** ▸ *Lydia asks you to modify the JobsEntry form by adding command buttons to help users complete common tasks.*

1. **Right-click the** JobsEntry form **in the Navigation Pane, click** Design View, **click the Button button** [icon] **in the Controls group of the ribbon, then click in the** Form Header **section at about the 3" mark on the horizontal ruler**

   The Command Button Wizard opens, listing 28 of the most popular actions for the command button, organized within six categories as identified in TABLE 6-7 and shown in FIGURE 6-18.

2. **Click** Record Operations **in the Categories list, click** Print Record **in the Actions list, click** Next, **click the** Text option button, **click** Next **to accept the default text of Print Record, type** PrintRecord **as the meaningful button name, then click** Finish

   Adding a command button to print only the *current* record prevents the user from using the Print option on the File tab, which prints all records. You also want to add a command button to add a new record.

3. **Click the** Button button [icon], **then click to the** right of the Print Record button **in the Form Header section**

4. **Click** Record Operations **in the Categories list, confirm that** Add New Record **is selected in the Actions list, click** Next, **click the** Text option button, **click** Next **to accept the default text of Add Record, type** AddRecord **as the meaningful button name, then click** Finish

   Format and then test your command buttons in Form View.

5. **Click the** Close command button, **click the** Home tab **on the ribbon, double-click the** Format Painter button, **click the** Print Record command button **in the Form Header section, click the** Add Record command button **in the Form Header section, click the** Save button [icon], **then click the** View button [icon]

   The Format Painter makes it easy to apply a number of formats quickly from one control to another. You test the Add Record button.

6. **Click the** Add Record button **in the Form Header section, then enter the four field values for the new record as shown in** FIGURE 6-19

   You test the Print Record button next.

7. **Click the** Print Record button, **confirm that only the Selected Record option button is selected in the Print dialog box, then click** Cancel **in the Print dialog box**

   Not only do the command buttons make common tasks easier, they also help the user avoid unintended actions such as printing all records in the form or accidentally closing the entire Access application.

FIGURE 6-18: Using the Command Button Wizard

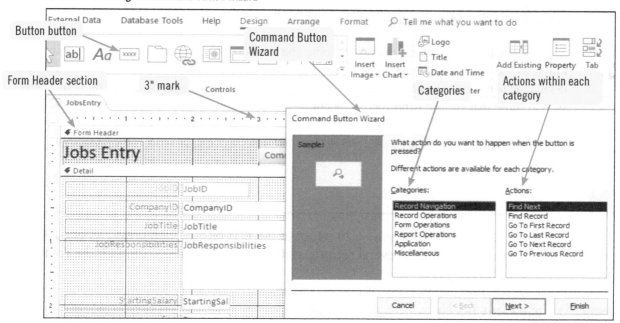

FIGURE 6-19: JobsEntry form with three command buttons

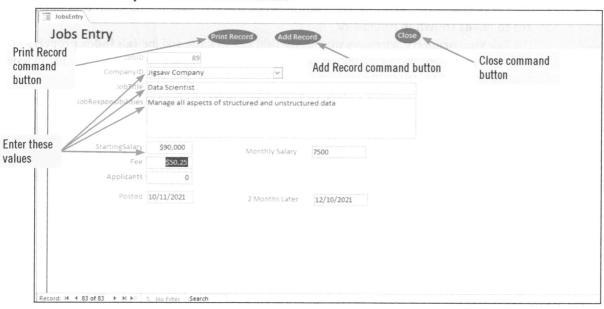

TABLE 6-7: Common actions provided by the Command Button Wizard

categories	common actions within this category
Record Navigation	Finding and navigating through records
Record Operations	Adding, deleting, copying, printing, or saving a record
Form Operations	Opening, closing, printing a form
Report Operations	Opening, emailing, printing a report
Application	Close the database and exit Access
Miscellaneous	Run a macro or open a query

Modify Tab Order

After positioning all of the controls on the form, you should check the **tab order**, the order the focus moves as you press TAB in Form View. A **tab stop** refers to whether a control can receive the focus. By default, all text boxes and combo boxes are set to automatically have a tab stop, but some text boxes, such as those that contain expressions, will not be used for data entry and therefore users do not need to tab into those controls. Unbound controls such as labels and lines do not have tab stops because they cannot receive the focus. **CASE** *Lydia suggests that you check the tab order of the JobsEntry and CompanyEntry forms.*

STEPS

1. **Click the** First record button **to return to the first record, then press** TAB **enough times to move through several records, watching the focus move through the controls of the JobsEntry form**

   There is no need to have a tab stop in either of the text boxes that contain calculations.

   QUICK TIP
   You can also switch between views using the View buttons in the lower-right corner of the window.

2. **Right-click the** JobsEntry form tab, **click** Design View, **click the** text box with the =[StartingSalary]/12 expression, **click the** Other tab **in the Property Sheet, double-click the** Tab Stop property **to toggle it from Yes to No, click the** text box with the =[FirstPosted]+60 expression, **then double-click the** Tab Stop property **to toggle it from Yes to No as shown in** FIGURE 6-20

   The **Tab Stop property** determines whether the field accepts focus, and the **Tab Index property** indicates the numeric tab order for all controls on the form that have the Tab Stop property set to Yes. To review your tab stop changes, return to Form View.

   QUICK TIP
   In Form Design View, press CTRL+. (period) to switch to Form View. In Form View, press CTRL+, (comma) to switch to Form Design View.

3. **Click the** View button **to switch to Form View, press** TAB **enough times to move to the next record, click the** Save button **, right-click the** JobsEntry form tab, **then click** Close

   You check the tab order for the CompanyEntry form.

4. **Double-click the** CompanyEntry form **in the Navigation Pane, then press** TAB **enough times to tab through all of the fields of a record**

   In this case, you want to change the tab stop order to move from top to bottom.

   QUICK TIP
   You can also modify tab order in Form Layout View.

5. **Right-click the** CompanyEntry form tab, **click** Design View, **click the** Tab Order button **in the Tools group to open the Tab Order dialog box, then click the** Auto Order button

   The Tab Order dialog box allows you to view and change the tab order by dragging fields up or down using the **field selector** to the left of the field name, or by automatically reordering the controls with the Auto Order button. Two of the entries, however, have vague names, Toggle## and Check##. To fix this, you modify their **Name property**, which helps you to reference the control elsewhere in the database application.

6. **Click** OK **in the Tab Order dialog box to close it, click the** More toggle button, **double-click** Toggle## **in the Name property in the Property Sheet, type** MoreToggle, **click the** check box, **double-click** Check## **in the Name property, type** InternshipsCheckBox, **click the** Save button **to save your work, then click the** Tab Order button

   Your screen should look like FIGURE 6-21. The Tab Order dialog box now shows descriptive names for all of the controls in the Detail section that can receive the focus.

7. **Click** OK **in the Tab Order dialog box, click** **to switch to Form View, press** TAB **enough times to test the top-to-bottom order of your tab stops, then close the CompanyEntry form**

FIGURE 6-20: Changing the Tab Stop property

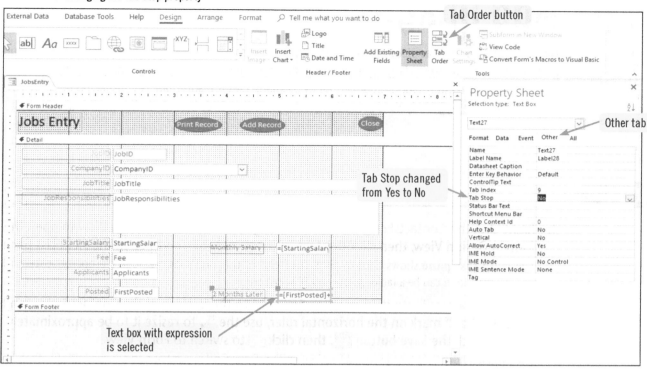

FIGURE 6-21: Modifying tab order

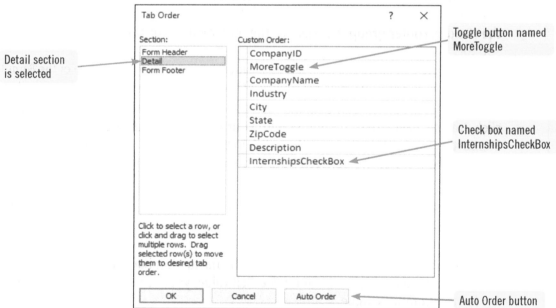

Naming conventions

Using a commonly accepted naming convention for the objects, fields, and controls in your database improves the logic and maintainability of your application. The **Leszynski/Reddick** **naming convention** uses a three-character prefix such as frm for form and txt for text box.

Add Images

Graphic images, such as pictures, logos, clip art, or background images, can add information, style, and professionalism to a form. Many types of files in an Attachment field display an image on the form. See TABLE 6-8 for more information on which types of image files are automatically displayed on an Access form or report. **CASE** *Lydia suggests that you improve the JCL ContactsEntry form with images.*

STEPS

1. **Right-click the** ContactsEntry form **in the Navigation Pane, click** Design View **to open the form in Design View, then click the** Add Existing Fields button **to open the Field List pane**

   The **Field List pane** shows a list of all of the fields in the form's Record Source property. A **Record Source** for a form can be a table, query, or SQL statement.

2. **Drag the** ContactPhoto field **from the Field List to the bottom of the ContactsEntry form at about the 2" mark on the horizontal ruler, use the ↖ to resize it to be approximately 2" by 2", click the** Save button 🖫**, then click** 🖾 **to switch to Form View**

   The ContactPhoto field for the record for ContactID 1, Doug Griffey, contains an attached JPG file that displays the photo in Form View. You also want to add a logo to the form.

3. **Right-click the** ContactsEntry form tab, **click** Design View, **use the move pointer** 🕏 **to move the existing Contacts Entry label in the Form Header section to the right so that the left edge is at about the 1.5" mark on the horizontal ruler, click the** Logo button **in the Header/Footer group, navigate to the folder with your Data Files, then double-click** Support_AC_6_jcl.png

   When you insert an image as a logo, it is automatically inserted into the left side of the Form Header section in a small layout. To specifically position an image on the form, use the Insert Image button.

4. **Click the** Detail section bar, **click the** Insert Image button **in the Controls group, click** Browse, **navigate to the folder with your Data Files, double-click** Support_AC_6_confidential.jpg, **then click in the lower-right corner of the form, to the right of the ContactPhoto control, as shown in** FIGURE 6-22

   You switch to Form View to observe the changes.

5. **Click the** Save button 🖫**, click the** Home tab, **then click the** View button 🖾 **to switch to Form View, as shown in** FIGURE 6-23

   You decide to add a new record.

6. **Click the** New (blank) record button ⏵ **in the navigation bar, then enter a new record using your name, (555)999-8800 for the Cell value, your school email address, and** Alark Inc **for the Company value**

   The EntryDate, ContactID, and other company information should fill in automatically.

7. **Double-click the** ContactPhoto control, **click** Add, **browse to a folder that contains a picture of yourself and double-click the picture to add it to the record or double-click the** Support_AC_6_man.jpg **or** Support_AC_6_woman.jpg **file supplied with your Data Files, then save and close the ContactsEntry form**

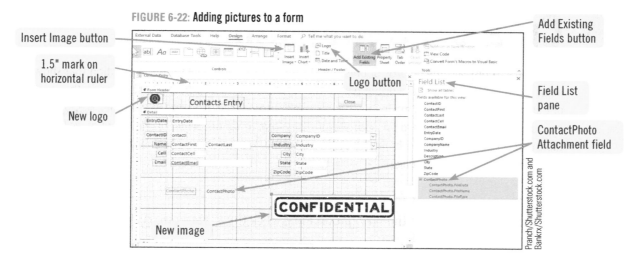

FIGURE 6-22: Adding pictures to a form

Insert Image button

1.5" mark on horizontal ruler

New logo

Logo button

Add Existing Fields button

Field List pane

ContactPhoto Attachment field

New image

Pranch/Shutterstock.com and Bankrx/Shutterstock.com

FIGURE 6-23: Final ContactsEntry form

New logo

Attachment field automatically displays JPG files

New image

aastock/Shutterstock.com, Pranch/Shutterstock.com, and Bankrx/Shutterstock.com

TABLE 6-8: Image file formats that can be displayed in an Access form or report

file extension	extension description
BMP	Windows Bitmap
RLE	Run Length Encoded Bitmap
DIB	Device Independent Bitmap
GIF	Graphics Interchange Format
JPEG, JPG, JPE	Joint Photographic Experts Group
EXIF	Exchangeable File Format
PNG	Portable Network Graphics
TIFF, TIF	Tagged Image File Format
ICON, ICO	Icon
WMF	Windows Metafile
EMF	Enhanced Metafile

Applying a background image

A **background image** is an image that fills the entire form or report, appearing "behind" the other controls. A background image is sometimes called a **watermark** image. To add a background image, use the **Picture property** for the form or report.

Create a Split Form

A **split form** displays the records of one table or query in a traditional form presentation that shows the fields of only one record in the upper half of the window, and a datasheet presentation in the lower half of the window. Any changes made in either pane are automatically updated in the other. **CASE** ▶ *Lydia has commented that she likes to use both the JobsEntry form to see the details of one record as well as the Jobs table datasheet to see several Jobs records at the same time. You will create a split form based on the Jobs table to give her both views in one object.*

STEPS

1. **Click the** Jobs table **in the Navigation Pane, click the** Create tab**, click the** More Forms **button, then click** Split Form

   The Jobs data appears in a split form with the top half in Layout View. The benefit of a split form is that the upper pane allows you to display the fields of one record in any arrangement, and the lower pane maintains a datasheet view of the first few records.

2. **Right-click the** Jobs form tab**, then click** Form View

   If you edit, sort, or filter records in the upper pane, the lower pane is automatically updated, and vice versa.

3. **Select** Customer Service **in the JobTitle field in the upper pane, type** Product **so that the JobTitle value reads Product Representative, then press** ENTER

   Note that "Product Representative" is now the entry in the JobTitle field in both the upper and lower panes, as shown in **FIGURE 6-24**.

4. **Click the** Next Record button ▶ **in the navigation bar four times to move to the record for JobID 6, Bank of the Midwest, Registered Client Associate**

   Note that as you move through one record at a time in the upper pane, the current record in the datasheet is also selected, as shown in **FIGURE 6-25**.

5. **Click the** Save button 🖫**, type** JobsSplit **as the form name, press ENTER, right-click the JobsSplit form tab, then click** Close

FIGURE 6-24: Editing data in a split form

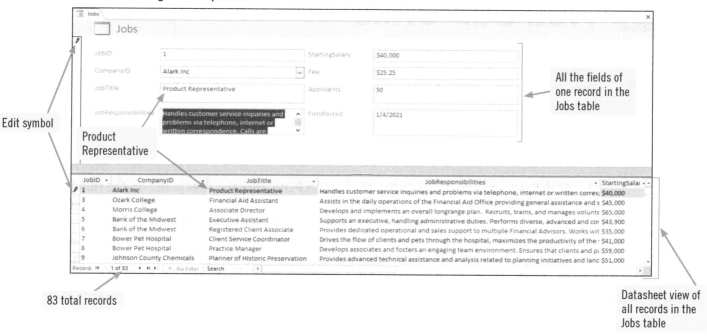

Edit symbol

Product
Representative

83 total records

All the fields of
one record in the
Jobs table

Datasheet view of
all records in the
Jobs table

FIGURE 6-25: Navigating through records in a split form

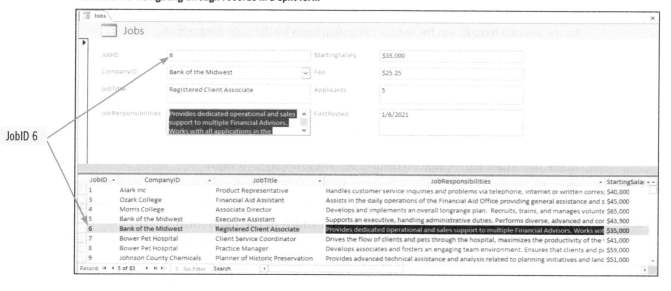

JobID 6

Add Subforms

A **subform** is a form within a form. The form that contains the subform is called the **main form**. A main form/subform combination displays the records of two tables that are related in a one-to-many relationship. The main form shows data from the table on the "one" side of the relationship, and the subform shows the records from the table on the "many" side of the relationship. **CASE** ▶ *Lydia asks you to create a form that displays the contacts for each company. A form/subform works well for this task.*

STEPS

1. **Click the** Companies table **in the Navigation Pane, click the** Create tab **on the ribbon, click the** Form Wizard button, **click the** Select Single Field button ⊳ **twice to select the** CompanyID **and** CompanyName fields **from the Companies table, click the** Tables/Queries list arrow, **click** Contacts, **click the** Select Single Field button ⊳ **seven times to select all of the fields from the Contacts table except those that start with** ContactPhoto, **then click** Next

   Because the Companies table has a one-to-many relationship with the Contacts table, the Form Wizard already knows how to organize the main form with fields from the Companies table and the subform with fields from the Contacts table as shown in FIGURE 6-26.

2. **Click** Next, **click** Next **again to accept a Datasheet layout for the subform, edit the titles to be** CompaniesMain **and** ContactsSubform, **then click** Finish

   The first company, ABA Solutions, has seven records as shown in FIGURE 6-27. The inside navigation bar is for the subform records, and the outside navigation bar is for the main form records.

3. **Click the** Next Record button ▶ **twice to move to the CompanyID 3 (AIT Group) in the main form**

   As you move through the records of the main form, the subform displays the related records for that company from the Contacts table.

4. **Click the** Save button 🖫, **right-click the** CompaniesMain form tab, **then click** Design View

   You can modify a form and subform in Form Design View just like any other forms and controls. The Contacts label is not needed and the subform needs to be wider to display more fields.

5. **Click the** Contacts label, **press** DELETE **to delete it, click the** subform **to select it, then use the horizontal resize pointer** ↔ **to drag the middle-left sizing handle as far as possible to the left to widen the subform to the full width of the main form**

   In Design View, you modify subforms like any other form. They appear like a datasheet in Form View because the subform's **Default View property** is set to Datasheet.

6. **Click the** Save button 🖫, **right-click the** CompaniesMain form tab, **then click** Form View

   Widening the subform helps it display more fields. Note that the CompanyID field in the last column of the subform is the common field that links the main form and subform.

7. **Right-click the** CompaniesMain form tab, **then click** Close

FIGURE 6-26: Using the Form Wizard to create a form with a subform

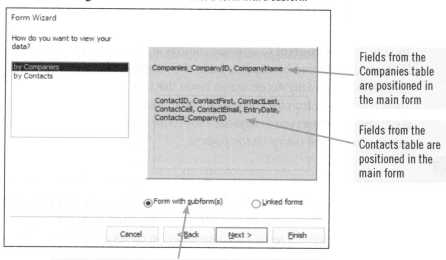

Fields from the Companies table are positioned in the main form

Fields from the Contacts table are positioned in the main form

The Form Wizard automatically suggests a form with a subform based on the relationship between the Companies and Contacts tables

FIGURE 6-27: CompaniesMain form with ContactsSubform

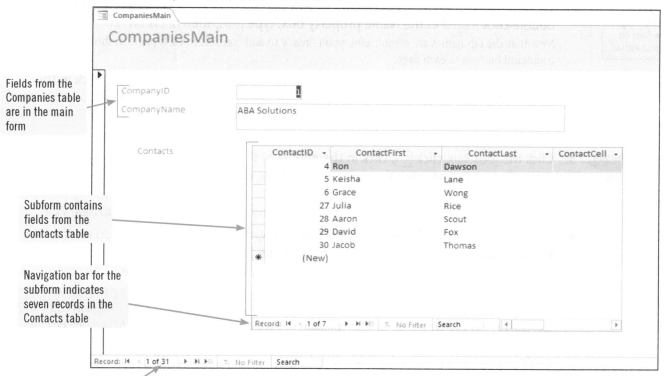

Fields from the Companies table are in the main form

Subform contains fields from the Contacts table

Navigation bar for the subform indicates seven records in the Contacts table

Navigation bar for the main form indicates 31 records in the Companies table

Linking the form and subform

If the form and subform do not appear to be correctly linked, examine the subform's Property Sheet, paying special attention to the **Link Child Fields** and **Link Master Fields** properties on the Data tab. These properties tell you which fields serve as the link between the main form and subform.

Add Tab Controls

Learning
Outcomes
• Add a tab control
  to a form
• Modify tab control
  properties

You use the **tab control** to organize controls in a three-dimensional or layered presentation on a form. Different controls can be organized and then displayed by clicking the tabs. You have already used tab controls because many Access dialog boxes use tabs to organize information. For example, the Property Sheet uses tab controls to organize properties into the categories of Format, Data, Event, Other, and All.

CASE ▸ *Lydia asks you to organize entry forms based on two subjects: Companies and Jobs. You create a new form with a tab control for this purpose.*

STEPS

1. **Click the Create tab, click the Blank Form button in the Forms group, click the Tab Control button ⬒ in the Controls group, then click the form**

   A new tab control is positioned in the upper-left corner of the new form with two tabs. You rename the tabs to clarify their purpose.

2. **Click the Page1 tab to select it, click the Property Sheet button in the Tools group, click the Other tab in the Property Sheet, double-click Page1 in the Name property, type Companies, then press ENTER**

   You also give Page2 a meaningful name.

3. **Click Page2 to open its Property Sheet, click the Other tab (if it is not already selected), double-click Page2 in the Name property box, type Jobs, then press ENTER**

   Now that the tab names are meaningful, you're ready to add controls to each page. In this case, you add command buttons to each page.

4. **Click the Companies tab, click the Button button ▦ in the Controls group, click in the middle of the Companies page, click the Form Operations category, click the Open Form action, click Next, click CompanyEntry, click Next, then click Finish**

   You add a command button to the Jobs tab to open the Jobs form.

5. **Click the Jobs tab, click ▦, click in the middle of the Jobs page, click the Form Operations category, click the Open Form action, click Next, click JobsEntry, click Next, then click Finish**

   Your new form should look like **FIGURE 6-28**. To test your command buttons, you switch to Form View.

6. **Click the View button ▦ to switch to Form View, click the command button on the Jobs tab, click the Close command button to close the JobsEntry form, click the Companies page, click the command button on the Companies page, then click the Close command button to close the CompanyEntry form**

   Your screen should look like **FIGURE 6-29**. The two command buttons opened the CompanyEntry and JobsEntry forms and are placed on different pages of a tab control in the form. In a fully developed database, you would add many more command buttons on each page to make other database objects (tables, queries, forms, and reports) easy to find and open.

7. **Click the Save button ▦, type JCLNavigation as the form name, then click OK**

FIGURE 6-28: Adding command buttons to a tab control in Form Layout View

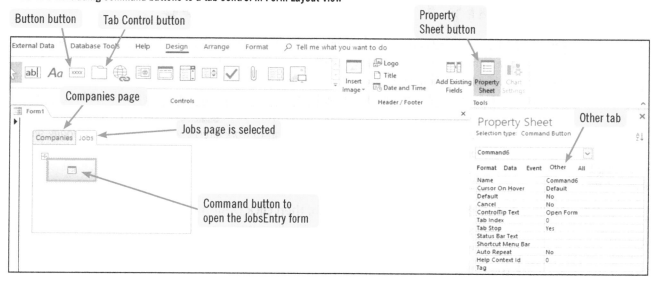

FIGURE 6-29: Using a tab control in Form View

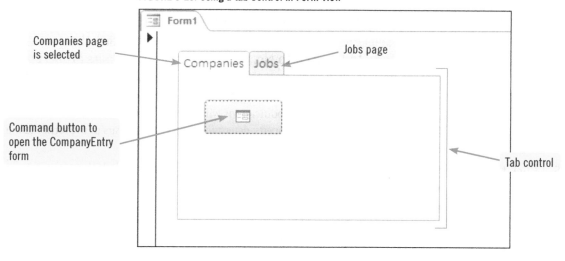

Create a group in the Navigation Pane

Another way to organize objects is to group them in the Navigation Pane. Right-click the Navigation Pane title bar, click Navigation Options, then click the Add Item button to add a custom group to the Navigation pane. Objects added to custom groups are shortcuts to the actual object.

Modify Form Properties

Forms, like all objects and controls, have properties that describe their characteristics. The most important property of a form or report is the **Record Source** property, which identifies the fields and records that the form will display as identified by a table name, query name, or SQL statement. Other form properties, such as **Caption**, the text that appears in the form's tab, and **Scroll Bars**, whether scroll bars appear in Form View, can be modified in Form Design or Form Layout View. **CASE** ▶ *Given the JCLNavigation form is used to help navigate through the database rather than to work directly with data, you will modify several other JCLNavigation form properties to make it easier to use.*

STEPS

TROUBLE
If the Property Sheet
doesn't display the
properties for the
form, click the Form
Selector button ☐ .

1. **Right-click the** JCLNavigation form tab, **then click** Design View

   The JCLNavigation form opens in Design View. The Property Sheet for the form displays the current properties, many of which have default values.

2. **Click the** Data tab **in the Property Sheet**

   Note that the Record Source property is blank. When you create a form using the Blank Form tool, the Record Source property is blank, but when you create a form using the Form Wizard, the Record Source property contains a table name, query name, or SQL statement that represents the fields and records you selected in the wizard.

3. **Click the** Format tab **in the Property Sheet**

   When using a form as a navigational tool such as the JCLNavigation form, it's helpful to modify the properties on the Format tab to remove items on the form that are not needed.

4. **Double-click the** Record Selectors property **to toggle it to** No, **double-click the** Navigation Buttons property **to toggle it to** No, **double-click the** Scroll Bars property **to toggle it to** Neither, **double-click the** Control Box property **to toggle it to** No, **then double-click the** Min Max Buttons property **to toggle it to** None

   Your screen should look like FIGURE 6-30. These modifications will help the form work better as a navigation form versus a data-entry form. The Caption property determines what text appears in the form's tab. If left blank, it will display the actual form name.

5. **Click the** Caption property, **type** JCL, **click the** Save button **■**, **right-click the** JCLNavigation tab, **then click** Form View

   The final JCLNavigation form is shown in FIGURE 6-31. It no longer displays a record selector, navigation buttons, scroll bars, a control box, or Min and Max buttons, items which are not needed for a navigational form. The form tab displays JCL versus the form name.

6. **sam⬆ Right-click the** JCL form tab, **click** Close, **compact and repair the database, then exit Access**

FIGURE 6-30: Modifying the JCLNavigation form's properties

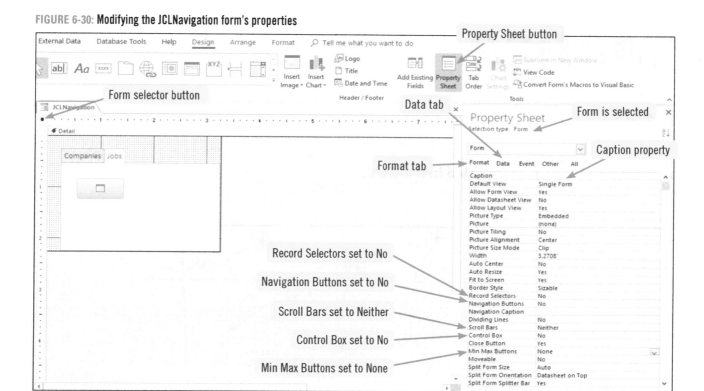

FIGURE 6-31: Final JCLNavigation form

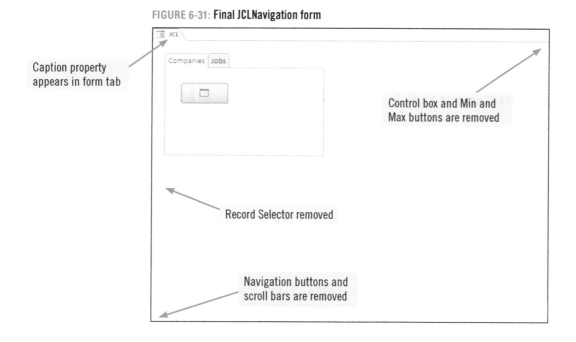

Practice

Concepts Review

Name the type of controls identified in FIGURE 6-32.

FIGURE 6-32

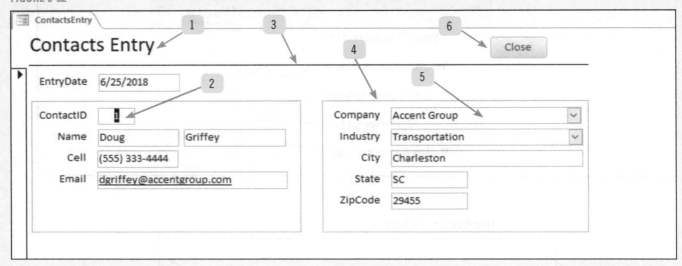

Match each term with the statement that best describes it.

7. **Tab order**
8. **Calculated control**
9. **Detail section**
10. **Split form**
11. **Bound control**
12. **Option buttons**
13. **Hyperlink**
14. **Check Box**
15. **Subform**

a. Created by entering an expression in a text box
b. Controls placed here print once for every record in the underlying record source
c. Used to display mutually exclusive values within an option group
d. Displays a single record in a traditional form in the upper pane and a datasheet of the records in the lower pane
e. Used on a form to display data from a field
f. A form within a form
g. Used to identify "yes" or "no" for a Yes/No field
h. Can be a created from a label or a command button
i. The way the focus moves from one bound control to the next in Form View

Select the best answer from the list of choices.

16. **Every element on a form is called a(n):**
   a. property.
   b. control.
   c. tool.
   d. item.

17. **Which of the following is probably *not* a graphic image?**
   a. Logo
   b. Calculation
   c. Clip art
   d. Picture

18. The most common bound control is the:
   a. text box.
   c. list box.
   b. combo box.
   d. label.

19. The most common unbound control is the:
   a. text box.
   c. combo box.
   b. label.
   d. command button.

20. Which form view cannot be used to view data?
   a. Design
   c. Datasheet
   b. Layout
   d. Preview

Skills Review

1. Add labels and text boxes.

   a. Start Access, open the IL_AC_6-2.accdb database from the location where you store your Data Files, then save it as **IL_AC_6_SupportDesk**. Enable content if prompted.

   b. Open the EmployeeMaster form in Design View, then add a text box control below the Salary text box control.

   c. Modify the Text## label to read **Dependents**. (*Hint*: You may modify the label directly on the form, or use its Caption property in the Property Sheet.)

   d. The text box should be bound to the Dependents field. (*Hint*: You may modify the text box directly on the form or use its Control Source property in the Property Sheet.)

   e. Add a second text box below the Dependents controls.

   f. Modify the Text## label to read **Emergency** and bind the text box to the **EmergencyPhone** field. (*Hint*: **FIGURE 6-33** shows the final EmployeeMaster form after Step 11.)

   g. Save the EmployeeMaster form and display it in Form View.

FIGURE 6-33

2. Resize and align controls.

   a. Switch to Form Design View for the EmployeeMaster form, then right-align the right edges of the labels in the first column.

   b. Left-align all of the left edges of the text boxes in the second column.

   c. Resize the EmployeeID text box and Dependents text box to be about half as wide as they currently are.

   d. Center the information within the EmployeeID and Dependents text boxes.

   e. Modify the text color for *all* controls (all labels and all text boxes) to be black.

3. Create calculations on forms.

   a. Add a text box to the right of the Salary text box at about the 4" mark on the horizontal ruler.

   b. Modify the Text## label to read **Monthly**, and move it closer to the text box. Modify the Control Source property of the new text box to an expression that calculates the monthly salary, **=[Salary]/12** then change the Format property for the new text box to **Currency** and the Decimal Places property to **2**.

   c. Align the top edges of the Salary label, Salary text box, Monthly label, and monthly expression text box.

   d. Set the text color for the new Monthly label and text box expression to black.

   e. Save the form, view it in Form View, and navigate through several records. Be sure the new text box correctly calculates the monthly salary.

Skills Review (continued)

4. Add check boxes and toggle buttons.

a. Switch to Design View for the EmployeeMaster form and add a check box control below the EmergencyPhone text box.

b. Modify the Control Source property for the check box to be **Veteran**.

c. Modify the Caption property for the new label to be **Veteran?**

d. Add a toggle button control to the upper-right corner of the Detail section of the form at about the 4.5" mark on the horizontal ruler.

e. On the Format tab of the Property Sheet, modify the Caption property for the new toggle button to be **ID**.

f. On the Event tab of the Property Sheet, modify the On Click property for the new toggle button to select the **ShowHideEmployeeID** macro.

g. Save the EmployeeMaster form and display it in Form View.

h. Click the ID button several times to test that it alternatively shows and hides the Employee ID label and text box when clicked.

5. Add combo boxes to enter data.

a. Switch to Design View for the EmployeeMaster form, right-click the Department text box, then change it into a combo box.

b. On the Data tab of the Property Sheet, change the Row Source property for the combo box to **Departments**.

c. Save the EmployeeMaster form and display it in Form View.

d. Test the combo box by changing the Department value for the first record (Employee ID 3 Aaron Cabrera) to Executive.

6. Add combo boxes to find records.

a. Switch to Form Design View of the EmployeeMaster form then add a new combo box to the Form Header section of the form at about the 4" mark on the horizontal ruler.

b. Choose the "Find a record..." option in the Combo Box Wizard.

c. Choose the LastName and FirstName fields for the combo box, hide the key column, then enter **FIND** as the label for the combo box.

d. On the Format tab of the Property Sheet, modify the List Rows property of the new combo box to be **30** and the Width property to be **2"**.

e. Change the text color of the FIND label to black, then position the controls so that they do not extend beyond the 5" mark on the horizontal ruler.

f. Move controls and narrow the form as needed so that the right edge of the form does not extend past the 5" mark on the horizontal ruler.

g. Save the EmployeeMaster form then display it in Form View.

h. Test the new FIND combo box in the form header to find the Mindi Perez record. Note that the list in the new combo box is not sorted.

i. Return to Design View, then click the new combo box in the Form Header section.

j. On the Data tab of the Property Sheet, click the Row Source property, then click the Build button. Add an ascending sort order to the LastName field. (*Hint*: The Combo Box Wizard automatically added the EmployeeID field back in Step c. Do not delete it.)

k. Close and save the Query Builder, then save the form and display it in Form View.

l. Test the updated FIND combo box in the form header to find the Samantha Wells record.

7. Add option groups.

a. Switch to Form Design View of the EmployeeMaster form and use the Option Group Wizard to add a new option group just below the Veteran check box.

b. The label names should be **Lot 1**, **Lot 2**, and **Lot 3**.

c. The default choice should be Lot 1, and the values of **1**, **2**, and **3** should correspond to the three parking lots.

Skills Review (continued)

   d. Store the value in the ParkingLot field using option buttons and an etched style.

   e. The caption for the group should be **Parking Lot Assignment**.

   f. Change the font color for all labels to black.

   g. Save the EmployeeMaster form and display it in Form View.

8. Add lines and rectangles.

   a. Return to Form Design View and add a rectangle control around the four Dependents and Emergency controls (two labels and two text boxes).

   b. Add a horizontal line control across the width of the form at the bottom of the Form Header section.

   c. Save the form and display it in Form View.

9. Add hyperlink controls.

   a. Return to Design View of the EmployeeMaster form, then add a label control to the lower-left corner of the form at about the 0.5" mark on the horizontal ruler.

   b. Modify the Caption property of the new label to be **Employee Master**.

   c. Change the font color to black.

   d. On the Format tab of the Property Sheet for the label, click the Build button for the Hyperlink Address property to open the Insert Hyperlink dialog box.

   e. Click the Object in this Database button on the left, then click the expand button for Reports to show the existing reports in the database.

   f. Click the EmployeeMasterList report, then click OK in the Insert Hyperlink dialog box.

   g. Save the EmployeeMaster form then display it in Form View.

   h. Test the Employee Master hyperlink label by clicking it, then close the EmployeeMasterList report to return to the EmployeeMaster form.

10. Add command buttons.

   a. Switch to Form Design View of the EmployeeMaster form, then drag the bottom edge of the Form Footer section down about 0.5" to open it.

   b. Use the Command Button Wizard to add a new command button to the Form Footer section at about the 3" mark on the horizontal ruler.

   c. In the Record Operations category, choose the Add New Record action. Select the Text option using **Add Record** as the text, then give the button the meaningful name of **AddRecord**.

   d. Use the Command Button Wizard to add a second command button to the Form Footer section at about the 4" mark on the horizontal ruler.

   e. In the Form Operations category, choose the Close Form action. Select the Text option button with **Close Form** as the text, then give the button the meaningful name of **CloseForm**.

   f. Align the top edges of the two command buttons in the Form Footer section.

   g. Save the EmployeeMaster form then display it in Form View.

   h. Test the Add Record command button by clicking it, then pressing TAB several times to move through the controls on the form. Notice that the tab order is illogical.

   i. Without entering a new record, click the Close Form command button.

11. Modify tab order.

   a. Reopen the EmployeeMaster form in Form Design View, then open the Tab Order dialog box.

   b. Click the Auto Order button, then click OK in the Tab Order dialog box to close it.

   c. Click the EmployeeID text box to select it, then set its Tab Stop property on the Other tab of the Property Sheet to **No**.

   d. Click the ID toggle button to select it, then set its Tab Stop property to **No**.

   e. Click the text box with the =[Salary]/12 expression to select it, then set its Tab Stop property to **No**.

   f. Save the EmployeeMaster form then open it in Form View.

g. Click the Add Record command button to add a new record with your name in the Last Name and First Name boxes. Note that the Employee ID field is an AutoNumber field that is automatically incremented as you enter your first and last names. Enter **Research** for your department, **$70,000** for your salary, **1** for dependents, and your school's telephone number for the emergency value. Click the Veteran? check box if you are a veteran, then accept the default Parking Lot Assignment value of 1 as shown in FIGURE 6-33.

h. Click the Close Form command button to close the EmployeeMaster form.

12. Add images.

a. Open the EmployeesByDepartment form in Form Design View, then add the Support_AC_6_computer.png image provided with your Data Files as a logo to the form.

b. Open the Field List, then add the Photo field directly under the FirstName text box. Resize the Photo control to be about 2" by 2".

c. Because this form is a work in progress, below the Photo control, insert an image with the Support_AC_6_draft.jpg file provided with your Data Files. Resize the Support_AC_6_draft.jpg photo to be about 1" tall by about 3" wide and change its Size Mode property to Stretch.

d. Save the form, display it in Form View, find the record with your name, double-click the Photo control, navigate to a folder that contains your picture, double-click your picture file, or navigate to the location of your Data Files, then double-click the Support_AC_6_man.jpg or Support_AC_6_woman.jpg file to attach it to that record.

e. Close the EmployeesByDepartment form.

13. Create a split form.

a. Click the CaseListing query in the Navigation Pane, click the Create tab, click the More Forms button, then click Split Form.

b. Close the Property Sheet if it opens, then switch to Form View.

c. Drag the split bar between the upper and lower portions up, to view as many records in the lower pane as possible without covering up any of the controls in the upper pane.

d. Click the CaseTitle value for Record 5 in the datasheet and modify the entry to be **Email attachment problem with large video file**. Note that the upper pane automatically displays that record.

e. Save the form with the name **CaseListingSplit** then close the form.

14. Add subforms.

a. Use the Form Wizard to create a form with the EmployeeID, FirstName, and LastName fields from the Employees table, all of the fields from the Cases table, and all of the fields from the Calls table.

b. View the data by Employees, which presents two subforms given one employee can be related to many cases in the first subform and one case can be related to many calls in the second subform.

c. Use a Datasheet layout for both subforms.

d. Title the forms **EmployeesMain**, **CasesSubform**, and **CallsSubform**.

e. Switch to Form Design View, then delete the Cases and Calls labels to the left of their respective subforms.

f. Widen the two subforms to start at the left edge of the main form and stop at the 8" mark on the horizontal ruler.

g. Save the forms then switch to Form View.

h. EmployeeID 3, Aaron Cabrera, has two records in the Cases subform. The first case is selected and displays one call in the Calls subform.

i. Click the CaseID 2 record in the subform. Notice that the Calls subform changes to display two calls for the second case.

j. Close the EmployeesMain form.

15. Add tab controls.

a. Use the Blank Form tool to create a new, blank form.

b. In Design View, add a tab control.

c. Change the Name property for the Page1 tab to **Queries**.

d. Change the Name property for the Page2 tab to **Forms**.

Skills Review (continued)

e. Right-click the Forms tab on the tab control, click Insert Page, then change the Name property for the Page# tab to **Reports**.

f. On the Queries tab, use the Command Button Wizard to add a command button to the page. From the Miscellaneous category, choose the Run Query action and the CaseDetails query. Choose the Text option button with **Case Details** as the text. Name the button **CaseDetails**.

g. On the Forms page, use the Command Button Wizard to add a command button to the page. From the Form Operations category, choose the Open Form action and the EmployeeMaster form. Open the form to show all the records, choose the Text option with the **Employee Master** as the text, and **EmployeeMaster** as the meaningful name.

h. On the Reports page, use the Command Button Wizard to add a command button to the page. From the Report Operations category, choose the Preview Report action and the CallLog report. Choose the Text option with the **Call Log** as the text and **CallLog** as the meaningful name.

i. Save the form with the name **Nav** then switch to Form view. Test all three command buttons then close all open objects.

16. Modify form properties.

a. Open the Nav form in Form Design View.

b. Open the Property Sheet for the Nav form and change the following properties on the Format tab of the Property Sheet:

Caption: **Navigation**
Record Selectors: **No**
Navigation Buttons: **No**
Scroll Bars: **Neither**
Control Box: **No**
Min Max Buttons: **None**

c. Save the Nav form then view it in Form View to review the property changes.

d. Close the Nav form, compact and close the IL_AC_6_SupportDesk database, then exit Access.

Independent Challenge 1

As the manager of Riverwalk, a multispecialty health clinic, you have created a database to manage the schedules that connect each healthcare provider with the nurses that provider needs to efficiently handle patient visits. In this exercise you will create a form that will help users find the objects (queries, forms, and reports) that they use to manage nurse and provider information.

a. Start Access, open the IL_AC_6-3.accdb database from the location where you store your Data Files, then save it as **IL_AC_6_Riverwalk**. Enable content if prompted.

b. Use the Blank Form tool to create a new, blank form.

c. In Design View, add a tab control.

d. Change the Name property for the Page1 tab to **Nurse Info**.

e. Change the Name property for the Page2 tab to **Provider Info**.

f. On the Nurse Info tab, use the Command Button Wizard to add two command buttons, side by side in the middle of the page to do the following:
- Open the NurseEntry form to show all of the records. Use the MS Access Form picture and a meaningful name of **NurseEntryForm**.
- Preview the ScheduleByNurse report. Use the Preview picture and a meaningful name of **PreviewScheduleByNurseReport**.
- Align the tops of the command buttons.

Independent Challenge 1 (continued)

g. On the Provider Info tab, use the Command Button Wizard to add two command buttons side by side in the middle of the page to do the following:
- Open the ProviderEntry form to show all of the records. Use the MS Access Form picture and a meaningful name of **ProviderEntryForm**.
- Preview the Schedule report. Use the Preview picture and a meaningful name of **PreviewScheduleReport**.
- Align the tops of the command buttons.

h. Save the form with the name **Switchboard** then switch to Form view. Test all four command buttons then close all open objects.

i. Open the Switchboard form in Form Design View.

j. Open the Property Sheet for the Switchboard form and change the following properties on the Format tab of the Property Sheet:

Record Selectors: **No**

Navigation Buttons: **No**

Scroll Bars: **Neither**

Control Box: **No**

Min Max Buttons: **None**

k. Save the Switchboard form then view it in Form View to review the property changes, as shown in FIGURE 6-34. Close the Switchboard form, compact and close the IL_AC_6_SupportDesk database, then exit Access.

FIGURE 6-34

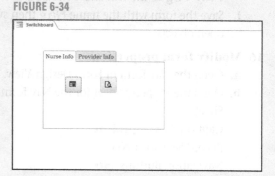

Independent Challenge 2

You are working for a city to coordinate a series of community-wide preparedness activities. You have created a database to track the activities and volunteers who are attending the activities. In this exercise you will create a form/subform to provide information about the volunteers who worked at each activity.

a. Start Access, open the IL_AC_6-4.accdb database from the location where you store your Data Files, then save it as **IL_AC_6_Volunteers**. Enable content if prompted.

b. Using the Form Wizard, create a form based on all of the fields of the Volunteers and Activities tables.

c. When asked how you want to view the data, click by Activities, click by Volunteers, then click by Activities again. Note that with both options, the Form Wizard wants to create a main form/subform using the data selected. This is because both the Activities and Volunteers tables have a one-to-many relationship with the same junction table, Attendance. One volunteer can attend many activities. One activity can have many volunteers. So the decision on which table to use for the main form and which for the subform is based on how you want to view the data. Click by Activities.

d. Choose a Datasheet layout for the subform, then enter **ActivitiesMain** as the title of the main form and **VolunteersSubform** for the subform.

e. Delete, move, and edit the labels, text boxes, and subform as shown in FIGURE 6-35.

f. Use the column resize pointer to resize the columns of the subform as shown in FIGURE 6-35.

Independent Challenge 2 (continued)

FIGURE 6-35

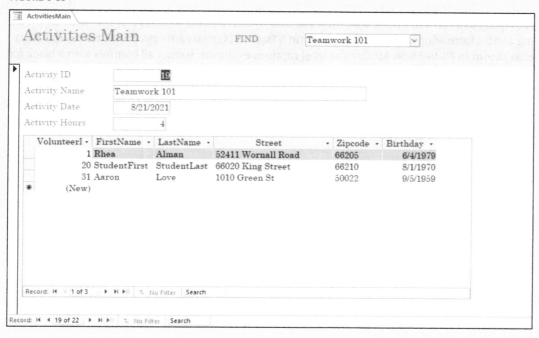

g. Save the form and in Form Design View, add a combo box in the Form Header section at about the 5" mark to find records. Select the ActivityName field for the list, hide the key column, and use **FIND** for the label.

h. Modify the properties of the new combo box to make the Column Widths **0"; 2"**, the List Width **2"**, and Width **2"**.

i. Modify the Row Source property so that the list is sorted in ascending order based on the ActivityName field.

j. Save the form, display it in Form View, then use the new combo box to find the record for Teamwork 101.

k. Change the name of Katrina Margolis to your own name in the subform. Close the ActivitiesMain form, compact and close the IL_AC_6_Volunteers database, then exit Access.

Visual Workshop

Start Access, open the IL_AC_6-5.accdb database from the location where you store your Data Files, then save it as **IL_AC_6_CollegeCourses**. Enable content if prompted. Use the Form Wizard to create a new form based on all of the fields in the StudentGrades query as shown in FIGURE 6-36. View the data by Enrollments so that all of the fields are on the main form versus creating a main form with subforms. Title the form **StudentGradeEntry**. Move, resize, and align the labels and text boxes as shown in FIGURE 6-36. Modify the label captions as shown. Format all controls with a black font color. Change the Grade text box into a combo box control. Set the Row Source property to: **"A";"B";"C";"D";"F"** and the Row Source Type property to **Value List** to display those values in the list versus selecting the list from an existing table. Set the Scroll Bars property for each of the text boxes to **None** and be sure that the tab order moves through the controls in a logical way. Change the name of Aaron Scout to your own first and last names and change the grade for the ENGR131 course to an **A** as shown in FIGURE 6-36.

FIGURE 6-36

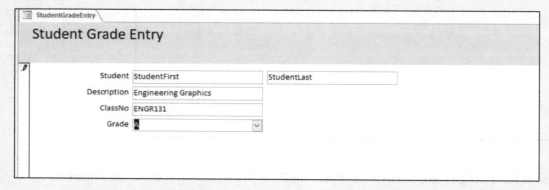

Creating Reports

CASE ▶ You are working with Lydia Snyder, vice president of operations at JCL Talent, to build a research database to manage industry, company, and job data. In this module, you'll create and modify reports that are used to analyze, subtotal, and interact with information.

Module Objectives

After completing this module, you will be able to:

- Create and preview a report
- Modify report layout
- Add fields and lines
- Group and sort records
- Add calculations and subtotals

- Resize and align controls
- Modify report sections
- Create multicolumn reports
- Add a subreport
- Add command buttons

Files You Will Need

IL_AC_7-1.accdb	IL_AC_7-4.accdb
IL_AC_7-2.accdb	IL_AC_7-5.accdb
IL_AC_7-3.accdb	

Create and Preview a Report

Learning Outcomes
- Set report properties
- Add the date and time to a report
- Preview and print a report

Reports are used to subtotal, analyze, and distribute information. Both reports and forms use label controls for descriptive text and text box controls to display data. See TABLE 7-1 for more information on common report controls. A big difference between a form and report, however, is that you use forms for data entry, whereas report data is **read-only**. You cannot enter or edit data on a report. **CASE** *Lydia Snyder asks you to create a report to display company information. You create the report using Report Design View and preview it in Print Preview.*

STEPS

QUICK TIP
If you use the Report Wizard, the Record Source property is automatically added to the report.

1. **sam ↓ Start Access, open the IL_AC_7-1.accdb database from the location where you store your Data Files, save it as IL_AC_7_Jobs, enable content if prompted, click the Create tab, then click the Report Design button**

   You can create a new report from scratch in Report Design or Report Layout View. The benefit of using Report Design View is that all report modification features are available, including ruler and report section information. The benefit of using Report Layout View is that it displays live data as you are building the report. Regardless of the view, the first task in creating a report from scratch is setting the **Record Source** property that identifies the table, query, or SQL statement that selects the fields and records for the report.

QUICK TIP
In Design View, and in other views if the object does not have a Caption property, the object's name appears in the tab.

2. **Click the Property Sheet button in the Tools group, click the Data tab in the Property Sheet, click the Record Source list arrow, then click Companies**

   The Record Source property can be a table, query, or SQL statement. If you use the Build button [...], you use the Query Builder to build an SQL statement using Query Design View. You also want to set the **Caption** property for the report, the text that will appear in the report tab when the report is opened a view other than Design View.

3. **Save the report as CompanyInfo, click the Format tab in the Property Sheet, click the Caption property box, type Company Information, then press ENTER**

   You next add the fields from the Companies table to the report.

4. **Click the Add Existing Fields button, click the CompanyID field in the Field List, drag it to the Detail section at about the 2" mark on the horizontal ruler, then drag each of the other fields to the report Detail section, as shown in FIGURE 7-1**

   Next, add the date and time to the report, then save and preview it.

5. **Click the Date and Time button in the Header/Footer group, click OK in the Date and Time dialog box, right-click the CompanyInfo report tab, then click Print Preview**

   Print Preview shows you how the report will look if printed, including page breaks, margins, and headers and footers.

QUICK TIP
To quickly move to a specific page, enter a number in the Current Page box.

6. **Click the Next Page button ▶ in the navigation bar, click the Previous Page button ◀, click the Last Page button ▶│, then click the First Page button │◀**

   By navigating through several pages of a report in Print Preview, you can see exactly how the report will look if printed or distributed. You can change the report margins in Print Preview.

7. **Click the Margins button, click the Narrow option (if it is not already selected) as shown in FIGURE 7-2, right-click the Company Information report tab, click Close, then click Yes to save the report**

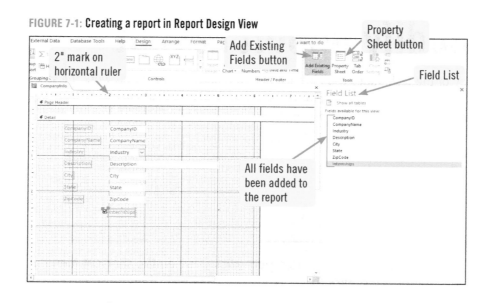

FIGURE 7-1: Creating a report in Report Design View

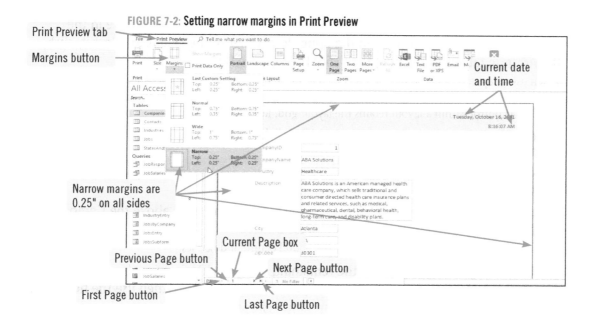

FIGURE 7-2: Setting narrow margins in Print Preview

TABLE 7-1: Common report controls

name	button	used to	bound or unbound
Label	Aa	Provide consistent descriptive text; the most common type of unbound control on a report	Unbound
Text box	abl	Display data or a calculation; the most common type of bound control on a report	Bound
Line		Draw lines, used to indicate subtotals and grand totals	Unbound
Command button		Provide an easy way to initiate a command or run a macro in Report View	Unbound

Modify Report Layout

Many of the techniques you have learned to modify form controls work the same way with reports, including moving, resizing, and deleting controls and control layouts. **CASE** ▶ *You create a copy of the CompanyInfo report to show Lydia an alternative layout.*

STEPS

1. **Right-click the** CompanyInfo report, **click** Copy **on the shortcut menu, right-click in the** Navigation Pane, **click** Paste, **type** CompanyInfo2, **then press** ENTER

   Creating a copy of an object creates a quick backup of the original, which is helpful if you want to experiment with the copy.

2. **Right-click the** CompanyInfo2 report, **click** Design View, **click the** Add Existing Fields **button, click the** =Time() text box, **press** DELETE **to delete it, click anywhere in the** Report Header section, **click** ⊞ **in the upper-left corner of the layout to select it, click the** Arrange tab **on the ribbon, then click the** Remove Layout button

   When using report- or object-creation tools such as the Report Wizard or the Date and Time button, Access often organizes controls in a **layout**, a grid that automatically moves and resizes all controls in the layout. Deleting a control within a layout retains the layout grid. Removing the layout removes the grid.

3. **Click the** Description text box, **press** DELETE, **click the** Internships check box, **then press** DELETE

   In both forms and reports, if you delete a bound control such as a text box or check box, Access deletes the accompanying label as well.

4. **Drag a** selection box **around the labels on the report (drag from above the** CompanyID **label to below the** ZipCode **label), then press** DELETE

   Deleting a label does *not* automatically delete the bound control it describes.

5. **Use the move pointer** ⟨ᵏ⟩ **to move the remaining** CompanyID, CompanyName, Industry, City, State, **and** ZipCode **text box controls, as shown in** FIGURE 7-3, **then use the horizontal resize pointer** ↔ **to resize the** CompanyName text box

   Mouse pointers in Report Design View have the same functionality as in Form Design View and are described in TABLE 7-2.

6. **Use the vertical resize pointer** ‡ **to drag the** top edge of the Page Footer section **up to the text boxes, right-click the** CompanyInfo2 report tab, **then click** Print Preview

   A portion of the first page of the new report, which now presents the data in a horizontal versus vertical layout, is shown in FIGURE 7-4. The horizontal layout of each record's data reduces the number of pages in the report to one or two pages depending on the height of the Detail section.

7. **Click the** Save button ⊟ **on the Quick Access Toolbar, right-click the** Company Information report tab, **then click** Close

FIGURE 7-3: Moving and resizing controls in Report Design View

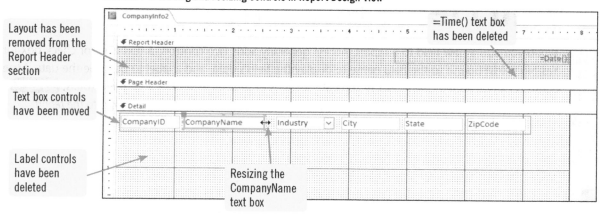

Layout has been removed from the Report Header section

=Time() text box has been deleted

Text box controls have been moved

Label controls have been deleted

Resizing the CompanyName text box

FIGURE 7-4: Previewing the new report layout

Bound controls have been moved into a horizontal layout, making the report much shorter

TABLE 7-2: Mouse pointer shapes in Report Design View

shape	when does this shape appear?	action
⌖	When you point to any unselected control on the report (the default mouse pointer)	Single-clicking with this mouse pointer selects a control. Dragging with this pointer selects all controls in the selection box.
✥	When you point to the upper-left corner or edge of a selected control in Report Design View or the middle of the control in Report Layout View	Dragging with this mouse pointer moves the selected control(s).
↕ ↔ ↖ ↗	When you point to any sizing handle (except the larger one in the upper-left corner in Report Design View)	Dragging with one of these mouse pointers resizes the control.
‡	When you point to the top edge of any report section or the bottom edge of the report	Dragging with this mouse pointer resizes the section above it.
↔	When you point to the right edge of the report	Dragging with this mouse pointer resizes the width of the report.

Add Fields and Lines

When you add a new field to a report, Access generally adds two controls, a text box (or check box for Yes/No fields) bound to the field name to display the field's data, and a label to describe the data. **Line** controls can be added to a report to separate sections or indicate subtotals and grand totals. **CASE** *Lydia asks you to modify the JobSalaries report by adding a new label, a new field, and lines to the report.*

STEPS

1. **Right-click the** JobSalaries report **in the Navigation Pane, click** Design View, **click the** Label button [Aa] **in the Controls group, click in the** Report Header section at about the 5" mark **on the horizontal ruler, type** JCL Internal Use Only, **press ENTER, click the** Format tab **on the ribbon, click the** Font Color list arrow [A ▾], **then click** Automatic (black)

   With the new label in place, you add the new field to the right side of the report.

2. **Click the** Design tab **on the ribbon, click the** Add Existing Fields button, **drag the** Applicants field **to the Detail section at about the 8.5" mark on the horizontal ruler, then click the** Add Existing Fields button **to toggle the Field List pane off**

   A text box with an accompanying label has been added to the Detail section. Report **sections** determine where and how often controls in that section print in the final report. TABLE 7-3 reviews report sections. In this case, you want the Applicants text box to remain in the Detail section, but the Applicants label should be positioned in the Page Header section as a column heading for each page.

3. **Right-click the** Applicants label, **click** Cut, **right-click the** Page Header section bar, **click** Paste, **then use the move pointer** ⇱ **to move the Applicants label above the Applicants text box, as shown in** FIGURE 7-5, **right-click the** Applicants label, **point to** Font/Fore Color **on the shortcut menu, then click the** black sample box **(first row, second column)**

   With the new field including the bound text box and descriptive label positioned correctly, you decide to add a line above the text box that contains the =Count(*) expression in the Report Footer to indicate a total.

4. **Click the** More button [▼] **in the Controls group, click the** Line button [◻], **press and hold** SHIFT, **drag a line from above the left edge of the text box in the Report Footer section to the right edge of the text box, then release** SHIFT

   Pressing SHIFT while dragging a line control creates a perfectly horizontal or vertical line.

5. **Click the** Save button [🖫] **on the Quick Access Toolbar, right-click the** JobSalaries report tab, **click** Print Preview, **then click the** Last Page button [▶|]

   The last page of the report should look like FIGURE 7-6.

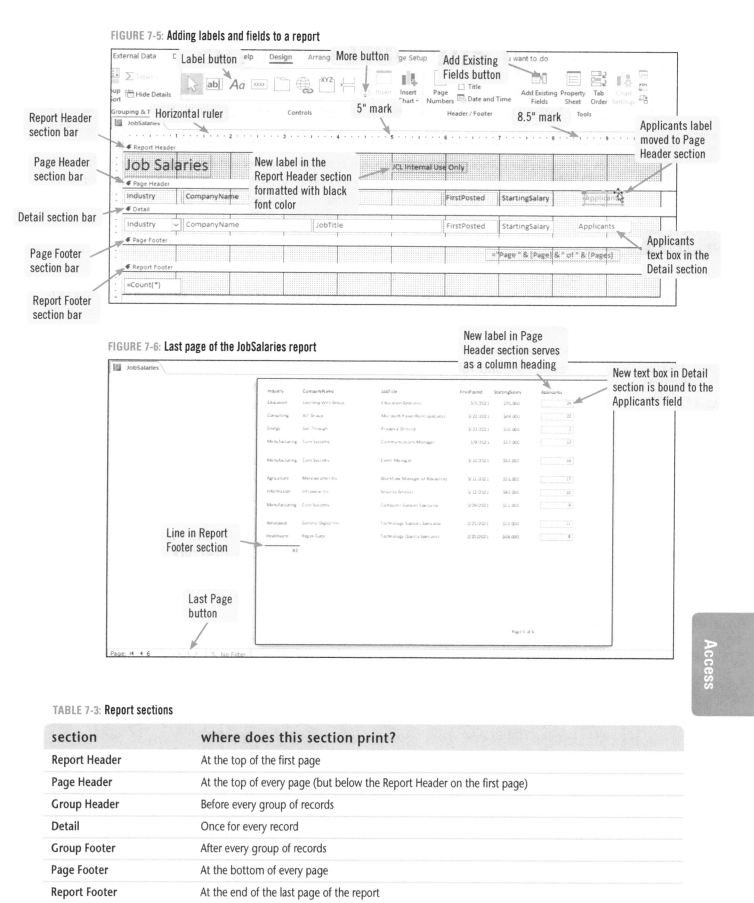

FIGURE 7-5: Adding labels and fields to a report

FIGURE 7-6: Last page of the JobSalaries report

TABLE 7-3: Report sections

section	where does this section print?
Report Header	At the top of the first page
Page Header	At the top of every page (but below the Report Header on the first page)
Group Header	Before every group of records
Detail	Once for every record
Group Footer	After every group of records
Page Footer	At the bottom of every page
Report Footer	At the end of the last page of the report

Group and Sort Records

Learning
Outcomes
• Group records
• Sort records
• Modify group
  report sections

You use the Group, Sort, and Total pane to identify the way the records on a report will be grouped and sorted. **Sorting** means to place the records in ascending or descending order based on the value of a field. **Grouping** means to sort records in a particular order plus provide a report section above or below that group of records. Fields that have a common value in several records are good candidates to use as a grouping field. After grouping records, it is common to further sort the records within each group.

CASE ➤ *Lydia Snyder asks you to organize the information in the JobSalaries report by industry and salary. You decide to group the records by Industry, then further sort them by StartingSalary.*

STEPS

1. **Right-click the** JobSalaries tab, **then click** Design View

   Grouping both sorts the records and provides a Group Header or Group Footer section before and after each group of records. The word *Group* is generic; it is replaced by the field name that is used for grouping on the report.

TROUBLE
Use the Move up
, Move down
, and Delete
buttons to
reorder the fields
in the Group, Sort,
and Total pane as
needed.

2. **Click the** Group and Sort button **on the Design tab, click the** Add a group button **in the Group, Sort, and Total pane, click** Industry, **click the** Add a sort button **in the Group, Sort, and Total pane, then click** StartingSalary, **as shown in** FIGURE 7-7

   The new Group Header section, Industry Header, prints only once per group of records. After grouping the records by a particular field, it is common to move the grouping field to the Group Header section to "announce" that group of records.

3. **Right-click the** Industry combo box **in the Detail section, click** Cut **on the shortcut menu, right-click the** Industry Header section bar, **then click** Paste

   You also need to open the Industry Footer section, the section that prints after each group of records, a logical location for subtotals that will be added in the next lesson.

4. **In the Group, Sort, and Total pane, click the** Industry group, **click the** Industry group More button, **click the** without a footer section list arrow, **then click** with a footer section

   The Industry Footer section opens in Report Design View and is a great location to add expressions that subtotal or count groups of records, as shown in FIGURE 7-8.

5. **Click the** Save button 🖫 **on the Quick Access Toolbar**

FIGURE 7-7: Grouping and sorting records in Report Design View

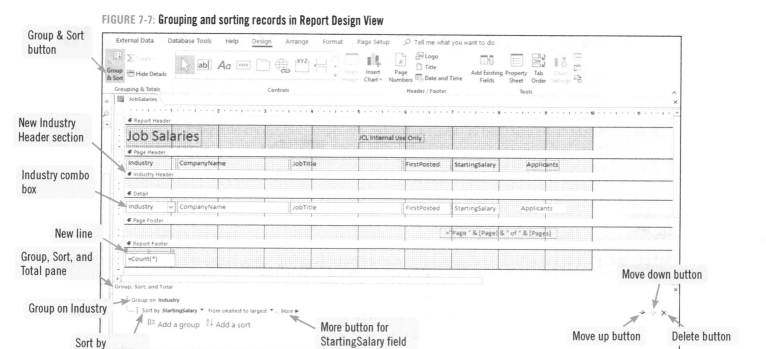

- Group & Sort button
- New Industry Header section
- Industry combo box
- New line
- Group, Sort, and Total pane
- Group on Industry
- Sort by StartingSalary
- More button for StartingSalary field
- Move down button
- Move up button
- Delete button

FIGURE 7-8: Opening the Group Footer section

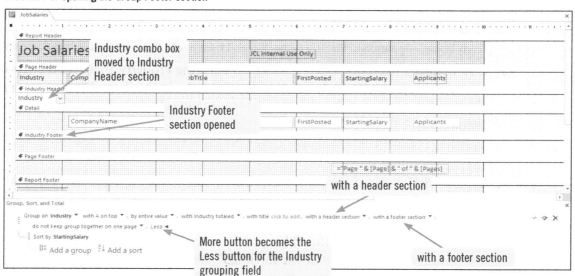

- Industry combo box moved to Industry Header section
- Industry Footer section opened
- with a header section
- More button becomes the Less button for the Industry grouping field
- with a footer section

Combo boxes versus text boxes on a report

If a field has been defined with Lookup properties in Table Design View, it will automatically be added as a combo box control to a form or report. But given that the data on a report is read-only, users cannot interact with a combo box control on a report to enter or edit data. Therefore, the combo box and text box controls function the same way on a report.

Add Calculations and Subtotals

Learning Outcomes
- Use functions in expressions
- Build subtotals on a report
- Create calculations in a query

In reports and forms, calculations are created by expressions. The expression is stored in the **Control Source** property of a text box control. Calculations on reports often use Access **functions**, built-in formulas that help build common expressions to subtotal or count groups of records. A few common Access functions are described in TABLE 7-4. You can also create calculations on reports as calculated fields in the query in the **Record Source** property for the report. **CASE** ▶ *Lydia Snyder asks you to add subtotals and calculations to the JobSalaries report.*

STEPS

QUICK TIP
The number portion of the caption of a new label is based on the number of previous controls added to the report. The instructions use ## to indicate any number.

1. **Click the** Text Box button [abl] **in the Controls group, click in the** Industry Footer section **at about the 1" mark on the horizontal ruler, click** Unbound **in the new text box, type** =Count(*), **press ENTER, click the accompanying** Text## label, **press DELETE, then use the move pointer** ▿ **to move the new text box to the left edge of the Industry Footer**

   All expressions start with an equal sign (=). When using the Count function, you can insert an asterisk (*) in place of a field name. You also want to subtotal the number of applicants within each industry.

2. **Click the** Text Box button [abl], **click in the** Industry Footer section **at about the 8.5" mark on the horizontal ruler, double-click** Text## **in the new label, type** Subtotal, **press ENTER, click** Unbound **in the new text box, type** =Sum([Applicants]), **then press ENTER, as shown in** FIGURE 7-9

   When referencing a field name within an expression, use [square brackets]—(not parentheses) and not {curly braces}—to surround the field name. You also want to add the monthly salary to the report.

3. **Double-click the** report selector box [■] **to open the Property Sheet for the report, click the** Data tab **in the Property Sheet, click** JobSalaries **in the Record Source property, click the** Build button [⋯], **right-click the** first blank field cell, **then click** Build **on the shortcut menu**

   By adding a calculated field to the query, any other forms or reports that are based on this query will also have access to this calculation.

QUICK TIP
You can also right-click a field cell, then click Zoom to create or edit a calculated field.

4. **Double-click** StartingSalary **in the Expression Categories list, type** /12, **click before** [StartingSalary], **type** Monthly: **as shown in** FIGURE 7-10, **then click** OK

   Monthly is the new calculated field name. The new field name is always followed by a colon.

5. **Click the** Close button **on the ribbon, click** Yes **to save changes, drag the** top edge of the Industry Footer section **down about 0.5", click the** Design tab **on the ribbon, click the** Add Existing Fields button, **then drag the** Monthly field **from the field list below the StartingSalary field in the Detail section**

   Any field added to the JobSalaries query is available to the report, including calculated fields. You format the Monthly field to display its values as currency with no digits to the right of the decimal point.

QUICK TIP
The Format property list provides examples of common formats such as Euro, Standard, Percent, and Scientific.

6. **Click the** Monthly text box, **click the** Property Sheet button **on the Design tab, click the** Format tab **in the Property Sheet, click the** Format property list arrow, **click** Currency, **click** Auto **in the Decimal Places property, click the** Decimal Places list arrow, **then click** 0

7. **Click the** Save button [■], **right-click the** JobSalaries report tab, **click** Report View, **then scroll down to see the entire Consulting group, as shown in** FIGURE 7-11

   Report View shows the entire report in one long view without page breaks. The basic information, subtotals, and calculations are now on the report.

FIGURE 7-9: Adding counts and subtotals to a report

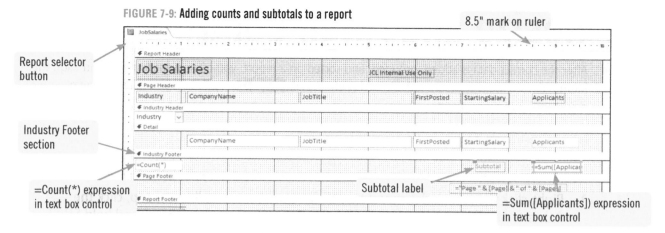

Report selector button

8.5" mark on ruler

Industry Footer section

=Count(*) expression in text box control

Subtotal label

=Sum([Applicants]) expression in text box control

FIGURE 7-10: Using the Expression Builder

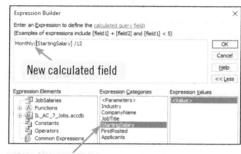

New calculated field

StartingSalary field

FIGURE 7-11: Previewing subtotals, counts, and calculations

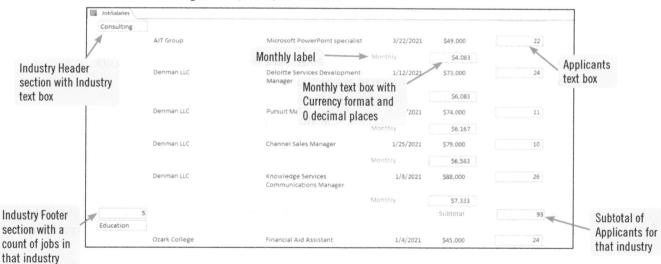

Industry Header section with Industry text box

Monthly label

Monthly text box with Currency format and 0 decimal places

Applicants text box

Industry Footer section with a count of jobs in that industry

Subtotal of Applicants for that industry

TABLE 7-4: Sample expressions using common Access functions

sample expression	function description
=Sum([Salary])	Uses the **Sum function** to add the values in the Salary field
=Avg([Freight])	Uses the **Avg function** to display an average of the values in the Freight field
=Date()	Uses the **Date function** to display the current date in the form of mm-dd-yy
=Left([ProductNumber],2)	Uses the **Left function** to display the first two characters in the ProductNumber field
=Count(*)	Uses the **Count function** to count the records

Resize and Align Controls

Learning Outcomes
• Resize controls and sections
• Align controls

After the correct data is added, grouped, and sorted on a report, you often want to resize and align the information to make it more readable and professional. **CASE** *Lydia asks you to resize and align the data on the JobSalaries report.*

STEPS

1. **Right-click the** JobSalaries report tab, **click** Layout View, **scroll to the top, click the** Property Sheet button **to close it, click the** CompanyName label, **press and hold** SHIFT, **click** General Digital Inc, **release** SHIFT, **then use the horizontal resize pointer** ↔ **on the right side to narrow the column to be only as wide as needed to display the data**

   Most modifications, such as resizing, aligning, and formatting controls, can be accomplished the same way in both Design and Layout Views. The benefit of resizing controls in Layout View is that you can see the data as you are modifying the controls.

   TROUBLE
   Use the Undo button ↶ to undo multiple actions in Report Layout or Design View.

2. **Click any occurrence of the** Monthly label, **press** DELETE, **then continue resizing and moving controls until all the data for one record is on the same line, as shown in** FIGURE 7-12

   The benefit of modifying controls in Design View is that you have access to the rulers and section bars.

3. **Right-click the** JobSalaries report tab, **click** Design View, **click the** Group & Sort button **to toggle off the Group, Sort, and Total pane if it is still visible, then use the resize pointer** ╪ **to drag the** top edge of the Industry Footer section bar **up to remove the extra vertical space in the Detail section**

   Recall that the Detail section prints once for each record in the record source. Keeping the Detail section as short as possible helps minimize the overall length of the report.

4. **Click in the** vertical ruler to the left of the Detail section **to select all controls in that section, click the** Arrange tab **on the ribbon, click the** Size/Space button, **click** To Tallest, **click the** Align button **as shown in** FIGURE 7-13, **then click** Top

   You also want to align the data in the Applicants column.

5. **Click the** =Sum([Applicants]) text box **in the Industry Footer section, press** SHIFT, **click the** Applicants text box **in the Detail section, click the** Applicants label **in the Page Header section, release** SHIFT, **click the** Align button, **click** Right, **click the** Format tab **on the ribbon, then click the** Align Right button ▤

   Recall that the alignment buttons on the Format tab align content *within* the control, whereas the Align button on the Arrange tab aligns the *edges* of the selected controls. Now that the controls in the Detail and Industry Footer sections are perfectly sized and aligned, you decide to remove the border on all controls in the report.

6. **Press** CTRL+A **to select all controls on the report, click the** Shape Outline button **in the Control Formatting group, click** Transparent, **click the** Report Footer section bar, **click the** line control **in the Report Footer section to select it by itself, click the** Shape Outline button, **then click** Automatic (black)

   Save and preview your changes.

7. **Click the** Save button 🖫, **right-click the** JobSalaries report tab, **then click** Print Preview

   The report is much shorter and more professional now that all the controls in the Detail and Report Footer sections are aligned and resized.

FIGURE 7-12: Resizing and moving controls in Report Layout View

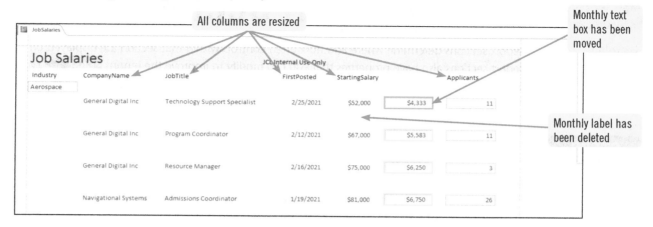

All columns are resized

Monthly text box has been moved

Monthly label has been deleted

FIGURE 7-13: Aligning controls in Report Design View

Arrange tab

Format tab

Size/Space button

Align button

Top option

Applicants label in Page Header section

Applicants text box in Detail section

Vertical ruler

Top edge of Industry Footer section bar

All controls in the Detail section are selected

Text box with =Sum([Applicants]) expression in Industry Footer section

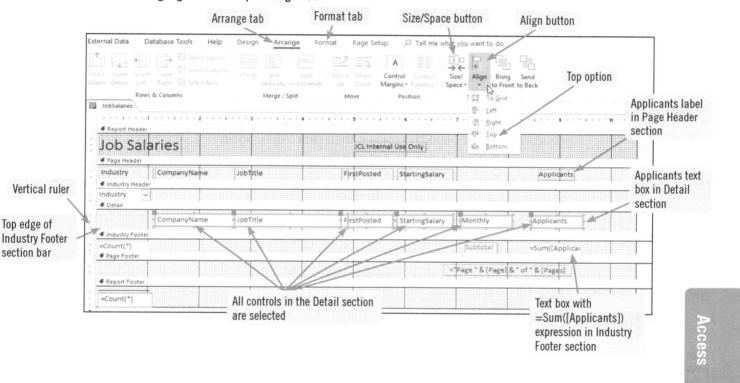

Modify Report Sections

Learning Outcome
• Modify section properties

Report sections determine where and how often controls within that section are displayed on the report. Report sections also have properties that you can modify to improve the report. **CASE** ▶ *Lydia asks you to continue improving the JobSalaries report by changing the way each industry group appears on the printout. You work with report section properties to make the changes.*

STEPS

TROUBLE
Be sure to click the Industry Header section bar versus the Industry Footer section bar.

1. **Right-click the** JobSalaries report tab, **click** Design View, **double-click the** Industry Header section bar **to open its Property Sheet, then click the** Format tab **if it is not already selected**

   The **Back Color** and **Alternate Back Color** properties determine the background color for every other Industry Header section. You change this to white for every Industry Header.

2. **Click the** Back Color property **in the Property Sheet, click the** Build button ▦, **click** White **in the Standard Colors palette (first column, first row), click the** Alternate Back Color property, **click the** Build button ▦, **then click** White **again**

   You modify section properties the same way for forms and reports, but modifying sections is more common in reports because they have extra Group Header and Group Footer sections for grouping and subtotaling records. You decide to make the same background color modifications for the Industry Footer section.

TROUBLE
Be sure to click the Industry Footer section bar versus the Industry Header section bar.

3. **Click the** Industry Footer section bar, **click the** Back Color property, **click the** Build button ▦, **click** White **in the Standard Colors palette, click the** Alternate Back Color property, **click the** Build button ▦, **then click** White **again**

   You also want each new Industry to start on its own page.

4. **With the Industry Footer section still selected, click the** Force New Page property, **click the** Force New Page list arrow, **then click** After section

   When an Industry spans more than one page, you want the Industry Header section to repeat at the top of that page.

5. **Click the** Industry Header section bar, **then double-click the** Repeat Section property **to toggle it from No to Yes, as shown in** FIGURE 7-14

   Save and preview the report.

QUICK TIP
Report View does not show page breaks, so you cannot test the Repeat Section or Force New Page section properties in Report View, only in Print Preview.

6. **Click Save** ▦, **right-click the** JobSalaries report tab, **click** Print Preview, **click the** Next Page button ▸ **twice to move to Page 3, then click the report to zoom in, as shown in** FIGURE 7-15

   No industries have enough records to span more than one page yet, but as the database grows, this report will repeat the Industry Header section as needed and start each industry at the top of a new page.

7. **Right-click the** JobSalaries report tab, **then click** Close

FIGURE 7-14: Modifying section properties

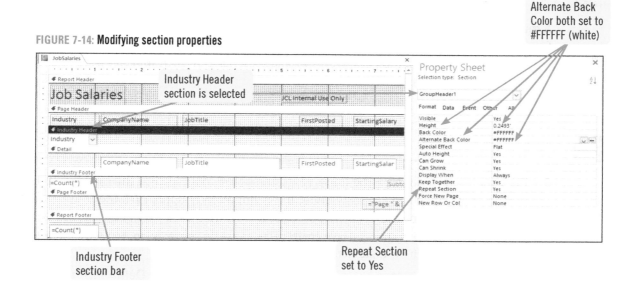

Industry Header section is selected

Back Color and Alternate Back Color both set to #FFFFFF (white)

Industry Footer section bar

Repeat Section set to Yes

FIGURE 7-15: Previewing the final JobSalaries report

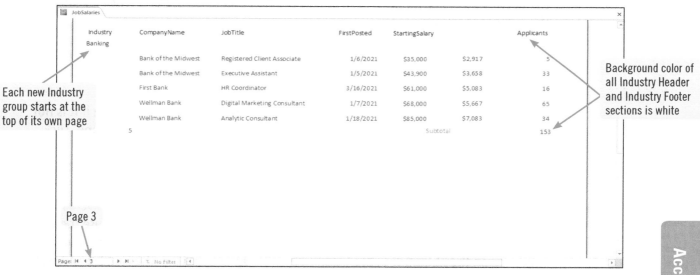

Each new Industry group starts at the top of its own page

Page 3

Background color of all Industry Header and Industry Footer sections is white

Hexadecimal color values

Hexadecimal color values are six-digit representations of color using two digits for each of the three colors of light: red, green, and blue (also sometimes called **RGB values** for red-green-blue). Each digit ranges from 0–9, then A–F for a total of 16 different values for each digit. #000000 represents no color in each of the three color positions, which yields black. #FFFFFF represents maximum amounts of red, green, and blue light, which represents white. #FF0000 represents maximum red, no green, and no blue, which defines red, and so forth. An equal mix of red, green, and blue such as #D8D8D8 is a shade of gray.

Inserting page breaks

If you want to force a page break at a certain point in a form or report, use the **Insert Page Break button** to insert a **page break control**, which forces any content after the control to start at the top of a new page when the form or report is previewed or printed.

Create Multicolumn Reports

Learning
Outcomes
• Add and modify
  columns
• Add page
  numbers to a
  report

A **multicolumn report** repeats information in more than one column on the page. You use the Page Setup dialog box to create and define multiple columns. **CASE** ▸ *Lydia asks you to create a report that lists contact names sorted in ascending order by contact last name. A report with only a few fields is a good candidate for a multicolumn report.*

STEPS

1. **Click the** Create tab, **click the** Report Design button, **double-click the** report selector button ▪ **to open the Property Sheet if it is not already open, click the** Data tab **in the Property Sheet, click the** Record Source list arrow, **then click** Contacts

   You decide to combine the first and last contact names into a single expression. You add a text box control to the report to contain the expression.

QUICK TIP
Be sure to insert a space after the comma in the new expression.

2. **Click the** Text Box button ⌨ **in the Controls group, click in the** Detail section, **click the** Text## label, **press** DELETE, **click the new** text box **to select it, click** Unbound **in the text box, type the expression** =[ContactLast] & ", " & [ContactFirst], **press** ENTER, **then use the horizontal resize pointer** ↔ **to widen the text box to be about 3" wide to display the entire expression**

   When building an expression that concatenates text, use the ampersand character (&) to combine the parts. In this case, the ContactLast value is concatenated to a comma and a space, which are then concatenated to the ContactFirst value. To make sure that the records sort in ContactLast, then ContactFirst order, you will set the report sort options in the Group, Sort, and Total pane.

3. **Click the** Group & Sort button **to toggle on the Group, Sort, and Total pane if it is not already opened, click the** Add a sort button **in the Group, Sort, and Total pane, click** ContactLast, **click the** Add a sort button **again, then click** ContactFirst

   With the desired information added and sorted on the report, you turn your attention to setting up the columns for the report.

QUICK TIP
You must use Print Preview to view report columns. Report View doesn't display multiple columns.

4. **Use the move pointer** 🖑 **to drag the** text box **into the upper-left corner of the Detail section, use the** ↔ **pointer to drag the** right edge of the report **as far left as possible, use the** ‡ **pointer to drag the** top edge of the Page Footer section **up to the text box, click the** Page Setup tab **on the ribbon, click the** Columns button, **double-click** 1 **in the Number of Columns box, type** 2, **then click the** Down, **then** Across option button, **as shown in** FIGURE 7-16

   When designing a multicolumn report, Report Design View should display the width of only the first column. The Columns tab of the Page Setup dialog box provides options to change column settings. You also want this report to have page numbers.

TROUBLE
If your data doesn't look like FIGURE 7-17, return to Report Design View and check your expression and sort orders.

5. **Click** OK **in the Page Setup dialog box, click the** Design tab **on the ribbon, click the** Page Numbers button, **click the** Page N of M option button, **click the** Alignment list arrow, **click** Right, **then click** OK **in the Page Numbers dialog box**

   The page number expression was added in a text box control to the right side of the Page Header section.

6. **Right-click the** Report1 report tab, **then click** Print Preview, **as shown in** FIGURE 7-17

   Contact names are now set in two columns, sorted by the ContactLast, then by the ContactFirst fields.

7. **Click the** Save button 🖫, **type** ContactList, **click** OK **in the Save as dialog box, right-click the** ContactList report tab, **then click** Close

FIGURE 7-16: Setting column properties

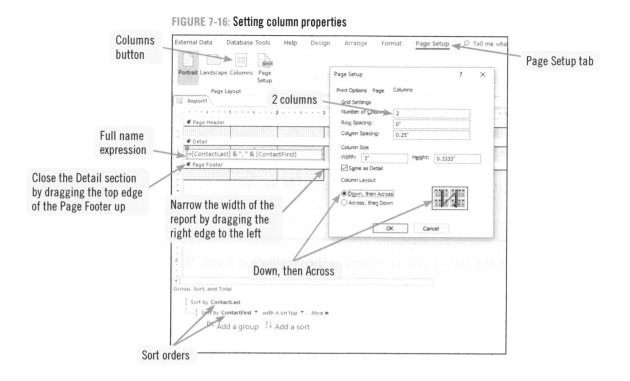

Columns button

Page Setup tab

2 columns

Full name expression

Close the Detail section by dragging the top edge of the Page Footer up

Narrow the width of the report by dragging the right edge to the left

Down, then Across

Sort orders

FIGURE 7-17: Previewing a multicolumn report

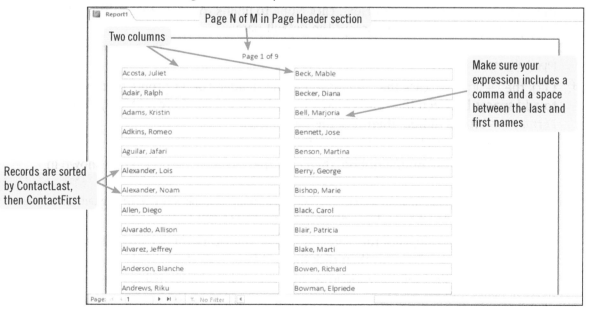

Page N of M in Page Header section

Two columns

Make sure your expression includes a comma and a space between the last and first names

Records are sorted by ContactLast, then ContactFirst

Add a Subreport

Learning
Outcomes
• Add a subreport
• Remove sections
• Add a title

A **subreport** is a report within another report. The report that contains the subreport is called the **main report**. You can use subreports when you want to chain together several reports for printing or electronic distribution. Using a common field in the main report and the subreport, you can also use a subreport to display only those records in the subreport that relate to the current parent record in the main report, similar to how a subform is related to a main form. **CASE** ▶ *Lydia asks you to distribute the IndustryIndex report with the JobsByHighestSalary report. You prepare the IndustryIndex report, then add it as a subreport to the JobsByHighestSalary Report Footer section to handle this request.*

STEPS

1. **Right-click the IndustryIndex report in the Navigation Pane, click Design View, right-click the Report Header section bar, then click Report Header/Footer to remove those sections from the report**

   If sections are empty or contain unwanted controls, it is best to delete them to simplify Design View. Report and page sections can always be added back to a report using the same right-click technique.

2. **Click the Save button 🖫, right-click the IndustryIndex report tab, click Close, click the Database Tools tab, then click Compact and Repair Database**

   Compacting and repairing your database at regular intervals helps it stay organized. Next, add the IndustryIndex report as a subreport to the JobsByHighestSalary report. The subreport and subform controls share the same button in the Controls group of the Design tab.

3. **Right-click the JobsByHighestSalary report in the Navigation Pane, click Design View, click the More button ⤓ in the Controls group, click the Subform/Subreport button 🖾, click at about the 1" mark on the horizontal ruler in the Report Footer section, click the IndustryIndex report, click Next, click None to unlink the main report from the subreport, then click Finish to accept the default name**

   The IndustryIndex report will be displayed after the JobsByHighestSalary report. The JobsByHighestSalary report also needs a title.

4. **Click the Design tab, click the Title button in the Header/Footer group, modify the title to add spaces between the words as in Jobs By Highest Salary, press ENTER, click the Format tab on the ribbon, then click the Bold button ⬛**

   The label is in a layout grid that consists of several cells.

5. **Click the Arrange tab on the ribbon, then click the Select Layout button, as shown in FIGURE 7-18**

   See TABLE 7-5 for more information on selecting, adding, merging, and splitting cells in a layout. Given you are using only one cell in the layout, you decide to merge all cells together.

6. **Click the Merge button, click the Save button 🖫, right-click the JobsByHighestSalary report tab, click Print Preview, then click the Last Page button ▶|**

   After the last page of the JobsByHighestSalary report is displayed, the IndustryIndex report is displayed, as shown in FIGURE 7-19.

7. **Right-click the JobsByHighestSalary report tab, then click Close**

FIGURE 7-18: Main report with subreport

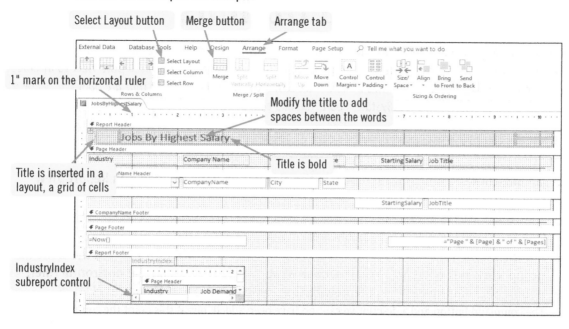

Select Layout button   Merge button   Arrange tab

1" mark on the horizontal ruler

Modify the title to add spaces between the words

Title is bold

Title is inserted in a layout, a grid of cells

IndustryIndex subreport control

FIGURE 7-19: Previewing a subreport

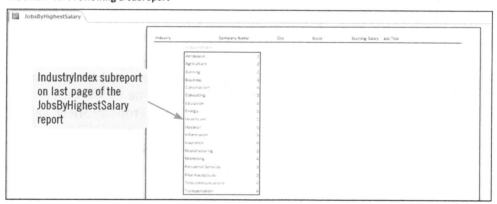

IndustryIndex subreport on last page of the JobsByHighestSalary report

TABLE 7-5: Modifying cells in a layout

button	description
	Inserts a row cell above or below the layout
	Inserts a column cell to the left or right of the layout
	Selects all cells in the layout
	Selects all cells in the current column or row
	Merges selected cells
	Splits selected cells into two cells vertically or horizontally

Add Command Buttons

Learning
Outcome
• Add a command
  button to a report

You have already used a **command button** to perform common actions in Form View such as printing the current record and closing the form. You can also use command buttons in Report View to interact with the report. **CASE** ▸ *Lydia asks if there is an easy way to display the jobs that are above or below a $50,000 starting salary in the JobsByState report. You add command buttons to achieve this.*

STEPS

1. **Double-click the** JobsByState report **in the Navigation Pane to open it in Report View, then scroll through the report**

   The starting salary data in the last column ranges from $35,000 to $95,000. You want to add two command buttons that will help you view only those jobs with a starting salary value above or below $50,000.

2. **Right-click the** JobsByState report tab, **click** Design View, **click** Button 🔲 **in the Controls group, click in the** Report Header section at about the 4" mark **on the horizontal ruler, double-click** Command## **in the new button, type** Below $50K, **then press** ENTER

   The command button and a descriptive caption have been added, but at this point the command button doesn't do anything when clicked. To add this functionality, use the command button's Property Sheet.

3. **With the command button still selected, click the** Property Sheet button **to open it if it isn't already open, click the** Event tab **in the Property Sheet, click the** On Click list arrow, **then click** LessThan50K

   LessThan50K is a previously created macro that applies a filter to display only those records where the StartingSalary field value is less than $50,000. You will learn how to create macros in a future module.

4. **Right-click the** Below $50K command button, **click** Copy, **right-click in the** Report Header section, **click** Paste, **use the move pointer** ⁚ᵗᵣ **to move the new command button to the right of the Below $50K command button, click the** On Click list arrow, **click** GreaterThanOrEqualTo50K, **click the** Format tab **in the Property Sheet, select** Below $50K **in the** Caption property, **type** $50K or More, **then press** ENTER

   Your screen should look like FIGURE 7-20. GreaterThanOrEqualTo50K is another previously created macro stored in the database that applies a filter to display only those records where the StartingSalary field value is greater than or equal to $50,000.

5. **Click** Save 🔲, **right-click the** JobsByState report tab, **click** Report View, **click the** Below $50K command button, **then click the** $50K or More command button, **as shown in** FIGURE 7-21

   Command buttons make a report flexible and interactive.

6. **Right-click the** JobsByState report tab, **click** Close, **double-click the** Contacts table **to open it in Datasheet View, add your name as a new record with a CompanyID value of 1, then close the Contacts table**

7. **sam↑ Compact and repair the database, then close the IL_AC_7_Jobs.accdb database and exit Access**

FIGURE 7-20: Adding command buttons to a report

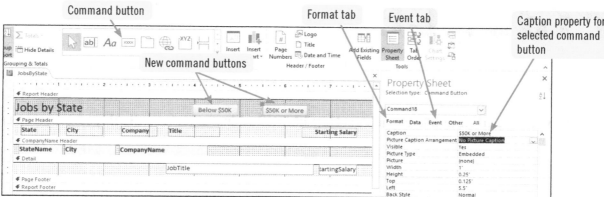

Command button · Format tab · Event tab · Caption property for selected command button · New command buttons

FIGURE 7-21: Filtering the records on a report with a command button

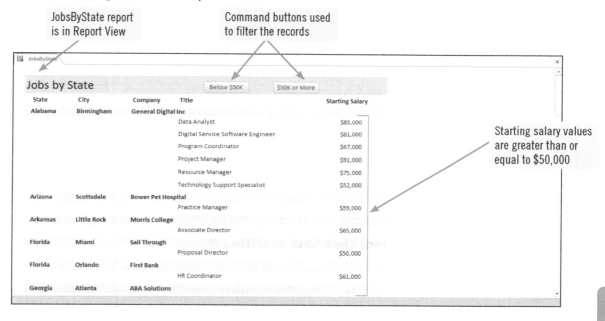

JobsByState report is in Report View · Command buttons used to filter the records · Starting salary values are greater than or equal to $50,000

Rich Text formatting

By default every text box on a form or report has a **Text Format property** of **Plain Text**, which stores only text, not formatting instructions. The **Rich Text** value for the Text Format property allows you to mix formatting for the content of one text box using **HTML (HyperText Markup Language)** tags such as <b> for bold and <i> for italic. If you need to format the content of one text box in multiple ways, explore the capabilities of Rich Text.

Practice

Concepts Review

Explain where and how often each section identified in FIGURE 7-22 **is displayed on a report.**

FIGURE 7-22

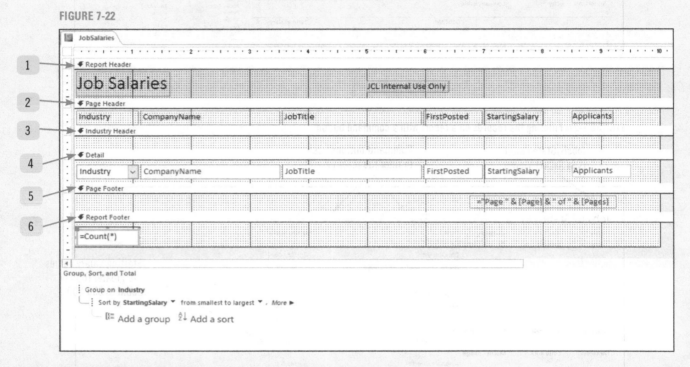

Match each term with the statement that best describes it.

7. **Text box**

8. **Grouping**

9. **Sorting**

10. **Record Source**

11. **Label**

12. **Read-only**

13. **Control Source**

14. **Layout**

15. **Main report**

a. A control used to display descriptive text on a report

b. To place the records in ascending or descending order based on the value of a field

c. A grid that automatically moves and resizes the controls it contains

d. To sort records in a particular order, plus provide a report section above and/or below the group of records

e. A control used to display data or a calculation on a report

f. A text box property where expressions are stored

g. A report that contains the subreport

h. A property that identifies the table, query, or SQL statement that selects the fields and records for the report

i. Not used for data entry or edits

Select the best answer from the list of choices.

16. **Which report view allows you to click a command button to execute an action?**

    a. Design View

    b. Layout View

    c. Print Preview

    d. Report View

17. Which report view displays data and allows you to resize controls?
  a. Design View
  b. Layout View
  c. Print Preview
  d. Report View

18. Which report view displays rulers and section bars?
  a. Design View
  b. Layout View
  c. Print Preview
  d. Report View

19. Which report view shows margins and page breaks?
  a. Design View
  b. Layout View
  c. Print Preview
  d. Report View

20. Which of the following expressions would subtotal a field named Cost?
  a. =Sum([Cost])
  b. =Subtotal{Cost}
  c. =Sub[Cost]
  d. =Total(Cost)

Skills Review

1. Create and preview a report.

  a. Start Access, open the IL_AC_7-2.accdb database from the location where you store your Data Files, then save it as **IL_AC_7_SupportDesk**. Enable content if prompted.

  b. Use the Report Design button to create a blank report in Report Design View. Set the report's Record Source property to the **EmployeeCalls** query and enter **Employee Calls** for the report's Caption property.

  c. Select the four fields LastName, FirstName, CaseTitle, and CallDateTime in the Field List, then drag them as a group or one at a time to the top of the Detail section at about the 1" mark on the horizontal ruler.

  d. Use the Date and Time button to add the current date and time to the report using a 30-Sep-21 format for the date and a 10:24 AM format for the time.

  e. Drag the top edge of the Page Footer section up to the text boxes in the Detail section, then save the report with the name **EmployeeCalls**.

  f. Switch to Print Preview, confirm that the report's margins are set to Narrow, then navigate through each of the report's pages to observe the length of the report.

  g. Close the EmployeeCalls report.

2. Modify report layout.

  a. Copy the EmployeeCalls report and paste it in the Navigation Pane with the name **EmployeeCalls2**.

  b. Open the EmployeeCalls2 report in Design View, then move, edit, and format the labels, as shown in FIGURE 7-23. The labels are positioned in the Page Header section, their captions have been edited to include spaces between words, and the labels have a bold and black font color.

  c. Move and format the text boxes, as shown in FIGURE 7-23. Note that the text boxes are positioned horizontally in the Detail section and that the CaseTitle text box has been widened to display more information.

  d. Drag the top edge of the Page Footer section up to the text boxes to remove vertical space in the Detail section.

  e. Remove the control layout from the controls in the Report Header section, then narrow and move the =Date() and =Time() text boxes side by side, as shown in FIGURE 7-23.

  f. Add a label to the Report Header section with **Employee Call List**, format it with bold, black font color, and 14-point font size, as shown in FIGURE 7-23.

  g. Save the report and preview all pages in Print Preview to make sure all information is clearly displayed, as shown in FIGURE 7-23. Note the difference in report page size between the EmployeeCalls report and EmployeeCalls2 report.

  h. Close the EmployeeCalls2 report.

Skills Review (continued)

FIGURE 7-23

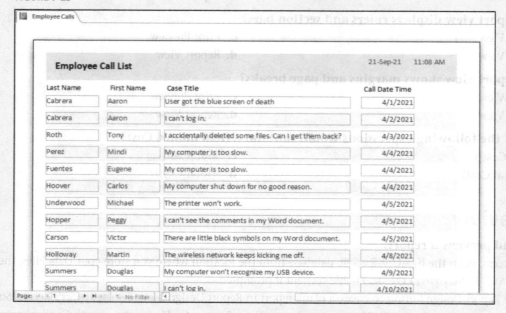

3. Add fields and lines.

a. Open the CaseInfo report in Design View, then delete the EmployeeID label and EmployeeID text box.

b. Open the Field List and add the LastName field to the report.

c. Move the LastName label to the Page Header section between the CaseID and OpenedDate labels and modify it to be **Last Name**. Use the Format Painter to copy the formatting from the CaseID label to the Last Name label. Widen the Last Name label as needed to clearly display the entire label.

d. Move the LastName text box in the Detail section between the existing CaseID and OpenedDate text boxes. Use the Format Painter to copy the formatting from the CaseID text box to the LastName text box and widen the LastName text box to fill the available space.

e. Expand the height of the Report Footer section enough to move the =Count(*) text box down about 0.25", then add a horizontal line above the =Count(*) text box to indicate a total.

f. Resize the Detail section to eliminate any extra blank space, then save the CaseInfo report, noting that the final report is shown in FIGURE 7-24.

FIGURE 7-24

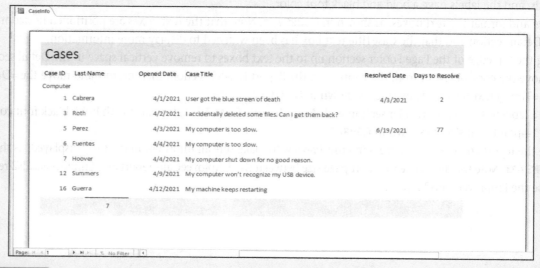

Skills Review (continued)

4. Group and sort records.

   a. Open the Group, Sort, and Total pane for the CaseInfo report. Add Category as a grouping field and OpenedDate as a sort field in that order.

   b. Move the Category text box to the left side of the Category Header section and delete the Category label in the Page Header section.

   c. Open the Category Footer section.

   d. Save the CaseInfo report.

5. Add calculations and subtotals.

   a. Copy the line and the =Count(*) text box from the Report Footer section, then paste the two controls into the Category Footer section.

   b. Move the Resolved Date and Days to Resolve labels in the Page Header section to the left, beside the Case Title label.

   c. Move the ResolvedDate text box in the Detail section to the left next to the CaseTitle text box.

   d. Add a text box control to the right of the ResolvedDate text box with the expression **=[ResolvedDate]-[OpenedDate]** to calculate the number of days between the date the case was opened and the date it was resolved.

   e. Delete the accompanying Text## label, then right-align the content within the =[ResolvedDate]-[OpenedDate] text box.

   f. Move and resize the =[ResolvedDate]-[OpenedDate] text box to make sure that it is positioned under the Days to Resolve label and to the left of the 10" mark on the horizontal ruler. Drag the right edge of the report to the left to make sure the report is not wider than the 10" mark on the horizontal ruler.

   g. Save and preview the CaseInfo report.

6. Resize and align controls.

   a. Return to Design View of the CaseInfo report, then size all the labels in the Page Header section to the Tallest and align their Top edges.

   b. Size all the text boxes in the Detail section to the Tallest, and align their Top edges.

   c. In the Report Footer section, align the left edges of the two controls (the line and the =Count(*) text box) with the left edges of the two controls in the Category Footer section.

   d. Select all controls and use the Shape Outline button to set the border to Transparent. Select the two line controls and use the Shape Outline button to set the border to black.

   e. Save and preview the CaseInfo report.

7. Modify report sections.

   a. Return to Design View of the CaseInfo report, then change the Back Color and Alternate Back Color to white (**#FFFFFF**) for the Category Header section.

   b. Change the Back Color and Alternate Back Color to white (**#FFFFFF**) for the Detail section.

   c. Change the Back Color and Alternate Back Color to Light Gray 1 (**#ECECEC**) for the Category Footer section.

   d. Set the Repeat Section property of the Category Header section to **Yes**.

   e. Set the Force New Page property of the Category Footer section to **After Section**.

   f. Save and preview the CaseInfo report, the first page of which is shown in FIGURE 7-24, then close the CaseInfo report.

8. Create multicolumn reports.

   a. Create a new report in Report Design View and set the Record Source property to the Employees table.

   b. Add page numbers using the Page N of M format to the left side of the Page Footer.

   c. Add a text box to the Detail section with the expression **=[LastName]&", "&[FirstName]** as the Control Source property. Be careful to include both a comma (,) and a space between the quotation marks so that the expression produces Cabrera, Aaron versus Cabrera,Aaron on the report.

Skills Review (continued)

d. Resize the text box to be about 2" wide. Delete the accompanying label and move the text box to the upper-left corner of the Detail section.

e. Drag the top edge of the Page Footer section up to the bottom of the text box in the Detail section.

f. Drag the right edge of the report as far as possible to the left so that the report is no wider than 2.5".

g. Save the report with the name **EmployeeList**, then display it in Print Preview.

h. Change the columns to **3** in an Across, then Down format.

i. Save, then close the EmployeeList report.

9. **Add a subreport.**

a. Open the CallLog report in Report Design View and use the Group, Sort, and Total Pane to remove the Department Header section. (*Hint*: Use the More button to specify "without a header section" for the Department group field.)

b. Open the Report Footer section by dragging the bottom edge of the Report Footer section bar down about 0.5", then add the EmployeeList report as a subreport at the far-left edge of the Report Footer section using the None option for the link.

c. Delete the label that accompanies the subreport control, and widen the subreport to be as wide as the report, but do not push out the right edge of the main report beyond 8".

d. Delete the label in the Report Header section, then use the Title button to add a title to the report. Modify the title to read **Call Log**.

e. Save and preview the CallLog report, then close it.

10. **Add command buttons.**

a. Double-click the EmployeeMasterList report to open it in Report View, then test the four command buttons in the Report Header section.

b. Open the EmployeeMasterList report in Report Design View, then add two new command buttons to the right of the Human Resources command button.

c. Change the new command button captions to be **Marketing** and **Production**.

d. The On Click event property of the Marketing button should be the **FilterMarketing** macro and the On Click event property of the Production button should be the **FilterProduction** macro.

e. Make sure that all command buttons are wide enough to clearly read their captions but not so wide as to push out the right edge of the report beyond the 10" mark on the horizontal ruler. Resize and move the command buttons as necessary to keep the report width at 10" or less.

f. Size the command buttons to the shortest button, then align the top edges of all the command buttons in the Report Header section.

g. Save the EmployeeMasterList report, then view it in Report View. Test the new Marketing and Production command buttons, then close the EmployeeMasterList report.

h. Double-click the Employees table, add *your name* as a new record, **9876** as the PhoneExtension field value, then complete the rest of the record with fictitious yet realistic data. Close the Employees table.

i. Compact and repair then close the IL_AC_7_SupportDesk.accdb database and exit Access 2019.

Independent Challenge 1

As the manager of Riverwalk, a multispecialty health clinic, you have created a database to manage nurse and doctor schedules to efficiently handle patient visits. In this exercise, you will create a report that will analyze nurse schedules at the different clinic locations.

a. Start Access, open the IL_AC_7-3.accdb database from the location where you store your Data Files, then save it as **IL_AC_7_Riverwalk**. Enable content if prompted.

b. Use the Report Wizard to create a new report on the ScheduleDetails query. Use all the fields and view the records by LocationNo.

Independent Challenge 1 (continued)

c. Do not add any more grouping levels, then sort the records by ScheduleDate.

d. Use a Stepped layout and a portrait orientation, and title the report **Schedule by Location**.

e. In Layout View, delete the LocationNo label and text box as well as the DoctorNo label and text box. Note that the final report is shown in FIGURE 7-25.

f. Save the report and switch to Design View. Add NurseName as second sort order below the LocationNo grouping field and ScheduleDate sort field.

g. Open the LocationNo Footer section and add a text box at about the 1" mark on the horizontal ruler. Add **=Count(*)** as the Control Source property and use **Count** as the Caption for the Text## label.

h. Open the ScheduleDate Header and Footer sections, move the ScheduleDate text box directly up into the ScheduleDate Header section, then copy and align the controls from the LocationNo Footer section in the ScheduleDate Footer section so that both sections count the number of records in that group.

i. Select all controls, then apply a transparent border and black font color.

j. Modify the labels in the Page Header section, as shown in FIGURE 7-25.

k. Save the Schedule By Location report, then view it in Report View, as shown in FIGURE 7-25.

l. Close the Schedule By Location report, right-click it, and rename it to be **ScheduleByLocation** to be consistent with the other objects in the database.

m. Double-click the Providers table, add *your last name* as a new record with the DrPA field value of MD, then close the Providers table.

n. Compact and close the IL_AC_7_Riverwalk.accdb and exit Access 2019.

FIGURE 7-25

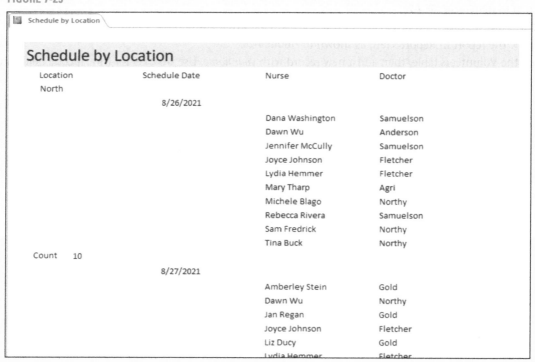

Independent Challenge 2

You are working for a city to coordinate a series of community-wide preparedness activities. You have created a database to track the activities and volunteers who are attending the activities. In this exercise, you will create a report to calculate information about the total number of volunteer hours at each activity.

a. Start Access, open the IL_AC_7-4.accdb database from the location where you store your Data Files, then save it as **IL_AC_7_Volunteers**. Enable content if prompted.

b. Create a new report in Report Design View. Set the Record Source property to the ActivityList query.

c. Group the report by ActivityName, then sort it by LastName.

d. Add the ActivityName and ActivityDate fields to the ActivityName Header section, as shown in FIGURE 7-26. Note that no labels are needed to describe these fields.

e. Add the LastName and ActivityHours fields to the Detail section, as shown in FIGURE 7-26. Note that no labels are needed to describe these fields.

f. Open the ActivityName Footer section and add a text box to subtotal (not count) the number of ActivityHours within each activity using the **=Sum([ActivityHours])** expression. Delete the accompanying Text## label.

g. Close the Page Header and Page Footer sections, then open the Report Header and Report Footer sections.

h. Copy the text box that subtotals the ActivityHours from the ActivityName Footer section to the Report Footer section and right-align the edges of the two controls plus the ActivityHours text box in the Detail section.

i. Right-align the content within the ActivityHours text box in the Detail section and the two text boxes that contain the expressions to sum the ActivityHours.

j. Add a title to the report with the text **Activity Totals**, merge all cells in the layout in the Report Header section, then save the report with the name **ActivityData**.

k. Select all controls, apply a transparent outline, then move, resize, and modify controls and section heights as needed to match FIGURE 7-26.

l. Add a short subtotal line above each of the two text boxes that contain the =Sum([ActivityHours]) expressions, then preview the report in Report View, as shown in FIGURE 7-26.

m. Open the Volunteers table, then add a new record with *your name*. Use **66215** for the Zipcode field value and fill in the rest of the record with fictitious yet realistic values. Close the Volunteers table.

n. Close the ActivityData report, compact and close the IL_AC_7_Volunteers.accdb database, and exit Access 2019.

FIGURE 7-26

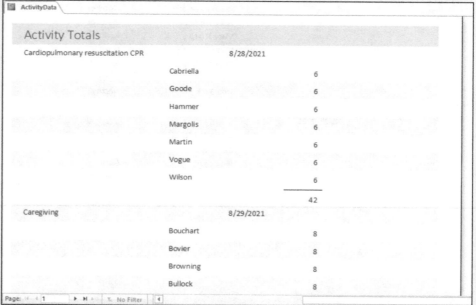

Visual Workshop

Start Access, open the IL_AC_7-5.accdb database from the location where you store your Data Files, then save it as **IL_AC_7_CollegeCourses**. Enable content if prompted. In Design View of the StudentGradeListing report, add four command buttons in the Report Header section with the captions shown in FIGURE 7-27. Use the On Click event of each command button to attach the command button to the corresponding macro. Size and align the command buttons as shown. Save the report and test your command buttons in Report View to filter the records for grade of A or B, C, D or F, and All, as shown in FIGURE 7-27. Close the StudentGradeListing report. Open the Students table and add your name as a new record with the StudentID value of **999**. Use fictitious yet realistic data for the other field values. Compact and close the IL_AC_7_CollegeCourses.accdb database and exit Access 2019.

FIGURE 7-27

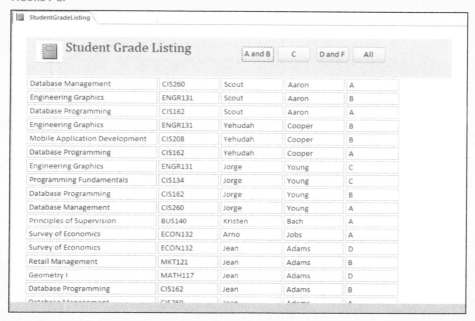

Importing and Exporting Data

CASE You are working with Lydia Snyder, vice president of operations at JCL Talent, to build a research database to manage industry, company, and job data. In this module, you'll learn how to import and export data with other Access databases and file formats. You will build charts to better visualize information, and you will explore database templates.

Module Objectives

After completing this module, you will be able to:

- Import Access objects
- Import or export text files
- Export to Excel
- Export to PDF
- Export to HTML or XML

- Merge to Word
- Create charts
- Modify charts
- Use a database template
- Use Application Parts

Files You Will Need

IL_AC_8-1.accdb
Support_AC_8_JCL_Development.accdb
Support_AC_8_Jobs.txt
IL_AC_8-2.accdb
Support_AC_8_SupportDesk_Dev.accdb

Support_AC_8_Employees.txt
IL_AC_8-3.accdb
IL_AC_8-4.accdb
IL_AC_8-5.accdb

Import Access Objects

Access gives you the ability to import and export Access objects from one database to another. **Importing** means to copy an object *into* the current database. **Exporting** means to copy an object *from* the current database to another database. Importing and exporting Access objects is especially helpful for a database developer. The developer can build and test objects in a development database and when ready, copy them into the production database. **CASE** *You have been working with a development copy of the JCL database to create two new reports. Lydia has reviewed and approved the reports, and has asked you to add them to the production database.*

STEPS

QUICK TIP
You can also right-
click in the table
section of the
Navigation Pane,
point to Import,
then click Access
Database.

1. **sam ↓ Start Access, open the** IL_AC_8-1.accdb database **from the location where you store your Data Files, save it as** IL_AC_8_Jobs, **enable content if prompted, click the** External Data tab, **click the** New Data Source button, **point to** From Database, **then click** Access

   The Get External Data – Access Database dialog box opens, prompting you for the location of the development database that contains the objects you want to import into the current database.

2. **Click the** Browse button, **navigate to the location where you store your Data Files, click** Support_AC_8_JCL_Development.accdb, **click** Open, **then click** OK

   The Import Objects dialog box opens. Each tab displays a list of that type of object from the selected database. You want to import two reports. You also need to import the two queries that support the reports referenced in the Record Source property for the reports.

3. **Click the** Queries tab, **click the** ContactsByCompany query, **click the** JobsByCompany query, **click the** Reports tab, **click the** ContactsByCompany report, **click the** JobsByCompany report **as shown in** FIGURE 8-1, **then click** OK

   As a final step, the Get External Data – Access Database dialog box prompts you to save the import steps. If you needed to repeat this import process on a regular basis, it would be a good idea to save the import steps to complete the next import process faster. In this case, you do not need to save the import steps.

4. **Click** Close **in the Get External Data – Access Database dialog box, double-click the** ContactsByCompany report, **then double-click the** JobsByCompany report

   The two imported reports open in Report View, as shown in FIGURE 8-2. In this case, the queries that served as the Record Source property for the reports were given the same name as their corresponding report, but that is not required.

5. **Right-click the** JobsByCompany report tab, **click** Close, **right-click the** ContactsByCompany report tab, **then click** Close

   A second way to share objects between two databases is to open both at the same time and work in the Navigation Pane to copy and paste objects between the two databases. An object must be closed before it can be cut, copied, renamed, or deleted.

   Yet a third way to share objects between two databases is to right-click the object in the Navigation Pane, point to Export, click Access, then follow the prompts provided by the Export – Access Database dialog boxes to export any object from one database to another.

FIGURE 8-1: **Import Objects dialog box**

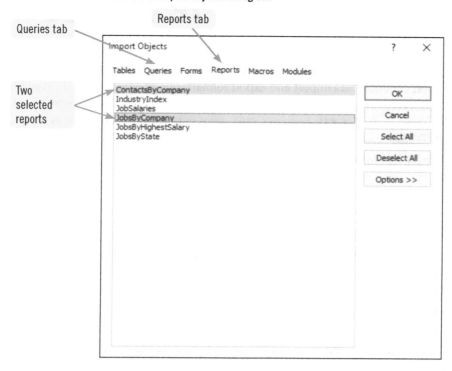

Queries tab

Reports tab

Two
selected
reports

FIGURE 8-2: **Imported queries and reports**

New reports opened in Report View

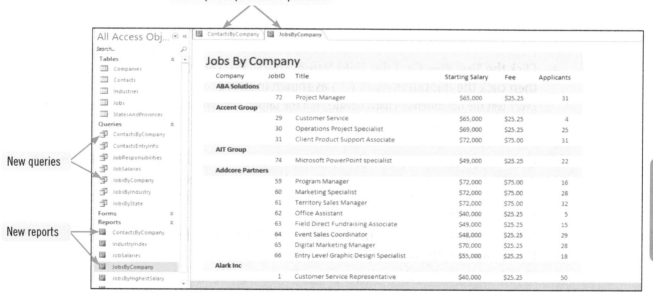

New queries

New reports

Access

Import or Export Text Files

Learning Outcomes
- Append data from a text file
- Review data import, link, and export file formats

Importing data means to copy data from an external file into an Access table. **Exporting** copies data in the opposite direction, from an Access table, query, form, or report to an external file. See TABLE 8-1 for information on common data import and export formats, one of which is a **delimited text file**, which organizes one record on each row. Field values are separated by a common character, the **delimiter**, such as a comma, tab, or dash. A **CSV (comma-separated value)** file is a common example of a delimited text file. **CASE** ▶ *New records for the Jobs table have been provided as a text file. You import and append the records to the Jobs table.*

STEPS

QUICK TIP

Files with a csv suffix (comma separated values) are a special type of text file that uses commas as the delimiter instead of tabs. They are imported the same way as other text files.

1. **Double-click the** Jobs table **in the Navigation Pane, click the** Last record button ▶ **in the navigation bar to observe that there are 82 records, then close the Jobs table**

   It's a good idea to confirm that an append process completed successfully by reviewing the data and number of records before and after the process.

2. **Click the** External Data tab, **click the** New Data Source button, **point to** From File, **then click** Text File

   The Get External Data – Text File dialog box opens, prompting you for the location of the text file.

3. **Click the** Browse button, **navigate to the location where you store your Data Files, double-click** Support_AC_8_Jobs.txt, **click the** Append a copy to the records to the table **option button, click the** table list arrow, **click** Jobs, **click** OK, **then click** Next **to confirm that the data is in a delimited format**

   The Import Text Wizard dialog box shows you a sample of the data with the fields separated with the Tab delimiter.

4. **Click the** First Row Contains Field Names check box, **click the** Text Qualifier list arrow, **then click the** quotation mark (") **as shown in** FIGURE 8-3

   Every text file has different characteristics, but the Import Text Wizard allows you to view the data as you complete the import process. In this case, it helps you see the field names and the eight records of data you want to append to the Jobs table.

5. **Click** Next, **click** Finish, **click the** Save import steps check box, **then click** Save Import

   Saved imports are accessed by the Saved Imports button on the External Data tab of the ribbon. If you need to run the same import on a regular basis, saving the import steps provides a consistent and fast way to repeat the process.

6. **Double-click the** Jobs table **to open it in Datasheet View, click the** Last Record button ▶, **then close the Jobs table**

   The Jobs table now has 90 records as expected after the append process.

FIGURE 8-3: Import Text Wizard dialog box

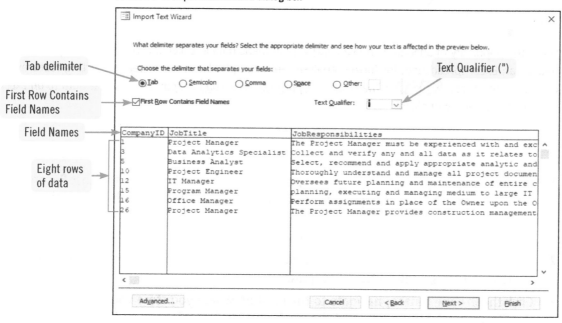

TABLE 8-1: File formats that Access can import, link, and export

category	file format	import	link	export
Microsoft Office	Excel	•	•	•
	Word			•
	Outlook address book	•	•	•
	Access	•	•	•
Online services	SharePoint	•	•	•
	Dynamics 365	•	•	•
	SalesForce	•	•	•
Database Management Software (DBMS)	SQL Server	•	•	•
	dBASE	•	•	•
	Azure Database	•		
	ODBC (Open Database Connectivity) Database	•	•	•
Other	Email file attachments			•
	HTML document	•	•	•
	PDF or XPS file			•
	Delimited text file such as CSV file	•	•	•
	XML file	•		•

Imported data must be structured

Before data can be imported into a new Access table, it must be structured properly. For example, before data can be appended to an existing Access table, its field names and data types must match those in the existing table. It is common to **scrub** data, which means to fix errors and inconsistencies by working with a text file in Excel before that data can be successfully imported into Access.

Export to Excel

Learning Outcomes
• Export data to Excel
• Save export steps

Given the popularity of analyzing and working with numeric data in Excel, it is common to export Access data to an Excel spreadsheet for further analysis. For example, Excel has superior charting features as compared to Access. **CASE** ▶ *The Finance Department asks you to export some Access data to an Excel spreadsheet for further analysis.*

STEPS

1. **Double-click the** JobSalaries query **to open it in Datasheet View, click the** Last Record **button** ▶ **to note that the query contains six fields and 90 records, then close the JobSalaries query**

   It's a good idea to review the data you are about to export to compare it to the final export.

QUICK TIP
You can also use the Excel button in the Export group of the External Data tab on the ribbon to export the data from a selected table, query, form, or report to Excel.

2. **Right-click the** JobSalaries query **in the Navigation Pane, point to** Export, **then click** Excel

   The Export – Excel Spreadsheet dialog box opens.

3. **Click the** Browse button, **navigate to the location where you store your Data Files, save the file as** IL_AC_8_JobSalaries, **click** Save **in the File Save dialog box, then click** OK

   To quickly repeat any export process, you can save the export steps with a name, then run the export using the Saved Exports button on the External Data tab of the ribbon.

4. **Click the** Save export steps check box, **edit the Save as description to be** Export-JobSalaries to Excel, **then click** Save Export

   You access and run a **saved export** using the Saved Exports button on the External Data tab. Saving the export steps provides a fast and consistent way to repeat an export process.

   To view the data, start Excel and open the exported JobSalaries.xlsx file.

TROUBLE
Some of the columns display ########, but that is easily resolved by widening the column.

5. **Start Excel, click the** File tab **on the ribbon, click** Open, **click** Browse, **navigate to the location where you store your Data Files, then double-click** IL_AC_8_JobSalaries.xlsx

   The IL_AC_8_JobSalaries.xlsx file opens, as shown in **FIGURE 8-4**, where you can further analyze, chart, and manipulate the data. Note that the Excel file contains six fields and that the first row contains field names.

6. **Scroll to the bottom of the data to note that the spreadsheet contains 91 total rows, then close the** IL_AC_8_JobSalaries.xlsx **file, close Excel, and return to Access**

   You can export the data from any Access table, query, form, or report to Excel using these steps.

FIGURE 8-4: IL_AC_8_JobSalaries.xlsx workbook

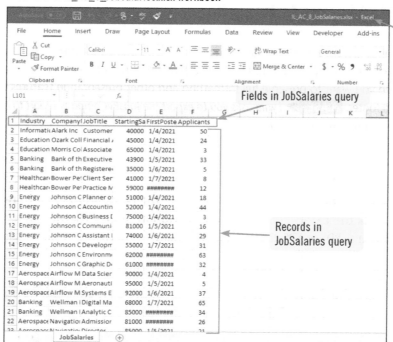

JobSalaries query exported as an Excel file

Fields in JobSalaries query

Records in JobSalaries query

Export to PDF

Learning
Outcomes
• Export a report
  to PDF
• Export other
  objects to PDF

Access objects can be exported to a PDF document. **PDF** stands for **Portable Document Format**, a file format developed by Adobe that has become a standard format for exchanging documents. PDF files are useful when you want to preserve full formatting and other presentation features of an object such as its header and footer. **CASE** ▶ *Lydia asks you to export the JobsByCompany report to a PDF document for later distribution as an email file attachment.*

STEPS

1. **Double-click the** JobsByCompany report **in the Navigation Pane to review it in Report View, click the** External Data tab **on the ribbon, then click the** PDF or XPS button

   The Publish as PDF or XPS dialog box opens, asking you to choose a name and location for the file. **XPS** (structured XML) is a file format that is similar to a PDF file but is based on the **XML** (Extensible Markup Language) instead of the PostScript language used by PDF files.

2. **Make sure the** Open file after publishing check box **is checked, navigate to the location where you store your Data Files, name the file** IL_AC_8_JobsByCompany, **then click** Publish

   The PDF opens in the program on your computer that is associated with PDF files. Several programs, including browsers such as Chrome, Firefox, and Edge as well as Adobe Reader, can open PDF files so the program that automatically opens the JobsByCompany.pdf file will vary from computer to computer and you may be asked to choose from more than one program that can open PDF files. The main thing to notice is that the PDF file is formatted and the data is arranged exactly as it looked in the Access report, as shown in FIGURE 8-5.

3. **Close the** PDF window, **return to Access, click the** Save export steps check box, **modify the Save as text to be** Export-JobsByCompany to PDF, **click** Save Export, **then close the** JobsByCompany report

   The IL_AC_8_JobsByCompany.pdf file is now available for you to distribute. For example, you could attach it to an email. Because it is a PDF file, users can open, view, and print the formatted report even if they don't have Access on their computers.

   Export to Excel when you want to give users the ability to further analyze and manipulate the data. Export to PDF when you do not want to allow users to manipulate the data but want to retain the formatting, layout, and style of the report.

FIGURE 8-5: Previewing the IL_AC_8_JobsByCompany.pdf file

IL_AC_8_
JobsByCompany.pdf
file is formatted like
the JobsByCompany
report in Access

Jobs By Company

Company	JobID	Title	Starting Salary	Fee	Applicants
ABA Solutions					
	72	Project Manager	$65,000	$25.25	31
	83	Project Manager	$65,000	$50.25	0
Accent Group					
	29	Customer Service	$65,000	$25.25	4
	30	Operations Project Specialist	$69,000	$25.25	25
	31	Client Product Support Associate	$72,000	$75.00	31
AIT Group					
	74	Microsoft PowerPoint specialist	$49,000	$25.25	22
	84	Data Analytics Specialist	$52,000	$50.25	0
Addcore Partners					
	59	Program Manager	$72,000	$75.00	16
	60	Marketing Specialist	$72,000	$75.00	28
	61	Territory Sales Manager	$72,000	$75.00	32
	62	Office Assistant	$40,000	$25.25	5
	63	Field Direct Fundraising Associate	$49,000	$25.25	15
	64	Event Sales Coordinator	$48,000	$25.25	29
	65	Digital Marketing Manager	$70,000	$25.25	28
	66	Entry Level Graphic Design Specialist	$55,000	$25.25	18
Alark Inc					
	1	Customer Service Representative	$40,000	$25.25	50
	85	Business Analyst	$55,000	$50.25	0
Artwell Corp					

Emailing an Access report

Another way to email an Access report (or any other Access object) as a PDF file is to click the report in the Navigation Pane, then click the Email button in the Export group of the External Data tab on the ribbon. You are presented with the Send Object As dialog box, which allows you to choose the desired file format, such as .xlsx, .pdf, .htm, or .rtf, for the report as shown in FIGURE 8-6. After you select the desired file format and click OK, Outlook opens with the report attached to the email in the chosen file format. You must have Microsoft Outlook installed and configured to use this option.

FIGURE 8-6: Emailing an Access report

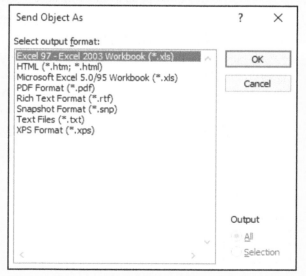

Access

Export to HTML or XML

You can export an Access object to an **HTML (HyperText Markup Language)** or **XML (eXtensible Markup Language)** file, which are both common for sharing information over the Internet. An XML file precisely defines data using descriptive tags to mark up the beginning and end of rows (records) and columns (fields), so it is often used to send only data across the Internet. If you want a person to be able to view the data in a browser like a regular webpage, use an HTML file. **CASE** *Lydia asks you to export the Companies table as an HTML file and the JobsByState query as an XML file.*

STEPS

1. **Right-click the** Companies table, **point to** Export, **then click** HTML Document

   The Export – HTML Document dialog box opens, prompting you for a location for the exported HTML file.

2. **Click the** Browse button, **navigate to the location where you store your Data Files, save the file as** IL_AC_8_Companies, **click** Save, **click** OK, **click the** Save export steps check box, **modify the Save as text to be** Export-Companies **to HTML, then click** Save Export

   Next, export the JobsByState query as an XML file.

3. **Right-click the** JobsByState query, **point to** Export, **then click** XML File

   The Export – XML Document dialog box opens, prompting you for a location for the exported XML file.

4. **Click the** Browse button, **navigate to the location where you store your Data Files, save the file as** IL_AC_8_JobsByState, **click** Save, **click** OK, **click** OK **to export the data XML and schema XSD files, click the** Save export steps check box, **modify the Save as text to be** Export-JobsByState **to XML, then click** Save Export

   The **XSD (XML Schema Definition)** file further describes how the individual pieces of data in the XML file are defined. To confirm that the HTML and XML files were exported successfully, view them in a browser.

5. **Open** File Explorer, **navigate to the location where you store your Data Files, then double-click the** IL_AC_8_Companies.html **file**

   The IL_AC_8_Companies.html file opens in whatever program is associated with HTML files on your computer, probably a browser such as Google Chrome, Firefox, or Microsoft Edge. The records from the Companies table appear as an HTML table in a regular webpage, as shown in **FIGURE 8-7**.

6. **Close the** IL_AC_8_Companies.html **file, return to** File Explorer, **then double-click the** IL_AC_8_JobsByState.xml **file**

   The IL_AC_8_JobsByState.xml file opens in whatever program is associated with XML files on your computer, which may be a code editor or browser. **FIGURE 8-8** shows the IL_AC_8_JobsByState.xml file open in Google Chrome. An XML file's purpose is to describe and successfully transfer the data to another program, not to create a webpage that is easy for a human to read.

7. **Close the window with the** IL_AC_8_JobsByState.xml **file and return to Access**

FIGURE 8-7: Companies table exported to HTML IL_AC_8_Companies.html

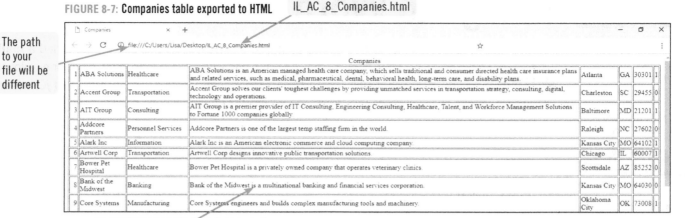

The path to your file will be different

Data from the Companies table is formatted as a table in a regular webpage to share information with a human

FIGURE 8-8: JobsByState query exported to XML

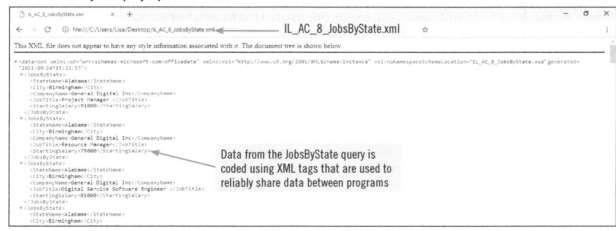

IL_AC_8_JobsByState.xml

Data from the JobsByState query is coded using XML tags that are used to reliably share data between programs

Merge to Word

**Learning
Outcomes**
• Merge table or
query data to
Word
• Use the Word Mail
Merge Wizard

Another way to export Access data is to merge it into a Word document. Sometimes called a **mail merge**, data from an Access table or query may be combined with a Word form letter, label, or envelope. **CASE** ▶ *Lydia asks if you can combine contact and company names with a welcome letter that JCL will be giving each contact at an upcoming conference. You will practice merging data to Word to handle her request.*

STEPS

TROUBLE
Click the Word
button [■] on
the taskbar if
Word doesn't
automatically open.

1. **Right-click the** ContactsByCompany query, **point to** Export, **then click** Word Merge
   The **Microsoft Word Mail Merge Wizard** dialog box opens, asking whether you want to link to an existing document or create a new one. The Word merge process works the same way whether you export a table or query object.

QUICK TIP
The "Next" and
"Previous" links are
at the bottom of the
Mail Merge task pane.

2. **Click the** Create a new document and then link the data to it option button, **then click** OK
   Word starts and opens the **Mail Merge task pane**, which steps you through the mail-merge process. Before you merge the Access data with the Word document, you must create the **main document**, the Word document that contains the standard text for each form letter.

TROUBLE
If you open the
Insert Merge Field
dialog box, use the
Insert and Close
buttons to insert a
field and return to
the document.

3. **Type** Welcome to the JCL annual conference! **and press** ENTER **in the Word document, click the** Next: Starting document link **in the bottom of the Mail Merge task pane, click the** Next: Select recipients link **to use the current document, then click the** Next: Write your letter link **to use the existing list of names**

4. **Click the** Insert Merge Field arrow **in the Write & Insert Fields group on the Mailings tab**
   The Insert Merge Field list shows all of the fields in the original data source, the ContactsByCompany query. You use this list to insert **merge fields**, codes that are replaced with the values in the field that the code represents when the mail merge is processed.

TROUBLE
You cannot type the
merge codes directly
into the document.
You must use the
Insert Merge Field
button.

5. **Click** ContactFirst, **press** SPACEBAR, **click the** Insert Merge Field arrow, **click** ContactLast, **press** ENTER, **click the** Insert Merge Field arrow, **click** CompanyName **as shown in** FIGURE 8-9, **then click the** Next: Preview your letters link **at the bottom of the Mail Merge task pane**
   You are ready to complete the mail merge.

6. **Click the** Next: Complete the merge link, **click the** Edit individual letters link **in the middle of the Mail Merge task pane to view the letters on the screen, then click** OK **to merge all records, as shown in** FIGURE 8-10
   The mail-merge process combines the ContactFirst, ContactLast, and CompanyName field values from the ContactsByCompany query with the main document, creating a 443-page document using section breaks between pages.

QUICK TIP
The total number
of pages in the
document is
displayed in the
lower-left corner of
the Word window.

7. **Press** PAGE DOWN **several times to view several pages of the merged document, then close the merged document (currently named Letters1) without saving it**
   You generally don't need to save the final merged document. Saving the one-page *main document*, however, is a good idea in case you want to make a change and remerge it (versus starting the merge process of creating a main document from scratch).

8. **Click the** Save button [■] **on the Quick Access Toolbar, click the** Browse button, **navigate to the location where you store your Data Files, enter** IL_AC_8_Welcome **in the File name text box, click** Save, **then close Word**

FIGURE 8-9: Merging Access data to Word

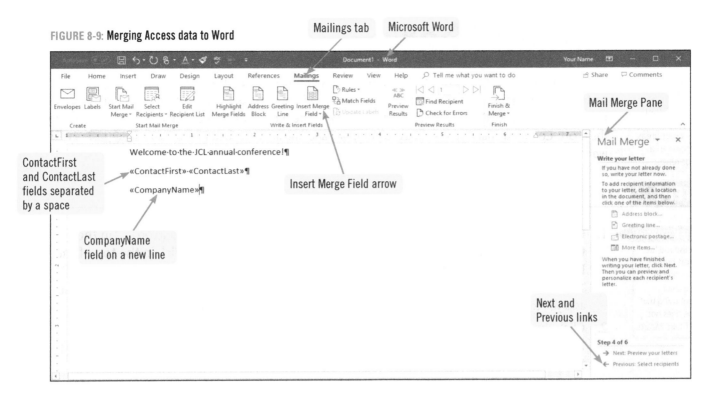

FIGURE 8-10: Access data merged into a Word document

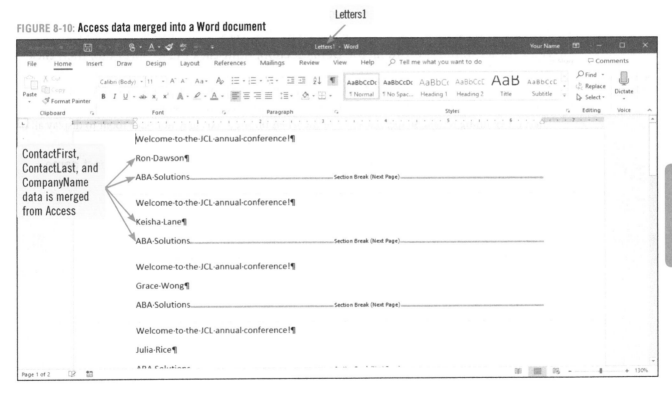

Access

Create Charts

Learning Outcomes
- Define common chart types
- Define chart areas
- Add charts to a form or report

Charts, also called graphs, are visual representations of numeric data that help users see comparisons, patterns, and trends in data. Charts can be inserted on a form or report. Access provides a **Chart Wizard** that helps you create the chart. Common **chart types** determine the presentation of data markers on the chart. Common chart types such as column, pie, and line are described in TABLE 8-2. **CASE** ▶ *Lydia wants you to create a chart of the total number of jobs by industry for a report.*

STEPS

QUICK TIP
You can also use the Insert Chart button on the Design tab to insert a chart object, but using that technique does not start the Chart Wizard.

1. **Click the** Create **tab, click the** Report Design **button, click the** More button ⏬ **in the Controls group on the Design tab, click the** Chart button 📊**, then click in the top of the Detail section at about the 0.5" mark on the horizontal ruler**

   The Chart Wizard starts by asking which table or query holds the fields you want to add to the chart, then asks you to select a chart type. The Chart Wizard works in the same way in Form Design View.

2. **Click the** Queries **option button, click** Query: JobSalaries**, click** Next**, double-click** Industry**, double-click** JobTitle**, click** Next**, click** Next **to accept Column Chart, then drag the** JobTitle **field from the Series area to the Data area, as shown in** FIGURE 8-11

   The **Axis area** identifies which field is positioned on the x-axis, the **Series area** sets the legend for the chart, and the **Data area** determines what field is measured by the data markers within the chart. If you drag a Number or Currency field to the Data area, the Chart Wizard automatically sums the values in the field. For Text or AutoNumber fields (such as JobTitle), the Chart Wizard automatically counts the values in the field. See TABLE 8-3 for more information on chart areas.

QUICK TIP
Double-click the Data area field to change the way the data in that field is summarized.

3. **Click** Next**, type** Jobs by Industry **as the chart title, click** Finish**, use** ↖ **to drag the lower-right corner of the chart to fill the Detail section, right-click the** Report1 **tab, then click** Print Preview

   When charts are displayed in Design View, they often appear as a generic Microsoft chart placeholder. When you switch to Print Preview, the actual data is loaded into the chart, which should look like FIGURE 8-12. The chart is beginning to take shape, but some of the labels on the x-axis may not have room to display all of their text. You fix this problem and modify the chart in the next lesson.

4. **Right-click the** Report1 **tab, click** Save**, type** JobsByIndustryChart **as the report name, then click** OK

FIGURE 8-11: Using the Chart Wizard to add a chart to a report

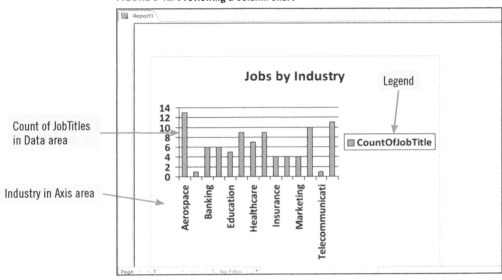

FIGURE 8-12: Previewing a column chart

TABLE 8-2: Common chart types

chart type	chart icon	commonly used to show	example
Column		Comparisons of values (vertical bars)	Each vertical bar represents the sales for a different product.
Bar		Comparisons of values (horizontal bars)	Each horizontal bar represents the sales for a different product.
Line		Trends over time	Each point on the line represents monthly sales for one product.
Pie		Parts of a whole	Each slice represents quarterly sales for the entire company.
Area		Cumulative totals	Each section represents monthly sales by product, stacked to show the cumulative total sales effort.

TABLE 8-3: Chart areas

chart area	description
Data	Determines what field the data markers on the chart represent
Axis	The x-axis (horizontal axis) or y-axis (vertical axis) on the chart
Series	Displays the legend when multiple series of data are charted

Access

Modify Charts

You modify charts in Design View of the form or report that contains the chart. To modify the chart, you modify the chart elements within the chart placeholder. See TABLE 8-4 for more information on chart elements. To view the changes as they apply to the real data you are charting, return to either Form View for a form or Print Preview for a report. **CASE** *Lydia wants you to change the color of the bars and remove the legend to better display the values on the x-axis.*

STEPS

1. Right-click the report tab, **then click** Design View

To make changes to chart elements, you first must open the chart in Edit mode by double-clicking it. Use **Edit mode** to select and modify individual chart elements, such as the title, legend, bars, or axes.

2. Double-click the chart

The hashed border of the chart placeholder control indicates that the chart is in Edit mode, as shown in FIGURE 8-13. The Chart Standard and Chart Formatting toolbars also appear and may be on one row or stacked. The chart datasheet may be opened or closed. You can modify individual chart elements using the menu options, the buttons on the toolbars, right-clicking the element to use the shortcut menu, or by double-clicking the element to open its Format dialog box.

Because only one series of bars counts the industries, you can describe the data with the chart title and don't need a legend.

3. Click the Legend button ▤ **to remove the legend**

Removing the legend provides more room for the x-axis labels.

4. Click any bar **on the chart in the first series to select them all, click the** Fill Color arrow ◇▾ **on the Chart Formatting toolbar, click the** Bright Green box, **click** Format **on the menu bar, click** Selected Data series, **click** Data Labels, **click the** Value check box, **then click** OK

Clicking any bar selects all bars in that data series, as evidenced by the sizing handle in each of the bars. The bars change to bright green in the chart placeholder, and data labels showing the value of the bar appear above each bar.

You also decide to modify the labels on the x-axis so they fit better.

5. Double-click any label on the x-axis **to open the Format Axis dialog box, click the** Font tab, **click** 8 **in the Size area, then click** OK

Preview the updated chart.

6. Click outside the hashed border **to return to Report Design View, click the** Save button 🖫 **on the Quick Access toolbar, right-click the** JobsByIndustryChart tab, **then click** Print Preview

The final chart is shown in FIGURE 8-14.

7. sam⬆ Close the JobsByIndustryChart report, **double-click the** Contacts table, **add your name at CompanyID** 1 **as a new record, close the Contacts table, compact and close the IL_AC_8_Jobs.accdb database, then exit Access**

FIGURE 8-13: **Modifying a chart in Edit mode**

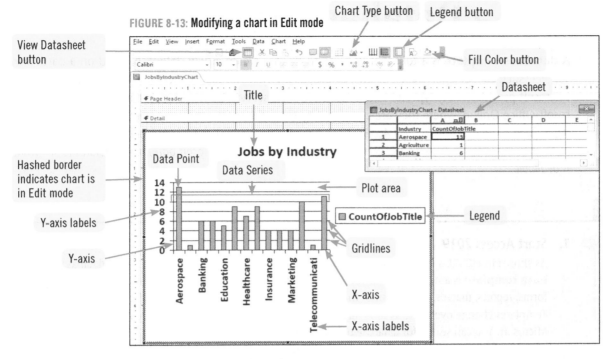

FIGURE 8-14: **Formatted column chart**

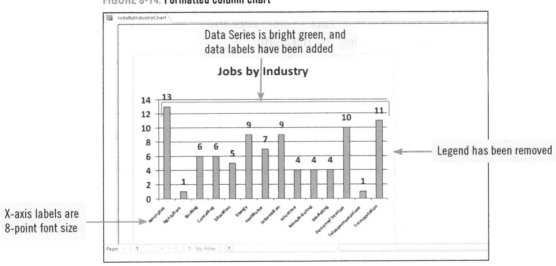

TABLE 8-4: **Chart elements**

chart element	description
Chart title	Determines what field the bars (lines, wedges, etc.) on the chart represent
X-axis	On a column chart, the horizontal axis
Y-axis	On a column chart, the vertical axis
Legend	Displays a color sample for each series of data markers
Data markers	The bars, wedges, points, or other symbol used to represent the data in the chart
Data labels	Optional values or text that describe each data marker
Data point	An individual bar, wedge, point, or symbol used to identify one data marker on the chart
Gridlines	On a column chart, the horizontal bars that help indicate where the data markers are in relationship to the y-axis
Plot area	On a column chart, the rectangle defined by the x-axis and y-axis behind the data markers

Use a Database Template

Learning Outcome
• Explore Access database templates

A **database template** is a tool that you use to quickly create a new database based on a particular subject, such as assets, contacts, events, or projects. When you install Access 2019 on your computer, Microsoft provides many types of templates for you to use. Additional templates are available from Microsoft Office Online, where they are organized by category, such as business, personal, and education.

CASE ▸ *Lydia asks you to see if Access might be useful for a group of JCL employees who have developed a support group that meets to discuss personal nutrition. You explore Microsoft database templates to see what is available.*

STEPS

QUICK TIP
One way to start Access is to type Access in the search box on your Windows taskbar.

1. **Start Access 2019**

   As shown in **FIGURE 8-15**, Microsoft provides many templates to help you create a new database. A **database template** is a new Access database file that may contain many objects of each type (tables, queries, forms, reports, macros, and modules) that build a sample application for that subject.

   Templates change over time as more are added and enhancements to existing templates are provided by Microsoft. You can search for database templates using the Search text box.

TROUBLE
Templates are constantly changing, so if you cannot find the Nutrition database or if it has changed, explore other templates and forms of your choice.

2. **Click the** Nutrition tracking database, **click the** Browse button 🗁, **navigate to where you store your Data Files, enter** IL_AC_8_Nutrition **in the File name box, click** OK **in the File New Database dialog box, click** Create, **click the** Enable Content button, **then click** OK **if prompted about sharing the database**

   The Nutrition tracking database template builds a new database that includes several sample tables, queries, forms, and macros. You can use or modify these objects to meet your needs.

   A form to track today's information opens automatically, and the other objects in the database are presented in the Navigation Pane, as shown in **FIGURE 8-16**.

3. **Right-click the** Today at a glance form tab, **click** Close, **then locate and double-click the** My Profile form **in the Navigation Pane**

   Objects created by database templates are rich in functionality and can be modified for your specific needs or analyzed to learn more about Access.

4. **Close the** My Profile form, **then double-click the** Search form **to open it**

   The Search form searches over 6,000 records stored in the Foods table that records calories, fat, protein, and other useful nutrition statistics for each record.

5. **Close the** Search form, **then open, explore, and close the other objects of the database**

   The Foods and Tips tables contain many records, and the other objects create the full application. You can learn a great deal about Access by exploring database templates. You will continue using this sample database to learn about Application Parts.

FIGURE 8-15: Access database templates

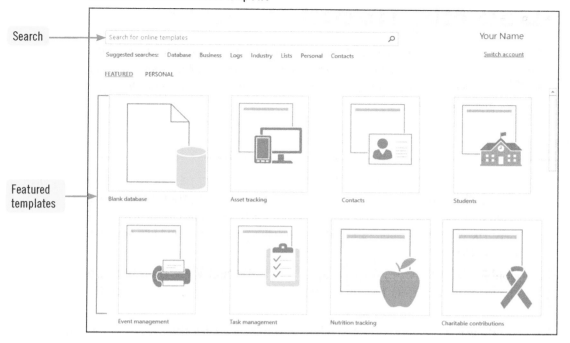

FIGURE 8-16: A sample form in the IL_AC_8_Nutrition.accdb database

Use Application Parts

Application Parts are templates that create individual objects such as tables and forms *within* an existing database. As with database templates, Microsoft is constantly updating and improving this part of Access.

CASE ▸ *Lydia asks you to continue your study of templates by exploring the Access 2019 Application Parts using the Nutrition database.*

STEPS

1. **Click the** Create tab, **click the** Application Parts button, **as shown in** FIGURE 8-17, **click** Issues, **click the** There is no relationship option button, **then click** Create

   Application Parts include templates for several subjects, including comments, contacts, issues, tasks, and users. The Issues Application Part created a new table named Issues and two new forms named IssueDetail and IssueNew.

2. **Double-click the** Issues table **to open it in Datasheet View, then tab across the fields**

   The Issues table has four Lookup fields: Status, Priority, Category, and Project. Explore them in Table Design View.

3. **Right-click the** Issues table tab, **click** Design View, **click the** Category field, **click the** Lookup tab, **then modify the Row Source property to be** "Health";"Food";"Exercise" **as shown in** FIGURE 8-18

   Modifying the Lookup properties of the Category field in Table Design View will affect the forms that use that field.

4. **Right-click the** Issues table tab, **click** Close, **click** Yes **when prompted to save the table, double-click the** IssueNew form, **then click the** Category combo box arrow **as shown in** FIGURE 8-19

   The change you made to the Category field in the Issues table is displayed in the IssueNew form. You might want to make many other modifications to use the objects created by an Access database template or Application Parts. These features provide an exciting way to learn more about Access features and possibilities.

5. **Compact and close the** IL_AC_8_Nutrition.accdb database, **then close Access 2019**

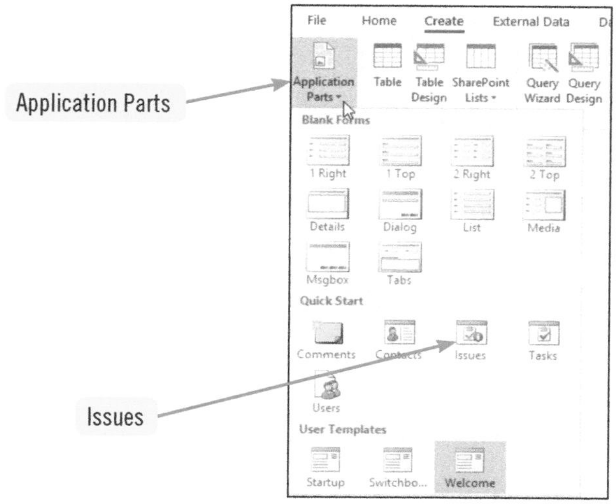

FIGURE 8-17: Exploring Application Parts

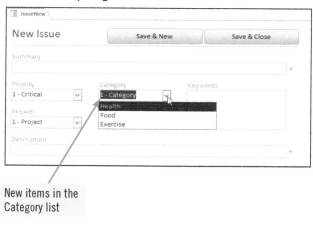

FIGURE 8-19: Exploring the IssueNew form

FIGURE 8-18: Modifying the Issues table

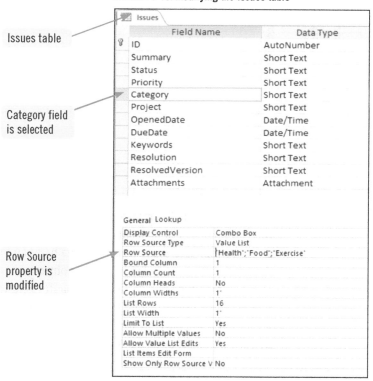

Creating custom Application Parts

To create a custom Application Part from the objects of an existing database, click the File tab on the ribbon, click Save As, click Template, then click the Save As button. The Create New Template from Database dialog box provides options to describe your new Application Part including its name, description, icon, and other details.

Access

Practice

Concepts Review

Identify each chart button or chart element shown in FIGURE 8-20.

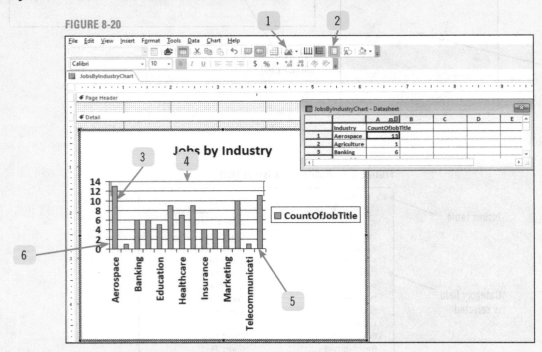

FIGURE 8-20

Match each term with the statement that best describes it.

7. **Application Part**
8. **HTML**
9. **export**
10. **PDF**
11. **XML**
12. **import**
13. **Excel**
14. **CSV**

a. a program that is commonly used to scrub data
b. copy an object or data *out of* the current database
c. file format used mainly to share data between programs on the web
d. a template for an individual Access object
e. a common type of text file that separates field values with commas
f. file format used to retain the formatting of a report
g. common webpage file format
h. copy an object or data *into* the current database

Select the best answer from the list of choices.

15. Which chart type is commonly used to show trends over time?

a. Pie
b. Line

c. Gantt
d. Scatter

16. Which chart type is commonly used to show cumulative values?

a. Bar
b. Line

c. Pareto
d. Area

17. **Which chart element contains color samples for each series of data markers?**
   a. Legend
   b. X-axis
   c. Y-axis
   d. Plot area

18. **Why would you use an Application Part?**
   a. to quickly create new objects
   b. to import and export data
   c. to email a report
   d. to start the Chart Wizard

19. **When a table or query is exported to an HTML file, how is the data presented on the page?**
   a. as an ordered single column
   b. using XML markup tags
   c. as an HTML table
   d. as an unordered list

20. **Which of the following types of objects may *not* be copied between two Access databases?**
   a. tables
   b. queries
   c. forms
   d. Every type of Access object can be copied between two databases.

Skills Review

1. **Import Access objects.**
   a. Start Access, open the IL_AC_8-2.accdb database from the location where you store your Data Files, then save it as **IL_AC_8_SupportDesk**. Enable content if prompted.
   b. Import the 50States table and the StateEntry form from the Support_AC_8_SupportDesk_Dev.accdb database in the location where you store your Data Files. Do not save the import steps.
   c. Verify that the 50States table and StateEntry form have been successfully imported into your database by opening them. Both should show 50 records.
   d. Close the 50States table and StateEntry form.

2. **Import or export text files.**
   a. Open the Employees table, then note the total number of records, 26. Close the Employees table.
   b. Import the Support_AC_8_Employees.txt file from the location where you store your Data Files, then append the records to the Employees table. Note that the data is tab delimited, that the first row contains field names, and that there are five data records. Do not save the import steps.
   c. Open the Employees table to confirm that there are now 31 records, add a new record with **your name**, Department value of **Information Systems**, Salary value of **$80,000**, and Dependents value of **1**, then close the table.

3. **Export to Excel.**
   a. Open the CaseInfo report in Report View to scroll through and view the data, noting that it contains 22 total records, then close the report.
   b. Export the CaseInfo report to Excel using the file name of **IL_AC_8_CaseInfo** in the location where you store your Data Files.
   c. Open the IL_AC_8_CaseInfo.xls file in Excel, confirm that the Excel file contains 23 rows of data (the first row will contain column headings), then save and close Excel and return to the IL_AC_8_SupportDesk.accdb database in Access.
   d. Save the export steps with the name **Export-CaseInfo to Excel**.

4. **Export to PDF.**
   a. Open the EmployeeMasterList report to review the information, then close the report.
   b. Export the EmployeeMasterList report to PDF using the file name of **IL_AC_8_EmployeeMasterList** in the location where you store your Data Files.
   c. Review the PDF file, then close it and return to Access.
   d. Save the export steps with the name **Export-EmployeeMasterList to PDF**.

Skills Review (continued)

5. Export to HTML or XML.

a. Open the Cases table to review the fields and records, then close the table.

b. Export the Cases table to XML using the file name of **IL_AC_8_Cases** in the location where you store your Data Files. Export both the XML and XSD files.

c. Save the export steps with the name **Export-Cases to XML**.

d. Export the Employees table to HTML using the file name of **IL_AC_8_Employees** in the location where you store your Data Files. Do not include formatting.

e. Save the export steps with the name **Export-Employees to HTML**.

6. Merge to Word.

a. Merge the Employees table to a new document in Word.

b. Create the main document in Word with the merge fields and text as shown in FIGURE 8-21. Be careful to add a space between the FirstName and LastName merge fields.

c. Complete the merge process. Close the Letters1 document, which is the final merged result with 32 pages, without saving it.

d. Save the main document with the name **IL_AC_8_TuitionMemo** in the location where you store your Data Files, then close Word and return to Access.

FIGURE 8-21

To: → «FirstName»·«LastName»¶

Re: → New·Employee·Benefits¶

Date: → (Insert·current·date)¶

Today·we·are·pleased·to·announce·a·new·employee·tuition·reimbursement·plan!··Call·Chris·Guerra·in·Human·Resources·for·details!¶

7. Create charts.

a. Open the EmployeeMasterList report in Design view, then add a chart control using the Chart button in the Controls group to the top of the Report Footer section at about the 0.5" mark on the horizontal ruler.

b. Select the EmployeesByDepartment query, the Department field, and the LastName field for the chart.

c. Choose a column chart with the Department in the Axis area and move the LastName to the Data area. The LastName field will be counted in the Data area.

d. Choose <No Field> for both the Report and Chart fields.

e. Accept the default title and do not display a legend on the chart.

f. Save the report and preview the chart on the last page returning to Design View as necessary to resize the chart so that all of the labels on the x-axis are clearly visible.

8. Modify charts.

a. Return to Design View of the EmployeeMasterList report, double-click the chart to edit it, then modify the title to be **Employees By Department**.

b. Change the bar color of the first set of bars to blue.

c. Save the report, then preview the chart on the last page as shown in FIGURE 8-22.

d. Compact and close the IL_AC_8_SupportDesk.accdb database, then close Access.

FIGURE 8-22

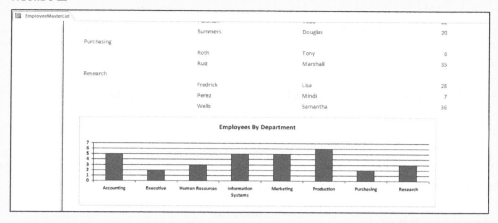

9. **Use a database template.**

   a. Start Access and build a new database based on the Charitable Contributions template. (If that template is not available, choose another.)

   b. Save the database with the name **IL_AC_8_Charity** in the location where you store your Data Files.

   c. Enable content, press F11 to open the Navigation Pane, then notice that the objects are organized by subject instead of by object type.

   d. Right-click the Navigation Pane title bar, point to Category, then click Object type.

   e. Enter your name in the Last Name and First Name fields of the Contributors table, then explore the rest of the objects in the database and be ready to discuss something new that you learned about Access in class.

10. **Use Application Parts.**

   a. If you cannot see the ribbon in the IL_AC_8_Charity database, close it, press SHIFT, reopen the IL_AC_8_Charity database and do not release SHIFT until the database is open. (*Hint*: Pressing SHIFT overrides startup options such as custom toolbars and hiding the Navigation Pane.)

   b. On the Create tab of the ribbon, use the Application Parts button to add a Comments table. There is no relationship to the new Comments table.

   c. Open the Comments table to review the fields, then close it.

   d. Compact and repair then close the IL_AC_8_Charity.accdb database and exit Access 2019.

Independent Challenge 1

As the manager of Riverwalk, a multispecialty health clinic, you have created a database to manage nurse and doctor schedules to efficiently handle patient visits. In this exercise you will export Access data to three common file formats in order to discuss the reasons you may need or want to use each format.

   a. Start Access, open the IL_AC_8-3.accdb database from the location where you store your Data Files, then save it as **IL_AC_8_Riverwalk**. Enable content if prompted.

   b. Add your last name and a DrPA field value of **MD** to the Providers table.

   c. Export the Providers table to Excel using the file name of **IL_AC_8_Providers** in the location where you store your Data Files. Do not include formatting. Save the export with the name **Export-Providers to Excel**.

   d. Export the Providers table to HTML using the file name of **IL_AC_8_Providers** in the location where you store your Data Files. Do not include formatting. Save the export with the name **Export-Providers to HTML**.

   e. Export the Providers table to PDF using the file name of **IL_AC_8_Providers** in the location where you store your Data Files. Do not include formatting. Save the export with the name **Export-Providers to PDF**.

   f. Open and review the data in each of the three exported files. Be prepared to give a reason you would choose to export data to each of these three different file formats.

   g. Close all open exported files, then compact and close the IL_AC_8_Riverwalk.accdb and Access 2019.

Independent Challenge 2

You are working for a city to coordinate a series of community-wide preparedness activities. You have created a database to track the activities and volunteers who are attending the activities. In this exercise you will create a report to calculate information about the total number of volunteer hours at each activity.

a. Start Access, open the IL_AC_8-4.accdb database from the location where you store your Data Files, then save it as **IL_AC_8_Volunteers**. Enable content if prompted.

b. Add your name as a new record in the Volunteers table with a Street value of **12345 College Blvd**, a Zipcode value of **66215**, and a Birthday value of **1/1/1991**. Close the Volunteers table.

c. In Design View of the VolunteerList report, use the Chart control from the Controls group on the ribbon to add a chart to the upper area of the Report Footer section at about the 0.5" mark on the horizontal ruler.

d. Base the report on the ActivityList query using the ActivityName and ActivityHours fields.

e. Use a column chart with the ActivityName in the Axis area and the ActivityHours (which will be summed) in the Data area.

f. Choose <No Field> for the Report and Chart Fields and use **Hours by Activity** for the chart title. Do not display a legend.

g. Resize the chart, change the data markers fill color to red, change the x-axis label font size to **8** point, and add the **value** as the data labels as shown in FIGURE 8-23.

h. Save and close the VolunteerList report.

i. Compact and close the IL_AC_8_Volunteers.accdb database, then close Access 2019.

FIGURE 8-23

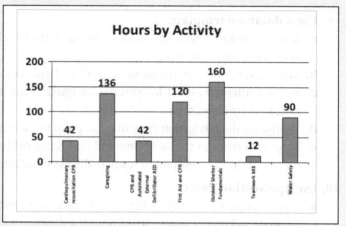

Visual Workshop

Start Access, open the IL_AC_8-5.accdb database from the location where you store your Data Files, then save it as **IL_AC_8_CollegeCourses**. Enable content if prompted. Add your name to the Students table as a new record using **999** as the StudentID, your own first and last names, and other fictitious but realistic data. Add a chart to the upper-left corner of the Report Footer section of the StudentGradeListing report based on the StudentGrades query. Include the ClassNo and PassOrFail fields. Use a column chart, then add the PassOrFail field to the Data area, where it will be counted. (Note that the PassOrFail field is used in both the Data and Series areas.) Choose <No Field> when asked to link the Report and Chart fields, title the chart **Pass or Fail by Class**, and display a legend. Format the first series (fail) with a red fill color and the second series (pass) with a blue fill color as shown in FIGURE 8-24. Widen the chart and change the font size to **10** point for the x axis (category axis) so that all of the ClassNo field values are clearly visible as shown in FIGURE 8-24. Save and close the StudentGradeListing report. Compact and close the IL_AC_8_CollegeCourses.accdb database, then exit Access 2019.

FIGURE 8-24

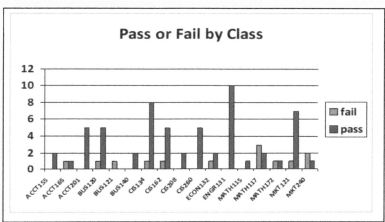

Pass or Fail by Class

FIGURE 4-27

Integrating Word and Access

CASE ▶ At JCL Talent, Inc., you work with files created in several applications, including Word and Access. You need to merge an Access database with a form letter, and then create a document in Word that includes a report that you export from Access.

Module Objectives

After completing this module, you will be able to:

- Merge from Access to Word
- Export an Access report to Word

Files You Will Need

IL_INT_5-1.docx	IL_INT_5-5.docx
IL_INT_5-2.accdb	IL_INT_5-6.accdb
IL_INT_5-3.docx	IL_INT_5-7.accdb
IL_INT_5-4.accdb	

Merge from Access to Word

You can merge data from an Access database with a Word document to create a series of individually addressed form letters. **CASE** ▸ *You want to merge Access data with a form letter that welcomes job seekers who have signed up for one of JCL Talent's job skills workshops. You create a query datasheet containing all the fields needed for the form letter, merge the data with a form letter in Word, then filter the results.*

STEPS

1. **Start Word, open** IL_INT_5-1.docx **from the location where you store your Data Files, save the document as** IL_INT_5_WorkshopLetter, **then close it**
   You use the letter in a mail merge after you prepare the Access database.

2. **Start Access, open** IL_INT_5-2.accdb **from the location where you store your Data Files, save the file as a database called** IL_INT_5_JobSkillsWorkshops, **then click** Enable Content
   You create a query for the form letter that contains fields from all three related tables.

3. **Click** Participants: Table **in the list of tables, click the** Create tab, **click the** Query Wizard **button in the Queries group, click OK, click the** Select All Fields button `>>`, **scroll up and click** Participant ID, **click the** Remove Single Field button `<`, **click the** Tables/Queries arrow, **click** Table: Trainers, **scroll to and click** Workshop **at the bottom of the Selected Fields list, click** Trainer Name **in the Available Fields list, click the** Add Single Field button `>`, **click the** Tables/Queries arrow, **click** Table: Workshops, **then add the** Workshop Title **and** Start Date **fields**
   The Simple Query Wizard dialog box lists fields from all three tables as shown in FIGURE 5-1.

4. **Click** Next, **click** Next, **click** Finish, **close the Participants Query datasheet, click any instance of** Participants Query **in the Navigation Pane, click the** External Data tab, **click** Word Merge **in the Export group, click OK, navigate to the location where you store your Data Files, double-click** IL_INT_5_WorkshopLetter.docx, **click OK, click the** Word icon **on the taskbar, then maximize the Word document window**

5. **Close the Mail Merge pane, type the** current date **and** your name **where indicated, click the** Edit Recipient List button **in the Start Mail Merge group, then click** Filter

6. **Click the** Field arrow, **scroll to and click** Workshop Title, **type** Skills Inventory **in the Compare to: text box, press TAB twice, select the** Trainer Name **field, type** Shelley Gable **as shown in FIGURE 5-2, click OK, then click OK**

7. **Delete** Address **below the date (but leave a blank line), click the** Address Block button **in the Write & Insert Fields group, click OK, delete** Greeting **(but leave a blank line), click the** Greeting Line button **in the Write & Insert Fields group, then click OK**

8. **Select** WORKSHOP_TITLE **in paragraph 1, click the** Insert Merge Field arrow **in the Write & Insert Fields group, click** Workshop_Title, **then as shown in FIGURE 5-3, insert merge fields to replace the** START_DATE, TRAINER_NAME, **and** FIRST_NAME **placeholders**

9. **Click the** Preview Results button **in the Preview Results group, select the name and address for Amir Baashi, click the** Layout tab, **change the After spacing to 0 in the Paragraph group, click after the zip code, then press ENTER**

10. **Click the** Mailings tab, **click the** Finish & Merge button **in the Finish group, click** Edit Individual Documents, **click OK, save the document as** IL_INT_5_WorkshopLetterMerged, **close the document, then save and close** IL_INT_5_WorkshopLetter

FIGURE 5-1: Fields entered from three tables

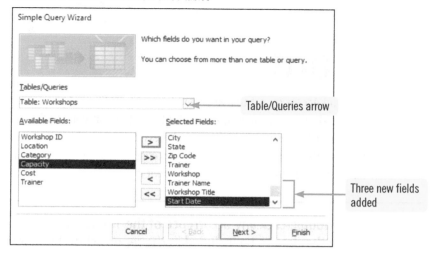

FIGURE 5-2: Filter and Sort dialog box

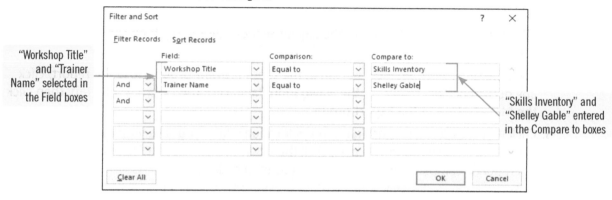

FIGURE 5-3: Merge Fields inserted

Export an Access Report to Word

Learning Outcomes
- Export an Access report to Word
- Convert an exported report to a Word table

You can export an Access report to a Rich Text Format (.rtf) file that you can open and modify in Word. You can then use Word tools to convert the report into a table that you can format easily. An Access report that you export to an .rtf file is not linked to the Access database. TABLE 5-1 summarizes the integration tasks you performed in this module. **CASE** ▶ *You create a report in Access based on the Trainers Report Query and then export it to a document in Word and format it as a Word table.*

STEPS

1. In Access, double-click any occurrence of the Trainers Report Query in the Navigation Pane, view the data to be included in the report, close the query datasheet, click the Create tab, then click the Report Wizard button in the Reports group

2. Click the Select All Fields button >> to add all four fields from the Trainers Report Query datasheet, then click Next four times

3. Click the Block option button in the Layout section, click Next, then click Finish
   The report appears in Print Preview as shown in FIGURE 5-4.

4. Click the Close Print Preview button in the Close Preview group, close the report, click any occurrence of Trainers in the Navigation Pane, click the External Data tab, then click the More button in the Export group

5. Click Word, click Browse, navigate to the location where you save your data files, save the file as IL_INT_5_WorkshopTrainers, click the Open the destination file after the export operation is complete check box to select it, then click OK
   In Word, the document is formatted with TAB characters that separate the data columns. You need to show the hidden formatting symbols so you can remove selected TAB characters and then convert the text into a table.

6. In Word, click the Show/Hide ¶ button ¶ in the Paragraph group to show the paragraph marks if they are not already showing, press DELETE to remove the TAB character to the left of "Trainers," then remove the TAB character to the left of "Trainer Name" and the name of each of the five trainers as shown in FIGURE 5-5

7. Scroll down to view the date at the bottom of the page, click to the left of the date to select the line, the paragraph mark, and the space above it, then press DELETE

8. Select the text from Trainer Name through the last instance of Resume Building, click the Insert tab, click the Table button in the Tables group, click Convert Text to Table, then click OK to accept four columns for the table

9. With the table still selected, click the Layout contextual tab to the right of the Table Design tab, click the AutoFit button in the Cell Size group, click AutoFit Contents, click the Table Design tab, click the More button ▼ in the Table Styles group, then click the Grid Table 2 - Accent 6 table design

10. Click the leftmost Layout tab, click the Margins button, click Normal, click below the table, press ENTER, type your name, save and close the document and exit Word, switch to Access, click Close, exit Access, then submit your files to your instructor

FIGURE 5-4: Report in Print Preview

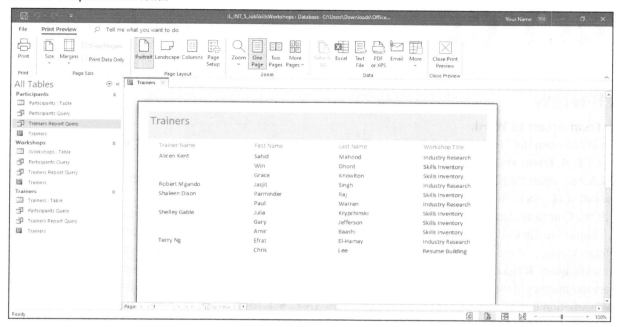

FIGURE 5-5: Access data pasted into Word document

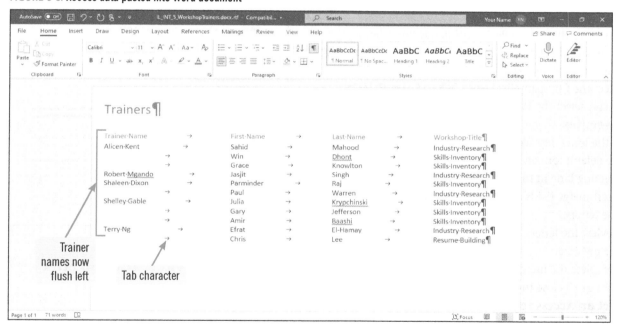

TABLE 5-1: Module 5 Integration tasks

object	command	source program	destination program	result	connection	page
Access query	Word Merge	Access	Word	The fields and records from the Access query datasheet merge into a letter created in Word	Linked	2
Access report	More button, then Word on the External Data tab	Access	Word	The Access report is saved in Rich Text Format with the structure defined with tabs; the .rtf file is opened in Word, where it was formatted with a table design	None	4

Practice

Skills Review

1. Merge from Access to Word.

a. Start Word, open the file IL_INT_5-3.docx from the location where you store your Data Files, save it as **IL_INT_5_GlobalChangeRegistrationLetter**, then close it.

b. Start Access, open the file IL_INT_5-4.accdb from the location where you store your Data Files, then save it as a database called **IL_INT_5_GlobalChangeConvention**. Enable content.

c. With the Company: Table selected, use the Query Wizard to create a query that includes the Company, Address1, City, State, and Zip Code fields from the Company table; the Title, First Name, and Last Name fields from the Delegates table; and the Workshop1, Time1, Workshop2, and Time2 fields from the Workshops table.

d. Name the query **Registration Letter Query**, then close the completed query datasheet.

e. Select any instance of the Registration Letter Query in the Navigation Pane, then use the Word Merge command to merge the Registration Letter Query with the Word document **IL_INT_5_GlobalChangeRegistrationLetter**.

f. Maximize the Word window, close the Mail Merge pane, then type the current date and your name where indicated.

FIGURE 5-6

g. Open the Mail Merge Recipients dialog box, view all the fields, then click Filter to open the Filter Records tab in the Filter and Sort dialog box.

h. Select the Company field, specify **Sustainability Now**, select the Workshop1 field, specify **Green Energies**, then close the dialog boxes.

i. In the letter, replace "Address" with the Address Block in the default format, and replace "Greeting" with the Greeting Line in the default format.

j. Insert merge fields over the placeholders shown in upper-case letters.

k. Preview the letters, then compare the letter for Lorna Chan to FIGURE 5-6.

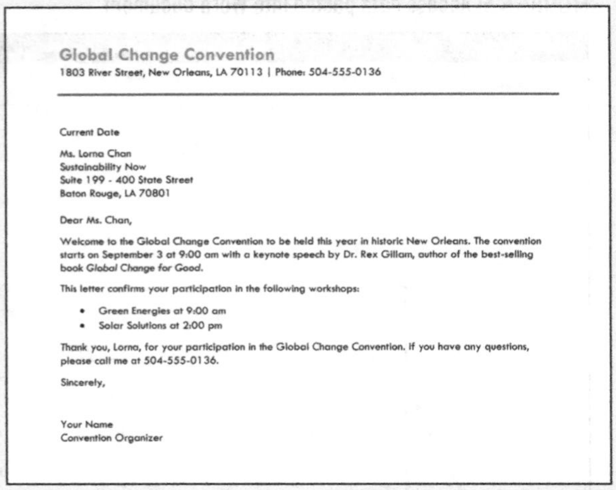

Global Change Convention
1803 River Street, New Orleans, LA 70113 | Phone: 504-555-0136

Current Date

Ms. Lorna Chan
Sustainability Now
Suite 199 - 400 State Street
Baton Rouge, LA 70801

Dear Ms. Chan,

Welcome to the Global Change Convention to be held this year in historic New Orleans. The convention starts on September 3 at 9:00 am with a keynote speech by Dr. Rex Gillam, author of the best-selling book Global Change for Good.

This letter confirms your participation in the following workshops:

- Green Energies at 9:00 am
- Solar Solutions at 2:00 pm

Thank you, Lorna, for your participation in the Global Change Convention. If you have any questions, please call me at 504-555-0136.

Sincerely,

Your Name
Convention Organizer

---

l. Complete the merge, save the two merged letters as **IL_INT_5_GlobalChangeRegistrationLetter_ Merged**, close the document, then save and close the Word source document.

2. Export an Access report to Word.

a. In Access, use the Report Wizard to create a report called **Delegates** from all the fields in the Report Query.

b. Close the Delegates report, then export it to an RTF file called **IL_INT_5_GlobalChangeConvention Delegates.rtf** that opens in Word, saving it in the location where you store your files.

Skills Review (continued)

c. In Word, show the formatting marks, delete the TAB character to the left of "Delegates" and "First Name" and the first names of each of the delegates, then delete the line containing the date and page number.

d. Select the text from First Name to the end of the text, convert the text to a table containing four columns, then autofit the table contents.

e. Apply the Grid Table 2 - Accent 2 table design.

f. Change the document margins to Normal, hide the paragraph marks and deselect the table, then compare the document to FIGURE 5-7.

g. Type your name below the table, save the document, then save and close all open files and programs and submit your files to your instructor.

FIGURE 5-7

Delegates			
First Name	Last Name	Company	State
Yani	Gruber	Global Solutions	LA
Filippa	Corelli	Earth Consultants	MS
Lorna	Chan	Sustainability Now	LA
Ibrahim	Halsi	Earth Consultants	MS
Sidney	Jefferson	Renfrew Consultants	LA
Maryann	Aguilar	Renfrew Consultants	LA
Jose	Sanchez	Sustainability Now	LA
Alvin	Bridges	Sustainability Now	LA
Augusta	Flores	Sustainability Now	LA
Fred	Bowen	Renfrew Consultants	LA
Ulrike	Leon	Renfrew Consultants	LA
Antonia	Sarducci	Global Solutions	LA

Independent Challenge 1

You are helping to organize an event called Fitness First as part of a community outreach program at the Riverwalk Medical Clinic in Cambridge, MA. You create a form letter in Word that welcomes people to the event, and then you create a report in Access that you publish and format in Word.

a. In Word, open IL_INT_5-5.docx from the location where you store your Data Files, save the document as **IL_INT_5_RiverwalkWelcomeLetter**, then close it.

b. In Access, open the file IL_INT_5-6.accdb from the location where you store your Data Files, enable content, then save the database as **IL_INT_5_RiverwalkClinicFitnessFirstEvent**.

c. Create a query called **Participants Query** that includes all the fields except the ID field from the Participants table and all the fields except the Specialty and Package ID fields from the Workshops table. Close the query datasheet.

d. Merge the Participants Query with **IL_INT_5_RiverwalkWelcomeLetter**.

e. In Word, replace the appropriate text with the Address Block and Greeting Line merge fields; use the Dear Joshua Greeting line format. Insert merge fields to replace the capitalized text, then add your name and the current date where shown.

f. Filter the Participants list to Salsa for Workshop1 and Jazz for Workshop2.

g. Preview the form letters and use the Spacing After option to close up the spacing in the address lines, add one blank line above the greeting line, complete the merge, save the merged document as **IL_INT_5_RiverwalkWelcomeLetterMerged**, close the document, then save and close the main document.

h. In Access, create a query called **Workshops Query** that includes the Specialty field from the Workshops table and the First Name, Last Name, and City fields from the Participants table.

i. Use the Report Wizard to create a report called **Workshops** from all the fields in the Workshops Query and using the Stepped Layout.

j. Close the report, then export it to Word as an .rtf file called **IL_INT_5_RiverwalkFitnessEvent Workshops.rtf**.

k. In Word, delete the date and page number at the bottom of the document, show the paragraph marks, delete extra TAB characters to the left of Workshops and at the beginning of each specialty category, convert selected text from "Specialty" to the last line of the text (ends with "Cambridge") to a four-column table separated at tabs, then autofit contents.

l. Click to the left of Workshops at the top of the document, press ENTER, press the up arrow and clear the formatting, then type the following sentence: **The fitness event hosted by Riverwalk Medical Clinic presented four fitness specialties: Aerobics, Dance, Healing, and Strength Training. The Dance workshops were the most popular with participants.**

m. Format the table using the Grid Table 4 - Accent 4 table design, then change the margins to Wide.

n. Type your name below the table, save and close all open files and programs, then submit your files to your instructor.

Visual Workshop

You manage the office for Atlantic Yarns, a wholesale distributor that sells yarn and textile arts accessories to small retail outlets in four states: North Carolina, South Carolina, Georgia, and Florida. In Access, open the file IL_INT_5-7.accdb from the location where you store your Data Files, then save it as **IL_INT_5_AtlanticYarns**. In Access, create a report from the Florida and South Carolina Sales query that includes all the fields except the ID field and uses the Tabular layout, then export the report to Word as **IL_INT_5_AtlanticYarns_FloridaandSouthCarolinaSales.rtf**. Remove the date and page number from the document, change the margins to Normal, convert all the text (including the title) to a table, then delete the blank first column and the "State" column from the table and format the table as shown in FIGURE 5-8 with Grid Table 4 - Accent 1, Autofit the contents, change the font in the header row to White, Background 1, merge the cells, and widen columns if necessary so none of the lines wrap. Type your name below the table. Close all open files and programs, then submit your files to your instructor.

FIGURE 5-8

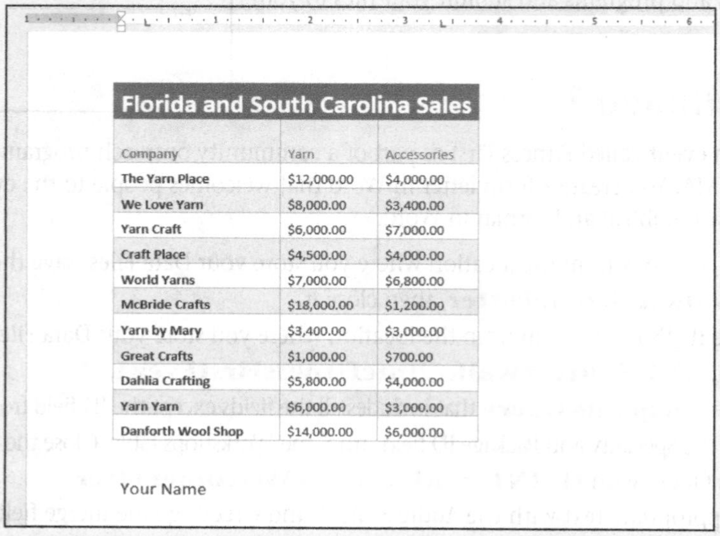

Florida and South Carolina Sales		
Company	Yarn	Accessories
The Yarn Place	$12,000.00	$4,000.00
We Love Yarn	$8,000.00	$3,400.00
Yarn Craft	$6,000.00	$7,000.00
Craft Place	$4,500.00	$4,000.00
World Yarns	$7,000.00	$6,800.00
McBride Crafts	$18,000.00	$1,200.00
Yarn by Mary	$3,400.00	$3,000.00
Great Crafts	$1,000.00	$700.00
Dahlia Crafting	$5,800.00	$4,000.00
Yarn Yarn	$6,000.00	$3,000.00
Danforth Wool Shop	$14,000.00	$6,000.00

Your Name

Formatting Slide Masters and Backgrounds

CASE ▶ You have reviewed your work and are pleased with the slides you created so far for the JCL presentation. Now you are ready to add some enhancements to the slides that include formatting the slide masters, creating custom layouts, and working with themes. You finalize the presentation by using the proofing and language tools and then inspecting the presentation for any issues. You then use advanced slide show commands to view the presentation.

Module Objectives

After completing this module, you will be able to:

- Apply design themes
- Modify masters
- Create custom slide layouts
- Customize the background and theme
- Use slide show commands
- Use proofing and language tools
- Inspect a presentation

Files You Will Need

IL_PPT_4-1.pptx	Support_PPT_4_Group.jpg
IL_PPT_4-2.pptx	Support_PPT_4_AI.jpg
IL_PPT_4-3.pptx	Support_PPT_4_R2G_Logo.jpg
IL_PPT_4-4.pptx	Support_PPT_4_Logo.jpg

Apply Design Themes

Learning Outcomes
- Apply a theme Modify the design theme
- Crop a picture to a shape

A design theme uses coordinated theme colors, lines, fills, shadows, and effects to transform your presentation. You can apply a theme to the whole presentation or to selected slides. Each theme has at least four custom coordinated variants that provides you with additional color options and effects. Theme variants are subtle deviations from the original theme, usually with slight color or text changes. Another way to alter the look of a slide is to use the PowerPoint Designer and apply a layout from the Design Ideas pane. As you enter content on your slides, PowerPoint Designer detects objects, key terms, and concepts and then provides several slide layouts that best match your content. **CASE** *You decide to change the design theme and variant on one slide, then you use the PowerPoint Designer.*

STEPS

1. **sam** ⬇ **Start PowerPoint, open the presentation** IL_PPT_4-1.pptx **from the location where you store your Data Files, save the presentation as** IL_PPT_4_JCL, **then click the** Design tab **on the Ribbon**

2. **Click the** Slide 3 thumbnail **on the Slides tab, click the** More button ⬇ **in the Themes group, then scroll to the bottom of the gallery**
   The Themes gallery opens.

QUICK TIP
One way to apply multiple themes to the same presentation is to click the Slide Sorter button on the status bar, select a slide or a group of slides, then click the theme.

3. **Right-click the** View theme, **then click** Apply to Selected Slides
   The new theme with a white background is applied to Slide 3.

4. **Slowly move your pointer** ⬆ **over the** variants **in the Variants group, then click the variant with the orange bar on the right side**
   The theme variant adds colored title text and background graphics to the slide, as shown in FIGURE 4-1. You can further modify the theme on Slide 3 by changing its color, font, or effects scheme.

5. **Click the** ⬇ **in the Variants group, point to** Colors, **then click** Green
   The title text color and background objects change color to reflect the new Green color scheme. Notice these changes only affect the design theme on Slide 3.

6. **Click the** Slide 2 thumbnail **on the Slides tab, then click the** Design Ideas button **in the Designer group**
   The Design Ideas pane opens. A list of slide layouts appears in the pane that the PowerPoint Designer identifies as being good matches for the content on Slide 2.

QUICK TIP
If Design Ideas is not active, and you are on the Internet, click the Turn on button in the Design Ideas pane.

7. **Locate and click the** slide layout **in the Design Ideas pane shown in** FIGURE 4-2, **then close the** Design Ideas pane
   Slide 2 changes to reflect the custom slide layout from the Design Ideas pane.

8. **Click the** picture, **click the** Picture Format tab **on the Ribbon, then click the** Crop button arrow **in the Size group**
   Pictures can be cropped to any shape found in the Shapes gallery.

9. **Point to** Crop to Shape, **click** Flowchart: Document **in the Flowchart section, then save your changes**

FIGURE 4-1: Slide showing a different design theme and variant

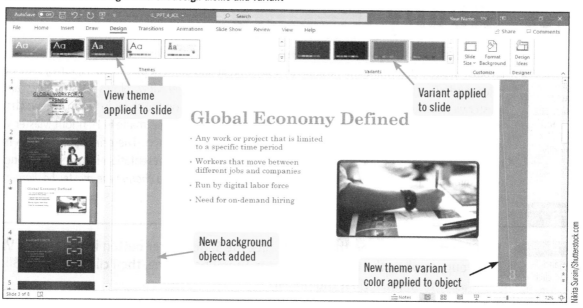

FIGURE 4-2: Slide 2 with new slide layout

Customizing themes

You are not limited to using the standard themes PowerPoint provides; you can also modify a theme to create your own custom theme. For example, you might want to incorporate your school's or company's colors on the slide background of the presentation or be able to type using fonts your company uses for brand recognition. To change an existing theme, click the View tab on the Ribbon, then click one of the Master buttons in the Master Views group. Click the Colors button, the Fonts button, or the Effects button in the Background group to make changes to the theme, save this new theme for future use by clicking the Themes button in the Edit Theme group, then click Save Current Theme. You also have the ability to create a new font theme or color theme from scratch by clicking the Fonts button or the Colors button and then clicking Customize Fonts or Customize Colors. You work in the Create New Theme Fonts or Create New Theme Colors dialog box to define the custom theme fonts or colors.

Modify Masters

Learning Outcomes
- Navigate Slide Master view
- Change the Master background and theme fonts
- Add and modify a picture

Each presentation in PowerPoint has a set of **masters** that store information about the theme and slide layouts. Masters determine the position and size of text and content placeholders, fonts, slide background, color, and effects. There are three Master views: Slide Master view, Notes Master view, and Handout Master view. Changes made in Slide Master view are reflected on the slides in Normal view; changes made in Notes Master view are reflected in Notes Page view; and changes made in Handout Master view appear when you print your presentation using a handout printing option. The primary benefit to modifying a master is that you can make universal changes to your whole presentation instead of making individual repetitive changes to each of your slides. **CASE** *You decide to change the master background style and font scheme to modify the look of the whole presentation.*

STEPS

QUICK TIP
You can press and hold SHIFT and click the Normal button on the status bar to display the slide master.

1. **Click the View tab on the Ribbon, click the Slide Master button in the Master Views group, scroll to the top of the Master Thumbnails pane, then click the Mesh Slide Master thumbnail (first thumbnail)**

   The Slide Master view appears with the slide master displayed in the Slide pane, as shown in FIGURE 4-3. A new tab, the Slide Master tab, appears next to the Home tab on the Ribbon. The slide master is the Mesh theme slide master. Each theme comes with its own slide master. Each master text placeholder on the slide master identifies the font size, style, color, and position of text placeholders on the slides in Normal view. For example, for the Mesh theme, the Master title placeholder positioned at the top of the slide uses a white, 32-point, Century Gothic font. Slide titles use this font style and formatting. Each slide master comes with associated slide layouts located below the slide master in the Master Thumbnails pane. Slide layouts follow the information on the slide master, and changes you make are reflected in all the slide layouts.

2. **Click the Title and Content Layout thumbnail in the Master Thumbnails pane**

   A ScreenTip appears identifying the slide layout by name and lists if any slides in the presentation are using the layout. Slides 4–8 are using the Title and Content Layout.

QUICK TIP
You can make sure the current master remains with the presentation by clicking the Preserve button in the Edit Master group.

3. **Click the Mesh Slide Master thumbnail, click the Background Styles button in the Background group, then click the Style 12 thumbnail**

   This background style darkens the background and makes the white placeholder text stand out. By modifying the slide master thumbnail, every associated master slide layout is also changed.

4. **Click the Fonts button in the Background group, scroll down, then click Cambria**

   The fonts for title and body text change on every master slide layout in the presentation.

5. **Click the Insert tab on the Ribbon, click the Pictures button in the Images group, then click This Device**

   The Insert Picture dialog box opens.

6. **Select the picture file Support_PPT_4_Logo.jpg from the location where you store your Data Files, then click Insert**

   The JCL logo picture is placed on the slide master and will now appear on all slides in the presentation.

7. **Click 2.45" in the Width text box in the Size group, type 1.00, press ENTER, click the Color button in the Adjust group, then click Orange, Accent color 6 Light in the Recolor section**

   The logo changes color.

8. **Drag the logo to the lower-right corner to align with the footer placeholder, as shown in FIGURE 4-4, then save your changes**

FIGURE 4-3: Slide Master view

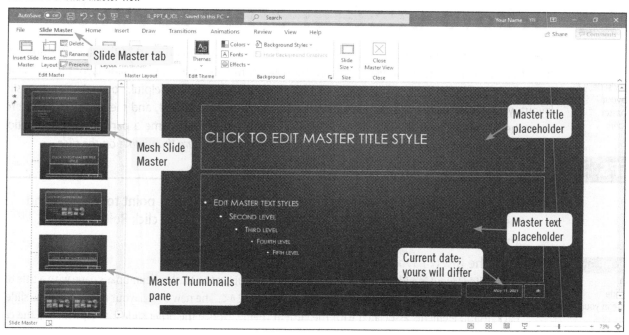

FIGURE 4-4: Customized slide master

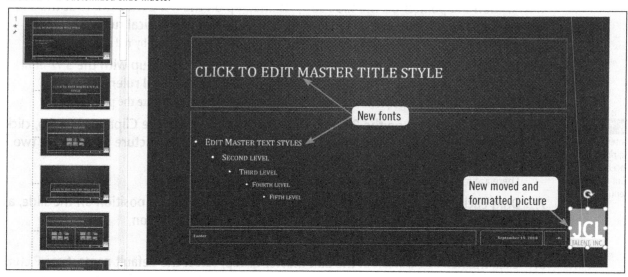

Understanding PowerPoint templates and themes

So what exactly is the difference between a PowerPoint template and a PowerPoint theme? A theme is a coordinated set of colors, fonts, and effects (such as shadows and reflections) that is used to modify the slide design of your presentation. For example, a theme is like the various colors a painter uses to paint the inside of a house where the walls are one color, the ceilings are a second color, and the window and door trim is a third color. A template, on the other hand, is a presentation that contains a theme and includes sample text about a specific subject matter, such as health and fitness. The sample text in a template provides you with the basic information that you can then use to modify the presentation with your own information. You can save any presentation as a template to use in the future by opening the Save As dialog box, then selecting PowerPoint Template in the Save as type text box. Your presentation is placed in the Custom Office Templates folder and can be accessed anytime.

Create Custom Slide Layouts

The standard slide layouts supplied in PowerPoint are adequate to design most of the slides for presentations that you will create. However, if you are consistently modifying a standard slide layout for presentations, having a custom slide layout that you created and saved would be helpful. To create a custom slide layout, you choose from eight different placeholders, including text, chart, and media placeholders. You draw the placeholder on the slide in Slide Master view; these then become a part of the presentation. **CASE** *You decide to create a custom slide layout that displays picture thumbnails on the slide.*

STEPS

1. **Right-click a blank area of the** slide master **in the slide pane, point to the** Grid and Guides arrow, **click** Guides, **right-click the** slide master, **then click** Ruler

   The guides and rulers are displayed on the slide master.

2. **Click the** Insert Layout button **in the Edit Master group**

   A new slide layout is added to the presentation and appears in the Master Thumbnails pane with a title text placeholder and footer placeholders, as shown in **FIGURE 4-5**. The new slide layout contains all the slide background elements associated with the current theme. Notice the other slide master, which is the customized master for Slide 3 of the presentation.

3. **Click the** Insert Placeholder arrow **in the Master Layout group, then click** Picture

   The pointer changes to ✛ when moved over the slide layout.

4. **Position the pointer on the slide so** ✛ **is lined up on the** horizontal guide **at the** 5 ½" mark **on the left side of the horizontal ruler and** 0" **on the vertical ruler**

   As you move the pointer on the slide its position is identified on the rulers by red dotted lines.

5. **Drag** ✛ **to draw a box down and to the right until** ✛ **is lined up with the** 3 ½" mark **on the horizontal ruler and the** 2" mark **below 0 on the vertical ruler**

   You drew a 2" × 2" square picture placeholder on the slide. You can duplicate the placeholder.

6. **Click the** Home tab **on the Ribbon, click the** Copy button **in the Clipboard group, click the** Paste button **in the Clipboard group, then duplicate the picture placeholder two more times**

   There are four picture placeholders on the slide.

7. **Drag each** picture placeholder **using the horizontal guide to a position on the slide, as shown in** FIGURE 4-6, **then click the** Slide Master tab **on the Ribbon**

   The placeholders are arranged on the slide layout.

8. **Click the** Rename button **in the Edit Master group, select the default name, type** Picture, **click** Rename, **then position** ⬚ **over the** slide layout **in the Master Thumbnails pane**

   The new name of the custom slide layout appears in the ScreenTip. The new Picture layout will appear when you click the Layout button or the New Slide list button in the Slides group on the Home tab.

9. **Right-click a blank area of the slide, click** Ruler, **right-click a blank area of the slide, point to the** Grid and Guides arrow, **then click** Guides

10. **Click the** Close Master View button **in the Close group, then save your changes**

    Slide 2 appears in Normal view.

FIGURE 4-5: New custom slide layout

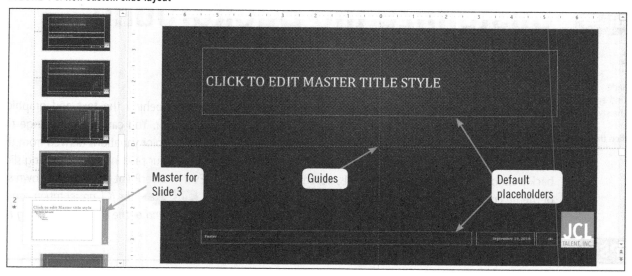

FIGURE 4-6: Custom slide layout with new placeholders

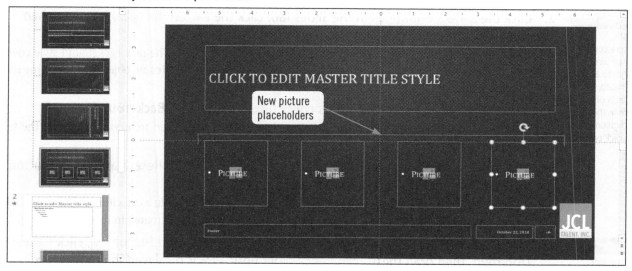

Restoring the slide master layout

If the slide master is missing a placeholder, open Slide Master view, then click the Master Layout button in the Master Layout group to reapply the placeholder. Clicking the Master Layout button opens the Master Layout dialog box, as shown in FIGURE 4-7. Click the placeholder check box to reapply the placeholder. To quickly apply or delete the title or footer placeholders on a slide master, click the Title or Footers check boxes in the Master Layout group on the Slide Master tab.

FIGURE 4-7: Master Layout dialog box

PowerPoint

Customize the Background and Theme

**Learning
Outcomes**
- Apply a slide
  background and
  change the style
- Modify
  presentation theme

Every slide in a PowerPoint presentation has a **background**, the area behind the text and graphics. You modify the background to enhance the slides using images and color. You can quickly change the background appearance by applying a background style, which is a set of color variations derived from the theme colors. Theme colors determine the colors for all slide elements in your presentation, including slide background, text and lines, shadows, fills, accents, and hyperlinks. Every PowerPoint theme has its own set of theme colors. See TABLE 4-1 for a description of the theme colors. **CASE** *The JCL presentation can be improved with some design enhancements. You decide to modify the background of the slides by changing the theme colors and fonts.*

STEPS

1. **Click the** Design tab **on the Ribbon, then click the** Format Background button **in the Customize group**

   The Format Background pane opens displaying the Fill options. The Picture or texture fill option button is selected indicating the slide has a picture background.

QUICK TIP

To add artistic
effects, picture cor-
rections, or picture
color changes to a
slide background,
click the Effects or
Picture icons in the
Format Background
pane, then click one
of the options.

2. **Click the** Slide 3 thumbnail **in the Slides tab, click the** Pattern fill option button, **then click the** Dotted: 25% pattern **(first row)**

   FIGURE 4-8 shows the new background on Slide 3 of the presentation. The new background style covers the slide behind the text and background graphics. **Background graphics** are objects placed on the slide master.

3. **Click the** Hide background graphics check box **in the Format Background pane**

   All the background objects, which include the colored shapes are hidden from view, and only the text objects, video object, and slide number remain visible.

4. **Click the** Hide background graphics check box, **then click the** Reset Background button **at the bottom of the Format Background pane**

   All the background objects and the solid fill slide background appear again as specified by the theme. The Reset Background button reverts the slide background to its original background, in this case a solid fill.

QUICK TIP

To change the slide
background to a
solid fill or a picture
fill, click the Solid fill
option button or the
Picture or texture fill
option button,
respectively.

5. **Click the** Picture or texture fill option button, **click the** Texture button 📷, **click** Canvas **(top row), then drag the** Transparency slider **until** 40% **is displayed in the text box**

   The new texture fills the slide background behind the background items.

6. **Click the** Gradient Fill option button

   A gradient fill now fills the slide background. PowerPoint splits the gradient background into four quadrants called **gradient stops** that can be individually customized.

7. **Click the** far-right gradient stop 4 of 4 🔲 **under Gradient stops, click the** Color button 🎨, **then click** Black, Text 1

   Changing the gradient stop color results in a shaded black color on the bottom of the slide. Compare your screen to FIGURE 4-9.

8. **Click the** Format Background pane Close button ❎, **then save your work**

FIGURE 4-8: New background style applied

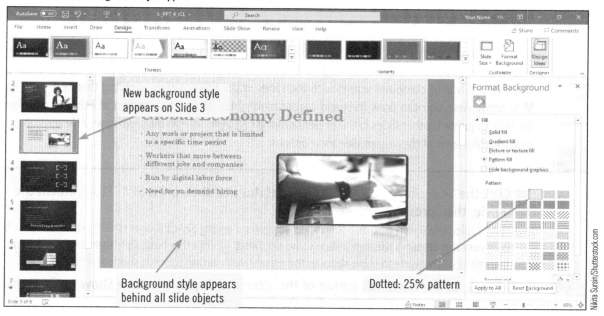

FIGURE 4-9: Slide with gradient fill background

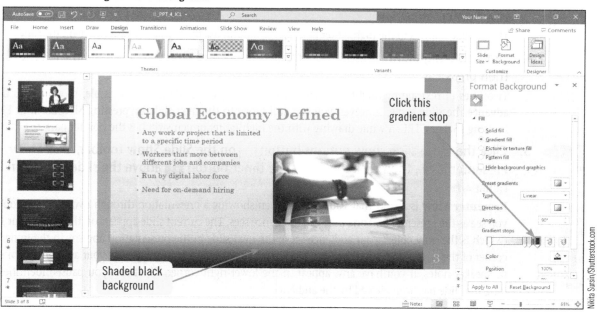

TABLE 4-1: Theme colors

color element	description
Text/Background colors	Contrasting colors for typed characters and the slide background
Accent colors	There are six accent colors used for shapes, drawn lines, and text; the shadow color for text and objects and the fill and outline color for shapes are all accent colors; all these colors contrast appropriately with background and text colors
Hyperlink color	Colors used for hyperlinks you insert
Followed Hyperlink color	Color used for hyperlinks after they have been clicked

Use Slide Show Commands

Learning Outcomes
• Preview a slide show
• Navigate a slide show
• Use slide show tools

With PowerPoint, Slide Show view is used primarily to deliver a presentation to an audience, either over the Internet using your computer or through a projector connected to your computer. As you've seen, Slide Show view fills your computer screen with the slides of the presentation, showing them one at a time. In Slide Show view, you can draw freehand pen or highlighter strokes, also known as **ink annotations**, on the slide or jump to other slides in the presentation. **CASE** > *You run the slide show of the presentation and practice using some of the custom slide show options.*

STEPS

1. **Click the Slide Show button 🖵 on the status bar, then press SPACEBAR, watch the movie, then press SPACEBAR again**

   Slide 3 filled the screen first, and then Slide 4 appears. Pressing SPACEBAR or clicking the left mouse button is an easy way to move through a slide show. See TABLE 4-2 for other basic slide show keyboard commands. You can easily navigate to other slides in the presentation during the slide show.

   TROUBLE
   The Slide Show tool-bar buttons are semitransparent and blend in with the background color on the slide.

2. **Move ⬚ to the lower-left corner of the screen to display the Slide Show toolbar, click the See all slides button 🔲, then click the Slide 2 thumbnail**

   Slide 2 appears on the screen. With the Slide Show toolbar you can emphasize points in your presentation by drawing highlighter strokes on the slide during a slide show.

3. **Click the Pen and laser pointer tools button 🖉, on the Slide Show toolbar, then click Highlighter**

   The pointer changes to the highlighter pointer ▯. You can use the highlighter anywhere on the slide.

4. **Drag ▯ to highlight Hiring practices since 2009 and Overseas workers in the text object, then press ESC**

   Two lines of text are highlighted, as shown in FIGURE 4-10. While the ▯ is visible, mouse clicks do not advance the slide show; however, you can still move to the next slide by pressing SPACEBAR or ENTER. Pressing ESC or CTRL+A while drawing with the highlighter or pen switches the pointer back to ⬚.

   QUICK TIP
   To advance a slide using a specified number of seconds, click the Transitions tab on the Ribbon, click the After check box in the Timing group, then enter the number of seconds in the After text box.

5. **Click the More slide show options button 🔲 on the Slide Show toolbar, click Show Presenter View, then click the Pause the timer button ❚❚ above the slide, as shown in FIGURE 4-11**

   Presenter view is a view that you can use when showing a presentation through two monitors; one that you see as the presenter and one that your audience sees. The current slide appears on the left of your screen (which is the only object your audience sees); the next slide in the presentation appears in the upper-right corner of the screen. If desired, you can black out the slide from view to prevent your audience from seeing it. Speaker notes, if you have any, appear in the lower-right corner. The timer you paused identifies how long the slide has been viewed by the audience.

6. **Click 🖵 Black or unblack slide show, click 🖵, click 🔲, click Hide Presenter View, then click the Advance to the next slide button ▶ on the Slide Show toolbar**

   Slide 3 appears.

7. **Press ENTER to advance through the entire slide show until you see a black slide, then press SPACEBAR**

   If there are ink annotations on your slides, you have the option of saving them when you quit the slide show. Saved ink annotations appear as drawn objects in Normal view.

8. **Click Discard, then save the presentation**

   The highlight ink annotation is deleted on Slide 2, and Slide 8 appears in Normal view.

FIGURE 4-10: Slide 2 in Slide Show view with highlighter strokes

FIGURE 4-11: Slide 2 in Presenter view

TABLE 4-2: Basic Slide Show view keyboard commands

keyboard commands	description
ENTER, SPACEBAR, PGDN, N, DOWN ARROW, or RIGHT ARROW	Advances to the next slide
E	Erases the ink annotation drawing
HOME, END	Moves to the first or last slide in the slide show
UP ARROW, PGUP, or LEFT ARROW	Returns to the previous slide
S	Pauses the slide show when using automatic timings; press again to continue
B	Changes the screen to black; press again to return
ESC	Stops the slide show

PowerPoint

Use Proofing and Language Tools

Learning Outcomes
- Spell check a presentation
- Translate slide text

PowerPoint has a number of language tools, including the Spell Checker, which compares the spelling of all the words in your presentation against the words contained in the dictionary. The **proofing language** is the language used by the spelling checker that you can specify. PowerPoint also has a tool, called the Translator, that translates words or phrases from your default language into one of 60 different languages. And, as you develop content, if you are having trouble coming up with just the right word, PowerPoint has a comprehensive **thesaurus** that can help you. **CASE** ▶ *You're finished working on the presentation for now, so it's a good time to check spelling. You then experiment with language translation because the final presentation will be translated into different languages.*

STEPS

QUICK TIP
To display the Revisions pane to compare and combine changes with your current presentation and another presentation, click the Review tab, then click the Compare button in the Compare group to open the Revisions pane.

1. **Click the Slide 1 thumbnail in the Slides tab, click the Review tab on the Ribbon, then click the Spelling button in the Proofing group**

   PowerPoint begins to check the spelling in your presentation and opens the Spelling pane. The Spell Checker identifies a name on Slide 7, but it does not recognize that is spelled correctly and suggests some replacement words.

2. **Click Ignore All in the Spelling pane**

   PowerPoint ignores all instances of this name and continues to check the rest of the presentation for errors. When the Spell Checker finishes checking your presentation, the Spelling pane closes, and an alert box opens with a message stating the spelling check is complete.

3. **Click OK in the Alert box, then click the Slide 4 thumbnail in the Slides tab**

   The alert box closes. Now you experiment with the language translation feature.

4. **Click the Translate button in the Language group, then click Turn on if you need to turn on Intelligent Services**

   The Translator pane opens.

TROUBLE
Do not select the space past the word "overhead" in the third line.

5. **Select the three indented lines of text in the text object, click the To down arrow in the Translator pane, then click Catalan**

   A Catalan translation of the text appears in the Translator pane shown in FIGURE 4-12. You have the option of inserting the translated text directly onto your slide.

6. **Click the Insert button in the Translator pane, then close the Translator pane**

   The translated text is inserted into the text object in place of the original English text. Now you use the thesaurus on Slide 5.

QUICK TIP
You can also right-click a word, point to Synonyms in the shortcut menu, then choose a new word.

7. **Click the Slide 5 thumbnail in the Slides tab, select the word committed in the text object, then click the Thesaurus button in the Proofing group**

   The Thesaurus pane opens and displays a list of synonyms, as shown in FIGURE 4-13.

8. **Point to dedicated in the list of words, click the down arrow, then click Insert**

   The word "committed" is replaced with the word "dedicated."

9. **Close the Thesaurus pane, then save your work**

FIGURE 4-12: Translated text in the Translator pane

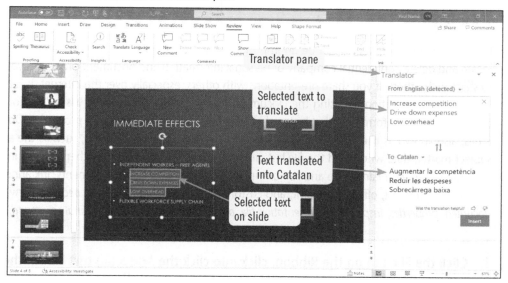

FIGURE 4-13: Window with open Thesaurus pane

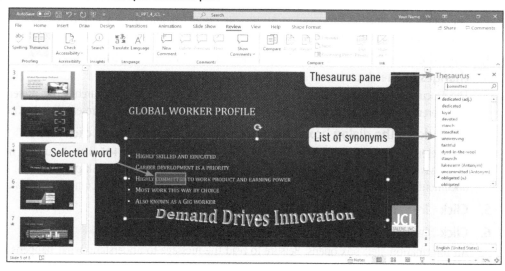

Rehearsing slide show timings

You can set different slide timings for each slide; for example, the title slide can appear for 20 seconds and the second slide for 1 minute. To set timings, click the Rehearse Timings button in the Set Up group on the Slide Show tab. Slide Show view opens and the Recording toolbar shown in FIGURE 4-14 opens. It contains buttons to pause between slides and to advance to the next slide. After opening the Recording toolbar, you can practice giving your presentation by manually advancing each slide in the presentation. When you are finished, PowerPoint displays the total recorded time for the presentation and you have the option to save the recorded

timings. The next time you run the slide show, you can use the timings you rehearsed.

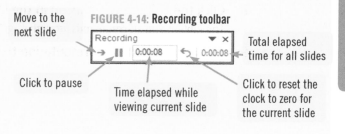

FIGURE 4-14: Recording toolbar

Inspect a Presentation

**Learning
Outcomes**
• Modify document
  properties
• Inspect and
  remove unwanted
  data

Reviewing your presentation can be an important step. You should not only find and fix errors, but also locate and delete confidential company or personal information and document properties you do not want to share with others. If you share presentations with others, especially over the Internet, it is a good idea to inspect the presentation file using the Document Inspector. The **Document Inspector** looks for hidden data and personal information that is stored in the file itself or in the document properties. Document properties, also known as **metadata**, include specific data about the presentation, such as the author's name, subject matter, title, who saved the file last, and when the file was created. Other types of information the Document Inspector can locate and remove include presentation notes, comments, ink annotations, invisible on-slide content, off-slide content, and custom XML data. **CASE** ▸ *You decide to view and add some document properties, inspect your presentation file, and learn about the Mark as Final command.*

STEPS

QUICK TIP
Click the Properties
list button, then click
Advanced Properties
to open the
Properties dialog box
to see or change
more document
properties.

1. **Click the** File tab **on the Ribbon, click** Info **click the** Add a tag text box **in the Properties section, type** Changing international labor force, **then click the** Add a category text box
   This data provides some descriptive keywords for the presentation.

2. **Type** Industry review, **then click the** Show All Properties link
   The information you enter here about the presentation file can be used to identify and organize your file. The Show All Properties link displays all the file properties and those you can change. You now use the Document Inspector to search for information you might want to delete in the presentation.

QUICK TIP
If you need to save a
presentation to run
in an earlier version
of PowerPoint, check
for unsupported
features using the
Check Compatibility
feature.

3. **Click the** Check for Issues button, **click** Inspect Document, **then click** Yes **to save the changes to the document**
   The Document Inspector dialog box opens. The Document Inspector searches the presentation file for 12 different types of information that you might want removed from the presentation before sharing it.

4. **Scroll down the dialog box, click any empty** check boxes, **then click** Inspect
   The presentation file is reviewed, and the results are shown in FIGURE 4-15. The Document Inspector found items having to do with document properties, which you just entered, task pane add-ins, and embedded documents which are the pictures in the file. You decide to leave all the document properties alone.

5. **Click** Close, **then click the** Protect Presentation button

6. **Click** Mark as Final, **then click** OK **in the alert box**
   An information alert box opens. Be sure to read the message to understand what happens to the file and how to recognize a marked-as-final presentation. You decide to complete this procedure.

7. **Click** OK, **click the** Home tab **on the Ribbon, then click anywhere in the title text object**
   When you select the title text object, the Ribbon closes automatically and an information alert box at the top of the window notes that the presentation is marked as final, making it a read-only file. Compare your screen to FIGURE 4-16. A **read-only** file is one that can't be edited or modified in any way. Anyone who has received a read-only presentation can only edit the presentation by changing its marked-as-final status. You still want to work on the presentation, so you remove the marked-as-final status.

8. **Click the** Edit Anyway button **in the information alert box, then save your changes**
   The Ribbon and all commands are active again, and the file can now be modified.

9. **sam**⬆ **Submit your presentation to your instructor, then exit PowerPoint**

FIGURE 4-15: Document Inspector dialog box

FIGURE 4-16: Marked as final presentation

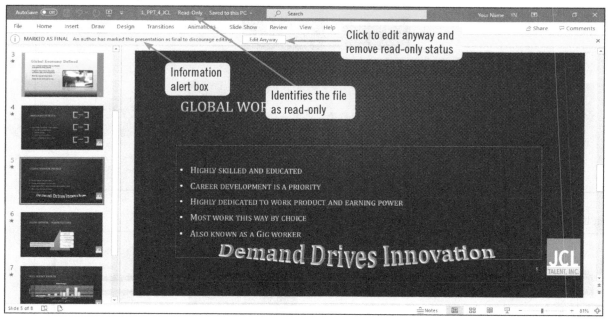

Practice

Skills Review

1. **Apply design themes.**

   a. Open the presentation IL_PPT_4-2.pptx from the location where you store your Data Files, then save the presentation as **IL_PPT_4_Jenlan**. You will work to create the completed presentation, as shown in FIGURE 4-17.

   b. Click the Slide 2 thumbnail in the Slides tab, then click the Design tab.

   c. Click the Themes group More button, locate the Circuit theme, then apply it to the selected slide only.

   d. Change the theme variant to the shaded black option.

   e. Click the More button in the Variants group, point to Colors, then change the color scheme to Paper.

   f. Go to Slide 3, then open the Design Ideas pane.

   g. Apply the slide layout shown in FIGURE 4-18, then close the Design Ideas pane. If the layout does not appear, then choose another layout.

FIGURE 4-17: Completed presentation

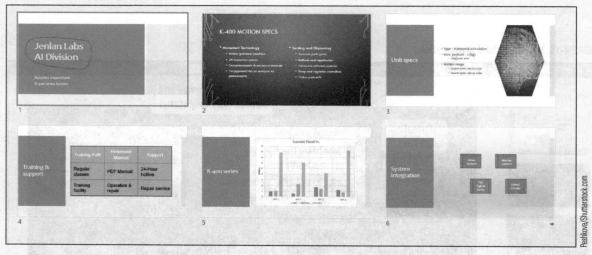

Peshkova/Shutterstock.com

FIGURE 4-18

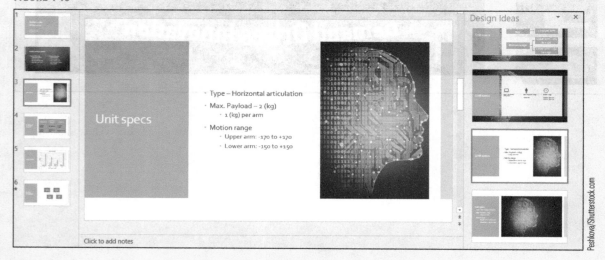

Peshkova/Shutterstock.com

Formatting Slide Masters and Backgrounds

Skills Review (continued)

h. Click the picture, click the Picture Format tab, click the Crop button list arrow, then crop the picture to a Hexagon shape.

i. Save your changes.

2. Modify masters.

a. Open Slide Master view using the View tab, then click the Frame Slide Master thumbnail in the Master Thumbnails pane.

b. Change the background style to Style 9.

c. Change the theme fonts to Candara, then change the theme Colors to Blue Green.

d. Save your changes.

3. Create custom slide layouts.

a. Insert a new slide layout, then display the ruler and the guides.

b. Add a Content placeholder the same size as the blue shape. Use the guides and rulers to help you create the placeholder.

c. Add a Media placeholder, approximately 3.5" wide by 2.5" high, then use Copy and Paste to create a second placeholder.

d. Position and align the placeholders, as shown in FIGURE 4-19.

e. Name the custom slide layout **Media**, turn off guides, then close rulers.

f. Save your changes, then switch to Normal view.

FIGURE 4-19

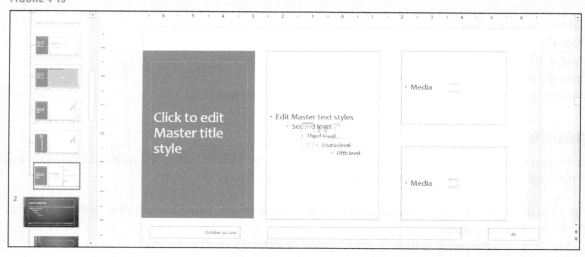

4. Customize the background and theme.

a. Go to Slide 6, then open the Format Background pane.

b. Click the Solid fill option button, then change the color to Aqua, Accent 1 Lighter 40%.

c. Change the color transparency to 40%, then click the Picture or texture fill option button.

d. Click the Texture button, then change the background to Blue tissue paper.

e. Click the Pattern fill option button, change the background to Small confetti, then click the Reset Background button at the bottom of the pane.

f. Click the Hide the background graphics check box, then click it again.

g. Select the Gradient fill option button, click the Preset gradients button, click Light Gradient - Accent 6 (top row), then close the Format Background pane.

Skills Review (continued)

5. **Use slide show commands.**

   a. Open Slide Show view, click the mouse twice, then go to Slide 1 using the See all slides button on the Slide Show toolbar.

   b. Use the Pen ink annotation tool to circle the slide title.

   c. Go to Slide 2, use the Highlighter to highlight any four points in the bulleted text on the slide, then press ESC.

   d. Open Presenter view, stop the timer, then click the Black or unblack slide show button twice.

   e. Advance the slides to Slide 6, then return to Slide 1.

   f. Hide Presenter view, advance through the slide show, save your ink and highlight annotations, then save your work.

6. **Use proofing and language tools.**

   a. Check the spelling of the document, and correct any misspelled words. There is one misspelled word in the presentation. Ignore any words that are correctly spelled but that the spell checker doesn't recognize. There is one word that spell checker does not recognize that is spelled correctly.

   b. On Slide 2, open the Translator pane.

   c. Select the last two bullet points in the left content placeholder, then change the To language in the Translator pane to Bulgarian.

   d. Click the Insert button in the Translator pane, then close the Translator pane.

   e. Go to Slide 3, right-click the word "Gesture" in the content placeholder, point to Synonyms, then click Motion.

   f. Save your changes.

7. **Inspect a presentation.**

   a. Go to the Info screen on the File tab, then in the Properties section, type information of your choosing in the Tags and Categories text fields.

   b. Open the Document Inspector dialog box.

   c. Make sure the Ink check box is selected, then inspect the presentation.

   d. Close the dialog box, then save your changes.

   e. Submit your presentation to your instructor, then close the presentation.

Independent Challenge 1

Riverwalk Medical Clinic (RMC) is a large medical facility in Cambridge, Massachusetts. You continue to work on a presentation on the latest emergency response procedures for a staff training later in the week.

   a. Open the file IL_PPT_4-3.pptx from the location where you store your Data Files, and save the presentation as **IL_PPT_4_Riverwalk**.

   b. Add the slide number and your name as the footer on all slides, except the title slide.

   c. Go to Slide 2, click the Design tab, then change the theme for the selected slide to Ion.

   d. If the Design Ideas pane is open, close it, then click the third variant from the left.

   e. Open the Slide Master view, click the Colors button, change the color scheme to Violet II, then change the background style to Style 3.

   f. Change the Font theme to Arial, then close the Slide Master view.

   g. Go to Slide 4, click the picture, click the Picture Format tab, then crop the picture to the Flowchart: Document shape.

   h. Go to Slide 5, click the Design Ideas button, select the first slide layout in the Design Ideas pane, then close the Design Ideas pane.

   i. Open Slide Show view, jump to Slide 1, then open Presenter view.

   j. Click the Pause the timer button, black the slide from view, make it appear again, then exit Presenter view.

   k. Proceed through the slide show to the end, then end the slide show.

Independent Challenge 1 (continued)

FIGURE 4-20

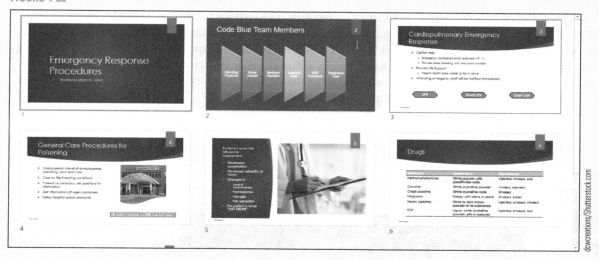

l. On Slide 5, right-click the word Alterations in the text object, point to Synonyms, then click the word Changes. An example of a finished presentation is shown in FIGURE 4-20.

m. Save your changes, submit your presentation to your instructor, close the presentation, then exit PowerPoint.

Independent Challenge 2

You are an associate at Global Systems, Inc., a manufacturer of civilian drone technology located in Santa Clara, California. Global Systems designs and manufactures personal drone systems largely used in the movie industry and in commercial business. You need to finish the work on a quarterly presentation that outlines the progress of the company's newest technologies by creating a custom slide layout, customizing the background, and using the Document Inspector.

a. Open the file IL_PPT_4-4.pptx from the location where you store your Data Files, and save the presentation as **IL_PPT_4_GSI**.

b. Go to Slide 2, then apply a gradient fill slide background using the Format Background pane.

c. Click the Preset gradients button, click Top Spotlight - Accent 3, then click the Hide background graphics check box.

d. Click the Hide background graphics check box again, then click the third gradient stop under Gradient stops.

e. Drag the Transparency slider to 40%, click Apply to All, then close the Format Background pane.

f. Open Slide Master view, insert a new slide layout, then create three 3" picture content placeholders.

g. On the vertical ruler, set a guide on the 1" mark above the 0, align the top edges of the placeholders on the guide, then distribute the placeholders horizontally.

h. Rename the new slide layout, **Picture**, close the Slide Master view, then open Slide Show view.

i. On Slide 3, use the highlighter to highlight two bullet points, move to Slide 4, use the pen to circle two bullet points, end the slide show, then save your annotations.

j. Run the Document Inspector with all the options selected, identify what items the Document Inspector finds, then close the Document Inspector dialog box.

k. Add your name and the slide number as a footer to all slides, check the spelling, fix any misspellings, close rulers and guides, then save your work.

l. Submit your presentation to your instructor, then close the presentation and exit PowerPoint.

PowerPoint

Visual Workshop

Create a presentation that looks like FIGURE 4-21, and FIGURE 4-22, which shows two slides with a specific slide layout. The theme used in this presentation is Berlin with a blue variant. Insert pictures **Support_PPT_4_Group.jpg** and **Support_PPT_4_AI.jpg** to the slides, then crop the first picture to the shape Rectangle: Diagonal Corners Rounded and the second picture to the shape Plaque. On the slide master, insert the picture **Support_PPT_4_R2G_Logo.jpg** to the Berlin Slide Master layout. Change the picture width to 1". Change the slide background of both slides to the Top Spotlight - Accent 1 preset gradient fill. Add your name as footer text to the slide, add slide number to the footer, save the presentation as **IL_PPT_4_R2G**, then submit your presentation to your instructor.

FIGURE 4-21

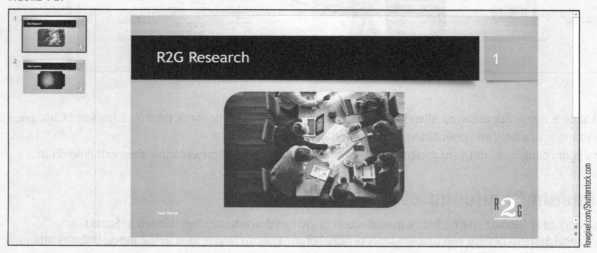

FIGURE 4-22

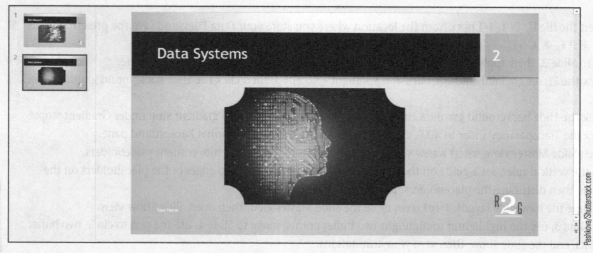

Formatting Slide Masters and Backgrounds

Working with Advanced Tools

CASE You continue working on the JCL Talent workforce trends presentation that details specific information on the labor force in the global economy. After receiving some initial feedback, you revise the presentation by formatting shapes, modifying pictures, customizing animations, using comments, customizing the master views, and combining reviewed presentations. You also add Zoom links to the presentation to facilitate navigation when you deliver the slide show.

Module Objectives

After completing this module, you will be able to:

- Use advanced formatting tools
- Insert and modify a picture
- Adjust and format text objects
- Customize animation effects

- Set advanced animation effects
- Use comments
- Combine reviewed presentations
- Insert Zoom links

Files You Will Need

IL_PPT_5-1.pptx

Support_PPT_5_Office_Group.jpg

Support_PPT_5_Review.pptx

IL_PPT_5-2.pptx

Support_PPT_5_TechRev.pptx

IL_PPT_5-3.pptx

IL_PPT_5-4.pptx

Support_PPT_5_Uganda.pptx

Use Advanced Formatting Tools

Learning Outcomes
- Apply 3D effects to objects
- Insert and modify connectors

With the advanced formatting tools available in PowerPoint, you can change the attributes of any object. You can format text and shapes using solid and texture fills, 3D effects, and shadows. To create a cohesive look on a slide with multiple objects, you can use the Format Painter to copy the attributes from one object and apply them to other objects. **CASE** ▶ *In this lesson, you draw and format a connector line on Slide 4 and then use the Format Painter to apply formatting to the connector line and to text on the slide.*

STEPS

1. **sam** ↓ **Start PowerPoint, open** IL_PPT_5-1.pptx **from the location where you store your Data Files, save the presentation as** IL_PPT_5_JCL, **then click** Slide 4 **in the Slides tab**

   Slide 4 appears in the Slide pane.

2. **Click the** arrow connector, **click the** Shape Format tab **on the Ribbon, click the** More button ⊡ **in the Shape Styles group, then click** Intense Line - Accent 2

   A gray theme style is added to the double-arrow connector line.

3. **Click the** Shape Effects button **in the Shape Styles group, point to** Glow, **then click** Glow: 8 point; Orange, Accent color 6 (last column, second row)

   An orange glow color is applied to the arrow connector line.

4. **Click a blank area of the slide, click the** Shapes button **in the Drawing group, then click the** Line Arrow: Double button ◥ **in the Lines section**

5. **Position** ✛ **on the** Supply shape connection site ◉ **as shown in** FIGURE 5-1, **press and hold the** left mouse button, **then drag** ✛ **to the right top-middle** ◉ **on the** Growth shape

   Green circle handles appear at each end of the connector line, indicating that it is attached to the two shapes. The connector line flows from the bottom left middle of the Supply shape to the top right middle of the Growth shape at a right diagonal.

6. **Click the** Home tab **on the Ribbon, click the** Trends to Supply connector arrow, **then click the** Format Painter button ◀ **in the Clipboard group**

   The pointer changes to ⬚ ♠. The Format Painter tool "picks up," or copies, attributes of an object and pastes them on the next object you select.

7. **Position** ⬚ ♠ **over the** Supply to Growth connector arrow, **click the** connector arrow, **then click a blank area of the slide**

   Both connector lines are formatted using the same theme style and glow effect.

8. **Click** Trends, **click the** Shape Format tab **on the Ribbon, click the** Text Effects button **in the WordArt Styles group, point to** Glow, **then click** Glow: 18 point; Orange, Accent color 6

   The Trends text in the shape is formatted with an orange glow text effect.

9. **Click the** Home tab **on the Ribbon, double-click** ◀ **in the Clipboard group, click** Supply, **click** Growth **in the rectangle shapes, then press ESC**

   Double-clicking the Format Painter button locks the Format Painter allowing you to apply the same formatting to multiple objects on the slide without having to reselect the tool.

10. **Click a blank area of the slide, then save your changes**

    Compare your screen with FIGURE 5-2.

FIGURE 5-1: Shape with connection sites displayed

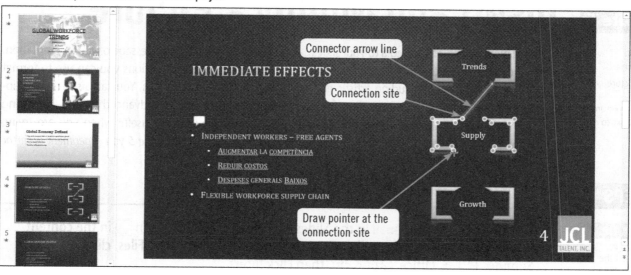

FIGURE 5-2: Formatted arrow connectors and shape text

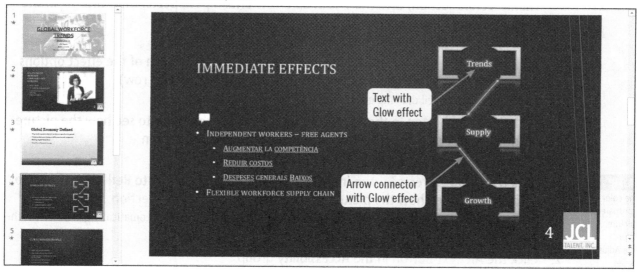

Creating columns in a text box

When the information you are working with fits better in a column format, you have the ability to format text into columns. Select the text object, click the Add or Remove Columns button in the Paragraph group on the Home tab, then click either One Column, Two Columns, Three Columns, or More Columns.

The More Columns option allows you to set up to 16 columns and customize the spacing between columns. You can display the ruler to set specific widths for the columns and further customize the columns.

Insert and Modify a Picture

**Learning
Outcomes**
• Apply picture
  effects
• Recolor a picture
• Add Alt text to a
  picture

Inserting pictures and other media to your slides can dynamically enhance the message of your presentation. When working with pictures in PowerPoint, you have a number of design options you can use to format pictures in creative ways, including artistic effects, recoloring, and border styles. You can also add descriptive text to a picture that can help those who are visually impaired. These advanced picture-formatting features can dramatically change how a picture appears, and they can be useful when you are trying to match the picture to other content in the presentation. **CASE** ▶ *On Slide 5 you experiment with the picture tools and accessibility features in PowerPoint.*

STEPS

QUICK TIP
To compress a
picture, select the
picture, click the
Compress Pictures
button in the Adjust
group, choose the
options you want,
then click OK.

1. **Click the** Slide 5 thumbnail **in the Slides tab, click the** Pictures icon 🖼 **in the content placeholder, navigate to the location where you store your Data Files, click** Support_PPT_5_Office_Group.jpg, **then click** Insert

   The picture fills the content placeholder and the Picture Format tab opens on the Ribbon.

2. **Click the** Picture Border button **in the Picture Styles group, point to** Weight, **then click** More Lines

   The Format Picture pane opens displaying border line style options.

3. **Click the** Solid line option button, **click the** Color button, **click** Orange, Accent 6 **in the Theme Colors section, click the** Width up arrow **until** 3 pt **appears, then click** ✕ **in the Format Picture pane**

   A three point orange border surrounds the picture.

4. **Click the** Artistic Effects button **in the Adjust group, point to each of the effect options to see how the picture changes, then click the** Pencil Sketch **(top row)**

   The picture has a pencil drawing quality now, as shown in FIGURE 5-3.

5. **Click the** Color button **in the Adjust group, point to each option to see how the picture changes, then click** Tan, Accent color 2 Dark **in the Recolor section**

   The picture is recolored with tan tones.

QUICK TIP
To make one color in
a picture transparent,
select the picture,
click the Color
button in the Adjust
group, click Set
Transparent Color,
then click the color
on the picture you
want to make
transparent.

6. **Click the** Picture Effects button **in the Picture Styles group, point to** Reflection, **point to each option to see how the picture changes, then click** Tight Reflection: Touching

   A reflection effect appears below the picture. Now edit the Alt text that was automatically generated for the picture using the Alt Text feature.

7. **Click the** Alt Text button **in the Accessibility group**

   The Alt Text pane opens. Use this pane to describe the picture for people who are visually impaired. Notice the automatically generated description of the picture.

8. **Click to the left of the word** people **in the text box, type** young, **press** SPACEBAR, **then click** ✕ **in the Alt Text pane**

   Text is edited and entered in the Alt Text pane providing a description of the picture.

9. **Click a blank area of the slide, then save your work**

   Compare your screen to FIGURE 5-4.

FIGURE 5-3: Pencil Sketch artistic effect applied to picture

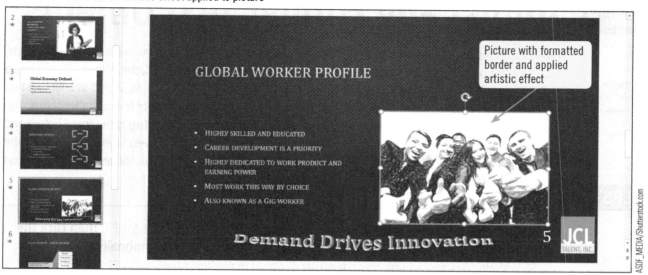

FIGURE 5-4: Color adjusted and reflection applied to picture

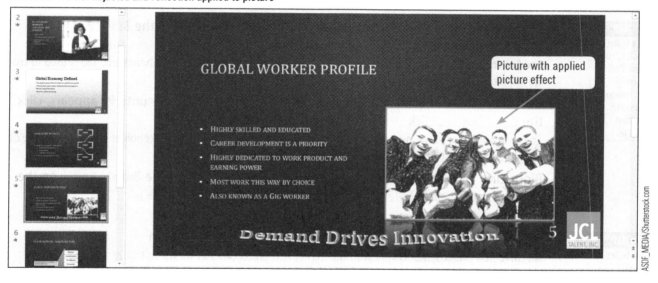

Using Paste Special

Paste Special is used to paste text or objects into PowerPoint using a specific format. For example, you may want to paste text as a picture or as plain text without formatting. Copy the text, or object, then in PowerPoint click the Home tab, click the Paste list arrow, click Paste Special, then select the appropriate format option. You can keep source formatting or apply the destination theme. You can also choose whether to embed or link an object or selected information from another program to PowerPoint using the Paste Special command. This technique is useful when you want to link part of an Excel worksheet or a chart from a workbook that contains both a worksheet and a chart. To link just the chart, open the Excel worksheet, then copy the chart. Leaving the Excel source file open, click the Paste list arrow, click Paste Special, click one of the Paste link options, then click OK.

Adjust and Format Text Objects

Having a consistent look in your presentation is important, so any changes you make to fonts or bullets, such as color or type, should be made to master text directly on the Slide Master. When you change a bullet type, you can use a character symbol, a picture, or an image that you have stored as a file. All text in PowerPoint is created within a text box that has space before and after lines of text or bullet points. You can modify this space between lines of text and paragraphs. **Paragraph spacing** is the space before and after paragraphs (bullet levels). **Leading** refers to the amount of space between lines of text within the same paragraph (bullet level). CASE ▶ *You decide to make a few formatting changes to the master text placeholder of your presentation.*

STEPS

1. **Press SHIFT, click the Normal button 🖿 on the status bar, release SHIFT, then click the Mesh Slide Master thumbnail (first thumbnail) in the Master Thumbnails pane**
   Slide Master view appears with the slide master displayed in the Slide pane.

2. **Right-click Edit Master Text Styles in the master text placeholder, point to the Numbering Arrow on the shortcut menu, then click 1. 2. 3.**
   The bullet for the first level of the master text placeholder changes to a number. You decide to modify the bullets further.

3. **Right-click Second Level in the master text placeholder, point to the Bullets Arrow on the shortcut menu, then click Bullets and Numbering**
   The Bullets and Numbering dialog box opens. The Bulleted tab is selected; the Numbered tab is used to create sequentially numbered or lettered bullets.

4. **Click the Hollow Square Bullets option, click the Size down arrow until 90 appears, click the Color button, click Orange, Accent 5, then click OK**
   The style and color of the new bullet in the second level of the master text placeholder changes. The size of the bullet is decreased to 90% of the size of the second-level text.

5. **Right-click Third Level in the master text placeholder, point to the Bullets Arrow on the shortcut menu, click Bullets and Numbering, then click Customize**
   The Symbol dialog box opens.

6. **Click the Double Dagger symbol ‡, click OK, then click OK again**
   All three new bullet symbols appear in the master text placeholder as shown in FIGURE 5-5.

7. **Click 🖿 on the status bar, click the Slide 2 thumbnail in the Slides tab, click the Global Trends text object, move the pointer over the text object border until it changes to ⇕, then click the border**
   The text object is selected and surrounded by a solid line border.

8. **Click the Line Spacing button ⸬▾ in the Paragraph group, then click 1.5**
   The space or leading between lines of text within the same bullet point increases to 1.5.

9. **Click ⸬▾ in the Paragraph group, click Line Spacing Options to open the Paragraph dialog box, click the Before up arrow in the Spacing section until 6 pt appears, click the After up arrow in the Spacing section until 18 pt appears, click OK, then save your work**
   The spacing before and after each bullet on Slide 2 changes. Compare your screen to FIGURE 5-6.

Working with Advanced Tools

FIGURE 5-5: **New bullets applied to the Slide Master**

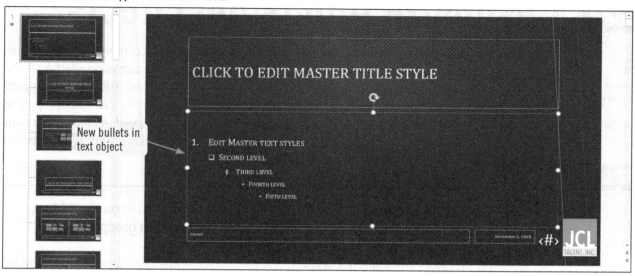

FIGURE 5-6: **Text object with changed paragraph and line spacing**

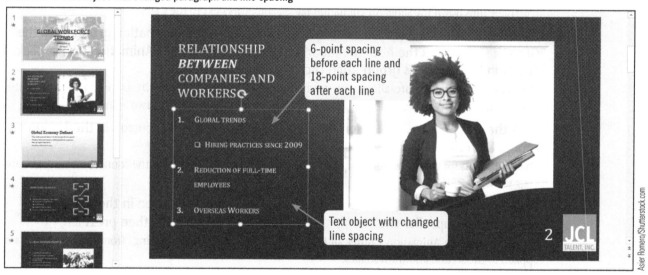

Changing text direction and margin space

Using the Text Direction button in the Paragraph group on the Home tab, you can change the direction of text and the margin space in a text object or shape. There are four text direction options available: Horizontal, Rotate all text 90°, Rotate all text 270°, and Stacked. The Horizontal option is the standard default text direction for all text in PowerPoint. The Rotate all text 90° text direction rotates text so it faces the right margin of a text object or shape. The Rotate all text 270° text direction rotates text so it faces the left margin of a text object or shape. The Stacked text direction stacks letters vertically on top of one another. Margins in a text object or shape determine the space between the edge of text and the edges of the text box. Click the Text Direction button, then click More Options to open the Format Shape pane. Four margin options are available to modify: Left margin, Right margin, Top margin, and Bottom margin.

PowerPoint

Customize Animation Effects

Learning Outcomes
- Apply multiple animations to an object
- Change animation order

Animating objects allows you to control how information flows and how objects move on the slide during a slide show. The simplest way to animate an object is to apply a standard animation effect from the Animation group on the Animations tab. There are additional entrance, emphasis, exit, and motion path animation effects available through the menu at the bottom of the Animation gallery that you can apply to objects. You can customize effect options including starting time, direction, and speed. And when you want to copy animation settings from one object to another, you can use the Animation Painter. **CASE** ▶ *You decide to animate the shapes and connector lines you created on Slide 4.*

STEPS

1. **Click the Slide 4 thumbnail in the Slides tab, click the Animations tab on the Ribbon, click the Growth shape, click the More button ⬇ in the Animation group, then click More Entrance Effects at the bottom of the gallery**

   The Change Entrance Effect dialog box opens. Effects are grouped by categories: Basic, Subtle, Moderate, and Exciting.

2. **Click Flip in the Exciting section, click OK, click the Duration up arrow in the Timing group until 01.50 appears in the text box, then click the Preview button in the Preview group**

   The shape flips down the slide. An animation tag ⬛1 appears next to the shape.

3. **Click the Growth to Supply connector line, click Wipe in the Animation group, click the Growth shape, click the Add Animation button in the Advanced Animation group, click Teeter in the Emphasis group, then click the Preview button**

   The Add Animation feature allows you to apply multiple animations to the same object. Notice the Animation tag 3 ⬛3 appears beside ⬛1 , which indicates the shape now has two animations.

4. **Click the Animation tag 2 ⬛2 on the slide, click the Move Later button in the Timing group, then click the Preview button**

   The animations for the shape now run consecutively before the animation for the connector line. Compare your screen to FIGURE 5-7.

5. **Click the Growth shape, double-click the Animation Painter button in the Advanced Animation group, click the Supply shape, click the Trends shape, then press ESC**

   When you use the Animation Painter all the animations and animation settings from the first shape are applied to the second and third shapes.

6. **Click the Growth to Supply connector line, click the Delay up arrow in the Timing group until 00.50 appears, then click the Preview button**

   The connector line's animation start time changes.

7. **With the connector line still selected, click the Animation Painter button in the Advanced Animation group, click the Supply to Trends connector line, then click the Preview button**

   Now both connector lines have the same animation and animation settings. The Supply to Trends connector line needs to play before the Trends shape.

8. **With the connector line still selected, click the Move Earlier button twice in the Timing group, click the Preview button, then save your changes**

   Compare your screen to FIGURE 5-8.

FIGURE 5-7: Animation effects applied to the objects

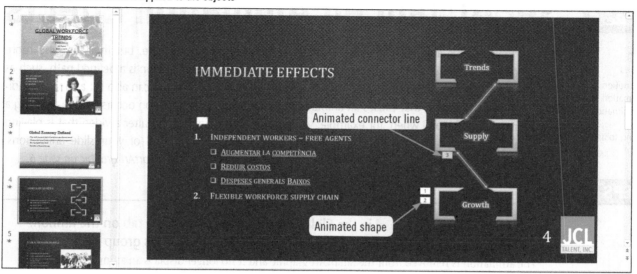

FIGURE 5-8: Completed animation effects

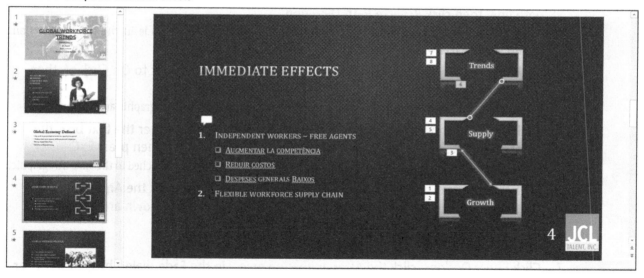

Understanding animation start timings

Each animated object on a slide has a starting time in relation to the other animated objects. There are three different starting time options: Start On Click, Start With Previous, and Start After Previous. The Start On Click timing option starts the animation effect when you click the mouse. The Start With Previous timing option begins the animation effect at the same time as the previous effect in the animation list, so two or more animation effects play at once. The Start After Previous timing option begins the animation immediately after the previous animation without clicking the mouse.

Set Advanced Animation Effects

Learning
Outcomes
• Apply a motion
  path animation
• Add an animation
  trigger
• Add sound to an
  animation

Most of PowerPoint's animation effects are simple actions like float in or fade, but there are also more advanced motion path effects that bring objects to life. A motion path animation is a defined path, such as a straight line or a loop, or a customized path that you draw on the slide. You can also set a special condition, known as a **trigger**, that causes an animation to play after a specific action occurs, such as clicking a shape. Triggers are helpful when, for example, you want an animation to play after a video that is playing during a slide show reaches a bookmark. Triggers allow you be in control of your slide animations.

CASE ⟩ *You add motion path animations, sound effects, and triggers to the SmartArt graphic on slide 6.*

STEPS

1. **Click the** Slide 6 thumbnail **in the Slides tab, click the** Animations tab **on the Ribbon, click the** SmartArt graphic, **then click the** None **in the Animations group**
   The animation is removed from the SmartArt graphic and it no longer displays an animation tag.

2. **Click the** More button ⊡ **in the Animation group, then click** Turns **in the Motion Paths section**
   The SmartArt graphic animates and a turn motion path object appears on the SmartArt graphic.

3. **Click the** Effect Options button **in the Animation group, click** Up, **right-click the** motion path line, **then click** Reverse Path Direction
   The SmartArt graphic now starts its animation up and moves down the slide in the reverse direction. Compare your screen to FIGURE 5-9.

4. **Click the** Trigger button **in the Advanced Animation group, point to** On Click of, **then click** TextBox 2
   The text box next to the SmartArt graphic is now the trigger for the SmartArt graphic animation.

5. **Click the** Slide Show view button ⊡ **in the status bar, move** ↳ **over the text box, the pointer changes to** 🖑, **click the** text box, **watch the animation, then press** ESC
   Clicking the text box in Slide Show view triggers the motion path animation attached to the SmartArt graphic.

6. **Click the** title text object, **click** Fade **in the Animation group, click the** Animation Pane button **in the Advanced Animation group, then click the** Title 1 down arrow **shown in** FIGURE 5-10
   The animation will dim the text on the slide as part of the animation.

7. **Click** Effect Options, **click the** After animation arrow **in the Fade dialog box, click the far right** color cell, **click the** Sound arrow, **scroll down the list, click** Chime, **then click** OK
   A chime sound now plays during the animation and the title text dims to an orange color when the animation finishes.

8. **Click the** Animation Pane Close button ✕, **click** ⊡ **on the status bar, click the** slide **twice, click the** text box, **press** ESC, **then save your changes**
   All the animations play during the slide show.

FIGURE 5-9: Motion path animation effect applied to SmartArt graphic

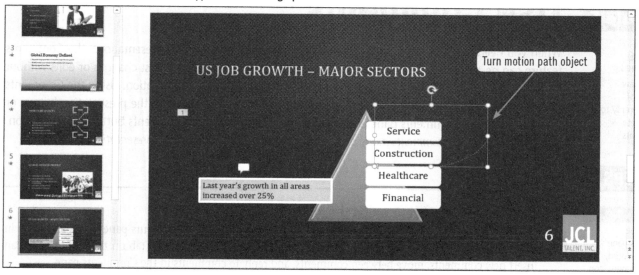

FIGURE 5-10: Slide with open Animation Pane

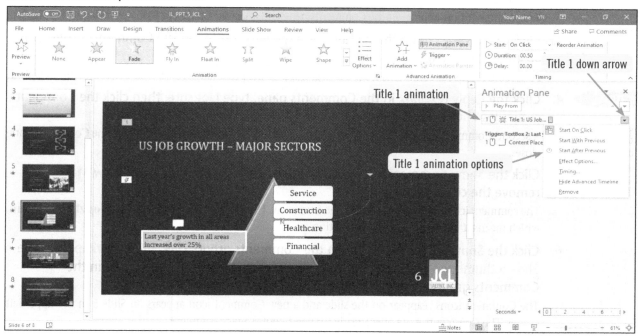

Animating objects with a custom motion path

Motion path animations provide you with a number of unique animations all of which follow a defined path, such as a loop, an arc, or a line. For a complete list of motion path animations click More Motion Paths at the bottom of the Animation gallery. If none of the defined motion paths provide the desired result, then you can draw a custom path. Custom motion paths can have both freeform and straight lines. Open the Animation gallery, then click Custom Path in the Motion Paths section. Drag ╋ to create a freeform motion path line or point and click ╋ to create a straight motion path line, then when you are finished, double-click the mouse. To change the route of the motion path, right-click the animation object, click Edit Points, then drag edit points as desired.

Use Comments

Learning Outcomes
• Add a new comment
• Review, reply to, and delete comments

When you need to review a presentation or when working with others on presentations, the Comments feature can be a useful tool to communicate ideas. Using comments to suggest changes or edits without disturbing the original content is an efficient way to collaborate on a presentation. Using the Comments Pane you can insert, reply, move between, and manage comments placed in the presentation by you or someone else. The Comments pane is easily accessible by clicking the Comments button on the Ribbon.

CASE ► *You review comments made by a colleague and add your own to the presentation.*

STEPS

1. **Click the Comments button on the Ribbon**

   The Comments icon indicates there is a comment on the slide. The Comments pane opens as shown in FIGURE 5-11. You can also access the Comments features through the Review tab on the Ribbon. You can insert new comments, move between comments, and reply to comments in the Comments pane.

2. **Click the Reply text box in the Comments pane, type Verified by marketing dept., then click the Next button 🗩 in the Comments pane**

   Your comment now appears in the Comments pane and a second Comment icon appears on the slide.

3. **Click the Review tab on the Ribbon, click the Next button in the Comments group until an alert box appears, then click Continue in the alert box**

   PowerPoint looks for comments from the beginning of the presentation and finds the comment on Slide 4.

4. **Click the Reply text box in the Comments pane, type Not sure, then click the Comments pane Close button ✕**

   A second Comment icon appears just behind the first Comment icon on the slide and the Comments pane closes.

5. **Click the Show Comments arrow in the Comments group, then click Show Markup to remove the checkmark**

   The comment icons are turned off or hidden from view. The Show Markup command is a **toggle command**, which means it has an on and an off position.

6. **Click the Show Comments arrow in the Comments group, click Show Markup, click the Slide 5 thumbnail in the Slides tab, then click the New Comment button in the Comments group**

   The Comment icons reappear on the slide and a new Comment icon appears on Slide 5 in the upper left corner. The Comments pane opens ready for you to enter a new comment.

7. **Type Is this list complete?, then click the Previous button in the Comments group**

   A new comment is placed on Slide 5 and Slide 4 appears with your previous comment open.

8. **Click Not sure in the Comment text box, then type Yes, Spanish and French**

   The comment is edited as shown in FIGURE 5-12.

9. **Click the Comments button on the Ribbon to close the Comments pane, then save your work**

FIGURE 5-11: Slide with open Comments pane

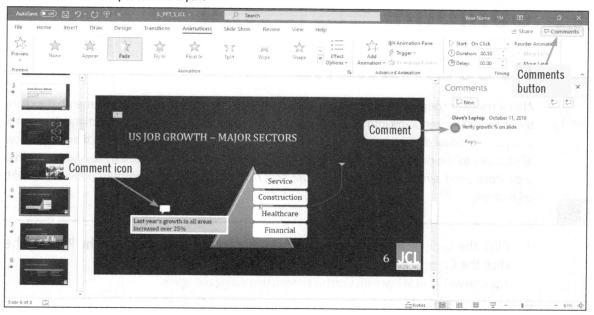

FIGURE 5-12: Edited comment in Comments pane

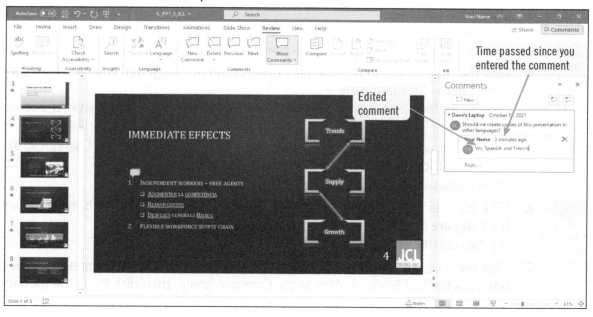

Replacing text and fonts

As you review your presentation, you may decide to replace certain text or fonts throughout the entire presentation using the Replace command. Text can be a word, phrase, or sentence. To replace specific text, click the Home tab on the Ribbon, then click the Replace button in the Editing group. In the Replace dialog box, enter the text you want to replace, then enter the text you want to use as its replacement.

You can also use the Replace command to replace one font for another. Simply click the Replace button list arrow in the Editing group, then click Replace Fonts to open the Replace Font dialog box. Finally, if you just want to find a word in your presentation, click the Find button in the Editing group, enter the word you want to find in the Find dialog box, then click Find Next.

PowerPoint

Combine Reviewed Presentations

Learning Outcomes
- Accept or reject changes from a reviewer
- Add and rename a section

After a reviewer completes reviewing your presentation and sends it back, you can merge the changes in the reviewer's presentation into your original presentation using the Compare command. You can accept or reject individual changes, changes by slides, changes by reviewer if there is more than one reviewer, or all changes to the presentation. **CASE** *You sent the presentation to a colleague who has reviewed the presentation and sent it back to you. You are now ready to combine the reviewed presentation with your original one.*

STEPS

1. **Click the Slide 1 thumbnail in the Slides tab, click the Review tab on the Ribbon, then click the Compare button in the Compare group**

   The Choose File to Merge with Current Presentation dialog box opens.

2. **Navigate to the location where you store your Data Files, click Support_PPT_5_Review.pptx, then click Merge**

   The reviewed presentation is merged with your original one, and the Revisions pane opens showing the reviewer's changes. Slide 2 is selected because it is the first slide with a change as shown in FIGURE 5-13.

QUICK TIP

To accept changes in the whole presentation, click the Accept button arrow in the Compare group, then click Accept All Changes to the Presentation.

3. **Click the All changes to Content Placeholder 2 check box, then review the changes in the text object**

   The change icon and both check boxes now have check marks indicating the changes are accepted.

4. **Click the Next button in the Compare group, read the suggested changes, then click SLIDES in the Revisions pane**

   Choosing the Slides option in the Revisions pane allows you to see changes the reviewer made to your original slide.

5. **Click the Accept button arrow in the Compare group, click Accept All Changes to This Slide, then click the Next button in the Compare group**

   All the changes on Slide 3 are accepted and Slide 5 appears with more changes.

QUICK TIP

To reject changes in the whole presentation, click the Reject button arrow, then click Reject All Changes to the Presentation.

6. **Click the Your Name check box in the Revisions pane, click the Reject button arrow in the Compare group, then click Reject All Changes to This Slide**

   The changes to the text object are rejected.

7. **Click the Next button twice in the Compare group, click Cancel in the message dialog box, click the End Review button in the Compare group, then click Yes in the message dialog box**

   The Revisions pane closes and applied changes are made. To help organize your presentation, you decide to create a section.

8. **Click the Slide 1 thumbnail in the Slides tab, click the Home tab on the Ribbon, click the Section button in the Slides group, then click Add Section**

   A section heading appears in the Slides tab above the Slide 1 thumbnail as shown in FIGURE 5-14.

9. **Type Intro in the Rename Section dialog box, click Rename, then save your work**

   The new section name appears in the Slides tab above Slide 1.

FIGURE 5-13: Open Revisions pane showing reviewer's changes

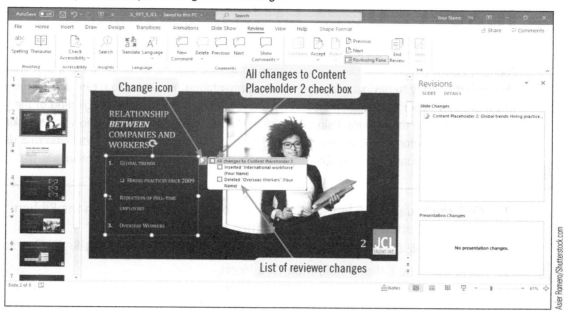

FIGURE 5-14: Slides tab showing new section

Changing page setup

When you need to customize the size of the slides in your presentation, you can do so using the Slide Size command in the Customize group on the Design tab. Click the Slide Size button to change the slide size to Widescreen (16:9) or Standard (4:3), or click Custom Slide Size to open the Slide Size dialog box. In the Slide Size dialog box, you can change the width and height of the slides to 13 different settings, including On-screen Show, Letter Paper, 35mm Slides, and Banner. You can also set a custom slide size by specifying the height and width of the slides.

PowerPoint

Insert Zoom Links

Learning
Outcomes
• Insert a Slide
Zoom
• Insert Summary
Zoom

If you want to creatively present information in a non-linear way during a slide show, you can create a Zoom. A **Zoom** is a link that allows you to jump to specific slides or sections during a slide show. Zoom gives you the ability to navigate anywhere in the presentation. You can also create a **Summary Zoom**, which organizes your presentation into sections and adds a new slide to the beginning of the presentation that displays all the sections. Using the Summary Zoom slide during a slide show you can skip around or revisit specific information as you like. **CASE** ▷ *In this lesson you create Zoom links to a slide and a section and then create a Summary Zoom, which adds a new section to the presentation.*

STEPS

1. **Click the** Slide 3 thumbnail **in the Slides tab, click the** Insert tab **on the Ribbon, click the** Zoom button **in the Links group, then click** Slide Zoom

   The Insert Slide Zoom dialog box opens with the eight slides in the presentation displayed as thumbnails.

2. **Click the** Slide 8 thumbnail, **then click** Insert

   A Zoom link of Slide 8 appears on the slide as shown in FIGURE 5-15. This thumbnail is the link that you click during a slide show to jump to Slide 8.

3. **Drag the** Zoom link **to the lower center of the slide, click the** Zoom tab **on the Ribbon, then click the** Return to Zoom check box **in the Zoom Options group**

   A Zoom link is created between Slides 3 and 8.

4. **Click the** Slide Show button ⌨ **on the status bar, click the** Slide 8 Zoom link, **press** ENTER, **then press** ESC

   The Zoom link jumps you from Slide 3 to Slide 8 and back again.

5. **Click the** Insert tab **on the Ribbon, click the** Zoom button **in the Links group, then click** Summary Zoom

   The Insert Summary Zoom dialog box opens with the Slide 1 thumbnail selected.

6. **Click the** Slide 4 thumbnail, **click the** Slide 7 thumbnail, **then click** Insert

   Each slide thumbnail selected in the Insert Summary Zoom dialog box creates a new section. A new summary slide with each section Zoom link is displayed in the Slide pane. Compare your screen to FIGURE 5-16.

7. **Click** ⌨ **on the status bar, click the** Slide 2 Zoom link, **press** ENTER **until the summary slide appears again, then press** ESC

   You viewed the slides in the Intro section and then jumped back to the summary slide.

8. **Click** ⌨ **on the status bar, watch the** Slide 5 and the Slide 8 Zoom links, **then press** ESC **to return to Normal view**

9. **Click the** Intro Collapse Section arrow ◢ **in the Slides tab, right-click** Intro **in the Slides tab, click** Move Section Up, **then click a blank area of the slide**

   The Intro section and associated slides move up above the Summary Section.

10. **sam** ↑ **Save your work, submit your presentation to your instructor, then exit PowerPoint**

FIGURE 5-15: Slide showing new Zoom slide

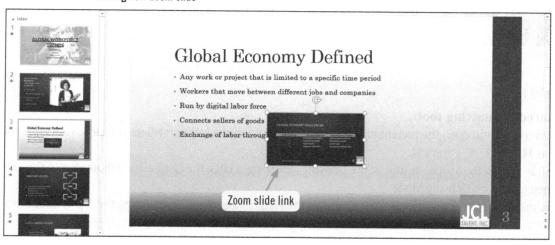

FIGURE 5-16: New Summary Section slide

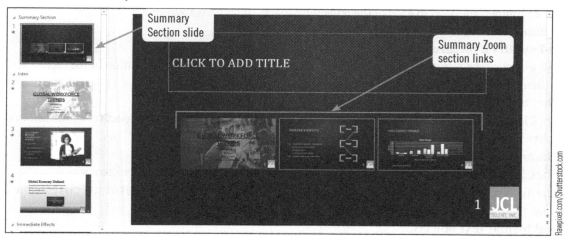

Dictating text on a slide

If you have a microphone and the Dictate feature is available in the Voice group on the Home tab, you can dictate text in text objects. Click in a text object where you want to begin dictating, click the Dictate button in the Voice group, then speak clearly into the microphone. When you are finished speaking, click the Dictate button again to turn off the feature. Using specific words and phrases, such as "comma" or "period," you can add punctuation to your text. Finally, if you want to dictate text in another (supported) language, click the Dictate button arrow, then select a language.

Practice

Skills Review

1. Use advanced formatting tools.

a. Start PowerPoint and open the presentation IL_PPT_5-2.pptx from the location where you store your Data Files, then save it as **IL_PPT_5_Powell**.

b. Go to Slide 3, click the Shapes button in the Drawing group, right-click the Connector: Elbow icon in the Lines section, then click Lock Drawing Mode.

c. Position the pointer over the left connection site on the Plant shape, then drag down to the top connection site on the Distribution Centers shape.

d. Position the pointer over the right connection site on the Plant shape, drag to the top connection site on the Consumer Sales shape, then press ESC.

e. Click the orange dotted line, click the Home tab, double-click the Format Painter button in the Clipboard group, click both elbow connector lines, then press ESC.

f. Double-click the text Plant in the circle shape, click the Shape Format tab, click the Text Effects button in the WordArt Styles group, point to Glow, then click Glow: 18 point; Gold, Accent color 3.

g. Click the Home tab, double-click the Format Painter button in the Clipboard group, click the text Distribution, Centers, Consumer, and Sales in each of the remaining shapes, then press ESC.

h. Click a blank area of the slide, then save the presentation.

2. Insert and modify a picture.

a. Go to Slide 5, click the picture, click the Picture Format tab, click the Picture Border button in the Picture Styles group, then click Orange under Standard Colors.

b. Click the Picture Border button, point to Weight, then click 4½ pt.

c. Click the Picture Effects button in the Picture Styles group, point to Shadow, click Perspective: Upper Left under Perspective.

d. Click the Artistic Effects button in the Adjust group, then click Cement (fourth row).

e. Click the Color button in the Adjust group, then click Aqua, Accent color 1 Dark under Recolor.

f. Click the Alt Text button in the Accessibility group, type **Picture of face as digital circuits**, close the Alt Text pane, then save your changes.

3. Adjust and format text objects.

a. Go to Slide 2, click the View tab, click the Slide Master button in the Master Views group, then click the Headlines Slide Master slide in the Master Thumbnails pane.

b. Right-click the Second level text, point to the Numbering arrow, then click 1) 2) 3).

c. Right-click Edit Master text styles, point to the Bullets arrow, then click Bullets and Numbering.

d. Click Arrow Bullets, click the Size up arrow until 110 appears in the text box, click the Color button, click Aqua, Accent 1 in the Theme Colors section, then click OK.

e. Right-click Third level, point to the Bullets arrow, click Bullets and Numbering, then click Customize.

f. Click the Fraction Slash symbol, click OK, then click OK again.

g. Close Slide Master view, right-click Baltimore, click Paragraph, click the Before down arrow until 0 pt appears, click the After up arrow until 6 pt appears, then click OK.

h. Click Philadelphia, click the Home tab, click the Line Spacing button in the Paragraph group, then click 1.5.

i. Save your changes.

Skills Review (continued)

4. **Customize animation effects.**

   a. Go to Slide 3.

   b. Click the Animations tab, click the Plant shape, click the More button in the Animation group, then click Shape in the Entrance section.

   c. Select the left elbow connector, click the More button in the Animation group, click More Entrance Effects, apply the Strips animation, click OK, then click the Duration up arrow until 1.00 appears.

   d. Click the left elbow arrow connector, click the Animation Painter button, then click the right elbow connector.

   e. Click the Effects Options button, click Right Down, then click the Preview button.

   f. Select the Distribution Centers shape, apply the Shape animation, click the Effect Options button in the Animation group, then click Diamond.

   g. Click the Move Earlier button in the Timing group, then click the Preview button.

   h. Use the Animation Painter to apply the Distribution Centers shape animation to the Consumer Sales shape, then click the Preview button.

   i. Select the dotted line between the Distribution Centers shape and the Consumer Sales shape, click Split in the Animation group, click the Delay button up arrow until 01.00 appears, then click the Duration up arrow until 01.00 appears.

   j. Click the Add Animation button, click Split, change the Effect Options to Vertical Out, click the Preview button, then save your changes.

5. **Set advanced animation effects.**

   a. Go to Slide 5, click the title text, apply the Swivel animation, then click the Animation Pane button in the Advanced Animation group.

   b. Click the Rectangle 2 animation down arrow in the Animation Pane, click Effect Options, click the After animation arrow, click the far right purple color, then click OK.

   c. Select the picture, click None in Animation group, click the More button in the Animation group, scroll down if necessary, then click Shapes in the Motion Paths section.

   d. Click the Effect Options button in the Animation group, then click Reverse Path Direction under Path.

   e. Click the Content Placeholder animation arrow in the Animation Pane, click Effect Options, click the Sound list arrow, scroll down, click Whoosh, then click OK.

   f. Close the Animation Pane, click the Trigger button in the Advanced Animation group, point to On Click of, then click Text Placeholder 4.

   g. Click the Slide Show button in the status bar, click the text object to trigger the picture animation, click through the title text object animation, then press ESC.

   h. Click a blank area of the slide, then save your changes.

6. **Use comments.**

   a. Go to Slide 1, click the Review tab, then click the Show Comments button in the Comments group.

   b. Click the Next button in the Comments pane, reply to the comment by typing **We should ask Brian**, click the Next button in the Comments pane until Slide 3 appears, then type **Thank you** in the comment Reply text box.

   c. Click the Previous button in the Comments pane until Slide 2 appears, select the text box with your comment, then type **or Jeri** at the end of your comment in the text box.

   d. Click the New button in the Comments pane, type **Can you check on distribution?**, click the Next button in the Comments group until Slide 4 appears.

   e. Click the Delete button in the Comments group, close the Comments pane, then go to Slide 3.

   f. Click the comment icon, click the Show Comments arrow in the Comments group, click Show Markup, click the Show Comments arrow again, then click Show Markup.

   g. Save your work.

7. **Combine reviewed presentations.**

   a. Go to Slide 1, click the Review tab, click the Compare button in the Compare group, navigate to the location where you store your Data Files, click **Support_PPT 5_TechRev.pptx**, then click **Merge**.

   b. Click the Accept arrow in the Compare group, then click Accept All Changes to This Slide.

   c. Click the Reject arrow in the Compare group, click Reject All Changes to This Slide, then click the Next button in the Compare group until Slide 3 appears.

   d. Click the Inserted "Direct" check box on the Consumer Sales shape, then click the Next button in the Compare group, then end the review.

   e. Go to Slide 1, click the Home tab, click the Section button in the Slides group, then click Add Section.

   f. Type **Intro Slide**, click Rename, then save your work.

8. **Insert Zoom links.**

   a. Go to Slide 2, click the Insert tab, click the Zoom button in the Links group, then click Slide Zoom.

   b. Click the Slide 4 thumbnail, click Insert, click the Zoom tab, then click the Return to Zoom check box in the Zoom Options group.

   c. Drag the Zoom link to the left just under the slide title, click the Slide Show button on the status bar, click the Zoom link, click again, then press ESC.

   d. Click the Insert tab, click the Zoom button in the Links group, then click Summary Zoom.

   e. Click the Slide 2 thumbnail, click the Slide 4 thumbnail, then click Insert.

   f. Scroll down the Slides tab, right-click the Quarterly Sales Report section in the Slides tab, then click Move Section Up.

   g. Go to Slide 1, then click the Slide Show button on the status bar.

   h. Click each section Zoom link, then press ESC when you are finished. Be sure to click through animations in each section Zoom link and the animation trigger on Latest Technology slide.

   i. Click the Intro Slide section Collapse Section arrow in the Slides tab, click the Intro Slide section Expand Section arrow in the Slides tab, then save your work.

   j. Submit your presentation to your instructor, close the presentation, then exit PowerPoint.

Independent Challenge 1

Riverwalk Medical Clinic (RMC), is a large medical facility in Cambridge Massachusetts. You continue to work on a presentation on the latest emergency response procedures for a staff training later in the week.

   a. Open the presentation IL_PPT_5-3.pptx from the location where you store your Data Files, then save it as **IL_PPT_5_RiverwalkMC**.

   b. Go to Slide 3, draw two Connector: Curved Double-Arrows (one between the left and the middle shape and one between the middle and the right shape).

   c. Select the left arrow, click the Shape Format tab, apply the Intense Line - Accent 2 style, then use the Format Painter to apply the new style to the right arrow.

   d. Select the text "CPR" in the left shape, click the Shape Format tab, then apply the text effect Glow: 18 point; Gold, Accent color 1.

   e. Use the Format Painter to apply the text effect in the CPR shape to the text in the other two shapes. (*Hint*: double-click the Format Painter to apply formatting to more than one item.)

   f. Go to Slide 5, apply a 3 pt Gold, Accent 1 picture border to the picture, then apply a Grayscale color to the picture.

   g. Apply the Round bevel picture effect to the picture, then apply the artistic effect Mosaic Bubbles to the picture.

   h. Click the Alt Text button, type **A picture containing a doctor** (some existing text may be present in the Alt Text pane, if so edit the text), then close the Alt Text pane.

   i. Insert three comments on the slides, use the Next and Previous buttons in the Comments group to move between comments, then edit one of your comments.

Independent Challenge 1 (continued)

j. Use the Show Comments button in the Comments group to hide comments and then show comments.

k. Insert a Zoom link on Slide 3 to Slide 7, move the Zoom link to a blank area of the slide, apply the option Return to Zoom to the link, then in Slide Show view watch the link.

l. Go to Slide 1, open the Insert Summary Zoom dialog box, click the Slide 3 thumbnail and the Slide 6 thumbnail, click Insert, then in the Slides tab move the Summary Section up.

m. Rename the Default Section in the Slides tab to Intro Slides, then collapse the Intro Slides section.

n. Save the presentation, then submit your presentation to your instructor.

o. Close the presentation and exit PowerPoint.

Independent Challenge 2

You are an assistant at International Solutions Inc., a company that works with government agencies in countries throughout the world to solve basic infrastructure problems, such as potable drinking water or agriculture production. You continue working on a presentation that you have been developing for an upcoming meeting with a delegation from Uganda.

a. Open the presentation IL_PPT_5-4.pptx from the location where you store your Data Files, then save it as **IL_PPT_5_Solutions**.

b. Open Slide Master view, click the Parcel Slide Master thumbnail, change the bullet in the first-level indent level to an arrow bullet 95% of text size, then change the bullet color to Aqua, Accent 1.

c. Change the second-level bullet to the a. b. c. bullet format, change the third-level bullet to the Double Dagger symbol, then close Slide Master view.

d. Go to Slide 9, press SHIFT, click anywhere in the text object, release SHIFT, click the Home tab, then apply a 2.0 line spacing to the text object.

e. Go to Slide 6, drag to select the four second-level bullet points, right-click the selected text, click Paragraph, then change the paragraph before spacing to 18 pt and the paragraph after spacing to 12 pt.

f. Go to Slide 5, click the Animations tab, remove the animation applied to the SmartArt graphic, then apply the Arcs motion path animation to the graphic.

g. Apply a 01.00 delay to the SmartArt graphic animation, add the Teeter animation as a second animation to the SmartArt graphic, then apply a trigger to the animation using the slide number placeholder.

h. Apply a Fade animation to the title text object, apply a dim after animation effect with a red color, then move the title text object animation so it happens first.

i. Use the Animation Painter to apply the title text object animation to all the slides in the presentation, except Slide 1.

j. Click the Review tab, merge your presentation with the presentation Support_PPT_5_Uganda.pptx, then accept all changes on Slide 2.

k. Use the Next button to move to the next change on Slide 6, accept the change on the slide, reject the change, then end your review.

l. Create one section, rename the new section, save the presentation, then submit your presentation to your instructor.

m. Close the presentation and exit PowerPoint.

Visual Workshop

Create a new presentation with slides that looks like the examples in FIGURE 5-17 and FIGURE 5-18. Locate and insert the picture Support_PPT_5_Office_Group.jpg on Slide 1. Close the Design Ideas pane if it opens. Then format the picture with a Rose, Accent 6, Darker 25% border that is 3 pt wide. Apply the picture effect Glow: 18 point; Rose, Accent color 6 to the picture. Review the Alt text that was applied and make any edits you believe are appropriate. On Slide 2 draw the shapes, format them with the shape style Moderate Effect—Rose, Accent 6, then apply a Tight Reflection: 8 point offset. Between shapes draw connector arrows using the Connector: Elbow Arrow, format them with the Single Arrow—Dark 1 shape style, then change the weight of the arrows to 3 pt. Use the Format Painter to apply the formatting objects. Add your name to the slide footer, then save the presentation as **IL_PPT_5_Process**. Submit your presentation to your instructor, then exit PowerPoint.

FIGURE 5-17

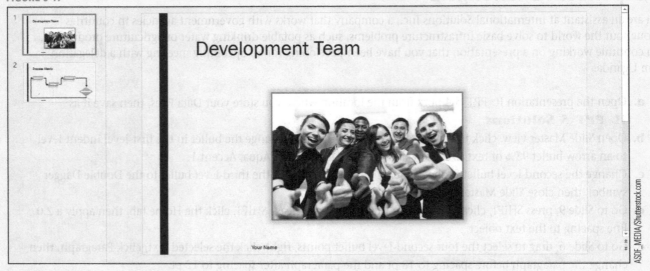

FIGURE 5-18

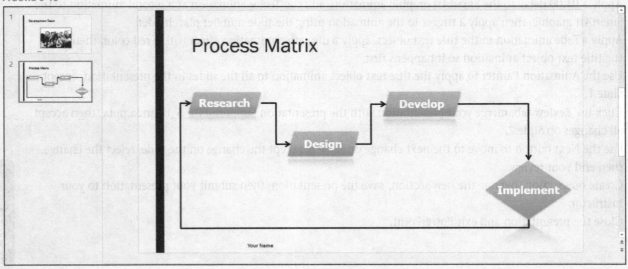

Enhancing Charts and Tables

CASE ▶ In this module, you continue to work on the global workforce project presentation for JCL Talent. You will focus on the slides that include charts and tables. You customize the chart layout, format chart elements, and create a custom table. To present the work done by the finance team, you embed an Excel chart, and then you link an Excel worksheet to the presentation so the presentation will always have the most recent data.

Module Objectives

After completing this module, you will be able to:

- Insert text from Microsoft Word
- Change chart design and style
- Customize a chart
- Modify chart elements
- Embed an Excel chart

- Link an Excel worksheet
- Create a custom table
- Modify data in a table
- Add effects to table data

Files You Will Need

IL_PPT_6-1.pptx	Support_PPT_6_Balance.xlsx
Support_PPT_6_Outline.docx	IL_PPT_6-3.pptx
Support_PPT_6_International.xlsx	Support_PPT_6_EMS.docx
Support_PPT_6_Account.xlsx	IL_PPT_6-4.pptx
IL_PPT_6-2.pptx	Support_PPT_6_G1.xlsx
Support_PPT_6_Alpine.docx	Support_PPT_6_G2.xlsx
Support_PPT_6_Chart.xlsx	Support_PPT_6_Trac.xlsx

Insert Text from Microsoft Word

It is easy to insert documents saved in Microsoft Word format (.docx), Rich Text Format (.rtf), plain text format (.txt), and HTML format (.htm) into a PowerPoint presentation. If you have an outline saved in a document file, you can import it into PowerPoint to create a new presentation or create additional slides in an existing presentation. When you import a document into a presentation, PowerPoint creates an outline structure based on the styles in the document. For example, a Heading 1 style in the Word document becomes a slide title, and a Heading 2 style becomes the first level of text in a bulleted list. If you insert a plain text format document into a presentation, PowerPoint creates an outline based on the tabs at the beginning of the document's paragraphs. Paragraphs without tabs become slide titles, and paragraphs with one tab indent become first-level text in bulleted lists. **CASE** ▶ *You have a Microsoft Word document with information that you want to insert into your presentation.*

STEPS

1. **sam ↓ Start PowerPoint, open the presentation IL_PPT_6-1.pptx from the location where you store your Data Files, save it as IL_PPT_6_JCL, click the View tab on the Ribbon, then click the Outline View button in the Presentation Views group**

2. **Click the Slide 8 icon ☐ in the Outline pane, click the Home tab on the Ribbon, click the New Slide button arrow in the Slides group, then click Slides from Outline**

   Slide 8 appears in the Slide pane. The Insert Outline dialog box opens. Before you insert an outline into a presentation, you need to determine where you want the new slides to be placed. You want the text from the Word document inserted as new slides after Slide 8.

3. **Navigate to the location where you store your Data Files, click the Word document file Support_PPT_6_Outline.docx, then click Insert**

   Two new slides (9 and 10) are added to the presentation, and the new Slide 9 appears in the Slide pane. Notice, the Notes pane automatically opens by default when you display your presentation in Outline view, as shown in **FIGURE 6-1**. The two new slides retain formatting from the Word document and need to be set to default format settings.

4. **Scroll down the Outline pane until Slide 10 appears, press and hold SHIFT, click the Slide 10 ☐, release SHIFT, then click the Reset button in the Slides group**

   The new slides now follow the presentation design and font themes.

5. **In the Outline pane on Slide 9, double-click to the right of the word "agents," press SPACEBAR, type and their expertise, then drag the Slide 9 ☐ above the Slide 8 ☐**

   New text is added to Slide 9. As you drag the slide in the Outline pane, a horizontal line appears to show you the new placement as Slide 9 becomes Slide 8.

6. **Click the Reading View button 🕮 on the status bar, click the Next button > on the status bar, then click the Normal button 🖵 on the status bar**

   You viewed the slides using Reading view navigating between Slides 8 and 9. Slide 1 appears in the Slide pane.

7. **Click the View tab on the Ribbon, click the Normal button in the Presentation Views group, click the Notes button in the Show group, then click the Home tab on the Ribbon**

   The Notes button is a toggle to open and close the Notes pane as needed. You return to Slide 1 in Normal view and close the Notes pane.

8. **Click the Slide 8 thumbnail in the Slides tab, then click the Save button 🖫 on the Quick Access toolbar**

   Compare your screen to **FIGURE 6-2**.

FIGURE 6-1: Outline pane showing imported text

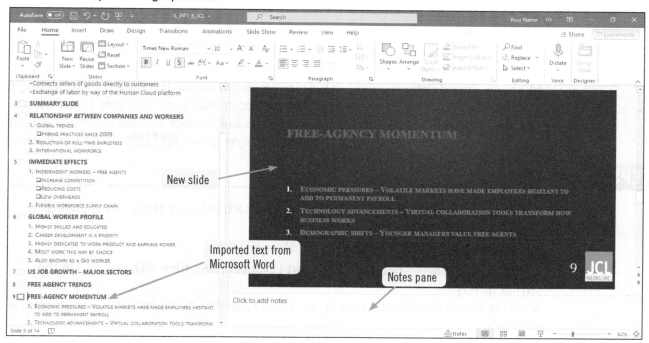

FIGURE 6-2: New slides from outline

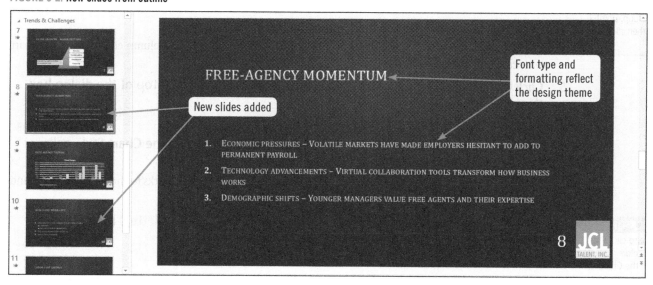

Recording a slide show

With the Record Slide Show feature you have the ability to record and save audio narrations, slide and animation timings, and laser pointer gestures for each slide during a slide show. This feature is great to use if you want to record audience comments so that people who were unable to attend the presentation live can view and listen to it later. To record a slide show, click the Slide Show tab, click the Record Slide Show button arrow in the Set Up group, then start recording from the beginning or the current slide. You then have to choose which elements you want to record during the slide show. If you choose to record audio narrations, you must have a microphone and speakers. A sound icon appears on every narrated slide.

Change Chart Design and Style

Being able to use Excel to create and modify charts in PowerPoint offers you many advantages, including the ability to use Excel Chart tools to customize chart design, layout, and formatting. After you create a chart, you can immediately alter the way it looks by changing individual chart elements or by applying a predefined chart layout or style. For example, you can select a chart layout that adds a chart title and moves the legend to the bottom of the chart. You can also easily change the color and effects of chart elements by applying one of the styles found in the Chart Styles gallery. **CASE** ▶ *You change the chart layout, style, and type of chart on Slide 9.*

STEPS

1. **Click the Slide 9 thumbnail in the Slides tab, click a blank area of the chart, then click the Chart Design tab on the Ribbon**

   The chart is selected and ready for you to make additional changes.

2. **Click the Quick Layout button in the Chart Layouts group, then click Layout 3 in the Layout gallery**

   ScreenTips identify each layout. Layout option 3 adds a legend to the bottom of the chart as shown in FIGURE 6-3.

3. **Click the Chart Elements button ⊞ on the slide next to the chart, click the Axis Titles arrow, click the Primary Vertical check box, click ⊞, select Axis Title on the chart, then type Percentage Change**

   The new axis title helps identify the meaning of the values in the chart.

4. **Click the Change Chart Type button in the Type group**

   The Change Chart Type dialog box opens. The current chart is a Clustered Column chart, which is a chart with column data series markers.

5. **Click Line in the left pane, make sure that Line is selected at the top of the dialog box, then click OK**

   All of the data series markers are now lines.

6. **Click the Chart Styles button ✐ next to the chart, scroll down the Chart Style gallery, then click Style 4**

   The Style 4 option changes the weight of the data series markers, adds tick marks to the horizontal axis, and enlarges the chart title.

7. **Click Color at the top of the Chart Style gallery, click Colorful Palette 4 in the Colorful section, then click ✐**

   The line colors change to reflect the new color scheme.

8. **Press and hold SHIFT, click the bottom-left sizing handle, drag down and to the left as shown in FIGURE 6-4, release the mouse, then release SHIFT**

   The chart is resized proportionally.

9. **Click a blank area of the slide, then save your presentation**

FIGURE 6-3: New layout applied to the chart

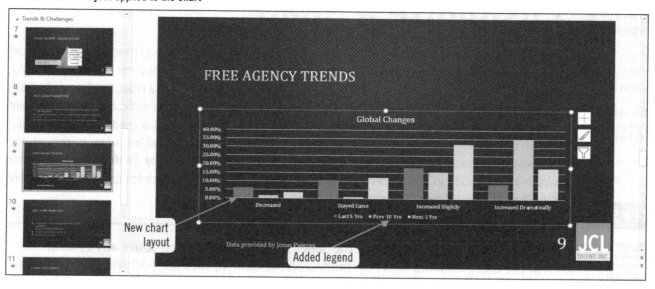

FIGURE 6-4: Resizing the chart

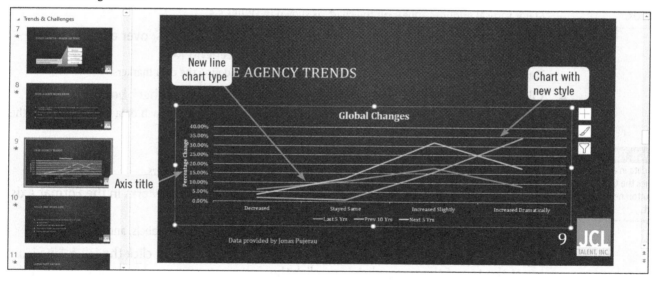

Using AutoFit Options to divide and fit body text

If the AutoFit Options button ⬛ appears while you are entering text in a body text object on a slide with either the Title and Content or the Content with Caption layout, you can click the button and choose from one of three options for dividing up the text in the object. The first option is to split text between two slides. If you choose this option, PowerPoint creates a second slide with the same title and then automatically divides the text

between the two slides. The second option is to continue the text on a new slide. Here again, PowerPoint creates a second slide with the same title, but instead of splitting the text between the slides, you are given a blank body text object on the new slide to insert more text. The final option on the AutoFit Options button for splitting text in a body text object is to change the body text object from one column to two columns.

Customize a Chart

**Learning
Outcomes**
- Add gridlines to a chart
- Add data labels to data markers
- Apply tick marks

One of the many advantages of creating charts in PowerPoint is the ability you have to customize chart elements, such as labels, axes, gridlines, and the chart background. For example, you can change the plot area color so the data markers are distinctly set off, or you can add gridlines to a chart. Gridlines help make the data easier to read in the chart and extend from the horizontal axis or the vertical axis across the plot area. There are two types of gridlines: major gridlines and minor gridlines. **Major gridlines** identify major units on the axis and are usually identified by a tick mark. **Tick marks** are small lines of measurement that intersect an axis and identify the categories, values, or series in a chart. **Minor gridlines** identify minor units on the axis and can also be identified by a tick mark. **CASE** *You decide to improve the appearance of the chart on Slide 14 by customizing some elements of the chart.*

STEPS

QUICK TIP
To switch values in chart rows and columns, click the Select Data button on the Chart Design tab, click the Switch Row/Column button in the Select Data Source dialog box, then click OK.

1. **Click the Slide 14 thumbnail in the Slides tab, click a blank area above any column in the chart, click the Chart Design tab on the Ribbon, click the Add Chart Element button in the Chart Layouts group, then point to Gridlines**

   The Gridlines gallery opens. Notice that Primary Major Horizontal is already selected indicating the chart already has major gridlines on the horizontal axis.

2. **Move ⌖ over each gridline option to see how the gridlines change on the chart, then click Primary Major Vertical**

   Major vertical gridlines appear on the chart, as shown in FIGURE 6-5.

3. **Click the Add Chart Element button, point to Data Table, move ⌖ over each data table option to see how the chart changes, then click No Legend Keys**

   You like seeing the data displayed in the chart because it helps define the data markers.

4. **Click the Chart Elements button ⊞, then click the Data Labels check box**

   Data labels, the actual value for each data series marker, appear just above each data marker. You like the data labels, but you want to move them to the inside of the data markers.

QUICK TIP
To filter data in a chart, click the Chart Filters button next to the chart.

5. **Click the Data Labels arrow, click Center, then click ⊞**

   The data labels are placed to the inside center of each of the data series markers.

6. **Right-click 25% on the vertical axis, click Format Axis, click Tick Marks in the Format Axis pane, then scroll down**

   The Format Axis pane opens with options for changing the axes, tick marks, labels, and numbers.

7. **In the Tick Marks section, click the Major type arrow, click Cross, click the Fill & Line icon ⬦ at the top of the pane, click Line, click the Color button arrow ✎·, click Red under Standard Colors, then close the Format Axis pane**

   The tick marks on the chart's vertical axis change to red and are easier to see.

8. **Click ⊞, click the Trendline arrow, click More Options, then click OK in the Add Trendline dialog box to add a Trendline based on the United States**

   The Format Trendline pane opens.

9. **Click ⬦, click the Width up arrow until 3 pt appears, click ✎·, click Red, close the Format Trendline pane, click a blank area of the slide, then save your presentation**

   Compare your screen to FIGURE 6-6.

FIGURE 6-5: Major vertical gridlines applied to the chart

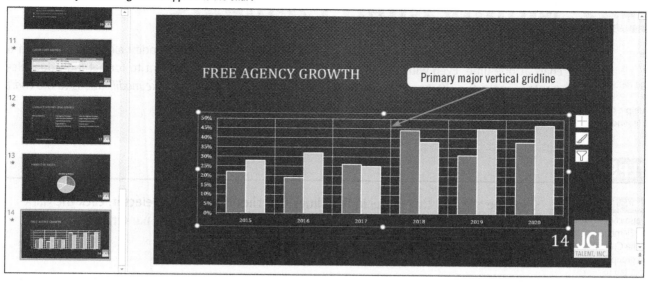

FIGURE 6-6: Chart with additional formatted elements

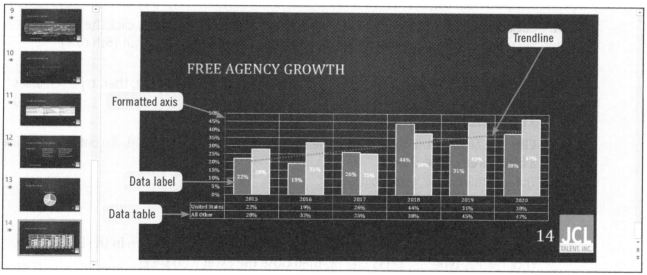

Using the Search pane

Sometimes when you are developing a presentation, you need help formulating your ideas or researching a particular subject. Using the Search pane, you can find information on a selected word or phrase, such as definitions, web articles, images, and other related information. To open and use the Search pane, click the Search button in the Insights group on the Review tab, type a word or phrase in the Search pane text box, then press ENTER. To see more information from a particular online source, click the More button in the Search pane, then select one of the options. The information that appears in the Search pane is generated by the Microsoft Bing search engine.

Modify Chart Elements

Learning Outcomes
- Change data series color
- Explode pie chart
- Add a legend to a chart

Quick Styles in PowerPoint provide you with a number of choices to modify all the elements in a chart at one time. Even with all the Quick Style choices, you still may want to format individual elements to make the chart easy to read and understand. **CASE** *You make modifications to the chart on Slide 13.*

STEPS

1. **Click the** Slide 13 thumbnail **in the Slides tab, click the chart to select it, click the** dark gray pie data series marker **twice, right-click the** dark gray data marker, **click the** Fill button **on the Mini toolbar, then click** Orange, Accent 6
   The data series marker now has an orange fill color.

2. **Right-click the** orange data marker, **then click** Format Data Point **on the Shortcut menu**
   The Format Data Point pane opens. Using this pane you can format an individual data point.

3. **Click the** Point Explosion up arrow **until 40% appears, click the** Angle of first slice up arrow **until 50° appears, then close the Format Data Point pane**
   The orange pie wedge explodes away from the pie chart and the chart is rotated to the right 50 degrees, as shown in FIGURE 6-7.

4. **Click a blank area of the chart, click the** Format tab **on the Ribbon, click the** Shape Fill button **in the Shape Styles group, point to** Texture, **then click** Walnut **(6th row)**
   A texture effect is added to the chart background.

5. **Click the** Chart Elements button ⊞, **click the** Chart Title check box, **then type** JCL Sales by Division
   A title is added to the top of the chart.

6. **Click the** Shape Outline button **in the Shape Styles group, click** Gold, Accent 4, **then click a blank area of the chart**
   The chart title now has a gold border.

7. **Click** ⊞, **click the** Legend arrow, **click** Left, **then click** ⊞
   A legend appears on the left side of the chart.

8. **Click the** Chart Design tab **on the Ribbon, click the** Edit Data button **in the Data group, click cell** B2, **type** 7.4, **press** ENTER, **then close the Excel worksheet**
   The National data value in the chart is changed.

9. **Click a blank area of the slide, then save the presentation**
   Compare your screen to FIGURE 6-8.

FIGURE 6-7: **Pie chart with exploded wedge**

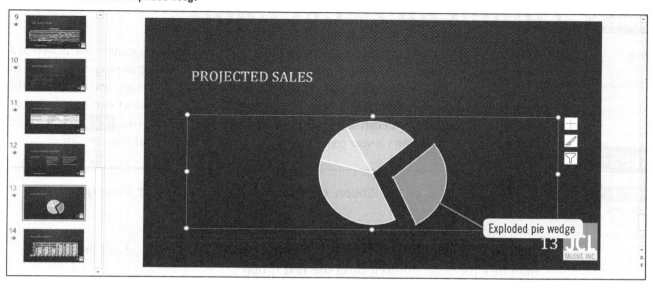

FIGURE 6-8: **Completed chart**

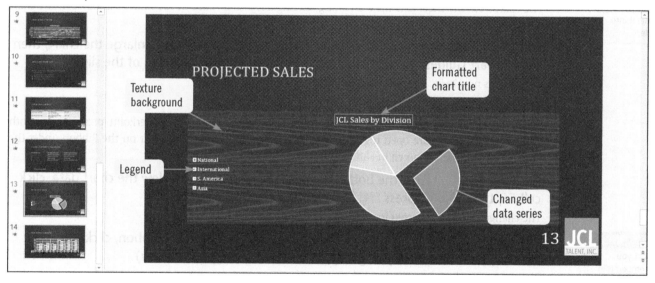

Changing PowerPoint options

You can customize your installation of PowerPoint by changing various settings and preferences. To change PowerPoint settings, click the File tab on the Ribbon, then click Options to open the PowerPoint Options dialog box. The sections in the left pane offer you ways to customize PowerPoint. For example, the General area includes options for viewing the Mini Toolbar, enabling Live Preview, and personalizing your copy of Office. You can also set Language options for editing and proofing as well as which language appears on buttons and ScreenTips.

PowerPoint

Embed an Excel Chart

Learning Outcomes
- Insert an Excel chart
- Modify an Excel chart

When a chart is the best way to present information on a slide, you can either create one within PowerPoint or you can embed an existing Excel chart directly to the slide. When you use another program to create an object, the program, Excel in this case, is known as the **source program**. The object you create with the source program is saved to a file called the **source file**. When you embed a chart into a presentation, the presentation file in which the chart is embedded becomes the **destination file**. **CASE** ▸ *You want to include last year's sales numbers in your presentation, so you embed an Excel chart in a new slide.*

STEPS

QUICK TIP

You can also press CTRL+D to duplicate a slide in the Slides tab.

1. **Click the** Home tab **on the Ribbon, click the** New Slide arrow **in the Slides group, then click the** Title Only layout

   A new slide with the Title Only layout is added to the presentation as Slide 14.

2. **Click the** slide title placeholder, **type** International, **click the** Insert tab **on the Ribbon, then click the** Object button ▣ **in the Text group**

   The Insert Object dialog box opens. Using this dialog box, you can create a new chart or locate an existing one to insert on a slide.

QUICK TIP

Another way to embed a chart is to open the chart in Excel, copy it, then paste it into your slide.

3. **Click the** Create from file option button, **click** Browse, **navigate to the location where you store your Data Files, click the file** Support_PPT_6_International.xlsx, **click** OK, **then click** OK **in the Insert Object dialog box**

   The chart from the Excel data file containing sales figures is embedded in the slide. You can open the chart and use the commands in Excel to make any changes to it.

4. **Drag the chart's** lower-left sizing handle **down and to the left to enlarge the chart, then using Smart Guides drag the** chart **to the middle of the blank area of the slide**

   The chart is now easier to read and is centered on the slide.

5. **Double-click the** chart **to open it in Excel**

   The chart appears inside an Excel worksheet on the slide of the open PowerPoint presentation. Both PowerPoint and Excel are open together, and Excel commands and tabs appear on the Ribbon under the PowerPoint title bar, as shown in FIGURE 6-9.

6. **Click the** Sheet 1 tab **at the bottom of the Excel worksheet to view the chart data, click cell** C6, **type** 45,660, **press** ENTER, **then click the** Sheet 2 tab

   The changed value is reflected for the Quarter 2 India data series in the chart.

QUICK TIP

If the chart you want to embed is in another presentation, open both presentations, then copy and paste the chart from one presentation to the other.

7. **Click the** chart **in Excel, click the** Chart Design tab **on the Excel Ribbon, click the** More button ▾ **in the Chart Styles group, then click** Style 9 (bottom row)

   The chart style changes with new data marker effects.

8. **Right-click the** Vertical (Value) Axis, **click** Font **on the shortcut menu, click the** Font style arrow, **click** Bold, **click** OK, **click the** Horizontal (Category) Axis, **then press** F4

   Pressing F4 repeats the last formatting action. Both the value and category axes labels are bold and now easier to read.

9. **Right-click the** legend, **click** Format Legend **on the shortcut menu, click the** Top option button, **then click** OK

   The legend moves to the top of the chart.

10. **Click outside the chart to exit Excel, click a blank area of the slide, then save the presentation**

    Compare your screen to FIGURE 6-10.

FIGURE 6-9: Embedded Excel chart

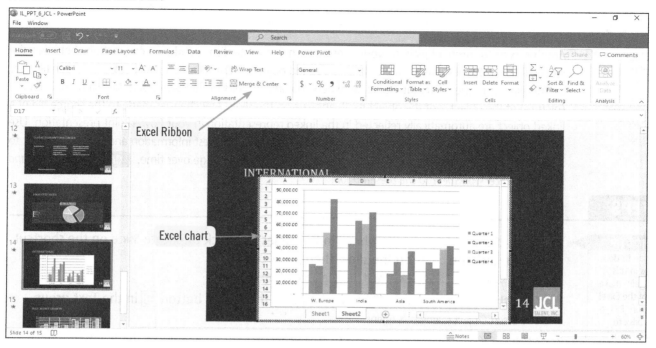

FIGURE 6-10: Formatted Excel chart

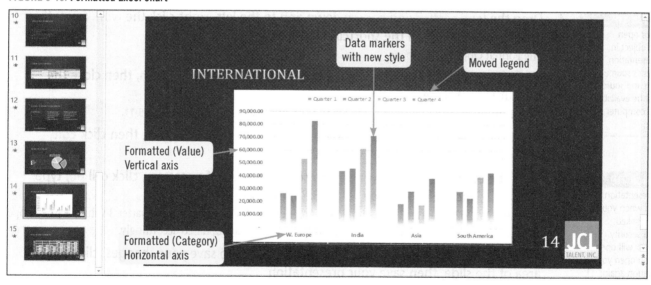

Embedding a worksheet

You can embed all or part of an Excel worksheet in a PowerPoint slide. To embed an entire worksheet, go to the slide where you want to place the worksheet. Click the Insert tab on the Ribbon, then click the Object button in the Text group. The Insert Object dialog box opens. Click the Create from file option button, click

Browse, locate and double-click the worksheet filename, then click OK. The worksheet is embedded in the slide. Double-click it to edit it using Excel commands as needed to work with the worksheet. To insert only a portion of a worksheet, open the Excel workbook and copy the cells you want to include in your presentation.

Link an Excel Worksheet

Learning Outcomes
- Link an Excel worksheet
- Format a linked worksheet

Another way to insert objects to your presentation is to establish a **link**, or connection, between the source file and the destination file. Unlike embedded objects, a linked object is stored in its source file, not on the slide or in the presentation file. So when you link an object to a PowerPoint slide, a representation (picture) of the object, not the object itself, appears on the slide. Any changes made to the source file of a linked object are automatically reflected in the linked representation in your PowerPoint presentation. Use linking when you want to be sure your presentation contains the latest information and when you want to include an object, such as an accounting spreadsheet, that may change over time. **CASE** *You link and format an Excel worksheet to the presentation.*

STEPS

QUICK TIP

If you plan to do the steps in this lesson again, make a copy of the Excel file Support_PPT_6_ Account.xlsx to keep the original data intact.

1. **Right-click the** Slide 14 thumbnail **in the Slides tab, click** Duplicate Slide **on the shortcut menu, click the** chart **on the slide, then press** DELETE

   A new slide, Slide 15, is created and the duplicated chart is deleted.

2. **Click the** Insert tab **on the Ribbon, then click the** Object button ▣ **in the Text group**

   The Insert Object dialog box opens.

3. **Click the** Create from file option button, **click** Browse, **navigate to the location where you store your Data Files, click the file** Support_PPT_6_Account.xlsx, **click** OK, **click the** Link check box, **then click** OK

   The Excel worksheet appears on the slide. The worksheet would be easier to read if it were larger and had a background fill color.

QUICK TIP

To edit or open a linked object in your presentation, the object's source program and source file must be available on your computer or network.

4. **Drag the** lower-left sizing handle **down and to the left, right-click the** worksheet, **then click** Format Object **on the shortcut menu**

   The Format Object pane opens.

5. **Click the** Fill & Line button ◇, **click the** Gradient fill option button, **then close the Format Object pane**

   A gradient fill background color is applied to the worksheet as shown in FIGURE 6-11.

6. **Right-click the** Excel worksheet, **point to** Linked Worksheet Object, **then click** Edit

   The linked worksheet opens in an Excel window.

QUICK TIP

If the presentation is closed when you update a linked object, a security dialog box will open when you open your presentation again; click Update Links to update the linked object.

7. **Drag the edge of the** Excel window **to see all the data if necessary, click cell B6, type** 99,897.66, **click cell D11, type** 180,453.83, **then press** ENTER

   The Fiscal Yr. 2020 Quarter 1 value for South America and the Fiscal Yr. 2021 Quarter 3 value for W. Europe change. All totals that include these values in the Total cells are updated accordingly.

8. **Click the** Excel window Close button ✕, **click** Save **to save your changes, click a blank area of the slide, then save your presentation**

   The Excel window closes. The Excel worksheet on Slide 15 is now updated with the new data. PowerPoint automatically makes all of the changes to the linked object. Compare your screen to FIGURE 6-12.

FIGURE 6-11: Linked Excel worksheet

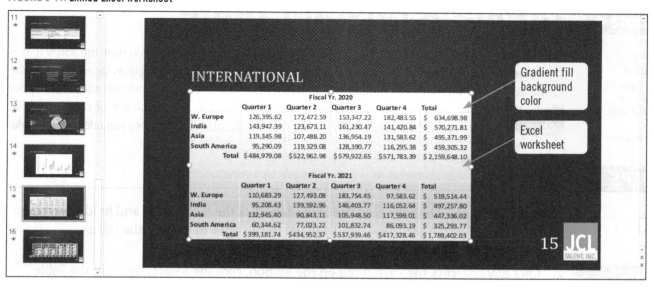

FIGURE 6-12: Updated linked worksheet

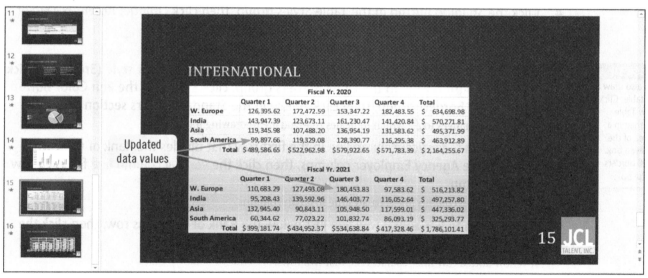

Editing links

Once you link an object to your presentation, you have the ability to edit its link. Using the Links dialog box, you can update a link, open or change a linked object's source file, break a link, and determine if a linked object is updated manually or automatically. The Links dialog box is the only place where you can change a linked object's source file, break a link, and change the link updating method. To open the Links dialog box, click the File tab on the Ribbon, click Info, then click Edit Links to Files button under Related Documents in the Info pane.

PowerPoint

Create a Custom Table

Learning Outcomes
- Add a table border
- Format a table border
- Resize a table

Tables provide a way to organize information for your audience. In PowerPoint, you have the ability to create vibrant tables. Tables you create in PowerPoint automatically display the style as determined by the theme assigned to the slide, including color combinations and shading, line styles and colors, and other effects. It is easy to customize the table border style, color, weight, and alignment of cells in a table.

CASE *You format a table on Slide 12 by adding color to the table cells and then you add a table border and format it.*

STEPS

1. **Click the** Slide 12 thumbnail **in the Slides tab, click the** table, **press and hold** SHIFT, **then drag the** bottom-right sizing handle **down to the right to enlarge the table**
   The table is resized proportionally.

QUICK TIP
To erase a cell border, click the Eraser button in the Draw Borders group, then click a table cell border.

2. **Click any** cell, **click the** Layout tab **on the Ribbon, click the** Select button **in the Table group, click** Select Table, **then click the** Table Design tab **on the Ribbon**
   The table object is selected.

3. **Click the** Borders button arrow **in the Table Styles group, then click** All Borders
   A border appears around the outside of the table and around all cells.

4. **Click the** Shading button **in the Table Styles group, then click** Orange, Accent 6, Darker 25%
   All the table cells have an orange background fill as shown in FIGURE 6-13.

QUICK TIP
You can also draw a custom table. Click the Draw Table button, then in a blank area of the slide, draw a box. Draw cell borders within the box.

5. **Click the** Pen Style button **in the Draw Borders group, click the** dot style (3rd style), **click the** Pen Weight button **in the Draw Borders group, click** 3 pt, **click the** Pen Color button **in the Draw Borders group, then click** Yellow **in the Standard Colors section**
   The pointer changes to ✏, which indicates that you are in drawing mode.

6. **Click the** white vertical column line **in the first row that divides the Rank of Concerns and the Free Agency Employer columns, then click the** vertical column line **for each row in that column**
   A yellow dotted column line separates the first two columns.

7. **Click the** white horizontal row line **just below the Rank of Concerns row, then click the** horizontal row line **for each column in that row**
   A yellow dotted row line separates the first two rows.

8. **Click the** Draw Table button **in the Draw Borders group, click outside the table, then save your presentation**
   Compare your screen to FIGURE 6-14.

FIGURE 6-13: **Formatted table**

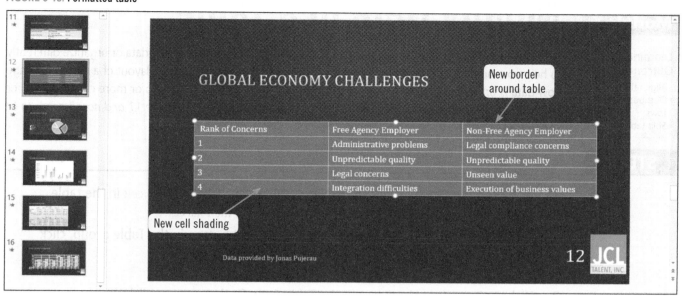

FIGURE 6-14: **Table with formatted table borders**

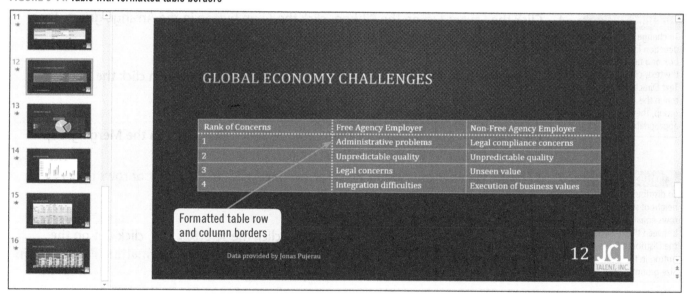

Resizing table rows and columns

Rows and columns in a table can be resized to approximate dimensions based on how the data is displayed in the table. To resize a row or column this way, select the row or column, then drag the row or column border to the desired position. If you want an exact row or column dimension, select the row or column, then adjust the row or column value in the Height or Width text boxes in the Cell Size group on the Layout tab.

Modify Data in a Table

Learning Outcomes
- Align table data
- Distribute table rows
- Split table cells

Once you have data entered in a table, you can modify it to emphasize certain data or organize differently to help your audience understand the information. It is easy to customize the layout of a table or change how data is organized. You can delete and insert rows or columns, merge two or more cells together, or split one cell into more cells. **CASE** ▶ *You have worked on the table on Slide 11 and now it needs to be customized.*

STEPS

1. **Click the** Slide 11 thumbnail **in the Slides tab, then click the** Total cell **in the table**
   Slide 11 appears in the Slide pane with the insertion point in the Total cell.

2. **Click the** Layout tab **on the Ribbon, click the** Select button **in the Table group, click** Select Row, **then click the** Table Design tab **on the Ribbon**
   The last row is selected.

3. **Click the** Total Row check box **in the Table Style Options group, click the** Shading button **in the Table Styles group, click** Orange, Accent 5, **then click the** Total cell
   Clicking the Total Row check box applies special formatting to the bottom row. Compare your screen to FIGURE 6-15.

4. **Click the** Layout tab **on the Ribbon, click the** Align button **in the Arrange group, then click** Align Middle
   The table moves up to the center of the slide aligned relative to the slide edge.

5. **Click the** Select button **in the Table group, click** Select Table, **then click the** Center button ☰ **in the Alignment group**
   The data in the table is centered in the table cells.

6. **Click the** 194 - Technology cell, **then click the** Split Cells button **in the Merge group**
   The Split Cells dialog box opens. The default setting is 2 columns and 1 row.

7. **Click the** Number of columns down arrow **once, click the** Number of rows up arrow **once, then click** OK
   You split the cell to create a new row in that cell.

8. **Drag to select** 351 - Non-Technology, **right-click the** selected text, **click** Cut **on the shortcut menu, right-click the** new row, **click the** Keep Source Formatting Paste Options button ⬚ **on the shortcut menu, then press** BACKSPACE
   The text 351 - Non-Technology is in a separate row. See TABLE 6-1 for Paste button options.

9. **In the last column drag to select the** 1832 cell **and the bottom** All cell, **then click the** Merge Cells button **in the Merge group**
   The two cells are merged together into one as shown in FIGURE 6-16.

10. **Click outside the table, then save your presentation**

FIGURE 6-15: Table with formatted total row

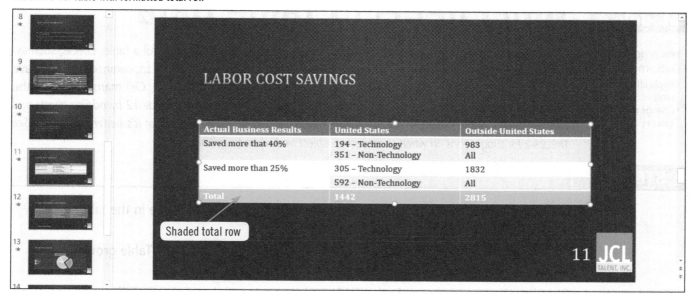

Shaded total row

FIGURE 6-16: Modified table

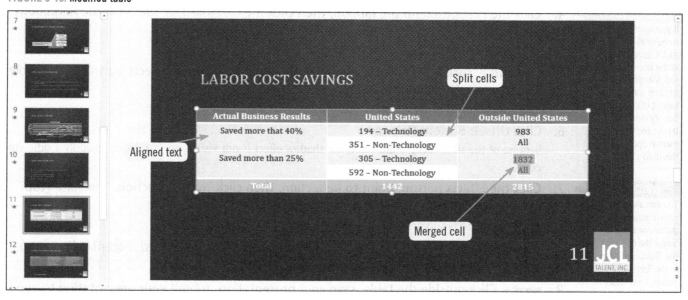

TABLE 6-1: Understanding common Paste button options

button	button name	result
	Use Destination Theme	Use the current theme of the presentation
	Keep Source Formatting	Use the formatting characteristics from the object's source file
	Picture	Insert the object as a picture
	Keep Text Only	Insert the object as text only with no formatting
	Embed	Insert the object as an embedded object

Add Effects to Table Data

Learning Outcomes
• Apply effects to a table
• Change margin spacing

PowerPoint has a number of formatting effects that you can apply to the cells of a table. Effects, such as, reflections and shadows allow you to create dynamic tables that have a unique appearance. You also have the ability to modify the space between table cells by changing cell margins. Cell margin refers to the space between cell text and the cell border. **CASE** ▶ *Modify the table on Slide 12 by adding effects and changing cell margins. You also review when it's better to link an object and when it's better to embed. See* TABLE 6-2 *for suggestions on when to embed an object and when to link an object.*

STEPS

1. **Click the** Slide 12 thumbnail **in the Slides tab, then click anywhere in the** table
   Slide 12 appears in the Slide pane with the table selected.

2. **Click the** Layout tab **on the Ribbon, click the** Select button **in the Table group, click** Select Table, **then click the** Table Design tab **on the Ribbon**

3. **Click the** Effects button **in the Table Styles group, point to** Cell Bevel, **then click** Round
   The round bevel effect is applied to all of the cells and the yellow dotted border lines that were present are removed as shown in FIGURE 6-17.

> **QUICK TIP**
> If you want to customize cell margins, click Custom Margins at the bottom of the Cell Margins menu to open the Cell Text Layout dialog box. Specify custom text layout and internal margin options in this dialog box.

4. **Click the** Layout tab **on the Ribbon, then click the** Cell Margins button **in the Alignment group**
   A list of cell margin options opens.

5. **Click** Wide, **click the** Table Design tab **on the Ribbon, click the** Effects button **in the Table Styles group, then point to** Shadow
   The Shadow effects menu opens.

6. **Click** Offset: Bottom **(top row)**
   Because of the slide background color, the shadow effect is not visible, so you decide to apply a different effect.

> **QUICK TIP**
> You can also fill a cell background with a picture or symbol. Select the cell, click the Shading button in the Table Styles group, then locate and insert a picture. Choose a picture from the Insert Pictures dialog box, then click Insert.

7. **Click the** Effects button, **point to** Reflection, **then click** Tight Reflection: Touching **(top row)**
   A reflection effects appears below the table.

8. **Click the** Shading button **in the Table Styles group, then click** Gold, Accent 4 **(top row)**
   The table is easier to read now as shown in FIGURE 6-18.

9. **sam⬆** **Click outside the table, save your presentation, submit your presentation to your instructor, then exit PowerPoint**

FIGURE 6-17: Table with bevel effect applied to cells

FIGURE 6-18: Table with distributed cells

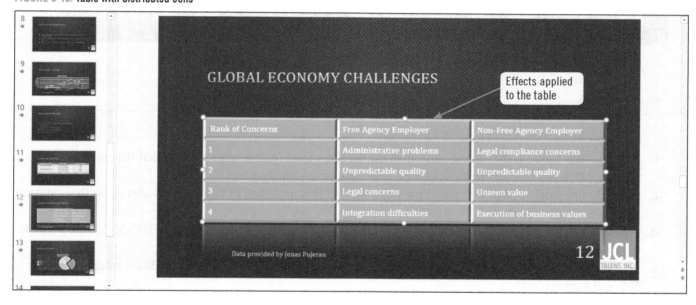

TABLE 6-2: Embedding vs. linking

situation	action
When you are the only user of an object and you want the object to be a part of your presentation	Embed
When you want to access the object in its source program, even if the original file is not available	Embed
When you want to update the object manually while working in PowerPoint	Embed
When you always want the latest information in your object	Link
When the object's source file is shared on a network for other users to access and change	Link
When you want to keep your presentation file size small	Link

PowerPoint

Practice

Skills Review

1. Insert text from Microsoft Word.

a. Open IL_PPT_6-2.pptx from the location where you store your Data Files, save it as **IL_PPT_6_Alpine**, then open Outline view. You will work to create the completed presentation as shown in FIGURE 6-19.

FIGURE 6-19

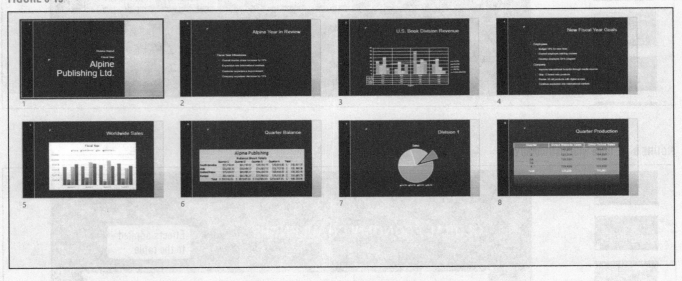

b. Click the Slide 2 icon in the Outline pane, then use the Slides from Outline command to insert the file Support_PPT_6_Alpine.docx from the location where you store your Data Files.

c. In the Outline pane on Slide 4 click after the word "access," then press ENTER to add a 4th bullet under the Company heading.

d. Type **Continue expansion into international markets**, press and hold SHIFT, click the Slide 3 icon in the Outline pane, then release SHIFT.

e. On the Home tab, click the Reset button in the Slides group, click the Layout button in the Slides group, then click Title and Content.

f. In the Outline pane, drag Slide 3 above Slide 2, then click the Slide 4 icon in the Outline pane.

g. Open Reading view, click the Next button until you return to Outline view, then click the Normal button in the status bar.

2. Change chart design and style.

a. Go to Slide 3, select the chart, then click the Chart Design tab.

b. Change the chart layout to Layout 10, then resize the chart proportionally smaller so the legend fits on the black background.

c. Change the chart type to Clustered Column, then add an axis title on the horizontal axis.

d. Type **Regions**, then change the chart color to Colorful Palette 1.

e. Click a blank area of the chart, then save your changes.

3. Customize a chart.

   a. Select the chart on Slide 3, then click the Chart Design tab.

   b. Click the Add Chart Element button in the Chart Layouts group, then add Primary Major Vertical gridlines to the chart.

   c. Click the Add Chart Element button in the Chart Layouts group, then add a data table with legend keys to the chart.

   d. Click the Chart Elements button next to the chart, then add data labels to the inside end of the data series markers.

   e. Add a linear trendline based on the 2nd quarter, then close the Chart Elements menu.

   f. Select the vertical axis, click the Format tab, click the Shape Outline button in the Shape Styles group, change the axis color to yellow, then change the axis weight to 2 1/4 pt.

   g. Click a blank area of the slide, then save your work.

4. Modify chart elements.

   a. Go to Slide 6, select the chart, click the 4th Qtr pie wedge (*Hint*: use ScreenTips to identify each wedge), right-click the pie wedge, then click Format Data Point.

   b. Change the angle of the first slice to 75 degrees, change the point explosion of the pie wedge to 35%, then close the Format Data Point pane.

   c. Click the Shape Fill button in the Shape Styles group, then change the pie wedge color to green.

   d. Click the Shape Outline button in the Shape Styles group, then add a 3 pt yellow border to the pie wedge.

   e. Add a legend to the bottom of the chart, add a chart title to the top of the chart, then, if necessary, type **Sales** in the chart title object.

   f. Click a blank area of the slide, then save your changes.

5. Embed an Excel chart.

   a. Go to Slide 5, click the Insert tab, then click the Object button in the Text group.

   b. Click the Create from file option button, click Browse, then locate and embed the file Support_PPT_6_Chart.xlsx from the location where you store your Data Files.

   c. Drag the lower-right sizing handle to increase the size of the chart so it fills most of the blank space between the title and the bottom of the slide and then center on the slide.

   d. Double-click the chart, click the Sheet1 tab in the worksheet that opens, change the value in cell D8 to **74820.33**, change the value in cell B6 to **21,473.53**, then click the Sheet2 tab. (*Note*: The hashtags indicate that the column isn't wide enough to display the full values in the cells, it won't affect your chart.)

   e. Right-click the legend, click Format Legend in the shortcut menu, click Top, then click OK.

   f. Click a blank area of the slide, then save your changes.

6. Link an Excel worksheet.

   a. Insert a new slide after Slide 5 with the Title Only layout.

   b. Type **Quarter Balance**, click the Insert tab, then click the Object button in the Text group.

   c. Click the Create from file option button, click Browse, locate the file Support_PPT_6_Balance.xlsx from the location where you store your Data Files, then link it to the slide. (*Hint*: Make a copy of the Excel file Support_PPT_6_Balance.xlsx to keep the original data intact.)

   d. Resize the worksheet object to fit in the blank area of the slide by dragging its sizing handles, then center-align it in the blank area of the slide.

   e. Right-click the worksheet, click Format Object, click the Solid fill option button, click the Color arrow, then click Gold, Accent 2.

   f. Close the Format Object pane, then double-click the worksheet.

   g. Drag to select cells B4 to E7, click the Number Format list arrow in the Number group, then click Currency.

   h. Click cell B6, type **75003.07**, click cell E5, type **31742.93**, then press ENTER.

   i. Close the Excel window, then click Save to save your changes to the Excel worksheet. The changes appear in the linked worksheet on the slide.

Skills Review (continued)

7. Create a custom table.

  a. Go to Slide 8, click in the table, then click the Table Design tab.

  b. Right-click the table, click Select Table in the shortcut menu, click the Borders button arrow in the Table Styles group, then add outside borders to the table.

  c. Click the Shading button in the Table Styles group, then change the color of the cells to Blue, Accent 4.

  d. Click the Pen Weight arrow in the Draw Borders group, click 3 pt, click the Pen Color button, click Red under Standard Colors, click the Pen Style arrow, then click the 4th option in the list.

  e. Click the bottom border of each cell in the first row, then click the Draw Table button in the Draw Borders group.

  f. Press and hold SHIFT, then drag the bottom-left sizing handle down to increase the size of the table so it touches the white vertical line.

  g. Click a blank area of the slide, then save your changes.

8. Modify data in a table.

  a. Click in the table, click the Table Design tab, then add a total row to the table.

  b. Right-click the table, click Select Table in the shortcut menu, click the Layout tab, then align the table cells to the center.

  c. Click the Distribute Columns button in the Cell Size group, click the Align button in the Arrange group, then align the table to the middle of the slide.

  d. Click the 3A cell, split the cell into 1 column and 2 rows, then type **3B** in the new cell.

  e. Click a blank area of the slide, then save your changes.

9. Add effects to table data.

  a. Select the first row in the table, click the Table Design tab, then apply the Round bevel effect.

  b. Click the 3B cell, then apply an Orange, Accent 1 shading to the cell.

  c. Apply the Inside Center shadow and the Tight Reflection: Touching effects to the table.

  d. Right-click the table, click Select Table in the shortcut menu, then change the cell margins to None.

  e. Save your work, submit your presentation to your instructor, close the presentation, and exit PowerPoint.

Independent Challenge 1

Riverwalk Medical Clinic (RMC), is a large medical facility in Cambridge Massachusetts. You have been asked by your supervisor to create a presentation on the Riverwalk Clinic EMS system. You have been working on the presentation and now you insert text from Microsoft Word and format charts to enhance the presentation.

   a. Start PowerPoint, open the presentation IL_PPT_6-3.pptx from the location where you store your Data Files, then save it as **IL_PPT_6_RMC**. You will work to create the completed presentation as shown in FIGURE 6-20.

   b. Insert the outline Support_PPT_6_EMS.docx after Slide 1, then open Outline view.

   c. In the Outline pane insert a new Slide 4 after Slide 3 using the Title and Content layout, then type **Purpose** in the title text object.

   d. In the text object, type **Standardization**, then type the following second level bullet text:
   - **Training programs**
   - **Levels of certification**
   - **Patient care**

   e. Select Slide 2 and Slide 3 in the Outline pane, reset the two slides, then change their layout to Title and Content.

   f. Move Slide 4 above Slide 2, then close Outline view.

   g. Switch to Reading view, then navigate the slides to the end of the presentation.

   h. Go to Slide 7, change the chart layout to Layout 1, then change the chart colors to Colorful Palette 3.

   i. Change the chart type to Line, add an axis title to the horizontal axis, then type **Response** in the axis title text box.

   j. Change the size of the chart so it is proportionally smaller, then add data labels above the data series markers.

   k. Add a data table with legend keys to the chart, then format the vertical axis outline with a 3 point red color.

   l. Add primary major vertical gridlines, go to Slide 6, then change the color of the largest pie wedge to Red, Accent 5.

   m. Explode the largest pie wedge to 25%, apply a 50 degree angle on the slice, then apply a legend on the right side of the chart.

   n. Apply a 4 point yellow border around the largest pie wedge, add a title to the top of the chart, then if necessary type **Systems** in chart title text box.

   o. Save the presentation, submit your presentation to your instructor, close the presentation, then exit PowerPoint.

FIGURE 6-20

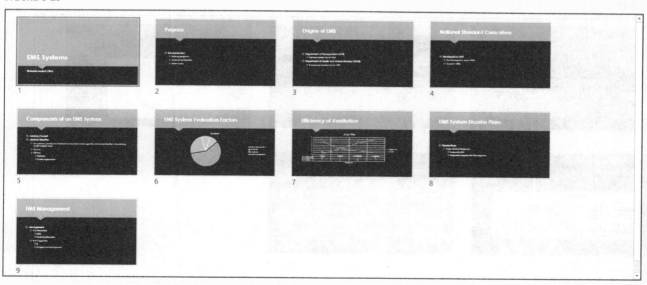

PowerPoint

Independent Challenge 2

Generac Products is a large company that develops and produces medical equipment and technical machines for operating and emergency rooms throughout the United States. You are one of the client representatives in the company, and one of your assignments is to prepare a presentation for the division management meetings on the profitability and efficiency of each division in the company. (*Hint:* Before you complete this step make a copy of the Data File Support_PPT_6_G2.xlsx.)

a. Open the file IL_PPT_6-4.pptx from the location where you store your Data Files, then save it as **IL_PPT_6_Generac**. You will work to create the completed presentation as shown in FIGURE 6-21.

b. Go to Slide 5, select the table, then shade the cells with Green, Accent 3.

c. Format the border between the first and second row with a 3 point dark red dotted line.

d. Resize the table proportionally so it fills the width of the slide, then center it in the blank area of the slide.

e. Split the cell System manager into two rows and one column, then type **Allegis UI** into the new cell.

f. Select the table, distribute the rows, then align the data in the cells to the center.

g. Select the top row, apply the Slant bevel, apply the Inside: Bottom shadow to the table, then apply the Tight Reflection: 4 point offset to the table.

h. Apply a Wide cell margin to all the cells, then go to Slide 3.

i. Embed the chart in the Excel file Support_PPT_6_G1.xlsx from the location where you store your Data Files.

j. Drag the corner sizing handles of the chart so it fills the blank area of the slide, double-click the chart, click the Sheet 1 tab, click cell C5, then type **-2**.

k. Click the Sheet 2 tab, click the Chart Design tab, click the Add Chart Element button in the Chart Layouts group, point to Legend, click Top, then click a blank area of the slide.

l. Go to Slide 4, then link the worksheet in the Excel file Support_PPT_6_G2.xlsx from the location where you store your Data Files.

m. Open the linked worksheet in Excel, select cells B4 through F10, click the Accounting Number Format button in the Number group, click cell B8, type **40,000.00**, save the changes to the worksheet, then close Excel.

n. Right-click the linked worksheet, click Format Object, click the Solid fill option button, if necessary, click the Color button, click White, Text 1, then close the Format Object pane.

o. Resize the worksheet to fill the slide, then view your presentation in Slide Show view.

p. Submit your presentation to your instructor, close the presentation, then exit PowerPoint.

FIGURE 6-21

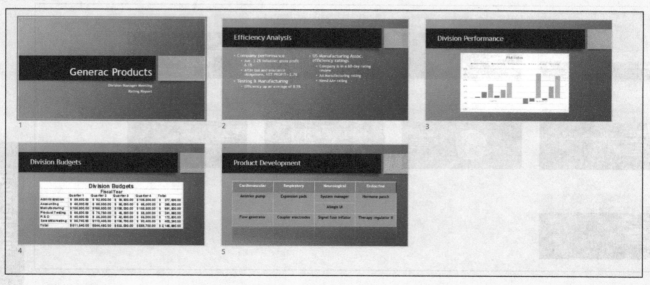

Visual Workshop

Create slides that look like the examples in FIGURE 6-22 and FIGURE 6-23. Start a new presentation, then embed the Excel chart Support_PPT_6_Trac.xlsx from the location where you store your Data Files. Resize the chart larger, then in Excel move the legend to the top of the chart. Format the first row in the table with a Round bevel effect, then center all the data in the center of the cells. Apply a wide margin to all the cells, proportionally resize the table larger, then align the table to the center of the slide. Save the presentation as **IL_PPT_6_TracTec**. Add the slide number as a footer to the slides, then submit your presentation to your instructor.

FIGURE 6-22

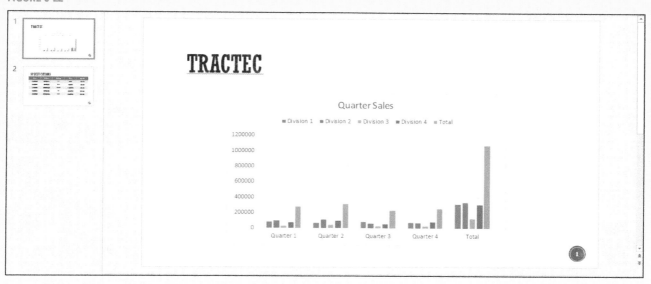

FIGURE 6-23

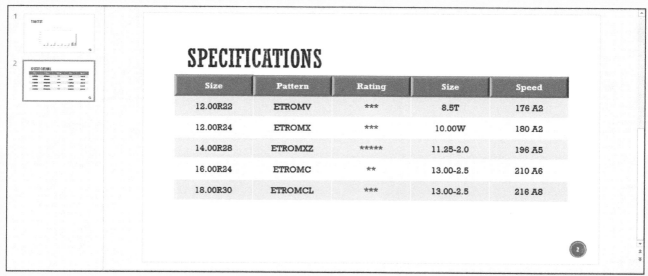

Inserting Graphics, Media, and Objects

CASE ▸ In this module, you work on a shortened version of the presentation you have been working on that describes global workforce trends. You use the advanced features in PowerPoint to customize a SmartArt graphic, a digital video, an audio clip, and a picture. You then insert action buttons and hyperlinks for better navigation. And finally, you insert and animate a 3-D model to enhance the presentation.

Module Objectives

After completing this module, you will be able to:

- Design a SmartArt graphic
- Enhance a SmartArt graphic
- Customize digital video
- Insert and trim audio

- Edit and adjust a picture
- Add action buttons
- Insert hyperlinks
- Insert and animate 3-D models

Files You Will Need

IL_PPT_7-1.pptx
Support_PPT_7_Desk.mp4
Support_PPT_7_Audio.mp3
Support_PPT_7_Woman.jpg
Support_PPT_7_Tables.docx
Support_PPT_7_Charts.pptx
IL_PPT_7-2.pptx
IL_PPT_7-3.pptx
Support_PPT_7_Office_Group.jpg
Support_PPT_7_Video.mp4

Support_PPT_7_Company.jpg
Support_PPT_7_Alpine.pptx
IL_PPT_7-4.pptx
Support_PPT_7_Doctor.mov
Support_PPT_7_ER.jpg
Support_PPT_7_RMC.pptx
IL_PPT_7-5.pptx
IL_PPT_7-6.pptx
Support_PPT_7_R2G.jpg

Design a SmartArt Graphic

SmartArt graphics improve your ability to create vibrant content on slides. SmartArt allows you to easily combine your content with an illustrative diagram, improving the overall quality of your presentation. Better presentations lead to improved understanding and retention by your audience. In a matter of minutes, and with little training, you can create a SmartArt graphic using slide content that would otherwise have been placed in a simple bulleted list. **CASE** *You continue working on the presentation by changing the graphic layout, adding a shape and text to the SmartArt graphic, and then changing its color and style.*

STEPS

1. **sam↓ Start PowerPoint, open the presentation IL_PPT_7-1.pptx from the location where you store your Data Files, save the presentation as IL_PPT_7_JCL, click the Slide 2 thumbnail in the Slides tab, then click the bottom shape in the SmartArt graphic**

   The SmartArt graphic is selected. Each shape in the SmartArt graphic is separate and distinct from the other shapes and can be individually edited, formatted, or moved within the boundaries of the SmartArt graphic. The bottom shape is selected.

2. **Click the SmartArt Design tab on the Ribbon, click the Text Pane control button [<] to open the Text pane, click the Add Bullet button in the Create Graphic group, then type Digital labor force in the Text pane**

   A new bullet appears indented beneath the bullet above it in the Text pane and in the graphic.

3. **Click the Promote button in the Create Graphic group, click the Move Up button in the Create Graphic group, then click the third shape in the graphic**

   The new bullet indents to the left, appears in its own shape, and moves up in the list. Compare your screen with FIGURE 7-1.

4. **Click the Add Shape arrow in the Create Graphic group, click Add Shape After, then click the Move Down button once in the Create Graphic group**

   A new shape in the same style appears with a new bullet in the Text pane and then is moved down in the Text pane.

5. **Type 75% increase in last 5 years, click the Demote button in the Create Graphic group, then click the top shape in the SmartArt graphic**

6. **Click Intense Effect in the SmartArt Styles group, then click the Right to Left button in the Create Graphic group**

   The style of the SmartArt graphic changes and the graphic layout switches from left to right. The new bullet point does not move, so you return the graphic to its original layout.

7. **Click the Right to Left button in the Create Graphic group, click the Change Colors button in the SmartArt Styles group, then click Colorful - Accent Colors in the Colorful section**

   Each shape now has a different color that follows the Theme colors of the presentation.

8. **Click the Text Pane button in the Create Graphic group to close the Text pane, then click a blank area of the slide**

   Compare your screen to FIGURE 7-2.

FIGURE 7-1: SmartArt graphic with added text

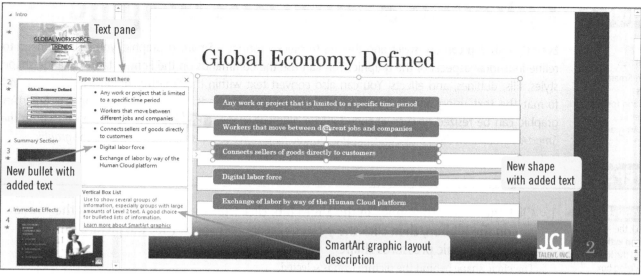

FIGURE 7-2: Formatted SmartArt graphic

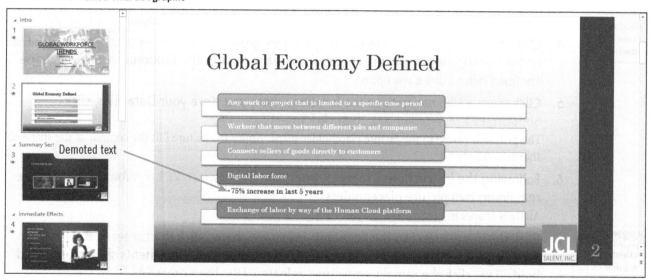

Creating mathematical equations

You can insert or create mathematical equations using the Equation button in the Symbols group on the Insert tab. Click the Equation button list arrow to access nine common equations, which include the area of a circle, the Pythagorean Theorem (my personal favorite), and the Quadratic Formula (my editor's favorite). To create your own equations, click the Equation button to open the Equation tab. On this tab you can use the Ink Equation button to insert an equation using your own handwriting, or you can create an equation using eight different types of mathematical symbols including basic math, geometry, operators, and scripts. You also have the ability to create mathematical structures such as integrals and functions.

Enhance a SmartArt Graphic

Learning
Outcomes
• Design SmartArt
  shapes
• Insert and format
  pictures in
  SmartArt graphics

Even though you can use styles and themes to quickly format a SmartArt graphic, you still may need to refine individual aspects of the graphic. You can use the commands on the Format tab to change shape styles, fills, outlines, and effects. You can also convert text within the SmartArt graphic to WordArt and format the text using any of the WordArt formatting commands. Individual shapes in the SmartArt graphic can be resized or even changed into a different shape. **CASE** *You continue working on the SmartArt graphic on Slide 8 by adjusting shapes, adding pictures to the shapes, and resizing the graphic.*

STEPS

TROUBLE
If you click the
Picture icon in the
shape and the Insert
Pictures dialog box
opens, close the
Insert Pictures dialog
box.

1. **Click the** Slide 8 thumbnail **in the Slides tab, click the** SmartArt graphic, **click the** Format tab **on the Ribbon, then click the** picture placeholder shape **(not the picture icon) next to the Economic pressures shape**

   The circle shape behind the picture icon is selected.

2. **Click the** Change Shape button **in the Shapes group, then click** Rectangle: Top Corners Rounded **in the Rectangles section**

   The form of the picture placeholder shape changes.

QUICK TIP
Click the SmartArt
graphic icon in a
Content placeholder
to insert a new
SmartArt graphic.

3. **Click the** middle placeholder shape, **press and hold** CTRL, **click the** bottom picture place-holder shape, **release** CTRL, **press** F4, **then click the** Technology advancements shape

   The picture placeholder shapes now have the top rounded corner rectangle shape.

4. **Click the** Shape Fill button **in the Shape Styles group, click** Gold, Accent 4, **then click the** picture icon ▣ **in the picture placeholder shape next to the Economic pressures shape**

   The Insert Pictures dialog box opens.

5. **Click** From a File, **navigate to the location where you store your Data Files, click** Support_PPT_7_Woman.jpg, **then click** Insert

   The picture is placed in the picture placeholder shape. Notice the picture fills the contour of the shape, as shown in FIGURE 7-3.

6. **Following the instructions in Step 5, insert the file** Support_PPT_7_Woman.jpg **into the remaining two picture placeholders**

   All three shapes in the SmartArt graphic have pictures in them.

QUICK TIP
You can convert
pictures on a slide to
a SmartArt graphic.
Select the pictures,
click the Picture
Format tab, click the
Picture Layout
button in the Picture
Styles group, then
click a layout.

7. **Click the** picture **next to the Economic pressures shape, click the** Larger button **in the Shapes group, click the** picture **next to the Technology advancements shape, press and hold** CTRL, **click the remaining** picture, **release** CTRL, **then press** F4

   The three pictures are a little larger now.

8. **Click a blank area inside the SmartArt graphic, click the** Shape Effects button **in the Shape Styles group, point to** 3-D Rotation, **then click** Perspective: Right **in the Perspective section**

   A 3-D effect is applied to the SmartArt graphic that turns it to the right.

9. **Click the** Size button, **click the** Shape Height up arrow **in the Size group until** 4 **appears, click a blank area of the slide, then save your work**

   The SmartArt graphic increases in size, as shown in FIGURE 7-4.

FIGURE 7-3: New shapes in SmartArt graphic

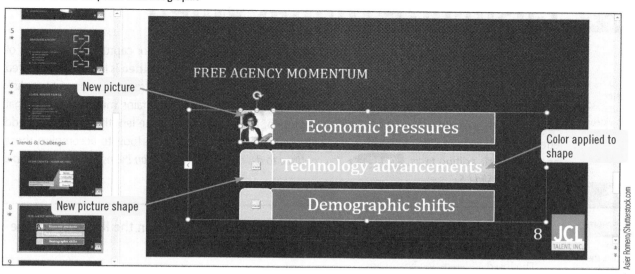

FIGURE 7-4: Completed SmartArt graphic

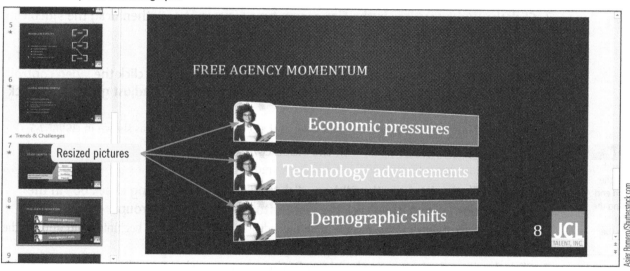

Saving a presentation in PDF, XPS, or other fixed file formats

In certain situations, such as when sharing sensitive or legal materials with others, you may find it necessary to save your presentation file in a fixed layout format. A **fixed layout format** is a specific file format that "locks" the file from future changes and allows others only the ability to view or print the presentation. To save a presentation in one of these fixed formats, click the File tab on the Ribbon, click Export, make sure Create PDF/XPS Document is selected, then click the Create PDF/XPS button. The Publish as PDF or XPS dialog box opens. Select the appropriate file type in the Save as type list box, choose other options (optimization), then publish your presentation in a fixed layout format. To view a fixed layout format presentation, you need appropriate viewer software that you can download from the Internet. Other common file formats supported in PowerPoint include PowerPoint Template (.potx), PowerPoint Show (.ppsx), OpenDocument Presentation (.odp), and PowerPoint Picture Presentation (.pptx). On the File tab, click Save As, then click the Change File Type arrow to save a file in another file format and to view descriptions of these and other supported file formats.

Customize Digital Video

**Learning
Outcomes**
• Insert a video
• Apply a poster
  frame
• Compress a video

In your presentation, you may want to use special effects to illustrate a point or capture the attention of your audience. You can do this by inserting digital or animated video. **Digital video** is live action captured in digital format by a video camera. You can embed or link a digital video file from your computer or link a digital video file from a webpage on the Internet. **Animated video** contains multiple images that stream together or move to give the illusion of motion. If you need to edit the length of a video or add effects or background color to a video, you can use PowerPoint video-editing tools to accomplish those and other basic editing tasks. **CASE** ▶ *You continue to develop your presentation by inserting and editing a video clip on Slide 6.*

STEPS

QUICK TIP

To insert a video from online, click the Video button, click Online Video, then enter the web address of the video from a supported video provider, such as YouTube.

1. **Click the Slide 6 thumbnail in the Slides tab, click the Insert tab on the Ribbon, click the Video button in the Media group, then click This Device**
   The Insert Video dialog box opens.

2. **Navigate to the location where you store your Data Files, click Support_PPT_7_Desk.mp4, then click Insert**
   The Support_PPT_7_Desk.mp4 video clip is inserted on the slide and fills the slide. You resize the video so it fits better on the slide.

3. **Click the Width text box in the Size group, type 6, press ENTER, then drag the video clip to the middle of the blank area on the right side of the slide**
   The video clip is proportionally smaller and fits better on the slide.

4. **Move ⌖ over the video control timeline located below the video, click the video control timeline at about 00:06.60, click the Poster Frame button in the Adjust group, then click Current Frame**
   The video frame at about 06 seconds is now set as the preview video image, as shown in FIGURE 7-5.

QUICK TIP

You can also add fade effects to the beginning and end of a video using the Fade Duration commands in the Editing group.

5. **Click the Play/Pause button ▶ in the video control bar**
   The short video plays through once but does not rewind to the beginning.

6. **Click the Playback tab on the Ribbon, click the Rewind after Playing check box in the Video Options group, then click the Play button in the Preview group**
   The video plays through once, and this time the video rewinds back to the beginning and displays the preview image.

7. **Click the Start list button in the Video Options group, click When Clicked On, then click the Play Full Screen check box in the Video Options group**
   Now the video will play full screen only when clicked during a slide show.

QUICK TIP

You can align two or more videos by clicking the Align button in the Arrange group on the Video Format tab.

8. **Click the Slide Show button 🖵 on the status bar, move ⌖ over the video, the pointer changes to 🖑, then click the video**
   The video clip fills the screen and plays and then Slide 6 appears in Slide Show view again.

9. **Press ESC, click the File tab on the Ribbon, click Info, click the Compress Media button, then click Standard (480p)**
   The Compress Media dialog box opens and the video is compressed.

10. **Click Close in the dialog box, click the Back button ⏴, click a blank area of the slide, then save your work**
    Compare your screen to FIGURE 7-6.

FIGURE 7-5: Video clip inserted on the slide

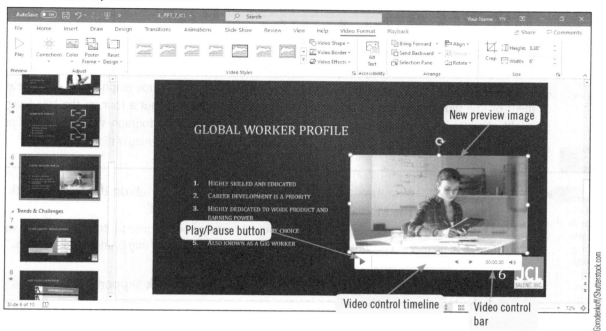

FIGURE 7-6: Edited video on slide

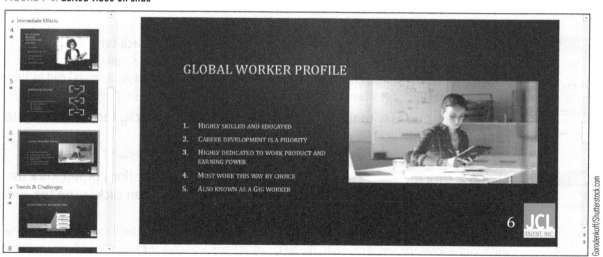

Trimming a video

After you watch a video clip, you may determine certain portions of the video are not relevant to your slide show. From PowerPoint, a video clip can be trimmed only from the beginning or the end of the clip; you can't use PowerPoint to trim out the middle of a clip. To trim a video clip, select the video, click the Playback tab, then click the Trim Video button in the Editing group. The Trim Video dialog box opens. To trim the beginning of the video clip, drag the start point (green marker) to the right until you reach a new starting point. To trim the end of a video clip, drag the end point (red marker) to the left until you reach a new ending point. If you want to precisely choose a new beginning or ending point for the video clip, you can click the up or down arrows on the Start Time and End Time text boxes.

PowerPoint

Insert and Trim Audio

**Learning
Outcomes**
• Insert, edit, and
play a sound file

PowerPoint allows you to insert sound files in your presentation to help narrate a slide or add audio effects. You can add sounds to your presentation from files on a removable storage device, the Internet, or a network drive. The primary use of sound in a presentation is to provide emphasis to a slide or an element on the slide. For example, if you are creating a presentation about a tour up the Nile River, you might consider inserting a rushing water sound on a slide with a photograph showing people on the Nile. **CASE** *You insert a recorded sound file on Slide 1 that will play during a slide show.*

STEPS

QUICK TIP
If you have two or
more audio clips on
the same slide, you
can group them by
clicking the Group
button in the
Arrange group on
the Audio Format
tab.

1. **Click the** Slide 1 thumbnail **in the Slides tab, click the** Insert tab **on the Ribbon, click the** Audio button **in the Media group, then click** Audio on My PC

   The Insert Audio dialog box opens. Common sound formats you can insert into a presentation include Windows audio files (waveform) (.wav), MP3 and MP4 audio files (.mp3 / .mp4), and Windows Media Audio Files (.wma).

2. **Navigate to the location where you store your Data Files, click** Support_PPT_7_Audio.mp3, **click the** Insert arrow, **then click** Link to File

   A sound icon with an audio control bar appears in the center of the slide, as shown in FIGURE 7-7.

3. **Drag the** sound icon ◁)) **to the lower-left corner of the slide, click the** Play button ▶ **in the audio control bar, listen to the music for about a minute, then click the** Pause button ❙❙

   You decide to trim the audio clip.

QUICK TIP
You can use
bookmarks to
manually start or end
an audio or jump to
a precise point in the
audio.

4. **Click the** Trim Audio button **in the Editing group on the Playback tab**

   The Trim Audio dialog box opens, as shown in FIGURE 7-8. Notice on the audio timeline there is a start point (green marker) and an end point (red marker), which identify the beginning and end of the audio. The blue marker identifies where you stopped listening. The audio is just over three minutes long.

5. **Drag the** start point ❘ **to the right to about** 00:09.135, **then drag the** end point ❘ **to the left to about** 02:07.221

   The audio will now start and end at the new selected points, as shown in FIGURE 7-9.

QUICK TIP
Click the Rewind
after Playing check
box in the Audio
options group to
rewind an audio clip
after playing.

6. **Click** OK, **click the** Play Across Slides check box **in the Audio options group, click the** Loop Until Stopped check box **in the Audio options group, then click** ▶ **on the audio control bar**

   The audio now plays between the new start and end points and then loops back to the beginning when the audio clip reaches the end. By default, the audio plays when you click the sound icon during a slide show.

7. **Click the** Pause button **in the Preview group, then click the** Play in Background button **in the Audio Styles group**

   Notice that by clicking the Play in Background button the Hide During Show check box is selected and the Start option is set to Automatically in the Audio Options group. The audio will now be hidden from view and run automatically as soon as the slide appears in Slide Show view.

8. **Click the** Volume button **in the Audio options group, click** Medium, **click the** Slide Show button 🖵 **on the status bar, then listen to the audio**

   The sound icon does not appear during the slide show.

9. **Click through each slide, watch all animations and the movie clip, press** ESC **on the last slide, then save your changes**

FIGURE 7-7: **Sound clip inserted on the slide**

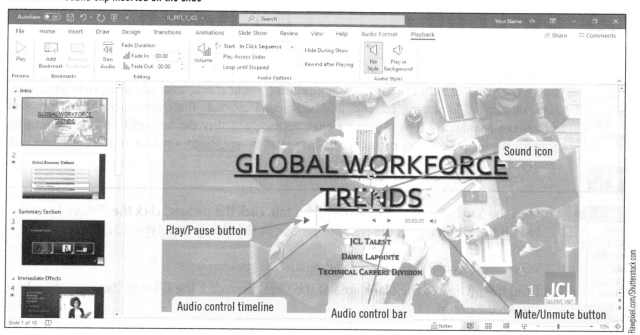

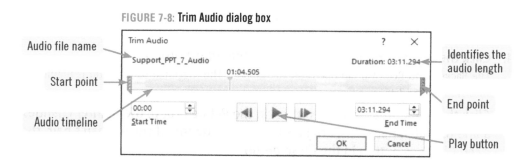

FIGURE 7-8: **Trim Audio dialog box**

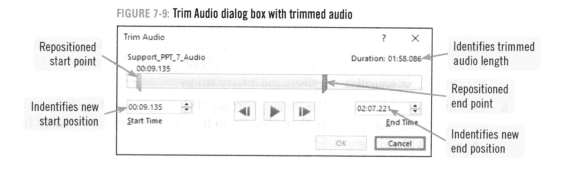

FIGURE 7-9: **Trim Audio dialog box with trimmed audio**

PowerPoint

Edit and Adjust a Picture

Learning Outcomes
- Replace a picture
- Remove picture background
- Convert picture to SmartArt graphic

Inserting pictures and other media to your slides can dynamically enhance the message of your presentation. When working with pictures in PowerPoint, you have a number of available design options you can use to format pictures in creative ways, including artistic effects, color saturation, color tone, recoloring, sharpening, brightness, contrast, and background removal. These advanced picture-formatting features can dramatically change how a picture appears, and they can be useful when you are trying to match the picture to other content in the presentation. **CASE** ▷ *On Slide 10 you experiment with PowerPoint picture tools.*

STEPS

QUICK TIP
To insert an online picture without a content placeholder, click the Pictures button in the Images group on the Insert tab, click Online Pictures, then locate a picture.

1. **Click the Slide 10 thumbnail in the Slides tab, click the picture, click the Picture Format tab on the Ribbon, click the Height text box in the Size group, type 3.5, then press ENTER**

   The picture proportionally increases slightly in size.

2. **Drag the picture to the blank area of the slide, then click the Change Picture button in the Adjust group**

   The Change Picture list box opens. Using this list you can search for a replacement picture from your computer or the Internet.

3. **Click From a File, navigate to the location where you store your Data Files in the Insert Picture dialog box, click Support_PPT_7_Woman.jpg, click Insert, review the Design Ideas pane, then close the Design Ideas pane**

   A new picture takes the place of the original picture. Eliminating the background of a picture can highlight the subject or remove distracting aspects of the picture.

4. **Click the Remove Background button in the Adjust group**

   The Background Removal tab opens on the Ribbon. The suggested background is highlighted in pink, as shown in FIGURE 7-10.

5. **Click the Mark Areas to Keep button in the Refine group, the pointer changes to ✐, drag a line to match FIGURE 7-11, drag a small line at the top of the woman's hair, then click the Keep Changes button in the Close group**

   Most of the background portion of the picture is removed from the picture.

6. **Click the Reset Picture button in the Adjust group, view the picture, then click the Undo button ↺ on the Quick Access toolbar**

   After looking at the picture in its original condition, you decide to keep the picture as is.

QUICK TIP
To make one color in a picture transparent, select the picture, click the Color button in the Adjust group, click Set Transparent Color, then click the color on the picture you want to make transparent.

7. **Click the Color button in the Adjust group, click Saturation: 66% in the Color Saturation section, click the Corrections button in the Adjust group, then click Brightness: +20% Contrast: 0% (Normal) in the Brightness/Contrast section (3rd row)**

   The picture color, saturation, brightness, and contrast change.

8. **Click the Rotate button in the Arrange group, click Flip Horizontal, click Compress Pictures in the Adjust group, then click OK in the Compress Pictures dialog box**

   The picture is flipped horizontally and compressed.

9. **Click a blank area of the slide, save your work, then compare your screen to FIGURE 7-12**

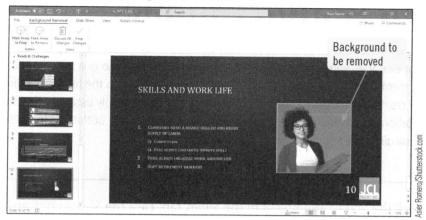

Background to be removed

FIGURE 7-11: Background removal line

Drag a line to here

Background area to be removed

FIGURE 7-12: Picture with removed background

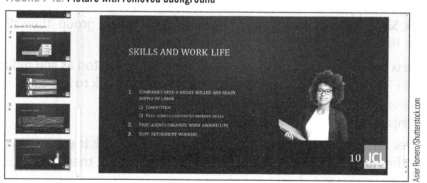

Compressing pictures

To compress all pictures in a presentation, select a picture, click the Compress Pictures button in the Adjust group, remove the Apply only to this picture check mark, then click OK. It's important to know that when you compress a picture you change the amount of detail in the picture, so it might look different than it did before the compression. By default, all inserted pictures in PowerPoint are automatically compressed based on default settings in the PowerPoint Options dialog box. To locate the compression settings, click the File tab, click Options, click Advanced in the left pane, then go to the Image Size and Quality section.

Add Action Buttons

Learning Outcomes
• Create action buttons
• Edit action buttons

An **action button** is an interactive button that you create from the Shapes gallery to perform a specific task. For example, you can create an action button to play a video or a sound, or to link to another slide in your presentation. Action buttons can also link to a webpage on the Internet, a different presentation, or any file created in another program. Action buttons are commonly used in self-running presentations and presentations published on the web. **CASE** ▷ *You add action buttons to the slides of your presentation, which will allow you to move from slide to slide in Slide Show view.*

STEPS

QUICK TIP

Any shape in the Shapes gallery as well as most objects can be an action button. Click the shape or object, click the Insert tab, click the Action button in the Links group, then select an action.

1. **Click the** Slide 1 thumbnail **in the Slides tab, click the** Shapes button **in the Drawing group, click** Action Button: Go Forward or Next ▷ **in the Action Buttons section, press and hold** SHIFT, **drag to create a button as shown in** FIGURE 7-13, **then release** SHIFT

   A small action button appears on the slide, and the Action Settings dialog box opens. Pressing and holding SHIFT while you create a shape maintains the shape's proportions as you change its size.

2. **Make sure** Next Slide **is selected in the Hyperlink to list, then click** OK

   The dialog box closes. The action button now has an action, in this case, linking to the next slide.

3. **Click the** Shape Format tab **on the Ribbon, click the** More button ⊽ **in the Shape Styles group, then click** Gradient Fill - Orange, Accent 6, No Outline **in the last row of the Presets section**

   The new theme fill makes the action button easier to see on the slide.

QUICK TIP

Use the arrow keys on your keyboard or press ALT while dragging the action button to nudge the action button into place.

4. **Drag the** action button **to the upper-left corner of the slide, click the** Home tab, **then click the** Copy button **in the Clipboard group**

5. **Click the** Slide 2 thumbnail **in the Slides tab, then click the** Paste button

   An exact copy of the action button, including the associated action, is placed on Slide 2.

TROUBLE

If you mistakenly paste a copy of the action button on Slide 3, select it, then press DELETE to delete it.

6. **Paste a copy of the** action button **on Slides 4 through 9, click the** Slide 10 thumbnail **in the Slides tab, click the** Shapes button **in the Drawing group, then click** Action Button: Go Home ⌂ **in the Action Buttons section**

7. **Press and hold** SHIFT, **create a similar-sized action button as you did for Slide 1, release** SHIFT, **make sure** First Slide **is selected in the Hyperlink to list, click** OK, **then drag the** action button **to the upper-left corner of the slide**

   Compare your screen to FIGURE 7-14.

8. **Click the** Slide 2 thumbnail **in the Slides tab, right-click the** action button, **click** Edit Link **in the shortcut menu, click the** Hyperlink to list arrow, **then click** Slide

   The Hyperlink to Slide dialog box opens.

9. **Click** 4. Relationship Between Companies, **click** OK, **click** OK **again, click the** Slide 1 thumbnail **in the Slides tab, then click the** Slide Show button ▭ **on the status bar**

10. **Click the** action buttons **on each slide, click the** Home action button **on Slide 10, press** ESC **to end the slide show, then save your changes**

    The pointer changes to 👆 when you click each action button.

FIGURE 7-13: **Inserted action button**

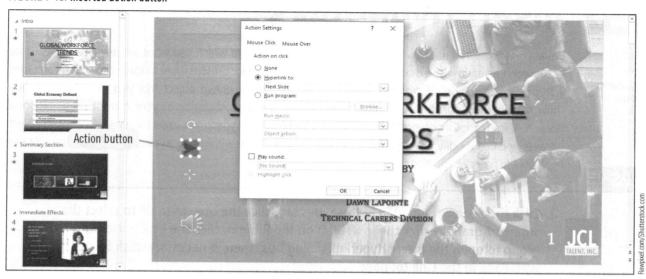

FIGURE 7-14: **Home action button on last slide**

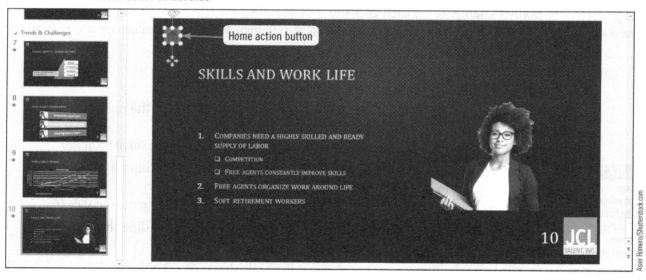

Changing the transparency of a picture

Pictures in PowerPoint are commonly used as slide backgrounds, individual objects on a slide, or inserted in another object, such as a SmartArt graphic. To change the transparency of a picture used as a slide background, insert the picture as a slide background using the Format Background button on the Design tab, then adjust the Transparency slider in the Format Background pane. To change the transparency of a picture on a slide, right-click the picture. Click Format picture on the shortcut menu, click Fill & Line, click the Picture or texture fill option button, then move the Transparency slider in the Format Picture pane.

Insert Hyperlinks

Learning Outcomes
• Create hyperlinks
• View and use hyperlinks

While creating a presentation, there might be a circumstance in which you want to view a document that either won't be easily viewed on a slide or is too detailed for your presentation. In these cases, you can insert a **hyperlink**, a specially formatted word, phrase, graphic, or drawn object that you click during a slide show to "jump to," or display, another slide or PowerPoint presentation in your current presentation; a document from another program, like Word; or a webpage. A hyperlinked object is similar to a linked object because you can modify the object in its source program from within PowerPoint. **CASE** *You add two hyperlinks to your presentation.*

STEPS

1. **Click the** Slide 7 thumbnail **in the Slides tab, click the** grey triangle **to select the SmartArt graphic, click the** Insert tab **on the Ribbon, click the** Link button **in the Links group to open the Insert Hyperlink dialog box, then, if necessary, click** Existing File or Web Page **in the Link to: pane**

   The Existing File or Web Page button is selected in the Link to: pane, and Current Folder is selected in the Look in pane. The location where you store your Data Files should be the open folder.

QUICK TIP
Links can also be established between slides of the same presentation, a new presentation, an email address, or any webpage.

2. **Click the file** Support_PPT_7_Tables.docx, **click** OK, **then click a blank area of the slide**

   Now you have made the grey triangle a hyperlink to the file Support_PPT_7_Tables.docx.

3. **Click the** Slide Show button ⬛ **on the status bar, point to the** grey triangle, **notice the pointer change to** 👆, **then click the** grey triangle

   Microsoft Word opens, and the Word document containing tables of information appears, as shown in FIGURE 7-15.

4. **Read the two-page document, then close the** Word window

   The PowerPoint slide reappears in Slide Show view.

5. **Press ESC, click the** Slide 10 thumbnail **in the Slides tab, right-click the** picture, **click** Link, **click** Support_PPT_7_Tables.docx, **then click** OK

   The picture is now linked to the Word document. You realize this is the wrong linked document.

QUICK TIP
To open, copy, or remove a hyperlink, right-click the hyperlink, then click the appropriate command on the shortcut menu.

6. **Right-click the** picture, **click** Edit Link **in the shortcut menu, click** Support_PPT_7_Charts.docx **as shown in** FIGURE 7-16, **then click** OK

   The PowerPoint presentation Support_PPT_7_Charts.pptx is now linked to the picture on Slide 10.

7. **Click the** Slide 1 thumbnail **in the Slides tab, click** ⬛ **to start the slide show, then click the** action buttons **to view the slides in the presentation**

   Be sure to watch the movie on Slide 6 and to trigger the animation on Slide 7 to move the SmartArt graphic.

8. **Click the** linked objects **on Slide 7 and Slide 10, press the** Home action button **on Slide 10, press ESC to end the slide show, then save your changes**

   The hyperlinks and action buttons all work correctly.

9. **sam ⬆ Submit your presentation to your instructor, then close the presentation but do not close PowerPoint**

FIGURE 7-15: Linked Word document

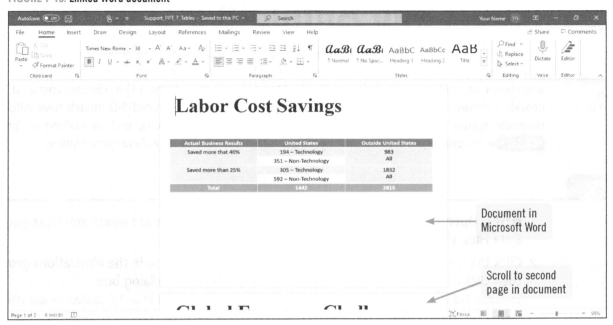

FIGURE 7-16: Open Edit Hyperlink dialog box

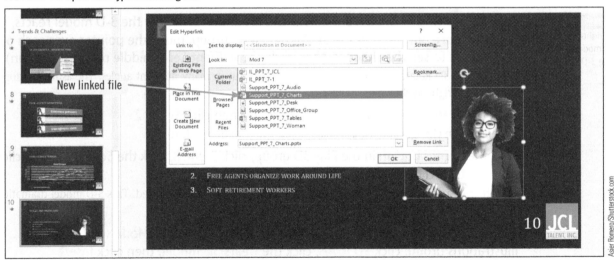

Inserting a screenshot

Using the Screenshot button in the Images group on the Insert tab, you can insert a picture, or screenshot, of an open program window or a specific part of the window. A screenshot is simply a picture of the window displayed on your screen. For example, you could use the screenshot feature to insert a picture of information you found on a webpage or found in other documents or programs that might not be easily transferable to

PowerPoint. Screenshots are static and are not able to be updated if the source information changes. Only open, nonminimized windows are available to be captured as a screenshot. When you click the Screenshot button, all open program windows appear in the Available Windows gallery. To take a screenshot of part of a window, click the Screenshot button, then click Screen Clipping.

Insert and Animate 3-D Models

Three-dimensional models are high-quality objects that you can modify by rotating or tilting to view different angles of the object to suit your needs. Once the 3-D model is inserted, you can manually adjust it or choose one of the standard views in the 3D Model Views group. Some 3-D models are animated and provide a dynamic way to display the model in your presentation. Animated 3-D models have different cinematic scenes that cause the 3-D model to perform different actions, such as walking or flying.

CASE ▶ *You open a presentation and experiment with 3-D models to use in future presentations.*

STEPS

1. **sam'** ↓ **Open the presentation** IL_PPT_7-2.pptx **from the location where you store your Data Files, then save the presentation as** IL_PPT_7_3DModel

2. **Click the** Insert tab **on the Ribbon, click the** 3D Models button **in the Illustrations group, then click** Animated for Education **in the Online 3D Models dialog box**
   The animated models in the Animated for Education group appear. All of these 3-D models are animated.

3. **Click the** astronaut, **then click** Insert
   The 3-D animated model of an astronaut appears in the middle of the slide. The astronaut appears to float on the slide, which is this 3-D model's animation movement. A 3D Rotate handle appears in the middle of the 3-D model.

4. **Drag the** 3D Rotate handle **up, down, and around, watch how the 3-D model reacts, click the** More button ⊡ **in the** 3D Model Views group, **move the pointer over each of the options to see the changes, then click** Above Front Left **(middle row, last column)**
   Dragging the 3D Rotate handle manipulates the astronaut in many different angles. The astronaut appears turned to the right, as shown in FIGURE 7-17.

5. **Click the** Scenes button **in the Play 3D group, then click** Scene 2
   The animation changes and the astronaut appears to turn from side to side.

6. **Click the** Scenes button **in the Play 3D group, click** Scene 3, **click the** Scenes button, **click** Scene 4, **then click the** Pause button **in the Play 3D group**
   The other two animation scenes play and then the 3-D animation is paused. This 3-D model dramatically increases the presentation file size, so you change the 3-D model.

7. **Press** DELETE, **click the** Insert tab **on the Ribbon, click the** 3D Models button **in the Illustrations group, click** 3D Icons, **click the** Gears 3D model, **then click** Insert
   The astronaut 3-D model is deleted and the gears 3-D model now appears, as shown in FIGURE 7-18.

8. **Drag the** 3-D model Rotate handle **so the model is in a new position, click the** Animations tab **on the Ribbon, click** Turntable, **click the** Slide Show button ⊡ **on the status bar, then click the** 3D Model
   The 3-D model animates by turning around.

9. **sam'** ↑ **Press** ESC, **submit your presentation to your instructor, close the presentation, then close PowerPoint**

FIGURE 7-17: Slide with astronaut 3-D model

FIGURE 7-17: Slide with astronaut 3-D model

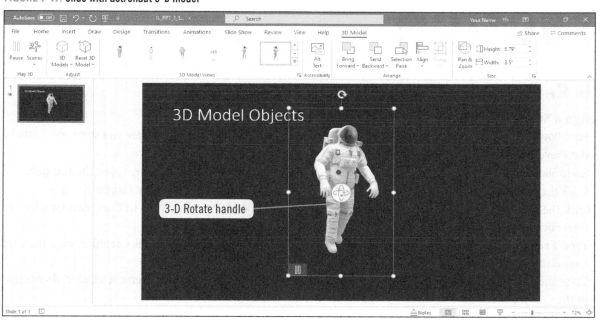

FIGURE 7-18: Slide with gears 3-D model

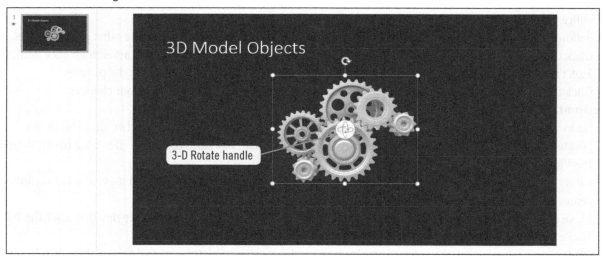

Zooming in on a 3-D model

With 3-D models you have the option of zooming in or out. You can also pan the 3-D model around to see a specific area. With the 3-D model selected, click the Pan & Zoom button in the Size group on the 3D Model tab. A magnifying glass appears on the right side of the 3-D model. To zoom in or out click the magnifying glass, then drag up or down depending on the direction you want to zoom. To pan the 3-D model, simply drag the 3-D model inside its selection box. When you are finished, click the Pan & Zoom button again.

Practice

Skills Review

1. Design a SmartArt graphic.
   a. Start PowerPoint, open the presentation **IL_PPT_7-3.pptx** from the location where you store your Data Files, then save it as **IL_PPT_7_Alpine**.
   b. Go to Slide 4, click the left shape in the SmartArt graphic, click the SmartArt Design tab, then open the Text pane.
   c. Click the Add Bullet button in the Create Graphic group, then type **Expand sales force by 5%**.
   d. Click the Promote button in the Create Graphic group, click the Add Shape list arrow in the Create Graphic group, then click Add Shape After.
   e. Type **Trim budget by 10%**, press ENTER, click the Demote button in the Create Graphic group, then type **Combine development projects**.
   f. Close the Text pane, click the Change Colors button in the SmartArt Styles group, then click Colorful - Accent Colors in the Colorful section.
   g. Click the left shape, click the Move Down button in the Create Graphic group, then click the right shape.
   h. Click the Move Up button in the Create Graphic group, then save your changes.

2. Enhance a SmartArt graphic.
   a. Click the Format tab, click the left picture shape in the SmartArt graphic, click the Larger button in the Shapes group, then increase the size of the other picture shapes.
   b. Click a blank area of the SmartArt graphic, click the Width text box, type **9.5**, then press ENTER.
   c. Click the Insert picture icon in the left picture shape, click From a File, then locate and insert the file Support_PPT_7_Office_Group.jpg from the location where you store your Data Files.
   d. Follow the above instructions and insert the file Support_PPT_7_Office_Group.jpg to the other picture shapes.
   e. Click the left picture, click the Shape Effects button in the Shape Styles group, point to Bevel, then click Round.
   f. Select the four other pictures, press F4, then select the light green colored shape behind the pictures.
   g. Click the Shape Fill button in the Shape Styles group, click Aqua, Accent 3, then save your changes.

3. Customize digital video.
   a. Go to Slide 2, click the Insert tab on the Ribbon, click the Video button in the Media group, then click This Device.
   b. Locate the file Support_PPT_7_Video.mp4 from the location where you store your Data Files, click Insert, then click the Video Format tab.
   c. Click the number in the Height text box in the Size group, type **3.5**, press ENTER, then move the video clip to the center of the blank area of the slide.
   d. Move the pointer over the video control timeline, click at approximately 00:09.02 in the timeline, click the Poster Frame button in the Adjust group, then click Current Frame.
   e. On the Playback tab, click the Rewind after Playing check box, then click the Play Full Screen check box in the Video options group.
   f. Click the File tab, click Info, click the Compress Media button, click Standard, then click Close in the Compress Media dialog box.
   g. Click the Back button, preview the video clip in Slide Show view, then save your presentation.

4. Insert and trim audio.
   a. Go to Slide 1, click the Insert tab, click the Audio button in the Media group, then click Audio on My PC.
   b. Locate the sound file Support_PPT_7_Audio.mp3 from the location where you store your Data Files, click the Insert arrow, then click Link to File.
   c. In the Audio Options group click the Play Across Slides check box, click the Loop until Stopped check box, then drag the sound icon to the lower-left corner of the slide.

Skills Review (continued)

d. Use the Trim Audio dialog box to change the start point of the audio clip to 02:04.800 and the end point to 03:05.900.

e. Click the Play in Background button in the Audio Styles group, click the Volume button in the Audio Options group, click Medium, then click the Slide Show button on the status bar.

f. Click through the slides in Slide Show view, review the movie on Slide 2, press ESC, then save your presentation.

5. Edit and adjust a picture.

a. Go to Slide 5, click the Picture, change the picture with Support_PPT_7_Company.jpg, review the designs in the Design Ideas pane, then close the Design Ideas pane.

b. Change the color saturation of the picture to Saturation: 0%, then correct the picture to Brightness: -20% Contrast: -20%.

c. Click the Remove Background button in the Adjust group, click the Mark Areas to Keep button in the Refine group, then draw small lines on all the people, the table, and the items on the table in the picture.

d. Reset the picture, click the Rotate Objects button in the Arrange group, then click Flip Horizontal.

e. Compress all the pictures in the presentation, click the Width text box in the Size group, type 6, then press ENTER.

f. Save your changes.

6. Add action buttons.

a. Go to Slide 1, click the Shapes button in the Drawing group, then click Action Button: Go Forward or Next.

b. Draw a small button, click OK in the Action Settings dialog box, then move the button to the left edge of the slide.

c. Click the Shape Format tab on the Ribbon, click the More button in the Shape Styles group, then click Colored Fill - Orange, Accent 5 in the second row.

d. Copy and paste the action button on all the other slides.

e. Right-click the action button on Slide 5, click Edit Link on the shortcut menu, click the Hyperlink to: arrow, click First Slide, then click OK.

f. Go to Slide 1, run the slide show, test the action buttons, exit the slide show, then save your work.

7. Insert hyperlinks.

a. Go to Slide 3, then click the green shape to select it.

b. Click the Insert tab on the Ribbon, click the Link button, locate the file Support_PPT_7_Alpine.pptx from the location where you store your Data Files, then click OK.

c. Go to Slide 4, right-click the left picture in the SmartArt graphic, then click Link in the shortcut menu.

d. In the Insert Hyperlink dialog box, click Place in This Document in the Link to: section, click 5. New Fiscal Year Goals in the Select a place in this document: section, then click OK.

e. Go to Slide 1, open Slide Show view, click the action buttons to Slide 3, then click the hyperlink shape.

f. Click through the slides of the linked presentation, click the action button to Slide 4, then click the hyperlink in the SmartArt graphic.

g. Press ESC, go to Slide 4, right-click the SmartArt picture with the hyperlink, click Edit Link, click 2. Alpine Year in Review in the Select a place in this document section, then click OK.

h. Go to Slide 1, open Slide Show view, click the action buttons to move between slides, watch the video on Slide 2, click the hyperlinks on Slides 3 and 4, press ESC when you are finished, then save your changes.

8. Insert and animate 3-D models.

a. Go to Slide 1, click the Insert tab, then click the 3D Models button in the Illustrations group.

Skills Review (continued)

b. Click 3D Icons, locate the 3-D model shown in FIGURE 7-19, then click Insert.

c. Drag the 3-D model to the lower-right corner of the slide, then drag the 3-D Rotate handle to change the angle of the model.

d. Click the Width text box in the Size group, type **3**, press ENTER, then reposition the model, if necessary.

e. Click the 3D Model Views More button, click Above Front Right, then click the Animations tab.

f. Click Jump & Turn in the Animation group, click the Effect Options button in the Animation group, then click Clockwise in the Direction section.

g. Click the Slide Show button on the status bar, view the animation on Slide 1, use the action buttons to go through the slide show, watch the video, view all hyperlinks, then press ESC when you are finished. The completed presentation is shown in FIGURE 7-20.

h. Save your work, submit your presentation to your instructor, then close the presentation.

FIGURE 7-19

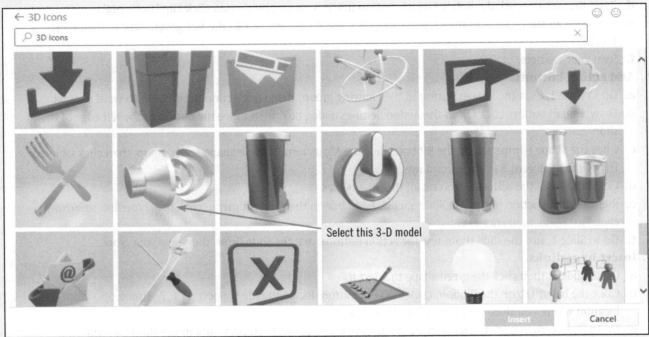

FIGURE 7-20

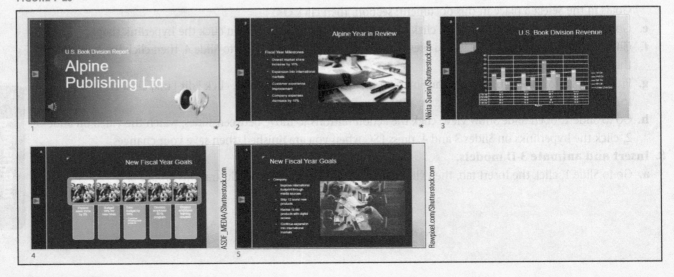

Independent Challenge 1

Riverwalk Medical Clinic (RMC), is a large medical facility in Cambridge, Massachusetts. Your supervisor has asked you to create a presentation on the Riverwalk Clinic EMS system. You have been working on the presentation and now you add video, audio, a hyperlink, and a 3-D model to the presentation.

a. Open the file IL_PPT_7-4.pptx, save it as **IL_PPT_7_RMC**, then go to Slide 6.

b. Locate and insert the video file Support_PPT_7_Doctor.mov from the location where you store your Data Files.

c. Resize the video to a width of 6.25", then drag the video to the middle of the blank area of the slide.

d. Apply a poster frame at about 00:10.00 in the video, then click the Playback tab.

e. Click the Play Full Screen check box, then click the Rewind after Playing check box.

f. Click the File tab, click Info, compress the video using the Standard (480p) format, then review the video in Slide Show view.

g. Go to Slide 1, locate and link the audio Support_PPT_7_Audio.mp3 from the location where you store your Data Files, then drag the audio icon to the lower-right corner of the slide.

h. Click the Playback tab, click the Play Across Slides check box, then click the Play in Background button.

i. Trim the audio clip so the start time is 00:06 and the end time is 02:17.200, then change the volume to Low.

j. Go to Slide 3, then change the existing picture to a new picture. Locate and insert the picture Support_PPT_7_ER.jpg from the location where you store your Data Files.

k. Change the picture color saturation to 200%, then change the brightness and contrast of the picture to Brightness: 0% (Normal) Contrast: -40%.

l. Resize the picture to a width of 7", using the Remove Background feature remove the parking lot from the picture, then keep your changes.

m. Reset the picture, then compress all pictures in the presentation.

n. Make sure the picture is still selected, click the Link button on the Insert tab, locate the file Support_PPT_7_ER.jpg from the location where you store your Data Files, then click OK.

o. Open Slide Show view, click the picture to view the linked picture, close the picture window, then press ESC when you return to Slide 3.

p. Right-click the picture, click Edit Link, locate the file Support_PPT_7_RMC.pptx from the location where you store your Data Files, then click OK.

q. Go to Slide 1, open Slide Show view, click through the presentation, click the linked picture on Slide 3, watch the video on Slide 6, then press ESC when you are finished. Your completed presentation should look similar to FIGURE 7-21.

r. Check the presentation spelling, submit your presentation to your instructor, then close the presentation and close PowerPoint.

FIGURE 7-21

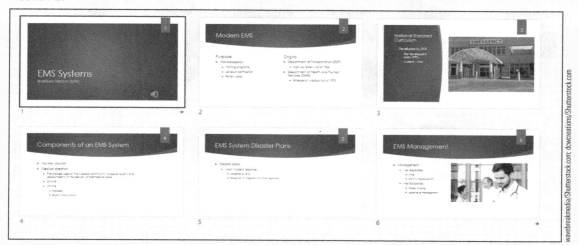

Independent Challenge 2

You work for JR Capital Group, a global financial services firm. You have been given the task of enhancing a presentation by modifying SmartArt graphics, adding action buttons, and adding a 3-D model.

a. Open the file IL_PPT_7-5.pptx from the location where you store your Data Files, then save it as **IL_PPT_7_JR**.

b. On Slide 2, open the SmartArt graphic Text pane, add a bullet to the first shape, type **U.S. Employees - 920**, then press ENTER.

c. Click the Promote button, type **30 years in business**, click the Move Up button, then click the Add Shape button to add a shape.

d. Type **Global reach**, then click the Move Down button, click the number 14 in the Text pane, then click the Move Up button.

e. Click the Change Colors button, click Colorful - Accent Colors, then click a blank area of the slide.

f. Go to Slide 4, click the middle shape in the SmartArt graphic, click the Format tab, click the Shape Fill button, then click Lavender, Accent 4.

g. Click the Larger button, click the Size button, click the number in the Height text box, then type **1.5**.

h. Click the picture icon in the top shape, then locate and insert the file Support_PPT_7_Company.jpg from the location where you store your Data Files.

i. Insert the same picture in the other two picture placeholders, then click a blank area of the SmartArt graphic.

j. Click the Shape Effects button, point to Preset, then click Preset 4.

k. Go to Slide 1, insert the shape Action Button: Go Forward or Next, make sure Next Slide appears in the Hyperlink to text box, then drag the shape to the upper middle of the slide.

l. Change the shape style of the action button to Subtle Effect - Red, Accent 3, then copy and paste the action button to the other three slides.

m. Right-click the action button on Slide 4, click Edit Link, click the Hyperlink to arrow, click First Slide, then click OK.

n. Open Slide Show view, click the action buttons to make sure they work correctly, then press ESC. The action button Slide 4 should return you to Slide 1.

o. Go to Slide 1, click the Insert tab, open the Online 3D Models dialog box, open the 3D Shapes section, then insert the dark red shape shown in FIGURE 7-22.

p. Change the width of the 3-D model to 2", then drag the model to the blank area to the right of the title text.

FIGURE 7-22

Independent Challenge 2 (continued)

q. Use the Rotate handle to change the angle of the model, then apply the Below Front 3D model view.

r. Apply the Turntable animation to the 3-D model, apply the effect option Continuous, click the Start list arrow in the Timing group, then click With Previous.

s. Open Slide Show view, watch the 3-D model animation, click the action buttons to view each slide, then press ESC when you are finished. Your completed presentation should look similar to FIGURE 7-23.

t. Submit your presentation to your instructor, close the presentation, then close PowerPoint.

FIGURE 7-23

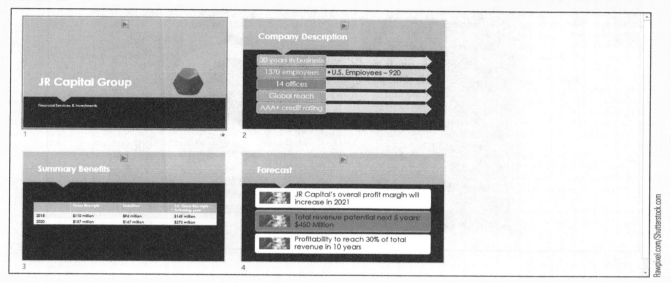

Rawpixel.com/Shutterstock.com

Visual Workshop

Open the file IL_PPT_7-6.pptx from the location where you store your Data Files, then save it as **IL_PPT_7_R2G**. Locate the file Support_PPT_7_R2G.jpg from the location where you store your Data Files, insert the picture, then close the Design Ideas pane. Change the slide background to solid Gold, Accent 4. Change the width of the picture to 7.2", then remove the background from the picture. On the Background Removal tab, click the Mark Areas to Keep button, then click the areas of the picture to keep it, as shown in FIGURE 7-24. Click the Keep Changes button in the Close group to save the changes to the picture and create a finished slide that looks like the example in FIGURE 7-25. Save the presentation, submit the presentation to your instructor, then close PowerPoint.

FIGURE 7-24

FIGURE 7-25

Integrating Word, Excel, Access, and PowerPoint

CASE At JCL Talent, Inc., you need to compile materials for a PowerPoint presentation and a Word report about job seeker workshops. The presentation includes an Access table, objects copied from Word, and a file linked to Excel. The Word report is created from handouts exported from PowerPoint and includes an embedded PowerPoint slide.

Module Objectives

After completing this module, you will be able to:

- Insert an Access table into PowerPoint
- Insert Word objects into PowerPoint
- Link an Excel file into PowerPoint
- Create PowerPoint handouts in Word
- Embed a PowerPoint slide in Word

Files You Will Need

IL_INT_6-1.pptx	IL_INT_6-4.xlsx
Support_INT_6_JobSeekerWorkshops.accdb	Support_INT_6_RenfrewCollegeOverview.docx
Support_INT_6_PopularWorkshops.docx	IL_INT_6-5.docx
IL_INT_6-2.xlsx	IL_INT_6-6.xlsx
Support_INT_6_ReportInformation.docx	IL_INT_6-7.pptx
IL_INT_6-3.pptx	Support_INT_6_AccommodationPartners.accdb
Support_INT_6_RenfrewCollegeData.accdb	Support_INT_6_WildlifeData.accdb
Support_INT_6_RenfrewCollegeTopPrograms.docx	IL_INT_6-8.xlsx

Insert an Access Table into PowerPoint

Learning Outcomes
- Paste an Access table in PowerPoint
- Format a pasted table in PowerPoint

You can copy a table or a query datasheet from Access and paste it on a PowerPoint slide. You can then use PowerPoint tools to modify the table attractively for use in a presentation. However, you cannot create a direct link between the Access table and the table copied to the PowerPoint presentation. **CASE** *You already have an Access database containing information about the job seeker workshops offered by JCL Talent, Inc. Because you don't need to link the database information to the presentation, you copy a query datasheet from the Access database, paste it directly into a PowerPoint slide, and then format it attractively.*

STEPS

1. **Start PowerPoint, open the file** IL_INT_6-1.pptx **from the location where you store your Data Files, save the presentation as** IL_INT_6_JobSeekerWorkshops, **then scroll through the presentation**

   The blank slides will contain objects that you import from other programs.

2. **Start Access, open the Data File** Support_INT_6_JobSeekerWorkshops.accdb **from the location where you store your Data Files, enable content if prompted, then double-click** Workshops Query **in the list of database objects to open it**

   The Workshops Query lists the workshops currently offered in various locations by JCL Talent, Inc.

3. **Close the Workshops Query, then with the** Workshops Query **still selected, click the** Copy **button in the Clipboard group**

4. **Switch to PowerPoint, go to** Slide 4 (Upcoming Workshops), **click the** content placeholder **to designate where the query datasheet will be pasted, click the** Paste arrow **in the Clipboard group, then move the mouse pointer over each of the Paste options to view how the pasted query datasheet will appear**

   The format of the query datasheet does not change to reflect Source or Destination themes because a query datasheet copied from Access does not use Office themes. The preview of the pasted query datasheet changes only when you move the mouse pointer over the Keep Text Only Paste option.

5. **Click the** Use Destination Theme button 🗋 **as shown in** FIGURE 6-1

   You can use PowerPoint tools to format the pasted table.

6. **Click the** Table Design tab, **click the** More button 🔽 **in the Table Styles group, then select the** Themed Style 1 - Accent 6 **design (gold in the top row)**

7. **Click anywhere in the table, press** CTRL+A **to select all the text in the table, click the** Home tab, **then click the** Increase Font Size button 🄰 **in the Font group until 18+ appears in the Font Size text box**

8. **Click anywhere in row 1, click the** right mouse button, **click the** Delete button **on the mini-toolbar, click** Delete Rows, **point to the left of row 1 to show** ➡, **click to select all the text in the new row 1, increase the font size to** 24 point, **then apply Bold formatting**

9. **Adjust column widths and position the table so that it appears as shown in** FIGURE 6-2, **save the presentation, switch to Access, then exit the program, answering** Yes **to empty the Clipboard, if prompted**

FIGURE 6-1: Viewing Paste Options for a copied Access table

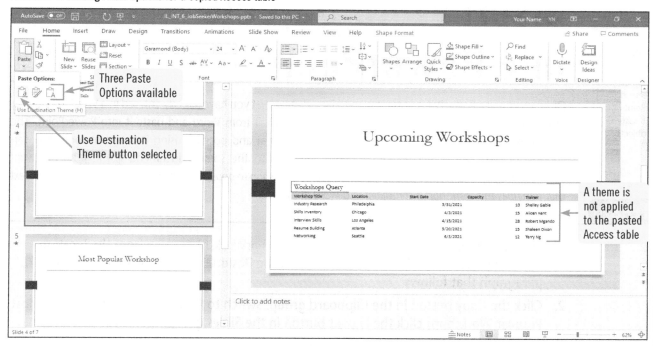

FIGURE 6-2: Access table formatted in PowerPoint

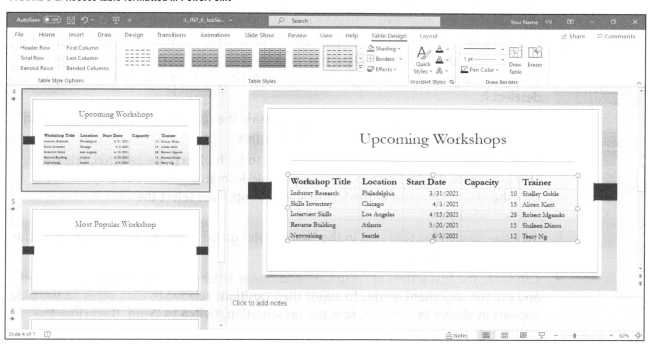

Insert Word Objects into PowerPoint

Learning Outcomes
- Paste copied text as objects in PowerPoint
- Format pasted Word objects

Often you need a PowerPoint presentation to include text that you have already entered in a Word document. Instead of retyping the text in PowerPoint, you can copy it from Word and paste it into PowerPoint. The pasted text becomes a text box that you can then format and position using PowerPoint tools. You can choose to paste the object with or without linking it to the source document. **CASE** *You want information about JCL Talent's most popular job seeker workshop to appear on Slide 5 of the presentation. The text that describes this workshop is contained in a Word document.*

STEPS

1. Start Word, open the file Support_INT_6_PopularWorkshops.docx from the location where you store your Data Files, then select the Resume Building heading and the paragraph that follows

2. Click the Copy button in the Clipboard group, switch to PowerPoint, go to Slide 5 (Most Popular Workshop) click the Layout button in the Slides group, then click Title Only

3. Click the Paste arrow in the Clipboard group, click the Use Destination Theme button 🗐, click the Quick Styles button in the Drawing group, click the Subtle Effect - Gold, Accent 6 quick style (far right column, fourth row), select all the text in the text box, then click the Increase Font Size button Aˆ in the Font group once (20+ appears)

4. Drag the left and right sizing handles and drag the text box edge to size and position it so it fills the slide as shown in FIGURE 6-3, then click outside the object to deselect it

5. Select the text resumes in the second line of the Resume Building description, click the Copy button, click outside the text box, click the Paste button (the object will appear within the large text box), drag the pasted object into the area below the text box, then deselect it

6. Copy cover letters from the text box, click outside the text box, paste the object, drag the pasted object into the area below the text box

7. Press and hold SHIFT, click the resumes object so both objects are selected, release SHIFT, increase the font size to 24 pt, apply Bold formatting, click the Shape Format tab, click the Shape Fill arrow in the Shape Styles group, then select the Gold Accent 6, Lighter 40% color

8. Click the Shape Effects button in the Shape Styles group, point to Bevel, then select the Slant bevel style as shown in FIGURE 6-4

9. Capitalize the first letters of "resumes" and "cover letters", resize the boxes as needed and use the alignment guides to adjust their positions relative to each other so the slide appears as shown in FIGURE 6-5, save the presentation, switch to Word, then close the document

FIGURE 6-3: Resized and repositioned text box

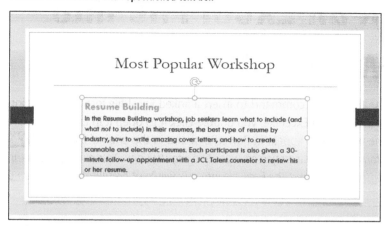

FIGURE 6-4: Selecting the Slant bevel style

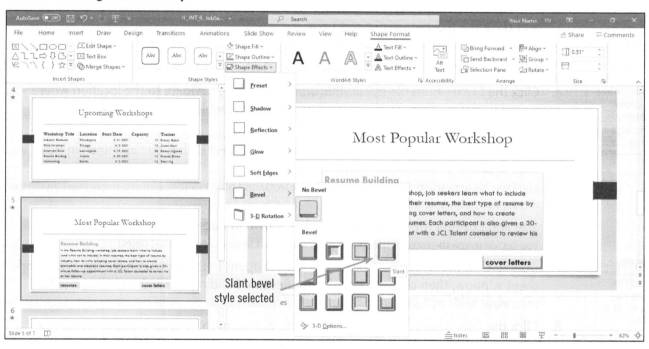

FIGURE 6-5: Completed slide with objects copied from Word

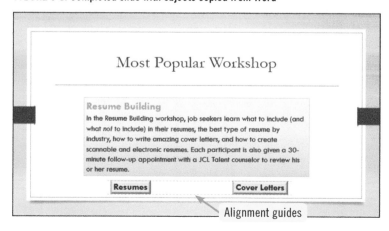

Link an Excel File into PowerPoint

Learning
Outcomes
• Insert a linked
  Excel file in
  PowerPoint
• Edit Excel data in
  PowerPoint

You can use the Object command to insert a linked Excel file into a PowerPoint presentation. To edit the content of the inserted Excel file, you double-click it to open it in Excel, the source program. Changes you make to the file in Excel appear in PowerPoint and in the original Excel file. **CASE** ▸ *You want Slide 7 to contain information about projected workshop registrations. You already have this information stored in an Excel spreadsheet. You insert the Excel file into a PowerPoint presentation and then update selected content.*

STEPS

1. **Start Excel, open the file** IL_INT_6-2.xlsx **from the location where you store your Data Files, then save it as** IL_INT_6_WorkshopRegistrations

2. **Click cell** E9, **click the** AutoSum button **in the Editing group twice, apply Bold, then save and close the file, but do not exit Excel**

> **QUICK TIP**
> Instead of applying the Title Only slide layout, you can just delete the lower placeholder by clicking its edge and pressing DELETE.

3. **In PowerPoint, go to** Slide 7 (Workshop Registrations), **change the layout to** Title Only, **click the** Insert tab, **then click the** Object button 🔲 **in the Text group**

4. **Click the** Create from file option button, **click** Browse, **navigate to the location where you stored** IL_INT_6_WorkshopRegistrations.xlsx, **then double-click** IL_INT_6_WorkshopRegistrations.xlsx

5. **Click the** Link check box **to select it in the Insert Object dialog box as shown in** FIGURE 6-6, **then click** OK

   The Excel file appears on the PowerPoint slide as a worksheet object formatted using the Banded theme that was applied to the source file.

6. **Size and position the worksheet object as shown in** FIGURE 6-7

   You decide to use the tools of the source program (Excel) to modify the linked object.

> **QUICK TIP**
> You can edit the linked object by opening the file in Excel or by double-clicking it in PowerPoint.

7. **Double-click the** worksheet object **(the object opens in Excel), maximize the Excel worksheet window, then change the price for Resume Building to** $800 **and the price for Interview Skills to** $550

8. **Click the** Page Layout tab, **click the** Themes button **in the Themes group, select the** Organic **theme, widen column D, then save and close the workbook and exit Excel**

9. **In PowerPoint, verify that the total projected sales are now** $43,950.00 **as shown in** FIGURE 6-8, **then save the presentation**

FIGURE 6-6: Insert Object dialog box

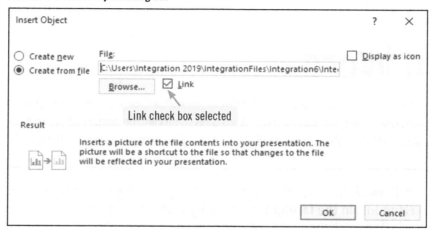

FIGURE 6-7: Excel worksheet object inserted into PowerPoint

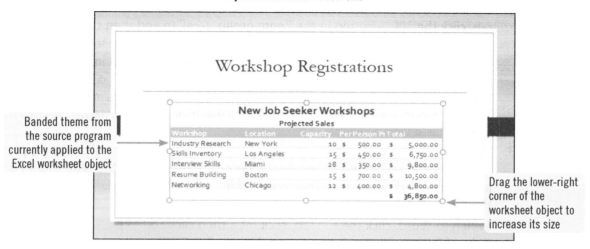

Banded theme from the source program currently applied to the Excel worksheet object

Drag the lower-right corner of the worksheet object to increase its size

FIGURE 6-8: Modified worksheet object in PowerPoint

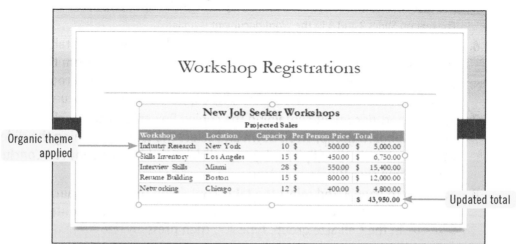

Organic theme applied

Updated total

Integration

Create PowerPoint Handouts in Word

Learning
Outcomes
• Send PowerPoint
slides to Word
• Edit linked slides
in Word

You can print slides as handouts directly from PowerPoint, or you can create handouts of PowerPoint slides in a Word document. You can then use Word tools to modify the document content and format. **CASE** ▸ *You create handouts of the PowerPoint slides in a Word document, and then add the report text to it.*

STEPS

1. In PowerPoint, click the File tab, click Export, click Create Handouts, click Create Handouts in the far-right pane, verify that the Notes next to slides option button is selected, click the Paste link option button, then click OK

TROUBLE
If the handouts are not created in Word, exit Word, then redo the steps.

2. Wait a few moments for the handout creation process to finish, click the Word button on the taskbar (it will be flashing) to view the three-column table in Word that contains the exported slides, save the Word document as IL_INT_6_WorkshopsReport, click the View tab, click the 100% button in the Zoom group, scroll to and then click to the left of the table row containing the Slide 6 text at the bottom of page 2 to select the entire row as shown in FIGURE 6-9, click the Home tab, then click the Cut button in the Clipboard group

   When you delete slide content from the Word document, that slide is not deleted from the PowerPoint presentation, even though the presentation and the document are linked. You must delete it manually from the PowerPoint presentation. Similarly, if you delete a slide from PowerPoint, you need to delete it manually from the linked Word document.

3. Switch to PowerPoint, click Slide 6 (Proposed Workshops) in the Slides pane, press DELETE, go to Slide 3, insert Job Seeker before "Workshop" in the slide title so it reads Job Seeker Workshop Focus, then go to Slide 2 and add Job Seeker at the beginning of the first bullet point

4. Switch to Word, click the File tab, click Info, then click Edit Links to Files in the bottom right of Backstage view (you may need to scroll down)

   In the Links dialog box, six entries appear. Each slide is linked separately to the PowerPoint presentation.

5. Press and hold SHIFT, click the bottom link to select all six links as shown in FIGURE 6-10, click Update Now, click OK, click ⊙ to exit Backstage view, change Slide 7 to Slide 6 in the last row of the table, then scroll up to see the updated slides

   The text on Slides 2 and 3 in the Word document is updated.

6. Press CTRL+HOME, press ENTER to insert a blank line above the table containing the slides, open the file Support_INT_6_ReportInformation.docx from the location where you store your Data Files, click the Select button in the Editing group, click Select All, click the Copy button in the Clipboard group, then close the document

TROUBLE
Make sure you select the entire table and not just the first row.

7. In the report document containing the copied PowerPoint slides, click the Paste button in the Clipboard group, scroll down and select the table containing the slides ⊞, click the Cut button in the Clipboard group, click in the blank line above "Conclusion" on page 1, then click the Paste button

8. Scroll up to page 1 and select the table containing the slides again, click the Layout contextual tab to the right of the Table Design tab, select the contents of the Height text box in the Cell Size group, type 1.7, then press ENTER

9. Deselect the table, click the View tab, click the Multiple Pages button in the Zoom group, save the document, then compare your screen to FIGURE 6-11

FIGURE 6-9: Selecting a table row

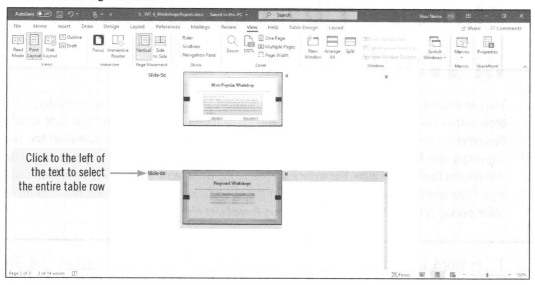

Click to the left of the text to select the entire table row

FIGURE 6-10: Selecting linked PowerPoint slides in the Links dialog box in Word

FIGURE 6-11: Word document containing slides exported from PowerPoint

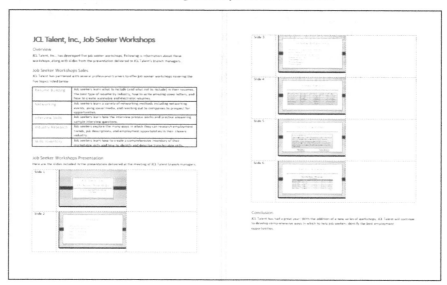

Embed a PowerPoint Slide in Word

Learning Outcomes
• Create a PowerPoint slide in Word
• Break links between linked files

You can embed a PowerPoint slide in a Word document and then, because it is embedded, use PowerPoint tools within Word to add text to the slide and apply formatting. The PowerPoint slide is not linked to a PowerPoint presentation. It exists only in the Word document. You can accomplish the same goal by copying a slide from PowerPoint, pasting it into Word, and then double-clicking it to make changes using PowerPoint tools. **CASE** ▶ *You replace the title of the Word report with a PowerPoint slide that includes the report title and then you break all the links to the presentation and report so you can send the document to other managers without sending the supporting PowerPoint file.*

STEPS

1. **In Word, return to 100% view, select the document title** JCL Talent, Inc., Job Seeker Workshops, **then press** DELETE

2. **Click the** Insert tab, **click the** Object button **in the Text group, scroll to and click** Microsoft PowerPoint Slide, **then click** OK

3. **Enter text on the embedded slide as shown in** FIGURE 6-12

4. **Click the** Design tab, **click the** More button ⊽ **in the Themes group, select the** Organic **theme, select the slide title, click the** Home tab **and reduce the font size to** 48 pt, **then click outside the embedded object to return to Word**

5. **Switch to PowerPoint, click the** File tab, **click** Info, **click** Edit Links to Files, **click the** link, **click** Break Link, **click** Close, **then click** ⬅ **to exit Backstage view**
   You've broken the link to the Excel workbook. Now if you make changes to the Excel workbook, the data in the worksheet object will not change.

6. **Switch to Word, click the** File tab, **click** Info, **click** Edit Links to Files, **select all the links (use** SHIFT**), click** Break Link, **then click** Yes

7. **Click** ⬅ **to exit Backstage view, click the** Design tab, **click the** Themes button **in the Document Formatting group, then click** Organic

8. **Click the** View tab, **click the** Multiples Pages button **in the Zoom group, press** CTRL+ENTER **to add a page break to the left of the "Job Seeker Workshops Presentation" heading, then compare the completed report to** FIGURE 6-13

9. **Save and close the document, exit Word, save and close the presentation, exit PowerPoint, then submit your files to your instructor**
   TABLE 6-1 summarizes the integration activities you performed in this module.

FIGURE 6-12: **Text entered on an embedded PowerPoint slide**

Word is the host program containing the embedded PowerPoint slide

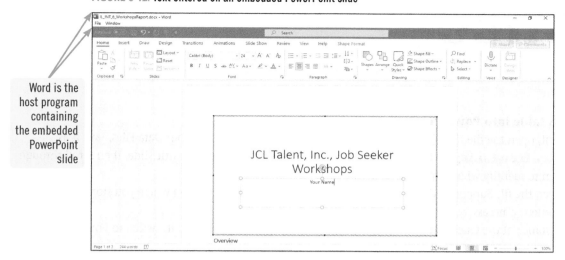

FIGURE 6-13: **Completed report**

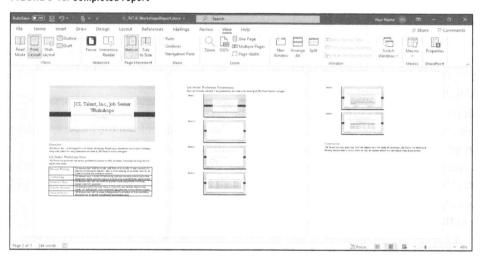

TABLE 6-1: **Module 6 integration tasks**

object	command(s)	source program	destination program	result	connection	page no.
Access table or query datasheet	Copy/Paste	Access	PowerPoint	Access table or query datasheet is pasted into the PowerPoint slide, then formatted with PowerPoint tools	None	2
Word text	Copy/Paste	Word	PowerPoint	Word text is pasted into the PowerPoint slide, then formatted with PowerPoint tools	None	4
Excel file	Insert/Object/ Paste Link	Excel	PowerPoint	Excel file is inserted into PowerPoint, then modified in Excel	Linked	6
PowerPoint slides	Create Handouts	PowerPoint	Word	PowerPoint slides are contained in a three-column table in Word	Linked	8
PowerPoint slide	Object button on the Insert tab	PowerPoint	Word	PowerPoint slide is embedded in a Word document and updated with PowerPoint tools	Embedded	10

Practice

Skills Review

1. Insert an Access table into PowerPoint.

a. Start PowerPoint, open the file IL_INT_6-3.pptx from the location where you store your Data Files, save it as **IL_INT_6_RenfrewCollegeReview**, add your name where indicated on the title slide, then scroll through the presentation to identify what information is required.

b. Start Access, open the file Support_INT_6_RenfrewCollegeData.accdb from the location where you store your Data Files. Enable content if necessary.

c. Select either instance of the Guest Lecturer Query in the list of database objects, copy it, switch to PowerPoint, then go to Slide 4.

d. Paste the Access query information on the slide using the Use Destination Theme Paste Option, then change the layout to Title Only.

e. Apply the Themed Style 1 - Accent 1 table style to the pasted datasheet. Select all the text in the table, then change the font size to **16+ pt**.

f. Delete row 1, increase the font size of the text in the new header row 1 to **18 pt**, then apply Bold formatting.

g. Adjust the column widths so none of the lines wrap and the table fits attractively on the slide, position the table so the left edge is even with the left edge of the slide title, save the presentation, switch to Access, then close the database and exit Access, answering Yes to empty the Clipboard, if prompted.

2. Insert Word objects into PowerPoint.

a. Start Word, open the file Support_INT_6_RenfrewCollegeTopPrograms.docx from the location where you store your Data Files, then select the Jazz Studies Diploma heading and the paragraph following.

b. Copy the text, switch to PowerPoint, go to Slide 5, apply the Title Only slide layout, then paste the text.

c. Apply the Subtle Effect - Lime, Accent 1 Shape Style to the text box, then increase the font size of all the text until **24+ pt** appears in the Font Size text box.

d. Size and position the object so it fills the area attractively, then deselect it.

e. Copy and paste the text "jazz performance," drag the pasted object below the text box, then deselect it.

f. Copy and paste the text "composition," then drag the pasted object below the text box.

g. Select both text boxes, reduce the width so the text fits, increase the font size to **24 pt**, fill the text boxes with the Lime, Accent 1, Lighter 60% shape fill, then apply the Round Bevel shape effect.

h. Capitalize each of the three words in the two text boxes, resize the text boxes so no lines wrap, use the alignment guides to position them attractively below the main text box, save the presentation, switch to Word, then close the document.

3. Link an Excel file into PowerPoint.

a. Start Excel, open the file IL_INT_6-4.xlsx from the location where you store your Data Files, and save it as **IL_INT_6_AnnualBudget**.

b. In cell F13, enter the formula **=F7-F12**, then save and close the file, but do not exit Excel.

c. In PowerPoint, go to Slide 7, change the layout to Title Only, then insert the IL_INT_6_AnnualBudget file as a linked object.

d. Enlarge the linked worksheet object and position it so it fills the slide attractively.

e. Double-click the worksheet object to open the source object in Excel, change the Donations income for Qtr 1 to **$3,500,000** and the Physical Plant expense for Qtr 2 to **$1,900,000**, then save and close the workbook and exit Excel.

f. In PowerPoint, verify that the two items were changed and that the total Profit/Loss is now $2,400,000.00. (*Hint*: If the Excel data did not update, open the Links dialog box from the File tab and click Update Now.)

g. Save the presentation.

4. Create PowerPoint handouts in Word.

a. In PowerPoint, create handouts in Word as pasted links, using the Notes next to slides layout and selecting the Paste link check box. (*Hint*: You may need to wait for several moments to allow the handout creation process to be completed.)

b. Save the new Word document as **IL_INT_6_RenfrewCollegeReport**, then use the Cut command to delete the row containing Slide 6.

c. Switch to PowerPoint, delete Slide 6 (New Freshman Workshops), then delete Freshman Year Workshops on Slide 2.

d. In Word, open the Links dialog box and update all the links.

e. Use CTRL+HOME to move to the top of the Word document, then insert a blank line above the table containing the linked slides.

f. Open the file Support_INT_6_RenfrewCollegeOverview.docx from the location where you store your Data Files, select all the text, then copy it.

g. Paste the copied text above the slides in the IL_INT_6_RenfrewCollegeReport document, then close the Support_INT_6_RenfrewCollegeOverview document.

h. Select the table containing the PowerPoint slides, cut the table, then paste it at the blank line above Conclusion on page 1.

i. Change the row height of all the rows in the table containing the linked PowerPoint slides to **1.8"**, then change Slide 7 to Slide 6 at the end of the document and save the document.

5. Embed a PowerPoint slide in Word.

a. Delete the document title Renfrew College, then insert a PowerPoint slide.

b. On the embedded slide, enter **Renfrew College Overview** as the slide title and your name as the subtitle.

c. Apply the same theme (the Retrospect theme) with the green variant to the embedded slide so it matches the slides you exported from PowerPoint.

d. Click outside the slide, then apply the Retrospect theme to the Word document.

e. In the Word document, break all the links, view all three pages of the report, add a page break, if necessary, to move "Annual Meeting" and the following paragraph to page 2, compare the document to FIGURE 6-14, then save and close the document.

f. In PowerPoint, break the link to the Excel worksheet, then save and close the presentation.

FIGURE 6-14

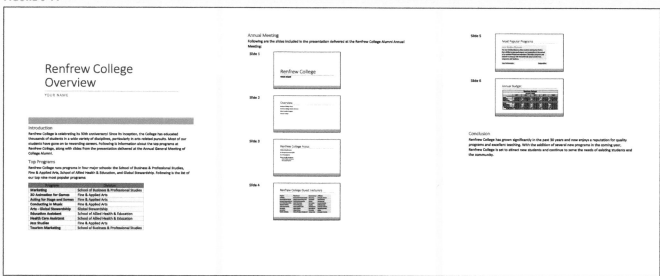

Independent Challenge 1

As part of your duties as an administrator at the Riverwalk Medical Clinic in Cambridge, MA, you meet monthly with a nonprofit organization called Family Place that finds accommodation for the families of patients coming from out of town to be treated at the clinic. At the last meeting, you were asked to assemble the meeting minutes. You create the minutes in Word from a selection of materials contained in PowerPoint, Excel, and Access files.

a. Open the file IL_INT_6-5.docx from the location where your Data Files are located, then save it as **IL_INT_6_ RiverwalkClinicandFamilyPlaceMeetingMinutes**.

b. At the beginning of the document, embed a PowerPoint slide, and enter **Family Place Meeting Minutes** as the title and your name as the subtitle. Apply the Ion Boardroom theme.

c. In Excel, open the file IL_INT_6-6.xlsx from the location where your Data Files are located, save it as **IL_INT_6_ FamilyPlaceExpenses**, calculate the required total in cell D6, apply Bold formatting to the total, then save and close the workbook.

d. In the Word document, replace the text "EXCEL WORKSHEET" but not the paragraph mark with the FamilyPlaceExpenses workbook inserted as a linked object. Edit the worksheet to change the nightly cost for accommodation in cell B4 to **$180**, then apply the Ion Boardroom theme. Save and close the workbook in Excel, and then update the link in Word. (*Hint*: Right-click the worksheet object, then click Update Link. The total should be $73,800.00.)

e. In PowerPoint, open IL_INT_6-7.pptx, then save it as **IL_INT_6_RiverwalkClinicFamilyPlacePresentation**.

f. In Access, open the file Support_INT_6_AccommodationPartners.accdb, copy the Accommodation Partners Query, then paste it on the appropriate slide in the PowerPoint presentation using the Use Destination Theme Paste option.

g. Apply the Themed Style 1 - Accent 1 table design, remove the first row, then increase the font size of the table text to **16 pt**, bold the top row and increase its font size to **20 pt**, and modify column widths so the table fills the space attractively and no lines wrap. Close the Access database.

h. In the Word minutes, copy the paragraph under the "Family Place Services" heading and paste it on Slide 2 in PowerPoint. Change the slide layout to Title Only, increase the font size of the pasted text to 24 pt., change the width of the object to approximately 10" wide, format the object with the Colored Outline, Plum - Accent 1 shape style, then center the object below the slide title.

i. Copy the phrase "caregiving seminars", paste it below the copied text, then increase the font size to **32 pt**, then reduce the width to fit only the text.

j. Format the pasted object with the Subtle Effect - Plum, Accent 1 shape style and the Angle bevel effect, capitalize the first letter of each word, resize the text box so the text doesn't wrap, then position the object so it appears centered below the table.

k. Save the presentation, then create handouts in Word, using the default style and selecting the Paste link option in the Send to Microsoft Word dialog box. In PowerPoint, change the title of the first slide to **Family Place Mission**, save the presentation, then verify that the slide updates in Word. Click in the table to show the Table Select handle, select and cut the table, paste the cut slides in the appropriate area of the minutes using the Use Destination Theme Paste option, answer No to update links, then reduce the height of the table rows to **2"**.

l. In Word, open the Links dialog box, then break all links.

m. Save the document, compare it to FIGURE 6-15, close the document, then close the Word document you copied the slides from without saving it.

n. Save and close the presentation, then submit your files to your instructor.

FIGURE 6-15

Family Place Report

Shari Warland circulated a report on the accommodations required by the families of patients in the first quarter of the year. The report includes information about the following topics:

- Accommodation costs
- Support activities for families provided by Riverwalk Medical Clinic in consultation with Family Place
- Presentations on family support delivered by Roger Ng

Accommodation Costs

Shown below is a summary of the costs for accommodation incurred in the first quarter. Accommodations are found and paid for by Family Place for a total of 80 families over a 90-day period.

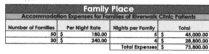

Family Place			
Accommodation Expenses for Families of Riverwalk Clinic Patients			
Number of Families	Per Night Rate	Nights per Family	Total
50	$ 180.00	5	$ 45,000.00
30	$ 240.00	4	$ 28,800.00
		Total Expenses	$ 73,800.00

Family Place Services

Family Place provides accommodations to families and sponsors a variety of activities designed to support families of patients being treated at Riverwalk Medical Clinic. Activities include movie nights, caregiving seminars, restaurant outings, and home support. Shown below are the slides that describe Family Place from a presentation recently delivered to potential accommodation partners.

Slide 1

Slide 2

Slide 3

Visual Workshop

As the resident naturalist for the municipality of Seacrest on the Oregon coast, you are responsible for putting together presentations about the local wildlife for school and community groups. You need to create two slides that you can later use to integrate into other presentations. One slide contains query data from Access, and another slide contains data from an Excel worksheet. Create a PowerPoint presentation and save it as **IL_INT_6_SeacrestMunicipalityPresentation**, then apply the Blank slide layout. Open the Access database called Support_INT_6_WildlifeData.accdb from the location where you store your Data Files, copy the Wildlife Sightings Query, paste it into the blank PowerPoint slide and apply the Title Only slide layout, close the Access database, then edit the slide and table text and format the slide and table as shown in FIGURE 6-16. (*Hint*: The slide uses the Basis design, and the table uses the Themed Style 1 - Accent 3 table style with the Header Row check box selected. Row 1 is deleted. The font size of the header row is **28 pt**, and the font size of the table text is **24 pt**.)

Open the Excel workbook called IL_INT_6_8.xlsx from the location where you store your Data Files, save it as **IL_INT_6_SeacrestMunicipalityNaturePreserveData**, change the number of Black Bear sightings to **10**, then save the workbook. Insert a new slide in the presentation using the Title Only layout, add the slide title text, insert the Excel file as an embedded object (not linked), apply the Basis theme to the embedded object in Excel, change the font size for all the data to **18 pt** and adjust column widths, then position the worksheet object as shown in FIGURE 6-17. Return to Excel, go to the Chart worksheet, copy the chart, then paste it using the Use Destination Theme & Embed Workbook Paste Option. Position the pasted chart as shown. Click the Chart Design tab, then apply Chart Style 4 to the chart. Insert a slide footer containing your name. (*Hint*: Click the Insert tab, click the Header & Footer button in the Text group, click the Footer check box, type your name in the Footer text box, then click Apply to All.) Save and close all files, exit all programs, and submit the files to your instructor.

FIGURE 6-16

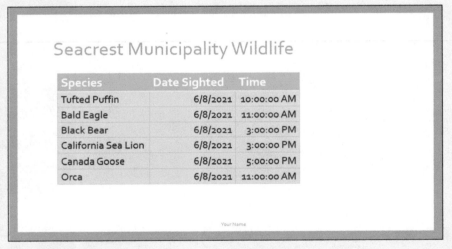

FIGURE 6-17

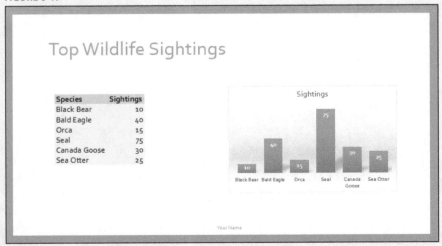

Index

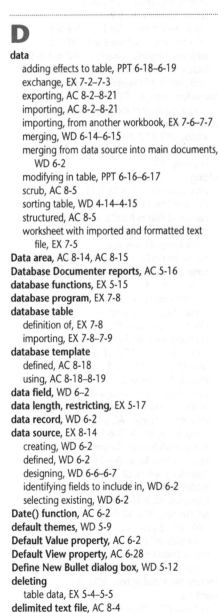